Making a Modern U.S. West

History of the American West

SERIES EDITOR

Richard W. Etulain, University of New Mexico

Making a Modern U.S. West

THE CONTESTED TERRAIN OF A REGION AND ITS BORDERS, 1898–1940

SARAH DEUTSCH

University of Nebraska Press | LINCOLN

Portions of chapter 3 previously appeared in "Being American in Boley, Oklahoma," in *Beyond Black and White: Race, Ethnicity, and Gender in the U.S. South and Southwest*, ed. Stephanie Cole and Alison M. Parker (College Station: Texas A&M University Press for the University of Texas at Arlington, 2004), 97–122. Used with permission.

Manufactured in the United States of America

Publication of this volume was assisted by the Virginia Faulkner Fund, established in memory of Virginia Faulkner, editor in chief of the University of Nebraska Press.

Library of Congress Cataloging-in-Publication Data
Names: Deutsch, Sarah, author.
Title: Making a modern U.S. West: the contested terrain of a region and its borders, 1898–1940 / Sarah Deutsch.
Description: Lincoln: University of Nebraska Press, [2022] | Series: History of the American West | Includes bibliographical references and index.
Identifiers: LCCN 2021007076
ISBN 9781496228611 (hardback)
ISBN 9781496229557 (epub)
ISBN 9781496229564 (pdf)
Subjects: LCSH: Economic development—West (U.S.)—History—20th century. | Borderlands—West (U.S.)—History—20th century. | Marginality, Social—West (U.S.)—History—20th century. | Migration, Internal—West (U.S.)—History—20th century. | West (U.S.)—History—1890–1945. | West (U.S.)—Social conditions—20th century. | West (U.S.)—Emigration and immigration—History—20th century. | BISAC: HISTORY / United States / State & Local / West (AK, CA, CO, HI, ID, MT, NV, UT, WY) | HISTORY / United States / 20th Century
Classification: LCC F595 .D48 2022 | DDC 978/.033—dc23
LC record available at https://lccn.loc.gov/2021007076

Set in New Baskerville ITC Pro by Laura Buis.

CONTENTS

SERIES EDITOR'S INTRODUCTION

RICHARD W. ETULAIN

Historical writing about the American West has undergone dramatic changes in the past half century and more. Specifically, historians have moved away from the frontier thesis of Frederick Jackson Turner and turned in new directions. Authors such as Henry Nash Smith and Earl Pomeroy helped us understand how the mythic West and western imitations of European and eastern American traditions shaped the history of the region. Other recent western histories highlight the roles of racial and ethnic groups, women and families, and urbanization in the development of the West. And widely recognized from the late 1980s onward is a New Western History that has brought forth the darker, more complex sides of the region's past.

These historiographical shifts compel us to ask new questions about the history of the American West and to reexamine the past in light of our experiences in the late twentieth and early twenty-first centuries. Fresh sociological, demographic, and environmental topics are being addressed; for many specialists in the field, the regional West has supplanted the frontier West, with *place* being emphasized more than *process*.

It's time for a new comprehensive history of the American West, one that reflects new scholarship without overlooking past perspectives. Volumes in the History of the West series do just that. A history of the region in six volumes, the series builds on these recent historiographical treatments of gender, ethnicity, and the environment. The volumes reflect current thoughts about the West as a region, provide a judicious blend of old and new subject matter, and offer narratives that appeal to specialists and general readers.

Sarah Deutsch achieves the large series goals in her book. Her expansive volume is now the most thorough examination we have of the American West from the late 1890s to the eve of World War II. Not only is the volume an extraordinarily thorough work, but it also provides a new reading of these four decades of western history. Readers will be drawn to the freshness of Deutsch's insights.

Several contributions of *Making a Modern U.S. West* deserve special mention. Making use of terms such as "borders," "boundaries," and "demarcations," Deutsch is especially provocative in her transnational coverage. Readers are given new readings of the U.S.-Mexican border and the cross-cultural influences, particularly across the southwestern region. Deutsch also uses metaphorical borders and boundaries to treat the racial, gender, and class differences and similarities over time among westerners. Her text is expansive on all these important topics. Migrants, miners, and other workers also receive much-merited attention. In addition, the author's insightful coverage keeps readers abreast of the West's contributions to national issues throughout these tense decades.

Overall, Sarah Deutsch provides an innovative interpretation of these western years. Earlier accounts often focused on political matters, but this volume uses a social history framework to provide striking and expansive results. Scholars and general readers will find inviting, fresh insights in this important book.

ACKNOWLEDGMENTS

This is a book long in the making, and it has piled up debts to more people than I can possibly name here. The unsung heroes of any research project, including this one, are the incredible librarians. I benefited greatly from the highly skilled and knowledgeable librarians at Clark University, the University of Arizona, and Duke University, where Carson Holloway was endlessly inventive and supportive. Generative audiences heard and improved portions of the book at various conferences and universities, including at the University of Texas, Arlington; University of London; University of California, Davis; University of Washington, Seattle; North Carolina State University; Colorado State University, Pueblo; and the LBJ Presidential Library.

I am grateful also to the generations of graduate and undergraduate students at the University of Arizona and Duke who have inspired me and whose insightful and original work has found its way into this book. They include, too, Brad Wood, research assistant par excellence, who enabled this manuscript to reach the finish line and did so with ingenuity, patience, good humor, and enthusiasm.

Stephanie Cole and Fawn Amber Montoya had a skilled hand in editing earlier versions of parts of this manuscript. Richard Etulain, the series editor, proved a model of patience, intellectual generosity, and support, even where we differed in emphasis and significance. At the University of Nebraska Press, Bridget Barry proved similarly patient and unfailingly reassuring and supportive, as well as equipped with an unerring literary scalpel.

The two anonymous readers and Katherine Benton Cohen, who endured a rough cut of the book, were more generous than I had any right to expect. Their comments without doubt strengthened the work.

Finally, I dedicate this book to my daughter, Sabrina, who has lived with this project her entire life, and to my husband, Reeve Huston, for whom it only felt that way, I'm sure, for his invaluable insight, ear, and brainstorming about thorny problems of emphasis and interpretation.

Making a Modern U.S. West

Introduction

How to Make the West Modern

By 1898 the United States had claimed the land west of the Mississippi for fifty years, yet New Mexico, Arizona, and Oklahoma were not yet states. Historian Frederick Jackson Turner had declared the frontier closed in a widely influential speech he gave during Chicago's Columbian Exposition in 1893, but vast spaces in the U.S. West remained sparsely inhabited. Settlers took out more homesteads after that speech than before it.[1] Sometimes the homesteader could not do much with the land. Failures ran rampant in every decade. But the promise of land for the taking retained incredible allure.

The promise of access to land, as old as the United States itself and seductive even in decades when farmers lost everything, was not about a love of farming. Rather, landholding represented security—having, literally, a place—a claim as important to dispossessed Native Americans and Mexican Americans as to aspirant immigrant, native white, and African American settlers. It represented at the most fundamental level a sense of belonging, whether to a local community or to a national myth. Landholders saw themselves as valiant contributors to the national good with commensurate claims on the state. In turn, congressmen, senators, and presidents remained as committed to an agrarian ideal of independent small farmers as Jefferson had been.[2]

Much of what transpired in the West between 1898 and 1940 concerned how to translate that dream into a self-consciously modern nation-state. To many Americans and would-be Americans, including policy makers, the West was simultaneously the greatest symbol of American opportunity, the greatest story of its past, and the imagined blank slate on which its future would be written. Turner had described the West as the crucible from which the U.S. democracy had been formed; at the same time, the disproportionate share of the West's landscape owned by the federal government enabled government planners to launch new "scientific" programs of land use and population management. Those programs made the region a showcase for the nation as a forward-looking modern state, ready to be a leader among global leaders. The same opportunities that drew individuals and planners drew transnational capital, and during these years ever larger corporations had their own visions of what constituted a modern landscape.

Making a Modern U.S. West is about the contests over both that vision of the past and the various visions of the future. Visions, in this sense, have material consequences. From the Spanish-American War in 1898 to the Great Depression's end, from the Mississippi to the Pacific, policy makers at various levels, large-scale corporate investors, and people on the ground struggled over who would get to define modernity, who would get to participate, and who would get excluded.

Shifting lines of inclusion and exclusion are central to this volume's story of the West and to the function it performed for the burgeoning U.S. nation. The story of the rise of Jim Crow in this era—of a segregated South and a depiction of the population as divided into two "races," Black and white—is usually told as a southern story. But the U.S. West played its own central and complicated role in the creation of that dominant national racial formation.[3]

The ability to segregate, to categorize and demarcate, was part of the function of a modern nation-state. It enabled the state to know its own resources, including human resources, to count the population, and to know the population to count on. In the United States the modern era of demarcating began with an imperial adventure. In the standard view among historians who took their cue from Turner, the Spanish-American War stands as a marker of the West's inability still to serve as the place of boundless opportunity, forcing the nation to seek newer frontiers of trade and commerce overseas. But crucial differences disrupted the seeming continuity of expansionism. What emerged from the congressional battles over how to deal with the people in the newly acquired territories was a reenvisioning of the American polity.

In 1898 the United States annexed Hawai'i and gained the Philippines, Guam, and Puerto Rico in the Treaty of Paris, which ended the Spanish-American War; in 1900 it acquired Samoa. For the first time, the United States gained territory with no intent fully to incorporate the territory or its inhabitants as citizens and participants in the republic. With the war, the United States shifted from a formal philosophy and policy of democratic incorporation of new territories and peoples (however imperfectly and slowly practiced) to an imperial philosophy of official colonization. There would remain deep differences between U.S. citizens and the nation's colonial subjects.

The policies and discourses that supported this shift both emerged from and affected relations on the mainland. Contestants in the twentieth-century West could take their cues from the new imperial culture. This creation of a nation-based empire required a new kind of logic around who could belong and who could not, around the borders of citizenship, around what made an "American" an "American." A series of cases came before the U.S. Supreme Court between 1901 and 1904, each dealing with the constitutional status of the territory acquired from Spain. In one of them, *Downes v. Bidwell* (1901), "the court wiped clean the long history of a continent peopled by diverse races." Erasing the prior residence and continued existence of Blacks, Mexicans, and Asians, Justice Henry Billings Brown, writing for the majority, contended that the continental United States was "inhabited only by people of the same race, or scattered bodies of native Indians." This erasure of the nation's heterogeneous past and present made it possible to pose the new territories as "a different case altogether, representing 'differences of race, habits, laws, and customs,'" language, and religion. The court rendered them analogous to the way it had come to see Native American peoples, as "domestic dependent nations."[4] By this means Justice Brown painted over the fact that Colorado had printed its official documents in German and Spanish, as well as in English; that the Dakotas and Nebraska had districts so heavily populated with German immigrants that schools were taught in that language; that Italians, far from being considered "people of the same race" as other inhabitants, were paid different wages from "white" men in many of the West's metal mines; and that myriad other differences shaped the history of the region and the nation. Redrawing the lines of difference, claiming a homogeneous population, made it easier to pose the colonized peoples as permanently outside the core nation; it enabled the "nation" to have "colonies."

Not only court cases but also the endless international fairs that littered the first decades of the twentieth century tied this lesson about difference, about the United States as a nation-based empire, to the history and future of the American West. American international expositions at the turn of the century explicitly linked nineteenth-century westward expansion, Anglo-Saxon racial development, and the new imperial policies. At Omaha, Nebraska, in 1898, 2.5 million people visited an exposition that featured mock battles between "Indians" and "whites," always ending with the Indians' surrender and promise to learn "civilized" behavior. The exposition also featured a Philippine village with sixteen "Manila warriors" who, the promoter told the *World Herald*, had cannibalistic tendencies. The Filipinos and Indians were joined by an African American village dubbed the "Old Plantation" and a postemancipation exhibit that featured Aunt Jemima serving pancakes. The fair's architects placed each of these peoples in a subordinate relationship to white Americans, ready and needing to be tutored. These carefully staged performances at the fairs made coherent the messy events and conflicts of the era; they created a single story and told it repeatedly to the vast number of visitors. These stories of pioneers, plantations, and progress along with judicial decisions clarified relations among the nation's inhabitants.[5]

The fairs that took place in the West allowed that region's white inhabitants to claim status as colonizers, not colonized, as part of the modern nation, the future, and not the past, having safely contained Native Americans and now putting the region in the context of the new U.S. empire. Visiting one such fair, President William McKinley insisted that America's continued grace and progress required assuming such tutelary "international responsibilities." At the Louisiana Purchase Exposition in St. Louis, Missouri, in 1904, the federal government and St. Louis civic leaders collaborated in juxtaposing an exhibit of just fewer than a thousand Filipinos (including one man labeled the "missing link") with a living ethnology exhibit of Native Americans. "White and Strong are synonymous terms," declared the fair's anthropological organizers, previously at the Bureau of American Ethnology. Such exhibits taught U.S. viewers that they already had successful experience ruling colonized peoples and cemented the presumptive eternal difference between white Americans and others. In these expositions and in countless historical pageants across the country, the new U.S. empire became the logical next chapter in a story of inevitable white progress.[6]

In short, the Spanish-American War marks the starting point for this volume because at the time it provided the nation's policy makers and promoters and their audience with a new framework for western struggles over land, rights, and the nature of democracy and relegitimized both white supremacy and the concept of whiteness. In this frame the United States—not in its identity as an experimental republic but in its identity as a "white" people—could assume its "rightful" place among the ruling, not the dependent, nations.[7]

Increasingly internally as well, the United States proved willing to draw lines within the boundaries of citizenship, separating citizenship from full rights. The federal government extended its dominion, unapologetically, to new realms. In 1903 the Supreme Court in *Lone Wolf v. Hitchcock* gave Congress full power over Indian property, including "the authority to unilaterally abrogate the terms of earlier treaties, provided only that its action toward its 'wards' was guided by 'perfect good faith.'"[8] As the United States enacted that "white" and "other" dichotomy at home, it dispossessed Indians and Mexican Americans, disenfranchised Blacks, created a sympathetic audience for the white disenfranchised Populists in Indian Territory, and created one particular version of the West for the twentieth century among the many possibilities available in 1900.

No one could better join the symbolic content of the West and the empire than Teddy Roosevelt. He made his reputation by writing up his dude ranch experience out west in the 1880s, authoring a series of books titled *The Winning of the West* (1889–96), and then leading the charge on San Juan Hill during the Spanish-American War. What would it mean to the West to have this cowboy unexpectedly assume office as president in the opening year of the new century? Roosevelt wrote in a book review that the "nineteenth century demands no more complete vindication for its existence than the fact that it has kept for the white race the best portions of the new world's surface, temperate America and Australia." It was no accident that Roosevelt vocally supported the theory of race suicide—that low birth rates among whites threatened white supremacy and so, in his view, the republic. To Roosevelt and others, taking the United States' rightful place in the "family" of nations as an imperial power and accepting its permanent responsibility for "lesser" races would reinvigorate American manhood and save the republic from decline. The Spanish-American War marked a crucial point in western history, in other words, not just because the United States gained the Philippines, Puerto Rico, and Guam but also because it redefined "frontier," "race," "citizenship," "manhood," "opportunity," and nationhood.[9]

Such categories as "race" and "citizenship" had long proved particularly unstable in the West. Federal, state, and even municipal governments struggled over whom to incorporate and to exclude, who could participate in the civilizing project of the "lesser races." How would they define racial categories? Given its role as the ultimate land of opportunity, the West may seem outside the racial paradigms that governed the rest of the nation. Yet the Supreme Court case ending legal segregation in schools, *Brown v. Board of Education*, was a Kansas case, one hundred years after battles over the enslavement of Black people earned the territory the label Bleeding Kansas. The West was a patchwork of different and incommensurate racial formations, but as early as 1909 the foreman of a company installing a gas line in Emporia, Kansas, had let it be known that "the color line is being strictly drawn."[10]

Strictly drawn . . . but where? The West's population raised many classificatory questions in acute form. Jim Crow rendered the key legal and social question in much of the country, Who is Black? But immigration, particularly in the West, made the legal and social question, Who is white? "Black" and "white" are categories in the U.S. Constitution. "Asian" is not. "Mexicans," people of Mexican descent, many with roots in the United States before the U.S. conquest in 1848, had citizenship rights by way of treaty, while their "racial" status evaded consensus. Before 1910 some

420 Japanese immigrants had succeeded in becoming naturalized citizens as "white." A 1906 act enabled Filipino naturalization, though courts consistently rejected applicants, insisting the law intended that only "white" or "Black" Filipinos could be naturalized. The myriad marriages joining a stunning array of dyads (Mexican, Chinese, Black, Indian, Japanese, Sikh, and others), along with their progeny, elicited erratic decisions from judges and consternation from census takers.[11] The instability of these categories led to repeated assertions and contestations over belonging and rights, including the right to property, as Pacific coast states passed laws in these years prohibiting landownership by "aliens ineligible for citizenship."

As governments at various levels struggled to draw clear lines around "race," the federal government struggled to draw clear lines around the nation's physical borders. Between the Spanish-American War and the Second World War, the United States went from having a loosely policed western frontier to a patrolled border that came to symbolize the coherence and strength of the nation. Such policing, like other regulatory reforms of the early twentieth century, required new government capacity. Not only was the West a showcase for the modern nation, but its governance helped generate the burgeoning bureaucratic state. Only in 1908 did the United States begin to keep land-based immigration records. It created the Border Patrol in 1924. This book is subtitled *The Contested Terrain of a Region and Its Borders* to highlight as central what is usually placed at the margin.

As with all histories, it is important to strike the right balance between continuity and discontinuity. What marks the beginning of the modern West? When I was an undergraduate in the mid-1970s, the nickname of the first half of the survey course of the American West was "Cowboys and Indians." The second half was called "Reds and Feds." In many ways, those titles still typify the ways in which popular culture presents the nineteenth- and twentieth-century Wests. The twentieth century became the time when the East disciplined the West, Indians disappeared, consolidation ruled the land, and the federal government, with a freer hand than in older states, more effectively imposed its will and shaped the landscape.[12]

Although I would agree with those who argue that the federal government exerted massive power west of the Mississippi in the twentieth century, that was also true in the nineteenth century. I would place the distinctiveness of the twentieth-century West elsewhere. It resides, at least in part, in Indians becoming cowboys, in the Fort Shaw Indian School women's basketball team beating all challengers in 1904, in the successful Teamsters Union formed by California's Concows and Yuki/Wailacki and white freighters in 1905, in short, in the adaptive Native American participation in capitalism and the dominant popular culture rather than in the disappearance of Indians and the end of the "frontier." Identities, as in "Indians" *versus* "cowboys," were unchanging only in Wild West shows and the popular imagination. In the non-Indian imagination, those imagined Indians could stand in for and even block the view of the Indians who actually lived and ranched in the West, attended its schools, and ran many of its businesses. Indeed, the federal government found it so unimaginable that Indians could become savvy capitalists that it labeled "mixed-blood" those who it believed could manage the market economy; it labeled "full-blood" those it saw as "real" Indians and "protected" them from the land sharks eager to purchase their allotments. It did so despite plentiful testimony that blood quantum was not at all the most accurate way to judge a person's market savvy.[13] This contest over who could participate in the modern West, whose claims to that participation would be seen as legitimate, whose identities could be fixed or erased is at the heart of the twentieth-century West.

The material transformations in daily life did not stop dreams and myths about the West as a limitless land of opportunity for those who did not already live there. And dreams of inclusion based on participating in that mythical western experience also continued to thrive and to structure the way that policy makers and western newcomers created their expectations and understood their experiences in the twentieth century.[14] African American Era Bell Thompson, for example, titled her autobiography of homesteading in the Dakotas *American Daughter*, as though that frontier experience rather than her birthplace legitimated her claims to Americanness. To lay claim to the West remained, in the most profound sense, as Thompson found, to claim to be "American." However, such claims flourished in the twentieth century within a new set of paradigms of race and citizenship that emerged not from the Mexican War, as in the nineteenth century, but from the Spanish-American War.

To just whom would the West provide its vaunted opportunity? Who would be cast as major players in its drama of the nation's future, and who would be consigned to bit parts or written out entirely? And above all, who would write the script? Would it be the nation-state? Or disaggregated collectives? Rebellious individuals, or some uneasy combination, perpetually fraught? The demarcating, agitating, speculating, and mobilizing that fill this volume were all manifestations of the contest—the attempt to map a particular future onto the western landscape. Different invocations of modernity called forth different notions of citizenship and indeed different citizens as its constituent parts.

In this period, the "frontier," with its seemingly limitless opportunity, became a place with borders. At the margins of their respective nations, borderlands can develop their own histories. They can and, as becomes apparent in this volume, they did become places where both ideas and people crossed national borders and refused the dictates of their central governments. "Borderlands" sets up a different paradigm for the history of the U.S. West than does the frontier, one that focuses on multidirectional flows and renarrates race, gender, capital formations, and nation in the making of the U.S. West. While Turner's frontier theory emerged in a context of nationalism and modernization, contemporary borderlands theory emerged instead in a context of transnationalism or postnationalism and postmodernism. Ironically, Turner's too was a day of global capitalism, when Dutch companies bought land grants in northern New Mexico and moved supervisors from Javanese plantations to manage them.[15] But the focus was on cementing a clear vision of the nation. National and imperial discourses demanded stabilized identities and clear categories. Such stability, such fixity, was part of what made them "modern."

Transnational flows of people, ideas, and capital can, by contrast, render identities unstable. The West from 1898 to 1940 was full of migrants, among them Sikhs and other South Asians in lumbering and farm labor, Japanese, Chinese, Germans, Greeks, Italians, Mexicans, and native-born U.S. citizens. Not all of them crossed national borders, but many did. They carried with them both ideas and goods. Their own political projects, their ways of understanding justice and hierarchy, crossed with them. What emerged was not an either/or identity—belonging to this homeland or that. What emerged was constant negotiation and multiple connection, creative appropriation of national identities and emblems. The migrants made common cause across national and other divides, and they refused to be bounded by an identity with a single nation-state or the increasing focus on borders, whether territorial or imagined, whether of Mexico, the United States, or Canada.[16]

This denial is precisely what allowed oppressed peoples and particularly migrant peoples to survive and pose an alternative future. Categories to these people and even to the federal government may have been essential, but they were more useful when they were fluid. As will become apparent in the succeeding chapters, the United States in this period moved the same people in and out of official national and racial categories at will. The nation they were creating was a project rather than a fact, rather than the imagined fixed entity. The migrants who created other visions of the region's future by both their movement and their actions disrupted and helped produce the modern nation.[17]

A running theme in this book is the tension between borders and borderlands, fixity and fluidity.[18] The new borderlands theory arose not only in the context of transnationalism but also in the context of Proposition 187 in California, which would have denied human services to undocumented immigrants, and of other nativist movements and a vastly increased border patrol. The idea of borderlands focuses on synergy, contests, and exchanges at a moment when border discourse is about exclusion, fear, safety, and "national security." Though they seem at odds, of course they constitute each other. Without borders, particularly policed borders, there are no borderlands.

As will become clear in succeeding chapters, this book is full of border crossers and border makers, official and unofficial. It includes federal and local officials who made and policed borders, as well as legal migrants. It includes vigilantes who patrolled the border, who constituted themselves the protectors of the nation and defined themselves by exclusion and domination, and migrants who crossed national and more abstract borders, who troubled the stark lines of demarcation and invoked a different kind of belonging and a different meaning for the region.

The book also recognizes that the borderlands is not a no-man's land—it is a contested masculinist space.[19] Manhood is continually evoked in these narratives. It was pervasively invoked at the time, from Teddy Roosevelt's faith in the frontier's ability to restore American manhood to vigor to white Populists living in Indian Territory claiming that their dependent status robbed them of manhood.

What this all meant for women was less clear. Almost every state west of the Mississippi granted women the vote before almost any state east of the river did. Yet that sense of women as equal partners, pervasive in agrarian movements in all parts of the nation, was not mirrored in other aspects of the region. The United States gave women access to homesteads more readily than did Canada, and Canadian women crossed into the United States seeking opportunity, but the U.S. government also considered women crossing into the United States more likely than men to become a public charge, a category that made them excludable.[20] Women in motion were seen as adventuring in the worst sense rather than the best. Not only were they more likely to become a public charge, they were more likely to become that other excludable category—a prostitute. No commensurate category banned men in motion. The nature of women's participation in both the material and mythic West proved more elusive and less secure and consistent than that of men.

On a resources frontier, the work available was largely men's extractive work (mining, farming, lumbering). Laboring men became the resource women extracted—men mined coal or copper, or silver or gold, and women mined men as prostitutes, boardinghouse keepers, and laundresses, for example, and sometimes as wives, teachers, or missionaries.[21]

Women traveled usually along the same circuits as men, if in smaller percentages, and they affected the ways men could organize and what they demanded, even when women did not organize separately and in their own right. The changes that rocked and/or were generated by working-class women are rarely integrated into the overarching narrative of the West. They are harder for the historian to see, but they are in the accounts of daily life. Ernesto Galarza's 1971 autobiography, *Barrio Boy*, covers most of the same years as this volume. He framed it with his mother's life—starting with her acquisition of a U.S.-made sewing machine in her Mexican village and ending with her death in the United States. In doing so, he created a narrative that linked global capital and women.[22]

The history of women in this volume is intimately tied to the national project that shaped the West and that the West helped shape. As they do in any racialized system, women became the bearers of the most pure expression of national identity and those with the most power to trouble it. In the United States, only women designated as white could bear white children. European American women could be missionaries, schoolteachers, bearers of the imperial message and of the national child, but they could create chaos by boundary crossing. Similarly, colonized women could signify to imperialists the need for empire (to protect them against their inadequate, primitive, and/or uncontained men) or seducers of imperialists, threatening their downfall. White women in Chinatown opium dens, for example, created moral panic. To deal with such threats, reformers increasingly succeeded in drawing boundaries around and cordoning off into set districts the West's sex trafficking. Western state laws against marriage between wildly differing designated groups proliferated. Montana in 1909 and Nebraska in 1913 banned marriage between whites and "Japanese" or "Chinese"; Missouri in 1909 and Idaho in 1921 banned marriage between whites and "Mongolians." Other Western states banned marriage between whites and "Malays," "Coreans," and/or "Hindus." Only five states west of the Mississippi had no such laws, and every state that did have such laws, among the other prohibitions, banned marriage between those they labeled white and those they labeled Black.[23] The delimiting symbolized, even where few such marriages occurred, the safeguarding of the imagined white race.

Defining borders went beyond policing individual behavior to creating a normative family. In the nineteenth century, this concern had meant, in part, opposing indigenous marriage practices, even marching couples, under armed guard, to a justice of the peace. In the twentieth century, the federal government wedded such concerns to health regimes erected in the colonies and brought home to the U.S. mainland. In new scientific discourses, health officials rendered the family structure of different groups of immigrants queer—out of the norm—by deploying a "science" of "race" and creating feminized men and overly fecund women, among other tropes, in groups they defined as racially "other." Rather than blame economic forces and legal restrictions, health officials blamed cultural and biological preferences and susceptibilities that led Japanese, Chinese, and Mexican immigrants to crowd together, that led women in those groups to have too many babies (and, in the case of the Chinese, for there to be sexually suspicious arrangements of too many men and too many prostitutes), and that led finally to too high an infant mortality rate (blamed on inadequate mothering and biological susceptibility to tuberculosis).[24] All sorts of action—intermarriage, white poverty, Black, Mexican, or Asian assertion—could endanger the security of white supremacy and so the legitimacy of empire. The modern empire required the fetishizing of borders.

Borderlands as a master narrative centers the edges and focuses on connection and contest rather than definitive conquest and the achievement of homogeneity. Borderlands inverts the site of invention, dynamism, players, and national identity. The migrations and displacements that create the borderlands are the products of the dramatically unequal processes of the frontier by uneven development and calculated incorporation. Borderlands and frontiers are in creative tension with each other; this is not a new binary of frontier or borderland, border or borderland. It is, instead, borders repeatedly redrawn and blurred.

This book proceeds in four parts. The first part, from roughly 1898 to 1910, attends to federal and local attempts to categorize and demarcate—to distinguish between modern man-made landscapes and the natural world; between the United States and its neighbors; between past and future; and among people by various means, including color, nativity, and sex—as a way to exert order and dominion over its territories and to make claims to and perform modernity on a wider stage.[25]

The second part follows challenges mounted to these purportedly neat categories, in particular, the 1910s radical democratic movements. The West experienced with particular ferocity the Mexican Revolution, strife between capital and labor (which contemporaries called "labor wars"), the woman suffrage movement, and the various rights movements surrounding the U.S. entry into World War I. The West also experienced a particularly ferocious repression of these movements, culminating in, among other places, Bisbee, Arizona; Houston, Texas; Everett, Washington; and Tulsa, Oklahoma.

The third part traces the shift from the movements for radical participatory democracy to an economic democracy characterized by easy access to speculative investment. Speculation was hardly new to the U.S. West, but in the 1920s the federal government encouraged, enabled, and tutored its citizens in the practice and took plunges itself, developing land on spec. Looking particularly at oil, land, and tourism, the part attends to the ways in which this state-endorsed speculation once again drew lines around past and future and defined a "modern" democracy and its participants with its attendant imprint on the land and the nation's borders.

The fourth and final part traces the mass mobilizations of the 1930s that simultaneously blurred and reinforced borders. It begins with the mass deportations of the late 1920s and continues through the mass labor and political movements of the middecade and the New Deal's resettling of people and animals.

By 1940 the West had taken on its contemporary contours. The region allowed the nation to develop a modern state with a modern state's capacities. It had federally owned resources unparalleled elsewhere in the nation; those resources, in turn, both required newly expanded bureaucracies to manage and financed that expansion. When western Populists in the 1890s had dreamed of their programs, they did not yet have the state that could enact and maintain them; it would take the progressives and the New Dealers (bureaucrats and technocrats) to build that state, and it would take the imagined blank slate of the West on which to build it. At the same time, the mass mobilizations of the era ensured the continued contest between frontier and borderlands and the determination of those excluded to share in and/or redefine the imaginary and the future.[26]

Part 1

Demarcating, 1898–1910

Historians can get obsessed with chronology. Did the twentieth-century West begin in 1893, when Frederick Jackson Turner declared the frontier closed? (How was he to know that more homesteads would be taken out after his pronouncement than before it?) Or did it begin in 1898, as I would argue, when the Spanish-American War redefined the role the West would play in the nation? In both cases, the issue is one of demarcation: How should the line that separates the nineteenth-century West from the twentieth-century West be drawn? It's a fitting dispute in some ways, since the early twentieth-century U.S. government was obsessed with demarcating. The government—its president, its congressmen, its bureaucrats—wanted to draw clear lines between the United States and Mexico and to enforce them, to police the border; it wanted to draw clear and yet inconsistent lines around who was or could be an "American," who belonged in what racial or ethnic categories the government invented; it wanted to draw lines between the "natural" world and man-controlled nature through conservation or irrigation.

All these distinctions served to mark the nation, to make an imagined, coherent community from a geographic entity. They enhanced both the illusion and the reality of governability, confusing the gathering and sorting of information with knowledge and control. The government and its allies enlisted new "sciences" of statistics, race, and anthropology, among others, and imposed the results on people and land. In the name of creating order out of chaos, the government replaced other systems of order. The process served as an emblem of the new nation's modernity. It served to validate the right of the United States to participate in the new nation-state-based imperialism, to be one of the family of white European empires along with Great Britain, France, and Germany, all engaged in similarly revising definitions of "race," "nation," and belonging.

In all these aspects of demarcation, the U.S. West played a special role. It was home to, in fact created by, the border with Mexico, which came to have a salience in this period that was entirely different from that of the border with Canada, so fraught in antebellum times. It was home to vast tracts of federally held lands on which new, large-scale experiments in controlling water—dams and irrigation—and forests and parks could be launched. It was home to the largest populations of Native Americans under federal governance, giving the federal government the power to define membership and civilization and to perform success as a caretaker of colonized peoples. And, like the Northeast in particular, it was home to a globally mobile population for whom national identity was not obvious. The following three chapters address different aspects of this process of demarcating. Chapter 1 turns to the enhanced demarcation between "man" and "nature," looking particularly at irrigation and conservation. Chapter 2 focuses on border crossers and hardening national borders. Chapter 3 uses the Black town of Boley, Oklahoma, to draw many of these threads together.

1

Man and Nature

When Frederick Jackson Turner declared the frontier closed in 1893, he based his declaration on the 1890 census finding that European American settlement had so spread over the western landscape that no single unbroken line separated what he defined as "civilization" from "savagery." In his influential address to the American Historical Association titled "The Significance of the Frontier in American History," he warned that the republic and its democracy were imperiled by the loss of the frontier. To many, the solution lay in empire and the creation of markets abroad, justifying the acquisitions of the Spanish-American War. Others found the conquest at home incomplete. To them, Americans had a choice. Conquer the Philippines, now waging a fierce anticolonial war against the United States as the successor to Spain in 1898, or conquer the arid lands at home. Consolidate the nation-state or go adventuring abroad. In 1898 a Nevada newspaper put it succinctly: "It is better and cheaper to reclaim land than to reclaim Filipinos."[1] In the end, the United States would make no such choice. It would complete its bloody conquest of the Philippines, and it would create an empire of irrigation at home.

In defining the nation's future, the West had as central a role as it had in defining the nation's past. On its vast tracts of federally held land, the government could launch large-scale experiments imposing its will on the region's water. Far from abandoning the idea of a line between "savagery" and "civilization," the government found in the region an arena where it could impose its will on both the landscape and its people and demarcate the border between the civilized and the "savage." Irrigation and preservation, the creation of dams and of wilderness areas, were part of the same project. This chapter turns first to the era's irrigation projects and then to conservation movements.

Irrigation

On the Great Plains, land suited to farming without irrigation was rapidly disappearing. Meanwhile, violent strikes raged in the industrial East, and rising tenancy and Populist unrest beset the West. Reclamation proponents saw the irrigated West as the solution. Arguing for federally funded irrigation, California lawyer George H. Maxwell wrote in 1899, "The wage-earners of the East want wider fields for labor. . . . The manufacturers of the East want new markets for their wares. Where can either get what they want so fully as by the development of the great arid West[?]" "Our irrigation empire," argued the president of the National Irrigation Congress in 1902, would give "a better chance to become useful men and women than boys and girls will have when raised in the city." Irrigation promised an ideal democracy of small-holders, ending the dire prospect of ever-increasing surplus labor, depressed wages, degraded workers, strikes and unemployment, urban and rural unrest. By 1900 both major political parties had proirrigation planks in their platforms.[2]

With such promises and urgency, it is not surprising that the history of irrigation in the twentieth-century West is the history of scientific hubris and unintended consequences. It is a story of an ambitious, burgeoning state, competing speculations, and the dismissal of local knowledge as atavistic. It is a story of great successes and costly failures. And in redistributing water, irrigation created a particular version of those elements that would be included in the West's future.

Americans were obsessed with the decline of farm ownership and the rise of tenancy throughout the country. In the West, large interests, often fueled by outside capital, gobbled up enormous acreage. Fraudulent use of homestead and other laws enabled corporations to scoop up holdings rich in coal and timber and control hundreds and thousands of acres of rangeland.[3] Cattle barons joined the rank of the Gilded Age's robber barons. They used similarly violent methods to control challengers and similarly monied efforts to control politics.

Things came to a head in the 1890s with the Johnson County Wars, fought in Wyoming between cattle barons and financial syndicates on the one side and small ranchers on the other. After a succession of cowboy strikes in the 1880s, large ranch owners had hired Pinkerton detectives and even created "dead lists," and with much the same language and tactics that white southerners were using in these peak lynching years to control Black labor in the South, they worked to eradicate cattle rustling and, inextricably, small ranchers, which many cowboys hoped to become.

The conflict culminated in 1892, the same year as the Pinkertons were involved in the great strike at Homestead, Pennsylvania. In that year, the stock growers recruited a small army of Texas gunslingers, who killed a local rancher, Nate Champion, and his partner, Nick Ray.

Two hundred angry citizens, sympathetic to Champion and Ray, responded to the sheriff's call for a posse. Meanwhile, the acting governor, with the help of one of the state's senators, called out the cavalry to protect the hired guns and bring them back to the cattle baron territory of Cheyenne, Wyoming.

The cattlemen hired good lawyers at an ultimate cost of $100,000. They spirited away the witnesses and strung out the case until the cost of feeding and housing the accused ($18,000) bankrupted Johnson County, a substantially poorer entity than the cattle barons. A Wyoming journalist fired off an account critical of the invaders only to have its publication legally suppressed in Wyoming. Copies were burned, and the author was driven out of the state.

Ten years later, the lesson that Owen Wister, friend to Teddy Roosevelt, drew in his spectacularly successful 1902 novel, *The Virginian,* favored scale over democracy. The hero of the novel is no lone individualist but a good ranch manager willing to work outside the law to serve the interests of his cattle baron boss against the forces of a too rampant democracy prone to acquit ranch hands who pilfered cattle from their bosses as the only way to enter the business.

Not everyone had drawn the same lesson. In the wake of those wars, a senator lost his seat in Congress, and Populists ousted Republicans from the state. The fear of monopoly at the turn of the century encompassed both the West and the East. In 1901

Alabama congressman Oscar Underwood, in a debate over irrigation, declared, "If this policy is not undertaken now, this great Western desert will ultimately be acquired by individuals and great corporations for the purpose of using it for grazing vast herds of cattle. They will acquire waterways and water rights for the purpose of watering stock and become land barons. Then it will be impossible to ever convert it into the homestead lands for our own people or to build up the population of this Western country." And, indeed, though the number of would-be homesteaders filing entries (the first step in claiming the land) on grazing lands more than tripled between 1898 and 1902, reaching sixteen million acres, as Underwood feared, ranchers controlled key water sites. By using public land as open range, these ranchers controlled vast swaths of the plains without having to fence or own anything but the watering hole.[4]

These cattle barons had no interest in converting public lands to private ownership—not their own, and particularly not others'. In the early twentieth century, they were just recovering from years of drought and low prices, a recovery aided by consolidation under such national syndicates as Swift & Company. Ranchers lobbied Congress for measures to safeguard their access to the open range in 1901 and 1902. They failed in that effort but ironically succeeded in cementing fears of a coming land monopoly, paving the way for federal irrigation legislation.[5]

Faced with declining opportunity to own arable land, even as Populism waned after its 1890s heyday, smallholders and those who wanted to join their ranks did not wait for federal action. Tenant farmers in Oklahoma Territory and Indian Territory joined the Socialist Party when it formed in 1901. They declared, "The renter is a slave. It makes no difference whether he is a subject of the Czar of Russia or an American citizen. His economic position is that of a slave." Others joined the Farmers Union, founded in 1902 in Texas. Impoverished dirt farmers, rural laborers, and their sympathizers made up the bulk of the membership. By 1905 the union had 120,000 members in Texas alone, with large memberships also in Arkansas, Oklahoma, and Indian Territory. Others still left the country altogether. A Canadian program begun in the late 1890s made it possible for irrigation companies to sell land at $5 to $8 per acre. It drew thousands of land-hungry U.S. residents, largely from the upper Midwest. Fifty thousand Americans took advantage of the program in 1902 alone.[6] These solutions found little favor in the halls of Congress. Senators and congressmen eager to build up the country hoped newly irrigated lands open for settlement would bring stability.

In the nineteenth century, the vast middle of the U.S. West, the area west of the one hundredth meridian, had been labeled the Great American Desert. It had been the place to which the U.S. government removed Indians, land it assumed U.S. settlers would not want. But irrigation had existed on this terrain long before Europeans set foot on the North American continent. In Arizona the Akimel O'odham harnessed the seasonal ebbs and flows of the Gila River to grow corn and cotton in the northern reaches of the Sonoran Desert as their ancestors had in the eleventh century. By the early nineteenth century, Hispano villagers in northern New Mexico and southern Colorado were electing mayordomos who oversaw collectively maintained and elaborate systems of ditches (acequias) and water gates. Early Mormon settlers established collective irrigation projects in Utah. Many of these communities continued to operate these systems well into the twentieth and even the twenty-first century.[7] Yet these sustainable, low cost, and democratic modes would not be the systems the federal government would choose to foster in the early twentieth century.

The federal foray into irrigation was not aimed at ameliorating the condition of what was seen to be a dying race of Native Americans. Rather, after one of the nation's, indeed the globe's, worst economic depressions, the administration's efforts arose from a determination to provide opportunity for working-class (and lower) white men, whom the West, after all, was destined to save along with the republic itself. New irrigation practices were predicated on the need to sustain opportunity for white workingmen and to do it on entrepreneurial white family farms. Indeed, the Newlands Act (1902) specified that "in all construction work eight hours shall constitute a day's work, and no Mongolian labor shall be employed thereon" and that the law's beneficiaries excluded "aliens ineligible for citizenship."[8]

The act bore the name of Nevada Democratic congressman Francis Newlands, a Populist, anti-imperialist native of Mississippi who favored a variety of progressive reforms. His vision of the United States as a white man's country would lead him later to suggest colonizing African Americans in the Caribbean and to urge the repeal of the Fifteenth Amendment. Some irrigation proponents favored a different approach. California's G. W. Burton acknowledged, "I may be speaking rank heresy on the Pacific Coast, but I don't care whether a man is black, yellow, or white, if he is *industrious*," but Newlands's was the more common view. A 1910 Medford, Oregon, booster of the irrigated Rogue River Valley bragged that it "is distinctly an American settlement . . . of the best class. There are no colonies of Japanese, Chinese, Hindoos, or Negroes to lower the standard of labor and of American civilization." On the Mexican border, the new "Valley Towns" created by the Lower Rio Grande Valley irrigation companies almost always had a section separating the overwhelmingly ethnic Mexican farm laborers from the new Anglo farmers, unlike the border towns that preceded them.[9]

Not only were the earlier irrigation systems in the wrong hands, they were largely outside the market. True, they had provided modest surpluses that allowed Native Americans to trade for Michigan copper and exotic South American feathers in the twelfth century and more recent practitioners to purchase modern cookstoves and sewing machines. These systems did not, however, fill railroad cars with commodities for eastern markets and raise the GNP.[10]

Finally, an irrigation system largely outside the market and shockingly bereft of machines could not stand as an emblem of the modernity of the region and the nation. It seemed more subordinate to nature than dominant. It lacked modern scientific expertise. Like the knowledge that generated it, its centralization was as local as its market. It belonged to a peasant past rather than a modern, nation-based, imperial future. R. L. Fulton, a Nevadan who favored irrigation, claimed in 1889, "We believe the Anglo-Saxon needs no example from Mexico, Spain or Lombardy, but will find in itself [*sic*] the intelligence, virtue, and grit to conquer this land as it has every country where it has ever set its foot."[11]

The arid West would provide a stage on which the United States could display its modernity in the guise of what it labeled "scientific knowledge." If the desert were not actually a blank slate, the irrigation project and its farmers would still wipe the slate clean, supplanting existing flora and fauna (sagebrush, greasewood, rabbitbrush, bunchgrass) with commercially viable alfalfa, potatoes, beets, and wheat. Cattle, sheep, pigs, and horses would replace jackrabbits (subject to collective rabbit hunts), coyotes, and deer—or so it was hoped.[12]

Westering Americans and immigrants had brought "modern" capital-based and capital-generating irrigation to the U.S. West in the mid-nineteenth century. Entrepreneurial schemes had begun to fill the California hinterland with privately financed irrigation systems that led to booms in the cultivation of fruit and vegetables. Spectacular profits resulted. In the 1870s San Joaquin Valley developer Timothy Paige paid sixty cents an acre for over 8,000 acres his neighbors deemed worthless. By the mid-1880s, when water became available, he sold 1,500 acres for nearly $90 an acre. Land in present-day Pasadena, California, sold for $7 an acre in the 1870s and returned as much as $1,000 per acre from its orchards within ten years. California was not alone. In the early 1890s farmers in Greeley, Colorado, and Yakima County, Washington, saw land values rise more than 90 percent thanks to irrigation.[13]

As these successes showed, not all irrigation in the West required federal aid. In 1898 one Robert Kleberg, while digging deep wells on his Santa Gertrudis ranch in South Texas, discovered an aquifer three times the size of Connecticut. The same year, farmer T. C. Nye experimented with planting Bermuda onions in Dimmit County, about one hundred miles northwest of Kleberg's ranch, and earned not the $10 to $15 he usually got per acre from cotton but over $1,000 per acre. Buoyed by Nye's findings, South Texas ranchers, faced with plummeting prices of livestock and persistent drought, broke their ranches into hundreds of small irrigated farm tracts. The sons of local rancher and former sheriff James G. Browne, for example, formed the Santa Helena Improvement Company in the early 1900s, selling small farm plots from their million plus acres in Cameron County. Over the next decades, aided by the aquifer and the burgeoning railroad lines, the number of farms exploded, while their size diminished.[14] Such an example, like the small irrigated farms of California, seemed proof positive of the efficacy of irrigation to provide opportunity for smallholders.

Most of the arid West, however, did not sit on such naturally abundant water. It would require more capital to develop, and success was far from universal. Private irrigation schemes had proven highly risky, particularly in years of depression and drought. According to agricultural economist Samuel Fortier in 1907, "95 per cent of the capital invested in canal enterprises from 1885 to 1895 produced no dividends and much of it was entirely lost." Companies built enormous projects costing well over half a million dollars, only to find few settlers. Even when drought did not rob the irrigation project of its waters, the settlers took years to bring in a crop worth enough to pay construction costs. Bankrupt companies could abandon their projects if they could not sell them (they often sold at a small fraction of the construction cost). The project might ultimately turn a handsome profit, but often not for the original investors. State-sponsored attempts in California, Nevada, and Colorado in the last decades of the nineteenth century fared little better. They, too, fell victim to insufficient funds, personnel, laws, and knowledge. Finally, private irrigation schemes had utterly failed to resolve legal issues regarding distribution. Residents of Arizona's Salt River Valley claimed to have rights to twenty-five times the water the river held. In September 1898 the Boise River carried thirty-five thousand miner's inches of water, but 151 residents claimed rights to over six million.[15]

In the face of these failures stood the Progressive Era's dauntless faith in modern engineering. As the most desirable properties for irrigation filled and private capital proved elusive, and in the context of continued immigration and urban and industrial unrest, the promoters of federally funded irrigation promised that it alone would keep the West open for the common man. They wrapped their fears of national decline in dreams of progress.

Irrigation promoters had to link irrigation to social reform because they knew irrigation could not pay for itself. By the century's end, there had been too many examples of failed irrigation schemes to attract new private capital, so irrigation promoter George Maxwell cultivated allies. He collected endorsements from a diverse array of organizations, including the Chicago Federation of Labor, the National Business League, the National Association of Manufacturers, the United Mine Workers, and others. One such ally was James J. Hill, railroad baron of the Great Northern and Northern Pacific. Hill knew that the nation's population growth far outstripped the growth in its wheat production (63 percent versus 25 percent) and was unsympathetic to eastern fears of agricultural competition. He feared revolution, and he also feared declining profits. In 1900 the Northern Pacific owned over thirteen million acres of land in Montana alone. During the drought from 1898 to 1901, the Red River Valley's famed wheat crop had declined by 50 percent, resulting in plummeting freight revenues. The Northern Pacific and other western lines contributed $30,000 a year to Maxwell's campaign. By early 1902 many major eastern newspapers favored federal reclamation, and so, it seemed, did everyone else. The Newlands Act passed with little debate.[16]

Irrigation promoters posed the arid West as a blank landscape, "manless, homeless, weedless, bugless," according to the *Idaho Republican* in 1907, a place where the farmer could "put everything on the land just to his liking." It was the perfect place to demonstrate the power of American modernity and its scientific knowledge. The *Twin Falls News* in 1904 declared, "Irrigation is the science of farming. . . . Rainfall farming is accidental farming." Four years earlier, Idaho's state engineer, D. W. Ross, claimed irrigation would allow farmers to "laugh at cloudless skies," having "much needed moisture under perfect control."[17]

Dry farming was not dead, it just was not sexy. In the same drought-ridden decade when the battle for federal irrigation funding was reaching a successful climax, Hardy Campbell began publishing on dry farming. In the 1890s, supported by railroads, he conducted experiments in the Dakotas and other plains states. Dry farming included mulching, deep plowing, soil compacting, and thin seeding. Unfortunately for Campbell, however, according to historian Donald Pisani, "dry farming preached the recognition of natural limits; irrigation emphasized the unlimited potential of western agriculture." Given the political imperatives of the age, dry farming was not likely to unseat irrigation. In 1893, when Campbell published his first pamphlet and Turner declared the frontier closed, the International Irrigation Congress met in

Los Angeles under a banner reading "Irrigation: Science, Not Chance." Claiming the mantle of science allowed those favoring irrigation to appropriate the dominant reform discourse of the era, with its faith in science and linking of science to modernity, science as the vehicle through which all ills of the age could be conquered.[18]

Dreams of this perfect convergence led Idaho's population to double between 1890 and 1900 and then again between 1900 and 1910, reaching a total of 325,000. Mormons, Quakers, Mennonites, Japanese, Germans from Russia, Indians on the Fort Hall Reservation, and other farmers from the South, Midwest, and Great Plains claimed land under the federal Carey Act of 1894, which granted up to a million acres of federally held public land to each of ten states or territories, provided the state or territory reclaimed the land and sold it to settlers (not speculators) in parcels of at most 160 acres, and the Newlands Reclamation Act of 1902, which authorized the secretary of the interior to construct reservoirs in the arid West financed by a fund from public land sales in those states and territories. As with the Carey Act, the public lands in the projects were for settlers only and in lots of at most 160 acres. Water users had to repay construction costs over ten years and continue to pay water costs. Unlike the Carey Act, the Newlands Act reserved major control of the projects and the land to the federal government and not the states. That decision, though fiercely contested by many of the states during the battle for the bill's passage, further reflected a vision of a modern, centralized state that established scientific knowledge, planning, and control over its dominion.[19] The West, in short, became a showcase for the nation's claim to be a modern state and its right to participate in modern, nation-state-based imperialism along with the European powers.

But this was no vision imposed on an unwilling western populace. The Newlands Act passed in the form it did partly because of the increasing strength of the region in the Senate: by 1900 the West provided 30 percent of the votes in that body. Western senators argued strenuously that the region had benefited proportionately little from the increase of federal spending on river and harbor infrastructure since the Civil War. Indeed, the 1899 bill funding those facilities provided only $2 million for the West but $28 million for the East. Failing to convince the Senate by other means, finally Senator Thomas Carter of Montana launched a twelve-hour filibuster of the 1901 Rivers and Harbors Bill. He succeeded. There was no rivers and harbors bill in 1901.[20] As a result, 1902 would bring the Newlands Act.

Little better illustrates the progressive vision, grandeur, and pitfalls of these schemes than ultimate western empresario Buffalo Bill Cody's attempts to partake of them. After his Wild West show's 1894 season ended, Cody headed back to Sheridan, Wyoming, where he owned an inn managed by his son-in-law. Together with a group of businessmen from New York and Omaha, he and his son-in-law invested in the latest of a long string of Cody's speculations, dating back to the 1880s. Envisioning a bustling basin that would double Wyoming's population, each partner contributed $5,000 to the Shoshone Land and Irrigation Company. Like so many speculators, they expected a railroad imminently to link their isolated valley to the world's markets. Cody dreamed big. He declared, "I propose to leave a monument of my work for the West by founding a colony in the Big Horn basin . . . which shall be to Wyoming what the Greeley Colony is to Colorado." By the end of 1896, however, the railroad had failed to appear, the company had spent $80,000 constructing fifteen miles of ditch, and only a dozen farmers had purchased land, watering about four hundred acres. While their application was wending its way through the secretary of the interior's office, moreover, other speculators had filed on about a thousand acres of the best land. Desperate for capital, the company sold bonds to Phoebe Hearst, the California heiress, at a 10 percent discount.

Despite ever better deals promised by the company to settlers, including perpetual water rights, a share in the company, and spectacular yields, and despite the company's attempt to entice philanthropic organizations to settle their constituents—from socialists to members of the Salvation Army—settlers refused to materialize. Cody poured profits from Buffalo Bill's Wild West show into the company to keep it afloat through the 1890s. He continued to develop the town of Cody, building a house, hotel, general store, and school, and he subsidized a newspaper. Turning himself into a commodity, he lured wealthy investors to the valley on hunting trips and promised to retire in the valley.

While Cody promised, "Yes, Cody will be a western metropolis and no mistake," in 1900 his Shoshone Land and Irrigation Company sold most of its water rights for $12 less per acre than the water cost to provide. In late 1901 the Burlington and Missouri Railroad finally extended its line to Cody. By then, despite Cody's eternal optimism, the other investors had lost interest and would neither extend nor maintain the ditches. Only the passage of the Newlands Act in 1902 and the amendment that made private lands eligible for inclusion in federal projects rescued Cody. Cody sold much of the land to the federal government, which irrigated the land and built the Buffalo Bill Dam eight miles southwest of the town of Cody, finally leading the basin's population to more than triple between 1900 and 1910. The federal government's Bureau of Reclamation spent almost $26 million to water less than one hundred thousand acres. In Cody's posthumously published autobiography of 1920, he claimed, "All my interests are still with the West—the modern West."[21] Modernity was expensive.

Cody's losses paled before those of the California Development Company and railroad mogul Edward Harriman's Southern Pacific Railroad. Their attempts to control the Colorado River in the Imperial Valley involved cross-border negotiations and recurrent floods that washed away jetties and dams. A flood in 1905 breached the riverbank, creating a four-hundred-square-mile inland sea with forty-foot-high waterfalls. In response, two thousand largely conscripted Native Americans from six tribes built a rock dam that also failed. Next, three thousand railroad cars spent two weeks carrying and dumping 5,765 loads of rock into the chasm; the river breached that wall in 1907. Tensions rose between Mexican and U.S. users of the Colorado River, between local users and the company, and between the company and the Bureau of Reclamation, which tried at one point to take over the project and the company. President Roosevelt's fury at the company's machinations and congressional resistance to bailing out a private company left the project's settlers literally on uncertain ground as the Mexican revolution began.[22]

There continued to be large-scale private-sector (like Bill Cody's and Harriman's) and state irrigation projects. As historian Mark

Fiege has written, however, despite the irrigators' conviction that they were somehow both conquering and working with nature, coaxing rivers into a different cycle and sometimes bed, they "never achieved the mastery that they promised. Behind their extravagant claims lay a complicated, difficult landscape in which farms did not function like laboratories and irrigators did not even attain their most basic objective: freedom from drought." The irrigators believed in their own technical expertise and that they were simply bringing nature to its full potential. This was the twentieth-century version of Manifest Destiny. Irrigation would "complete Nature," as the *Twin Falls* paper put it in 1904, to allow the U.S. West to continue to provide opportunity for the common (white) man and so allow the nation to escape the degradation and unrest of Europe.[23] But nature proved a fickle partner with its own destiny.

With the greater capital and technology of new federal projects and the appointment of state engineers in most western states, success seemed more assured. Their engineering expertise and funds did not, however, protect them from the vagaries of nature. Riverbeds shifted. Droughts persisted. Canals and reservoirs seeped and leaked into porous lava rock and soil, sometimes creating swamps out of fields. Since rivers often crossed state and national boundaries, states and even nations argued over water rights.[24]

Even the best-conceived plans for water distribution and appropriation shredded under such stress. With little water to distribute, was it better to distribute an inadequate supply to all users or to deliver sufficient water to very few? Older doctrines of prior appropriation favored those upriver; other doctrines that bound water rights to adjacent property rights created their own difficulties; and no one could effectively separate the stored water of the reclamation project from the stream water, though they measured them differently—in static measure (acre-feet) as opposed to flow (cubic feet per second).[25] From 1900 to 1910 farmers and irrigation companies filled the courts with lawsuits, while users created extralegal means on a daily basis.

In this uncertain environment, ambitious irrigation projects, particularly sizable dams, could take over a decade to break ground. Planning began for a Central Valley, California, dam in 1900 on the Upper San Joaquin River watershed, following a drought that had bankrupt the hydroelectric company serving Fresno. After hydraulic engineer John Eastman spent substantial hours moving hand over hand along cables strung thousands of feet above gorges and canyons trying to survey likely dam sites whose power could serve San Francisco and Los Angeles, as well as Fresno, after filing countless reports and trying to satisfy funders, including Henry Huntington, railroad heir and electric power and real estate tycoon, who blew hot and cold on the project, construction would not begin until the decade closed. Elephant Butte Dam in southern New Mexico, among the first substantial projects built under the Newlands Act, ran afoul of rivalries between downstream El Paso, Texas, and Las Cruces, New Mexico, after exhausting a variety of local, private, and public funding and location schemes that began even before the 1902 act and only finally completed construction in 1916.[26]

By the end of Theodore Roosevelt's presidency in 1909, the reclamation service had supported the creation of thirty irrigation projects containing about three million acres, including three projects on Indian reservations. Ironically, many of those acres had been irrigated already before 1902, and the three million were far fewer than the sixty to one hundred million promoters had promised. Moreover, about 30 percent of the project land remained vacant.

In attempting to restore opportunity to the smallholder, Newlands had opened fewer acres than imagined and had also failed to solve the dramatic rise in the price of farming—in which the cost of land was often the least of the expenses relative to the cost of irrigation, fencing, machinery, livestock, and buildings. Speculators raised the price of land, and irrigation raised the price of water. Tunneling through the mountains to bring the Gunnison's water to the Uncompahgre project, for example, raised the cost per acre of water from $9 to $30 by 1910, $50 in 1915, and $125 in 1925. Farmers who entered a project in Boise, Idaho, having understood the cost to be $25 per acre, found instead that at the end of construction the cost to the farmer was $80 per acre. This was not a new problem. In southern Idaho, settlers had started forty-two separate projects under the 1894 Carey Act, but the government engineers underestimated the costs and overestimated the amount of water, as they would continue to do, leaving farmers with vastly inflated taxes.[27]

Nor had Newlands resolved the problem of myriad competing constituencies in managing the water. Such conflicts often ended with the displacement of prior communities. In Tres Alamos, Arizona, community irrigation projects on the San Pedro River had crossed ethnic lines. Arizona had adopted Mexico's water doctrine of prior appropriation. Since the earliest farming settlers in the area were Mexicans, it behooved incoming Anglos to partner with them. John Montgomery owned his ditch with the Ruíz family and Antonio Grijalba. The Madríd family owned their ditch with the Dunbars. Digging a mile-long ditch could foster camaraderie. Families intermarried.[28]

Things had begun to change as early as the 1880s with the arrival of the railroad and a Mormon community upriver called St. David. The Mormon community's use of water depleted supplies for those downriver. In 1908 St. David's Mormons and a local politician created the Benson Canal Company. The Benson Canal, completed in 1912, dwarfed other irrigation efforts on the San Pedro River. With its water, a new Mormon community, Pomerene, blossomed. It sat across the river from Tres Alamos. The farmers of Tres Alamos found their water dwindling despite their technical "first rights." Their farms, as a result, began to fail. Government officials turned a blind eye. By 1920 Pomerene had fifty-two households, and Tres Alamos had nearly disappeared. Mexican American women and men would continue to farm and to take out homesteads, but in nearby Cascabel, Arizona, they would build a community more homogeneous and insular than that of Tres Alamos. Elsewhere, older patterns of collaborative, nonmarket, noncash irrigation projects often continued, but even when they existed largely outside market agriculture, the advent of higher taxes, let alone taxes for the reclamation projects if people were users, made it difficult for people who had lived in the area on other terms to survive. It was one of many avenues through which a diverse and multilayered past became a white man's West.[29]

People had named irrigation canals after the communities that carved them from the land, such as the People's Canal (1894) or the Farmers' Own Ditch Company (1896), or even after individuals or pairs of farmers, such as the Nielsen-Hansen or the Mace-Catlin. Those practices gave way to more corporate names, such as the Enterprise Canal Company (1903), created when farmers floated bonds to finance larger-scale irrigation and hire the hundreds of laborers it demanded. Some of the workers might be off-season farmers or their sons, but many more were itinerant contract laborers, Greeks, Austrians, Danes, Bohemians, Italians, Canadians, Irish, Japanese, Bulgarians, French, and others who could rarely become farm owners.[30] The canals and the labor to maintain them no longer reflected the preexisting communities.

Similar developments in South Texas found Anglo farmers coming en masse into new irrigation projects. The new arrivals contested the power of political bosses. The bosses were ranchers, often scions of mixed Mexican and Anglo families, who relied on Mexican voters. In 1903 the new residents helped make the direct primary law; in 1904 the State Democratic Executive Committee approved the practice of the White Man's Primary Association by suggesting county committees require primary voters to affirm, "I am a white person and a Democrat," effectively excluding most of the state's Mexican-heritage U.S. citizens.[31] By such practices, large-scale commercial and public irrigation projects narrowed what constituted appropriate economic and political participation in the region's future.

The constant struggle between extant farmers, new investors of various scales, and speculators converged in central Arizona's Salt River and its federal irrigation project. The valley was filled with existing small-acreage farms and fractious, cautious, but organized landowners who had long used the abandoned irrigation ditches of the ancient Hohokam. By 1900 the valley's Maricopa County had 20,457 residents farming about 113,000 acres with water from ten major canals. An Old Settlers Protective Association determined, from its founding in 1898, to protect the rights of prior appropriators in the face of any new capital-intensive irrigation schemes, rendering any such project unappealing to private investors.[32]

While just over half the Salt River farmers held 160 acres of irrigated land each, some held as many as 2,000 acres. For those wanting more consistent water supplies and more development, the Newlands Act was heaven-sent. Thanks to a late amendment, it would not only develop newly irrigated lands open for homesteading but also benefit extant farmers. The farmers split into two factions, "business" and smallholders. Both factions had at their head influential, well-connected easterners who had moved to the valley in the late nineteenth century for their health. On the business side was Dwight B. Heard, who had thousands of acres at stake and financial connections in Chicago and who was friend and ally of both Teddy Roosevelt and Gifford Pinchot. On the smallholder side was Benjamin Fowler, graduate of Phillips Academy and Yale University, formerly a publisher with Dodd, Mead and Company in New York and then with his own publishing house in Chicago.[33]

For over two years after the act passed, local landowners, with factions led by Heard in the interests of "business" and Fowler for the smallholder, struggled to come to an agreement. They fought over what constituted democratic practice and accountability. They disagreed over how to balance the financial requirements of the project, the desire to keep speculators from having any authority over the project, the needs of existing landowners of various size using the land in various ways (both ranching and farming), and the desire that those who took the risk by investing in shares of the project would benefit from their investment in cash and water and retain some control over both. They had no precedent on which to build.

The risks were considerable. Farmers guaranteed the government repayment of project costs by mortgaging their farms. Small farmers risking everything watched costs mount. They operated in an arena of extreme uncertainty. Even three years into the planning, they still had no firm sense of how much acreage would be served by the project. They resented absentee investors, including eastern companies that demanded high fees for the dam site. Bitter negotiations led a Phoenix daily to claim, "Few people believe . . . that these New Yorkers with a Phoenix assistant have any moral right to recover from the people of this section the money they spent in promoting a scheme of which they made a failure." Meanwhile, the river took matters into its own hands. In early 1905 the Salt River raged, washing out a 100-foot section of the twenty-eight-year-old, 1,100-foot Arizona Dam.[34]

The disaster seemed the necessary spur to move forward. Potential users found sufficient common ground to create the Salt River Valley Water Users Association. Its board was elected by eligible water users: those whose acreage to be watered by the project was fewer than 160 acres. Larger holders could own stock in the project but not vote. The sympathetic new territorial governor was simultaneously the attorney for the association. The project broke ground in 1905.[35]

In the end, the project produced not just a water storage facility with the potential for generating hydroelectric power but also a cement mill to provide for the innovative poured concrete pipes, 112 miles of permanent roads, a necessarily remote construction camp complete with electric and telephone lines, a vegetable garden, bath houses, and a small hospital.[36] Some local towns, including Mesa, Phoenix, and Tempe, had passed bonds to help defray the cost of the roads. Mexican and Apache workers poured the concrete. The required predam construction took until 1909. The dam finally stood complete in February 1911.

Along the way, the project had doubled its capacity, providing hydroelectric power and other improvements not in the original plan. Most landowners had enthusiastically lobbied for the expansion but apparently had not understood the impact on costs. The original estimate for the entire Salt River Project had stood at $3.75 million; by 1912 it was instead $10.5 million, with repayment by the farmers due to start. While all seemed to agree that the newly named Roosevelt Dam, the highest in the world, was a magnificent achievement, the farmers demanded a federal investigation of the costs. Farmers with preexisting water rights objected to the vastly inflated costs of their water. Typical was a Mrs. J. W. Stewart of Mesa, who, foreseeing the problem, wrote Teddy Roosevelt in 1908 explaining that she and her husband were both over fifty-five, with three daughters and a forty-acre farm. Her husband taught school for $600 a year and now faced project repayment costs of $1,200 to $1,600 per year in addition to water dues of $50 to $100 per year, irrigation expenses, regular farm labor, and taxes. Large landowners could sell surplus lands worth more than before the reclamation program, a luxury unavailable to small farmers. The projected per-acre repayment had more than doubled over the course of construction. Even allowing for the sale of hydroelectricity to apply to the reclamation fund debt, the costs outstripped the ability of many farmers to repay.[37]

By 1910 almost all the government-sponsored irrigation projects needed more cash, some as much as $2 million. Without the cash, the projects sat unfinished, and repayment could not commence. Congress agreed with President Taft's recommendation to loan the reclamation fund $20 million to be repaid with interest. Meanwhile, the head of the Reclamation Service continued to see the failure to adhere to a strict repayment program as a moral failure of the farmers, eliminating the "unfit" and speculator. It was as though he and his ilk believed that the ability to engineer a dam, what historian Karen Smith has called an "over-emphasis on the engineering side," was enough to create viable agriculture, regardless of crop prices and the nature of the land.[38]

Such irrigation projects did indeed fuel the region's population growth. Homestead claims rose, and populations in some counties tripled or rose even further from 1900 to 1910. Cheyenne County, Colorado, grew by 635 percent during the decade. Texas panhandle farms doubled, and the population quadrupled. Ultimately, the dam at Salt River allowed Phoenix to boom, though perhaps not with the originally intended yeoman farmers, and at least as much because of the hydroelectric power as the water storage. Over the next decades thousands of new acres came into cultivation both within the project served by the dam and outside it where the dam's hydroelectric power raised water from the aquifer. Major corporations, including Goodyear Rubber and Southwest Cotton Company, invested in the region.[39]

The earlier inhabitants of the land did not disappear. The Akimel O'odham and Maricopa sued the Salt River farmers who diverted the tribes' water.[40] But the land, the people who farmed it, and the way they farmed conformed more closely to the vision of those who framed the federal program. Project after project, across the West, resulted in the displacement of prior inhabitants, often but not always people of color who had successfully occupied the land for decades, even centuries. This was indeed modernity inscribed on the landscape, theoretically the triumph of science over nature, the Progressive Era's engineering of man and land.

Conservation

Not only farmers, developers, and ambitious politicians felt the West's thirst in the early twentieth century, but the region's burgeoning cities did as well. Los Angeles and San Francisco provide two examples with dramatically different results. Both cities struggled between private and public interests. But San Francisco's search for water set the stage for an epic early conservation battle that highlighted the ways in which irrigation, conservation, and preservation were all manifestations of the same demarcating impulse: to create artificial boundaries around what was pristine nature and what was human landscape, what was modern and scientific, and what was primitive and natural.

Los Angeles residents had lost patience with the city's private monopoly water company. They established the Board of Water Commissioners in 1903 and determined to hold on to city water rights unless two-thirds of qualified electors decided otherwise.[41] The city's population had doubled during the 1890s to one hundred thousand, and as it nearly doubled again by 1904, water superintendent William Mulholland quietly searched for new water sources.

However quietly he searched, others saw the writing on the wall. Mulholland, an Irish immigrant, scrappy former merchant seaman, and ditch digger, took on his erstwhile employer, former Los Angeles mayor Fred Eaton. Eaton, an engineer, had helped create Los Angeles City Water and had connections in the Reclamation Service.[42] Eaton, Mulholland, and the Reclamation Service had all done reconnaissance, and all landed on the Owens River, on the east side of the Sierra Nevada about 235 miles north of Los Angeles. The Reclamation Service had withdrawn all public lands in the area to protect them for a publicly owned Los Angeles water project and shared its studies with Mulholland. But Eaton had secured rights from a privately held ranch that boasted the valley's only possible reservoir site. The city had no choice but to fork over twice the property's value for a perpetual easement in 1905. The deal made Eaton rich, but the city would have water.

Congress granted the right-of-way on public lands in 1906, voters approved $23 million in funding in 1907, and construction began in 1908. Unlike the Salt River Valley, the project came in on time and within budget, with the first water reaching Los Angeles in 1913, by which time the population had reached five hundred thousand. Only the municipality had access to the water, leading to a pattern of annexation that tripled the city's size to 285 square miles by the end of 1915.[43] Mulholland became the highest-paid public official in the state.

San Francisco, on the other hand, faced not just a monopoly water company and land speculators but also rising interest in wilderness. The best site for San Francisco lay in a remote valley, just as it did for Los Angeles, and that valley (in this case, Yosemite) lay largely in public hands. But unlike the Owens Valley, Yosemite had already earned notoriety. The federal government had granted it status as a state park in 1864. Wilderness advocate John Muir, watching the plunder and neglect of the park, lobbied in 1890 to have Yosemite given back to the federal government for the park's greater protection. Congress responded to Muir by creating a federal reserve (later called a park) of the forest surrounding the state park, which left the state park intact but meant federal troops would protect its surroundings.[44]

As did the stock growers in Wyoming and farmers along the Salt River, however, local constituents had their own ideas. Rising rage from voters in the cattle, sheep, and timber industries at the withdrawal of land from the public domain led their congressman to mount the first of a series of challenges to the new forest boundary line.

The congressman's attempt to diminish the newly protected federal forests surrounding Yosemite State Park spurred Muir to found the Sierra Club in 1892. Scientists, particularly earth and life scientists, dominated the club's leadership for more than a decade (1892–1905).[45] In the irrigation movement, science weighed in on the side of making dramatic changes to the land. Science in this fight, by contrast, started on the side of wilderness.

Sierra Club members rallied to defend the boundaries on two seemingly contradictory grounds: future use and permanent preservation. They warned of possible damage to commercially significant watersheds, forests, and reservoir sites and to the unique geologic and scenic features. Muir called the eighty thousand sheep that grazed in the park "hoofed locusts." The club lobbied to preserve the park's value as a scientific and recreational resource of greater significance than lumber and sheep. After over a decade of lobbying on all sides, the Sierra Club won. In 1906 Yosemite and its forest became a single national park.[46] But that turned out to be the beginning rather than the end of the fight.

The battle exposed tensions within the forestry community. In 1896 Congress had "authorized the National Academy of Sciences to appoint a Forestry Commission to tour the national forest reserves and recommend an overall policy." Harvard professor Charles Sargent chaired the commission. As a botanist, he favored preservation of species. He was also an ally of Muir. A generation younger (at age twenty-nine), Gifford Pinchot was also a member of the commission. Though he admired Muir and was a Sargent protégé, his study in Europe had introduced him to scientific forestry, the idea that trees could be managed like other crops—grown and harvested for a sustainable yield. Nothing could be more at odds than Sargent's (and Muir's) notion that forests needed to be protected by the U.S. Army from human intervention.[47]

The commission had recommended in February that President Cleveland create thirteen new forest reserves in the West, which Cleveland did, ten days before leaving office. As usual, federal plans to remap the West fell afoul of local interests. The commission's well-educated members of elite families (Sargent was a Harvard professor and Boston Brahmin; Gifford, from a prominent Pennsylvania family, went to Yale) made them targets for western congressmen. Under their pressure, Congress passed an amendment that suspended the reserves for almost a year, allowing time for those who claimed land within the reserves to apply for comparable acreage in the public domain outside them and prohibiting the inclusion of valuable mining or agricultural land in the reserves. The Forestry Commission, including Pinchot, to Muir's disgust, supported the amendment as better than torpedoing the reserves entirely. Pinchot became the Interior Department's "confidential forest agent" to reform reserve policy, and on July 1, 1898, he became chief forester.[48]

Meanwhile, private acquisition of the nation's forests continued. In 1900 Frederick Weyerhauser of Minneapolis bought nine hundred thousand acres of timber from the Northern Pacific Railroad. By 1913 Weyerhauser would own more than a quarter of all timberlands in Washington and just under one-fifth of those in Oregon. The Northern Pacific held on to 30 percent of the timberlands in Montana.[49] Corruption ran rampant. Large corporations paid often transient individuals to take out homestead claims; the corporations then stripped the land of timber and five years later let the land revert to the federal government. Foresters began to warn of a coming "timber famine."

The federal government tried to outpace the speculators and fraudulent homesteaders by withdrawing millions of acres of forest land pending investigation. But the forests lay under the purview of the Department of Agriculture, which had no foresters. The Department of the Interior had foresters but no forest reserves. Finally, in 1905 Gifford Pinchot won control of the federal forest for the Department of the Interior and created the Forest Service.[50]

What has all this to do with water? By 1900 the residents of San Francisco, like the residents of Los Angeles, had had it with the water monopoly's stranglehold on the city. In that year San Francisco's new city charter, approved by the California legislature, mandated municipal ownership of utilities. With the monopoly (Spring Valley Water Company) demanding an outrageous price for its dwindling water supply, the city needed to find an alternative.

While Congress considered a bill to permit the construction of pipelines and water conduits through federal forest reserves, San Francisco mayor James Phelan secretly dispatched the city engineer (Carl Grunsky, also a Sierra Club member) to survey possible water sources. The congressional bill became law in 1901, and the city administration chose to focus on Hetch Hetchy Valley, a steeply walled, U-shaped valley complete with spectacular waterfall fifteen miles northwest of the Yosemite Valley, within the national park. The valley was perfect. Its steep walls made it a good candidate for a dam, it was remote enough to remove pollution as an issue, since it was in the public domain there would be no title nightmares, and, finally but significantly, it would generate hydroelectric power.[51]

At first, Washington DC saw things differently. The secretary of the interior denied the city's petition to dam Hetch Hetchy three times between January 1903 and February 1905. The secretary held that the 1890 mandate to preserve nature in the creation of Yosemite National Park remained paramount, despite the 1901 Right of Way Act.

But the city's lobbyists—foremost among them Sierra Club member and civil engineer Marsden Manson—were getting to Pinchot and Roosevelt. Like Muir, Manson favored preserving watershed forests to regulate water. Unlike Muir, he favored doing so by constructing reservoirs.[52] Thus began the battle that would not be resolved until the end of 1913, nearly a decade later.

Weighing in on the preservation side were not only Muir and the Sierra Club as an entity but also an array of mobilized women. They included those who mobilized as scientists, such as Alice Eastwood, curator of botany for the California Academy of Sciences and an active Sierra Club member who had led a successful campaign to create and maintain a state park for Mount Tamalpais, north of San Francisco. They also included those who mobilized as club women, usually elite nonprofessionals, including Carrie Stevens Walter of the San Jose Women's Club and Mrs. Lovell White of the California Club, instrumental in the successful campaign to create a state park to protect redwoods in Big Basin. That latter campaign had linked the women's clubs with the Sierra Club for the first time. It also marked the increasing emergence of women's organized lobbying as the women's club movement consolidated its myriad organizations into state federations across the country.[53]

The women's clubs tended to work with local officials, using connections and diplomacy, as well as publicity and alliances. Under Muir, the Sierra Club often instead used strong, sometimes polarizing, language and the national stage.[54] "Dam Hetch Hetchy!" wrote Muir in 1908. "As well dam for water-tanks the people's cathedrals and churches, for no holier temple has ever been consecrated by the heart of man." He accused those who threatened it of serving "the Prince of the powers of Darkness" and the "Almighty Dollar."[55]

Women's clubs and the preservationists largely differed in styles and tactics, but the proponents of a Hetch Hetchy reservoir succeeded in linking the two groups in the least flattering light. Though there were scientists, including women scientists, among the reservoir's opponents, and though there were women's clubs in favor of the reservoir, the San Francisco newspapers cast all the opponents as effeminate sentimentalists. Women's groups helped make the dam proposal a national issue by deploying a variety of rhetorical tactics, from claims of expertise to attacks on market mentalities. Yet their opponents cast them all as impractical, misguided, and hysterical. They lauded the dam's proponents, in contrast, as men of science, engineers whose credentials they listed at length.[56]

Muir and the preservationists wedded preservation to an ideology of evolution, seeing their opponents as those not yet sufficiently evolved to understand that "everybody needs beauty as well as bread, places to play in and pray in where Nature may heal and cheer and give strength to body and soul alike."[57]

In return, Muir's opponent Manson privately joined ideas of manhood, modernity, science, and development, describing his opponents as "short-haired women and long-haired men." To Manson, real men dominated nature, they did not worship it. By the early twentieth century, nature, religion, and sentiment had all been feminized. When San Francisco newspapers cast the opposition as sentimentalists in an era when most women still did not have the vote, they cast Muir and his allies as inappropriate participants in the development politics of the West. When the Sierra Club tried to fight fire with fire and hired an engineer lobbyist of its own, its members learned too late that he was on the payroll of the Spring Valley Water Company, which had a vested interest in discrediting the dam site. So damaging was this war of words that soon few engineers wanted to risk their reputations by siding against the reservoir publicly.[58]

Even those in favor of the dam tended to cast themselves as lovers of wilderness, but lovers of humankind more. Those arguing for the reservoir included wealthy William Kent, a congressman from California who had donated several hundred acres of virgin redwood forest to the federal government under the new Antiquities Act (1906) and had persuaded President Roosevelt in 1908 to designate the land Muir Woods National Monument. But Kent could not side with Muir in this fight. He saw Hetch Hetchy's hydroelectric potential as the one way to rescue the people of San Francisco from the clutches of the monopolistic Pacific Gas and Electric Company. In a midnight vote on December 6, 1913, the U.S. Senate gave approval for the Hetch Hetchy reservoir. Ironically, the Hetch Hetchy controversy turned scattered wilderness preservation sentiment into a powerful national movement. Fifty years earlier, the proposal to build such a dam would have raised little if any public opposition.[59]

Whose Wilderness?

Hetch Hetchy's dam was not the only fly in the ointment of Yosemite for the worshipers of pristine nature. Valuing the wilderness also meant defining it, demarcating it from "civilization," from that which was not wilderness, adopting, in short, the mid-nineteenth-century formula of George Perkins Marsh, founder of the conservation movement, of a stark division between the human and the natural world. That formula left in the park the vexed question of its Indian inhabitants. Like many of the nation's new wilderness parks, Yosemite was not, in fact, an uninhabited wilderness but part of a long-standing human environment. Of course, the parks could hardly function as therapy for overstressed, overcivilized white men if those men were in constant danger of running into Indians. Nor were Indians seen as the appropriate audience for the parks' grandeur—they were not civilized enough to appreciate it.[60] Indians had to disappear for the parks to provide true recreative value.

Regarding Yosemite, according to historian Mark Spence, Helen Hunt Jackson, an Indian advocate, found in the 1870s that "the presence of 'filthy' Indians only detracted from the sublimity of the scenery," and Muir confessed that he "could not feel the 'solemn calm' of the wilderness when he was in their presence." In 1897 complaints that Indians had killed many of the park's deer (presumably for subsistence) led to enforcement of new antihunting regulations by the cavalry. Already forced by whites into dwindling reservations with limited resources where even allotments, supposed by federal law to be 160 acres, could only be 10 acres because of insufficient land, Indians maintained their centuries-old pattern of exploiting and managing a multitude of resources to garner subsistence and income. They cultivated land where they could, fished, hunted, did wage work on and off reservations, and gathered food. Their ability to use what were now park lands was essential to their subsistence base.[61]

But with the newly imagined use of the parks, Indians could only remain in the parks by being "Indians," by playing Indians. They were not playing themselves. They were playing the romanticized Indian, appropriately costumed, supposedly disappearing. The wage-working Indians who carried luggage in national park lodges for white tourists were not seen as Indians. Only the Indians (also paid) who practiced traditional crafts (but not traditional practices such as hunting) in carefully demarcated spaces were "Indians."[62]

If they could no longer hunt in the park, they had to find other means to augment their living. In Yosemite, Indians became accustomed to posing for photographs and charging for their efforts. Their presence helped authenticate a visit to the park as a wilderness experience. At Yosemite also tourists became part of Native experience, folded into their migratory patterns of resource extraction. One park visitor noted that many Native families were "in the habit of repairing yearly to . . . Yosemite for the purpose of sharing in the double harvest—first of the tourists, later of the acorns."[63]

At Yellowstone, it had taken over twenty years and the U.S. Supreme Court to effect this transformation. Rich in game, Yellowstone had served as hunting grounds for at least four tribes. Their treaties with the U.S. government often stipulated their hunting rights in perpetuity. Such was the case for the Shoshones and the Bannocks, who annually left their reservations to hunt in Yellowstone and at Jackson Hole. Local white guides complained that the Native hunters frightened the whites' wealthy clients and reduced their hunting success. These complaints led Constable William Manning, with the support of Wyoming's governor, to lead local posses to arrest Indians found hunting in the Jackson Hole area as violating Wyoming's game laws. In July 1895 he deputized twenty-six men and set out to find his quarry. After three days, they surprised a camp of twenty-six Bannocks. They confiscated the Bannocks' property, including their tents, saddles, blankets, rifles, their one horse, and nine packs of elk meat. They placed them under arrest and forced them to march at gunpoint from dawn to nightfall. As they approached some woods, Manning ordered his men to load their weapons. The Bannock women panicked, the men bolted for the woods, and the posse opened fire. They killed Se-we-a-gat, an elderly man who was shot four times in the back, and injured another, and two children were lost. A passing party of Mormons found one; the other was never found. The surviving Bannocks hid until morning and then returned to their reservation.

Fears of retribution brought the U.S. Eighth Infantry. The two to three hundred Bannocks and Shoshones still off reservation, fearing white violence, also returned to the reservation. After consulting with government officials, tribal leaders decided to bring suit. Judge John Riner of the U.S. Circuit Court for the District of Wyoming decided that the Indians' treaty rights from 1868 took precedence over the laws of Wyoming, only established as a state in 1890. The Wyoming attorney general appealed to the U.S. Supreme Court.

It was a month of landmark decisions. Only a week after it issued its ruling in *Plessy v. Ferguson*, on May 25, 1896, the court decided *Ward v. Race Horse*, overturning the lower court's decision. The court argued that the 1868 treaty had to be viewed in its own context, that the United States in 1868 would have seen it as a temporary expedient, that they never intended the rights granted in the treaty to be perpetual, despite the treaty specifically stating they were. The court held that "the march of advancing civilization foreshadowed the fact that the wilderness which lay on all sides of . . . the reservation was destined to be occupied and settled by the white man, hence interfering with the hitherto untrammeled right of occupancy of the Indian." When Congress admitted Wyoming on "an equal footing with the original states," Wyoming had no more obligation than those states (i.e., none) to recognize treaty rights. The decision became the basis for arresting any Indian on public lands during closed hunting season.[64]

Indians became invisible in both international and national disputes about conservation. Native Americans on the Pacific Northwest coast practiced small-scale commercial seine fishing: the Makahs sold over $6,000 of salmon to a cannery in 1902, and in good years they sold as much as $20,000. They relied even more heavily on their sealing. But when the United States, Canada, Japan, and the British Empire sought to create treaties to protect the Pacific North's fur seals and manage dwindling salmon in the early twentieth century, no Native Americans sat at the table. Unable to "see" the Makahs of the Pacific Northwest coast as commercial sealers and fishers, the U.S. government denied that negotiations to outlaw commercial ocean sealing and restrict salmon fishing contradicted mid-nineteenth-century treaty rights guaranteeing Makah access to those waters they viewed as their country.[65]

Even without the Makahs, the negotiators found little unity within each nation, let alone between them. Salmon fishers declared that the best way to protect salmon was to kill seals, but photogenic fur seals, though ruthless predators, had doe eyes, generating a constituency salmon could not match. Rather than attack seals, U.S. legislators attacked the fishing methods used in neighboring states, reservations, or provinces and determined to turn the Makahs and other Indians from the sea altogether. David Starr Jordan, ichthyologist and president of Stanford University, worked on behalf of the U.S. government in the case of both fur seals (starting in 1896) and salmon but ran into difficulties. He made little headway on salmon while fishermen did not believe "they could exhaust such a vast resource base." Once conservationist Roosevelt left the White House and William Howard Taft moved in, the fishing treaty was doomed.[66]

The disappearance of the fur seals, on the other hand, was highly visible. As the various parties quarreled over how to manage the hunting on the high seas, "the seal population crashed 90%." The seal harvest netted the U.S. Treasury hundreds of thousands of dollars a year. The United States and Britain had every interest in maintaining the species, but it took Japan's victory over Russia and another three years before an agreement among Russia, the United States, Britain, Japan, and Canada was reached in 1911.[67]

Meanwhile, salmon fisheries remained highly profitable, and Canadian and U.S. firms expanded their fleets and surged into the market. As the fisheries began to manifest increasing stress, the legislators and white commercial fisheries targeted Washington's tribal nations, including the Makahs and Lummis, who fished for both consumption and the market. The treaties may have saved the seal and salmon population, but it ended the autonomy of these Pacific coast peoples as businessmen and turned them into precisely the image the government had of them as dependent laborers.[68]

Conclusion

The population of the trans-Mississippi West grew dramatically in the first decade of the twentieth century, spurred at least in part by irrigation. Irrigation schemes rarely went as planned, and as historian Louis Warren wrote, "The land is never really 'settled'"; droughts, floods, blights, and other elements "unsettle" the land.[69] Irrigation colonists likewise often unsettled previous inhabitants, only to find themselves unsettled when costs outran their ability to pay. Nonetheless, the projects and the settlers in the longer term rearranged the region's landscape and the nature of its opportunities.

Despite its unpredictable results, faith in irrigation as the solution to the nation's problems—increasing class conflict, dwindling arable land, and declining opportunity—remained unshaken. Irrigation remained the symbol of modern man's ability to complete the conquest of the continental United States through modern technology. This was a culturally specific vision of the West's future. It had no room for older systems of irrigation. The risky and capital-intensive irrigation schemes often resulted in consolidation of landholding rather than in multiplying opportunity for the small farmer, but those invested in the new schemes blamed feckless farmers. Successfully conforming to notions of modern farming meant the right to participate in the opportunities and governance the region offered and increasingly separated the farmer from "nature."

The increasing settlement of the West raised the demand for water, leading to new conflicts, including a newly organized wilderness lobby. "Wilderness" did not so much mark a place untouched by human hands as a place created by humans who carefully demarcated it from other places and, as with irrigation, from former human systems that ordered the natural world.

Many of the actors in this puzzle linked preservation to purity, whether preserving pure wilderness or preserving the white race, and saw the U.S. West as the last hope for both. Roosevelt would create 105 national forests between 1903 and 1909, all but five west of the Mississippi.[70] Theodore Roosevelt, Gifford Pinchot, and Madison Grant were all elites, educated at Yale and Harvard, and key players in the Boone and Crockett Club Roosevelt had founded in the late nineteenth century to preserve the habitat of game animals. The club's members saw hunting as a key to manliness and took up the cause of preservation to save the opportunity to hunt big game in the United States and so save American manhood.

From there, club members' thinking evolved, sometimes in different directions. Pinchot remained focused on preservation for future use. Grant became focused on preservation for its own sake. Stunned by the plunging number of bison in his own lifetime, from thirty million to only eighty-five remaining in the wild by 1903, Grant proposed legislation to protect them as an endangered species, a cause no one in 1903 seemed prepared to defend. By 1905, however, Congress had authorized the president to set aside part of the Wichita Forest Reserve as a game refuge. Roosevelt did so, and the government stocked it with selected bison from the Bronx Zoo.[71]

By that date, Roosevelt and Grant were concerned not only with dwindling bison but also with what they perceived as another endangered species much closer to home: what they defined as the white race. As early as 1901 social scientist Edward Ross had coined the term "race suicide" to describe what had ended the Roman Empire, overrun by enslaved captives from its imperial wars, and applied it to what he saw happening to the United States under the regime of open immigration. By 1907 Roosevelt had adopted the term, and by the middle of the next decade, Madison Grant would not only be working to save the California redwoods with Muir and his colleagues but also publish the highly influential volume *The Passing of the Great Race*.[72] By 1919 a Bureau of Reclamation circular had boldly declared, "'The primary purpose of the Reclamation Law' . . . was to create on these irrigated lands the 'gradual welding of all Aryan races in a final race' that 'will dominate the world.'"[73]

The twin trends of the decade—federal intervention to create large-scale irrigation systems and federal intervention to create wilderness—drew from the same logic. Both manifested a belief in the ability of planners to impose human design on the land and to demarcate clearly one sort of use from another and order them in evolutionary, temporal terms, the modern from the premodern, the human from the "natural." Together they created an American West as a refuge for white families and other species they saw as equally endangered.

2

The Changing Meaning of Crossing Lines

At the turn of the century, U.S. western land borders were loosely policed and mostly unmarked. The U.S. government kept no records of overland immigration. Capital flowed unimpeded across borders. Corporate and individual landholding straddled national divides. New forms of empire, capital, and labor recruitment entwined, leaving officials, businessmen, and workers with imperial circuits of knowledge.

But as the decade wore on, though there would be no Border Patrol until 1924, the border hardened regarding immigration. This hardening went hand in hand with the United States' imperial ambitions, the borderland's industrial development and labor strife, and the U.S. government's appropriation and invention of racialized categories.

This chapter turns first to landholding and development that crossed national borders, then to the patchwork quilt of changing racial formations at local, transnational, and imperial levels and the competing forces that deployed them, including colliding diasporas of workers. The chapter ends with the increasing federal policing of the border and its gender implications.

Transnational Landholding and Investing

In 1901 the Alamo Canal began irrigating a large, fertile, but arid valley in California called the Colorado Desert. The temperature there could reach 120 degrees Fahrenheit. The developer who engineered the canal renamed the area. He called it instead the Imperial Valley. The name change and the canal helped the previously desolate spot draw two thousand settlers in eight months.

In the previous chapter, the irrigation canal illuminates the difficulty of bending nature to human will. Here, the Alamo Canal exemplifies cross-border development. The canal, like the Alamo River, flowed north across the U.S.-Mexico border. In exchange for permitting the intake, Mexico demanded the right to take up to half the water from the river. With the population rising on both sides of the border, Imperial Valley residents found themselves rationing water. Though the water was intended to be suitable for both domestic and agricultural use, farmers found dead horses and even occasionally dead humans floating in the canal.

Settlers on the U.S. side began to demand an "all-American canal," one completely on the U.S. side of the border. But what kind of international conundrum was this? It turned out that 840,000 acres of the Mexican land belonged to a Los Angeles syndicate that included Harry Chandler, son-in-law of Harrison Gray Otis, soon to be publisher of the *Los Angeles Times*.[1] In ownership abutting the canal, it was already "all American."

This cross-border investment in the Imperial Valley came at a time when international financial syndicates from Europe and the United States built empires in the American West. They backed vast ranches in Montana and owned enormous land grants in New Mexico. Individuals' properties, like the Alamo Canal, crossed borders that seemed to exist only on maps. By 1910 U.S. citizens owned 27 percent of Mexico's land; another 8 percent was owned by other foreigners. Foreigners owned an even greater percentage of Mexico's coastline and border; U.S. citizens owned over half of the 60 percent that lay in foreign hands. One hundred sixty U.S. citizens owned at least one hundred thousand acres each, totaling ninety million acres of agricultural, ranch, mining, and timber lands.[2]

U.S. capitalists, and in these years, particularly capitalists from the U.S. West (Texas, California, Oregon, etc.), saw Mexico and the U.S. West as one and capital drawn from Mexican investments as essential to the development of the West. Not just large corporations but also citizens from Tacoma and Seattle, Washington, and from Greeley, Colorado, formed investor groups. Mormons seeking to escape restrictions on polygamy, Doukhobors escaping Canadian oppression, Cherokees, and Greeley, Colorado, residents colonized Mexico. They adopted Mexican labor practices, employing debt peons, and they opened small businesses.[3] But it was the large-scale investors who defined the territory.

Tombstone, Arizona, rancher William Cornell Greene built one such transnational empire. By 1905 he owned 30,000 acres in Arizona and 750,000 acres in Sonora, Mexico. The next year he acquired over two million acres in Sonora and Chihuahua. Within his holdings lay fifty miles of the U.S.-Mexico border, ranches, timberlands, dozens of mines, and a railroad running from El Paso, Texas, to Terrazas, Chihuahua.[4]

Greene had not always been so successful. His success came from a wealthy marriage and cross-border networks. He married Ella Roberts in 1884. While she built up their cattle herd from her own resources, he grew beans and cut hay for local markets in southern Arizona and established a ranch nearby on leased land. He cultivated relations with other ranchers on both sides of the unfenced border; they gathered each year at the Elías ranch for the spring roundup. When opportunity knocked, he used his connections. Pooling their resources, these men bought mines from the widow of the governor of Sonora and founded the Cananea Copper Company in 1896. The investors included a local rancher, local merchants, businessmen, and the widow's new husband. They used other connections (a local mining engineer with a New York lawyer friend) to get the legal expertise they needed to create both a Mexican corporation (the Cananea Consolidated Copper Company [CCCC]) and a U.S. holding company (the Greene Consolidated Copper Company, which controlled the Mexican company's operating stock) and, finally, to organize a stockholder base on Wall Street. Greene's strategies interwove the local and the transnational—and on the border, sometimes the local *was* the transnational.

It took the governments of both Mexico and the United States to create the symbiotic forms, collaborations, and rules that allowed such cross-border corporations to flourish. Greene's Mexican corporation was considered a Mexican citizen and subject to Mexican law, just as his U.S. corporation was considered a U.S. person in U.S. courts. The Mexican government exempted the CCCC and its salaried employees from taxes for twenty years; it also gave the company the right to expropriate land if it could not agree to a sale with the owner. In return, the corporation agreed to take students from Mexican state schools and pay them as apprentices.

The CCCC brought modern machines for mining and smelting, railroads and management, street lights and sewer lines. It created a technological and corporate spectacle incarnated in the built environment. The state and the corporation built each other's power in the name of both progress and profit.

Some local Mexican elites enthusiastically joined the venture, selling family lands to Greene, buying elegant haciendas, and raising crops for the animals that hauled goods for the company. Some belonged to families who had participated in U.S.-Mexico trade for generations.

Under Mexican president Porfirio Díaz (1876–1910) and U.S. presidents who identified as "progressive," international capital funded the building of railroads and mines and developed ranches and farms that drew on a labor force freely crossing national borders. It developed henequen plantations that linked farmers and prison labor on the plains and prairies of the United States and Canada with producers and consumers in the Yucatan, Europe, and the Caribbean. The same financial syndicates and corporations that mined copper in Arizona mined copper in northern Mexico's Sonora and Chihuahua. The North American West proved a particularly attractive market for global capital, and investors found Díaz and the U.S. government highly sympathetic to their needs.[5]

In both Mexico and the United States the large-scale accumulation of land came at the expense of communal and small landholders. Much of the Yucatan had been held communally by small farmers. The Mexican government, like the U.S. government, favored individual property titles instead. It allowed the communal owners to convert their titles by surveys, but the surveys were expensive, beyond the reach of many of the landholders, and so the owners sold to those more wealthy, including Yucatán's governor, Olegario Molina Solís, who by 1913 owned, with his clique, 247,000 acres and controlled 75 percent of the henequen trade. By 1912 there were no more ejidos (commons) in the henequen zone, only large plantations.[6]

In the same years, after decades of struggle, the U.S. Congress established the Court of Private Land Claims, hoping to settle disputes over landownership in the Southwest. The Treaty of Guadalupe Hidalgo, which ended the Mexican-American War, had guaranteed the property rights of those former Mexicans now encompassed by the United States. The government guaranteed those rights, but its citizens had other ideas. By a variety of means, Anglo newcomers claimed land apparently granted to those of Mexican descent individually or as communities. The court held the same views of progress and landholding as other parts of the U.S. and Mexican governments and increased the loss of land by the heirs of the original Mexican grantees. Of the over 35 million acres at stake, the court confirmed to Hispano claimants in New Mexico, Arizona, and Colorado only 2,051,526 acres, or less than 10 percent. The judges rejected even century-old grants with no prior dispute. And, as in the Yucatan, the process was costly. Even Hispanos who won in court could lose land to their lawyers.

From 1891 to 1910 every lawyer in the area had at least one land grant case at any time. As Hispano small farmers and villagers usually had no cash, lawyers accepted payment either in land or, if the decision was to partition the communal grant and sell it as the most "practical" remedy, in proceeds from the sale. Some lawyers received as much as half the grant. In the relatively small Anglo community of the early twentieth-century Southwest, the court-appointed land commissioners, new claimants, judges, and lawyers of both sides were often friends, if not partners. Thomas Catron had arrived in New Mexico with two wagons of flour in 1866. Within three years he had entered law practice with a college friend and served as attorney general of the territory. By 1894 he had amassed nearly two million acres of land and held part ownership or represented the owners of four million more.[7]

As in Wyoming and across the West, the open range was disappearing. The U.S. government removed over six million acres of New Mexico's land for national forests, and as early as 1900, homesteaders claimed one million acres more. Confined by Anglo settlement, corporations, and the federal lands, local sheep farmers now had to pay cash for grazing permits. In 1880 in northern New Mexico, to be a sheepherder was to be a youth. By 1900 roughly half the greatly increased number of shepherds and day laborers were heads of households. Sons could no longer expect to move from being a laborer to an owner. Instead, they went from their parents' or grandparents' ranches to work for other owners as buyers, foremen, or, most often, herders at $15 or $16 a month with board.[8]

Those with large financial resources benefited greatly from the open borders and welcoming governments at the turn of the century. They brought large-scale industry and industrial development and consolidated their hold on resources. Their consolidation of holdings, however, rendered smallholding more precarious, tipping many smallholders into wage labor and restricting the opportunity for would-be smallholders.

All Racial Politics Are Local—and Imperial: Arizona and New Mexico

The cross-border large-scale enterprises relied on collaborations among elites across national lines and within the United States across ethnic ones. By the 1880s many Anglos and Mexicans across the Southwest had found an uneasy modus vivendi, ranching side by side, intermarrying, and sharing electoral power.[9] Party rosters showed members of both groups.

By the end of the 1890s that system was showing increasing strain. Historians have found that the dynamics of imperialism and the demands of imperialists encouraged a reformulation of racial ideology. Instead of the nineteenth century's multitude of races and racial hierarchies, the world could now be divided into the empire builders (part of the "white" "European" *family* of nations) and the colonized ("other"). Historian Rosina Lozano has connected the rise of U.S. imperialism to a change in domestic language policies. Colorado and California had printed official documents in German and Spanish, as well as English; New Mexico practiced government in Spanish and English. According to Lozano, "National discourse regarding language politics changed as the nation's borders hardened (both racial and territorial), due in part to the addition of immigrants and insular subjects in 1898 who did not speak English. The more permissive language politics of the mid-nineteenth century largely disappeared as federal and educational policies explicitly favored English."[10]

To understand the shifts that did and did not take place (e.g., the lack of a comprehensive set of Jim Crow laws for Mexicans in the Southwest) and the resistance to the hegemony of new racial projects requires looking at a variety of levels or theaters—

international, local, and national. The accommodation struck by the white primary and poll tax in Texas (see chapter 1) differed from that of Arizona and New Mexico, and those two differed from each other. In their battles for statehood, fought with a new urgency to distance themselves from the new overseas territories, Arizona spent much of its effort defining itself as "not New Mexico."[11] Both territories found their fate and the meaning imputed to their populations colored by their entanglements with the Spanish-American War, their own histories of colonization, and their proximity to Mexico.

On the federal level, whatever its seeming continuity with earlier expansionist efforts, the Spanish-American War marked a severe departure from earlier episodes in its definition of the polity. In the Mexican-American War, treaty provisions had required that all inhabitants "except uncivilized tribes" receive U.S. citizenship. There had also been a clear expectation of eventual statehood, even if, in the case of territories with majority Spanish-speaking residents, it was taking an unconscionably long time. The Treaty of Paris, ending the Spanish-American War, had no such guarantees. It "explicitly left the 'civil rights and political status' of these territories' inhabitants to be 'determined by Congress.'" With the war, the United States shifted from a formal philosophy and policy of democratic incorporation of new territories and peoples (however imperfectly practiced) to empire and official colonization. The policies and discourses that supported this shift both emerged from and affected relations on the mainland, and both policies and discourses were heavily racialized and raised considerable anxiety in the mainland's remaining territories.[12] Contestants in the twentieth-century West could take their cues from the new imperial culture.

The young Republican senator from Indiana, Albert Beveridge, who would sit on the Senate committees charged with overseeing the Philippines and Puerto Rico, waxed poetic in his 1900 defense of the new American empire: "God has not been preparing the English-speaking and Teutonic peoples for a thousand years for nothing but vain and idle self-contemplation and self-admiration. No! He has made us the master organizers of the world . . . [h]as made us adepts at government that we may administer government among savage and senile peoples. . . . And of all our race He has marked the American people as his chosen nation to finally lead in the regeneration of the world." Following this declaration of the destiny of the "English-speaking and Teutonic peoples," the Industrial Commission on Immigration, reporting to the U.S. House of Representatives in 1901, declared, "The most important improvement since 1893 in the method of compiling statistics of immigration was introduced in 1899," just a year after the Spanish-American War, "when, instead of the preceding classification of immigrants according to the countries or political divisions from which they came, they were classified according to the races to which they belonged."[13] "Race" replaced "nation" in the way the federal government saw the world.

The destabilizing impact of the increasingly popular racial categorizing became clear in a Texas district court case that challenged Ricardo Rodriguez's citizenship status in 1897. "'As to color,' the case noted, Rodriguez 'may be classed with the copper colored or red men'"—a definite liability in a nation whose constitution mentioned only Blacks and whites as eligible for citizenship. Rodriguez's citizenship was saved only by the stipulations in the Treaty of Guadalupe Hidalgo that ended the Mexican-American War, based on nationality rather than "race."[14] That his citizenship could be challenged at all in the 1890s was a mark of the strength of the new racial project emerging. In the new era, treaty-based or nation-based rather than race-based claims to citizenship made Mexicans anomalous members of the new polity. In the new system, they became people who could simultaneously be inside and outside the polity—inside by treaty, outside by "race."

Mexico occupied an ambiguous position in the bipolar scheme of empire versus colonized. When the United States and the Spanish Empire went to war in 1898, Mexico declared neutrality. In spite of the declared neutrality, U.S. Anglo newspapers first cast the Mexicans as loyal members of a "sister republic" hostile to Spain. As the United States committed to becoming an empire, taking over Spain's possessions rather than liberating them, the Anglo press began casting Mexico more clearly as subordinate, more like a colony than a sister. The *Arizona Daily Star* posed President Díaz as demonstrating "fealty and gratitude" toward the United States.[15]

Articles posed the United States as the liberator of Mexico from the French incursion of the 1870s and reaping Mexican gratitude just as it purportedly would reap that of the Cubans.

The U.S. English-language territorial press studiously ignored the copious evidence from the Mexican press of substantial sympathy with and support for Spain. It consistently depicted Mexico as inhabited only by Mexican and U.S. nationals. The Mexican press, by contrast, showed the country as cosmopolitan, a world full of expatriates of various nations who occupied managerial positions, running railroads and other industries, reflecting the transnational capital investment in Mexico, and hooked into the Mexican state.[16] The image of a Mexican state subordinate to the United States only worked without this cosmopolitan element.

The resistance to the image of the United States as liberator rather than predatory capitalist not only was evident in the Mexican press but also showed up in New Mexico's Spanish-language press. *La Voz del Pueblo* in Las Vegas, New Mexico, a section of the territory dominated by those of Spanish and Mexican descent known as Hispanos or Neomexicanos, depicted the whole war as a Republican Party boondoggle. In New Mexico, Yankee aggression was no distant memory. By 1898 the Land Court at Santa Fe had rejected 5,540,294 acres and confirmed only 7,400 acres, or just over one-tenth of 1 percent of Neomexicano land claims. The paper called it unrealistic to expect Mexico "to forget or pardon" its "brutal dismemberment" at the hands of the "ambitious and aggressive Yankees."[17]

Nonetheless and despite its resentment, *La Voz del Pueblo*, with war on the horizon, was quick to assert the loyalty of the Neomexicanos to the United States. Though proud of their Iberian heritage, they loved their country, and they would fight against Spain to defend the United States. The paper reported on deaths and injuries of prominent Neomexicanos in the war and congratulated them for putting to rest the doubts some had cast "sin motivo, sin causa y sin razón" on the patriotism of the Neomexicanos.[18]

The English-language presses in New Mexico and Arizona also hastened to assure their readership of the loyalty of the U.S. citizens of Mexican descent. They claimed that "the number of those who sympathise with Spain in the impending conflict can be counted upon less than the fingers of one hand." All papers, in either English or Spanish, dismissed rumors of a pro-Spain revolt in northern New Mexico that had led to calls for federal troops.[19]

Yet it seemed there was some foundation to the accusation. Despite all the hoopla and the high percentage of New Mexican Anglos enlisting, Spanish-speaking citizens in New Mexico and Arizona failed to enlist in the U.S. Army in substantial numbers. The *Daily Optic* reported that in the New Mexico Battalion, according to one report, of 352 soldiers, only 7 "native citizens were recognized." On July 29, 1898, the *Arizona Daily Star* announced, "It is officially stated that not a single Mexican in Arizona offered his services as a volunteer in the present war." The *Daily Optic* rejected rumors of discrimination against New Mexicans of Spanish descent "because of their nationality": "Our understanding has been that they were not in the Battalion simply because they did not enlist."[20]

La Voz del Pueblo admitted the low enlistments and feared that accusations of disloyalty would hurt the territory's ambitions in Congress: "It was said in Congress that one of the reasons they would not grant statehood to New Mexico [despite the territory meeting the population requirement of at least sixty thousand people] was because most of the inhabitants were a people alien to American institutions and with very little sympathy for the United States." *La Voz* countered with a letter from one Juan José Herrera, who claimed that poverty rather than disloyalty kept people from enlisting. They could not leave their work and still feed their families. Whatever the cause of enlistment rates, they gave fodder to newspapers across the country that claimed that fifty years of U.S. citizenship had failed to turn Mexicans into Americans. Foreigners they remained. The sense of doomed hope for statehood was widespread.[21]

New Mexico was not alone in such dilemmas. A Texas attorney who had lived in the border town of Rio Grande City, Texas, during the Spanish-American War claimed that half the city's residents had supported Spain. They had resented the U.S. Army weighing in on behalf of the Mexican dictator, Díaz, against the Texas-launched 1895 effort of anti-Díaz revolutionary Catarino Garza and doubted U.S. claims that the Spanish-American War was one of liberation.[22]

Critics of the New Mexico Territory's Mexican-descent residents launched a movement to require English literacy for voting. "Thank god," wrote one, that New Mexico remained a territory rather than governed by these aliens. Only with a literacy requirement could the territory safely be admitted to the union. Others would add to the proposal the denial of the right to serve on juries or in the courts. One such proponent in Las Cruces signed himself "an American." One Republican paper in the territory in August offered that as long as the United States was considering annexing so much foreign territory, it might consider annexing New Mexico.[23] *La Voz* in the next weeks complained bitterly of the failure of even Hispano Republicans to defend the people against such attacks.

By August, however, the Republicans had retreated from support for an English-language and literacy voting requirement. Apparently the move had backfired in a territory with 150,000 Spanish-speaking citizens and only 60,000 English-speaking ones. But there had been a shift. While the New Mexico Democrats' platform framed Republican efforts as depriving "the native people of this Territory from the enjoyment of these privileges which pertain *by birth* to every American citizen," the Populist *Daily Optic* instead focused on their right to vote as guaranteed not by birth but by "the treaty of Guadalupe Hidalgo and the organic act of the Territory." And it added that "our young men and young women of Spanish descent are almost universally acquiring a mastery of the English language."[24]

That fall, when reporting on the campaign for territorial congressional delegates, the *Daily Optic* proclaimed, "The race issue is dead in New Mexico. . . . [W]e are all Americans." Republican Don Pedro Perea defeated incumbent Harvey Fergusson. Like the territorial governor, Miguel Otero, Perea heralded from a wealthy landholding family and was a longtime political officeholder (twenty-five years).[25]

Despite Perea's victory, the future had changed even for elite Republican "native Mexicans." Governor Otero, friend of McKinley and the first Mexican-descent U.S. governor of the territory, had raised a company for the war. A successful politician who, like Perea and many Republicans, opposed statehood for the Democrat-dominant territory, Otero had become accustomed to the promise of incorporation into the U.S. ruling class. His dreams of larger political horizons would dwindle into a minor ambassadorship. Speaking the language and claiming the heritage of the fallen enemy empire made elite Neomexicano participation in the U.S. polity problematic. With the Spanish-American War, they were relentlessly cast as "foreign."[26]

Worse, elites found even their racial category destabilized. Identifying as "Spanish," they found themselves cast by the federal government as "Mexican," with its implication of indigenous (colonized) mixing. At a moment when Italians, Poles, and other Europeans in the United States were beginning to be called "whites" rather than national "races," Mexicans and Mexican Americans of all classes found themselves being pushed to the far side of the white/other divide.

Early in the century, the issue was far from settled. In 1901 a federal Industrial Commission report included Mexicans and Indians under "foreign whites" and revealed a host of contradictory racialized hierarchies on western railroads, reflected in pay scale and job types. The Southern Pacific Railroad Company included all "other than Asiatics and Mexicans" as "Americans" even when they were foreign-born noncitizens. In contrast, northern railway lines counted Mexicans like any other foreign-born laboring group, listing them along with Irish, Germans, Chinese, Swedes, and many others.

As historians have shown, the discourse on race was pervasive and clearly structured but radically inconsistent. The burgeoning U.S. state spent increasing effort in an almost obsessive attempt to police and define these boundaries but appeared not at all concerned with inconsistency. The setting of boundaries, not their consistency, was the hallmark of modern governance. "Much to my surprise," wrote the author of one section of the report, "I found that in some of the principal mining states of the West . . . no attempt has been made to segregate the nationalities of those employed in the mining industry."[27]

Since European and Chinese immigrants dominated federal concerns, it is not surprising that the commission spent little ink on Mexican immigrants. It is more surprising that they spent any ink on them at all. In previous federal reports and discussions of immigration, though Mexicans had been migrating to the United States in large numbers since the 1880s, Mexicans had been invisible in the federal record. In government documents they appeared largely in the context of land grant cases. Mexico appeared as a potential source of goods, location of investments, and avenue of illegal Asian immigration. In 1901, surprised by finding that Mexicans formed about one-third of maintenance-of-way workers on railroads in the Southwest and up to that number, depending on the line, for other types of railroad labor, the commissioners devoted a paragraph of their over eight-hundred-page report to what they called "Mexican peon labor" and sounded the alarm.

Mexicans were working in the Southwest in far larger numbers than the Chinese or Japanese were. "As appears by the tables," the commissioners reported, "it will be seen that large numbers of Mexicans are employed on some of the lines. . . . A large percentage of such Mexicans are aliens who reside on the Mexican side of the line and who come into the United States as laborers." The going "American" wage rate was twice that of what the companies paid Mexicans. "The Mexican peon laborer," the report concluded, "is little if any better than the Japanese coolie, and the competition of the Mexican is quite as disastrous to white labor as is that of the Chinese and Japanese." This report did not yet define the Mexican immigrant as unassimilable, however, something it still limited to the "Mongolian races."[28]

Nine years later, the two-volume abstracts of the 1911 report of another Immigration Commission, the Dillingham Commission, continued the trend. The commissioners devoted nine pages, instead of one paragraph, to "Mexicans." They complained about the lack of good records for land-based immigration. Land-based immigration was not even recorded by the Bureau of Immigration before 1908, itself an indication that Mexican immigration was, like Canadian immigration, seen as a nonissue in the earlier federal racial regime. The numbers the commissioners did have indicated a rapid rise in Mexican immigration between 1899 and 1909. The report labeled Mexicans "as a race . . . unprogressive" but "sufficiently intelligent" for common labor "under close supervision." It also claimed that they provoked "less opposition . . . by white employees . . . than [employment] of the Japanese." But, the report concluded, "their progress toward assimilation has perhaps not been more rapid than that of the conservative Chinese," and "thus it is evident that in the case of the Mexican he is less desirable as a citizen than as a laborer." Mexicans are cast as a "race," and a race more akin to the excluded Chinese and the almost excluded Japanese than the European descent that Neomexicanos claimed. Moreover, unlike earlier reports, there is no sense here in the federal record of the substantial Mexican-descent U.S. citizenry already existing in the United States.[29]

These reports clarify that even before the Mexican Revolution dramatically increased the immigration of Mexicans and the federal suspicion of their character, the federal government's view of Mexican immigration was changing. Aided by the local dynamics around the Spanish-American War and the new racial paradigm, Mexican Americans were well on their way to becoming a permanently foreign "other," labeled "Mexican" even when they were U.S. citizens and not Mexican citizens.

Meanwhile, many Neomexicanos worked hard to place themselves on the side of the colonizers rather than the colonized. Governor Otero sent his territory's bilingual teachers and other officials to help Americanize and govern newly acquired Puerto Rico and the Philippines in 1901. In the same vein, at the 1904 Louisiana Purchase Exposition in St. Louis, Governor Otero promoted New Mexico's Spanish missionary heritage. Indeed, tourism became a vehicle through which to remake the meaning of New Mexico in the national fabric.[30]

Such efforts were helped immeasurably by Charles Fletcher Lummis. A classmate of Teddy Roosevelt, Lummis in 1893 penned *The Spanish Pioneers,* depicting a humane, progressive Spanish conquest; the book went through twelve editions. Through these pages New Mexico, no longer filled with permanently *alien* Spanish speakers, instead stood simultaneously as U.S. antiquity, displayed in the territory's ancient ruins and current Pueblo Indian villages, and as the earliest site of European American attempts to "civilize" the continent with the Spanish missions. By placing themselves as heirs to the conquistadores, as civilizers of the territory, in contrast to the Indians, Neomexicanos both elite and villagers placed themselves on a parallel with westering Anglos.

Those same Spanish speakers now could theoretically take their place alongside the descendants of the English pilgrims. Teddy Roosevelt applauded such moves, and it was one of his fellow Rough Riders, George Armijo, who would dress as the conquistador Diego de Vargas in the 1911 Santa Fe Fiesta, created to celebrate precisely this vision of history.[31]

To this end, particularly but not solely elite Neomexicanos increasingly explicitly claimed a purely European ancestry shared with the incoming Anglos, an identity as Spanish American. "Mexican" came to mean a mixed Indian and European heritage. They came to these terms as a way of resisting the new racial formations of the federal government. During a 1902 Senate hearing held in New Mexico to investigate its fitness for statehood, Senators William P. Dillingham (Vermont) and Albert Beveridge (Indiana) questioned probate clerk Isidor Armijo about his ancestry. He was, he averred, "of Spanish extraction . . . but I was born in the United States and I am an American." When pressed by Beveridge about possible Mexican roots, claiming the committee was "just getting at the racial blood; that is all," Armijo rejoined that indeed his parents were Mexicans, adding, "And yours were German, but that doesn't make you Dutch." Others made similar claims. One census enumerator labeled himself a "Spaniard" who had always lived in New Mexico, and another, when asked "to what race did those inhabitants [she enumerated] mainly belong, Mexican or American," replied, "Spanish; that is[,] not any Indians." By her lights, New Mexico had few Mexicans, that is, few Mexican immigrants or mestizos; similarly, when asked why he kept records in Spanish, a justice of the peace insisted, "Because the people here are Spanish."[32]

Before the rampant Americanization campaigns surrounding the U.S. entry into World War I, it was not always obvious to all that speaking Spanish was at odds with U.S. loyalty. Indeed, a newspaper in Nebraska, a state with a large German-speaking population, pointed to the continued use of French in Louisiana and Missouri, questioning the use of Spanish as grounds for denying New Mexico statehood in 1903.[33]

Ironically, despite their claims to be early participants in the civilizing mission, Neomexicanos were themselves targets or beneficiaries, depending on the view, of U.S. missionaries. Unlike the earlier Spanish efforts aimed at Native Americans, these missionaries were Protestant, almost entirely women, and focused on Neomexicanos. These women had learned to think of their New Mexico subjects from globe-trotting missionaries, particularly from Africa, to whom they listened spellbound in small and large salons across the nation. They measured the daring and significant quality of their work by the benighted level of their subjects and referenced "darkest Africa" on first arrival. When one of these women missionaries published a less than flattering account of the local Spanish-speaking residents, calling them "slovenly and semi-pagan, degraded and superstitious, of mixed ('Indian and Iberian') blood, a people who lived in mud huts and slept on piles of rags for beds," the editor of *La Voz* called for an indignation meeting that resulted in six hundred Neomexicanos marching through the streets of Las Vegas, New Mexico, in October 1901. Most of the women missionaries had far better relations with their villager neighbors, and some married into the villages, but such accusations stung. Young lawyer Eusebio Chacón told the crowd in 1901, "No other blood circulates through my veins but that which was brought by Don Juan de Oñate." Literally true or not, such a claim demonstrated the degree to which Neomexicanos understood what historian John Nieto-Phillips calls the "language of blood," which dominated the new empire's race-making.[34]

These New Mexican strategies came in stark contrast with those of Arizona. Anglo residents of that territory had resisted attempts to join the territory to New Mexico, as Oklahoma and Indian Territories were joined into a single state in 1907. Outnumbered by New Mexico's population, they resisted what they saw as the submerging of their own interests. At times they framed the issue in gendered and racist imagery, as in a December 6, 1905, cartoon in the *Arizona Republican* (Phoenix) that featured a kneeling young Anglo woman, identified as Arizona, pleading with Teddy Roosevelt, who wielded a club and sported a loincloth and who threatened to handcuff her to a sombrero-wearing male "New Mexico." At a congressional hearing in 1906, one Arizona resident asked, "Shall we join the Mexican greasers to Arizona and let them control it?" When Congress approved joint statehood in 1906 with Roosevelt's blessing, both territories rejected the option, Arizona overwhelmingly, 16,265 to 3,141.[35]

Seeking separate statehood, Arizona claimed that the Mexicans within its borders (unlike those of New Mexico) were docile transient laborers, safely controlled by the corporations that hired them. Whereas the Mexican-descent population in New Mexico would remain the majority until the 1920s, as early as the 1890s Arizona's Mexican-descent population had shrunk to about 20 percent of the whole, only about half of whom were U.S. citizens. When the territory's claims of Mexican workers' docility wavered in the dramatic 1903 copper miners' strike, fueled by Mexican workers, proponents of statehood focused more heavily on their Anglo identity, passing an English literacy requirement for voting over their governor's veto.[36]

Arizona had the same tourist strategies as New Mexico regarding its Indian population, with the Harvey Company setting up shop at the Grand Canyon and the Santa Fe Railroad's promotional pamphlets promising the opportunity to watch Hopi dances. But there was no counterpart to the conquistador focus. There was no "Spanish American" aspect to the tourist image. And when women on a civilizing mission stepped in to wrest the West from "Mexican" culture in Arizona, they were mining town women, wives of artisans and shop keepers, and a few ranchers, some of them only just beginning successfully to claim status as "white" in the aftermath of the 1903 strike. At the beginning of that strike, Mexican and other workers had joined together. The copper mining corporation Phelps Dodge had responded with a divide-and-conquer strategy, turning the strike into a Mexican revolt and bringing the Mexican workers' allies, including the Italians, over to the "white" side of the line. The next year, when a group of orphans from New York arrived at the homes of the Mexicans who had agreed to adopt them, the women, including Italians, engineered the "rescue" of the New York orphans from the Mexicans. The strike had helped move them into the "white" column, and the abduction would cement their new position and sharpen the border between "white" and "Mexican."[37]

New Yorkers, who had sent the orphans, drew "racial" lines

differently, as did Mexican-descent Arizona residents. While the rescuers posed the Mexican families in the most unsavory possible terms and posed themselves as rescuing fair-haired innocents from mongrel hordes, the New York press called the rescuers lawless barbarians and published a letter from Mariano Martinez of nearby Benson, who insisted the families had been carefully vetted by the local priest:

> Nearly all of the Mexican families referred to own their own farms, ranches, cattle, &c., and are better able financially to take care of themselves than the "Americans of Arizona." The heads of these Mexican families and their children were born and raised in Arizona under the American flag. They are able to write and speak both the Spanish and English languages, and they do not butcher it as do you so-called "Arizona Americans," who are composed of Swedes, Norwegians, Servians, Canadians, and Dutch, who have been shipped from the old country to work our mines and make out of this portion of the United States a dumping ground.

Himself born and raised in Tucson, the child of parents born in the territory, Martinez pointed out those "Arizona Americans" were "not even entitled to cast a vote because they have not been in this country long enough. Probably the only claim you have to call them 'Americans' is that they have blue eyes, red hair, a face full of freckles, and long feet."[38]

Regardless of the truth of Martinez's claims and the level of his frustration, the Supreme Court sided with the abductors. The case was *New York Foundling Hospital v. John Gatti*, who had led the abductors. At the trial, no Mexicans sat in the audience. The lawyers introduced no Mexican witnesses. The journalists interviewed no Mexicans.[39] The vigilantes would keep the children, and the new state's identity would be not-Mexican.

The divergent strategies of Arizona and New Mexico were starkly reflected in the territories' constitutional conventions that preceded statehood after President Taft signed enabling legislation in 1910 for two separate states. Although underrepresented at the convention, Neomexicanos still made up about one-third of the delegates for the New Mexico convention, with Solomon Luna, an esteemed wealthy rancher, chosen to chair the Committee on

Committees. The constitution would specify that no voter could be disqualified or kept from serving on juries or holding local offices on the basis of "religion, race, language, or color" and that all public documents would be printed in English and Spanish. In contrast, the Arizona constitutional convention boasted only a single member of Mexican descent, the prominent merchant Carlos Jácome, and he was given minor committee assignments. The constitution mandated that voting required the ability to "read the Constitution of the United States in the English language in such a manner as to show he is neither prompted nor reciting from memory, and to write his name." Jácome, like the other four Republican representatives from southern Arizona's Pima County, voted against the constitution. Despite their opposition, it passed handily.[40]

So we were clearly not "all just Americans," as the *Optic* had claimed. New Mexico and Arizona would not become states until fourteen years after the Spanish-American War, not until they were safely Anglo or on their way to being so. Migration to New Mexico in the first decade of the twentieth century was greater than that to California; the territory enjoyed a net gain of 60,000, and 120,000 residents of the territory had been born elsewhere in the United States.[41] By then the larger Anglo population that had entered was unaccustomed to having to accommodate an indigenous Mexican presence and understood Mexican immigration in the post-1898 framework. The Republicans had not disenfranchised the Spanish-speaking citizens of New Mexico, but soon enough they would not need to, having gained an Anglo majority. On the eve of the Spanish-American War, Anglos had limited and local nightmares about a revolt of Hispanos at home. On the eve of World War I, the federal government had far more substantial fears of a fifth column in the Southwest, though in that war the enemy was not even Spain. That fear measured "our" own success at othering the "Mexicans" within U.S. borders.

Transnational Workers and Transnational Organizing

The dynamics that drove former farmers and villagers to seek wage work were mirrored not just in other parts of North America but across the globe. That mobilization meant that when Hispanos and Native Americans, as well as Black and white small farmers, entered railroad construction camps, lumber camps, and copper and coal mines, they encountered Mexicans, Slavs, Italians, Irish, Poles, Scots, English, Greeks, Chinese, and others. In southern Colorado's coal camps, workers represented thirty-two nationalities and spoke twenty-seven different languages. Elsewhere, one ethnic group might dominate, as in Butte, Montana's copper mines. By 1900 Butte had the largest population, production, and labor force of any mining city in the world. At one-quarter Irish, the copper mining town was more Irish than Boston.[42]

At all these production centers, workers were highly mobile. Since so much of the American West's production of the era was extractive and often seasonal, transience characterized it even more than in other parts of the United States. Many of the western miners had first stopped in Michigan, Minnesota, Pennsylvania, and other states. Farm laborers from Italy traveled to Argentina, to the Great Plains, and back to Italy. Mexicans came to work on the ever-expanding railroad systems. Railroad routes, priorities, and subsidies in turn eased migration. From railroad work, Mexicans spread to other industries. The Americans who owned the land along the Alamo Canal in Mexico recruited Chinese immigrant labor, still legal in Mexico, for its cotton fields so as not to compete with the rising demand (including their own) for Mexican labor north of the border.[43]

In this swirling mass of travelers, sociability crossed many lines. Historian Julian Lim finds that the "multiethnic and multiracial population" traversing the border "came together dynamically through work and play, in the streets and in homes, through war and marriage, and in the very act of crossing the border." Even for Chinese immigrants, according to historian Beth Lew-Williams, "at the borderline, the federal government attempted to codify, standardize, and record the terms of exclusion, but within the nation the terms of inclusion were often informal, irregular, and unspoken until violated." In the rural West, Chinese tenants rented from white landowners and occasionally employed white widows and children. The children visited their houses and ate at their tables, and though exceptional cases led to sensational trials, for the most part in the rural West these visits raised no eyebrows.[44]

These workers carried their ethnic identities with them like a suitcase. The Ancient Order of Hibernians, for example, had chapters across the United States, aiding Irish immigrants in finding work, lodging with coethnics in boardinghouses, and finding bartenders who would cash their paychecks and serve as their bankers and officers who could introduce them to local politics and unions.[45]

Ethnic identity was not all they carried. To the harsh working conditions of western mines and fields they carried organizing experience. The fierce labor battles of the 1890s West that had radicalized so many workers and led to the founding of the Western Federation of Miners (WFM) carried into the twentieth century. By 1900 U.S. workers had carried the WFM with them into British Columbia. In 1903 nine hundred Mexican track workers in Los Angeles went on strike for higher wages, as did Mexican and Japanese agricultural workers in the region. In 1903–4 a sympathy strike by the WFM on behalf of smelter workers in four Colorado cities spread rapidly in response to draconian measures of mine and smelter owners and their sympathetic governor until WFM leader "Big Bill" Haywood claimed that "the entire state was in conflagration." When the company tried to import strikebreakers to Denver, two-thirds of the Joplin, Missouri, workers they imported refused to break the strike.[46]

The owners defeated the workers in large part by organizing and mobilizing the power of the state. Their government allies suspended the Bill of Rights, including free speech, freedom of the press, the right to bear arms, and rights of assembly. The companies used espionage, state militias, and the National Guard to arrest and drive out union workers even when strikes were reported as peaceful.

In response to these moves by powerful, often transnational corporations, workers increased the scale of their organizations and their aspirations. The regional WFM helped found the global Industrial Workers of the World (IWW) in 1905. The same year, a group of Mexican exiled revolutionaries in St. Louis, traveling in overlapping circles with the WFM and the IWW, established the Partido Liberal Mexicano (PLM). Their manifesto in 1906 called for the ouster of Díaz and for labor protections, political freedom, land redistribution, and the restoration of land rights.[47] The movements would converge in the borderlands' mining towns.

In that same year of the Colorado mining strikes, 1903, the dramatic strike at the Clifton-Morenci copper mines in Arizona that put Italians into the "white" column also demonstrated the connections between circulating capital and diasporic labor. Phelps Dodge employed about nine hundred men in the mines at Clifton-Morenci and at least an additional thousand in the smelter and mill that turned the mined ore into marketable copper. Clifton-Morenci was part of a growing Phelps Dodge copper empire that stretched across the U.S.-Mexico border. As did most mines, it drew its workers from both sides of the border and across Europe. Some came to the mines with experience in their home countries; some came with experience in the United States or Mexico. Since the company owned mines on both sides of the border, often workers had worked for the company at other sites.[48]

Coal mining was dangerous enough, with five major disasters in Wyoming alone between 1900 and 1910, killing 448 miners, and similar tragedies in other states. But hard rock mining was even more dangerous. In a single year, 1912, for example, as many as 27 percent of copper miners were injured; those who survived lost, on average, twenty-two working days. Survival could depend on the miner's work team, and if the accident proved fatal, the miner's family depended on the other miners as well. At Clifton's Sacred Heart Church, from 1900 to 1902, the years leading up to the strike, 45 percent of the men buried had died of mine accidents. Most accidents never got reported, and the company evaded responsibility wherever possible. The companies blamed the men's carelessness or inexperience; often, the companies blamed fate. The copper companies had far more power than the workers, and few workers or their survivors ever won a suit against them. Usually, the companies paid something to widows; Phelps Dodge in 1905 gave them about two months' pay, or $150, and thought itself generous.[49]

The hardships made mining a select fraternity. Hard rock miners had started organizing democratic unions in the U.S. West in the 1870s. They fought ferociously for better conditions and wages and more control over their work. They often won. Mining was among the highest-paid wage work in the West. The better organized the mine, the better the workers were paid. At Butte, Montana, the tight-knit Irish-dominated mining workforce had generated the WFM and received the highest copper mining wages in the world. They made double the wages of most industrial workers. At Clifton-Morenci workers had won wage increases, too, but not equally. Management divided workers into three wage groups: "Mexican," which included those of Mexican descent born on both sides of the border; "Italian"; and everyone else.[50]

Like the Irish in Butte, Mexicans in Clifton-Morenci were highly transient. In 1902 most Mexican mine workers quit three to six months after they started. Mine employers gave a distinct meaning to Mexican transience, however. It is true that many Mexicans had small farms and family obligations on one or the other side of the border and moved in and out of wage work to enable their families to hold on to the land. It is unlikely, however, that, as one piece of advice to mine employers ran, "the average Mexican cannot stand prosperity."[51]

In the early twentieth century, an increasing proportion of Mexican miners—more often than Anglo miners—brought their families and so proved less mobile. Although earning substantially lower wages than Anglos earned ($2.50 per day at most vs. $4.00 per day), Mexicans at Clifton still earned far more than in other industries, even copper mining in Mexico. These wages meant that miners could send their children to school; their wives could buy meat. They could afford to take in orphaned children and still meet some of their obligations to those who had stayed behind.[52]

In June 1903 a new territorial law went into effect in Arizona limiting underground miners to an eight-hour day.[53] Where mines employed only Anglo miners, the eight-hour day already prevailed. At Clifton-Morenci, the shift stood at ten hours. The Republican press denounced the law as interference with free enterprise. The Democratic press and the Anglo miners' union favored the law as a way to drive out "foreign" labor.

Who counted as "foreign" and "white" was in flux, but these lines, like so many other lines in the early twentieth century, were beginning to harden. As early as the 1880s, Bisbee, Arizona, another copper mining town, had a reputation as a "white man's camp," though at that point, as many as two-thirds of the camp's residents were Mexican. In contrast, from the days of the earliest gold strikes in California in the mid-nineteenth century, U.S.-born whites and European immigrants had struggled to make the potential wealth their exclusive prerogative. They resented the skill and experience of Mexicans who fared better in the early diggings. They drew up local codes excluding Chinese and Mexicans from mining; where they could, they passed laws taxing "foreign" miners. As mining shifted from prospecting to wage work, they carried their notions of entitlement with them down the shafts. The codes they created were riddled with inconsistencies from district to district and even within districts. One early code created a three-man committee to "decide who are & who are not Mexicans."[54]

"White" miners had a string of justifications for such provisions. They claimed to protect white women's virtue from unfair service sector labor competition, but often white women boardinghouse keepers relied on Chinese labor for laundry or cooking and were not fans of the rules. The miners claimed the distinction lay on natural grounds—that Mexicans and Chinese could survive on a lower wage, ate cheaper food, or did less work—claims that did not withstand scrutiny. Sometimes they simply admitted they wanted to keep the West's vaunted opportunities for whites. To curry favor with skilled white miners, as copper demand skyrocketed in the 1890s and Phelps Dodge consolidated its hold on borderlands copper mining, the company adopted Bisbee's preexisting rules as a "white man's camp." For a time, despite lowering the wages, this strategy successfully forestalled union organizing.[55]

While Bisbee had banned Mexicans from underground mining, Clifton had not. When mine owners responded to the new eight-hour law by cutting the pay proportionately, Clifton's workers began talking. Complaints about the pay cut quickly morphed into a larger set of issues. Mexican workers knew that their $2.50 daily wage was already lower than that of other workers. Anything even lower threatened their fragile hold on stability. But they also had other grievances. They wanted locker rooms where they could change their filthy, sweat-soaked clothes before going home; they wanted the companies to pay hospitalization costs and insurance for death or injury; they wanted an end to arbitrary firings of men and arbitrary price increases at company stores where they had to buy their provisions; and they wanted the companies to employ only men who would join their organization.[56]

The demands seemed reasonable to many of the townspeople, to the "American" workers, as well as the "Mexican" ones, to the sheriff and many of his deputies, and even to the captain of the Arizona Rangers. To the owners they seemed impossible. Working in a global competitive market, they claimed, including competition with other U.S. copper mines, they could not make the changes and remain profitable.

For weeks, both mine workers and mine managers and owners had been planning for the date the eight-hour law would take effect (June 1). While the miners met and drew up demands, the mine managers hired a detective agency, which placed Italian and Mexican operatives as informants among the workers in the mines. Phelps Dodge's top Arizona man, James Douglas, convened a meeting of all the operators in the district and secured an agreement not to waver on the wage cuts. The day before the law took effect, the mine operators posted notice of the changed hours and pay. That was Sunday, May 31. On Monday the miners walked out. They allowed no ore to move from the bins, and as a result, by Tuesday the smelters and mills had to shut down. On Wednesday the workers at the smelters called a sympathy strike. By the end of the week the workers had brought production in the district to a standstill.

Unable to believe that Mexicans were capable of leading such an effective strike, newspapers at first pointed to Italians as the strike leaders. If not the Italians, they thought, perhaps the Western Federation of Miners. But the WFM, despite the pleas of some of its members, largely excluded Mexicans; the WFM was as invested in the identity of manliness with whiteness and whiteness with western opportunity as earlier labor organizations. Moreover, at the time, the Mexican workers had created a movement in Mexico more developed than that of the U.S. Southwest, one that was intertwined with mutual aid organizations (as was the movement in Butte among Irish workers), and the workers in Clifton-Morenci called on Sonoran expertise in planning their strike.

Officers in the *mutualistas* served as three of the strike leaders. The mutual aid organizations had credibility with the workers, having long provided solidarity in hard times, respectability, insurance, death and sickness benefits, social activities, and meeting places. Indeed, during strikes, mutual aid association halls were often the only spaces open to strikers for meetings.

Ten to twenty percent of the strikers were Anglos. When it became clear the strike would not fade as quickly as they anticipated, they began to drift away, looking for work elsewhere. The Mexicans, Italians, and other strikers stayed. They began to challenge the dual wage system that created a "white" man's and a "Mexican's" wage. More inclusive voices began to impress the WFM, and they sent union men from Globe, Arizona. A telegram of support arrived from WFM's Big Bill Haywood, though no material aid.

Despite the lack of any disorder, with lines clearly drawn and over three thousand men on strike, the local sheriff deputized sixty men, largely drawn from local ranches—people suspicious and resentful of mine owners' political clout, capital, and the land and water that capital allowed them to monopolize. Not trusting such local law officers to represent their own notions of law and order, the companies prevailed on the territorial governor to call out the Arizona Rangers. It was the Rangers' first strike-breaking assignment. Created in 1901 to keep the border safe from cattle rustling and smuggling, they had cemented a heroic reputation by capturing the notorious bandit Augustín Chacón in late 1902. There were only twenty-four of them, many nonprofessionals, poorly paid (though at twice the rate of the miners on strike), and without uniforms. They supplied their own weapons, horses, and other equipment. Some had experience as Texas Rangers (used to break strikes since the 1880s) and were drawn to an itinerant life with little supervision. Not all were thrilled with this new turn in their work.

In the end, things did not go according to anyone's plan. The miners were better organized than the Rangers or the sheriff. On Monday, June 8, on the orders of Phelps Dodge, the Rangers stretched across the roads from Metcalf, where many strikers lived, creating a barrier around the mines at Morenci. The strikers simply took another route. The now horseless Rangers tried to head them off by climbing a steep mountain, only to find that about 150 miners had surrounded the sheriff and his 32 deputies and held them at gunpoint. Farther out, another thousand or so miners had surrounded a small party of Rangers. The sheriff had his deputies lay down their guns. Nor did the Rangers see any point in starting a battle. As one of them put it, "I see there wasn't noways any use all of us going down there and starting an all-round killing."

The sheriff tried to mediate, telling the Phelps Dodge manager the strikers' demands were reasonable. Mills, the manager, refused to budge. The strikers' speeches became more threatening, including threatening to take the sheriff and Mills hostage, whereupon Mills fled. As the rain poured down and strikers deployed along the hills the next day, the sheriff admitted he could no longer contain them, and Mills called on his friend and fellow Rough Rider, the territorial governor, who sent in the troops: six companies from Forts Grant and Huachuca, including the entire territorial militia and two hundred soldiers of the regular army, who arrived late on June 10, followed by a cavalry troop from Fort Apache the next day.

Yet it wasn't this accumulation of force that did in the strike. It was the torrential rain, which triggered the biggest flood Clifton-Morenci had ever seen. As strikers ducked under hillside crags, their families sought shelter in their canyon homes from the rain and hail. The flood rocketed down the canyon walls, broke through the company's inadequate tailings dam, and swept away houses, horses, wagons, and human beings, shattering them against canyon walls and drowning them in the muddy waters. Most of the thirty-nine dead were Mexican women, children, and the elderly who had lived along Chase Creek.

In the aftermath of the disaster, the army enforced martial law, prohibiting assemblies and searching Mexican homes for the weapons the company was so convinced the workers had stockpiled, only to find very few. Nonetheless, the army arrested those they identified as strike leaders. When strikers tried to meet, the army dispersed them. By June 12 most strikers had capitulated. The territorial supreme court issued an injunction against the strikers, and the cavalry stayed in town for the rest of the month.[57]

There were many outcomes to the strike. The company did its best to label it a "Mexican" strike, though at the start the strike and its issues had encompassed all the mine's workers. As the skilled and better-paid Anglo workers melted away, the company made the issue one of inferior and disorderly workers (Mexicans and their Euro-Latin allies) rather than legitimate issues, despite the sympathy of many nonminers in the area. In some ways, the strikers played into this strategy. The "Mexicans," like the Irish in Butte, saw no contradiction between calling on their ethnic solidarity as "Mexicans" and workers and their rights as "Americans." But the construction of "Mexicans" as disorderly and the cause of local unrest went hand in hand with the development of the Arizona Rangers as a cross-border disciplinary force, putting down Indian insurrections, strikes, and any other mobilization that threatened the growing corporate-state alliance north and south of the border.[58]

This southern border alliance was mirrored on the northern border, with the Canadian Mounties in the role of the Rangers. As elsewhere in Canada, the number of strikes jumped in the first decade of the twentieth century over the last decade of the nineteenth, more than tripling in the Canadian Northwest. In the 1906 Alberta Railway and Irrigation Company strike, the workers turned to the United Mine Workers of America, no doubt impressed by their string of victories in 1903 in Arkansas, Indian Territory, and northern Texas, rather than to the Western Federation of Miners, which they perceived as more radical. Like the miners at Clifton-Morenci, the Canadian workers wanted an eight-hour workday, a minimum wage, and union recognition. When the company's general manager rejected their proposals, almost all the 524 employees walked out. As had the mine manager at Clifton-Morenci, the general manager in Alberta called on government troops, in this case, the Mounties, whose commissioner sent his troops. They took up residence in company boxcars, ate company meals, and swore in eleven company employees as "special constables." They became, essentially, an arm of the company. The Mounties even infiltrated the union. The Mountie presence, their protection of strikebreaking workers, and their prevention of protests led to a stalemate until the coming of winter led Deputy Minister of Labour Mackenzie King to broker an agreement, as Teddy Roosevelt had three years earlier during the U.S. coal strike, giving strikers a wage increase and grievance procedure but none of their key demands, including union recognition and a closed shop.[59]

Where workers did win strikes in these years, the mobility of workers and their organizations and ideas had much to do with victory, even where employers tried to use that mobility to their own benefit. In 1903, for example, during the Texas and Pacific Coal Company strike, at a cost of $90,000, the company "brought in several trainloads of replacement workers, only to see all but three of the men turn around before reaching the mines." Those three then joined the union, becoming known as "$30,000 men." Anti-Díaz organizer Abrán Salcido helped workers organize in Clifton-Morenci in 1903 and Cananea, Mexico, in 1906.[60] Without land-based border controls, workers from the United States, Latin America, Europe, and Canada, like capital, flowed easily across North America.

Colliding Diasporas and the Borders of Whiteness

At the same time that Mexican workers were demanding to be treated on a par with their "white" counterparts in the Southwest, agitation among workers claiming to be "white" in the Pacific Northwest was coming to a head. Pushed by the same forces as workers in Mexico, Ireland, and elsewhere, South Asians left the subcontinent to work in Hong Kong and then Vancouver, Seattle, and their hinterlands. Labor contractors brought Japanese workers to plantations in Hawai'i, who then left the recently annexed U.S. territory for the Pacific coast of North America. There these groups encountered a workforce that had already successfully excluded Chinese workers, already identified itself as "white" and "free" in contrast to contracted and Asian labor.[61]

The collision of these diasporas was not a pretty sight. They collided in rapidly growing areas of the American West, whether in the mining towns of the Southwest, where places like Bisbee, Arizona, and Cananea, Sonora, grew as much as tenfold in population in the century's first decade, or in the lumber camps, mines, and cities of the Northwest. Washington's population grew at six times the rate of the national average, doubling in that decade, and in British Columbia nearly 80 percent of residents in 1900 were recent arrivals.[62]

Bill Haywood had announced in May 1903 that the WFM would henceforth organize among Chinese and Japanese laborers as a powerful symbol of international working-class solidarity, but it was a hard sell. For the Irish, the situation was particularly fraught. Coming from a colonized island off Great Britain in a world rapidly being divided into colonizers and colonized, their situation remained unstable. They asserted their rights not as "Englishmen," the way British laborers struggled. That claim would have been anathema to Irish struggling against British rule. Instead, they ferociously asserted their rights as "white" men. In the nineteenth century, such claims had contributed to the outlawing of most Chinese immigration to the United States. In the twentieth century, it combined with new imperatives in the United States and Canada to define themselves as white nations.[63]

For Canadians, the sense of standing at a crossroads must have been intense. How independent were they as a dominion? The British promised free circulation within the empire. Did Canada have the right to determine who could cross its borders? Would it be a participant in the empire on a par with England itself? Or would it be more like India, clearly subordinate? Could Canadians successfully demand a role as colonizers, not colonized, with certain rights of sovereignty, including whom to admit within their borders, and as members of the white "family" of nations? In the context of this instability and dramatic diversity, the nature of the future society seemed up for grabs.

In 1907 J. E. Wilton was a recent English immigrant to Vancouver and already secretary of the Vancouver Trades and Labour Council. He was also an advocate of Asian exclusion. Under his leadership, the Trades and Labour Council established the Canadian branch of the Asiatic Exclusion League. He had worked in Australia, New Zealand, and South Africa and had witnessed in Natal, South Africa, what he saw as the fruits of large-scale immigration of South Asians to the point that they outnumbered white settlers by 1900. He saw "honest working white men who fought for the country walking the streets by days, sleeping in the parks by nights" while South Asians prospered as merchants, artisans, and farmers. By contrast, he called exclusionary Australia and New Zealand a "veritable white man's paradise" where "the capitalists obeyed the law and employed white men at a white wage."[64]

Workers like Wilton carried their ethnicity with them, as well as the ideas they acquired in the global circuits of empire.

The Asiatic Exclusion League had its origins in San Francisco in 1905 as the Japanese and Korean Exclusion League. On Labor Day, September 2, 1907, amid the festivities, white workers in Bellingham, Washington, began attacking South Asians. Several hundred South Asians lived in the town, often in barracks; most mills employed some, paying them less than they paid white workers, $2.00 per day instead of $2.22. Two days later, between four hundred and five hundred white men marched on South Asian neighborhoods while local law enforcement officials basically stood aside. The violence of the attack drove South Asians from their homes en masse, some to Vancouver and others to California.[65] On September 7 Vancouver followed suit. The Japanese and Korean Exclusion League became the Asiatic Exclusion League.

Vancouver's Asiatic Exclusion League organized an anti-Asian protest that drew twenty-five thousand people, including representatives from fifty-eight labor organizations from both sides of the U.S.-Canada border. Their speakers demanded new immigration policies modeled on those of Australia and South Africa, and the roused participants marched into Vancouver's Chinese and Japanese neighborhoods, instigating several days of armed conflict. Better prepared than the South Asians in Bellingham, the Japanese and Chinese barricaded their quarters and, armed with guns, repelled their attackers. Not only were they not driven from the city, they successfully called a strike to bring home to their attackers and those who had failed to defend them their importance to the local economy.[66]

To quiet the rising disorder, the Canadian and U.S. governments separately negotiated what became known as "Gentlemen's Agreements" with Japan. Japan had demonstrated, with its victory in the Russo-Japanese War in 1905, that it could not be treated lightly. A unilateral arrangement like Chinese exclusion, first enacted in the United States in 1882 and repeatedly renewed, was risky. Nor was Britain likely to condone the extension to Japanese immigrants of the exorbitant per-head tax imposed on Chinese immigrants to Canada, $100 in 1900 and $500 (almost a year's wages for a worker) in 1902. Instead, the Japanese government agreed to limit passports it issued.[67]

Roosevelt feared Japanese political designs on California; he admitted it was one reason he had sent the fleet to the Pacific. Meeting with politicians from British Columbia, Roosevelt insisted, "We have got to build up our western country with our white civilization." Earlier in 1907 President Roosevelt had already issued an executive order authorizing immigration officials to refuse entrance to Japanese and Korean workers with passports issued for anywhere but the continental United States. In the first nine months of that year, more than eight thousand Asian immigrants had landed at Canadian Pacific ports, over half asking for admission to the United States.[68]

Well aware that labor contractors on both sides of the U.S.-Canada border smuggled workers back and forth, the U.S. and Canadian governments also collaborated in what historian Kornel Chang calls the "institutionalization" of the border, "a binational system of border policing and surveillance in the Pacific Northwest." U.S. immigration officials, who had been lobbying for more officers, got them.[69] For the first time, the United States began to keep records of land-based immigration.

One writer in the American Federation of Labor's newspaper claimed, "Men on both sides of the international line feel that the continent of North America is intended to afford the largest democratic development to the white men of the earth" and that the American West "is the region that the common man finds his last chance; it is the land of the . . . homestead, high wages, men at work on the soil, women toiling in the home, the scene of the square deal for every square fellow."[70]

There were dissenting voices to this depiction of racialized conflict that emerged from the West. Josiah Royce, who had grown up in the Grass Valley, California, gold fields, in 1906 gave a series of lectures to the Society for Ethical Culture in New York and Philadelphia on race prejudice, which he published in 1908. In them he condemned assertions of Black inferiority as ill-founded and misguided and wondered whether it is "a 'yellow peril' . . . or a 'black peril'—or perhaps, after all, is it not rather some form of 'white peril' which most threatens the future of humanity in this day of great struggles and complex issues." And despite the mayor's full-throated endorsement of anti-Asian policy, when San Francisco faced an outbreak of bubonic plague, its Citizens Health Committee determined not to repeat the 1900 outbreak, when a bungled quarantine demonized Chinese immigrants and sealed off Chinatown. Instead, they focused on killing every rat in the city, succeeding by 1909 in killing one million rats and finding only two cases of plague in Chinatown.[71]

These views did not prevail. Nor did the Gentlemen's Agreement quiet anti-Asian activism. In 1908 the *Vancouver Daily Post* printed a cartoon titled *Looking Ahead: What It May Come to If the Oriental Invasion Is Not Stopped.* It pictured, seated on a raised platform, an elderly "Homo Albus (White Man) At one time very numerous in this province may still be found east of the Rocky Mountains" as an Asian lecturer tells an audience of East and South Asians, "We have here gentlemen positively the last specimen of a white man known to exist in B.C." After Bellingham and Vancouver, expulsions of South Asians occurred as far north as Juneau, Alaska, and as far south as Live Oak, California. Many South Asians headed for the interior, where their coethnics had settled, European Americans had not yet organized, and the demand for agricultural labor was rising fast. In 1910 the United States established Angel Island, off San Francisco, as the counterpart to the East Coast's Ellis Island and there detained for prolonged periods would-be Asian immigrants.[72]

Federal Troops and Federales

If border policing was meant to preserve a white man's West, it was also meant to reduce labor unrest. Unlike the United States and Canada, Mexico would not police Asian immigration in the first decade of the twentieth century. Mexican enterprises, including those owned by U.S. investors, relied on Chinese labor.[73] On the other hand, when it came to Mexican dissident labor organizers and Yaqui nationalists, the United States and Mexico found common ground.

On June 1, 1906, three years to the day after the strike at Clifton-Morenci, four hundred miners (the same number as members of the PLM local) shut down one of Cananea's largest mines. As there was in the copper camps of southern Arizona, there was a dual wage system, with Mexicans paid less than Anglos. In Mexico the rate differential demarcating Anglo from Mexican vastly surpassed that in the United States.[74] Now Mexican miners demanded to be paid and promoted on the same terms as their U.S. counterparts, and they demanded an eight-hour day. The miners elected two PLM members to negotiate new labor contracts.[75]

William Greene, on behalf of CCCC, rejected the demands, and the strikers marched through town. The manager turned a fire hose on them. Gunfire ensued, killing several men on both sides within minutes. The manager and his brother were caught by the crowd and killed as they tried to escape. U.S. corporate elites whizzed through town in their new automobiles, deputized U.S. employees, and in the next clash, near Greene's mansion, U.S. employees killed half a dozen Mexicans.[76]

As they had at Clifton-Morenci in 1903, both the corporate leaders and the municipal elites who condemned those corporate leaders' actions as reckless reached for whatever troops they could get. They got quite a variety. The governor of Sonora, Rafael Izábal, sent *rurales*, or federal troops; he also sent the Russian émigré Emil Kosterlitzky and his border police force—more or less the equivalent of the Rangers. En route to the scene, the governor, traveling through southern Arizona as the fastest way to get to Cananea, ran into a group of Arizona Rangers and "volunteers." They wanted to join the fray. At Greene's request, Izábal allowed them in, but only if they disbanded as Rangers. They obliged, entering the country as individual civilians, and Izábal then accepted them as Mexican volunteers under his orders.[77]

The disbanded Rangers arrived first and dispersed the strikers but did not deter them. As Greene and Izábal made speeches to symbolize the restoration of order, the strikers ridiculed them and the "order" they claimed to represent, the privatized, corporate state. When the *rurales* (the government's rural police) finally arrived, they reinforced the notion of a state run amok with a drinking spree that led to gunfire and further casualties on both sides. Heavily outnumbered, Izábal and his men could do little. It was Kosterlitzky who restored order, partly by sending the thinly disguised Rangers home immediately. Normally, Kosterlitzky was quite happy to cooperate with the Rangers on both sides of the border, but he understood that in this case they represented to the local population an illegitimate invading force operating on behalf of foreign capital.[78]

The Mexican government created a permanent garrison at Cananea, and U.S. residents succeeded in having Kosterlitzky as its commanding officer. The CCCC even began to employ police through Kosterlitzky, who disbursed the wages and extended corporate control into the countryside.[79]

Infuriated by the Cananea strike, Greene and the Mexican government went after the PLM's leadership in the United States. They hired detectives, including Pinkertons. They ordered Mexican consuls to engage in surveillance. They put U.S. local sheriffs, police officers, and marshals on retainer. While Ricardo Flores Magón, leader of the PLM, continued to elude them, U.S. officials jailed PLM members. They held Tucson PLM members in jail for weeks. There and elsewhere, judges did not hand the PLM members over to the Mexican government. PLM actions had been political, not criminal, and so the men were not extraditable. But while judges did not extradite, they did deport ten of the Tucson rebels and many others in Arizona's mining districts, setting the precedent for future mass deportations of Mexicans.[80]

Magón meanwhile was captured with his confederates in 1907 in Los Angeles on charges of violating the U.S. Neutrality Act. At the Los Angeles County jail they became a sensation, a tourist attraction, and a focal point for leftist organizing. Officials transferred them to Arizona, where they remained imprisoned until 1910.[81]

In the same years, Yaquis elicited similar cross-border mobilizations. The war between the Yaquis and the Mexican government was already decades old by the turn of the century. As had the United States with its indigenous peoples, the Mexican government saw the Yaquis as an impediment to progress, and in the last decades of the nineteenth century, the governor of Sonora worked to bring in the railroad and confiscate Yaqui land, opening the way for Mexican and foreign colonies and investors, including those from the United States. Ironically, they included two colonies of Cherokees fleeing the increasing depredations on their land and rights in Indian Territory, soon to be Oklahoma. They fled south as Yaquis fled north across the border, establishing the Pascua colony in Tucson and others in Yuma and Los Angeles.[82]

The Yaquis had signed a treaty with the Mexican federal government in 1897, but the federal troops, or *federales*, had not left, triggering a further revolt early in the new century. The bloody battle of Mazocoba left four hundred Yaquis dead, almost a thousand prisoners, and nine hundred in flight. As the intensity of fighting grew, increasingly by guerrilla means, the Mexican government started arresting Yaquis wholesale and enlisted Colonel Emil Kosterlitzky, who would later that year be so helpful at the Cananea strike, to capture Yaquis fleeing to Arizona. Those captured were brutally treated, and in an effort to destroy the Yaquis as a people, families were split up, with children who survived adopted by Mexicans or used as servants in Mexican homes.[83] In 1907 the U.S. Department of Commerce joined the effort, enlisting the Arizona Rangers to hunt down Yaquis and deport them back to Mexico, despite the U.S. government's awareness of the conditions the Yaquis faced there.

Yaquis continued to resist depredations on their land, and they funded and armed that resistance by working in U.S. mines and using their wages to buy U.S. guns. In 1910 Arizona's governor, Joseph Henry Kibbey, prohibited the sale of arms to Yaquis. Since few could tell a Yaqui from a Mexican, however, and many Yaquis had Mexican relatives, and many residents of the border had both Yaqui and Mexican forebears, the law had minimal success. On the other hand, eager for peaceful conditions for their economic enterprises, U.S. investors secretly supplied Sonoran troops with weapons from Arizona.[84] As a result, both sides got arms from Arizona.

While the increasing involvement of Mexican federal and a variety of U.S. troops policing both sides of the U.S.-Mexico border sat well with some border interests, it sat less well with others. Many U.S. border towns still had a Mexican American majority, in contrast to the hinterland, which was rapidly filling with Anglo ranchers and farmers. In the border towns, Mexican American elites held sway, and Mexican Americans often dominated law enforcement. In Laredo, Texas, an immigration inspector complained that immigration agents in South Texas "can count on no cooperation from the City, County officials, including the Police Department, as nearly all of these people are hostile to the Immigration Service and the laws under which they work."[85] The era saw a string of border heroes whose defiance of the state and evasion of law officers became the stuff of ballads, or *corridos*, from Joaquín Murieta in nineteenth-century California to rancher Gregorio Cortez in early twentieth-century Texas.

At Brownsville, Texas, just over a decade after white U.S. troops fruitlessly scoured the Texas-Mexico border, searching for the anti-Díaz revolutionary leader Catarino Garza, and just months after the strike at Cananea, violence erupted between the U.S. federal troops stationed there (now Black) and the largely Mexican-descent citizens. Often interpreted by historians and certainly interpreted by Black activists at the time as a race riot, the violence makes more sense as the fruits of resistance to the growing federal policing of local life on the border.[86]

Local law enforcement, as well as local citizens, subjected soldiers to daily harassment. When soldiers of whatever color entered town on payday, heading for bars and other entertainments, they became an easy mark for just about everyone who stood to gain from relieving them of their funds. Dance hall girls, gamblers, bartenders, and sheriffs, colluding or not, took advantage of them. When Black troops returned to the border after the Spanish-American War, they replaced the white soldiers as targets. In 1899 at Rio Grande City, Texas, Private William Turner, a veteran of the Black Ninth Cavalry for five years, was arrested in town for carrying a pistol; he pleaded guilty and paid his $34 fine. About a month later, on payday, after a brawl in a gambling house where civilians claimed that drunken soldiers drew their weapons, sending the customers fleeing, Turner encountered a group of Mexicans who beat and shot him; he was not alone. Another five-year veteran was shot through the shoulder fleeing to the post, and Mexicans stabbed two other Black soldiers. Local authorities responded by arresting two soldiers who claimed to have been attacked by Mexican gamblers. They arrested no civilians. The inexperienced post commander responded to rumors of dozens of armed Mexicans planning to attack the fort by placing a Gatling gun near the fort's gate and firing several rounds. The investigation that ensued garnered a raft of such conflicting evidence that investigators could assign no clear blame.[87]

Was this hostility about race? The Seminole Negro Indian Scouts, who camped outside the fort at Brownsville rather than in it and all of whom spoke Spanish, had no trouble with the townspeople. Similarly, though such incidents occurred in El Paso and Laredo, El Paso's substantial civilian Black population escaped any damaging effects of the city residents' hostilities to the troops. On the other hand, U.S. federal forces had found their scouts singularly unhelpful when tracking Catarino Garza's forces from 1891 to 1893.[88] Local distrust of federal soldiers had long roots.

The Black Twenty-Fifth Infantry arrived in Brownsville in July 1906. Of the town's eight thousand inhabitants, the quarter of the town labeled "white" was comprised largely of "Spaniards"—local elites, businessmen or railroad developers who had settled there after 1900. The rest were "Mexican." The coinage was Mexican, and English speakers had to learn Spanish to survive. Most of the townspeople sympathized with anti-Díaz forces and resented the U.S. Army's role in putting down such revolts.[89]

Still, difficult as the border assignment was for white troops, it was worse for Black ones. Texas was a segregated state, with Blacks on one side and everyone else on the other. Brownsville's bars adhered to those requirements. Black soldiers faced not only regular police harassment but also racial slurs. Black soldiers were understandably affronted. Particularly after the Spanish-American War, with their service in Cuba and the Philippines as agents of the U.S. empire and with the increasingly professionalized army and its rising status, as one report explained, "the colored soldier is much more aggressive in his attitude on the social equality question than he used to be."[90] These Black soldiers would be policing the national border and pushing against the racial one.

As they were at Rio Grande City, the contours of the Brownsville violence are mired in contradictory testimony. A complaint that some of the soldiers had assaulted a white woman led the fort's commanding officer to confine all soldiers to the post by August 13. That night at midnight, in the space of ten minutes, someone or perhaps several people fired up to two hundred shots into homes and businesses near the fort. At one of the few saloons to serve the troops, a young bartender was killed. Though the commanding officer ordered a personnel check immediately after the shooting and found no men missing, the town's civilians blamed the troops.[91]

The ensuing investigation produced no physical evidence and only conflicting testimony. President Roosevelt chose to interpret the silence of the troops as proof of conspiracy. He delayed announcing his decision until after the midterm elections so as not to alienate Black voters' traditional support for Republican candidates. On November 6, 1906, Roosevelt announced the dishonorable discharges, without any formal court-martial or filing of official charges, of 167 men from the Twenty-Fifth Infantry.[92] With that dismissal, the complex Mexican border incident did indeed become an affair of Black and white.

After the Civil War, the United States had deployed its Black soldiers to police Indians, Mexicans, Filipinos, and "others" on the edges of its new empire. It had also occasionally deployed Black troops against strikers. At the heart of the empire, on the other hand, the situation of Black troops was marginal. The spectacle of twenty-year veterans dismissed without charges led Black newspapers such as the *New York Age* to condemn any Black man who would enlist in such an army. Even some white Texans shared their outrage. The outrage did nothing to change the discharge. Instead, within a year of the incident, the government shifted all the Black regiments to Cuba or the Philippines.[93]

The lesson of the Brownsville riot became the marginalization of Black soldiers. That lesson swamped any official recognition of ongoing local borderlands hostility to increasing federal policing of the national border, whether by Mexico or the United States.

Policing Women on the Border

While male workers were concerned with manliness and autonomy and corporations recruited male workers, women also crossed the West's national borders. They too found it virtually impossible to separate the threads tying together transborder capital moves, worker mobility, increasing nation-state assertion and capacity, and dissident mobilizations.

Teresa Urrea, the daughter of a Mexican rancher and a Tehueco Indian servant (Teresa was legitimized a dozen years later), became a *curandera* (healer) whose symbolic value overshadowed her actual deeds on both sides of the border. In 1889 a vision led Urrea to add spiritual to healing services; she amassed a following well beyond her father's estate and preached against clerical abuses in favor of equality and love. By April 1890 she was baptizing nearby Yaqui children at the moment the Díaz government was buying up their communal land. Despite her refusal to be drawn into the dispute, the village of Tomochic rebelled, defending their land in her name and fighting off the *rurales*, only to suffer slaughter at their hands.

With the Díaz regime suspecting her involvement, Urrea fled to Nogales, Arizona, where a crowd welcomed her. In southern Arizona, her father continued his sympathetic connections with anti-Díaz activists who began exploiting Urrea's popularity as La Santa de Cabora despite her repeated, published insistence that "I am not one who authorizes or at the same time interferes with these proceedings." In 1897 the family relocated to Clifton, Arizona, where in 1900 she embarked on a brief marriage to a Yaqui miner.

Clifton's elite knew a good enterprise when they saw one and engineered what promised but then failed to be a lucrative healing tour for Urrea, beginning in San Francisco with an audience of more than a thousand. After a stint in St. Louis, Urrea returned to California, settling in East Los Angeles's Sonoratown and coming to the aid of Mexican Pacific Electric Railway workers who had organized the Union Federal Mexicanos in 1903. Paid less than the Japanese, who were paid less than the Greek workers, seven hundred Mexican workers went on strike that April with the support of the AFL. African American, Chinese, and Japanese workers replaced them; the strikers moved to Oxnard, and Urrea returned to Clifton, Arizona, in the early fall of 1903. She died there in early 1906 at the age of thirty-three, donating her home to the Phelps Dodge company for a hospital.[94] Urrea's connections to capital and labor defy the neat boundaries between them, as did her cross-border appeal. Exceptional in her fame, she was typical in her inability to escape the era's entangled borders.

While Urrea had been able to cross borders without suspicion as to her virtue, vice was the lens through which the state most often saw autonomous women in motion. Ordinary women of all kinds were increasingly drawn into the market for the same reasons as men: dwindling resources at home. In the United States, if they had the resources, were over twenty-one, and had or intended to have citizenship, women could homestead, and single women from Canada, which offered them no such opportunity, headed for the United States to do so. Most women, however, lacked such resources. They entered the market in a variety of ways, including farm production; running mining camp boardinghouses; weaving, as did Navajo women; or using sewing machines, as did Mexican women, Neomexicanas, and others.[95]

Emblematic of women's place in the waged economy was the landmark *Muller v. Oregon* U.S. Supreme Court case, which upheld Oregon's 1903 law forbidding the employment of women for more than ten hours per day. The law, the fruit of a coalition of Oregon progressive groups, at once acknowledged the reality of women's non-family-based participation in the labor market and signaled its questionable acceptability by differentiating women's labor force participation from men's. Women, as more vulnerable and less organized, needed state protection, and the state needed to protect them. Legitimating government regulation was the state's interest in women's ability to produce healthy children. Other laws and regulations signaled that such reproduction should take place only in male-headed households. In Colorado's mining camps, widows and single women could not take in boarders. Housing unrelated male workers made the women's virtue suspect. The inability to take in boarders limited the ability of female heads of household to remain in the camps at all.[96]

The suspicion of women outside male-headed households (meaning women whose relation to the market was unmediated by the men in their families) was enshrined in immigration law. The 1907 Gentlemen's Agreement with Japan mandated that Japanese women could immigrate only if they were married to men resident in the United States. Starting in the same year and enhanced by succeeding statutes, immigration laws excluded not only prostitutes but also women or girls in the United States for any other "immoral purposes." Even if they turned to "immoral purposes" after their arrival in desperation or for whatever reason, they could still be deported, even after an ever-lengthening number of years. Japanese-descent sex workers born in Hawai'i before the United States annexed it were "deported" under the law. The vagueness of "immoral purposes" led to an increasing list of prohibited behaviors, including those outside the market entirely: fornication, premarital sex, adultery, and homosexuality.[97] Marking borders involved not only policing a fictive line but also creating a system of deportation that deeply implicated gender and family formations.

Vice was something imagined as excludable, something that happened on the other side of the border (and, indeed, prostitution was legal and regulated in Mexico). The rise of land-based border patrols and border regimes targeted solo women as potential prostitutes, not only Mexican women from the South but also Anglo women crossing into Canada and Chinese women going anywhere. Women on their own, with no husband or father, if self-sufficient were suspected of prostitution and if not self-sufficient were suspected of depending on the state. They were excluded by the category "likely to be a public charge."[98]

Keeping single and married men mobile and single women immobile was essential to the nation-building and labor demands of the United States, Mexico, and Canada. Women had a particular role to play in the nation the United States hoped to build in the West. Although the West's economy relied on highly transient male labor, as historian Nayan Shah has pointed out, the government increasingly saw migrants and the often transnational societies they built as disorderly and aberrant. Migrants seemed dangerous to the "nation" instead of alternatives to settled society. Officials in the United States and Canada targeted and raided neighborhoods designated as "Chinatown" as centers of vice. This rising suspicion of migrants and increasing investment in the white nuclear family as the ideal western settler came despite and because of the dependence of the region on creating and mobilizing large numbers of migrant workers. Such workers could, by asserting their rights, literally unsettle the region.[99]

The vice undeniable within U.S. borders was corralled in some cases and rendered invisible in others. Cities began to put borders around their sex districts. In Texas the court ruled that Houston's city charter could allow the creation of a sex district, though it could not create a licensing system, and Dallas city officials successfully defended a local ordinance mandating the segregation of prostitution to a limited area of the city. In New Orleans officials increasingly demarcated the red light district and forbid the serving of Blacks and whites in the same establishment. In San Francisco the city began to restrict legal prostitution to the area near the old Barbary Coast.[100]

Anglo women missionaries rescued Mexican, Mormon, Native American, and Asian women from men they characterized as lazy, oversexed, or exploitative, as the opposite of the appropriate domestic relations of protector and protected. That characterization justified the public performance and participation of Anglo women as imperial protectors of debased and vulnerable women. It elided the soldiers visiting brothels and domestic violence, alcoholism, and infidelity, including the debauching of domestic servants in their own households.[101]

Demarcating vice districts and policing women at the national border drew a line between vicious and virtuous women. Such delineating not only confined women to particular roles with limited autonomy in the service of creating a stable society built on white nuclear families but also simultaneously rendered migrants more vulnerable and excluded them as stakeholders.

Conclusion

The hardening of national borders in the U.S. West did not differ from the policing of borders in the company camps and sex districts in the region's cities. Like the determination to define "races" and to differentiate New Mexico from Arizona, those borders were part of the agenda for Beveridge's "master organizers of the world." As shown in the previous chapter, these demarcations evidenced the desire to create ordered space and distinguish it from what was defined as premodern and so disorderly. The "primitive" order lay at odds with the demands of a particular vision of a modern United States that would be tied in part to corporate industrialization, whether agricultural, mining, or other. A Los Angeles settlement house worker in 1906 wrote of "a tunnel in the heart of Los

Angeles connecting a Mexican pueblo, dirty, peaceful, unprogressive, with a handsome, bustling, modern city."[102]

That alternative order became invisible to the progressive industrial and political leaders *as* "order" at all. They determined to create a modern order legible to themselves and to the state, with an identifiable populace, workers, fighters, voters, women, and men neatly if inconsistently demarcated, and to define appropriate participation in the nation.

The great strikes of the middecade, the founding of the IWW and the revolutionary PLM in the same year, the Brownsville riot, the anti-Asian riots, and the enhanced border policing were all part of the same struggle. They resulted from the same collisions of transnational migrations and transnational investment. Some investigators at the time saw them as the last convulsive struggle of the democratic frontier, where power passed from settlers to managerial elites. When employers labeled their offensive against workers a "Citizens Alliance," as they did in Denver in 1903 among many other places across the country, they "implied a struggle, not between workers and employers, but between 'citizens' and the 'lawless element,'" as historian David Brundage points out.[103]

The West continued to rely heavily on migrant workers, but the needs of transnational capital and the capacity of nation-states had shaped new forms of policing and reshaped the meaning of transience. Those needs redefined populations. What, for example, did it mean to be "Mexican"? Theoretically fixed, these lines and borders had to be constantly made and as constantly contested.

3
Being American in Boley, Oklahoma

Boley, a Black town founded in 1903 on a railroad line in east-central Oklahoma, may seem to belong more to the nineteenth century than the twentieth—part of the history of newly freed Black people, called Exodusters, who headed west in the years just after Reconstruction and part of the history of the rise of transcontinental railroads in all their power. The town may seem to belong to the history of Gilded Age speculation, which filled the region with often ephemeral, mirage-like communities. In its violent confrontations with local Creek Indians, Boley may seem a nineteenth-century story of displacement and frontier settlement.

Instead, Boley provides a foundational story of the twentieth-century West and, inescapably, of the twentieth-century nation. Boley's story involves not only speculation and political and capital formation—standard facets of most twentieth-century West histories, as seen in the previous two chapters—but also the racial/ethnic formations, slippages, and re-formations that undergirded them and the related notions of manhood and citizenship. The dramatic and sometimes convoluted history of this early twentieth-century town, its peoples and surroundings, illuminates the complexities of the construction of race in the United States. It provides a culminating example of the early twentieth-century attempts to create order by carefully demarcating western spaces and peoples and a fitting case study to conclude this section of the book.

Oklahoma lies on the border between South and West, an ideal location to answer questions about "race" and "citizenship," incorporation and exclusion. These answers differ from those in New Mexico and Arizona, seen in the previous chapter. But here too they involve struggles over landownership, definitions of modernity, federal and local governance, and competing visions of the future of the West and its appropriate participants.

Boley resulted principally from a shift in U.S. relations with the Creeks, a change made official in the same year as the Spanish-American War (1898). Twelve years earlier, Congress had exempted the Five Civilized Tribes, including the Creeks, from the Dawes Severalty Act (1887), which had promoted the allotment of Indian tribal lands in fixed acreages to individual Indians and opened the "surplus" Indian lands to other settlers. That exemption had protected the Creeks' communal landholding, control over resources, and relative autonomy.

By 1893, however, decent "surplus" lands were scarce, and the Indian Territory of the Five Civilized Tribes, which adjoined Oklahoma Territory, was full of whites who leased Indian lands and fiercely resented their lack of political and economic rights. It was also full of Black and white townsite developers who harbored similar resentment.[1] Congress conceded to intense pressure by creating the Dawes Commission to negotiate with the Five Civilized Tribes for allotment. The Creeks, having witnessed the devastating effect of allotment on other Indian nations, determined allotment a total failure and rejected U.S. attempts to negotiate a new treaty.

In pressing the tribes for allotment, congressional advocates had claimed to be protecting the smallholder and would-be smallholder of whatever color from elite Creeks. Congressmen pointed to members of the Creek Nation, often former plantation owners, who, bereft of forced labor, had moved into less labor-intensive ranching and fenced large swaths of common lands. As seen in the previous two chapters, the concentration of landholding in the U.S. West was a hot-button issue. Like smallholders elsewhere, Creek smallholders cut the fences and contested claims. But neither they nor the elites favored allotment.[2]

Senator Henry L. Dawes, on the other hand, saw communal landholding as impeding progress, insisting it meant "there is no selfishness, which is at the bottom of civilization."[3] When the Creeks and other tribes refused allotment, Congress provided for surveying the lands anyway, and in 1896 Congress authorized the Dawes Commission to make an official roll of the members of each tribe. Such a roll would determine eligibility for allotted land, a clear sign that the commission intended to move ahead with or without tribal consent.

Those two federal moves—surveying and constructing an official roll—alarmed the Creeks, among others, into opening negotiations. When the Creeks nonetheless rejected the ensuing agreement at a special election, Congress in 1898 passed the Curtis Act, unilaterally dissolving the Creek, Chickasaw, Choctaw, and Cherokee Nations, converting their former citizens into U.S. citizens, and mandating the allotment of their lands.[4] Although the U.S. government had refused to allot southern freedmen forty acres each from white rebel-held lands after the Civil War, the federal government now required the Five Civilized Tribes to allot their freedmen forty acres each from the tribal lands.[5] The allotment that formed the townsite of Boley belonged to a child of Creek freedmen, Abigail Barnett. Her legal guardian, "full-blood" Josiah Looney, arranged the sale with developers working with the Fort Smith and Western Railroad.

Ironically, Looney would not have been able to sell his own land to developers. Only certain allottees were entitled to sell their lands immediately. The law's crafters assumed "full-blood" Creeks did not understand markets. They could not sell their allotments for twenty-five years. Creek freedmen and freedwomen and "mixed-bloods" could sell their allotments at will. Even though Creek freedmen often identified themselves as "Creek," only spoke Creek, and had no market experience, the U.S. government designation of them as freedmen—not Indians—allowed them to sell their lands. More Creek land became available to the new settlement when other Black migrants, such as the Turner brothers, obtained allotments by marrying Indian women. In turn, Boley's new Black entrepreneurs from the states (as opposed to Blacks from Indian or Oklahoma *Territory*) founded the Creek-Seminole College.[6]

In Boley, Oklahoma, Creeks who had been forced west more than sixty years earlier, dispossessing previous occupants, now found themselves being dispossessed in part by Boley's Black settlers.[7] The Creeks did not disappear into remote reservations or even into Wild West shows. Instead, they disappeared into a set of competing racial dualisms central to the twentieth-century West and revealed in the way various players narrated early conflicts in and around Boley.

Black Boley

The seeming Black-Creek alliance was more complicated than the founding picture of harmony would imply. To Booker T. Washington, Boley was about Blacks, not about Creeks. "Boley," wrote Washington in a 1908 *Outlook* article, "represents a dawning race consciousness, a wholesome desire to do something to make the race respected; something which shall demonstrate the right of the negro, not merely as an individual, but as a race to have a worthy and permanent place in the civilization that the American people are building."[8] Boley, then, would cement Black claims to be "American."

Washington differentiated between the Exodusters of the nineteenth century and the twentieth-century Boley migrants from the South and Midwest. These twentieth-century Black *civilized* settlers differed from earlier migrants, whom he described as a "helpless and ignorant horde of black people." The new arrivals included "land-seekers and home-builders, men [note only men] who have come prepared to build up the country." These Black migrants were "enterprising" and had "learned to build schools, to establish banks and conduct newspapers." This was not Frederick Jackson Turner's rough democracy on the frontier. Indeed, Washington gave his speech at Boley's new $35,000 Masonic Temple.[9] Education, commerce, and communication marked Boley's new settlers as worthy of being colonizers rather than colonized.

At the same time Washington claimed for them an "American" identity, he posed them as distinctively African, having "recovered something," Washington wrote, "of the knack for trade that their foreparents in Africa were famous for."[10] Theirs was a uniquely African American civilizing mission.

The civilizing mission would apply uniquely to Blacks as subjects and not just civilizers. Washington claimed to have achieved a "high respect" for Indians' "character and intelligence" during the last years of his stay at Hampton Institute, when, he wrote, "I had charge of the Indian students." By including that backdrop, he established a racial hierarchy that placed African Americans in custodial authority over Indians and simultaneously separated the two as distinct races, a project he was at pains to solidify elsewhere in the article, despite the presence of freedmen among the Creeks who identified themselves as Creeks and the presence of many Creeks, not freedmen, who had some African descent. Washington added, as evidence that Boley stood "on the edge of civilization," "You can still hear on summer nights, I am told, the wild notes of the Indian drums, and the shrill cries of the Indian dancers among the hills beyond the settlement."[11] Indians, as Washington portrayed them, were permanently beyond settlement, signifiers of the frontier.

To Washington, only Blacks could be brought into the fold of American civilization. He had been, he wrote, "particularly interested to see [Indians] in their own country [Oklahoma], where they still preserve to some extent their native institutions." However, he claimed that he rarely could catch sight of what he termed "a genuine native Indian." "When I inquired," he confessed, "as I frequently did, for the 'natives,' it almost invariably happened that I was introduced not to an Indian, but to a Negro." Stopping "at the home of one of the prominent 'natives' of the Creek Nation," the superintendent of the Tullahassee Mission, Washington pronounced, "But he is a negro. The negroes who are known in that locality as 'natives' are the descendants of slaves that the Indians brought with them from Alabama and Mississippi, when they migrated to this Territory." Other "natives" he met, he claimed, "as far as my observation went . . . were, on the contrary, white men." When he finally asked, "Where . . . are the Indians?" he repeatedly got the reply, "They have gone. . . . [T]hey have gone back."[12]

Despite the presence of the Creek-Seminole College and Agricultural Institute in Boley, in this article Washington participated in the classic dominant Anglo-American narrative of the disappearing Indian, ever retreating before the advance of civilization. "The Indians," he explained, "who own practically all the lands, and until recently had the local government largely in their own hands, are to a very large extent regarded by the white settlers, who are rapidly filling up the country, as almost a negligible quantity," a view further evidenced by the constitution of the new state of Oklahoma taking "no account of the Indians in drawing its distinctions among the races. For the constitution," he claimed, "there exist only the negro and the white man. The reason seems to be that the Indians have either receded—'gone back,' as the saying in that region is—on the advance of the white race" or have intermarried with whites and been absorbed by that race.[13] Either case foreclosed any distinct Indian presence.

In Washington's schema, Blacks formed part of this civilized advance rather than part of the retreat. "The negroes," he insisted, "immigrants to Indian Territory, have not, however 'gone back'" but instead were working alongside whites, with their banks, businesses, schools, and churches. Moreover, demonstrating the essentially progressive nature of the race, part of the future, not the past, of the nation, he claimed that even those Blacks labeled "natives" "do not shun the white man and his civilization, but, on the contrary, rather seek it, and enter, with the negro immigrants, into competition with the white man for its benefits." Indeed, in contrast to those Washington labeled as "genuine" Indians, "native negroes" he found, had been helpfully influenced by the Black southern migrants, not absorbed by whites, and not defeated. As Black troops of the U.S. Army had served in the Philippines during the Spanish-American War, here on the domestic frontier Blacks formed a part of that advance guard of "civilization." They were going forward, not back, not as a blended but as an alternative future. Indeed, Washington focused attention on Boley rather than the myriad other Black-founded towns because of its exclusion of whites. Whites could come to trade, but they could not stay, even overnight. Oklahoma was full of white-only towns, white-dominated towns, and Black-founded towns, but Boley stood as the single exclusively Black town. "In short," Washington concluded, "Boley is another chapter in the long struggle of the negro for moral, industrial, and political freedom."[14]

Mixing It Up

Washington was correct in noting that the Oklahoma constitution delineated only two categories: "Wherever in this Constitution and laws of this state the word or words, 'colored' or 'colored race,' 'negro' or 'negro race,' are used, the same shall be construed to mean or apply to all persons of African descent. The term 'white race' shall include all other persons." In other words, Oklahoma recognized only Black people and white people. Despite "Oklahoma" meaning "red man" in the Choctaw language, there was no room for an independent racial category "Indian" here. Was it because Indians had ceased to be a factor? The Black and white population of Indian Territory had increased more than 400 percent between 1890 and statehood, while the Indian population had held steady. By 1907 the roughly 61,000 Indians were vastly outnumbered by the more than 80,000 Black and 530,000 white people. Portions of Indian Territory were heavily Black, over 40 percent in some counties and over 80 percent in some townships.[15] In that context, perhaps Washington could be forgiven for casting the Indians as of dwindling import.

But Indians still mattered as voters and landholders. Oklahoma defined "race" in the context of creating laws about voting, schools, and marriage. Marriage and landholding were intimately connected in a territory where marriages had entwined people defined as white, Black, and Indian for a century or more. By the 1880s seven states had banned marriages between whites and Indians, leaving Indians free to marry Black people. If Oklahoma did so, it would not only upend existing marriages between whites and Indians and jeopardize white property-holding but also allow the means by which Boley was created, via collaborations, including marriage, between Creeks and freedmen, to be perpetually replicated, and the rapidly growing number of Black landholders in Oklahoma, already the majority in some districts, would increase.[16] Black-Creek alliances, marital and otherwise, would be fostered.

What, though, did it mean to categorize the Creeks as "white"? Such a categorization flew in the face of Creek diversity. In Washington's record, no people of African descent could be "genuine" Indians. Apparently, the Creeks themselves understood things differently, at least through the late nineteenth century. After all, Creeks and Cherokees would joke with each other before the Civil War, "You Cherokees are so mixed with whites we cannot tell you from whites," to which Cherokees would reply, "You Creeks are so mixed with Negroes we cannot tell you from Negroes." To those Creeks, "mixed-blood" could include both African and European ancestry. African Americans who had escaped slavery joined the

Creek Nation; African Americans whom Creeks enslaved before 1800 usually gained their freedom. Both groups often married Creeks. No lines prevented people of joint Indian and African descent from acceptance as "Creek." People, here labeled "Afro-Creeks," had long held important leadership positions, including the highly respected "old beloved woman" and chief. In 1900 Creeks with some African ancestors still held leadership positions, including the elected office of chief. Photographs of Creek leaders at the time bear out the wide range of Creek heritage.[17]

Yet even before Oklahoma statehood and despite the relatively full acceptance among Creeks of Afro-Creeks, Creek relations with freedmen were complicated and contradictory. The Exoduster and migrant towns were not, as it turns out, the only Black towns in Oklahoma. In 1903, when Boley was founded, there were already three towns of Creek freedmen (Arkansas Colored, Canadian Colored, and North Fork Colored), indicating a significant degree of preexisting segregation. Even those Creeks most disposed to define the nation by culture and affinity as a political unit began to shift toward a racialized definition based on indigenous Creek ancestry with allowances for some European but no African heritage. In 1883 Isparhecher, a leader of smallholder Creeks, had triumphed in the tribal election and told the council, "Every Muskogee [Creek] citizen, whether his skin be red, white or black, has equal rights and privileges in this nation, and the most abject, poor and ignorant is entitled to equal consideration with the most distinguished, rich and learned at the hands of our officers." He retained those views in 1891, but by 1898 he had excluded freedmen from the category "Indian." It had become clear to him that expanding membership in the Creek Nation would reduce the land available to each. While he argued for Indians receiving 160 acres each, freedmen, he concluded, should only receive 40.[18]

Freedmen, whether previously enslaved by Creeks or by others, usually had no Creek lineage. After the Civil War and under pressure from the U.S. government, Creeks had granted citizenship to Creek freedmen. Freedmen disagreed among themselves as to how eagerly the Creeks had done so. Even when they had some African ancestry, as did Confederate veteran Pleasant Porter, Creeks who identified with southern white culture and had owned numerous enslaved people tended be more hostile toward freedmen than did smallholders. Even the smallholders, however, occasionally resented the increasing freedman presence and voting power in Creek Territory, as Isparhecher had come to do. Blacks from the southeastern United States and by the 1890s from Kansas, Missouri, and Texas fled post–Civil War racial violence and were welcomed into Creek freedmen towns where the elected Creek freedmen chiefs facilitated their acceptance as Creek citizens. Such acceptance swelled the towns' population and hence their political heft within the Creek tribal council, as well as their claims to Creek lands.[19]

Amid rising tensions, Creek criminal codes exacted harsher penalties for freedmen than for Creeks, and civil laws taxed freedmen, but only those who were not tribal members. Moreover, Creek law made it unlawful for Creek men to marry Black women. These laws were clear signals that the acceptance of freedmen among Creeks was not universal.[20]

Unquestionably, however, the Creeks had continued their greater openness to Blacks than had other groups. Unlike the Cherokees, they granted the freedmen property rights in the nation. Although Creek men could not marry Black women, Creek women could marry Black men. All children of Creek women and Black men, when the children were not more than half Black, were counted as Creek citizens (retaining the matrilineal character of tribal identity).[21] Such unions were common. Relations between freedmen and Creeks, in short, may at least for some have been more about tribal identity than about color hostility. There were, after all, also laws that governed the terms of incorporating whites.

Indeed, terminology regarding race may obscure more than it reveals. Whites had adopted something they thought of as blood quantum as a way of judging racial and ethnic identity, particularly in the South before the Civil War. Indians had not. Many Indians who dealt with whites demonstrated that they had become adept at manipulating the whites' language regarding such matters. Others demonstrated clearly that such criteria were meaningless to them. A man named Redbird Smith testified before the 1905–6 Senate Committee investigating the chaos in Indian Territory that resulted from the 1901 settlement. The committee asked, "Are you a full-blood Indian?" "I am a Cherokee," Smith responded. The senators repeated and, they thought, clarified, "Are you a full blood or part blood?" The question stumped the witness. The interpreter interjected, "From my experience he must be a full blood." The witness chimed in, "I think I must be a full blood; I don't know, but I think I am." At this point even the senators clearly became confused, agreeing with the interpreter that blood quantum was a matter of experience, not biology: "From your experience you must be a full-blood Cherokee Indian?" Answer: "Yes, sir." The senators were in good company. By 1900 the U.S. Census Bureau defined "full-blood," when referring to Creeks, as one-quarter Creek Indian.[22]

Rivalries

Despite Washington's dismissal of Indians as significant actors in Oklahoma's future, Boley's own settlers knew better. Black newcomers deplored the failure of the Native population to see the benefit of an alliance by which "negroes and Indians would have the political balance of power in the future state of Oklahoma." At the same time, Boley's booster paper seemed oblivious to Indian fears of dispossession. The *Boley Progress* repeatedly advertised the newly available "surplus lands," twenty thousand acres "of the finest land in the Creek Nation surrounding Boley to be leased and bought by Negroes."[23]

The Boley southern migrant town fathers were chagrined to find that even Creek freedmen, the "native negroes," were often less than welcoming. Washington admitted that, in the first years of the settlement, "native negroes" had occasionally come in to "shoot up" the town. He framed it as a case of savage drunken revelry. Creek freedmen reasoned differently, however. "I was eating out the same pot with the Indians . . . while they was still licking the master's boots in Texas," claimed one, signifying the higher status and inclusion granted even enslaved Blacks among the Creeks than among southern whites. The dissidents' shooting frequently broke up church services and other public gatherings, and they shot out windows late at night. Creek freedmen labeled the newcomers "state negroes," saw them as inferior, and recognized them as a threat to their own tribal position. Their suspicions were borne out when, in 1904, only a year after Boley's founding, the Creek Nation's school board introduced segregation, stipulating separate schools for all Blacks—whether tribal members or new arrivals—and Creek students.[24]

But strictly racial terms may not be the best way to understand even that segregation. In his testimony before the Senate committee, Creek witness Eufala Harjo complained, "As long as the Indian had his own schools they were good schools and they were proud of them; but they can't say that anymore." "The white men came in and crowded us out and took our schools away from us," he explained, adding, "It seems to me that the little white children and the little negro children should not be made to go to the Indian schools that the Indians made with their own money." The issue was not simply the overcrowding of schools and strained budgets. The issue was also cultural behavior. Harjo offered this analogy: "I came in here a good while ago, and I was sitting back there a long time. . . . You saw me sitting back there, and I don't like to come forward. Now, when I take a little Indian child to school the white man and the negroes will go before me to school with their children and they will put their children first and they will push mine out of school, and that is the way it will go." In Creek eyes, including those of Creek freedmen, white and Black interlopers shared an aggression that pushed Indians aside.[25]

Many among the Five Civilized Tribes in Indian Territory favored a two-state solution, with Oklahoma Territory becoming Oklahoma and Indian Territory becoming the state of Sequoyah. In 1903 the principal chief of the Choctaws, Green McCurtain, called for a constitutional convention. "It seems to me," he declared, "in the light of our history, it would be fitting and just to permit the Indian to have a voice in the erection of at least one state, on a continent to which he once lay claim." In 1905 the Five Civilized Tribes met in the Sequoyah Convention, and Indian Territory then ratified its proceedings.[26] Prosperous ex-Confederates dominated the convention's leadership, including General Pleasant Porter, principal chief of the Creek Nation, whom attendees elected as president, and William H. Murray, a white segregationist and intermarried citizen of the Chickasaw Nation. Not everyone in Indian Territory agreed with them. White tenants in Indian Territory feared their disenfranchisement would be made permanent and their hope of achieving yeoman status foreclosed if they were no longer ruled by Washington DC but directly by Indians. Some Indians opposed statehood, favoring the preservation of separate tribes over a joint identity. Others, in the context of the growing Black Creek population, feared tribal members would lose control to freedmen. Nonetheless, the vast majority voted for statehood. Congress refused even to consider it. Roosevelt too opposed it.[27]

Toward a White Oklahoma

Even before the much-resisted 1901 agreement allowing for the allotment of Creek lands, the Snakes, a Creek society, had been meeting at their traditional gathering spot, Hickory Ground. In 1900, in protest against the negotiations delegates of the tribal council had begun with the federal government, the Snakes created an alternative Creek government. Although some contemporaries and historians have labeled that government a restoration of traditional Creek systems and the Snakes as "full-bloods," those terms are misleading. The Snakes included some Afro-Creeks, and the racial makeup becomes crucial later in the story. Also, "traditional" clearly did not mean a precontact version of Creek identity. Chitto Harjo, the group's leader, dressed much as his European American neighbors did, adhered to syncretic forms of government, and demanded adherence to mid-nineteenth-century treaties. The Snakes defined "traditional" as refusing to divide up Creek land into individual allotments and refusing to abandon Creek nationhood.[28]

In 1901 the new dissident Creek government—a principal chief (Chitto Harjo, whose name the press translated as "Crazy Snake"), a second chief, and a two-house legislature—reenacted the Creek laws suspended by the Curtis Act and formed a police corps to enforce them. They sent an ultimatum to President McKinley and roamed the countryside confiscating allotment certificates from Creeks; they whipped Creeks who took allotments, employed whites (note, not Blacks), or rented lands to non-Creek citizens. The chief U.S. marshal soon called out the Eighth Cavalry, and federal marshals arrested nearly a hundred Indians.[29]

Two years later, in 1903, southern Black migrants and Creek

freedmen together founded Boley, a founding made possible in part by allotment and the destruction of Creek sovereignty in exchange for Creek citizenship in the United States. Incoming African Americans valued U.S. citizenship more highly than Creek citizenship. To the Creeks, becoming U.S. citizens signified the annihilation of the Creek Nation and autonomous Creek citizenship. Conversely, African Americans saw citizenship as the opposite of annihilation; it was instead the dawning of political visibility and autonomy.

Meanwhile, the federal government reduced the categories available to Creeks. Federal officials determined eligibility for allotment, meaning they defined who was and who was not "Creek." Unlike the Creek Nation, the Dawes Commission sought to quantify and racialize Creek identity. They interviewed each applicant about his or her ancestry. Based on those responses, the commission determined "blood quantum," how much Creek "blood" the applicant had. The commission made "freedman" and "Creek" mutually exclusive terms. Anyone with African descent the commission labeled "freedman." To Creeks, the child of a Creek woman and a freedman was Creek; to the Dawes Commission, the child was a freedman. The commission granted exceptions among prominent Creeks, including former chiefs, with some African heritage, but such exceptions were rare. The Dawes rolls recognized "intermarried whites" but had no such category for intermarried Blacks.[30]

The redrawing of lines accompanied the deterioration of Black-white race relations in Oklahoma. While Boley's booster paper boasted of Black freedom and enfranchisement when soliciting more southern migrants, whites in the same county swiftly acted to minimize potential Black political power even before statehood. White farmworkers and miners threatened a race war over the importation of Black workers; unions excluded them, and whites organized to ostracize farmers hiring Blacks. Whites forced Blacks out of white-dominated mixed communities, sometimes with only twenty-four-hour notice; in 1905 Guthrie crowed over the triumph of an all-white ticket in city elections. A mixed-race Republican coalition enjoyed one last flowering. In 1906 Boley, which held the balance of power in the county, helped carry the Republican candidates to victory. The Republican county convention elected a white president and a Black secretary, O. H. Bradley, former editor of the *Boley Progress.* Several whites then broke with the convention and formed a rival slate. When the official convention went further and nominated two Blacks for county offices, the *Weleetka American* warned its readers, "STOP! LOOK! LISTEN! TO A RAILROAD DANGER SIGNAL! THE COUNTY IS IN DANGER OF NEGRO DOMINATION—WHITE VOTERS, CRUSH THE INSOLENCE OF THE NEGRO! PROTECT YOUR HOMES WITH YOUR BALLOT."[31] Whites feared Black political and economic encroachment at least as much as Indian resistance.

Oklahoma territorial governor Thomas B. Ferguson had called on the militia to protect Black voters in Lawton in 1902, and Black voters had responded to the rising violence by creating the Negro Voters Protection League. Republicans had dominated territorial politics because of the Black vote. But now some white Republicans moved toward the "lily-white" party strategy, and even a few Black Republicans saw whitening the slate of candidates as the only way to preserve Republican rule.[32]

Native Americans, on the other hand, tended to belong to the Democratic Party, seeing the Republicans as the party of the freedmen. By the 1906 election for the constitutional convention, it seemed both whites and Native Americans saw the contest as one over "negro domination." Democrats sported buttons reading "Democracy = White Man and Indian Against Negro and Carpetbagger." In return for their electoral support, as well as ensuring white access to Native American property, the Democrats made Native Americans "white." When Democrats won the majority of delegates—99 out of 112—to the convention, the *Daily Oklahoma* declared, "The election of delegates has settled the negro question. This is a white man's country."[33]

The convention elected as its president known white supremacist William Murray, who had attended the Sequoyah Convention, and now pushed for segregation, on which 90 percent of its delegates had campaigned. Oklahoma's Enabling Act, however, like that of all recently admitted states, had a clause forbidding color discrimination. Roosevelt had lost too much Black support over Brownsville to break with that precedent in an election year. He met with a Black delegation from Oklahoma and Indian Territories but offered little support to either side. The constitution came in without a discrimination clause, but the triumphant Democratic candidate for governor, Charles N. Haskell, emphasized the danger of "negro domination" and on taking office immediately asked for and received Jim Crow laws as the first act of the new state in 1907. In the same month, the legislature required Jim Crow cars on all railroads operating in the state and in May 1908 enacted a law forbidding marriage between Blacks and whites. At Haskell's inauguration, a mock wedding followed the ceremony in which the white governor, Haskell, dressed in formal trousers and a black suit coat, took as his "bride" Anna Trainor Bennett from Muskogee, a woman of Cherokee descent, in a floor-length satin dress. Cowboy married Indian; Oklahoma Territory married Indian Territory.[34]

For Creek couples who would now be declared illegally intermarried, the transition was particularly traumatic. The official Oklahoma designations led to the spectacle of courts invalidating a marriage between two Creeks, each three-quarters Creek, but the husband a quarter Black and the wife, according to her testimony, a quarter "white, I guess."[35]

Some of the African American press lashed out, enraged that the law ousted highly educated Blacks in favor of the "gut eating Apache Indian, and our constitution calls him white." Many Black Indians left the new state, seeking a safer haven. Some went to Canada, responding to immigration promotions there as did whites from the United States, mostly headed for the newly (1905) established province of Alberta. This influx so alarmed the Canadians that they sent an immigration inspector on a fact-finding tour of Oklahoma. There he found many Black landowners being pressured to sell and leave by their white neighbors. Hysterical, the Canadian Immigration Branch hired an itinerant Black clergyman "to stump the black belt against any migration to Canada" and a Black doctor from Chicago to tour Oklahoma with horror stories about the weather and other hardships.[36]

In Oklahoma the Democrats' triumph signaled the beginning of open violence against Blacks in the county. In late 1907 the new state witnessed its first lynching, at Henryetta. A Black man killed a white livery stable owner for refusing to rent him a rig. A white mob hanged the Black man from a telephone pole and riddled his body with bullets. Many Blacks fled Henryetta for other towns. Many white towns prohibited Blacks from being in the town after dark. Boley Blacks, secure in their Black town, remained enfranchised, but well before Oklahoma's 1910 grandfather clause, violence, white-controlled registration, and gerrymandering had destroyed any greater Black political power.[37]

What does all this have to do with Creeks? The failure of the 1901 and 1905 resistance movements had not ended the struggle. Followers of Harjo continued to refuse their allotments. In July 1908 Creek freedmen and Black migrants came together at the traditional Snake "stomp," or meeting, grounds, Hickory Ground. They were still there when a large group of Snakes came to the place for their annual council. No simple pattern explains Creek-freedmen relations. The history of African descendants and Creeks reveals not only mergers and alliances but also friction. And the increasing violence against Black people led to Black alliances of Creek and non-Creek freedmen and Afro-Creeks. With some Afro-Creeks in the Snake police, the presence of a large group of armed and organized Blacks and Indians alarmed nearby whites.

After this council, apparently some of the Creek freedmen and the "state negroes," that is, the southern Black migrants, remained on Hickory Ground, intending to create a permanent town. They erected some twenty-five tents, each with a stone chimney, along with a wooden store and a restaurant near the Snake Council House. Both white and other Black townspeople labeled the group ruffians, fugitives from the law, and troublemakers. White Indian agents trying to avoid conflict advised Harjo to distance his group from the new Black settlement. Harjo, who had gone on record in 1906 with his resentment of freedmen, readily complied.[38] He had apparently already taken literal steps to do so, holding his 1908 council a mile from the encampment. Despite his efforts, the presence of a Black encampment on Snake grounds would offer whites a useful opportunity to blur lines.

In March 1909, a little more than a year after Washington's article in the *Outlook* and eight months after Harjo's council meeting, a constable from Henryetta came to the southern migrant and Creek freedmen encampment at Hickory Ground, looking for thieves who had robbed a neighboring white farmer's smokehouse. A most unfriendly reception forced him to leave. He returned to Henryetta to form a posse, and armed skirmishes began almost immediately. Before dawn the next day, a posse of fourteen attacked the encampment, forcing some Blacks to flee and arresting forty others, including some Creek freedmen, one person labeled "white," and one labeled a "mixed-blood" of "unsavory reputation."[39] They killed one Black man. The local sheriff and his men then occupied the campsite and ordered the remaining women and children to leave within an hour. The next day the Snake Council House, an emblem of Creek, not southern, freedmen presence in the area, was torched. The sheriff denied responsibility but was seen leaving the scene. Similarly, an "unknown" arsonist burned all the wooden structures, tents, and household effects. Hickory Ground was just east of racist Weleetka and south of Henryetta, the site of the lynching. Whites had succeeded in literally redrawing the map and erasing the settlement.

By torching the Snake Council House, the posse had encompassed Snakes—allotment resisters—in its attack on disruptive elements at Hickory Ground. Anxious to extend their victories and as clear evidence of their ability to cast this fight with Hickory Ground "ruffians" onto the Snakes, a group of deputies went to arrest Harjo, holding him responsible for the encampment that he had tried to avoid. When Harjo and his fellow Snakes returned gunfire, two men, including the son of the sheriff, died in the battle. The white newspapers had a field day, vastly inflating the numbers killed and declaring "WAR WITH SNAKES." Posses roamed the countryside arresting Indians and Blacks. They burned Harjo's house and looted others under the guise of putting down a rebellion. White papers demanded "protection and Indian suppression"; the mayor of Henryetta declared, "The Snake Indians and the negroes affiliated with them are a menace to the country and should be captured." The local federal Indian agent maintained that Harjo would have to admit that "this was going to be a white man's country."[40]

The white posse and its allies had strategically conflated freedmen from everywhere, Blacks of all sorts, and Creek resisters. Such a conflation created a two-race system: whites and "others." In this case, “Blacks” (unlike in the state’s constitution) became “Indians.” Engaging the script of Anglo western conquest allowed these whites to pose the eradication of a Black settlement as a final Indian engagement, a legitimized whitening of the West against a known external enemy.

Most players read the script with hearty skepticism. A federal investigating commission blamed whites for the unrest. The editor of the *Indian Journal* at nearby Eufaula, with heavy sarcasm, wrote, “The Spanish-American war was never more vividly pictured, and the number killed, wounded and captured is generally larger than was Taft’s majority.” The *Boley Progress* also saw the numbers and the conflict as absurdly inflated but took a different direction, trivializing the resistance to allotment and doubting Harjo ever had more than a dozen followers at any time, whereas sources in the Senate testimony had placed his following in the thousands.[41] Neither white nor Black promoters wished to pose this developing section as unduly riddled with violent contestants.

It is important in this context to look briefly at iconography. A cartoon, *War in Oklahoma*, from the *Oklahoma City Times* of March 31, 1909, depicts a band of white easterners who echoed Teddy Roosevelt’s look, including the “Indiana Rough Riders,” Rough Riders being the name of Roosevelt’s Spanish-American War troops. They are all men, and all but the journalist wear Stetsons as they triumphantly march out of Hickory Ground, now for rent to picnickers, parading their captured Indian, clearly depicted as Black. The meaning of the West in 1909 was clearly inseparable from national racial issues as recodified in the wake of the Spanish-American War.

Where Were the Women?

The absence of women in the picture raises some final questions about citizenship and manhood in the events surrounding Boley and in the polity of the New West. Despite the earlier arrival of woman suffrage in the West than in the East, signs indicate that whites, Creeks, and Blacks in Oklahoma differed in their notions of gender as in so much else. The paucity of the sources makes it impossible to do more than venture some hints and suggestions in this regard.

For whites, posing Oklahoma as militarized terrain, as in the cartoon, identified it as undoubtedly male space (despite the presence of journalists and actual homesteaders who were white women).[42] Whites, the conquerors, intentionally selected one of their own to play the groom in the inaugural pageant of Oklahoma Territory's marrying Indian Territory. The rhetoric around the Spanish-American War illustrated that asserting authority and dominion over "lesser" races bolstered white American manhood. It is clear how whites used the West as a site for deploying these notions of manhood, but it is less clear how shifting notions of manhood and political participation played out in nonwhite communities in the West in the first decades of the century.

White reports of the attack on the encampment at Hickory Ground and the burning of the tents mention only male fighters and passive women and children. Similarly, reports of the aftermath of the pitched battle with Harjo and his supporters in 1909 only depict noncombatant women and children as opposed to male warrior-citizens. Yet when Chitto Harjo was struggling to evade the white troops after the 1909 fracas, women were among those who aided him, and while the men fled their homes to avoid arrest, the women stayed, though being female offered them no protection. Investigators reported tales of "brutality in the treatment of blacks and Indians—mostly involving women," because the men were in hiding.[43] The complicity of women in Harjo's escape and the presence of women at the Black tent colony would argue that these were more participatory communities than the depictions allow. As in the cartoon, these depictions largely omit women from the actors in the drama. The frontier remains a place where men fight for territory and women keep the home fires burning.

Did Harjo restore a measure of female power in the Creek community? Had it ever been lost? What bits of evidence there are on Creek women show that at least those women vocal in Harjo's support were savvy commercial farmers. Court cases also prove that Creek women insisted on controlling their own allotments and on what would happen to the property after they died. They retained the system of Creek casual marriage and serial monogamy to a degree that virtually forced U.S. courts well after statehood to accept it. Formal legal marriage would have meant that the current partner rather than the children inherited the allotment.[44]

Similarly, in Boley, women not only ran the Ladies Commercial Club (although it was not open to single and divorced women) but also bought allotments, ran businesses, and participated in political meetings. Amid its Victorian-style appeals to women's higher moral character and its declaration that in Boley "every man is a man" because he raises and is free to dispose of the entirety of his own crop, Boley's paper also promoted commercial opportunities that would "allow our boys and girls to become business men and women." Even Booker T. Washington, though he only mentioned "men" coming out to build up the country, when referring to the African commercial heritage chose the word "foreparents," not "forefathers."[45]

Women could not vote in Oklahoma, but Boley's leaders called open meetings to debate issues or gauge public opinion. All adult members of the community, of whatever sex or economic standing, took part in the general discussion. Such a system echoes Elsa Barkley Brown's description of Reconstruction-era Black political meetings in Virginia, where women and children, as well as men, instructed their elected representatives in equal measure. Similarly, descriptions of Cherokee council meetings identified participants as both women and men. And in 1900 representatives of the Creek Nation sent a document to the federal government protesting against the ratification of the agreement with the United States. It argued that ratification by the Creek National Council (men elected by a male electorate) was "not right. Every man, woman, and child among the Creeks has a right to be heard upon the question."[46]

In 1900 few white men clamored for business opportunities for their women in the same breath they did for their men, and Oklahoma would be far from the first western state to offer women the vote. Indeed, whites often considered not only battle but also commerce and development explicitly manly, as when the (white) Commercial Club of Muskogee, Indian Territory, referred to itself as "the most virile and progressive commercial organization of the Southwest" in an address to the Senate.[47] The triumph of the imperial United States may have succeeded more completely in imposing a new racial than a new gender order in Oklahoma.

Conclusion: The Twentieth-Century West

Black town builders, with sixty some communities in Oklahoma by 1907, had dreamed of a Black county or even a Black state. Indians had been given to understand that Oklahoma was their territory. With the twentieth century those dreams gasped their last breath. In 1905 at a summer carnival in Boley, a Black band and Indian ball games between Creek and Seminole players had entertained the crowds. By 1909 that picture of a multicultural Oklahoma was hard to find. Snake bands without Black allies, such as Eufala Harjo's, as opposed to Chitto Harjo's, experienced no violence during the rebellion.[48] The Black press's dream of a united front of people of color in the state may have presented local whites a sufficient nightmare that white actions concentrated not only on Blacks but also on Blacks with Indian allies.

All these groups—Creeks, Blacks, and whites—were themselves hybrid groups, invented ethnicities/races: "Creeks" invented two hundred years earlier in the Southeast, "Blacks" a mélange of African groups intermingled with Europeans and Indians, and "whites" from various parts of Europe and the United States. None of them was native to Oklahoma, itself an invented concept. The fact that all the racial categories in the story have to be put in quotation marks is itself significant. Booker T. Washington's search for and/or creation of the "genuine" Indian, the elision of Afro-Creeks but the depiction of Creek freedmen, and the creation of categories such as "full-blood" and "Native" versus "state" Negroes mark the striving for a clearly racialized world essential to the early twentieth-century imperial United States. The particular contests over and constructions of these categories in the West had everything to do with the meaning of establishing settlements in Oklahoma for the various groups and individuals involved.

It is crucial to see Jim Crow as a western and not just a southern phenomenon, to see the differently disenfranchised "Indians" and "Blacks" as securing a white man's West. African Americans fleeing the increasingly repressive South in the decades after the Civil War had headed to Kansas and then on to Indian Territory. Now, discouraged by developments in the West, Blacks as a proportion of the region's population fell. The same Oklahoma constitutional convention that encouraged segregation also emphasized antimonopoly provisions and increased participatory democracy for whites. As historian David Chang has noted, by the early twentieth century, U.S. policies in Indian Territory "made land ownable and made race a fixed and powerful legal category. Policy made a world where all land was owned, where some people were propertied and others were propertyless, where some could be landlords and others would be tenants." It had done so in the name of guaranteeing opportunity for the nation's white inhabitants. The federal official who insisted that Chitto Harjo would have to admit that "this was going to be a white man's country" showed how imperfect and unstable was the new state's inclusion of Indians in the category "white." Coming in the context of Harjo's revolt, it also showed the ways in which "white man's country" was not just about who benefited from the region's resources. It was, as Chang points out, about the triumph of a whole system of individual property holding and the governance of white-dominated institutions. With the eradication of Creek autonomous government and the restrictions on Black suffrage, Indians and Blacks were excluded from the polity more thoroughly than they ever had been during the second half of the nineteenth century, and "populist" and "progressive" measures aimed at leveling the economic playing field and expanding political and economic opportunity, albeit in diluted form, served only "whites."[49]

Part 2

Agitating, 1910–21

The 1910s was a decade of upheaval in the U.S. West and the world. The decade opened with the Mexican Revolution on the U.S. southern border and closed with revolution in Russia, the Great War and its aftermath, and the victory of the woman suffrage movement in the U.S. In the U.S. West, the order seemingly established in the century's first decades, the careful demarcations, generated continuing challenges on the ground. Those excluded did not disappear, and boundaries blurred. The upheavals of this second decade concerned the nature of the economy and of democracy itself. Who would participate, what would governance encompass, who would decide?

The simmering discontent in Mexico burst into full-scale revolution, dramatically affecting not just relations in the borderlands but also the sense of possibility for structural change across the United States. Frustrations over the power of large corporations and defeated expectations of small farmers fostered the rise of the Socialist Party in the West. There it had both agrarian and industrial roots. It built on the Western Federation of Miners and the Farmers Union, the Women's Christian Temperance Union and the Populists. The two major political parties, Democratic and Republican, continued to dominate electoral contests in the West, particularly at the state level, but the Socialist Party's strength forced them to the left.

The following three chapters explore the dramatic conflicts of the 1910s as they emerged in and shaped the region. Chapter 4 discusses the revolution on the U.S. West's southern border and the ways in which it spilled over and shared dynamics with demands for change in the West. Chapter 5 hones in on the region's political movements for a more radically participatory democracy, focusing on women and their allies. Finally, chapter 6 follows the region into the World War and its aftermath.

4

Revolution and Revolutionaries

In August 1911 at a slaughterhouse in the small town of Oroville, California, a butcher surprised a man lurking in the shadows. Convinced the man had taken the meat that had been disappearing in recent weeks, the butcher, Adolph Kessler, tackled him. The man wore only a shirt and had bits of buckskin threaded through his ears and nose. Kessler, thinking the man was Mexican, tried Spanish but got no response. While the other three butchers stood guard, Kessler phoned the sheriff, who came, handcuffed the silent man, and took him away.

Oroville was small but typically western. It had fewer than a thousand people, but those people had the language skills to try not only Spanish but also English, Chinese, and the Indian language Maidu. Nothing worked. The press had a field day. The *Oroville Daily Register* declared "Aboriginal Indian, the Last of the Deer Creeks, Captured near Oroville," the "last surviving member . . . [of a] . . . proud tribe of warriors." Despite the man's shirt, the paper claimed he was "still untouched by [the] civilization that destroyed his people." The *San Francisco Examiner* called him "a savage of the most primitive type."[1]

This man's story, the casting of him as "the last" Indian, fit within the paradigm of demarcations that characterized the century's first decade. Indians were gone; "modern" civilization had triumphed. But it was an artificial separation. It was a distinction desired by many western white people and their government but denied by the persistence of Indians and their pursuit of their rights. The narrative that marked him as "the last" also separated the United States' battles with Indians over their land from the "modern" labor wars and revolutionary movements that dominated the 1910s. That too is a false demarcation. The battles over labor and land, over the nature of the economy and governance, were bound together in both the United States and Mexico. After looking more closely at this story and its framing, the chapter moves to the Mexican Revolution and its U.S. entanglements and finally to labor wars and revolutionary movements within the U.S. West.

Beginnings and Framings

The apprehension of the backwoods "savage" thrilled Alfred Kroeber, chair of the University of California, Berkeley's anthropology department. When Kroeber came to California from Columbia University in New York in 1900, he plunged into the back country, hoping to find remote, surviving Indians, holdovers from precontact language and customs. He had only found Indians who dressed like any other backcountry resident and spoke the same way. Now he wanted this Indian. Enlisting the help of an elderly resident of Redding, California, who spoke a California Native dialect, Kroeber met with the man. He called him Ishi, the Yahi word for "man."[2]

At Kroeber's instigation, Ishi moved into the new anthropology museum at the University of California, Berkeley, where he became a janitor and an exhibit, as well as a resident. He dramatically increased the museum's attendance figures. Indians had been exhibited for over a decade as curiosities at "world's" fairs and expositions not as part of the contemporary world but as artifacts of a world gone by, as living history, as beings on the edge of extinction. Exhibitors worked to showcase Indians' exoticism and not their familiarity. They were sometimes literally exhibited as the "missing link" in human evolution during this, the heyday of Darwinian evolution and the pseudosciences it spawned, including eugenics and anthropometrics.[3] Such exhibits, along with the California universities elbowing their way onto the stage by using them, were profoundly reassuring (to many white western inhabitants) evidence that the West was now safely "modern." The vanishing of Ishi's "race" marked the blameless ascent of the modern West.

Ishi had a more complicated story. There had been about 150,000 Indians in California in the mid-nineteenth century when large-scale white migration to the territory began. Forced labor, disease, enslavement, and massacres followed. By 1900 there were only about twenty thousand. Like many other Indians in California, Ishi had steered clear of people he thought were "white" because, having witnessed the events of the nineteenth century, he decided it was safer to do so. Ishi may have avoided whites for his own safety, but he lived a more complicated and eclectic life than the stories people wanted to tell about him. Moreover, there were still Indians around Oroville, the town near where Ishi was captured. One of the Indians who visited Ishi soon after his "discovery" had actually run into Ishi and a friend weeks earlier. The encounter had seemed unremarkable, and the Konkow fruit picker and his son had not reported it. In fact, Ishi had for a time hidden out in the barn of a mixed family, according to the memories of Vera Clark McKeen, a child at the time whose family of farmers and loggers included her Maida grandmother and her Scots and English ancestors. Those Indians wore Anglo-style clothes, spoke English, and had European names.[4]

Anthropologists had been on the trail of Ishi for some years. They wanted to find an Indian who did not wear overalls, but while they took evidence from the Indians they did find (a rabbitskin blanket, arrows, mortars, and other essential goods, just as winter was setting in), despite using guides and tracking dogs, they had found no Indians.[5] What does it mean that they could imagine a human group as "extinct," that those hunters could not see as "Indians" the people around them? How could they define them as "extinct" rather than intermarried and living down the road?

According to anthropologist Orin Starn, Ishi rapidly acquired an English vocabulary and manners. He was no captive. He roamed San Francisco on his days off, visited his neighbors, carved dolls for the girls who liked to accompany him to the grocery store, and eagerly shared his stories, myths, and customs with anthropologists. Nor did he accommodate every desire of his hosts. On his first day at the museum, the press wanted to photograph him shirtless. He refused. He said, according to the translator and the *San Francisco Call,* which reported the incident, that "he not see any other people go without." So the *San Francisco Chronicle* had to show the last "wild" Indian in a shirt and tie. And he never gave his name. Yet more enduring, perhaps, certainly more widely distributed, was the image he did not want to leave—not his stories but the stories that others wove about him for their own ends, as well as the photograph, finally with his chest bared, from 1913, published with over a hundred others from a variety of Indian nations in Joseph Dixon's collection titled *The Vanishing Race*.[6]

Ishi was supposed to stand for the passing of one kind of conflict in the U.S. West, for the triumph of the modern and the disappearance of the primitive. The Indians' putative "disappearance" made it harder for them to fight effectively to retain their lands and treaty rights, harder for them to be seen. At ever-increasing rates, they faced dispossession by the federal government and the unilateral disavowing of treaty rights in the name of freeing the Indians to enter the dominant society, forcing more rapid assimilation, and aiding regional development. Yet their fight over land and their sense of themselves as distinct peoples persisted alongside their participation in what became known as the decade's labor wars. In 1911 a group of well-educated Indians, some of whom had grown up embedded in tribes and others who had not, created the first pan-Indian civil rights group, the Society of American Indians. The founders included doctors Charles Eastman (Dakota) and Carlos Montezuma (Yavapai), attorney Thomas Sloan (Omaha), Episcopalian minister Sherman Coolidge (Arapaho), anthropologist Arthur C. Parker (Seneca), and writer Gertrude Bonnin, who published her memoirs as Zitkála-Šá (Dakota).[7]

For others, resistance was more direct. Well into the 1910s, when Yaquis working in the United States bought arms to defend their lands in Mexico, U.S. reporters and authorities framed the trafficking as Yaqui miners supporting their traditional cousins, just as they liked to distinguish between "wild" and other Indians in the United States. But the same Yaquis were both copper miners and freedom fighters, battling both Mexican and U.S. troops. In Arizona, advocates for the Tohono O'odham successfully fended off a 1913 attack on their lands by arguing that Salt River Valley cotton growers depended on Tohono O'odham seasonal laborers. While those speaking on behalf of the reservation touted the Tohono O'odham workers as docile and disciplined, the Tohono O'odham proved just as capable of fighting for their rights as workers as they did fighting for their land as Indians. In December 1916, when copper miners in Ajo, Arizona, called a strike in support of pegging wages to the rising price of copper, the strikers included 130 Tohono O'odham.[8]

It is tempting to see the land wars as the frontier past and the labor wars as the product of the region's emerging modernity. My favorite such story is the one about the family who take the exit from the highway to the Ludlow monument, erected by the American Federation of Labor, and then are chagrined to discover that the Ludlow Massacre did not involve Native Americans but rather the 1914 gunning down of coal strikers' families in Ludlow, Colorado. Those misguided tourists, the implication is, were swept up in a different version of national history, the one that poses the significance of the U.S. West to the nation as lying in the contest for land between European Americans and Indians rather than in a history of conflict between capital and labor. Yet to the Tohono O'odham farmers, cotton pickers, and miners, to the Hispano/a land grant heirs working in the coal mines, to the Sonoran peasants who joined with revolutionary Pancho Villa, and to the Yaqui farmers and copper miners, the land wars and the labor wars formed part of the same struggle.

Massive strikes were not new to the twentieth-century U.S. West or even to the nation as a whole. Two decades earlier, western governors had called out the National Guard on behalf of mining corporations to battle organized workers in massive hard rock mining strikes that gave birth to the Western Federation of Miners. Less than a decade earlier, the 1902 Pennsylvania coal strike had threatened to bring industry to a standstill and leave millions without the ability to heat their homes. That strike had led President Theodore Roosevelt to take the unprecedented step of calling representatives of the unions and corporations involved to the White House so that he could take a hand in resolving the dispute himself.

But the scope, scale, and even intent of the 1910s strikes seemed different. Workers faced ever-larger national and multinational corporations. By the 1910s, many western states were virtually wholly owned subsidiaries of corporations: Arizona with Phelps Dodge, Washington with Weyerhauser lumber, Montana with Anaconda Copper, southern California with the Southern Pacific Railroad, Wyoming with the oil companies, North Dakota and the Canadian Prairies with Minneapolis millers, and Colorado with John D. Rockefeller's Colorado Fuel and Iron Company (CF&I).[9]

Mine owners employed their own police forces, rivaling small armies, and controlled schools, churches, and even towns and counties. In response to this level of dominion, strikes could become revolutions. Coal miners, for example, organized and conquered huge swaths of territory—much of Colorado in one strike. Workers joined in seemingly unprecedented alliances: at Wheatland, California, agricultural workers organized Japanese, Mexican, Anglo, and other workers into a single body to fight Japanese and U.S.-born growers. Organized women, many of them middle class and elite, fighting for the vote and winning it in most western states before 1920, marched into state offices, agitating on behalf of the strikers and their families. Socialists accrued ever-increasing numbers in local, state, and even national elections, and the relatively new Industrial Workers of the World, organizing across skill level, race, and gender with its radical democratic philosophy, challenged the American Federation of Labor for leadership of organized workers. At stake were not just wages and hours. What the activists proposed was a radical redefinition of democracy. Who would lead? Who would participate? Who would shape the future?

Revolution

Nowhere in the early part of the decade was the battle over democracy and its meaning more fraught and violent than on the U.S. southern border, in Mexico. Decades of exiles' organizing in the U.S. borderlands reached a high point in 1911. By April 1911 some eight thousand people had joined the fight against Díaz in Chihuahua and Sonora alone, with as many more in the rest of Mexico. Wealthy landowning reformer Francisco Madero from Coahuila drew adherents across class lines, including the working-class rebel Francisco "Pancho" Villa from Durango and the muleteer son of a shopkeeper Pascual Orozco from Chihuahua. In May 1911, with arms smuggled through El Paso, Texas, together they captured the critical railroad hub of Ciudad Juárez, just across the border from El Paso. After over three decades in power, Díaz agreed to resign. Madero handily won the ensuing election.[10]

Not everyone so easily capitulated. A bloody contest for power and the future of Mexico ensued, ineluctably drawing in the U.S. West. For a decade Mexico and the U.S. Southwest suffered from the violence and chaos of regime change. Revolutionary rivals and counterrevolutionary leaders plotted in Texas, Arizona, and California. Supporters sent arms and funds to their favored generals. Arms smuggling boomed; former Laredo, Texas, mayor Amador Sánchez used the county jail to store weapons destined for Victoriano Huerta in late 1911; he paid the $1,200 fine for violating U.S. neutrality and returned to work as county sheriff. Generals used border cities to stage military incursions and smuggle arms.[11]

The generals ran the gamut from Díaz-like dictators (Huerta) to socialists determined to seize properties on behalf of the people. A dizzying array of revolutionary platforms and practices in Mexican states differing in population, geography, and economy emerged. In Morelos, Governor Emiliano Zapata rapidly erected a legal framework for land reform known as the Plan of Ayala: unused land went to peasants for cultivation, and big landlords fled. In Coahuila, Governor Venustiano Carranza focused on labor conditions, equalizing taxation and extending educational work. In Nuevo León, ex-Magonista governor Antonio Villareal abolished debt peonage and supported striking streetcar workers; he favored socialist land reform and state-run corporations and supported the Mexican workers' organization linked with the IWW. In Sonora, Villa's was a peasant revolution.[12]

Rivals fought fiercely along the border between Mexico and the United States. Pascual Orozco captured territories from the Maderistas; Carranza and Villa captured territory from Huerta, who had assassinated Madero and seized power; Villa and Carranza split, and Villa attacked Carranza's forces; Alvaro Obregón also took territory from Carranza. Three of the primary revolutionary leaders died by assassins—Madero in 1913, Carranza in 1920, and Villa in 1923.[13] In the United States, Mexico went from being a "sister republic" to a source of terror or inspiration.

Tens of thousands of U.S. expatriates headed home, some after witnessing the deaths of family members and the destruction of their property. Many ordinary Mexicans eagerly joined the fight; others fled; and still others, unable to escape, found themselves forcibly pressed into one army or another. Approximately two million Mexican combatants and noncombatants would die during the revolution, and another million fled to the United States.[14]

Yet cross-border ties built over decades did not wither with revolution. Southwestern mines continued to rely on Mexican workers, now suspected revolutionaries. Border towns continued to rely on trade with Mexico. El Paso's dramatic growth in the century's first decade had depended not just on the six railroads that crossed it but also on Mexican ore for its smelter, lumber for its mills, and cattle for its stockyards. With its paved streets and multistory brick buildings, El Paso had become a symbol of the region's modernity. When the revolution disrupted the delivery of cattle and ore, the city's merchants nimbly shifted to arms sales. Selling arms itself was legal, but selling arms to foreign revolutionaries was not. Attempts to crack down on the smuggling proved largely futile. Local resentment of U.S. federal agents and Mexican *federales* along with the city's dependence on arms commerce meant juries would not convict those accused of violating neutrality laws.[15]

The stakes for the United States and its citizens went beyond border town commerce. Southern California's water supply relied on security in the Mexican territory through which it ran. U.S. armed forces had come to rely on the Mexican Petroleum Company, created by California oilman Edward L. Doheny and his partners as U.S. output declined and demand exploded. Doheny had bought 450,000 acres south of Tampico, struck oil, and bought more land.[16] Altogether, U.S. citizens owned over 20 percent of Mexico's surface in 1910, including huge swaths—millions of acres—of ranchland and immense amounts of subsurface mineral rights, timberland, and railroad track.

Those cross-border connections mirrored connections between large investors from the U.S. West and the U.S. government. U.S. businessmen worried about the security of their investments in Mexico, worth $1.5 billion. In the Senate, New Mexico senator Albert Fall demanded an invasion. Outside the Senate, Colonel Edwin Mandell House of Houston linked the investors to President Wilson. House was a major stockholder of an oil company that was a bastion of regional elitism, wealth, and power, the Texas Company. He also ran the Texas Democratic Party machine, which helped elect Wilson. In April 1914 he helped bring Wilson on board to invade and occupy Veracruz, the key oil port for U.S. investors.[17]

The invasion further strained diplomatic relations between the United States and Mexico. Rival generals struggled for arms and resources. They simultaneously resented and solicited U.S. involvement, and the United States struggled to negotiate the shifting sands of revolution. Wilson, unable to stomach the authoritarian dictator after his assassination of Madero and assumption of power, had invaded partly to block Huerta's access to a shipment of German arms. But Wilson had not anticipated the level of popular fury at the U.S. incursion. The invasion of Veracruz engendered an attack on the U.S. embassy. The United States withdrew from Veracruz but not from the revolution. Uneasy about Villa's attitude toward private property, Wilson favored the constitutionalist liberal, Carranza. Wilson engineered arms deliveries to Carranza when the United States withdrew from Veracruz while denying arms to Villa, embittering the former U.S. darling and helping engender Villa's subsequent anti-U.S. raids.[18]

Ordinary cross-border friction exponentially multiplied. Ranchers had long allowed their cattle to cross the international border, where they at times fell into the hands of "bandits." Now ranchers on the border found that their livestock had fallen prey to desperate revolutionaries facing an ever more barren northern Mexico landscape as rival armies swept back and forth across the northern Mexican states. U.S. borderlands ranchers and city dwellers called on the U.S. Army. More raiding led to more fear. The residents of Bisbee, Arizona, fearing Yaquis and revolutionaries, petitioned the U.S. government for two cavalry troops in the fall of 1915 to protect them from "one thousand hungry desperate irresponsible Indians and renegade Mexicans" at nearby Naco, Sonora.[19]

In Texas, a toxic combination of factors—cross-border raiding and revolutionaries, risky investments, and racism—led to a bloodbath. Texas elites—ranchers, oil men, and bankers—had invested heavily in costly irrigation projects, which found few takers, with borderlands violence making national news. The portrayal of the Mexican Revolution in the United States posed Mexicans as lawless, short-sighted, treacherous bandits. White Texans in particular used that image to justify indiscriminate brutality against Tejanos and Mexicans, citizens of the United States or not, raiders or not, in the name of restoring order.[20]

Tejanos resisted the terrorism aimed at them. They resisted the pressure to sign over their property deeds at gunpoint. They resisted with arms and in court, in the press, and in the legislature. In Laredo, a year after the revolution began, Mexicans led by journalist and labor activist Nicasio Idar formed El Primer Congreso Mexicanista with the aim of defending their rights and property and building a regional federation that, in their words, "would be socially significant here as well as in Mexico and would excite interest throughout the world." Representatives of sixteen South Texas cities attended the first Mexican Congress meeting.[21]

Texas violence peaked with the Plan de San Diego. Named for the small town of San Diego, Texas, where the plan was promulgated in January 1915, it called for killing all Anglos over the age of sixteen; creating an independent republic out of Texas, New Mexico, Arizona, Colorado, and California; and aiding African Americans in seizing contiguous territory to establish their own nation. Indians, too, would be liberated. The plan's raids lasted from May until October.[22] As many as five thousand people in the Texas borderlands purportedly joined the plan, rebelling against dispossession and the impunity with which Anglos meted out "justice."

Texas Anglos had already stepped up a regime of terror and discrimination against Mexican workers. Now their fears of revolution were realized as the plan's participants murdered Americans on at least one train and seemed to attack isolated ranches almost daily. White Texans' reprisals were out of all proportion to their own dozens of casualties. Some killed anyone of Mexican descent who crossed their path. Hundreds died. There was, as a contemporary journalist explained, "an open gun season on Mexicans along the border," and "no jury along the border would ever convict a white man for shooting a Mexican." The countryside emptied. Meanwhile, the Plan de San Diego raids stopped in October 1915, coinciding with the U.S. recognition of Venustiano Carranza, whose complicity has been suspected.[23]

In New Mexico as in Texas, revolution refused to stay south of the border. In early March 1916 Carranza's rival Francisco Villa and five hundred of his men capped off a series of border raids by sweeping into Columbus, New Mexico. They had already taken from a train and killed sixteen American mining engineers en route to reopen a mine and had attacked an English-speaking Mormon colony in Mexico. Now they moved on to the military encampment and town center across the border in Columbus.[24]

Villa's revolutionaries were hungry and exhausted. Many were unwilling members of Villa's army, uncertain even where they were. In the rosier days of 1913 and 1914, then popular Villa had kept an office in Columbus, spreading a penumbra of safety about the locals.[25] Now the Villistas expected help from Columbus's "Mexican" residents. They got it. To Columbus's Mexican-heritage population, Villa stood for the dispossessed. Labor and land were deeply linked for New Mexicans. At statehood in 1912, the Spanish-heritage population remained the majority. As the years passed, small farmers and workers, often the same people, struggled to hold their own as agribusiness joined the state's mining interests. For Villa, Columbus Mexicans distinguished Anglo from Mexican residences and businesses. Villa's men attacked only the "gringos."

The local Mexican consul took advantage of that fact to protect Anglo women in the town's hotel, claiming it held only "our people." The women escaped. When the ruse was discovered, Villa's men shot the consul and torched the hotel. By the time the U.S. soldiers sent Villa back across the border, at least sixteen Anglos and a much larger number of Villa's raiders lay dead, and a large part of the town had been burned. The *Albuquerque Morning Journal* called it a massacre and Villa's men "bandits." Over a hundred Villistas died in the reprisals.[26]

New Mexico's English-language press saw the Villa raid as an extension of the Plan de San Diego. The U.S. Army had done nothing officially to end those raids. But now U.S. troops were massing on the border. Wilson was sending General John J. Pershing and his men to pursue Villa in Mexico in what became known as the Punitive Expedition.[27]

Villa's former status as the favored revolutionary leader, the subject of a laudatory film by D. W. Griffith released in the spring of 1914, before Wilson switched to backing the more moderate Carranza exclusively, seemed forgotten. Spectators gathered, whistled, and cheered for hours as General Pershing's 11,000 Black and white troops (in segregated units) crossed into Mexico. Before the Columbus raid, 20,600 U.S. soldiers, one-quarter of the whole army, patrolled the border. After Villa's raid, Wilson added 100,000 National Guard troops, who remained on the border until February 1917.[28]

The expedition was a debacle. Pershing utterly failed to capture Villa. Mexican popular resentment of the U.S. incursion reversed the descending arc of Villa's popularity, and he gathered support once again. Pushed to the left by Villa's renewed popularity, the constitutional convention inserted into the new Mexican constitution a proworker labor code, the legal basis for land reform, and government power to regulate, tax, and even expropriate foreign-owned oil properties, endangering the U.S. $500 million investment in petroleum.[29]

Just as it seemed that little more was needed to convince the U.S. public that Mexicans were enemies, whether by virtue of U.S. aggression or Mexican, on March 1, 1917, less than two months after Pershing finally withdrew his increasingly bedraggled troops from Mexico, newspapers printed the Zimmermann telegram. Wilson's earlier refusal to withdraw Pershing had led Carranza to approach Germany, whose foreign secretary in turn secretly sent a telegram to his ambassador in Mexico. Arriving in late January 1917, the Zimmermann telegram, as it came to be known, promised Mexico the return of the U.S. Southwest in exchange for an active alliance. On top of the Plan de San Diego and Neomexicano collaboration with Villa, the telegram raised the specter of a possible fifth column: the stubbornly persistent Spanish-speaking community of the U.S. Southwest.[30]

The Mexican Revolution laid bare that the history of the Mexican North and the U.S. Southwest were inseparable. The consolidation of Anglo business and enterprise on both sides of the border, beginning with the coming of the railroads in the 1880s, had reduced the economic power and land base of the Mexican population. By the 1910s it had generated sufficient rancor that Mexican revolutionaries could plausibly imagine the support of U.S. citizens of Mexican descent, as Villa did—and whether or not they consistently received it, the imagined scenario was equally plausible to the region's newer Anglo residents. The Plan de San Diego, the

Columbus raid, and the Zimmermann telegram seemed to show that, given the interwoven nature of life in the vicinity of the border, there was no possibility of quarantining revolution, despite the presence of U.S. troops. Rising fears, particularly among Anglos in the Southwest but also spread nationally by newspaper coverage, depicted the border and its peoples as violent, dangerous, and in need of suppression. And the confusion and inadequacy of the U.S. response relative to its ambitions only enhanced the fear and suspicion. But chaos in Mexico was not the only lesson; the promise of revolution—redistribution of power and land—also sounded across the border.

Revolutionaries at Home? Land, Liberty, and Labor

The Mexican Revolution made credible the possibility of radical change in the United States. The growth of large-scale, heavily capitalized and mechanized farming had not only dispossessed Mexicans on either side of the border. Even in Oklahoma, where the victory of the white man's West had seemed most clear, farmers' investment in whiteness did not protect them from dispossession. The Panic of 1907 wreaked havoc, and by the end of the decade, over half of Oklahoma's farmers worked as tenants rather than owners. Dispossession of the state's Indians and Black residents had followed swiftly from the various allotment measures. But in former Indian Territory, white tenancy rates exceeded those of every other group. The "surplus lands" had largely enriched a relatively few white lawyers and speculators, helped by corruption on an almost unimaginable scale, and as in New Mexico, their growing wealth and influence made those lawyers and speculators even more powerful.[31]

Other factors contributed to the dire condition of small farmers. Even in good years, the luck was uneven. The 1910s saw the highest number of acres successfully filed and proven up under the Homestead Act and therefore transferred from federal to sole proprietors, but during that same period, six years of drought in Montana from 1916 to 1922 forced three-quarters of those who had arrived since 1909 to leave.[32]

In this context, Socialist Party organizers found fertile ground. They brought together former agrarian Populists from Oklahoma

Territory with tenants and coal miners from former Indian Territory. Tenants barred from the established churches by the townspeople and wealthier farmers, who considered them "crude, immoral, and unsuitable church members," flocked to socialist camp meetings in 1908 that gathered as many as ten thousand people each. That year the Farmers Union, founded in 1902 and bringing together small farmers and rural laborers along with sympathetic teachers, doctors, and country newspaper editors, now numbering about seventy thousand, moved toward the socialists. Oklahoma had the highest rate of tenancy in the United States, at 80 percent. In some Oklahoma counties, 24 percent of voters chose the Socialist Party. In 1912 16.6 percent of the state presidential vote went to Socialist Party candidate Eugene Debs. In 1914 Oklahoma voters elected 175 Socialist Party candidates to local offices and six state legislators. Oklahoma's cotton gins became public utilities in 1915. The Democrats responded by pushing for a literacy law, largely to keep the socialists from the polls. But by World War I the socialist vote had doubled in every election since the party's founding in the territory.[33]

Oklahoma was far from unique politically. In many western states, the Socialist Party had gained strength when voters found the major parties unresponsive. North Dakota by 1912 housed 175 socialist clubs, and socialists held the top offices in Minot, Hissboro, and Rugby. In 1911 Portland, Oregon, elected a small business owner who belonged to the Socialist Party to its city council. Butte, Montana, elected a Socialist Party mayor and city government in 1911, as did Anaconda, Montana, leading the Anaconda Copper Mining Company to fire every actual or alleged socialist, damaging the party and the union. Colorado and Arizona mining districts also elected socialists on the local level.[34]

Doubting the Socialist Party could win nationally, most voters stayed with the dominant parties in congressional and presidential elections, but only when courted. In state after state, voters pushed both the Democratic and Republican Parties to the left, the wings labeled "progressive." In Kansas, William Allen White claimed the progressives had "caught the Populists in swimming and stole all of their clothing except the frayed underdrawers of free silver." In the West, as White also acknowledged, progressives showed the influence of both socialists and Populists. Gone were the demands for the unlimited monetization of silver that had dominated Rocky Mountain state Populism, but remaining were direct democracy in the form of initiative, referendum, and recall, as well as laws regulating hours and wages for women and conditions of work and hazard (including workmen's compensation laws), measures to protect wage workers and farmers and to enfranchise women, calls for municipal ownership of streetcar systems and utilities, and limits on the power of large, often monopoly corporations. When corporations such as Anaconda in Montana, Phelps Dodge in Arizona, and the Southern Pacific Railroad in California bought legislatures, direct democracy—the ability to introduce and pass legislation by initiative and referendum—bypassed elected officials.[35]

Whether Republicans or Democrats won Great Plains states usually depended on who represented the more progressive alternative. In 1912 all three presidential candidates claimed the label "progressive," but with the Republican Taft on the most conservative end of that spectrum, every state in the region went for Woodrow Wilson except South Dakota, which voted for the Progressive Party's candidate, Teddy Roosevelt. Roosevelt's running mate was California's Hiram Johnson. Johnson had risen as an anti-municipal-corruption Republican in San Francisco in 1906, becoming governor in 1910 and representing California in the U.S. Senate from 1917 to 1945. In South Dakota, Nebraska, and Montana, Republicans won progressive measures that limited the power of large corporations and enhanced direct democracy. Wyoming Democrats essayed similar reforms in 1910 under Joseph Carey, previously a Republican and then a progressive. In 1913 Arizona's Democrat governor saw himself as indebted to the socialists. By 1912 Colorado seemed to many in the labor movement to be the country's most successful trade union / Democratic Party alliance. Idaho elected progressive senator William S. Borah, and the state gained electoral reform, employer liability, workmen's compensation, woman suffrage, and laws regulating child and women's labor. William U'Ren had worked in Colorado's mines as a youth, studied law, worked as a reporter, and then worked on his parents' ranch in eastern Oregon. His only elected office was in the state

House of Representatives as a Populist, but later, as a Republican operative, he helped get initiative and referendum into Oregon's 1902 constitution, direct primary in 1904, and recall in 1908. In 1912 Colorado voters passed an amendment that allowed for the popular recall of not just a judge but his decision, which the state's supreme court later declared unconstitutional.[36]

These measures were in no way antithetical to the white man's West. Western states embraced eugenics more than any other region of the era, with eight states passing eugenic sterilization laws. California and other Pacific coast states passed laws prohibiting landownership by immigrants ineligible for citizenship. Progressive governor Hiram Johnson had quashed such legislation in 1911 on behalf of the Taft administration in Washington DC, which feared a diplomatic breach in the delicate era after the Gentlemen's Agreement of 1907. Now, in 1913, with a Wilson White House, Johnson signed a law that barred Japanese and Chinese immigrants from owning land and allowed them to lease land only for a maximum of three years.[37]

Socialists struggled to find common cause in economic status rather than color as southwestern states found new ways to disenfranchise voters labeled nonwhite. In Texas, led by the White Men's Primary Association, Anglos excluded Mexican Americans from meaningful participation in electoral politics in the commercial agricultural counties southwest of San Antonio in 1913 and 1914. In these counties, which generated the U.S. leaders of the Plan de San Diego, irrigated development had soared from 54,000 acres in 1909 to 228,000 acres in 1919. But not all Texans had benefited equally. Tejano families who were unable to get water because of diversions by others sold their land at bargain prices to developers who then got water and sold to Anglo newcomers. Texas then created seven new counties in the region to enhance the power of farming and ranching elites.[38]

But as in Oklahoma, not all Anglos benefited. The two-hundred-thousand-acre Taft Ranch in Texas shifted to industrial farming and from Anglo tenants to Mexican wage labor, housing them in closely controlled company towns. Other tenants who, like most renters, had hoped to turn into landowners rather than wage laborers feared the same prospect awaited them. Such fears moved them toward socialism. Those fears proved greater than fears of endangering their racial status and helped the white socialist tenants who founded the Texas Renters' Union in 1911 to abandon their whites-only clause in 1912.[39]

Across the Southwest, socialist summer encampments brought hundreds of families together in the 1910s as they had in Oklahoma in the previous decade to hear the socialist analysis of their plight. Texas alone had 125 summer encampments in 1914. They educated and entertained the often isolated farmers. In western Oklahoma, where Mexican politics was a frequent topic of conversation, such gatherings might feature a rodeo and carnival. Small-town merchants sponsored the gatherings, glad to benefit from the thousands of attendees, who vastly outnumbered the local villagers.[40]

But the organizing was far from limited to rural farm towns. By 1910 about thirty thousand coal miners worked the mines of Oklahoma, Arkansas, Texas, and Kansas, the vast majority of them United Mine Workers members and early supporters of the Socialist Party. Timber workers in the region, like the United Mine Workers, organized by industry rather than skill and included Black, white, and Mexican workers. Housewives, tenant farmers, tradesmen, and others would join their struggle against the companies and the Democrats who worked for them.[41]

The connecting threads between the Mexican Revolution and the West's insurgent politics showed most clearly in Texas. The Anglo tenant farmers who formed the debt-ridden majority of the Texas Socialist Party adopted the Magonista slogan, "Land and Liberty." They won 12 percent of the vote—twice that of the Republican candidate—in the 1914 Texas governor's race. Geographically mobile workers made, as historian Neil Foley writes, "radical ideas about land distribution and ownership . . . a transnational and global phenomenon"; socialist organizers in the Southwest had come from Ireland, Mexico, and Germany, as well as the United States, "in search of land they could call their own." As Mexican workers crossed back and forth across the border over the course of the decade, their experiences proved mutually reinforcing. Mexican refugees from Porfirio Díaz's dictatorship had run newspapers and organized an international group of rebels from Los Angeles, California, to Laredo, Texas, since the 1880s. They provided an articulate radical presence with a larger-than-national vision.[42]

Radical Unions and Labor Wars

As voters turned to direct democracy at the ballot box, western workers turned to unions to bring democracy to the workplace. Amid intensifying questions about who counted as true Americans, polyglot unions claimed that their conditions and their organizing were native to the region. The most explicitly radical of the unions were those of the Industrial Workers of the World (IWW or Wobblies), but even unions affiliated with more conservative federations pressed for radical change.

William Dudley "Big Bill" Haywood was born in Salt Lake City, Utah, in 1869. At the age of nine he lost an eye and as a youth knocked about as a hard rock miner, cowboy, and homesteader in Utah, Nevada, and Idaho. In 1896 he joined the Western Federation of Miners (WFM) and quickly rose to a leadership position. As secretary of the WFM Haywood went on trial in 1907 after Harry Orchard, convicted of murdering Idaho governor Frank Stunenberg, implicated him and other WFM leaders. Defended by famous Chicago civil rights lawyer Clarence Darrow and prosecuted by future progressive and later New Deal liberal senator William Borah, they gained national attention, and Haywood won acquittal. It seemed a trial of labor against capital. Haywood emerged from this triumph as the personification of the radical labor movement in the U.S. West. When the WFM took a turn to the right, exiting the IWW it had helped found, Haywood stayed on to lead the fledgling organization.

Haywood's prototypical tour through iconic western occupations gave him added credibility when he argued that this radicalism had its roots in a particularly American economic system and the conditions of work it generated. The idea behind the IWW was "One Big Union," with the motto and journal *Solidarity* and the long-range goal of industrial democracy: worker ownership and governance of factories and other means of production. Its focus on democracy put it perfectly in step with the democratic movements sweeping the western United States, Mexico, and western Canada, to which the IWW also spread.

The IWW's reach was transnational, but its structure particularly suited the West's disproportionately large share of transient workers, those generally considered unorganizable. Youths coming from the interior met an ever-larger array of diverse young single men who jumped ship on the West Coast. American, Japanese, Chinese, Dutch, Norwegian, and English ships carried Japanese, Malay, Chinese, Filipino, "Hindoo," anarchist, polygamist, and illiterate crews—excluded classes by U.S. law—who then jumped ship while in port, bribing the ship owner when necessary.[43] Their numbers and the ideas they carried swelled the workforce and the possibility of change made credible by the Mexican Revolution.

The IWW included Asians among its members, in distinction to unions that promised a "white man's camp." Those latter unions had linked white workers and organizers traveling to the West via the routes of the British Empire—from Ireland to Australia, South Africa, and Canada—for whom whiteness was central to their sense of identity, privilege, and security. The IWW seemed to travel different circuits. Its members included those who came from and through the Philippines, Spain, and South and East Asia to the U.S. West, Mexico, and Canada. They created unions that often included Asian and Mexican migrants alongside the European and U.S. ones, and they often organized women as well. They created spaces where anticolonial movements converged with revolutionary movements. Indian nationalists, Filipino insurgents, and Mexican revolutionaries mingled in revolutionary Mexico, in the lumber camps of the Pacific Northwest, and in the fields of California.[44]

The same forces of development and displacement, the eradication of the small producers and the rise of global capitalism, set them in motion. The roving transnational managerial class they encountered differed from the early settler colonialists like those of California, Arizona, New Mexico, and Texas who had married Mexicans without thinking of it as "going native." By the 1900s, in contrast, the ex-Panama overseer who settled in South Texas and the mining technocrats who moved from the United States to Australia and back did not identify with the people who harvested the crops and removed the ore.[45]

The IWW had low or no dues, and with "One Big Union" a member was a member wherever he or she went. "Big Bill" Haywood, at about six feet, four inches tall and powerfully built, towered over the men he led and used a charismatic presence to persuade workers of all types—agricultural, lumber, mining, millworkers (both smelter and textile)—to join a union, to see a strike through, and to unite in a common cause. Itinerant workers, often male and young, had little to lose. They loved their reputation as rugged frontier individualists, egalitarian and antiauthoritarian, comprising a grassroots organization. The IWW did not always win, but it amassed a string of victories from 1907 forward, improving pay and conditions in British Columbia, Washington, Oregon, Colorado, California, and elsewhere among lumber and sawmill workers, smelter workers, sewer and gas diggers, bridge workers, diamond workers, harvest workers, and others.[46]

Despite the IWW's reputation, for the most part its actions were nonviolent. Wobblies did believe in direct action: strikes, free speech fights, mass picketing, and striking on the job (e.g., occupying mines so the employer could not send in strikebreaking workers). Unlike the American Federation of Labor (AFL), however, the IWW uncompromisingly rejected the capitalist system, and it was Wobblies' ideals and rhetoric that in part accounted for the fear and revulsion felt by businessmen and industrialists and even the AFL toward the IWW.

By 1913 Wobblies had demonstrated strength in California when they asserted their vision of a democratic West in two free speech fights in San Diego and Fresno. Fresno was the center of agricultural labor in California, the heart of the San Joaquin Valley. There the Wobblies had fought for the right to maintain their headquarters, distribute literature, and hold public meetings throughout 1910, battling the Fresno authorities, who wanted to shut them down and ride them out of town. As soon as authorities crushed the Wobblies, they launched a new campaign and finally got an unwilling local tolerance for their activities.[47]

San Diego was more violent. Starting in January 1912, San Diego authorities began to suppress Wobbly meetings, aided by an ordinance outlawing free speech in this city of forty thousand. Wobblies from throughout the West started descending on the city, growing to a group of 150. The press, controlled by the growers, threatened that thousands would converge, leading the authorities to sponsor a local vigilance committee, which established camps and posted armed guards on highways leading to San Diego, turning back all transients.[48]

In San Diego proper, the vigilantes rounded up all people remotely suspected of being Wobblies and drove them one night to Sorrento. The vigilantes made the Wobblies mount a platform, kiss an American flag, and sing the national anthem in front of hundreds of vigilantes armed with revolvers, knives, clubs, blackjacks, and whips. They then marched the Wobblies to San Onofre and drove them into a cattle pen, where they systematically slugged and beat them. One died of these injuries in jail. All this activity met with approval by the civil authorities and enthusiastic resolutions by the Merchants Association and the Chamber of Commerce.[49]

Far from being driven underground by these actions, the Wobblies established locals throughout California at Fresno, Bakersfield, Los Angeles, San Francisco, Sacramento, and even San Diego and from these locals sent delegates into the fields to organize workers on the job. Many resultant strikes were successful, including that of agricultural workers at Brawley, California, in July 1913. The reputation of the Wobblies grew, though formal membership was still fewer than five thousand in the state, less than 8 percent of the state's migratory farmworkers.[50]

The organizing culminated at Wheatland that summer. As most growers usually did, hops grower Ralph H. Durst had advertised in newspapers in California and Nevada for workers, asking for 2,700, though he knew he could only employ about 1,500. It was a recession year. Within four days of the advertising, about 2,800 job seekers had responded. Of the 2,800, about 1,500 were women and children, and over half were noncitizens. About a third of the workers came from California towns and cities and were usually of Anglo or Mexican descent; about a third came from the Sierra foothills with wagons and carts; the rest were migrant workers of longer circuits, including Japanese, South Asian, and Puerto Rican workers. At one later meeting, seven interpreters had to be used, and note was made of twenty-seven nationalities represented in a work gang of 235 men on the ranch.[51]

Many of the 2,800 had no blankets. They slept in tents rented from Durst at seventy-five cents per week. Those who could not afford the rent slept in the fields. Forty-five men, women, and children slept on a single pile of straw. With nine outdoor toilets for 2,800 people, the camp was not a pleasant place. Vomiting and dysentery were common. Durst admitted later that he allowed the camp to stay filthy in the hope that some of the workers would leave before the season was over, forfeiting the 10 percent of their wages he held until the end of the season.

They started work about 4:00 a.m., working through 105 degree heat, with no means provided for bringing water to the fields. Durst's cousin had a lemonade concession and sold the drink to workers at a nickel a glass. Local Wheatland stores were forbidden to send delivery wagons into camp so, as they did in the mining towns, workers bought from a similar "store" on the ranch. Earnings varied from seventy-eight cents to a dollar a day, depending on how many workers there were that day.

About one hundred of the men had at some time been card-carrying IWW members, including a few veterans of the free speech movement and a few organizers from the timber camps of the Northwest who had drifted south to the agricultural fields.[52] About four hundred of the workers knew something of the IWW philosophy and some of the songs. As resentment in the camp steadily mounted over living conditions, on August 3, 1913, the Wobblies among the workers called a mass meeting. An unarmed former IWW organizer, Blackie Ford, addressed the workers. He took a sick baby from its mother's arms, held it up, and shouted, "It's for the kids we are doing this." He closed the meeting with a Wobbly song, at which point the sheriff and his posse arrived with the district attorney, who happened also to be Durst's private attorney. The sheriff and his men started pushing through the crowd to arrest Ford. A deputy on the fringe of the crowd fired a shot into the air to sober the quiet "mob," and as he fired, fighting started. The district attorney, deputy sheriff, and two workers, one Puerto Rican man and one English boy, were killed. The posse fled, astonished that the workers had resisted. The governor dispatched four companies of the National Guard, who marched to the workers' camp, surrounded it, and helped local officers arrest about one hundred workers. Most of the workers fled that night, but the National Guard remained for a week.

Reaction was harsh and sweeping. Local authorities were convinced it was a revolution. Wobblies were arrested in every part of California and often held incommunicado for months. Among the hundreds arrested was a man detectives followed into Arizona, arrested, put on a boxcar, brought back to California, and prevented from contacting a lawyer by moving him from hotel to hotel and beating him with rubber bludgeons to elicit a confession, though he had not been present at the riot. His attorney found him weeks later. After such treatment one Wobbly committed suicide and another went insane. Ford, eight months later, was convicted of murder and sentenced to life in prison.

The episode spurred the creation of the California Commission on Immigration and Housing. California progressives hoped the new housing commission would turn aside immigrant workers from revolution and "Americanize" them. But though the commission's frequent investigations exposed horrendous conditions, they led to little action.[53] By 1914 there were seventy-five thousand migrant farmworkers in California working on ranches without even the kind of accommodations provided for livestock.

Meanwhile, the agricultural workers continued to organize. In the winter of 1914, some two thousand of the seventy-five thousand agricultural workers prepared to march on the state capitol. At Sacramento they met a force of eight hundred special deputy sheriffs, who drove them back across the river, "burned their blankets and equipment, and mounted an armed guard along the bridge to keep them out." Despite such defeats, the IWW in the next few years won victories for lumber workers, iron workers, and even agricultural workers in the West. In April 1915 it chartered what became the Agricultural Workers Industrial Union in Kansas City. It doubled its membership in 1917.[54]

While the IWW workers were striking in Wheatland, California, the coal miners in southern Colorado battled for workplace democracy as well. Led by the United Mine Workers of America, they went out on strike in the autumn of 1913. In the face of monopoly capitalists in the coal industry who attempted to control every aspect of the workers' lives in their new company towns, they struck for better wages and conditions and for union recognition. Since many lived in company towns, they were evicted and set up domestic life and union organization in strategically located tent colonies, from which they hoped to bar the entrance of strikebreaking workers.[55]

Production in the southern coal fields of Colorado by both of the major producers (Victor-American Fuel Company and CF&I) had already gone flat years before the strike. With labor among the few costs the corporations could control, coal companies opted for increasingly draconian labor relations—building closed company camps, hiring more company guards, letting wages lag behind the rising cost of living by 50 percent—and for ignoring state laws forbidding pay in scrip and mandating an eight-hour day. In the face of the union organizing drive in 1913, CF&I and Victor-American raised wages and abolished scrip, but in the context of the holistic control companies now exercised over the lives of their workers, the workers held out for union recognition. These companies, with enormous war chests and a lack of competition within the state, settled back to outlast the strikers.[56]

The Colorado governor called out the National Guard to keep order, but the National Guard, like local politicians, was far from even-handed. Determined to allow strikebreakers to reach the mines and with guns trained on the tent colony at Ludlow, the National Guard murdered strike leader Louis Tikas and several others on April 20, 1914, and then set fire to the colony, smothering a group of women and children who had taken refuge from flying bullets beneath the floorboards of their tent. This was the Ludlow Massacre.

Making sense of the massacre, even in the context of continued violence on both sides, turned into a public relations battle. The epic shift at the time to coal and the energy economy that swirled around it led to an insatiable demand for energy and a panicky willingness to go to great lengths, including trampling on various liberties, to avoid stoppages in energy supply.[57] On the other hand, the widespread appeal of socialism reflected a broad swath of citizens who feared a runaway state that, in cahoots with powerful corporations, would trample on civil liberties. They feared the loss of sovereignty, both national and individual. They were prepared to suspect the motives and power of the coal company.

Coal companies tried to control the narrative. As it did at Wheatland, diversity characterized the workforce. CF&I's miners heralded from roughly thirty-two nations and spoke twenty-seven different languages, with roughly two-thirds of the workers being non-U.S. citizens and a hefty proportion of the citizens being Hispanos native to the region. A CF&I executive blamed mine accidents on outside agitators and, though he employed them, disdained "these foreigners who do not intend to make America their home, and who live like rats in order to save money." They "are over here for the purpose of selling their labor in the highest market in the world, and when they have a few hundred dollars to their credit in the banks of the countries from which they came, they will go back there to enjoy their bread and beer."[58] In this paradigm, it is the immigrants rather than those who employ them for substandard wages who exploit the nation.

On the other hand, the workers' demands—though often posed by the press at the time as radical—were seen by the workers as the ultimate American demands of self-determination and liberty in the face of an oppressive corporate regime that tried to control not only their labor but also the intimate spaces of their daily lives, including in company-built houses and towns, designed after the 1894 coal miners' strike to prevent the resurgence of union identity.[59] Like the agricultural workers at Wheatland, these strikers understood the larger economic world in which they struggled. They made common cause despite the barriers of language and culture, staking out their territory literally and, despite their relatively small numbers and financial backing, posing a significant threat to the status quo.

Following the massacre at Ludlow, a ten-day armed uprising of enraged, polyglot strikers merged into a tornado-like force and took over and occupied a huge swath of southern Colorado. They destroyed mine property and in some places killed company employees and state militiamen. Reporters called it the beginning of a civil war. President Wilson, whose government had already begun investigating the strike before the massacre, called in the federal troops. To their supporters, labor radicalism and violence appeared as the necessary pushback to the increased power and wealth of corporations and the state's willingness to operate as an arm of the corporation. The National Guard was inseparable, by the end of the strike, from the company mine guards it inducted. The strike and its aftermath called attention to relations between labor, capital, politics, and economics.[60]

Ultimately, the companies' corporate owners won the strike, but they lost the media war. Journalist Scott Martelle takes apart the loaded terms of coverage (e.g., "massacre," with its implication of intentional genocide) and meticulously follows the newspaper and local source trails to find that the miners killed nearly twice as many men as they lost in their battle with what he agrees was corporate feudalism. But the miners succeeded in dominating the media war. The image of the miners as victims of corporate violence, of the women and children smothered in the flames at Ludlow, prevailed, though few would argue they were intentionally killed. That image overwhelmed the coverage of the ten days of violence that followed both in the media and in the historical record. This dominant image was far more likely to garner sympathy for the labor movement and outrage against monopoly capital than would the image of roving bands of armed immigrant strikers.[61]

Had women and children not been killed at Ludlow, it might have had no larger profile than any other violent strike. The ability to pose the women and children (who were seldom named lest the Italian and Mexican names interfere with compassion) as "innocent" victims of state and corporate-sponsored violence was critical to the media war. Yet women, like the men of the strike, were everywhere, and not just under the tents. They were strategists (e.g., national labor leader and icon Mother Jones), protesters, warriors, and marchers. They kept house in the tent colonies, fought strikebreakers, and marched on the governor's office and the National Guard. They reported on Ludlow for the state and national press and served as state legislative representatives and as commissary managers.

Women in Colorado had been voting since 1896. Helen Ring Robinson represented them in the state senate, only the second woman in the country to be elected to such an office. Senator Robinson, former president of the Denver Women's Press Club, the daughter of a laborer, and long an advocate for the rights of labor and working women in particular, shortly before the massacre had been commissioned by the *New York American* to investigate the coal fields owned by the CF&I. She had produced a scathing account of corporate tyranny, writing, "In the city of Trinidad the Rockefeller interests are all powerful. The officials of the company control the courts, control the sheriff's office, control the County Commissioners. A word from these officials . . . has caused licenses to be revoked from men believed to be unfriendly to the Colorado Fuel and Iron Company. And another word has opened the doors of jails to freedom for notorious thugs and outlaws." She called the region "a barony or a principality of the Colorado Fuel and Iron Co.," adding, "And I don't wish to say that the Colorado Fuel and Iron Co. have limited their efforts to Las Animas and Huerfano Counties . . . but they have in time past reached out beyond the boundaries of their principality and made and unmade governors." On Saturday, April 25, 1914, five days after the massacre, Senator Robinson assembled a thousand women in the rotunda of the state capitol and then marched them to the House of Representatives' chamber. When the governor failed to appear, a committee of the women confronted him in his den and forced him to meet with the crowd; when he slipped away again, Senator Robinson and the committee followed him back to his office and refused to leave until, ten hours later, he caved in to their demands and sent a telegram to President Wilson asking for federal troops.[62]

The men who opposed them placed the marchers on the governor's office in the context of wild women and suffragettes, meaning to align them with yet more of the radical dangers of the era.[63] It is key to recognize, as their opponents did and as becomes apparent in the next chapter, that the radicalism of woman suffrage was not separate from the other radicalism of the era: the broader demand for an expansion and redefinition of democracy. Woman suffragists were deeply implicated in most radical and reform groups across a wide spectrum.

Conclusion

Different visions of western modernity collided violently in the 1910s. Revolutionary ideas of democracy in politics and economics converged in a West crisscrossed by migrant streams from around the globe. By middecade these violent confrontations had fractured progressive coalitions not because of the weakness of the mass movements but because of their heft. In the Pacific Northwest, for example, the IWW included Chinese, Japanese, and South Asian workers, radical Finns and other Scandinavians, and footloose young men born across the United States. In Everett, Washington, a free speech fight in 1916 led to yet another massacre as business leaders mobilized the government to fight organized labor. With the sheriff and a deputy among the casualties, widespread middle-class support for organized labor evaporated.[64] In 1917 President Woodrow Wilson would claim the United States entered what became World War I to make the world safe for democracy, but the citizens of the U.S. West had already joined a global battle for democracy, whose sites included their own backyard.

The rise of the Socialist Party and the events at Wheatland, Ludlow, and Everett occurred in a period when radicals in the West had some clout at the ballot box, held some governors in their sway, and found more acceptance for divergent views of what constituted true Americanism than would be the case four years later. Corporations had greeted with disgust the election of Woodrow Wilson in 1912 as president and, to them, worse still, his choice of a former United Mine Worker secretary-treasurer, William B. Wilson, for the first ever secretary of labor in 1913, the year the strike at Ludlow began. These years marked both an almost unimaginable ideological tolerance and unspeakable vigilantism. Embedded in this wider ideological dialogue, workers went on strike as political and not just labor actors.[65]

The region's probusiness boosters held strong to their depiction of their complicated region as a homogeneous white haven. The swirling, noisy, and international democratic insurgencies posed a public relations problem in Washington, California, and elsewhere just as the border raids did in Texas. California boosters had already forced the removal of Indian villages in order to develop hot springs, and they now turned their attention to organizing two world's fairs, one at San Francisco and the other at San Diego. They would put forward a different vision of international order and California's place in it. Those in San Diego were keen to distance the city from Mexico and to counter the visibility of the 1912 IWW free speech movement. Timed to open in 1915 with the completion of the Panama Canal, the fair would highlight the mission theme, the aristocratic Spanish fantasy heritage, and the benign bringing of civilization. No California tribes would grace the fairgrounds. Pueblo Indians would perform their peaceful identity, never "in white man's clothing," and thrilling exhibits, including a Chinese opium parlor, highlighted eroticism, drugs, violence, and the backwardness of nonwhite people elsewhere.[66] The fight over how to depict the West was inseparable from the battle for democracy.

Revolution in this era was a spectacle and not just a political movement. Already in the 1910s the structure of spectacle was well ingrained. Middle-class crowds with no direct relation to the struggle gathered on an adjacent hilltop to watch the labor clashes at Ludlow in 1914. U.S. crowds gathered at the border, whether at El Paso, where a river marked the line, or at the featureless, barrierless border in Tijuana, to watch opposing Mexican forces in battle. After the Magonista victory at Tijuana, which crowds had watched from a sort of natural amphitheater, the victors allowed the spectators to tour the battle site for twenty-five cents each. In Brownsville in 1913 crowds gathered around the International Bridge on hotel and store roofs to watch the impending battle. From his perch atop the customs house, one William A. Neale recalled, "It was a beautiful sight to see how the invaders advanced towards the breastworks where their foes were waiting for them." Robert Runyon made a good living selling photographs and postcards he produced of the carnage for the U.S. market. According to his chroniclers, "Graphic scenes of destruction sold particularly well."[67]

The careful demarcations built up in the century's first decade blurred in the second. Revolutions and revolutionaries crossed national borders. Native Americans fought for land and freedom. Workers crossed seas and national borders and prescribed "racial" lines to assert their rights to participate in the ordering of their economic lives. Women stormed statehouses. States developed ever-greater capacities to reinscribe the lines. They called out the National Guard, blended their forces with those of corporations, and chose allies among an array of labor associations. They created new lines of exclusion at every level, from immigration to property ownership to suffrage requirements. The marketing of these contests as spectacles helped to create them as containable, legible, comprehensible, and apart from the spectator. At the same time, that distance was illusory. Spectators on the U.S. side of the border during the Mexican Revolution occasionally got shot.

5

Women and Their Alliances

The morning after the election of 1920, the town of Yoncalla, Oregon, woke to what one newspaper called a "feminist revolution." Women had swept the elections. Yoncalla had 323 residents. Men outnumbered women almost two to one. And men, comfortable in their majority, had run the town inefficiently. The women had organized in secret. Only other women knew, and they prevailed. Longtime resident and university graduate Mrs. Mary Burt was the new mayor. Also elected to the town council was Mrs. Laswell, wife of the ousted mayor. Mr. Laswell could only say to the press that he was "much surprised."[1]

But the same thing had happened in Umatilla, Oregon, at the other end of the state, four years earlier. In 1916, four years after gaining the ballot in the state, the women of Umatilla grew tired of the minimalist town government. Ordinances went unenforced. Bills went unpaid. Turning off the streetlights was the last straw. Mrs. C. G. Brownell held a card party, hatched a plot, and triumphed at the polls. Mrs. Laura Starcher trounced her husband, Mayor E. E. Starcher, and became the new mayor. Brownell served on the town council with two other women. They promised a "business administration and a progressive administration," and they delivered. The streets were lit, cleaned, and policed. Then, four years later, their job done, the women disappeared as suddenly as they had come. The town returned to its all-male rule, and women disappeared from the ranks of the candidates.[2] It was a sort of Lone Ranger model of politics.

Women in Oregon clearly wielded their new political power in ways that allowed them to control their environment, at least for a while. Power-sharing was real. And these women fulfilled the expectations of those who had seen them as fit to rule because they stood above narrow economic interests and for civic order and welfare. Yet Umatilla and Yoncalla set an example singularly unmatched in the eastern part of the country, even after 1920. Umatilla had a population of about two hundred. In the late 1910s it was a town where almost as many people ran for office as voted. Candidacies did not have to be announced. Candidates could win with write-in campaigns.

The women's victories may have been unusual, but the mobilization was not. Umatilla and Yoncalla were the fruits of radically democratic winds that swept the western United States and its borders in the 1910s. It was also the fruit of its limits. A relatively homogeneous electorate helped the women into office. What was radical about this democratic fire was not always its politics. It was the belief in mass participation, the same mindset that generated initiative and referendum beginning in the 1890s, taking legislative power directly to the people—termed "direct democracy." Expanding the franchise followed that logic. But not everyone agreed on who "the people" were.

Woman suffrage was the largest expansion of the electorate since the dawn of the republic. It doubled the number of potential voters. Women of all political persuasions fought for the vote, and many conservative women opposed it. Whatever their stance, giving women the vote was a radical proposition. It recognized women as autonomous political actors. It has usually been treated in histories in isolation, as tangential at best to the other insurgencies of the decade. But particularly in the West, the women who fought for suffrage saw it as part and parcel of what one of them called "the greatest movement of the age—the fight for a wider democracy."[3] This chapter focuses on those connections, the deeply entwined nature of the movements in the West, and their mutually shaping implications. It begins by looking at who these women were in the American West, then at their allies on the northern border, and finally at the dynamics on the southern border.

Defining "the People"

The women elected in Umatilla and Yoncalla were clubwomen, college graduates, property owners, schoolteachers, and sometimes telegraph operators—they were not poor or even industrial working class, and they were all clearly marked as white. "Oregon"—that is, those settlers who claimed to embody that imaginary—had been since its origins as part of the United States invested in its identity as white. Its white inhabitants had fought to displace and contain Native Americans and voted to exclude Black settlers even before the Civil War. They had been hostile to Chinese workers who showed up in their port cities and railroad towns.[4]

These women's ability not only to enact an identity as "Oregon" and "white" but also to claim an identity as civic-minded clubwomen emerged, as it did for their cohort across the nation, from a national concern with the health of the country in the context of labor and racial unrest, border troubles, imperial adventures, and immigration. Faced with this context, white middle-class and elite men and women demanded and drew increasingly sharp boundaries around the nation-state—both geographic and demographic. Many of the western woman suffrage leaders claimed a "pioneer" identity. To claim "pioneer" status, to claim to have been an early settler, ignored those already quite settled in these territories—Native Americans. In the Southwest that claim also excluded Mexican Americans, who were rarely endowed with "pioneer" status or memberships in the pioneer associations that proliferated at the turn of the century.[5] A claim to pioneer status was a claim to have participated in the white conquest of the West and to have endured the hardships accompanying conquest, to have labored in ways usually associated with men, and so to have a claim on full citizenship.

In the struggle to create a defined and bounded citizenry, marriage became a central concern. State-level miscegenation laws multiplied. There had long been miscegenation laws on the books in various states. Most southern states had laws banning marriages between whites and Blacks from at least the eighteenth century. As racial categories multiplied, laws grew more elaborate, and new states (Oklahoma in 1907, Arkansas in 1911, Tennessee in 1917, Virginia in 1924, Alabama in 1927, and Georgia in 1927) adopted a one-drop standard (any African heritage at all) to define "Negro." Almost three-quarters of the states to add new groups to banned intermarriages between 1909 and 1933 were west of the Mississippi (Montana and Missouri in 1909, Nevada in 1911, Nebraska and

Wyoming in 1913, Idaho in 1921, Arizona in 1931, and California in 1933).[6] The groups added included Japanese, Chinese, Mongolians, Malays, "Coreans," and Hindus. Finally, also inseparable from drawing the "nation's" borders was the rising pervasiveness of Black/white segregation labeled Jim Crow, widespread in many western states even when not encoded in state laws. These efforts were all manifestations of the same tendency of making and marking borders, and this border marking was the context for the rise of reform women to political power.

Those who could do so not only insisted on drawing these borders around "race" and "nation" but also drew borders around gender and sexuality. Only manly men and womanly women, after all, were fit to have dominion over those defined as "lesser breeds" by the new imperialists, including Rudyard Kipling, who used the term in his poem *The White Man's Burden,* urging the United States to empire.[7] Similar to developments in other late nineteenth-century imperializing nations, distinctions between men and women in the United States, of which fashion was only one manifestation, sharpened. Despite and because of the challenge of the New Woman—that late nineteenth-century professional and public creature—woman suffrage in the United States would not be won on the grounds of *human* rights, the identity of males and females as individuals, but instead on the grounds of women's essential virtue. It would be won not on the grounds of sameness but on the grounds of difference—hence the women's reform administration victories in Umatilla and Yoncalla. Women would not be creatures of political machines. They would be above "politics."

Simultaneously, the growth of a "science" of race was joined by a rising "science" of sex. Those "scientists" invented, multiplied, and delimited categories, and they defined "normal" and "deviant." Concerned about declining "manliness," men, including Teddy Roosevelt, created hunting clubs, boosted men's physical fitness, and gave manliness a martial definition. The federal government worked along the same lines. On a Crow reservation, for example, the U.S. agent imprisoned and forced haircutting and physical labor on a person perfectly acceptable to the Crow as a man-woman.[8]

In late 1912 a scandal exploded in Portland, Oregon. A terrified nineteen-year-old named Benjamin Trout, U.S. born and white and arrested for a petty crime, not only confessed to the crime but also exposed a whole world to the eyes of a horrified readership, a homosexual subculture that linked major West Coast cities from Vancouver to Los Angeles. It had its own secret codes, male brothels, drag parties, local sites, and national networks. The news filled the papers for weeks.

Portland and other Pacific Northwest coastal cities were used to occasional stories of same-sex practices among the transient workers who seasonally flooded their more seamy neighborhoods and bars. The region had the largest proportion of transient labor in North America, and distant from their families, these workers found alternative modes of intimacy, emotional support, and kinship. The stories had worried local reformers about sex that transgressed racial boundaries and imperiled white youth and so imperiled the middle-class family, but this scandal was different. This scandal originated in the white, native-born middle class, in the YMCA and its respectable patrons. These men weren't just having occasional sex with other men; these men were that newly defined being: the homosexual.[9]

The response highlighted the anxieties of the era. As prospective suspects fled Portland, law officials up and down the coast cooperated in hunting them down. Reformers who aligned themselves with progressives strengthened existing laws, passed new laws, and ratcheted up punishments in what they refused to see as a futile determination to eradicate homosexuality from the body politic. Portland police arrested dozens of men. This harsher regime was not even-handed. Authorities still targeted particularly working-class men and particularly those men defined as nonwhite, which included Greek migrant laborers in a fresh scandal in the spring of the following year. Obsessions with defining race, sex, and gender were manifestations of the same impulses.[10]

These borders did not exclude those sexed and gendered as women from office, but they dictated the terms by which they might enter. Women could enter as true "women"—white, middle-class or elite, reform women who would clean up the town, as did those of Umatilla. And they could only do so where the territory had safely already been won by white men, as it had in Oregon. Umatilla had no African American residents, but it did have a longstanding Chinese and Japanese immigrant population in 1910.[11] Defined as ineligible for citizenship and with a sharply controlled immigration, they stood outside the electoral system.

The years of establishing Jim Crow (racial segregation and Black disenfranchisement) were the same years in the United States in which women suffragists won no state victories. Suffragists labeled the long dry spell "the doldrums." In those years women had occasionally won the right to vote for school boards or municipal officers. They regrouped, fought with each other, tried and failed in ballot initiatives and legislatures. Finally, with Jim Crow in place and the rumblings of revolution in Mexico and at home, women won the vote in Washington in 1910 by a margin of almost two to one.[12] The next years saw a succession of victories, all, until 1917, west of the Mississippi. The movement became part of the decade's great mobilization for expanding democracy.

This climax is usually treated as totally distinct from the other mass mobilizations of the decade, but the relationship is intimate. It was men who had to vote women into power. With the rise of socialism, progressive men turned to women like those in Umatilla and Yoncalla as ballast against the tilt toward more radical change. Yet suffragists and socialists were often one and the same. Shifting coalitions and alliances with socialists and progressives, "good government" forces and organized labor, along with their own improved organizing skills, garnered hard-fought victories for women. In southern California, the socialist-feminist alliance swept Los Angeles into the suffrage column and so won California for woman suffrage in 1911, outweighing the more polarized forces of conservatism and a more immigrant labor machine in San Francisco. In Kansas, socialists played a leading role in the woman suffrage victory. In Arizona, the joint movement bypassed a legislature beholden to party machinery and took the issue to the people in a referendum, sweeping to victory the year after statehood.[13] By 1915 eleven states, all west of the Mississippi, had granted women full suffrage.

These western suffrage leaders and early women officeholders tended to be "New Women," like the women in Yoncalla and

Umatilla. They not always but sometimes deployed their "pioneer" status; they led unorthodox lives and had college educations and careers. They were journalists, doctors, and lawyers. Helen Duett Ellison was born in Texas and moved to Arizona with her rancher family in 1885. She and her sister drove cattle, and she served as the foreman of the Ellison ranch. She roped, tied, and branded longhorn cattle, was a crack shot, and never allowed her cowboys to curse, chew tobacco, or wear their chaps or spurs in her home. She married woman suffrage supporter and future progressive Arizona governor George Hunt.[14]

Frances Willard Munds won election to the Arizona Senate in 1914, the first election after women had won the vote in Arizona. Five feet tall, red-haired, and never timid, she had demanded a secondary education. She alone of her eleven siblings got it. Afterward, she taught school in various Arizona towns, including a Mormon community, where she lodged with a Mormon family. She came to respect those Mormons far more than the men of Jerome, Arizona, who were disposed to wander drunkenly into her schoolroom, wedged as it was between two saloons. She married John Munds, a rancher, miner, and homesteader, in 1890, cut her hair short to spare herself the fuss, and rode around Arizona on her own. A thorough New Woman, her politics demonstrated a complex drawing of inclusions and exclusions. As her husband won political office, she worked to ensure that the woman suffrage movement stayed on the side of labor unions and progressive reformers but also to exclude non-English-speaking Mexican American voters. She favored the election of Mormon candidates; Mormons composed by 1910 only about 10–15 percent of the population of Arizona but almost half the thirty-two members of the Arizona Equal Suffrage Association campaign committee. In 1914 she narrowly won the Democratic primary against four male contenders for state senate, and buoyed by a large female turnout in the Democratic county, she swept to victory.[15]

The most successful on the national level was Jeanette Rankin. Rankin epitomizes both the organic ways in which social concerns led to women's political activism and the alliances that brought them success. Born in Montana in 1880, the oldest of seven, Rankin graduated with a degree in biology in 1902 with a class of only eighteen from what would become the University of Montana in Missoula. All of Rankin's sisters followed in her footsteps, but her brother went east to Harvard College and Harvard Law School. Like many women graduates in an extremely restricted job market, she taught school. Hers was a one-room schoolhouse, and she did not enjoy it. In 1904 she quit to take care of her father in what turned out to be a fatal case of Rocky Mountain spotted fever. Then she floundered. She grabbed the chance to go to Cambridge to care for her brother when he fell ill, and when he recovered, she headed down to Washington DC in 1905 to attend an inaugural ball, which she thoroughly enjoyed. Nevertheless, what she saw of eastern poverty disturbed her. She read on social issues; she took a course in furniture design; she became depressed; she developed rheumatism; she went to San Francisco in 1907 to visit an uncle and stayed to work in a settlement house among Italians on Telegraph Hill. The house provided classes in English, health, and citizenship; day care for the children of working mothers; and after-school programs. While working there, Rankin attended meetings on labor conditions and labor legislation. In 1908 she headed east to enroll in the New York School of Philanthropy.[16] She spent part of her time in the night police courts, helping young girls arrested for prostitution find other jobs, often in factories that turned out to be at least as dangerous as the streets.

When she graduated in 1909, she returned to Missoula and investigated the county jail, ultimately leading a successful campaign to improve conditions there. She moved on to a position as a professional children's social worker at the Washington Children's Home Society, first in Spokane, then in Seattle. Frustrated that all the interesting work was monopolized by the male staff and disheartened by the home conditions of the children, the low placement rates, the high return rates, and the high mortality rates, she left the job in a matter of weeks and enrolled at the University of Washington with the aim of preparing herself to work for social legislation. She studied economics, political science, and public speaking and supported herself by dressmaking.[17] Her experience had led her to believe that the answer to social ills lay not in social services but in politics.

Rankin's brother, Wellington, had meanwhile returned to Montana, where he ran a law practice and made millions as a businessman, rancher, and criminal lawyer. He became the largest individual landholder in the United States. In 1909, listening to her talk endlessly about the woman suffrage work she had seen in the East, he had suggested to Jeanette that she might prefer woman suffrage work to social work as a career. The spring of 1910 found her plastering the university neighborhood with suffrage posters, leading to her recruitment by the College Equal Suffrage League for a position that would pay her expenses beginning in the fall. Overcoming splits between the eastern U.S. suffrage leadership and the western leaders and among the Washington suffragists, winning over Norwegian lumber mill workers, addressing farmers' organizations and unions, and traveling to nearly every county west of the Cascade Mountains, Rankin experienced success. Women won every county in the state.[18] Rankin learned to build alliances among like-minded voters.

Impressed, the suffrage leadership recommended her for a position at the New York headquarters. Jeanette would remain a paid suffrage worker for the next five years. She worked on campaigns in California, North Dakota, and finally Montana. Then she took a break from mobilization and from the fractious politics within the movement. She went to New Zealand, where women had voted since 1893 and had put into place an extensive system of social welfare. She again supported herself by dressmaking while she studied labor and welfare conditions and programs. It was part of a trend historical sociologist Elisabeth Clemens labeled "policy tourism."[19]

When she came back refreshed in 1916, she decided to run for Congress. Friends, neighbors, and suffrage movement leaders thought she was crazy, but her brother, Wellington, said, "You run and I'll elect you." Wellington's own ambitions for office met with less success. He ran seven times and won only once, for state attorney general, in 1920. But he always supported his sister and woman suffrage, even after, contrary to his advice, she voted against the U.S. entry into World War I.[20]

Choosing Allies

While Rankin educated herself on issues and organizing, the Nonpartisan League (NPL) emerged on the ground from the worsening conditions of North Dakota wheat farmers. Between 1890 and 1910 the percentage of farms, largely family farms, that were mortgaged rose from 31.4 to 50.9; the percentage of farms run by tenants rather than owners more than doubled. Debt spiraled. Farmers felt squeezed between conditions on the ground and the middlemen who controlled the price of grain. The grade of wheat determined the price the farmer got, and grain elevator managers determined the grade. Lowering the wheat crop one grade meant a $5 million loss to North Dakota farmers in 1915.[21]

Farmers fought to gain more control over the process. In the Farmers Union and the American Society of Equity, a progressive farmers' group, they fought for state-owned terminal elevators and state power over weighing, inspecting, and grading. They had come close when the legislature passed a levy for the purpose in 1913, and state residents voted overwhelmingly in favor, but the 1915 legislature killed the project. The death met with outrage at the annual convention of the North Dakota Union of the American Society of Equity, meeting in the state capital, Bismarck, at the same time. In attendance, too, were members of the Farmers Union. It was like an alternative general assembly. After all, the state was at the time 70 percent rural. No city had even twenty thousand inhabitants. Twenty-seven percent of its six hundred thousand people were foreign-born, and about the same number were U.S.-born children of immigrants. Most had acquired their farms by homestead or preemption.[22] The legislators' votes did not represent the small farmers' interests.

The issue was not only middlemen. Farmers across the country had long proposed and agitated for measures that would smooth out the unpredictable upheavals of the business (principally, weather and international competition), as well as reduce the power of middlemen and railroads. Many of those mortgage-carrying farmers had run up debt due to the vagaries of the weather. Even the smallest-scale and most careful farmers could run afoul of early frosts, grasshoppers, and global gluts. Larger-scale farmers risked more. Arthur C. Townley, born into a farm family in Minnesota, was one of them. After a stint as a schoolteacher, he struck out for the West and his fortune. Farming in North Dakota with his brother, working as a plasterer's helper, and failing with a consortium in large-scale wheat farming in Colorado followed. In 1907 he began raising flax with his brother in North Dakota. By 1912, on his own, he had become, according to railroad land agents, the "flax king of the Northwest." That year he threw all he owned into the venture, sowing eight thousand acres in flax and buying ten traction engines and other equipment on credit to handle the expected crop. With flax at $3 a bushel, he could clear $100,000. Then came an early crop and, despite the smaller yield, market speculation, which dropped the price to under $1 a bushel. By the end of the season he stood $80,000 in debt.[23]

Townley determined to change the system. He headed first for the Socialist Party, well-organized in North Dakota, and ran for the legislature on its ticket in 1914. He lost. He participated in a party experiment to get a sense of the difference in numbers between those who supported the *party* and those who supported its *platform*. The lesson was clear: the platform was popular. After attending the 1915 Equity Society convention, Townley recruited collaborators, many of them socialists, and at the age of thirty-five launched a movement to create a nonpartisan political alliance of farmers with a clear, limited agenda: to control the state's primaries, endorsing primary candidates who committed to the alliance's platform. Membership dues of $6, often paid in checks dated after the harvest, supported the organization. The NPL used its own publication, *Nonpartisan Leader*, launched in 1915, to press for public ownership, already in practice in New Orleans and Seattle. They won the endorsement of the Equity Society and newspapers that claimed, as the *Fargo Forum* did, "These men will not be radicals, or socialists or anarchists as some people seem to believe. They will be the farmers of the state in convention assembled."[24]

The organization's structure was entirely grassroots. In March 1916 the NPL held delegate conventions in almost all the state's forty-nine legislative districts to choose candidates to endorse, with no regard for party affiliation. The state convention of about forty-five delegates met in Fargo at the end of the month. After hours of discussion on the qualifications of the various candidates unearthed by the district conventions, the delegates voted by secret ballot. Those endorsed were heavily Republican but included socialists and Democrats as well. For governor they endorsed Lynn J. Frazier, a farmer, former township supervisor, and local school board member who, when called with the news on a trip to town, later recalled, "I told them I couldn't come that night, because I had my overalls on and no suitable clothing with me."[25]

Born in Minnesota like Townley, Frazier had come as a child with his parents to homestead in North Dakota. He wanted to become a doctor and taught in rural schools to earn money for tuition. He graduated in 1901, a star football player with high academic honors, but when his father and brother both died, he acceded to his mother's wishes and returned to run the farm. He was a rugged, portly, bald man who never smoked or drank, a plain speaker with a deep bass voice, and the worst the opposition could find to say about him was that he was relatively unknown. This relative unknown carried forty-six of fifty-three counties for the Republican nomination. The Republican press refused to endorse NPL candidates, but when the election came in November, Frazier won in every county of the state, his overall majority over four to one. The NPL failed to take control of the state senate but succeeded by winning 81 seats in the house out of a total 113. NPL membership stood at approximately forty thousand, with an organizational income of $270,000.[26]

While the NPL—without control of the senate or many of the committees—could not accomplish all its goals in that first legislature, it did establish a state grain grading system, a state bank deposit guarantee law, a reduced rate of assessment on farm machinery and improvements, a moneys and credits tax law, a number of laws forbidding discriminatory railroad rates, a virtual tripling of state aid for rural education, and the authorization of negotiable warehouse receipts, among other measures. It was enough to awaken the interest of farmers in other states and requests for help in organizing, including in Minnesota, Idaho, Wisconsin, Texas, and Kansas. Simultaneously, Socialist Party activists from across the Southwest and Midwest flocked to the NPL, ultimately forming part of its core leadership.[27]

The NPL spread into the Canadian prairies. Canada's electoral system had no primaries, so the NPL could not adopt the U.S. tactic of capturing primaries, and in a parliamentary system, partisanship ruled. In Canada the NPL became a political party. The

Saskatchewan NPL elected only one candidate in 1917. In Alberta the NPL did better. One theory on the growth of the NPL in Alberta holds that it was really populated by U.S. immigrants to Alberta. One of the ironies of firmer borders is that it is possible to imagine that one's desires foreclosed at home could be met across the border. In the first decade of the twentieth century, eager to settle their own West with white farmers, Canada launched a propaganda campaign aimed at encouraging disillusioned U.S. settlers to move to lands farther north. A small flood of settlers followed. White farmers, many discouraged by the retreat from populism on the northern U.S. plains, crossed paths with single women, ineligible to homestead in Canada, coming south for the purpose.[28] In Canada the U.S. migrants found the dominant political alternatives (Liberal and Conservative) alienating. They had brought in their baggage from the United States their experience with Populism and the similarly minded, nascent NPL.

Organized womanhood and organized farmers made a powerful combination. In North Dakota NPL victories included the proposal of an amendment for complete woman suffrage and the granting of immediate woman suffrage on the election of presidential electors and a number of other offices and appropriations. In Alberta, where women won the vote in 1916, the NPL chose Louise McKinney as its candidate and then voted her into office. Her victory made her one of the first two women elected to a legislative body in the British Empire, along with fellow Albertan Roberta Macadams. In 1916 also Montana's Jeanette Rankin, with ties to the NPL, became the first woman to win election to the U.S. Congress.[29]

The NPL was a northern U.S. plains / Canadian prairies phenomenon, but its connection to leftist and women's reform movements is, in this context, more than regionally important. The connection between the leftist NPL and organized women and the NPL's choice to have women candidates was not aberrant or incidental or even tokenistic. It was a logical requirement of a mutually beneficial alliance between like-minded mass movements. McKinney had lived in North Dakota as a farm wife before heading for Alberta. It was she who called "the greatest movement of the age—the fight for a wider democracy," and she chose the NPL as the best vehicle for it. A year earlier, when Jeanette Rankin set her sights on Congress in Montana, the NPL did not yet exist as a political party. Nominated by the Good Government League, she announced for the Republican nomination. She had grown up in a Republican family, and her brother was active in the progressive wing of the party. Running her campaign as she had the suffrage campaigns, with stump speeches, bands, telephone brigades, visits to remote areas, and grassroots mobilization, she trounced her Republican primary opponents. Nonetheless, she ran as close to an NPL campaign as she could. According to her biographer, she "adopted most of the platform of the Montana Society of Equity." Though she ran on the Republican ticket, she "was never," she later said, "a Republican." Many Democrat suffragists crossed over and helped sweep Rankin into office.[30]

While many women's rights campaigners sought the vote as a tool to remake society, the specific link here is the Woman's Christian Temperance Union (WCTU). The combination of the WCTU and the NPL was potent. The WCTU was the largest voluntary association in the nation. It would be hard to overestimate the popularity of temperance in the early twentieth century. Activists had successfully linked excessive drinking to poverty, domestic violence, violent crime in general, and industrial accidents, and scientists had linked it to ill health and a shortened lifespan. By 1900 the WCTU was interested in a broader array of social reforms, with branches supporting pensions for mothers and workers, educational reform, and social justice and the vote for women to achieve them. By the early twentieth century, the major suffrage organization in the Canadian West was the WCTU, and Louise McKinney presided over the Alberta branch.[31]

In Alberta the greatest concentration of WCTU members was in the same area as the NPL: the wheat-farming areas south of Edmonton. The WCTU in many rural parts of the U.S. West, including Kansas, Oklahoma, and California, was also a forerunner of the Socialist Party. Frances Willard, long president of the national WCTU, was an avowed socialist, and with her extremely decentralized "do everything" organization, where branches could choose their own focus from the dozens of WCTU departments, her brand of radical Christian socialism echoed across the rural plains and prairies, as well as in more urban sites, including Los Angeles, for more than a decade after her death in 1898. Scratch the surface of many of the NPL leaders, suffrage leaders, and labor activists in the early twentieth-century U.S. and Canadian Wests, and you find someone with roots in the WCTU.[32]

In the WCTU women learned political mobilization, campaigning, activism, and that prohibition was the beginning, not the end, of their efforts; for some branches, it wasn't even the main event. Although Rankin had exiled the WCTU forces in the Montana suffrage campaign to avoid rousing the liquor interests, which had proved so powerful in California, the newly elected legislature in 1915 had approved a state referendum on prohibition, and in her own congressional campaign, Rankin supported it. In 1918 she would have the endorsement of the new NPL and the WCTU, but her opposition to U.S. entry into World War I and her attempt to mediate an IWW strike cost her the Republican nomination. When she lost that nomination, she decided to run (and lost) on a third-party ticket, the National Party ticket, a coalition of socialists, progressives, prohibitionists, and the state Nonpartisan League.[33]

Women in Public and Public Women: Protecting the Nation?

The WCTU had branches in Mexico, some run by U.S. expatriates but many not. Little else is known about the Mexican WCTU or about whom exiled socialist general Salvador Alvarado was hanging around with in Arizona, where he ran a small business before he returned to revolutionary Mexico and launched his dramatic and feminist reforms in 1915. But Alvarado's actions linked socialism, prohibition, and women's rights. He had gone into exile after participating in the 1906 Cananea strike, around the same time he began supporting the PLM. From its first party convention, in San Luis Potosí, the PLM had supported equal rights for women and men, including in work and pay. Alvarado's exile years in Arizona coincided with that territory's (and then state's) most progressive years. Labor was in the ascendant, and women won the vote in 1912 with heavy labor and socialist support, led by Frances Willard Munds, who adored her distant relative, Frances Willard, WCTU president, for whom she was named. The new state and its newly enfranchised women then enacted prohibition. When Alvarado returned to Mexico, he led a group of radical socialist governors in Mexico who lined up behind women's rights.[34]

Many of the women active in the Mexican Revolution had been, like their North American feminist counterparts, rebels since their youths, unconventional women. And, as in the United States and Canada, they wedded socialism and women's rights, and they crossed borders. Flores de Andrade inherited part of her grandparents' estate at the age of thirteen and immediately forgave the debt of the peons on her portion of the estate; she then divided the lands among them. Widowed as a young woman, she organized a semisecret organization, the Hijas de Cuauhtémoc (named after the Aztec emperor Cortés had tortured), across Chihuahua to work with the revolutionary Mexican Magón brothers' PLM against Díaz. In dire poverty by 1906, she headed for El Paso, Texas, hoping to better her economic situation. In 1909 she became president of a new women's group in El Paso to support the revolution, taking "charge of collecting money, clothes, medicines, and even ammunition and arms." In 1911 she helped hide Francisco Madero in El Paso for three months, using her clubwomen as a screen and later facilitating his reentry to Mexico, for which she was arrested and almost killed by U.S. authorities.[35]

Former PLM member Dolores Jiménez y Muro presided over the Hijas de Cuauhtémoc when, on September 11, 1910, the organization "sponsored a huge march in Mexico City" protesting Díaz's policies, calling on women to take up both rights and obligations outside of the home, and demanding the "enfranchisement of Mexican women in their 'economic, physical, intellectual and moral struggles,'" an event for which the regime threw her in jail. By May 1911 the *New York Times* reported Mexican women's widespread participation in the revolution. As the revolution became a civil war, armies displaced women, and women struggled to survive while their husbands, brothers, and fathers served at the front. Some women joined the labor force, while others, on their own or with their families, voluntarily or conscripted, joined the armies ranging across the country, cooking, laundering, and bearing arms as *soldaderas* and sometimes even as officers.[36] Having construed the civic woman as a bounded category, the United States now witnessed her bounding across borders.

As the decade wore on and the unrest within and across national boundaries grew more intense, efforts to police borders, to safeguard the nation from contagion, grew ever more extreme. Since the end of the nineteenth century, faith in public health agencies, like public faith in science, had been rising. In the 1910s that faith, wedded to the decade's anxious desire to draw boundaries, led to what one scholar has called the medicalization of the U.S.-Mexico border. Typhus provided one justification. The disease was terrifying. Along the Texas-Mexico border in 1917 the mortality rate among adults over forty years of age with typhus was 70 percent. By 1910 public health professionals knew that lice carried on rats bore the germ that spread the disease.[37] Lice do not respect human social class, but public health officials did. They looked at neighborhoods of poor Mexicans increasingly crowded with refugees, neighborhoods that provided few or no sanitary facilities, neighborhoods where their laundresses and house cleaners lived, and they concluded, without a trace of irony, that those who kept the houses and clothes of the middle class and elites clean were themselves inherently prone to filth, laziness, and disease, that is, prone to be "lousy." Rather than neighborhoods and conditions, lice and the people officials believed carried them became the targets.

The modernist Porfirian Mexican state had instituted a public health regime on the Mexican side of the border decades earlier and had launched a campaign for inoculation against smallpox that had proven more successful in generating compliance than had that of the United States, but the Mexican state's health regime fell into disarray during the revolution. The way was open for the assertion of U.S. dominion over its border through the relatively new expertise and state capacity of the U.S. Public Health Service (USPHS). There were already tensions over the USPHS regime regarding smallpox beginning in early 1916. At Rio Grande City, for example, the USPHS inspected and vaccinated regardless of evidence of prior vaccination at the will of the inspector, and at least one man, Miguel Barrera, a Mexican businessman based in Texas, had been vaccinated against his will. The U.S. rejection of this evidence signaled a denial of Mexico's identity as a modern state and Mexicans as a modern people. When Mexican authorities mimicked U.S. practices, imposing their own inspection requirements in Piedras Negras on March 6, 1916, the U.S. local military, responding to horror on the U.S. side that "respectable American ladies" would be exposed to Mexican soldiers, threatened President Venustiano Carranza's access to essential resources, and the Mexicans backed down.[38]

U.S. imposition of a health regime at the border signified the marking of these border towns as U.S. terrain. The populations had risen dramatically during the Mexican Revolution, receiving an influx of both U.S. military personnel and investors, as well as Mexican refugees. The border towns, even on the U.S. side, before the 1910s revolution, had been largely uncontested "Mexican" space. The majority of the population, though U.S. citizens, were usually of Mexican descent, as were their locally elected officials.[39] In the context of revolution in Mexico, the Mexican nature of the U.S. border towns became fraught. Anglo federal officials found themselves often at odds with local "Mexican" ones.

As word of a typhus outbreak in Mexico spread and a health inspector in El Paso died of typhus, in 1916 the USPHS began setting up and improving inspection and quarantine facilities on the Mexican border. To those convinced that Mexicans bore the disease vector, the outbreak pointed out the dangers of the casual mixing and unpoliced borders within El Paso, as well as across the national line. On the bridges from Mexico to the United States, the USPHS separated immigrants into two groups: those the USPHS deemed white and respectable, and those it labeled "peons," who tended to be poor and have darker skin. The USPHS officials required the latter to strip before fumigating their clothes, inspecting their bodies, and dousing them with a mixture of kerosene and vinegar. In El Paso itself officials moved more quickly, targeting those already in public control: the Mexican men in the city jail and hospital. On March 6, 1916, as fifty male prisoners stripped in a central courtyard and gathered for a dousing, a spark ignited the kerosene vapors. The windows and doors of the prison hospital exploded. Those not instantly killed by the flames fled. Eleven were killed in the carnage; the fumes overwhelmed would-be rescuers.[40]

The people of Ciudad Juárez, El Paso's cross-border twin, were enraged. Already resentful of the treatment at the border, the kerosene-vinegar baths, and the stigmatization, they attacked "everyday signs of U.S. intrusion." They attacked Americans in the city's commercial and entertainment districts. They attacked the streetcars that carried the sporting men of El Paso to the racetrack in Ciudad Juárez. The U.S. Army demanded that Mexican troops protect the circuit to the racetrack. The Carranza government declined to intervene. The U.S. Customs office closed the Santa Fe Bridge to automobiles and streetcars en route to Ciudad Juárez. The unrest lasted for days.[41]

In El Paso a crowd gathered, expecting to hear the indictment of the USPHS agents from a grand jury convened by the city's mayor and judge. Instead they heard of Pancho Villa's raid on Columbus, New Mexico. Many Mexican locals interpreted Villa's raid as a reprisal for the holocaust at El Paso. Villa, whose star had been descending, rose in their estimation. Anglos in the crowd, in contrast, blamed El Paso's Mexican residents for the Anglo deaths at Columbus. They swarmed to the nearest "Mexican" neighborhood and attacked anyone who looked Mexican. General George Bell Jr. moved his troops from the Santa Fe Bridge where they had protected U.S. public health officers from angry Mexicans, to fend off the mobs attacking neighborhoods deemed Mexican.[42]

While Bell succeeded in fending off the crowds, over the next two weeks USPHS agents brought people from South El Paso to the disinfecting baths, stripped them, and bathed them while public health authorities burned or fumigated their residences and belongings. They destroyed housing, not rats. Nellie Quinn, a Mexican immigrant laundress, recalled,

> Some inspectors came to the neighborhood and started boarding up a lot of the shacks as unsanitary and unsafe. The women and children began crying as they were literally put out on the streets. . . . The block we were living in was condemned. . . . [T]here was no house to be had anywhere. Everyone in El Paso was afraid to take anyone in from the contaminated neighborhood. I took [the] children and went to live under a tree in the outskirts of town. It was nice weather at the time. Thank God there were a lot of trees because other people got the same idea. Families just went out and found a tree to live under. I would say we lived there three or four months.[43]

Despite the disaster, officials maintained their inspection regime with vinegar-kerosene baths. Those who could afford to ride the streetcar across the bridge escaped such surveillance, though they witnessed it. Those who had to walk across the bridge, whether for day labor or more permanent immigration, faced inspection and forced bathing. Though it was clear by early 1917 that the majority of El Paso cases of typhus emerged after a month's residence and the incubation period for typhus was at most two weeks, local USPHS officials continued to blame national origin and not neighborhood conditions. When city health officer W. C. Klutz succumbed to typhus, dying on January 4, 1917, the mayor wanted to close the border. Under pressure, President Wilson imposed a full quarantine instead, requiring full inspection and full disinfection of all border crossers.[44] The women rebelled.

The *New York Times* called them "Quarantine Riots." "Women Lead Demonstration against American Regulation" was the headline. On the day the mandatory inspections went into effect, the women refused to submit to them. U.S. newspapers labeled Carmela Torres, a leader of the group, "Auburn Haired Amazon" and "Red Haired Chief of Woman Mob." According to the *El Paso Times*, these "servant girls" had heard that quarantine officers photographed the stripped bathers. Prevented from respectable entry to the United States, the women stopped southbound traffic. They attacked and stripped automobiles and sometimes their drivers and seized streetcars. They particularly targeted El Paso's leisure class coming to enjoy the sporting life in Ciudad Juárez. They laughingly turned aside the Mexican cavalry, whose attempts to restore order in the face of the U.S. dictum must have been half-hearted. Mexican working men played a supporting role in the riot; it was clear women were the leaders. These were working women whose lives were defined by their ability to cross the U.S.-Mexico border, whose lives denied the stability and reality of that boundary's distinctions. The U.S. press posed them as unruly women. As Villa eluded Pershing, and Pershing finally withdrew, the USPHS—the federal agency—posed the issue of inspection as one of sovereignty. Mexican general Francisco Murguía arrested Carmela Torres and two men alleged to be ringleaders and turned them over to the local El Paso authorities, but the city judge dismissed the charges, declaring that El Paso had no legal jurisdiction over events in Ciudad Juárez.[45]

Notions of protecting inviolate citizens of the United States, controlling unruly women, reinscribing perpetually challenged boundaries between good women and bad (as more and more women won the vote and achieved official status as "the public"), and, finally, preserving U.S.-Mexico relations all came together with the Selective Service Act of 1917, which governed drafting young men into the armed forces. Congress, appalled when rumors of drunken revelry among troops at the border in 1916 turned out to be exceeded by reality and struck by the need to have soldiers "fit to fight," as the term went, included in the act sweeping powers for the secretary of war to eradicate prostitution around military camps. Many cities in the U.S. West had a long history of profiting from their red light districts. In a region heavily peopled by male workers in extractive industries, many towns' and even cities' budgets relied on a regular routine of arresting and fining sex workers and brothel owners. Experiments in eradicating such districts often fell afoul of budgetary necessity and the preference for taxing vice over taxing virtue. Some western cities, including San Francisco and New Orleans, experimented with regulated vice districts.[46]

The economic benefits of a military encampment, however, far exceeded those of a red light district, and across the region even the most famous of red light districts were officially eradicated, though often they reemerged underground. By driving sex workers indoors, supplanting the madam with the male pimp soliciting on the street, the measures also offered clearer ways of demarcating between "good" women and "bad." For the many encampments on the border, the closing of red light districts in the United States in tandem with the enactment of nationwide prohibition of alcohol simply made official fact the fantasy that vice, disorder, and unruly women lay on the other side of the U.S.-Mexico border.[47]

Conclusion

Just as white supremacy traveled the circuits of the British Empire, the movements for radical democracy did not stop at the borders of nation-states. Anarchism traveled the circuits of the Spanish

Empire, and populism left its mark on the prairies and plains of Canada and the United States. Both Canadian and Mexican newspapers covered women's rights battles in the United States.[48] Like the ideas of white supremacy and direct democracy, the ideas of the women's rights movement circulated in cross-border traffic north and south, culminating by 1916 in a series of convergences. In 1916 the United States elected its first woman to Congress and Canadians elected the first women to sit in an elected legislative body in the British Empire, and in 1915 and 1916 radical socialist governors of Chiapas and the Yucatán held Mexico's first national women's congresses and in the Yucatán dramatically expanded coeducation and women's labor rights and opportunities.

At least in the United States, women's entry into public space without the assumption of lost virtue for the first time occurred at the very moment when public space became more heterogeneous in other ways. No sooner, in other words, had those boundaries of Jim Crow and worthy women been seemingly set than they faced a new onslaught. Having these women in power simultaneously manifested and undercut the borders so carefully and constantly erected in these decades. Many of these mobilized women, like many of the farm men, working men, and immigrant men, had a radically different vision of American democracy, from Mexico to Canada, in the 1910s.[49] These different visions and the people who held them clashed, often violently.

While various laws and sciences demonstrated an official desire to create and police borders, they also demonstrated how unnatural such borders were and how constantly eroding. After all, if no one married across fictive "racial" lines, then no law would be necessary. Indeed, throughout this period, the "transgressions" that evoked these borders were ever more frequent. A sense of desperation took hold. With upheaval on every side and a war threatening in Europe, in 1913 only eight states in the United States neither had miscegenation laws nor introduced them to the state legislatures. The Portland homosexuality scandal had broken in the context of dire warnings in the press that, with the completion of the Panama Canal, the city would soon be deluged with "aliens."[50]

Organized women served as engines and cocreators of a revolutionary vision of the U.S. West. They were no monolith. There were conservatives in the woman suffrage campaign in the U.S. West and in the WCTU. Not all of them sought what the NPL called "economic democracy." And even among the Left-leaning women, as among the men, that revolutionary vision was not always at odds with a racist vision of a white "man's" country. But the collective action of organized women shifted the ground in the region. The large contingent of women who marched on the Colorado governor's office in 1914 successfully urged the use of federal troops after the National Guard massacred the strikers at Ludlow. The women's groups who allied with the labor movement in Los Angeles and in Seattle shifted the possibilities and content of reform in those cities and even those states. They won a range of measures, from equal pay for equal work clauses in contracts to mothers' pensions. And through these alliances elsewhere, they generated the two leftist, suffrage movement, temperance women who were the first women elected to serve in the U.S. Congress and any legislative body in the British Empire.[51]

These movements have been treated in isolation from each other both across borders and within borders across sexes, but their convergences are far more illuminating when placed in the same frame. Women's mobilizations in the U.S. West were neither auxiliary nor simply coincident with the larger story of the decade's radical democracy—the Mexican Revolution, the IWW, the labor wars, and woman suffrage. Women's determination radically to expand democratic participation, in part with their own enfranchisement, had a shaping role in the concerns of the era as much as that of other constituents of these movements. They made alliances and they were sought as allies, and together they changed the meaning and content of that democratic revolution. The measures they sought in tandem with their labor and agrarian allies reshaped the relationship of women to men and women to the state in much the same way it reshaped the relationship of workers to employers and workers to the state, as well as farmers to middlemen and farmers to the state. In each case these measures created a more level playing field, reduced dependency on private individuals and corporations, and increased the possibility of democratic participation.[52]

6

Global Conflict and Local Strife

In early 1917 massive upheaval pervaded the West. Battles over the vote for women, over labor in coal, timber, and copper, and over land between ranchers and Native Americans pitted westerners against each other. At stake was the nature of democracy in the West.

That spring the United States entered the war in Europe, joining the Allies against the Germans and the Austro-Hungarian and Ottoman Empires. With war on the horizon, controlling the seeming chaos at home became a high priority. Though Woodrow Wilson had won reelection in 1916 by promising to keep the United States out of the war, there was no shortage of patriotic zeal once the United States entered it. Some people volunteered for military service. Other citizens bought Liberty bonds to finance the war and flocked to self-described patriotic societies to serve in a variety of ways on the home front. But despite the patriotic zeal and economic benefits the war brought to the American West, these zealots faced continuing upheaval.

A greater proportion of people in the U.S. West opposed the war than did people of other regions.[1] The West's mines were filled with refugees who had fled conscription in the Austro-Hungarian Empire and Irish who had no desire to fight for the British one; its plains were full of Germans now suspect as potential enemy aliens, and throughout the region workers of various backgrounds saw themselves as conscripted to fight on behalf of capital. Wilson claimed that the war aimed to make the world safe for democracy and launched the United States into the war to defend freedom of commerce. The two were not necessarily at odds, but in this context, the struggle over competing visions of a "modern" U.S.

West acquired existential dimensions. Just what was the order the United States needed to establish in the West to prosecute the war?

The United States had to mobilize its population for military service abroad and war production at home. The question of what it meant to be a true American and who could claim that status came instantly to the fore. Who could be trusted to produce war matériel? Who could be trusted to serve in the armed forces? Everything became framed as a question of loyalty. Dissent, the hallmark of democracy, became increasingly dangerous. Governors who identified themselves as progressives, including those of Kansas, New Mexico, Washington, and Arizona, found it increasingly difficult to uphold individual rights when the government at all levels mobilized to regulate not only action but also speech and even thought.[2]

These questions and the wartime apparatus outlasted the war and shaped the postwar possibilities.

Wartime Government: The Councils of Defense

Eight months before the United States entered the war, in August 1916 Congress authorized the formation of the Council of National Defense. The council's mission was to organize the production of food and munitions and assess the possibilities of mobilization. Once the United States entered the war, states also formed councils of defense, and some counties and communities followed suit. These councils and the local draft boards, which managed the first call-up in June 1917, shaped the way most people in the West encountered the war.

The state councils had enormous power—so much power in New Mexico that the legislature adjourned for the duration of the war. Governors filled the councils with prominent men and a few women they saw as representing myriad constituencies. California's council included twenty-nine progressive and Republican men and three women, numbering among them members of the University of California and Stanford, labor leaders, major agriculturalists and oil producers, bankers, attorneys, military officers, utility and transport company executives, state officials, and clubwomen. Local California councils included judges, law enforcement officers, and often county farm advisors.[3]

Unlike in the legislature, these representatives were appointed, not elected. State and local councils of defense did their best to collaborate with corporate giants, including lumber and copper companies. Some struggled to balance the outsized power of the region's corporations on the councils; others did not. Even when they did try to balance power at the state level, at the local level the councils often became tools of corporations. In Gallup, Deming, and McKinley County, New Mexico, the council agenda was union busting.[4]

Wartime governments and their allied corporations acquired new tools to suppress dissent. States followed the example of the federal government in passing sedition acts and set their own examples with antisyndicalist ones. Corporations framed union organizing as disloyal, impeding the war effort. Corporations and state governments could now attack the IWW as both a labor and an antiwar organization. Frances Willard Munds, victorious suffragist and member of the Arizona legislature, wrote to Governor George Hunt in 1918, "It is getting so that every working man who dares to say his life is his own is called and denounced as an IWW."[5] Towns banned the display of red banners.

The pressures to conform to a unitary, imagined, "American" identity grew. Governments at every level and many private philanthropies and individuals displayed a willingness to deploy a coercive intensity in favor of their brand of "Americanization." In a nation at war and with a president wedded to "Americanism," Americanization rapidly found not only increased popular support but also official federal government support. The National Council of Defense designated the state councils as responsible for Americanization. Even the "heartland" turned out to be filled with foreigners. Colorado had only recently stopped printing its government proceedings in German, as well as in Spanish and English. North Dakota in 1890 had the highest proportion of foreign-born of any state in the union. Great swaths of the plains were populated with German heritage people; in some towns, schools were taught in German. That practice ended with the war. Colorado, Montana, Nebraska, and South Dakota "restricted or banned the teaching of German in public schools and pressured parochial schools to cease instruction in German."[6]

The government imprisoned conscientious objectors, including pacifist Mennonites, whom prison guards at Leavenworth, Kansas, tortured; when two of the Mennonites died from the treatment, the prison guards dressed them in military uniforms and returned the bodies to their pacifist brethren in South Dakota. Many Mennonites along with German-speaking Americans and Scandinavian dissenters fled the United States for Canada.[7]

The violence of mining strikes, the Mexican Revolution, and U.S.-Mexico relations made Mexican Americans vulnerable to the same repressive nativist trends as enemy aliens were. Discontent was defined as disloyalty and alienation, and the cure for alienation lay in Americanization. As it did elsewhere in the United States and for other ethnic groups, Americanization became intimately tied to the war effort, and "100 percent Americanism" became the only way to prove loyalty and ensure national security. Presbyterian mission administrator Robert McLean relayed in 1918 "a cry . . . from the Southwest, from the thin line there on guard: come and help us to redeem the Mexico within our borders, that America may be made safe!"[8]

"Redeeming" this internal Mexico required turning its inhabitants into Americans, unhyphenated. From 1910 to 1920 approximately 230 Spanish-language newspapers originated in the U.S. Southwest, ranging across the political spectrum. Despite the friction between "Spanish Americans" (those Spanish-speaking residents of New Mexico and Colorado whose ancestors had resided in that territory before U.S. conquest) and Mexican immigrants, the majority of Americanizers were unable or unwilling to draw the distinction. Despite Hispano service records and repeated testimonials to the loyalty of the Spanish Americans, church woman Katharine Bennett was not alone in her thoughts that "in this day when hyphenated Americans are unpopular it is a curious fact that here in the Southwest the form Spanish-American is constantly used." *Literary Digest* declared the "hyphenate issue" the most vital of the day, and Woodrow Wilson proclaimed, "Any man who carries a hyphen about with him carries a dagger that he is ready to plunge into the vitals of this Republic." In this context, the retention of not only a hyphen but also the Spanish language and a distinct culture seemed to Anglos evidence of divided loyalty on the part of U.S.-born Hispanos, evidence of a continued inability "to forget the wrong which they consider the United States inflicted on their country" in 1848. Spanish Americans and Mexican Americans became ever more firmly tied to Mexicans in the Anglo mind. They seemed to the Anglos more alike than not: equally alien, dangerous, and candidates for Americanization.[9]

At the same time, Mexican Americans pushed back, finding ways to use the war mobilization to promote civil rights. In Texas former socialist organizer F. A. Hernández informed on German and Mexican Americans who vocally opposed the war, but he also reported incidents of discrimination against Mexicans, arguing to the authorities that such treatment made them more receptive to antiwar agitators. Colorado and New Mexico councils of defense similarly found that recognition of Hispano cultural distinction proved a more effective integrating force than attempts to eradicate it did. They included Hispanos on their councils and held special meetings for their Spanish-speaking constituents. Not everyone got the message. In September 1918 at a Democratic Party County Convention in New Mexico, a Mississippi transplant, impatient with his Spanish translator, stormed, "I don't want to talk to anybody but Americans." The *Santa Fe New Mexican* reported that an audible gasp escaped the approximately 40 percent Neomexicano audience, and the paper claimed that not even "'a group of Bolsheviki [that] had thrown a bomb' could have caused more commotion." Newspaperman Antonio Lucero spoke next, first in English and then in Spanish, "with a scathing critique" of the preceding speaker. To tumultuous applause, he described "'Spanish-American' New Mexicans as '100 percent loyal Americans' who fought and died on the battlefields of Europe at a higher rate than Anglos."[10]

The Draft in the West

Many residents of all stripes rushed to volunteer for military service, including some Native American men for whom it offered, finally, a route to join the prestigious warrior societies of their people. Congressmen submitted bills to create separate Native American units. Some Native Americans and Anglos who spoke in favor of the measure pointed to pride in tribal identity and cohesion. Both General John J. Pershing, who would command the American Expeditionary Force, and Interior Secretary Franklin Lane, within whose purview lay the Bureau of Indian Affairs, supported the idea. Pershing had gotten permission in 1916 to enlist a separate company of Apache Scouts as part of his Punitive Expedition into Mexico, and he had been impressed. But Cato Sells, head of the Bureau of Indian Affairs, opposed it on assimilationist grounds, as did the civil rights group Society of Indian Affairs, which called such units "walking reservations." The bills failed, and Native Americans would serve alongside whites, Mexican Americans, Asian Americans, and others. Only African Americans would serve in segregated units.[11]

Despite some initial enthusiasm, voluntary enlistment fell far short of military target numbers, triggering the first round of a national draft in July 1917. All men aged twenty-one to thirty-one had been required to register for the draft in June. Each state had to meet a quota of enlistees based on the number registered. Most of those inducted were white, but in Texas the government disproportionately drafted African Americans. In New Mexico the government similarly disproportionately drafted Hispanos.[12] Across the country, it disproportionately drafted Native Americans.

In the summer of 1917 a member of the Sioux Nation presented himself, as required, to his local draft board. A member of the board then asked the required questions. The following dialogue ensued: "Are you an alien?" "No," he responded, "I was born in the United States." "Then you are a citizen," the board member informed him. "No," he responded again, "I am not a citizen. I am not an alien." "What are you then?" the board member inquired. "I am an Indian," he said. "I have neither the rights of an alien nor of a citizen, yet I was born in the United States. My father is a full blood Sioux Chieftain . . . and I must offer myself up for service."[13]

All Native American men of appropriate age were required to present themselves to their local draft board, but only those with citizenship were eligible for the draft. In 1831 the United States Supreme Court had declared tribes "distinct independent political communities" and "domestic dependent nations," whose members were not U.S. citizens. Since that time, several measures had granted citizenship to various Native Americans, but more than one-third of Native Americans in 1917 were still not U.S. citizens.

Determining citizenship status could be tricky. Two separate federal acts, guidelines about property control and competency, and vague language about living apart from one's people and adopting the habits of "civilized life"—whether Native Americans requested citizenship or not—governed granting them citizenship. In these circumstances, not all Indians, let alone anyone else, knew for certain their citizenship status. Local draft boards had enormous discretion. Their practices varied wildly. Because a state's quota of soldiers depended on the registrants, citizen or not, eligible or not, if Indians were ineligible, then a higher proportion of whites would be drafted. Yet the provost marshal found that the ratio of Indian registrants inducted was twice the average of all registrants.[14]

Not all Native Americans easily stepped into line. "Jails Papago Chief," reported the *Albuquerque Morning Journal* when Juan Kahn-A-Rone, head of the Santa Rosa village, "was locked in the county jail today on a complaint that the chief had advised and prevented young Indians in his village from registering for the draft." Dr. Joseph Peck was detailed to examine draftees elsewhere in the arid Southwest. "When the three or four boys of draft age at the [Goshute] Reservation received greetings from the Draft Board," he recalled, "I was ordered to go over there and examine them." "These Indians had never achieved citizenship," he continued. "Probably they never would have been disturbed if the agent had not developed a patriotic brainstorm and insisted to the Department that these boys be called to serve the country to which they owed so little." When Peck tried to explain to a baffled tribal elder why the United States had entered the war, he ran into a logical brick wall. After suggesting that if we had entered the war because the Germans sank our boats, then perhaps we should keep our boats at home until things quieted down, the elder asked what Germans looked like. Peck replied, "Germans looked like other white people and that because of his name I was sure the agent was of German parentage." The elder offered, "You tell white father we kill him for free and any other Germans that come around here too. You go fight your war. Gosiutes will stand behind you and keep Germans from capturing Ibapah valley. . . . We keep boys at home. Anybody come here you want killed we do it—Germans, Paiutes or Indian agents."[15]

It is tempting to write this account off as a humorous misrepresentation, but other sources show the Gosiutes or Goshutes as reluctant indeed. Their reservation population on the Nevada-Utah border numbered 150. They had long complained of corruption in the Bureau of Indian Affairs administration, and they opposed registration for the draft. In response, newspapers printed rumors that German agents were inciting this resistance. The BIA dispatched an inspector, who ignored the complaints and threatened arrest, imprisonment, and conscription. Fearing the resistance would spread to other nearby reservations, the agent, with the permission of the War Department, took fifty enlisted men and launched a dawn raid on the reservation. Going house to house, they arrested all seventy-five Goshute men. The BIA inspector held them under armed guard until they promised to respect the authority of the reservation superintendent they had accused of corruption.[16]

Neither were the Creeks in Oklahoma enthusiastic. Ellen Perryman, whose father had fought for the Union in the Civil War, gathered people at the Hickory Ground in June 1918. At this site, where a decade earlier the "Crazy Snake" uprising had reached a climax, she encouraged the thirty people in attendance to resist the draft. Newspapers went wild. From Tulsa to Louisville to the *New York Times*, they exaggerated the numbers and invented German agents and murderous Indians. As they had done with the Goshutes, federal agents arrested her, released her when she promised to obey, and characterized her as a "disordered mind."[17]

The war was a hard sell in other quarters, too. In New Mexico villages impoverished in terms of both cash and government services, reactions to the war itself, according to contemporary observers, ranged from people "much opposed" on whom the food regulations worked real hardship to "great indifference" among others who seemed focused on "how to avoid going or allowing others to go into the service." Some Hispano villagers had never heard the Pledge of Allegiance, and in the first conscription of 1917, thirty-eight of forty-six draftees from Taos and Mora Counties, New Mexico, could not understand "enough English to attempt to drill." Elsewhere in the United States, as many as two-thirds of the workforce was born in or had parents born in what were now enemy lands. If they had even begun the process of naturalization in order to become U.S. citizens, they were eligible for the draft. As many as one in five draftees were foreign-born. Roughly 12 percent of draftees simply dodged the draft. Only half were caught.[18]

In Oklahoma many citizens saw the war as fought on behalf of the very capitalists who dispossessed them. Though they knew success was unlikely, they turned to armed refusal of the draft. On July 27, 1917, eight hundred to a thousand white, African American, and Native American farmers gathered at John Spears's farm, where he raised both the U.S. flag and the red socialist banner. They intended to march to Washington to present their case to President Wilson. Within a week, posses engaged the group in pitched battle, killing three men and, after scouring the countryside, taking 450 men prisoner; 150 were convicted and sentenced to terms ranging from sixty days to ten years.[19]

This "Green Corn" rebellion provided the perfect excuse for local and federal officials to arrest any socialist or IWW member they could find. Without feeling the need for proof, authorities blamed the IWW for any and every crime in the region. When a bomb exploded at the Tulsa home of a wealthy oilman just as ten thousand oil workers in Texas and Louisiana went on strike, within days the Tulsa police raided the IWW hall, arrested nearly a dozen men on vagrancy charges (since no evidence connected them with the bombing), arrested the six IWW members who came to testify for their defense, convicted them all, and allowed a vigilante mob to take the prisoners outside the city and beat and tar them. The *Tulsa World* applauded the action, defining the perpetrators as a "sterling element of citizenship, that class of taxpaying and orderly people who are most of all committed to the observance of the law."[20]

What the War Did for the West's Economy

In 1913 the region, like the nation, had found itself in an economic slump. Where employers still hired, they enjoyed a labor surplus despite the decline in immigration from Europe caused by the war in the Balkans and then the broader conflict. Western railroads came to rely increasingly on Mexican labor. Small farmers along the new irrigation developments also looked to this labor as they continued to expand their acreage in sugar beets and cotton despite the declining profitability caused by the general economic slump and the threat of gradual removal of all tariff protection on sugar. In fact, the ever-rising Mexican immigration, coupled with the slump, created a southwestern farmer, according to one labor recruiter, "satisfied by the thought that he can hunt up some Mexican any time."[21]

In just a few years, however, the situation changed drastically. With the onset of a wider conflict in Europe came an unparalleled increase in industrial and agricultural activity throughout the United States to meet European belligerents' demands. The U.S. West went from slump to peak times. The specter of a free market in sugar disappeared along with beet sugar from central Europe. Wheat rose to three or four times its prewar price. Urged to participate in the "Great Plow Up" to provision the Allies, farmers borrowed money to buy additional land and machinery to work it. Wheat production skyrocketed, with the federal government guaranteeing to purchase all wheat harvested and setting commodity prices above prewar levels. In eastern New Mexico alone acreage in wheat grew from 113,000 to 283,000 acres between 1916 and 1919.[22] Ranchers, too, benefited. The Stock-Raising Homestead Act of 1916 allowed homesteading ranchers to claim 640 acres, and in New Mexico the federal government opened an additional 950,000 acres of the public domain and proved generous with credit as well, encouraging stockmen to expand their ranches.

Commissioner of Indian Affairs Cato Sells speeded up both the competency commissions giving individual title to former tribal members and the opening of Indian lands to non-Indians through large-scale leasing and purchase. He and western boosters remained convinced the land would produce more in non-Indian hands. Just fifteen days after Wilson declared war, Sells advocated reducing appropriations for Indians despite treaties guaranteeing the funds. He saw the move as creating "'more self-respect and independence for the Indian' leading to 'the ultimate absorption of the Indian race into the body politic of the Nation' and 'the beginning of the end of the Indian problem.'" Bureau of Indian Affairs agents encouraged Indians to sell their herds, even when they had raised cattle for decades, believing once they had sold the cattle, they would no longer refuse to lease reservation lands. Non-Indian ranchers and farmers leased ever-larger reservation spreads.[23]

Manufacturing, too, boomed. The military presence in the region, particularly on the West Coast, reached an unprecedented scale. The region dramatically expanded its shipbuilding capacity, more than tripling manufacturing employment in Seattle, including thirty-five thousand shipyard workers. The military also invested in the region's infrastructure. It bought land to build barracks and depots; it spent millions to construct camps and facilities. It revived San Diego's economy by spending over $4 million on navy barracks and $6 million on land, in addition to almost half a million dollars to fit out an aerial gunnery school. The military spent large though lesser sums up the West Coast collaborating with state and municipal governments. California's State Harbor Board dredged San Francisco Bay and built sheds, wharves, and warehouses, paved roads, and invested in other infrastructure, while Los Angeles dredged channels and basins and built wharves, warehouses, bridges, and roads to enhance the capacity of its port. Pacific Ocean trade and shipbuilding rose dramatically.[24]

Farm owners, ranchers, and manufacturers raked in money during the war. Corporate consolidation grew, fueled by wartime opportunity, access to private capital, connection to public officials, professional expertise, and interlocking directorships until in California corporations owned 26.2 percent of businesses by 1919, employed 81.9 percent of wage earners, and controlled 83.1 percent of the total value of products.[25]

Not all farm owners benefited. Continuing dispossession and consolidation meant that many former small farmers could not reap the benefits of the more-than-doubled price of wheat and corn or the boom in livestock prices. Meanwhile, rampant wartime inflation made the cost of living skyrocket. Rural migrants across the country found the increased wages for common labor during the war an additional drawing factor. Beet work wages, for example, rose by 50 percent. Both pushed and pulled, many rural residents headed to fields, mines, and smelters, as one missionary put it, so that "they may earn enough money to keep the wolf from the door." Their hometowns became increasingly dependent on their migrant labor.[26]

The war also brought new government services to remote areas. As the government reached into every village, plaza, town, and reservation, "bringing the war home," what it found there could be disquieting. Government-aided studies exposed many Anglos for the first time to the conditions in Hispano villages, for example. As the investigators found "the death rate appallingly high," they brought the villages a new allotment of health services. Similarly, the government vastly expanded its agricultural extension and home demonstration services, encouraged lessees to plant crops on state land, and offered seed at cost or on mortgage. For previously alienated rural citizens, the new services, recognition, and above all their actual experiences or their sons' experience in arms as active and solicited participants in a common cause could instill a new identification with the United States.[27]

Wartime Workers

The slump was gone, but so was the abundant cheap labor. In the name of patriotism, employers and state officials sent schoolboys, patriotic women, Chinese former sex workers living in Presbyterian missions, and wards of the state into the fields. One rancher called his teenaged hired hands the "kindergarten outfit." The employers claimed these new workers enjoyed the outdoor life, toasted marshmallows, and sang songs. Perhaps, but those patriotic women, the California Division of the Women's Land Army, began to make demands, including an eight-hour day, overtime, and camp inspection, and when the war emergency was over, the growers were not sorry to see the last of them.[28]

More employers began to recruit actively and vie for Mexican and Mexican American labor, formerly their labor of last resort. As cotton and beet growers in California, Arizona, and Texas and railroad and mining enterprises increased the competition for this labor, increasing numbers of recruiting agencies, processing companies, and farmers' associations sought labor directly from Mexico.[29]

The Immigration Act of February 1917 had seemed to the commissioner-general of immigration "an eminently satisfactory piece of legislation," but it provoked, in the commissioner's own assessment, "no little hysteria" on the part of southwestern employers. The law contained a literacy test, as well as a doubled head tax. It threatened to halt the immigration of impoverished and largely illiterate Mexicans at a time when southwesterners planted record crops; resident Mexicans, spurred by threats of conscription, fled the United States in droves; and Black field workers raced to newly available and better-paying industrial work in the North. Farmers warned of lost harvests, and railroad employers claimed that with half their summer construction workers barred, disrepair of tracks could endanger troop and supply movements.[30]

At the urgent behest of southwestern employers, the U.S. federal government negotiated its first guest worker program with Mexico. A series of administrative decrees temporarily exempted, in theoretically regulated numbers, Mexican agricultural labor from the head tax and literacy test and even from much older contract labor provisions. Local federal officials set the number of exempted laborers based on their estimate of the amount of labor already available on the site. Employers guaranteed they would match prevailing wage rates and return the exempted labor to Mexico within the year. The plan rapidly expanded to include railroad and certain coal labor and later included laborers in government construction.[31]

How It Came Together: War, Labor, and the Military

With the revolution on the southern border, labor wars throughout the country, and fears about the war in Europe, it was all too easy to associate workers asserting their labor rights with enemies of the country allied with Germany. General Pershing, only recently returned from his failed Mexican mission to capture Pancho Villa and now named to lead the American Expeditionary Force in Europe, saw Mexican revolutionaries, IWW members, labor unionists of all stripes, and any striking workers as one and the same. Labor upheaval permeated the production of essential war materials (e.g., copper and the spruce essential to build airplanes), as well as wheat and other food crops. Pershing blamed Mexican revolutionaries for spreading a virus of discontent via migrant IWW members.[32]

Faced with the demands of mobilization, including the need to rapidly build barracks, and faced with what appeared to be the rising might of the IWW, Woodrow Wilson reached out to the rival labor federation, the American Federation of Labor (AFL). To get barracks built and avoid price gouging and labor strife, Secretary of War Newton Baker and the head of the AFL, Samuel Gompers, compromised: they signed an open shop agreement (i.e., workers were not required to join the relevant union) that also included union standards in terms of wages, hours, and conditions. The agreement created a three-person commission, with one representative chosen by Baker, one chosen by Gompers, and a public delegate. The agreement led to smoothly running construction, rising wages, and no-strike pledges; it spread to other industries.[33]

Some industries proved more intransigent than others. When management dug in its heels and where the IWW rather than the AFL held sway, things could get ugly. New migrants swelled the ranks of workers now well practiced in demanding better conditions, a say at the workplace, and economic democracy. While some businessmen favored increasing coercion because they feared vulnerability to foreign enemies, for others the war had merely newly legitimated older desires to extend more control over the workforce.

The new Espionage Act (June 1917) and the Sedition Act (May 1918), which extended its scope, meant that the Bill of Rights would no longer protect workers relying on freedom of speech, and with a nation convinced it was beset by spies and in a region dangerously close to that dangerously and newly socialist republic, Mexico, little public sympathy would reach the Wobblies. After the Zimmermann telegram was exposed, asking Mexico to join Germany against the United States to win back lost territory in the Southwest, many in the United States felt they could not be too careful; all those Mexican Americans, German Americans, and Irish Americans could be a potentially dangerous fifth column. Beginning in July 1917, three months after the United States entered the war, the new demands for conformity and the older mobilizations came together explosively across the region.

On June 28, 1917, 2,000 of the 4,500 copper miners employed at Bisbee, Arizona, went on strike. Over the next two weeks, as tensions rose in Bisbee, papers reported on pervasive unrest: southern Colorado coal miners, nine thousand strong, prepared to go on strike in a renewed "labor war"; woman suffragists picketing the White House in Washington DC had been jailed; brutal race riots had erupted in East St. Louis; hundreds of socialists had marched in a peace demonstration in Boston; Globe, Arizona, copper miners had joined those on strike; and, finally, federal troops might be sent to Arizona's strike zones.[34]

On July 10, 1917, the mayor of Jerome, Arizona, backed by fifty townspeople claiming the label "citizens," forced sixty-seven IWW members into cattle cars and "deported" them to Needles, California. Two days later, Bisbee followed suit. The Citizens' Protective League forced 1,140 unarmed strikers (labeled "IWW") at gunpoint into freight cars and dumped them unceremoniously in the southern New Mexico desert near the town of Columbus. Bisbee became a police state. The mayor threw his support behind those who claimed to protect the nation and its women. Using vagrancy laws, city officials continued the deportations, and the vigilantes, turned into the Loyalty League, monitored the return of any deportees, requiring from them letters of reference and loyalty oaths not only to the United States but also to the company. Only about 6 percent of the deportees returned.[35]

The war against the IWW reached such a fever pitch that it trammeled civil liberties, targeting more than miners. As Rosa McKay, a suffragist elected as state representative of Cochise County, ran into the Western Union telegraph office to cable President Wilson and Arizona's U.S. senator "asking protection for the women and children before we have another Ludlow, Colorado," a gunman knocked her down. Her fellow representative opposing deportation, Tom Foster, found himself deported as well. Crowds in New Mexico cheered McKay when she showed up with supplies for the deportees gathered by women back home, but on her return, vigilantes at the state border fired on the train.[36]

The deportations did not end the labor unrest in Arizona, New Mexico, or elsewhere. A riot at Miami, Arizona, resulted from a failed police attempt to break up an IWW meeting among the copper miners and required two U.S. Cavalry troops, rushed over from Globe, to quell. The same day, coal miners threatened a strike at Madrid, New Mexico. In response, Sheriff Celso Lopez swore in twenty-five deputies to protect properties owned by Senator George

A. Kaseman of Albuquerque.[37] In Butte, Montana, another copper strike led to the lynching of IWW organizer Frank Little.

The Justice Department began to identify "radical" with "alien," despite most strikers being U.S. citizens. Frustrated at its inability to deport those it could not, the government deported all those it could as the United States began to use beliefs as a criteria for citizenship. Before the war, IWW actions and beliefs had not been defined by law as un-American. Now not only beliefs but also membership or aid of any sort, including lending a meeting place to the IWW, became grounds for arrest and deportation. The union's head, Bill Haywood, saw the IWW as the most American of institutions, arising from domestic conditions and political faith in democracy. Haywood, homegrown as he was, found himself fleeing the country of his birth. The U.S. postmaster general, Albert S. Burleson, former congressman from central Texas, a heavy investor in Mexico, and a pioneer in replacing tenant cotton farmers with convict labor, banned socialist newspapers from the mail.[38]

On September 7, 1917, the federal government, targeting the IWW, launched prosecutions in Wichita, Sacramento, and Chicago. Federal officers arrested 500 people and convicted 160. On the following days, they conducted raids throughout the United States. In Sacramento, when the prisoners came on trial in December, five had already died of the flu, and the remaining forty-two refused to enter any kind of plea after issuing a statement that they knew they would be convicted no matter what they said or did. At the end of the trial they stood up and sang the left-wing anthem, "The Internationale."[39] To Americans fueled by wartime patriotism, they seemed evil saboteurs, keeping vital crops from being harvested by demanding better conditions.

Amid all the chaos, there were moments of calm. In Columbus the Bisbee deportees set up camp under the watchful eye of federal troops. It was called Camp Wobbley. According to the *Albuquerque Morning Journal*, "they presented one of the strangest sights Columbus has seen since Villa's Mexican bandits dashed into the town on March 9, 1916." Montenegrins, Slavs, Italians, Serbs, Austrians, Welshmen, Mexicans, U.S.-born citizens, and others among the 1,140 deported miners, mill men, and small merchants worked together in 100 degree heat. The exhausted deportees declared,

"We are rearing to go back to Bisbee but not until the soldiers go along to protect us." Meanwhile, the deportees "discussed plans for filing a blanket suit against the operators, officials and others responsible for the wholesale deportation from Arizona of those held to be members or sympathizers of the IWW movement."[40]

Ironically, these men, so despised for their presumed disloyalty by Bisbee's Citizens' Protective League, rejected the notion of a prayer for their release through a writ of habeas corpus "on the ground that it would embarrass the federal government." That Sunday passed quietly. The men bathed and did their laundry in a horse trough. "Eleven wives of deported miners came from Bisbee to visit," some bringing small children. The men, who had been charged with breaking no laws, ate "Mulligan stew" prepared from leftover scraps of their rations, and a thousand of them attended outdoor church services led by the cavalry chaplain, who "spoke on the subject of man's honest convictions." A few days later, the protective troops began overseeing vaccinations and military training of the camp residents.[41]

While the Bisbee deportees awaited their fate, a federal mediator prepared to meet with the miners from Madrid, New Mexico, to head off an impending strike. The paper reported that "the Spanish-American miners are not joining in the movement to unionize the camp." Two days later, the *Albuquerque Morning Journal* reported that the Madrid miners had organized a union but for patriotic reasons would ask neither for recognition nor for improved wages and hours.[42]

Ironically, the less controversial United Mine Workers did go on strike at the end of July and into August at Gallup, New Mexico, coal mines with a large Mexican heritage contingent. Similar "deportations," imported gunmen (who boasted of victories at Ludlow), and an entirely Anglo local council of defense followed. By the end of 1917, *El Excelsior,* a Mexican paper, claimed the prisons of New Mexico and Arizona held four thousand Mexican strikers.[43]

To the north, in Montana, miners battled the Anaconda Copper Mining Company. The copper mines around Butte produced a fifth of the country's copper, and the country needed the copper to produce arms. As it had in Bisbee, a strike here became a national security issue. The mining company, benefiting from high copper prices, kept total control over labor, denying a job to any man with known union experience. But in early June 1917 a fire in a mine killed more than 167 men. The miners blamed the company, particularly when they discovered that in violation of state law, the company had blocked some of the mine exits with concrete bulkheads. Five thousand miners walked off the job and organized into a new union. By the end of the month, fifteen thousand men were on strike.[44]

Montana congresswoman Jeannette Rankin went to Bernard Baruch, head of the federal war metals division, and President Wilson. Neither would act. Nor would the secretary of labor or the attorney general. At the end of July, Rankin got a telegram; the miners feared violence. On August 1 Frank Little, an IWW organizer who had come from Arizona's copper field to help the effort in Montana, was found nearly naked and hanging from a railroad trestle with the placard "Others Take Notice. First and Last Warning." Four days later, in the largest funeral procession Butte had ever seen, three thousand people "escorted Little's casket on a four mile march past thousands of onlookers." The incident catapulted the IWW into the strike's leadership.[45]

Rankin responded. She introduced a joint resolution in Congress authorizing the president to seize and operate metal mines essential to the war effort as the government operated the railroads. She, along with the federal troops ordered to the district, then headed for Butte. Since the company would meet with neither Rankin nor the union, she went directly to the public. On August 18 she spoke to a crowd of fifteen thousand people in a park outside the city. She criticized the company for unfair hiring practices and unsafe conditions, and she criticized the IWW for its policy of sabotage, urging it not to destroy the country's supply of wheat during its current strike in Oregon's wheat fields. She condemned Little's lynching but urged the men to return to work at their old wages if the company instituted safety measures and fair hiring practices. But there was to be no compromise by either party. The government raided IWW headquarters and found nothing subversive. The strikers' money ran out, and the men drifted back to work. It is a measure of the widespread unrest in the region that despite the fury of the all-controlling copper company and Rankin's vote against entry into the war, not to mention rising antipathy toward the Nonpartisan League in some Montana towns that barred members from public speaking and deported their members, Rankin only narrowly lost the Republican nomination for the U.S. Senate in 1918. The NPL fared better in North Dakota and Minnesota, winning sweeping victories in 1918, and in Canada, instead of disappearing, the NPL merged with the United Farmers of Alberta "and ultimately forced it into politics."[46]

Things went less well for labor in Washington. In 1916 Seattle schools had resisted the militarization of the curriculum in the preparedness campaign. In 1917 the Seattle Central Labor Council, 250 to 0, voted to oppose the U.S. entry into the war within days of Wilson's declaration to do so and demanded the repeal of conscription. Seattle's workers publicly endorsed the Bolshevik Revolution of 1917. Workers on the waterfront, in the forests, and in the mines of the state and region engaged in general strikes, slowdowns, and sabotage. They met "the U.S. Immigration Service in Seattle . . . at the cutting edge of state anti-radicalism." Using the new Espionage Act and civilian allies in the Klan and American Legion, the Immigration Service identified more potential deportees in Seattle than in any other region and indicted the leader of the state Grange.[47]

Anna Louise Strong, daughter of a progressive, antidraft minister expelled from the Municipal League, was elected to the Seattle school board in 1916 at the urging of progressives and clubwomen. Strong defended free speech and Wobblies and found those same clubwomen now demanded her removal from the school board, charging her with antiwar activities. The local press attacked her and refused to print her own statement even when she offered it as a paid advertisement. Many of the women's groups still supported her but not publicly, lest "they be charged with being unpatriotic," a friend wrote. She was recalled from office in March 1918 by over two thousand votes.[48]

Government repression grew steadily during wartime; federal officials and city leaders raided and destroyed IWW headquarters, and Seattle's Minute Men physically attacked Wobblies and broke up meetings. More than one historian concluded, "It was probably safer to be a German agent in the Northwest than to be a Wobbly."

In California in the summer of 1917, four years after Wheatland, steady attacks on the IWW and its offices failed to deter the union; in the context of labor shortage, the union won workers' demands in raisins, grapes, and citrus. The press accused them of being German agents, and U.S. federal agents raided IWW headquarters in Fresno in September, arresting the eighteen members they found there. As the IWW moved on to organize in other places, including the oil fields of Oklahoma and Kansas, controversy followed them. The Tulsa U.S. attorney would not prosecute them, seeing the agitation as a legitimate dispute over wages, but the Kansas City attorney arrested one hundred IWW members in November 1917 and held them for a year without going to trial.[49]

Late in 1917 the federal Immigration Service loosened its standards of evidence. Now local inspectors could detain immigrants for deportation simply because they belonged to the IWW. Possessing IWW literature became equivalent to advocating illegal principles; ultimately, dues paying itself became advocacy. In court, when the IWW claimed nonviolent principles, the Immigration Service shifted its logic, claiming that a slowdown on the job was dangerous and illegal. Finally, the migrant, seasonal nature of the Wobblies' work became fodder for a claim that itinerant Wobblies were likely to become a public charge.[50] A rule used disproportionately to deport independent women (see chapter 2) could now be turned against independent workers.

In this context, the federal government put its mind to producing enough lumber to meet war needs, including the hard-to-harvest spruce necessary for the airplanes the government and its allies believed would end the stalemate and horror of trench warfare. In the lumber industry, the government faced itinerant workers, more often IWW than AFL members, and intransigent owners. The federal government wanted to avoid another Bisbee debacle. The owners wanted to avoid nationalization.

The Northwest's forests, covering an area including eastern Washington and Oregon, northern Idaho, and western Montana, provided over one-sixth of the U.S. peacetime annual supply of lumber. Overproduction had led to fierce competition and consolidation but no monopoly. Lumbermen owned huge tracts of timberland. They had faced narrow margins and dramatic price fluctuations until they joined in the West Coast Lumbermen's Association in 1905. In 1917 they watched prices for pine and fir soar. These trees formed the heart of their industry. But airplanes required spruce. Lightweight and strong, spruce grew in scattered clumps and required milling different from that used for the more commonly used trees surrounding it. Almost all of the world's supply of spruce trees grew in this region. Lumbermen had mostly ignored them. They were not inclined to change their habits and invest in massive new infrastructure for what they believed would be a brief demand in a short war.[51]

The lumbermen also had no intention of changing their treatment of workers. They refused to deal with any union in their strike-prone industry. They had seen forty-four strikes in lumber in 1916 and over twice as many in the first months of 1917. The lumbermen's intransigence and violence, including the Everett massacre, in the face of appalling labor conditions and hours in lumber camps led to dwindling public support and growing sympathy for labor. The federal government approached veteran Brice P. Disque, who had transformed Army Land Transport Corral, Canal, and Shops in Manila into a smooth-running machine. The government hoped he could perform the same miracle with timber in the Northwest. On his first exposure to labor conditions in timber, he reported, "We treated captured Moros better in the Philippines during a war." "I thought radical propaganda had inspired the reports on these conditions," he continued. "They defied exaggeration." In March 1917 the first IWW local formed, the Lumber Workers Industrial Union (LWIU), whose offshoots quickly spread from eastern Washington to Oregon and California. Despite constant harassment from law officers, patriotic organizations, and federal attorneys, both the LWIU and the relevant AFL unions planned a strike for July.[52]

Pershing needed the region's National Guard units to head for France in August, but as tensions rose in the West, the man tasked with creating order in wartime lumber production estimated keeping order would take at least 125,000 combat-ready soldiers. And, indeed, lumber production in five western states ground to a halt; sympathy strikes and slowdowns in shipbuilding and barracks building followed, along with violence and intimidation. This situation was Pershing's worst fear—that the soldiers he needed to head to Europe would instead be bound to peacekeeping in the West. And indeed, congressmen and senators called for martial law to crush the strikes. Idaho's progressive senator William Borah opposed martial law, as did the secretary of war and the president. As timber workers on strike left for other industries, the IWW spread. Shipyard and farmworkers suffering from inflation, newsboys, domestic servants, and others talked of organizing. Sixty thousand western shipyard workers went on strike just as lumber workers exchanged striking for something they called a "strike on the job," that is, a deliberate slowdown. The slowdown made them less vulnerable and kept them paid.[53]

Lumbermen dominated the region's American Protective League and used it to fight unions. They seemed less interested in getting spruce or, indeed, any lumber cut than in keeping organized workers out of their timber. So many lumber workers held membership in the IWW or sympathized with it that blacklisting them from the industry meant severe labor shortages. Yet lumbermen used their connections with the APL to ensure these unionized workers got drafted. As a result, undercover agents reported, Wobblies infested the army, bringing their ideas into the hurriedly built, crowded training camps.[54]

Labor turnover in the lumber industry reached 1,000 percent a year in 1917. Disque confessed, "My wonder . . . was not that production was low but that there was any production at all." He and his allies thought that only the army, despite its past use in strikebreaking, had the credibility to convince labor, management, and owners of their neutrality. They created the Loyal League of Loggers and Lumbermen (4L), a unit under military supervision, encompassing owners and workers, improving conditions and hours despite resistance from owners, and endowing the workers with stability, status, and the aura of patriotism. Without the word "union" in its title, it still provided representation for workers in managing conditions in timber, and IWW members, unless they recruited actively, were hired, keeping them out of the army. The new unit had enrolled twenty-five thousand members by January 1918. By June they had built eighty-seven miles of logging roads and twenty-five miles of industrial rail lines, and they had reduced the cost of harvesting and milling spruce to a tenth of what it had been. The lumbermen expressed their unhappiness with what they saw as a drift toward a permanent democratic organization, but by August 1, 1918, the 4L had enrolled over 115,000 members and had a monopoly on the Northwest's labor in lumber. Steady work, better hours, wages, food, health care, housing, and local respect for the previously disdained migrant workers made for uninterrupted production. For the first time, timber workers had community roots, possessions, families, and debts.[55]

Borders and Borders: Black Troops and the Houston Mutiny

While the exclusionary AFL strengthened its hand against the IWW and Disque quieted unrest in the Northwest by turning loggers into troops and troops into loggers, the U.S. troops tasked with keeping order at the Mexico border were disproportionately African Americans. Pershing, in particular, had long championed his Black soldiers.[56] Though segregation pervaded the Southwest, Black residents at the border often fared better than in the rest of the country. W. E. B. Du Bois in 1914 noted "several large property owners among the colored people" of Nogales, Arizona. Blacks similarly prospered in segregated El Paso, Texas, where Black physicians served Mexican patients.[57]

El Paso marked two kinds of borders: the international one and the Jim Crow border. Trains traveling east from El Paso had Jim Crow cars; trains traveling west did not. Texas was a state full of contradictions for African Americans. The United States stationed over sixty thousand troops there by 1916; these troops often joined local Anglos in violence against Mexicans, and in January 1916 troops and Mexicans engaged in a riot. The situation only deteriorated after Villa's Columbus raid. One dark-skinned Mexican-descent resident sought to escape injury by yelling back to the pursuing Anglos, "I'm a n——; I'm a n——."[58]

Texas ports and border cities had similarly complicated Black-white relations. The port of Galveston, whose native son Jack Johnson had successfully challenged white supremacy in the boxing ring in 1910 only to be arrested two years later because he transported a white woman, with her consent, across state lines, hosted a community of particularly assertive Black and white longshoremen who worked together in their union. Houston replaced Galveston as the state's major port after dredging enabled oceangoing vessels in 1914. That year Black dockworkers organized the city's first International Longshoremen's Association local.[59]

With the war, demand for cotton and oil exploded, and these cities grew. Petroleum shipments from Houston increased from 31,584 short tons in 1915 to 293,400 a year later. At a time when towns across Texas lost population to the North, El Paso's and Houston's Black population skyrocketed. Texas Blacks fleeing violence in other towns found Houston a relative refuge with a thriving Black community, including a substantial Black middle class.[60]

Black soldiers were keenly aware of the contradictions not only in Texas but also in their army service more generally. Black soldiers at Columbus, New Mexico, chased Pancho Villa and guarded Bisbee deportees. They also subscribed to *The Crisis*, the journal of the National Association for the Advancement of Colored People, the radical civil rights organization of its time, and they raised funds for the victims of racial violence in East St. Louis and elsewhere.[61]

These contradictions came to a head in August 1917. As new war industry opportunities opened in the North, Black Texans left the state en masse, precipitating a labor shortage that, paradoxically, gave Black workers who remained unprecedented bargaining power. Farm laborers withheld their labor and tripled their wages; washerwomen organized and got higher pay. Toward the end of that month, two white policemen in Houston, accustomed to virtually unchallenged dominion over the Black parts of town, roughed up a housewife who had simply dared to ask them what they wanted when they barged into her house in pursuit of someone they thought had run across her backyard. Refusing to let her change from her nightclothes, they threw off the child for whom she reached and began to drag her to jail. Word spread as the police waited for a paddy wagon. A crowd formed, and at its head, approaching the officers, was a uniformed Black soldier from the Twenty-Fourth Infantry, stationed since the end of July in Houston. Houston's racial politics demanded that military police go unarmed, so Corporal Charles Baltimore carried no weapons as he asked the two policemen to let Mrs. Sara Travers dress and be remanded to his custody. Armed or not, to the two white policemen, Baltimore was an even greater threat than Mrs. Travers. Who would govern the city—the white police or the Black soldiers? They raised their guns and beat him; he ran, wounded; they pursued, beat, and arrested him.[62]

To white Houston, the military encampment on its outskirts threatened to upend the social order. The encampment came only two years after the Plan de San Diego's perpetrators had recruited Blacks in South Texas and Oklahoma to join Mexicans in the reconquest of the U.S. Southwest. Now, despite the southern origins of most Black soldiers, the threat made southern whites see the soldiers as a northern invasion, a federal imposition of a different social world on the state of Texas. Conflict was daily—over bus seats, leisure spaces, and just the right to hold up their heads. Many of the soldiers in Houston had already risked their lives for their country. They had fought in the Philippines and felt keenly the betrayal of the Black troops at Brownsville a dozen years earlier. Others, eager to fight in France, had entered the army to escape the daily indignities of living Black in the South, only to be mired in Houston's contempt. The United States' entry into World War I and the propaganda that labeled it a "war for democracy" highlighted the disparity between the war aims abroad and behavior at home. In Texas African Americans could not vote in the Democratic primaries, which determined the election's outcome in that single-party state. They did not have equal rights to public accommodation, education, or services or even the safety of their own persons. As Black soldiers had defended the border, they heard the steady drumbeat of lynchings in Arkansas, Texas, and elsewhere. The number of Blacks lynched rose dramatically with U.S. entry into the war.[63] Corporal Baltimore's beating and arrest were for many of the Twenty-Fourth the last straw. The government for which they fought would not fight for them. They would, then, fight for themselves.

The incident fractured the Black officers and men until a sizeable contingent marched, orderly, four abreast, on Houston in full mutiny. They attacked those who stood in their way; stray bullets hit victims through walls and behind doors. They killed one of the policemen who had manhandled Mrs. Travers. They battled with local whites who had grabbed guns. They battled with police. Some African American bystanders applauded them. Some mutineers, including Corporal Baltimore, turned back, knowing the Illinois National Guard unit, also stationed in Houston, was mobilizing, until Sergeant Vida Henry, who had helped lead the rebellion, alone remained. He was found dead the next day. The riot, the fruit of years of frustration, had lasted two hours. It left seventeen whites and two Black soldiers dead.[64]

Interpretations of the riot varied. One Houstonian equated the rioters with world heavyweight champion Jack Johnson, seeing the rioters as wanting "social equality." A Georgia editorial saw the fight as a battle over access to public space on equal terms. Few if any white accounts included the assault on Mrs. Travers as a cause, but at least one Texas teacher valued the fact that they had "dared protect a Negro woman from the insult of a southern brute" and found it preferable "than to have you forced to go to Europe to fight for a liberty you cannot enjoy."[65] White papers did not mention the years of frustrations and white violence central to the understanding of the Black press.

The military sent the accused to Fort Bliss in El Paso and the rest of the Third Battalion back to Columbus, New Mexico. The sixty-three charged with mutiny awaited their trial in San Antonio. Tried, sentenced, and hanged in secrecy in December 1917, with no opportunity to appeal, thirteen of the mutineers, including Corporal Baltimore, who, though he had marched downtown, had not committed any violence, met their fate without flinching. Of the rest, five were acquitted, forty-one were sentenced to life, and nine received shorter sentences. Ninety-three more men were tried early the next year; eleven received death sentences, and eighteen received jail terms. Convinced that the nation had again refused to protect those who served to protect, Black communities across the country went into mourning. Editors and writers who published dissenting views of the riot were arrested under the Espionage Act. Black Texans founded twelve new branches of the NAACP in Texas in 1918 and twenty-one more in 1919; membership soared. Concerned about maintaining the loyalty of the Black troops at the border and in the face of Black protests across the country, towns in neighboring Arizona decided against allowing the wildly popular white supremacist film, *The Birth of a Nation,* to show.[66]

Amid such unrest, fears of insurrection, and continued cross-border raids by Mexicans on farmers and ranchers in Texas, New Mexico, and Arizona, as well as cross-border forays by U.S. troops and law enforcement officials to pursue the raiders (to the protest of the Carranza government), in mid-1918 the United States issued the Passport Control Act, which remained in effect until 1921. It limited legal entry to those with an official passport, complete with photographs, issued only in Washington DC. Complaints by border residents led to the issuance of tightly controlled border-crossing cards to locals. Daily crossings for work became virtually impossible. Customs inspections also tightened. Finally, in August 1918 the tensions inherent in U.S. fears of revolutionary incursions and Mexican resentments of U.S. military incursions, land grabs, and economic exploitation burst into a gun battle at Nogales. For over two hours, U.S. soldiers fired into Nogales, Mexico, and Mexican customs and immigration officers fired into Nogales, Arizona. It had all started with one man calmly walking across the border, an artifact of a behavior apparently no longer possible. The U.S. customs inspector suspected smuggling and ordered him to halt, but the Mexican officials waved him on. The U.S. officer, along with two U.S. soldiers, raised their weapons, and the Mexicans did in turn, one of them firing and hitting a U.S. sentry in the face. The other U.S. soldier returned fire, and the battle was on. By the end of the battle, U.S. soldiers occupied the Mexican side and twelve people lay dead, including the mayor of Nogales, Sonora.[67]

Ironically, that same mayor had ordered the construction of a six-foot wire fence through town to decrease border conflict by channeling traffic through particular crossing points. He had urged the United States to do the same. To the west, in Calexico and Mexicali, officials trying to determine whether a Mexican had been shot on U.S. or Mexican soil discovered that nobody, including themselves, was sure of the placement of the international border. The finding prompted a joint consensus on the wisdom of determining the border and marking it with a fence. By the 1920s most border towns had such fences.[68]

The war had not quieted the decade's unrest. Contending forces pressed with new urgency and a sense of heightened stakes where the nation's survival seemed on the line. New wartime measures calculated to suppress dissent had led to mass deportations, increased surveillance, gun battles, riots, and even mutiny. Amid the unrest, the economy flourished, new services penetrated the hinterland, and migrant loggers found new respectability. The West's people emerged from a war repeatedly invoked as making the world safe for democracy but with no consensus on what that term meant and for whom.

Aftermath

The war in Europe ended in November 1918. It took longer for the war at home to end. Competing voices wanted a determining role in the emergent postwar order. The decade's grassroots agitation for a radically participatory democracy continued unabated, despite massive repression by local, state, and federal officials and vigilantes to match. The rhetoric of the war (fighting for democracy), the wartime services reaching into remote rural areas, the experience not only of combat but also of encampments and life abroad with modern conveniences all raised expectations for a more abundant and equitable postwar world. The withdrawal of those wartime services, dislocations from the end of military contracts and spending, and the restoration of peacetime global economies upended those expectations. It was a combustible mix. In 1919, across the country, one out of every five workers would go on strike, dozens of race riots would erupt, and nearly one hundred African Americans would be lynched, many wearing their military uniforms. Among farmers, smallholders renewed their battle against dispossession.[69] Farmers, wage workers, and small and large businessmen of all types struggled over the meaning of democracy in the West and the meaning of the West for the nation.

State governments and their allies mobilized to suppress dissent. They continued to use state criminal syndicalist laws passed during the war. They arrested over five thousand people in California, Oregon, Kansas, Oklahoma, and Idaho. Oklahoma's governor called for a revival of the KKK "unless there is a change for the better" after strikers in Drumwright disarmed the local sheriff and threatened to lynch him. The Better America Federation attacked institutions apparently run amok, including the Los Angeles YMCA and YWCA for encouraging working women to organize and the California Commission on Immigration and Housing for being "a friend of the IWW." The federation agitated with some success to oust liberals from state commissions and universities.[70] IWW membership peaked between 1919 and 1923 at about one hundred thousand, but by 1921 the most effective IWW leaders had been deported or jailed.

The contest came together powerfully in Seattle. Despite or because of the rampant anti-IWW violence, the AFL flourished. The war's end found 20 percent of Seattle's residents belonging to the AFL. Though the AFL privileged organization by craft, not industry, the Seattle workers created ever-denser networks of cooperation that were in no way limited to the workplace.[71]

As elsewhere, the shift from military to peacetime economy assailed Seattle's prosperity. Demobilized soldiers and sailors and dislocated shipyard workers formed councils, and the AFL moved left. Wages dropped in the shipyards, and on January 21, 1919, seventeen unions belonging to the Seattle Metal Trades Council went on strike. Well aware of their weak bargaining position, the unions called on the city's central labor council to make the walkout citywide. The council's 110 union affiliates agreed, and at 10:00 in the morning of February 6, nearly sixty-five thousand workers began the first general strike ever held in the United States.[72]

Two days in advance of the strike, the U.S. attorney general relayed his reading of the situation to the Department of Justice in a telegram composed in the heightened terms of the now-ended wartime: "Intention of strike is revolution led by extreme element openly advocating overthrow of Government." But when Robert Whitaker reported on the strike for *The Nation*, he found the "Seattle Revolution" less alarming. "A 'revolution' in the sense of intending any bodily harm to anybody it was not," he concluded. "The actual conduct of it was as orderly as a Quaker Quarterly Meeting. It was revolutionary only in the sense that it revealed to a startled public . . . the unrealized dependence of a modern community upon the least and poorest of the workers, and showed what the economic power of workers means once they move and act with a common purpose." The tight networks of workers emerging from the war made it possible to maintain order in the city, create emergency kitchens to feed workers, union members or not, and deliver milk for babies and hospitals. Having demonstrated their ability to run the city, the strikers ended their action after a few days, pressed by the AFL's national leadership.[73]

While the workers avoided the inflammatory language of revolution, their opponents did not, and middle-class support for organized labor evaporated. Former progressive and now mayor Ole Hanson justified closing printing plants, infringing on free speech, and arresting dozens of Wobblies because of the purportedly revolutionary sentiment, and employers formed the Associated Industries of Seattle to launch an open-shop drive to destroy the collective power of workers; their tactics included using labor spies and printing their own magazine. They helped battle the nineteen strikes waged in Seattle from late 1919 to mid-1920.[74]

But that was not the only legacy of the general strike; there was a new wave of workers' cooperatives and alliances with farmers who also engaged in cooperative organizing. As reform politics continued to suffer attacks and reform leaders were purged from parties and imprisoned under state criminal-syndicalism laws, such nonpolitical organizations seemed an ever-more-attractive way to pursue political aims.[75]

The alliances climaxed with the One Big Union movement and then the Triple Alliance, a coalition of radical workers, railroad brotherhoods, and the Washington state Grange. A voter registration drive in working-class neighborhoods proved promising until vigilante American Legionnaires used an Armistice Day parade in Centralia, Washington, to provide the culmination of their violent attacks on the IWW. As they paraded, armed, toward the IWW hall, shots struck two of the Legionnaires. Unlike in previous attacks, the IWW leaders had also armed themselves and intended to fight back. Undeterred, the Legionnaires stormed the hall, captured what Wobblies they could, and pursued those in flight. World War I veteran Wesley Everest was captured despite killing one of his pursuers. That night, men broke into the Centralia jail, seized Everest, castrated him, and hanged him from a local bridge. When Harry Ault of the *Union Record* editorialized, "Don't Shoot in the Dark!" federal officials arrested him, along with Anna Louise Strong (erstwhile women reformers' candidate for school board) and other officers of the paper, and shut it down for a few days. On Election

Day, a grand jury indicted the *Union Record* officers, voters rejected the Triple Alliance candidates, and no official investigated the lynching of Everest.[76] Insurgent democracy seemed foreclosed in Washington in or out of electoral politics.

Women numbered among the myriad workers exiting the war with heightened expectations that erupted into the 1919 strike wave. With the medicalization of the U.S.-Mexico border (see chapter 5) and the increasing association of sanitation with citizenship came ever-rising demands of cleanliness. More cleanliness meant demand for more domestic workers, particularly on the border. Despite border restrictions, inspections, and resistance, Mexican women continued to provide these services to Anglos on and across the border. In October 1919 they went on strike. In El Paso, in the midst of an organizing drive, the Acme Laundry had fired two veteran workers and organizers. Their coworkers shut down the plant. Almost immediately, five hundred Mexican women laundry workers from five other El Paso laundries joined them. They picketed not only in front of the laundries but also on the transnational Santa Fe Bridge. All "Mexican," but many of them U.S. citizens, they picketed the bridge to prevent other Mexican women from coming to take their jobs. As the women negotiated with the companies, the El Paso Federation of Labor abandoned its anti-Asian and anti-Mexican policies to support the drive as part of a broader claim for a worker citizenship that included unions.[77]

Elsewhere on the border, Brownsville's state legislator, J. T. Canales, appalled at the impunity with which Texas Rangers continued to mow down Tejanos under the guise of suppressing revolution, spurred an official investigation by the state legislature from January through February 1919. It filled over 1,600 pages with testimony from men and women witnesses of every class, ethnic group, and occupational background, and it led to a dramatic overhaul and reduction in force of the Rangers.[78]

The war had clearly not ended tensions at the border or the marking of borders inside the West. To many white Texans, African Americans and Mexican Americans who threatened the racial status quo merged—Mexican revolutionaries were depicted in Texas newspaper cartoons as caricatured African Americans, with thick lips, kinky hair, and dark skin. White citizens in particular fiercely reimposed demarcations in the face of repeated challenges. The increasing assertion of African Americans for civil rights and simple dignity met with harsh reprisals in the West as elsewhere in the United States. Their assertion and the reprisals were inseparable from their demands not only as citizens but also as workers. Waco Blacks circulated a petition that proclaimed that the "last war made [Blacks] the equals of the white race, and that this stand must be enforced." After a Black man accused local officials of covering up a lynching in Longview, Texas—a town with a slim white majority—in the summer of 1919, white mobs burned stores and homes. White and Black longshoremen battled at Port Arthur.[79]

Texas governor William P. Hobby, the same progressive governor with whom white women had allied in 1917 to gain the vote in the state's primaries, now turned to the federal government to save the state from "Race Riot propaganda in Texas." Convinced such agitation came from outside Bolshevik radicals and apparently failing sufficiently to arouse the federal government, in the summer of 1919 he unleashed the Texas Rangers on a fact-finding tour, particularly targeting the Black press and the NAACP. The Rangers pressed local sheriffs, less alarmed than they, to prepare for race war. The Fort Worth sheriff responded, obligingly ordering "a dozen sawed off pump shot guns." Others created white vigilance committees to save white supremacy. As NAACP membership in the state soared, the state government went after the newly officially chartered state NAACP with a vengeance. The state attorney general accused it of operating in violation of state law, and when the white national executive secretary of the NAACP, John R. Shillady, came to the branch's defense in August, a county judge, local constable, and other Austin men waylaid him and beat him to a pulp, threatening to kill him if he ever returned to the state.[80]

The West's efforts to reinforce its demarcations were hardly limited to Texas. In Omaha, Nebraska, whose Black population had doubled during the war, amid labor unrest and rumors of Black strikebreakers, a corrupt city machine politician used the pervasive desire to reassert white supremacy to oust a new city reform administration. He successfully framed a Black citizen for rape, manipulating the press and the public, fostering a lynching and race riot. In Bisbee, Arizona, white men launched a gun battle with members of the Tenth Cavalry, a Black unit on leave enjoying a dance at the Silver Leaf, a Black club. Yet the next day saw the unit parade, safely demarcated in the town's July Fourth celebration, without incident.[81]

Black soldiers uncontained seemed dangerous to the survival of white supremacy in the West as they did in the South; Black veterans were no safer. In Phillips County, Arkansas, Black sharecroppers, many of them ex-servicemen, beset by vagrancy laws and unscrupulous farm owners, found themselves bound by debt peonage. They organized a union and hired a lawyer to force equitable crop settlements from landlords. Meeting at night in a church near Elaine, Arkansas, in late September 1919, members carried arms, suspecting white landlords would attack. In the pitch-black darkness of 11:00 p.m., a car packed with white officials drove up, turned on flashlights, and shouted at those meeting to disperse. Gunfire opened on all sides, killing one of the officials and wounding another. Claiming to fear an insurrection, the region's white leaders requested and secured over 2,500 federal troops. White vigilantes joined the troops in a massacre of as many as 250 sharecroppers. According to historian Steven Reich, "Delta officials arrested over 1,000 Black men and women, indicted 122, convicted 79, and sentenced 12 Black men to death."[82] On every front, the deck seemed stacked in favor of the forces of reaction.

Mexican Workers / "Mexican" Citizens

In the context of this massive unrest, the prospect of an unlimited number of extremely vulnerable workers had great appeal to employers. Employers of Mexican labor—commercial farms, mines, railroads, and smelters—had justified the wartime immigration exemptions by pointing to new global demands for cotton, wheat, fruit, and sugar from southern, southwestern, and midwestern states. They labeled the measures strictly a wartime expediency. But the demand for labor, like Mexican immigration, had emerged before the United States became directly involved in the conflict, and it, like the exemptions, continued after the conflict ended. Many employers had come to rely increasingly on this supplementary Mexican labor.[83]

As the time limit for the Immigration Act exemptions metamorphosed from a matter of months to the duration of the war and then, for agricultural workers, to a season or two beyond that, the exemptions looked less and less temporary and limited. In fact, the number of Mexicans entering under the exemptions for agricultural labor increased over 100 percent in the first year after the war and continued to grow.[84]

Even during the war, the regulations governing this vital labor had operated haphazardly. The situation did not change afterward. Not only was illegal recruiting commonplace, but legally recruited labor easily "escaped" the confining terms of its contract. At the end of 1920, of the 50,852 Mexicans legally admitted under the exemptions in the previous three years, over 10,000 had disappeared from official view. Only 17,186 had returned to Mexico.[85]

While the overall numbers of new Mexican residents remained low relative to state populations in the United States, many residents of small agricultural towns were struck most forcibly by the change in scale. In Weld County, Colorado, for example, the number of Mexican-born inhabitants had increased over 700 percent in ten years, from 90 to 756, and these were accompanied by an even larger number of U.S. citizens of Mexican descent in this formerly almost entirely Anglo county. Local Anglos voiced fears of "this invasion of aliens."[86]

This "invasion" spelled danger to observers who ignored the long history of a Mexican presence and warned that "the creation of a distinct nationality of another speech within our borders may constitute as real a menace as that which we hope has been overthrown by the war with Germany." Anglos whose heads still rang with the importance of "100 percent Americanism" saw the immigration as a threat to whatever fragile unity they had found during the war, a threat against which they stood exposed and disarmed by the removal of wartime federal support and controls. As New Mexico's Mexican-born governor, Octaviano Larrazolo, demanded of New Mexico's educators in 1919, "Wouldn't it be well for every English-speaking child also to know Spanish?" these anxious patriots saw evidence of corruption, degradation, and anarchy on all sides, including Larrazolo's educational proposals. In a year of unprecedented labor uprisings in the United States, Mexican Americans and Mexican nationals numbered among the miners on strike at

Gallup, New Mexico, leading to the imposition of martial law in November 1919. "We must remember that the only government of which they have any knowledge," reported a *New York Times* correspondent, "is one of license and misrule."[87]

The debate over Mexican immigration culminated in the hearings before the House Committee on Immigration and Naturalization and the Senate Committee on Immigration in 1920. These hearings bore witness to the gradual ascendance of "race" in the United States over the nativism of the war. Increasingly, Americans decided that factors they saw as biological would or should permanently prevent the assimilation of certain groups, among whom they included Mexicans. Men on these congressional committees called "race-mingling" "the greatest of all our problems" and labeled Mexican "intermixture or intermarriage . . . a mistake, a crime, and a damage to whatever population it touches"; it was even "an absolute tragedy," because "the product is a Mexican." They did not hear with sympathy witnesses who queried, "What objection, if he is a serviceable man, is there to assimilating him[?]" or with credulity claims of his childlike and tractable nature.[88]

As race riots exploded across the country in 1919, most Anglos seemed to feel, with Secretary of Labor Wilson, that "we have all the race problems in the United States that it is advisable for us to undertake at the present time." Particularly dangerous was permanent immigration to farm and rural regions where "there are not enough people," experts declared, "to keep up good social institutions unless all the people are of one race so that there are not impassable social barriers." Even advocates of continued exemptions, such as Representative Claude Hudspeth of Texas, hastily assured the committee, "If I believed by bringing these people in you were going to permanently increase the Mexican population down there, I would say to keep them out."[89]

This impermanence and marginality had justified the exemptions, and it was here that advocates of continued Mexican immigration took their strongest stand. Despite the evidence of an increased resident Mexican population in the United States, the AFL's complaints, the use of Mexicans to break steel strikes in the Southwest and elsewhere, and evidence of increasing numbers of Mexicans in Colorado's coal mines, a congressional investigating committee in 1920 found the number of Mexicans displacing "white" labor "negligible." "Our investigation proves beyond a reasonable doubt," reported the committee, "that white men are averse to accepting, and refuse to accept (as they have the right to do), employment as unskilled or common laborers, except, perhaps, where that employment is within the limits of towns or cities."[90]

The committee implied that Mexicans did not displace white labor, because Mexicans had a limited and defined role in the American economy: rural manual and stoop labor, labor Anglos did not want.[91] In arguing for continued unrestricted Mexican immigration, John Davis of Laredo, Texas, told the House committee, "I really think we can not get a more desirable citizen to occupy the place that he can occupy." When the chairman asked, "That is, a No. 2 place?" Davis responded, "I would modify that by saying, to occupy the place that somebody must occupy." It had grown increasingly difficult in rural America to move up the agricultural ladder from laborer to tenant to owner. With the positions on the ladder fixed, some group had to be found to occupy the lower rungs permanently. In addition, Theodore Roosevelt's Country Life Commission had exposed the gap in the standard of living between the farm and the city. As migration from the farms to the cities continued to rise, efforts had been made to increase the comfort and perfect the economy of the small farm in order to save the nation's backbone, the yeoman farmer. And, as important, to keep that farmer conservative rather than a rural insurgent.

But the new conveniences demanded in the modern home had made "the American home an expensive proposition," according to the president of the National Sugar Company. "It means," he continued, "a little automobile for the farmer; it means running water in the house and victrola for the wife[;] . . . and it means the ambition of the parents for the children that they shall have their education and equal opportunity to advance in the world as far as any other citizen of the United States."[92]

Advancing in the world did not mean common labor. "We have got beyond soiling our hands," Texas cotton farmer John Davis explained, "and we want somebody else to do the real work." "Do any of you," Davis challenged his unresponsive audience, "want to give up your places as members of this committee and go back and soil your hands in the dirt, cultivating cotton, picking cotton to make the clothes we have got to wear, or do you want to shear the sheep or slaughter the beef?" To these southwestern small farmers with their marginally profitable land, raising the standard of living on the farm to match that of towns required cheap labor. Common labor had become for them a threat to hold over schoolboys to make them study, while education, in turn, ruined a man for common labor. Even the Black man, Davis asserted, had been educated "beyond his capacity to serve the land and he wants to live in town," and it was possible that resident Mexicans would eventually be so educated.[93]

The perpetually migrant Mexican would form a permanent underclass, with Mexico, as committee member John Raker baldly put it, "the breeding ground for more second-class cotton pickers and beet diggers, hoers and toppers." "This is not work the white man cannot do," admitted W. B. Mandeville regarding Colorado beet work, but he also asserted, "We have made an absolute class distinction in labor." It seemed they were willing to make it a caste distinction as well. These southwestern employers would create a distinct group to form a permanent laboring force that would minimize the differences in living standards among Anglo participants in American democracy. A system of perpetually cheap migrant labor would boost the income and diminish the manual labor of the farmer and his family, while at the same time it would exclude the poorest class in the vicinity from the Anglo comity.[94]

By early 1921 the war boom had finally ended. Unemployment reached the highest level in U.S. history. At least 150,000 Mexicans returned home. In Colorado the Great Western Sugar Company reaped, in a glutted market, the financial disaster of its postwar expansion. Labor demand plummeted. Denver, according to one news headline, was "crowded with Mexicans who are near starving." The deputy city attorney estimated that "70 percent of the 5,000 Mexicans now in the city are without means of support and must be fed by charity." In March the secretary of labor finally rescinded the immigration exemption orders and called upon the importers "to return to Mexico all such aliens then in their employ," while federal officials tracked and deported those they could find of the 21,400 deserters.[95]

The marginality and vulnerability of the newly augmented Mexican labor force was harshly illuminated for this brief season as workers moved across the border at the convenience of Anglo employers and the government that represented them. But this depression proved only an ill-fitting prelude to the economic expansion of the 1920s. The renewed expansion would not be hindered by the lack of overt government sanction for the importation of Mexican labor. The government had withdrawn the exemptions that had permitted virtually unrestricted immigration but had failed to appropriate money to restore the wartime policing of the border. Without this border patrol, the supervising inspector on the Mexican border had warned in 1920 that "practically any alien desirous of entering the United States and possessed of ordinary intelligence and persistence could readily find the means of doing so without fear of detection." By 1923 Mexican immigration, largely illegal now, surpassed its wartime rate, and the number of Mexicans and Mexican Americans in the Southwest's mines and fields and on its railroad crews again began to rise.[96] When the Border Patrol was finally created in 1924, it had only a small fraction of the size and resources of the wartime force.[97]

The war years had witnessed the establishment of Mexican labor as a permanent and significant factor in the United States as a whole. During the war, Mexican migratory patterns, already essential to migrants' home place survival, had become equally essential in the eyes of many Anglos to maintenance of the western Anglo small farmer's standard of living and corporate farming profits. Federal mobilization had helped bring Mexicans into the public eye and then had abandoned them there. For U.S. citizens of Mexican descent, the new services, the wartime clubs, the Hispano demonstration agents, and the federal funds that had begun to integrate them into the larger American polity disappeared.[98]

Wartime policies and rhetoric had also further obscured the distinction between U.S. citizens of Mexican descent and Mexican nationals. A significant minority of the migrants ceased their peregrinations and began, in new parts of Colorado, in Chicago, and elsewhere, to form an increasingly persistent contingent. They stayed in increasing numbers (e.g., by 1920 about a quarter of Mexican and Mexican American workers in the mines and fields of northern Colorado now stayed through the year), but they were set apart, often literally, in housing as in the types of jobs they could hold.[99] The American Beet Sugar Company had planned its thirty-two colonies "where the residence of Mexican people would be least objectionable to people prejudiced against them."[100] In Bisbee the copper mining corporation launched a new homeownership campaign for workers with corporate mortgage plans; it excluded Mexicans, who instead were directed to rental "tenements" separated from the "American" neighborhoods.[101]

The unarticulated compromise that had emerged from the 1920 hearings lay in the blind eye of the immigration officials, in the admission, however illegally, of permanently marginal laborers. Though those admitted were Mexican, the racial ideology demanded the identification of all those of Mexican descent and of whatever citizenship as "Mexican," while the determination to avoid the re-creation of the racial problems of the South demanded the myth that all these "Mexicans" disappeared below the border each year and were no part of the U.S. polity. The 1920 hearings had made clear that what the Anglo employers now wanted, as the chairman of the House committee summarized it for them, was "first class labor, but No. 2 men." And it did not augur well for the new migrants and would-be settlers that a Colorado congressman expressed his determination to make "this country . . . as much as I can help to make it so . . . a white man's country."[102]

Black Dreams, White Nightmares

The violent climax of the commitment to a white man's West came in the same year the immigration exemptions ended, in Tulsa, Oklahoma. Tulsa was simultaneously the capital of the burgeoning, highly speculative domestic oil industry and the capital of African American westward migration. Blacks may no longer have dreamed of a Black state on Oklahoma land, but they had dared to build a Black utopia in Tulsa. When massive oil strikes suddenly goosed Tulsa to life after 1900, Blacks participated in its meteoric rise. In 1900 the town, on land in the Creek Nation, boasted all of 1,300 inhabitants. By 1910, now in the new state of Oklahoma, it had over

18,000 and by 1920 over 72,000. As early as 1899, word of Tulsa as a land of opportunity had reached the border states of the South. Black entrepreneurs found Tulsa unsegregated. Black businesses sat on downtown land; Black lawyers there employed a white stenographer. Black and white residents shared a rooming house.[103]

But Black real estate speculators who had imbibed Booker T. Washington's message of Black enterprise and separate development opted to create a Black town alongside the white one. J. B. Stradford, son of an enslaved man who emancipated himself by escaping to Ontario, Canada, graduate of Oberlin College and Indiana Law School, and business owner in Kentucky and Indiana, arrived in Tulsa in 1899 and bought large tracts of land north of the city's railroad tracks and sold it only to fellow African Americans. Others followed suit. They named the area Greenwood, after a town in Mississippi. By 1907, the year of statehood, the area had two physicians, a dentist, a minister, a newspaper (that essential item of real estate development), and three grocers among its denizens. Though Blacks were shut out of oil work, Greenwood benefited from the boom indirectly. The work they could get paid higher wages, and oil workers spent their dollars in Greenwood's vice district. Tulsa annexed the approximately four-square-mile valley that held Greenwood in 1909, and in the next decade of explosive growth, Tulsa's Black population grew, in proportion, even faster than the exponential rate of its white population, rising from just under two thousand to almost nine thousand, reaching 12.3 percent of the town.[104]

White boosters were less than pleased. Already in 1912 the lead story in the *Tulsa Democrat* worried, "Tulsa appears now to be in danger of losing its prestige as the whitest town in Oklahoma." While Stradford and his colleagues had created a Black city by choice, Tulsa whites strove to make it law. In 1916 the city passed an ordinance forbidding members of either of the two races recognized in Oklahoma (Black and not-Black, or white) from residing on any block where three-quarters or more of the residents were of the other race. Though the U.S. Supreme Court invalidated the ordinance in 1917, Tulsa never repealed it.[105]

Meanwhile, Greenwood flourished. Its multistory business district had a confectionery with a twelve-foot fountain and a movie house. It had assertive lawyers, including B. C. Franklin, father of historian John Hope Franklin, who successfully fought the city's effort to move Black Tulsa farther north; a Black newspaper, the *Tulsa Star*, whose publisher and owner declared at the top of his paper, "THE MOTTO OF EVERY NEGRO SHOULD BE: YOU PUSH ME AND I PUSH YOU"; and A. C. Jackson, whom the founders of the prestigious Mayo Clinic called "the most able Negro surgeon in America." It had a four-story Black high school, named Booker T. Washington High School, and the three-story brick Mount Zion Baptist Church. And it had the Stradford Hotel. The $50,000 three-story hotel, finished in mid-1918, had elegant chandeliers, modern conveniences, and respectability. Just as the Hotel Tulsa symbolized white Tulsa's aspirations as a modern, prosperous city, the Stradford Hotel, the church, and the school made concrete the city's Black dreams of first-class citizenship.[106]

What, then, could go wrong? The immediate postwar years brought massive displacement of the countryside's white farmers and workers. As cotton and grain prices had skyrocketed during the war, more than doubling in the case of cotton, newly prospering small farmers across the country borrowed heavily to put as many acres as they could into their cash crops, buying more land when possible. Landlords pushed tenants and sharecroppers to devote increasing proportions of their acreage to grain and cotton. It was not just greed; government propaganda made clear the dire need, encouraging the expansion. But greed definitely played a role. Government-appointed guardians for Oklahoma's Native Americans sold off land to relatives and colleagues, ignoring their mandated duty to protect the interests of their "wards." Land prices spiraled upward.

With the end of the war, it all came crashing down. Farmers had to sell their cotton crops at a loss, making it impossible for them to meet their debt obligations. Often they lost not only their newly acquired land but all their land. Farm ownership fell dramatically among whites. As they failed, they watched the relative success of nonwhite farmers around them. With little or no access to credit, Native American and African American farmers had been less likely to acquire debt from wartime speculation. Now they had cash and could buy land when it came on the market. Their gains were not evenly spread geographically. In the hardest-hit county for whites, nonwhite owner-operators fell in number by almost the same proportion as whites. Elsewhere, however, the trends parted. In one extreme case, the number of nonwhite owner-operators rose by over two-thirds, from 490 to 728.[107]

These displaced white farmers headed for Tulsa, where they found yet more economic distress. Oil prices in 1921 plummeted. Oil fetched $3 a barrel in 1920. A year later the price was only $1 a barrel. By one estimate, almost two-thirds of Oklahoma's oil industry shut down. Even in affluent neighborhoods, a third of the homes were for sale.[108]

On Memorial Day 1921, 90 degrees and humid, crowds gathered for parades, bands, and salutes to men in uniform. Handsome, dapper, nineteen-year-old "Diamond Dick" Rowland, who shined shoes at a downtown pool hall, headed into the Drexel Building, which held one of the only "colored" bathrooms in segregated downtown Tulsa. It was on the top floor, and operating the elevator was a seventeen-year-old white divorcée, Sarah Page, new to Tulsa, having moved from Kansas City. Page screamed. A white clerk ran to the elevator, saw Rowland fleeing, and called the police, labeling the encounter an attempted sexual assault. When police interviewed Page at the station, she hedged and implied she would not press charges. The police made no arrests.[109]

Word on the street took a nasty turn, since most people were ignorant of Page's interview, and in response, the police sent one Black and one white officer to arrest Rowland. It is not clear whether they wanted to accommodate the sentiment or protect Rowland. In either case, the afternoon edition of Tulsa's *Tribune* hit the streets at 3:00 with newsboys hawking, "Negro assaults a white girl!" The newspaper account had him clawing at her skin and tearing her clothes, and it posed her as an orphan working to pay her way through business college. With rumors of a planned lynching, Tulsa's police chief removed Rowland to a more secure jail. There he was guarded by the unflappable Sheriff McCullough, who disabled the elevator and placed six deputies behind a steel door at the top of the staircase, the only access to the cell.[110]

While young Tulsa Black men, many of them veterans, argued with their elders about the proper course of action, the sheriff managed peacefully to discourage an angry white crowd and to disperse armed groups of Black men.[111] But remnants of the white crowd lingered on the courthouse lawn, where they were joined by younger men, including the city's transient oil workers, who hooted at the sheriff when he urged them to disperse. The white crowd turned their attention from the imagined threat posed to white womanhood by Rowland to the threat posed by armed Black men invading white Tulsa. By 10:00 p.m. about 1,500 whites, some armed, had gathered at an intersection next to the courthouse. At 10:15 another contingent of Blacks, about seventy-five of them, armed, arrived from Greenwood. A scuffle broke out between a white and a Black man over a gun, which then went off.[112]

Within seconds, whites and Blacks lay dead or dying, and the vastly outnumbered remaining Blacks fled toward Greenwood. Whites hunted down the Blacks and broke into sporting goods stores, pawnshops, and anywhere they could find weapons and ammunition. Some also took advantage of the disorder to sweep up $43,000 in stolen property. The police deputized five hundred men to put down what they and their mayor seemed to see as a Black insurrection. What followed was a pitched battle by vastly unequal forces. As thousands of white Tulsa men invaded Greenwood, Greenwood's Blacks fought back, exchanging fire. Whites set fire to buildings along the tracks. In the early hours of June 1, 1921, as the scale of the white assault became clear, Blacks streamed out of Greenwood into the countryside, and while some whites hid them and some churches gave them refuge, thousands of whites, including members of the police and the local National Guard units called out for the occasion, rioted, looted, battled those who remained, and burned Greenwood to the ground. The fire department had orders not to respond.[113]

Greenwood's remaining citizens were treated like prisoners of war, lined up on the street with their hands raised and marched out of the district. When the city jail was full, they were taken to the Convention Hall. When the Convention Hall was full, Blacks were marched through Tulsa with guards shooting at the heels of any laggards. They were imprisoned in the city's baseball facilities and, finally, at the city's fairgrounds, where six thousand of them slept on platforms normally used to groom cows.[114]

A chorus of contrition, horror, and dismay among whites across the country and outrage among Blacks immediately followed the riot, even in Tulsa. Among whites, at least, it was short-lived. While one local judge declared the city and county "legally liable" for all damages, that declaration had no legal standing. Instead, court proceedings began against those labeled "Negro instigators." Greenwood's refugees faced the elements in army tents for over a year as the federal government thought better of its initial impulse to launch an investigation of the riot and the city and insurance companies successfully declared themselves without liability for the loss of property. Tulsa's white city leaders created the Business Man's Protective League, instructing its 250 men to patrol the major roads within and en route to Tulsa, stopping any African American they deemed suspicious, and firing if the person did not stop. In white accounts, the victims had brought destruction on themselves, and their vice-ridden neighborhood must never revive.[115] In Tulsa, among the city's white boosters, this picture of upstanding whites putting Blacks in their place was far more palatable than the alternative, that of a lawless West.

Conclusion

While demarcating seemed to be triumphing over the agitation for radical democracy by 1920 and the assertion of the white man's West inseparably with it, radical protest survived and, at certain times and places, prospered, providing an alternative vision of a modern West. In Tonopah Divide, Nevada, and Butte, Montana, despite repeated calls by mine owners for the federal government to arrest and deport IWW organizers, despite the influence of two Nevada senators and an ex-governor of Delaware with investments at stake, and despite mine owners resorting to blacklists, mob violence, bribery, false affidavits, labor spies, and private gunmen, federal investigations found no cause for action and no immigrants advocating destruction of property or the government, and local juries refused to rule for the corporations and against the workers. In New Mexico in 1919 Governor Larrazolo made the controversial decision to pardon twenty-one Villistas taken in the wake of the Columbus raid. Despite being kidnapped by American Legionnaires and dumped in the desert, Ida Crouch Hazlett, suffragist and socialist, continued touring the West on behalf of the movement. In 1920, running for president of the United States from his federal prison cell for his opposition to the war, Eugene V. Debs garnered nearly a million votes, tripling the number the socialists polled two years earlier. He fared best in New York and Wisconsin, but six western states gave him returns above the national average. In that same election, over 19 percent of Washington and South Dakota voters went for the Farmer-Labor Party. And even in Tulsa, Black lawyer B. C. Franklin won his lawsuit and saved Greenwood for African Americans against Tulsa's white elites' desire to turn the district into an industrial zone.[116]

Similarly in North Dakota, bucking the trend elsewhere in the country, the Nonpartisan League successfully fought off attacks.[117] At particular issue was the Bank of North Dakota. It had originated in the struggling Scandinavian-American Bank of Fargo, taken over by the NPL to provide a credit system for farmers more in harmony with farm economics and NPL principles than had been available elsewhere. It accepted farmers' notes and postdated checks, for example. When it became the Bank of North Dakota in 1919, the state required all state and local funds be deposited in the bank; any individual or corporation could also make deposits, which the state would guarantee and render exempt from any state, county, or municipal taxes. It was seen as the flagship of a fleet of 1919 measures that created a variety of state enterprises to be managed in the interests of the people. In poor shape when acquired and operated on a shoestring (with the notes and checks handled "almost entirely by one woman who maintained most inadequate records," according to one historian), the bank came under heavy scrutiny, and the interpretation of its health tended to be at least as political as statistical.

In response, as antiradicalism rode an ascending arc, the rabid anti-NPL periodical the *Red Flame (That Is Burning the Heart Out of North Dakota)* hit the newsstands, with red covers and dramatic cartoons in which a giant "Bolshevism" wreaked havoc and destruction on village churches and squares. The fracas culminated in a lawsuit that wended its way to the United States Supreme Court. The issue at stake was whether a state could operate a bank. Corporate lawyers, including counsels for the Northern Pacific and the

Great Northern Railroads, milling and power corporations, and telephone companies, spoke on behalf of the "42 taxpayers" who brought the suit. They tried to draw a clear line between public purpose and enterprise they saw as, by its nature, private. "Well," replied Justice James Clark McReynolds, "and why should not the state go into business?" The defendants argued that the citizens of North Dakota had amended their state constitution to enable various enterprises, and the people had repeatedly approved them. "The People," their attorney concluded, "have full authority, and the people of North Dakota have spoken." And the United States Supreme Court heard them. On June 1, 1920, it handed down the decision, concluding the Supreme Court had no jurisdiction in the case: "If the State sees fit to enter upon such enterprises as are here involved, with the sanction of its constitution, its legislature, and its people, we are not prepared to say that it is within the authority of this Court, in enforcing the observance of the Fourteenth Amendment, to set aside such actions by judicial decision." Despite the bruising election season that followed, the NPL prevailed at the polls as well.[118]

North Dakota's victory was in harmony with the radical democratic insurgencies of the decade that linked economic and political democracy—the Mexican Revolution, the NPL, woman suffrage, the IWW, and others. The determination to retain a white man's country had proved a less powerful antiradical tool in a state defined as overwhelmingly white. Elsewhere, the coalitions that had sustained the radical democratic movements fared less well. The antiradical democracy tools seen as wartime measures and so as temporary, as well as the pervasive policing and repression, had lasting effects, tipping the balance and allowing, for most of the region, the opposing forces to wrest control of the meaning of the region and the nature of the postwar order—who's American, and whose America. The IWW never fully recovered. Alien Land Laws deprived Asian immigrants and ultimately even their citizen children of property rights on the West Coast. The U.S. Supreme Court definitively put Asians on the nonwhite side of an imagined line.[119] "Mexicans" could be U.S. citizens but never dependably "Americans," depending on whether the United States was trying to recruit Mexican labor or repatriate it. The set of institutional compromises that included the creation of a Border Patrol with a blind eye meant the continuing commitment to a vision of the U.S. West as always intended as a proving ground and opportunity for white men at the same time that it primarily advantaged large-scale agriculture, ranching, mining, and other businesses and did nothing to halt the ongoing dispossession of the smallholder. The "modern" U.S. West emerged from the war with its capital and racial formations shaken but not overthrown by the decade's agitation. The racial formation that emerged was not a product of the Jim Crow South, with its Black/white binary. In the multiplicity of the West, defendants of white supremacy faced a more varied set of challengers. Instead, the racial formation emerged from the West, abetted by the federal and state governments, an imagined West made material by those with the power to do so. The dream of a broadly participatory democracy would be channeled into other streams.

Part 3

Speculating, 1920–29

The postwar recession hit western states hard, and for many people good times only returned with the rain in middecade; for some, they never returned. The Southwest in the 1920s witnessed recurring drought, tight capital, and falling prices. In one northeastern New Mexico district, a third of the population had left by 1924. On the Great Plains, wheat proved a fickle friend. Eastern Oklahoma enjoyed a wheat boom. Oklahoma became second only to Kansas in the amount of wheat produced. It lasted, like the rains there, until 1927. Other states fared less well. The cost of living rose, and wheat prices declined. By 1926 more than half of Montana's banks had failed; over half of Nebraska's did so by 1932 and 71 percent of those in South Dakota. In 1929 North Dakota's per capita income was a little over half the national average, at $375.[1]

In the Pacific Northwest, as prices for wheat, potatoes, and sugar beets fell, those with capital to mechanize and acquire failing farms accumulated land. Even where wheat boomed, farms dwindled in number but grew in size, requiring fewer farmers, and Idaho, for example, had the second greatest outmigration among western states.

With lumber once again a glut on the market, timberland owners turned against the Loyal League of Loggers and Lumbermen, which would never recover its wartime strength. The owners helped Washington's Republicans elect Roland Hartley governor, and he in turn ousted the University of Washington's president, Henry Suzzallo, so instrumental in bringing the 4L into being, with its costly labor provisions and worker empowerment. That ouster, of course, failed to halt the steady decline of lumber, wheat, cattle, and wool prices in the 1920s or the persistent bank failures that resulted.[2] Mining suffered as well. Metal prices declined, including gold, silver, and copper, while coal rode a roller coaster.[3]

Yet there was no return of the massive 1910s unrest. That decade's movements for radically participatory democracy had stretched across the North American West from the Mexican Revolution to the northern plains' triumph of the Nonpartisan League. Women allied with socialists had won the vote in the West; socialists had played a major role in western urban centers from Seattle to Los Angeles; strikers had taken over large swaths of Colorado in what the press called labor wars; and the NPL not only sent the first women representatives to the federal governments of the United States and Canada but also opened state enterprises and successfully defended them before the Supreme Court.

Corporate, state, and municipal attempts to squash these triumphant movements had enjoyed limited success until they were authorized and joined by the wartime federal government in often bloody reprisals, imprisonments, and deportations that only ended with the opening of the 1920s.[4] This pattern of the evisceration of radical democracy in western states was coupled with corporate deregulation and the rising influence of western senators, who, if they agreed on anything, agreed on the benefits of development. Together, they enabled state actors to reframe government to enhance speculation. They helped create a citizenship defined in relation to a highly speculative market rather than a highly partisan ballot box.

Investment in the market became tied to the rights of every American. The New York Stock Exchange also had a hand in the vastly expanded number of investors and the reshaping of the meaning of investment. In the wake of the congressional investigation in 1913 that had accused a "money trust" of manipulating prices and endangering democracy, the NYSE launched a publicity campaign that equated government securities regulation with inhibiting the freedom of the small investor. The NYSE equated freedom with "the *possibility* of trading," and beginning in 1922, it aggressively sought to widen its shareholder base. It created an ideology that historian Julia Ott calls "direct economic democracy," in which, in contrast to corporate hierarchies and secret boardrooms, any individual had equal access to participating in corporate ownership through stocks on the open market. No longer would a bright line separate capital and labor. Its proponents contrasted this "democratic type of capitalism" with a Soviet Union "under which speculation would not be permitted." They defined this speculative market not only as freedom but also as modern: this direct economic democracy was "modern American capitalism"; it was a modernization of the founding mythology of the yeoman farmer; now Everyman would own shares of stock, not a farm.[5] This economic democracy, in short, would substitute for the radical social democracy advocated in so much of the West in the previous decade and repressed so violently at the decade's end—and now defined as premodern. What these small investors bought, in other words, was not risk; this speculation was patriotism, citizenship, and equal participation in modern democracy.

Amid this frenzy, powerful progressive reformers found themselves increasingly challenged by business Republicans. What was the proper relationship of the federal government to the market? And what was the proper vision of the relationship between the West and opportunity, citizenship and speculation? The relevant congressional hearings in the early 1920s over various issues and scandals—oil in the Red River's bed, restrictions on Osage Indian oil revenues, Pueblo land rights, irrigation developments, and corruption surrounding the development of naval reserves at Teapot Dome, Wyoming, among others—were messy and contradictory. "States must 'puzzle before they power,'" commented a historian, and often they first puzzle through a problem that surfaces tangentially in relation to other problems, so these hearings dealt with federal holdings and Indian policy rather than directly with the financial markets.[6]

In these hearings, through their discussions, the congressmen and witnesses produced concepts and categories of speculation, and by defining illegitimate speculation, they defined speculation itself as legitimate. They produced regulations to police the boundaries between legitimate and illegitimate speculation, but the way they enforced those regulations did as much to construct categories and behaviors, as well as norms of citizenship, as the regulations themselves. These categories in turn helped determine rights and benefits, in this case, economic rights and benefits, who had them, and who did not. Would-be participants in the market conformed to market identities.[7]

By defining who was a legitimate participant and who was not, who had the capacity to participate in a speculative market and who did not, the state constituted not only a speculator citizenship but also a stratified one. This new hierarchy was layered over older ones and could obscure them. Indians were "protected" not only from loss but also from gain. Indians designated as "full-blood" were denied the ability to manage their own wealth and property for a period of decades, by which time, presumably, they would acquire the necessary market acumen. And their exclusion marked again the West as the arena of opportunity for white people, and white men, in particular, as peculiarly suited for both the speculation and the responsible enjoyment of the wealth that followed. The concept of capacity was clearly rooted in racist thinking—blood quantum, for example, in the case of Indians—but it did not require that racist criteria be explicit; the concept was framed as an issue of market savvy, not race.

The early 1920s was a time of concentrated redefinition of U.S. citizenship. In 1924 alone Congress enacted the National Origins Act, providing quotas based on immigrant origins; the Oriental Exclusion Act, excluding all immigrants ineligible for citizenship; and the Indian Citizenship Act, providing citizenship even for Indians still enrolled as tribal members and living on reservations. While most historians and theorists define citizenship as either status (something static that you either have or do not have) or practice (something you enact and so claim or perform and so justify), historian Cherstin Lyon sees citizenship as process. Citizenship is worked out in constant negotiations at various levels of government and community between individuals, communities, and the state. In Lyon's reading, "citizenship" is fluid, which better explains the flux in hearings and experience, in inconsistent inclusions and exclusions that often mirrors the fuzzy racial categories in anti-interracial marriage law.[8]

The differentiation is both internal and external. Political theorist Lisa J. Disch writes, "Citizenship fosters 'internal differentiation and hierarchy' . . . by incorporating some into citizenship in a way that highlights their subordination or 'degraded status.'"[9]

Certainly this kind of incorporation characterized African Americans in the Jim Crow United States at the same time that incorporation was coming to define the citizenship of Native Americans in the early twentieth century with limitations on their property rights. In other words, a person could be an outsider and a citizen at the same time, and the subordinated inclusion could be necessary to the defining of the body politic.

The following three chapters examine different manifestations of this new speculator state and citizenry in the West and the ways in which they shaped the region's landscape and opportunities. Chapter 7 focuses on the rampant oil craze; chapter 8 on federal agricultural and land policy; and chapter 9 on tourism, real estate development, and Hollywood.

7

Oil

Early on the morning of January 26, 1920, the employees of the Burke Divide Company, holding leases from the state of Oklahoma, struck oil in the southern part of the bed of the Red River. The river sat between Oklahoma and Texas. Within hours, twenty-eight armed Texas Rangers came down from the bluffs overlooking the riverbed and drove off the Burk Divide employees and officers. They had been waiting until the oilmen struck oil, and then "they pounced on them." According to a company representative, "Their commissary was taken; their groceries were taken. . . . Their tools were taken and the clothes of the employees of this company were taken, and have not been recovered to this day."[1]

The Burke men had known they were under surveillance. Elsewhere on the riverbed the previous fall, a surveyor hired by another group of claimants had to battle not only high winds and floods but also Texas claimants who, under cover of darkness, cut the guy wires on the derricks, which then fell over at the first hard wind. They also shot at the surveyor and his men from the river's south bank. Around the same time, according to former congressman Henry D. Green, Thomas Testerman turned over his property to a district judge from Oklahoma who had been appointed a receiver when Texans contested Testerman's claims, but that receiver fared no better, overpowered in November by "a bunch of fellows who said they were representing the court of Texas." Even a U.S. government surveyor investigating the claims "was beaten over the head by one of those Texas officials." An Oklahoma government attorney claimed, "If *our* governor had been as flighty, I might say, as the governor of Texas," they might have faced "a little civil war down there between Texas and Oklahoma."[2]

The Supreme Court was left to fix the ownership of the heavily disputed southern half of the riverbed and the southern boundary of the river—a task made trickier by the river's propensity to shift its bed and collapse its banks on a regular basis. Not only did the warring states of Texas and Oklahoma make their case, but the federal government staked a claim on its own behalf, as did Kiowa allottees and, more fleetingly, the state of Arkansas. Oil, it seemed, had many fathers. Even when the court declared the U.S. government the true owner, the rival claimants—individual, corporate, state, and everything between—pursued their case before the House Committee on Public Lands, arguing that their good-faith efforts deserved compensation from the flowing crude. The hearings reveal not only the free-for-all oil rush in the 1920s but also the shifting terrain of western investment—highly speculative since the beginning—and its meaning for the general polity.[3]

These hearings occurred in the context of the formation of a speculator state, that is, a state that is organized to promote and protect speculation and that creates the normative, virtuous citizen, the most desirable citizen, the modern citizen as a speculator. The label seems most evident in relation to oil, but it also emerges in relation to restrictions on Indian property rights, themselves in many cases enmeshed in the promise of greater resources. In the early twentieth century, Congress decided, as a largely futile attempt to halt the mass dispossession of Indians by hands other than Congress's own, to define Indian property rights by a concept equally foreign to most Indian groups: blood quantum. "Half-bloods" or less could control their own allotted land; "full-bloods" would enjoy their property under guardianship for the next twenty-five years, to expire in 1931. Although there was always some confusion over whether "blood" meant genetics or experience, there was an explicit connection between the full property rights usually seen as part of citizenship and market savvy. The state (i.e., any aggregate of people authorized to define and enforce what a citizen is and what that citizen's rights are) defined citizenship in relation to the market.

Even at the earliest moment of the United States as a nation, there was some ideal connection between citizenship and economics. The ideal citizen, the yeoman farmer, was self-sufficient, economically dependent on no man, and so offered a vote free of untoward influence. But the laws that limited the access of members of the Five Civilized Tribes and later some others to their property were not concerned with economic dependence and its impact on politics. Particularly by the early 1920s, the laws referred to understanding a speculative market in land. Their ideal citizen was a savvy participant in a speculative market. Indians were culturally constructed by whites as genetically ill-suited to profit maximization and speculation. By these restrictions, full citizenship required economic citizenship.

Neither speculation nor oil was new to the 1920s, and both were national phenomena linked to the consumer fever that swept the nation in the wake of wartime austerity and the accumulation of wartime wages. What is western about oil in the 1920s is, first, that most of the oil and most of the oil booms occurred west of the Mississippi. Particularly intense booms occurred in the late 1910s and early 1920s in Los Angeles; Hot Springs, Wyoming; northeastern Oklahoma (Osage County); Eldorado, Texas; southwestern Arkansas; northern Louisiana; Goose Creek and Damon Mound on the Texas Gulf Coast; and eastern Kentucky. In 1909 states west of the Mississippi were extracting almost two-thirds of the oil extracted in the United States. By 1919 the figure was over four-fifths, where it remained in 1939. California was the largest oil producer much of the period, with just over 52 million barrels in 1909, over 97 million in 1919, and almost 224 million in 1939. Oklahoma was the second largest in 1909 and 1919, growing from over 45 million to over 81 million barrels in 1919 and over 153 million barrels in 1939. Texas had surpassed both states by 1939. Texas output grew exponentially, up 740 percent between 1909 and 1919 and up 541 percent between 1919 and 1939, reaching at that latter date over 467 million barrels. By 1939 other western state producers included Arizona, Colorado, Louisiana, Kansas, Montana, New Mexico, and Wyoming.[4]

Second, the West played a role in how oil investment was imagined. Promoters relied on a largely false East/West financial dichotomy. When attempting to reassure suspicious investors, securities promoters promised that a listing on the New York exchange was imminent—the New York Stock Exchange, not the Los Angeles

Stock Exchange, founded as the Los Angeles Oil Exchange in 1899 and developing dramatically in the 1920s. Eastern capital and institutions still stood for stability; they could rescue investors from the unruly risk of western investments even when, in actuality, the eastern and western financial markets and investors were deeply integrated.[5]

Third, the hearings, the popular press, and the promotional materials were all saturated with ideas of opportunity linked to the mythology of the American West. Those protagonists enmeshed in oil dealings struggled to narrate their behavior in a way that put them in the mold of the ultimate American virtue: opening up the country, building up the nation, creating growth and progress from a barren landscape.

Fourth and finally, disproportionately, the congressional committeemen dealing with oil issues, whether on public lands committees or Indian affairs committees, hailed from the West and represented western constituencies. Republicans swept the West in presidential elections throughout the 1920s. Only Arizona, Texas, Oklahoma, Arkansas, and Missouri among western states resisted the party's call. But state and local politics were more complicated. The decade saw a mix of reactionary and progressive politicians win office in the region. In 1922 Iowa and Nebraska elected progressive Republicans to high office, voters placed progressive Democrats in the governor's office in Colorado and Arizona and in the Senate in Washington and Montana, and Minnesota elected a Farmer-Labor Party senator. Politicians ousted at the state level during World War I for their progressive proclivities often regained office in the 1920s. Having lost his Montana state office during World War I, Democrat Burton K. Wheeler won his Senate race in 1922 and ran as the vice presidential candidate on the national Progressive Party ticket with Robert LaFollette in 1924. That party, labeled by *The Nation* as "the first formal alliance of organized labor in America with farmers and Socialists," took 30–54 percent of the vote in ten states, all but one of them west of the Mississippi, and took 20–30 percent of the vote in six other western states. Montana's Thomas Walsh, a Wilsonian Democrat, retained his Senate seat, and a progressive Republican won the governorship but failed to combat the power of the Anaconda Copper Mining Company.

Wyoming went Republican with the exception of the Democrat senator John Kendrick, a wealthy rancher attentive to the state's agricultural interests. North Dakota's Nonpartisan League governor, Lynn Frazier, suffered recall in 1921 as part of a general purging of the NPL in that state but was elected to the U.S. Senate the following year. Nebraska, Kansas, Oklahoma, and South Dakota suffered similar anti-NPL sentiment carrying over from the anti-radicalism of the war. But in South Dakota progressive Republicans won office by co-opting the NPL agenda, and in Oklahoma NPL affiliates headed for the Farmer-Labor Reconstruction League, which enjoyed a brief success early in the decade when it captured the state's Democratic Party. Its influence in the state legislature led to the increased power and role of farmer cooperatives, regulated warehouses, marketing inspection laws, more funding for schools, and $3 million for highways, though it failed to get a state bank and was plagued by corruption and ultimately a brief alliance with the KKK.[6] Wheeler, Walsh, Kendrick, Frazier, and other westerners would play an outsize role in the congressional hearings.

So this 1920s oil story was a western story from beginning to end, from the shoot-out at the Red River to the showdown at the Senate hearings on oil leases at Teapot Dome that threatened to topple the administration of President Warren G. Harding.

The Market in Oil

The oil boom was concentrated in the late 1910s to early 1920s, precisely the years in which the federal government began to expand its bureaucratic capacity.[7] Government bureaucracy had expanded dramatically during World War I not only to deal with conscription and fight a war but also to impose newly legal income taxes, to sell Liberty bonds, to manage food shortages, and to control military morals, drinking, and venereal disease. The wartime federal government took over the nation's railroads and telecommunications. It dramatically expanded its surveillance machinery and its ability to police political conformity. And with Liberty bonds it aggressively entered the securities market. All this activity by the federal government provided a context for western speculation different from the previous booms.

Though the federal government pulled back from some of these activities after the war, it had done a masterful job preparing the ground for the mass speculations of the 1920s. Wartime elevated wages and restrictions on consumption that limited everything from the amount of wheat consumed to the amount of cloth in a suit meant that despite wartime inflation, most U.S. citizens found themselves with an unaccustomed amount of cash on hand in the late 1910s. Moreover, the slickly produced, celebrity-rich Liberty bond campaigns aimed at mass audiences of small means created the idea of accessible investment, attached glamor to it, and promised security through it. Thirty million Americans bought small-denomination Liberty bonds, nearly a third of those investors with annual incomes at most of $2,000. By the war's end "more than 18 million Americans [had become] securities owners *for the first time*."[8]

These audiences across the nation were ripe indeed for the oil salesmen's pitch. Nor was their enthusiasm dampened by the sharp postwar recession of 1921–22. What the recession seemed most to demonstrate was the fragility of prosperity and the lack of connection between effort and reward. After all, another federal piece in laying the groundwork for a speculator citizenship was the government's encouragement of expansion in wheat and cotton farming and coal and oil for the benefit of the battles abroad. Farmers enjoying peak prices patriotically purchased ever more machinery and acreage, plowing their profits back into the land. Oil production skyrocketed in response to rising prices and national fears of scarcity, with consumption outstripping production during the war. The production in 1921 at over 472 million barrels was more than double that of 1911. When the collapse came, as it did even for coal and oil prices by 1921 (in the first half of 1921, oil prices crashed from a peak of $3 per barrel in 1920 to an average price per barrel of $1), the only answer to many seemed another speculative gamble. That year in Henry County, Missouri, forced to choose between the Missouri College of Agriculture's exhibition of scientific stock breeding and a competing barbeque offered by strangers selling shares in a risky tire and rubber company, the farmers flocked to the barbeque, and the promoters raked in $100,000 in sales.[9]

Hundreds, even thousands of new companies, including smaller firms, partnerships, and common-law trusts that did not require state charters, materialized as if by magic (and some seemed to have more magical than material assets). Almost anyone could organize an oil company; not only ranchers and lawyers, bankers and insurance salesmen but also printers and even Arctic explorers did. In the year after the armistice, investment in oil securities rose from $1.8 billion to $3.2 billion. Farmers and others traded their Liberty bonds to banks as security for loans or for shares promising more spectacular earnings. Liberty bonds, in short, provided the route for many new investors into greater speculative ventures.[10]

Meanwhile, the demand for energy sources continued to skyrocket. Americans' romance with the automobile resulted in farmers who bought cars during their boom years before they bought indoor plumbing or central heat. In 1916 there were 3.5 million cars on the road; in 1921 10.5 million. The advent of the radio and other electronic goods fueled the expansion of electric power until by 1928 two-thirds of all U.S. families had electricity.[11]

But few farm families numbered among them. Farm income never recovered from that severe recession that opened the decade. Farmers were far better off if they could exploit what lay beneath the soil, particularly in Oklahoma. By 1920 Oklahoma had hosted a number of oil rushes. In that year the United States produced almost two-thirds of the world's oil, and half of U.S. production came from Oklahoma's midcontinent field. By 1923 over five hundred farmers took in between $100 and $5,000 a month from oil royalties at a time when average per capita farm income rested below $300 a year.[12]

Farmers became oilmen. Alva Varner, a farmer living near Grandfield, Oklahoma, located four claims on the riverbed in January 1919 for himself and his thirty-one associates. But rarely were farmers drillers. Drilling was immensely capital intensive; instead, farmers sold leases on their acreage to explorers, adventurers, speculators, and companies that either had the capital (big oil) or turned to a broad array of investors to find it or that flipped the leases themselves for a hefty profit. While oil giants, including Rockefeller's Standard Oil, could fund their own exploratory drilling, small independent oilmen had long relied on the sale of shares through promoters to raise revenue, and their investors in turn made possible the vast expansion of U.S. oil production during the 1920s.[13]

Basically, everyone in the 1920s, from multimillionaire Andrew Mellon to retired schoolteachers, enjoyed the new national pastime of taking a plunge in some market. Oil in particular remained a favorite of small investors throughout the decade. All the major fields discovered in the early twentieth century had produced "oil kings," and their highly publicized success made for eager emulators. The Burke Divide Company's investors included its farmer president, a taxicab company manager as secretary and treasurer, the proprietor of a Terre Haute, Indiana, restaurant, a railroad employee, a lumber dealer, and a lawyer. The company spent over $100,000 drilling, and just over a thousand stockholders invested almost another $800,000 about the time the federal government stepped in and appointed a receiver.[14]

The investors could be a local group of prospectors, as in the original set of claimants with Testerman, or a localized group of investors targeted by a smoothly successful promoter, as was the Red River claimant Buckeye Petroleum Company and the Southwest Petroleum Company, with their 200 stockholders from two counties in western Pennsylvania and about 150 in Ohio and Indiana. Similarly, when the Burke Divide Company's original investors needed more capital for drilling equipment and labor at the height of the oil boom, ultimately sinking $102,000 into drilling, they recruited 1,114 stockholders, about 700 of them from Vigo County, Indiana.[15]

Some oilmen, most famously C. C. Julian in California, wrote their own copy and sold their shares directly, but most hired "pens" who used the decade's new advertising techniques, mass mailing using purchased "sucker lists," traveling salesmen and brokers on commission, celebrity endorsements, and mass media to put across their ideas to the small investor. Newspaper readers were accustomed to reading fictional serials among the news. The line between fiction and news could indeed be fine and stretchy. Julian and others paid for regular columns of intimate narratives about the trials, tribulations, and triumphs of their drilling ventures, addressed to their investors. Here was no impersonal exchange. Small investors, who did not interest reputable bankers, received flattering and reassuring attention from both reputable and disreputable oil promoters.[16]

It was easy to tip over from legal to illegal promotions by offering promises instead of shared risk, overcapitalizing, overvaluing (usually immensely) the lease and/or the equipment, and misleading investors as to the share of the proceeds they would receive. Many oilmen who started as honest bankers, merchants, and lawyers, swept up in the excitement of the chase and desperate for cash when drilling costs mounted, found themselves traveling down dark roads, hiring shady associates, and luring their investors after them. Such a case was that of the Lubbock Oil Corporation, organized by a bank director, a retired merchant, and a local rancher. They wanted to drill just one wildcat well in Wise County, Texas, at the edge of a corridor smoking with oil activity. They had no clue as to what they were doing. They leased acreage, planning to sell subleases to raise funds, and promised the lessor to drill to 3,500 feet. During an oil boom, experienced men are scarce on the ground, so they hired men as inexperienced as they were to drill and manage, including the young pastor of the First Christian Church of Lubbock, scion of a prominent cattle family, and his brother-in-law. When the leases sold too slowly to raise funds for drilling, they missed their drilling deadline and forfeited their bond; with a check that bounced, they bought a rig that turned out to be missing parts. Saltwater came into the well, the rig collapsed, they lost tools down the well, and they needed more funds. They could have called it quits at that point and cut their losses. Instead, they converted their trust to a public corporation so they could sell securities; grossly inflating their assets and issuing overly optimistic financial statements, they dug ever deeper. In March 1921 they finally liquidated, among much mutual recrimination.[17]

This was indeed a free market. Was there an obligation of the state to protect its citizens from such fraud? What was, again, the proper relation between the state and its speculating citizens in this 1920s moment? The answer was regulation—sort of. States passed "blue-sky" laws—a reference to securities backed by nothing but blue sky—to regulate these speculative industries, and the federal government expressed its intent to wield the power of the post office and the Department of Justice. But it chose to provide little funding, signaling a distinct ambivalence. And so aside from a few sensational cases, the federal government left the laws unenforced or easily evaded and the industry unpoliced. In 1920 federal attorneys in Kentucky and Texas, under public pressure, investigated ninety oil companies and ten brokerage houses but tried only four cases. In Houston the federal government tried only twelve cases of mail fraud between 1917 and 1922. In Dallas the caseload rarely exceeded six cases a year. Federal law officers in Dallas preferred going after violators of the antivice Mann (sex trafficking) and Volstead (alcohol prohibition) Acts to prosecuting fraudulent speculative ventures. Like the securities it was meant to regulate, the 1913 Texas blue-sky law had "more loopholes than substance."[18]

The variety of investment instruments made evasion easier. Enforcement also suffered from local federal judges known to be sympathetic to entrepreneurs of "most stripes." When agents did succeed, like the oil promoters, they inflated their claims. In 1923 federal attorney Henry Zweifel told the press that those he indicted had sold a total of $200 million in stock to over two million individuals; the postmaster general, on the other hand, claimed it was half as much to a quarter as many. Zweifel claimed to have shut down about 85 percent of the worthless oil companies and was closing in on the last 15 percent, making it safe to invest in oil again. By the nature of this enforcement, the state structured a speculator economy and a population fallaciously convinced that a government-issued license to sell stock was an endorsement of probity and that the speculative market was safe.[19]

The New "Pioneers"

It is not an accident that the oil promoters who wrote their journals into their newspaper advertisements posed themselves as selfless, using their own resources and risking all in the service of their investors. In an earlier age, the yeoman farmer and then the home-bound woman had stood outside the selfish individualism of the market to protect national virtue. But how to define republican virtue in the new speculator state? Now women had the vote and invested in oil like everyone else. This tension at least in part explains the reaching in the congressional hearings for the proper narrative, the proper framing of this adventure. In Teapot Dome,

Red River, and the Osage hearings, there was a battle for the soul of the West and the nation.

The central issue of the Red River hearings, for example, was what constituted "good faith." Those Red River investors in good faith could look forward to some reimbursement from the oil pumped out of the ground during the time the federal government operated the field in receivership. In trying to define "good faith," the contestants brought into the discussion not only speculation and pioneering but also risk and responsibility. These qualities were all connected. To the claimants, the heroes who deserved reimbursement were precisely the risk-takers—not only those who did the labor of locating and drilling but also those who risked only their hard-earned money. Like a remote cousin, the proceeds of the investment were hard-earned once removed. Now the money did the labor. A Houston, Texas, attorney representing the receiver of General Oil Company found the Justice Department "hard-hearted. . . . [It] would take the net proceeds made by somebody's hard earned money." "What greater faith" could "a man show in anything," asked the attorney, whose clients had responded to a lurid newspaper and circular campaign, than investing deeply?[20]

Even the claimants, however, drew distinctions between "speculators" and others. Attorney Henry Green, former member of Congress and now a lumber and oil developer on public lands (and often in court, it seems), testified, "There is not a man that has come or will come before this committee, that does not consider that Tom Testerman" and his "people are all right. They are not speculators." He contrasted their virtue with the nature of their Texan rivals: "These men . . . are speculators." Unlike those Texans, who had simply flipped the leases, Testerman had developed the country and "made 55,000 acres . . . potentially valuable for oil" by his drilling, and he did so, moreover, "for the United States." "Oil," Green continued, "is a big benefit to the general public." Similarly, according to Colonel Jesse B. Roote, testifying on behalf of the Burke Divide Company, the claim locators were "pioneers."[21]

Testerman stood for the heroic, pioneering type of the ultimate American Everyman—in this case, an oil prospector. His advocate labeled him many things: a pioneer, "a plain, practical man" (as opposed to a lawyer), "an ordinary farmer," a "rough and ready old frontiersman," a "white man." "He is one of the men who has made Oklahoma what it is," this advocate continued. "He has helped to build a commonwealth and to establish a seat of civilization, than what there is no greater service to this country or to the people of this country." He was "a sort of Davy Crockett. . . . Now, the men who have redeemed this country from the wilderness . . . who have carried our flag and our institutions from the eastern to the western seas were not jurists . . . but they knew how to do things . . . how to carry forward the vanguard of civilization and how to make America the greatest land the sun shines upon. Thomas Testerman is of that mold."[22]

This "practical man" was actually a member of the state senate when the oil rush in the Red River took off, with several terms in the state legislature under his belt. A close friend of the sitting governor and former chief justice of the state, Testerman had looked to his friend's authority, and his friend held that the southern half of the riverbed lay in Oklahoma's jurisdiction. Testerman also consulted boundary markers on bridges, tax policies for toll bridges, and whiskey arrests. Very practical. He did not, however, consult legal precedent, which his advocate held that Testerman the farmer would not have understood. Nor did he consult placer mining laws (which it may be supposed that Testerman the legislator might have understood). He could "pass judgment on a herd of cattle or drove of mules" and "have a wizard's eye in searching out the treasures of this earth," but he could not decipher legal technicalities or men's duplicity. In the only invocation of race in the entire hearing, his advocate concluded, as a clincher, that Testerman "was the first white man to go in this oil field in Red River. That is undisputed."[23]

While the congressmen were inclined to be sympathetic to the oilmen, they knew speculation when they saw it. The Justice Department and the committee chair agreed that at stake was a moral issue. "The moral right, the moral claim to some consideration," the assistant to the attorney general insisted, "is not based on the mere act of going out and trying to get something for nothing, where the law says that act is utterly illegal." The committee chairman agreed. "On any moral question, here are men who rushed into this situation, knowing they were up against a fight against three or four parties; they risked their money on finding oil there; they risked their money on the Texas title being good; they risked their money on the Oklahoma claim being good; they risked their money on the north shore claims being good, and then they risked some more money. . . . [W]hy don't they stand their losses just as the rest of the people do?"[24] The moral flaw here was not speculation—getting something for nothing—but refusing to accept risk.

Nor would Major W. W. Dyar of the Justice Department allow the oilmen to claim moral superiority as pioneers who opened up the country. "They *all* claim to be pioneers," he said. Had the Burk Divide Company people so operated? "No," said Dyar. "As soon as they got there, they turned their guns against every other man in every direction, and the others who were to follow and who stood on the bank and wanted to do their share of pioneering, were kept off by force."[25]

Had they only been prudent, Dyar averred, "unwilling to take big risks in the face of opposing claims, and had kept off the river bed," the Interior Department and Justice Department could have settled the questions, the United States would have gotten more revenue, and the area would have gotten orderly development. At this point, Representative Olger B. Burtness of North Dakota chimed in: "Do prudent men, as a rule, go in the oil business?" which garnered him a round of laughter.[26] "Prudence" was not the watchword of the decade. In this battle between prudent and speculator citizenship, the speculators ultimately won; they were awarded a percent of the oil revenue from the contested claims the Supreme Court bestowed on the United States.

The risks were, indeed, high. There was no reimbursement for the many dry holes prospectors drilled and investors paid for. To one witness, referring to federal legislation on oil and mineral leasing, these investors and their men on the ground were simply fulfilling a Supreme Court mandate to develop the West: "The Supreme Court of the United States has said in reference to [the mining law of 1872, which declared that 'all valuable mineral deposits in lands belonging to the United States, both surveyed and unsurveyed, are hereby declared to be free and open to exploration and purchase,' that] this section, gentlemen, . . . was an invitation by Congress to the pioneer citizens of this country . . . to go out on the public lands and explore them and bring the hidden wealth in the earth to the surface, and to thus increase the general wealth of this country."[27]

"Orderly Development" or Development and Disorder?

Testerman and his companions invested in the midst of riotous activity. Oil prices had reached an all-time high by the late 1910s. Wichita Falls, Texas, about twenty-five miles across a broad prairie from the riverbed, "was at that time the Mecca of all the oil men in the United States." "This whole country," claimed Dyar, "was wild with excitement." The sale of leases was fast and furious, and clear title was hard to establish. In May 1919 the superintendent of the Kiowa and Comanche Reservation, eager to capitalize on the excitement on behalf of the tribes, sold leases at auction, with one-eighth royalty on oil produced returning to the tribe, with bids reaching $150 to $175 an acre, or $25,000 to $26,000 (nearly $400,000 in 2020 dollars) for 160 acres. Oil exchanges blossomed in Wichita Falls, Shreveport, Dallas, Fort Worth, and Tulsa to handle the traffic in leases.[28]

With demand at an all-time high, wells sprouted like weeds, and equipment and labor were hard to come by. Workers responded to the high wages no longer available for war work, and strangers flooded into small prairie towns. They built roads to bring oil to market. When they could, they worked in the oil fields themselves. In one county alone eight thousand came to work in oil. They earned $125 a month as roustabouts, $12 a day as drillers, and $13 a day as carpenters' base pay at a time when, nationwide, union carpenters averaged $31 a week. An additional five thousand worked as teamsters. Merchants were not far behind, opening the bars and rooming houses and providing the services necessary to feed and create a social world for a transient population overwhelmingly young and male. At the other end of the scale, construction boomed, and leisure and luxury goods served the newly rich and those who hoped to become rich. In that county seat, three banks holding $1 million before oil held $13 million by 1927.[29]

As U.S. agricultural goods failed to recapture European markets, increasing differences marked farm and nonfarm lives: by 1929 the average farm per capita annual income remained $223, while nonfarm had risen to $870. During the war, white tenants had taken out loans to buy their own farms at peak prices, driven up by oil speculation and high cotton prices. As cotton prices fell below production costs, they lost their farms to foreclosures or sold at a loss. Oil speculation was highly localized around currently producing wells or likely geological formations, and few farmers benefited directly from it. At the same time, in some eastern Oklahoma counties, nonwhite farm ownership rose in some places by as much as two-thirds. Ironically, discrimination in lending meant that people of color had to pay cash for their farms, insulating them from foreclosure. As farmers struggled in Oklahoma, they watched the oil workers and their world take over their towns. Work in coal and oil was irregular and short-lived. Workers came and went without putting down roots in the town, and their means of sociability could lead to what farmers saw as social mayhem.[30]

But it wasn't the farmers who called in the KKK. The Ku Klux Klan, resurgent since the late 1910s, hit its peak in the first half of the 1920s. Spurred by an extremely successful sales and publicity campaign, the Klan organized across the country. It found fertile soil in the West, capturing governorships in Oregon and Colorado and pervasive power elsewhere, including Oklahoma's oil and coal counties. The fierce antiradicalism of the war years and the grim economics of agriculture, lumber, and mining after them created a volatile legacy. Vigilante violence had reached new levels of acceptability during the war, and the Oklahoma governor's invocation of a Klan revival in 1919 turned out to be prescient. With dispossessed farmers heading to the cities encountering roving migrant oil and other workers, as in Tulsa, longer-term residents felt a dramatic loss of control over not just their future but also their environs. The KKK denounced immigrants, Catholics, Jews, and radicals and claimed to uphold Protestant morality, paternal authority, and American family values. Its middle-class white voters organized against what they perceived of as disorder.[31]

In the West, though the Klan committed violent acts on Blacks, it more often targeted Catholics, Asians, organized labor, the NPL, Mexicans, and hard-living whites. In California it murdered Mexican American farmworkers; in Washington it bombed Japanese farms and forcefully deported Filipino farmworkers. In the early 1920s it helped elect KKK dues-paying member Walter Pierce as Oregon's governor, and with heavy Klan influence the Oregon legislature attacked parochial schools and Japanese immigrants, including passing in 1923 the Alien Property Act, which prohibited noncitizens from owning land in the state. In Texas, as elsewhere, the Klan included many Protestant ministers, as well as police and city officials. Texans elected a Klansman to the U.S. Senate, and the Klan controlled the state legislature's lower house. In 1922 the Dallas KKK flogged sixty-eight people for moral transgressions. In Kansas, where the state membership numbered about one hundred thousand, these vigilante advocates of law and order invaded homes to stop Sunday card-playing, searched cars for liquor, and flogged violators. In Colorado the Klan co-opted the Republican Party and elected the state's governor and Denver's mayor, and in South Dakota, with the Klan in every major town, tar and featherings grew common.[32]

In oil-rich Oklahoma, Klan strongholds tended to be in the relatively prosperous towns of northeastern Oklahoma rather than the countryside. Beggs, Oklahoma, in Okmulgee County, at the center of the old Creek Nation, had about eight hundred residents in early 1918. Then came oil. By 1920 the town had over two thousand. Land adjoining producing wells had sold for $15 to $20 an acre; now it leased for over $1,000 an acre. As "roughnecks" and "roustabouts" flooded into town, so did sex workers and bootleggers. They hijacked cars, fought, and sometimes killed each other. Farmers sent their daughters out of town. But farmers did not join the Klan. Beginning in 1921, a garage manager and hotel manager, a grocer, a school principal and a teacher, a doctor and a druggist, ministers and policemen, including the chief of police, donned white robes and attacked urban oil workers and rural socialists. They kidnapped white oil field worker Norman Chesser, drove him out of town, and whipped him for neglecting his widowed mother, selling whiskey, and sporting a gun. They threatened bootleggers, dope peddlers, brothels, pimps, and unwed couples, particularly white ones. Certainly, they committed heinous violence on Blacks, beating and killing Blacks they saw as subverting the racial order, but most often the Klan targeted whites who also, by their behavior, threatened the racial order that legitimated the white man's West. White men who associated with Black men or women could be and sometimes were kidnapped and beaten.[33]

From its arrival in 1920 with Texas organizers in Tulsa, the Klan had grown rapidly in Oklahoma. In 1923, a year after the Tulsa race riot, it claimed about one hundred thousand members, or over one out of every five native-born white men of native white parentage. The Klan had members and endorsed politicians in both major parties, and word had it that the majority of state legislators were Klansmen; more had Klan support. Their raids targeted working-class whites, bootleggers, brothels and the men who patronized them, men who failed to support their families, and people involved in radical politics (including those discontented farmers) in the name of "the protection of our homes" and "the chastity of our women." They flogged native-born white Protestant women, teenagers, and men. While the Klan unmistakably associated "American" with "white," proclaiming to an audience of 2,500 gathered in Muskogee, Oklahoma, in May 1923 that "the salvation of the country today relies on the native born, white protestant Americans," by one estimate, only 3 of 147 Klan incidents between 1919 and 1923 in Oklahoma had mainly racial origins; indeed, much of the violence targeted only those misbehaving white Protestants.[34]

In 1922 rural Oklahoma's white farmers and workers revolted. Both the moderate Farmers Union and the radical Farmer-Labor Party supported Democratic Oklahoma City mayor Jack Walton for governor, and joined by labor activists, they swept him to victory. When a Klansman murdered three people in Okmulgee County, Walton declared martial law there, then in Tulsa County, and finally in the state as a whole to crush the Klan. It was not that Walton opposed white supremacy; according to Walton, "The supremacy of the white race needs no advocacy." Walton opposed, rather, the Klan's attack on religious freedom and ethnic minorities, including German Americans. "There cannot be two governments in Oklahoma while I am governor," Walton proclaimed. "When the sheriff, the county attorney, the district judge, and the jury commission are all in the hands of an organization responsible for mob activities, what can be done? You have no law, and you have no courts worthy of the name." But after the state indicted thirty-one Klansmen, and only ten months into his governorship, the Klan orchestrated Walton's impeachment and removal from office.[35]

Only a series of sexual and financial scandals within the organization and the passage of immigration restrictions at the federal level broke the Klan's hold. In 1924 Texans elected Miriam "Ma" Ferguson governor and an attorney general on an anti-Klan platform. In 1927 Oregon finally repealed the law written into its constitution (and voided by the Fourteenth and Fifteenth Amendments) that forbade Blacks from residing in the state.[36]

Spectacle

In the same year that Oregon repealed its anti-Black law, the Teapot Dome scandal reached its denouement. Albert Fall, key figure in the scandal, erstwhile senator from New Mexico, land speculator, rancher, corporate lawyer, and interventionist regarding Mexico, was not a proponent of "orderly development." He had long stood for unrestrained development of the West. Over a decade before the scandal broke, he had proclaimed himself less troubled by illegal actions of robber barons than by unexploited resources. Alarmed by the rising power of the conservation movement, in 1912 he told a journalist that conservationists and preservationists "would convert the Western settlers into a lot of peasants." They protected bears, mountain lions, and timber wolves instead of livestock, farmers, and business. Fall put reservations for forests and for Indians in the same category: equally detrimental to economic development. They kept western states impoverished. The vast federal landholdings west of the Mississippi instead belonged in the hands of state governments, which would use them to bring their territories into modern industrial development. On becoming secretary of the interior in 1921, Fall declared, "All natural resources should be made as easy of access as possible to the present generation. . . . Man can not exhaust the resources of nature and never will."[37]

The eagerness to cash in on natural resources became a spectacle in its own right. Oil became conflated with entertainment. People toured oil regions in the hopes of watching a gusher come in. People filled courtrooms at the more notorious trials. And people became part of the spectacle when they crowded into boom towns looking for leases or into tents on as-yet-undeveloped fields to be swayed by the performance of fervent salesmen. In 1919 the world's largest film company, Pathé Weekly, sent a film crew from California to Fort Worth, Texas, to film the spectacle for national audiences. Even remote areas could participate in such activities, and most oil lay in a barren and featureless, sparsely populated landscape.[38]

But when Edward Doheny discovered an oil field around what is now Dodger Stadium in Los Angeles in 1892 he opened up a new world of possibilities. Real estate salesmen turned easily to oil, applying the same techniques. People passed derricks on the way to work, saw wells on town lots, heard stories of quick riches, saw and heard of success all around them. Promoters hired men and women to canvass the neighborhoods and fill the seats on oil promotion tour buses. They drove their potential investors by mansions they claimed oil had built and mentioned Hollywood investors such as Buster Keaton, and when they reached their destination, they accepted not only Liberty bonds but also jewelry and fur coats. An August 1923 oil tour included Iowa and Missouri farmers, a New York realtor, a middle-aged female voice teacher, a mechanic, a boardinghouse mistress, an elderly man who frequently invested in oil, and many working women of modest means—those whom observing journalists described as "drab" and "ignorant." The modest means were signaled by the shift in promotion trappings from the luxurious special rail cars, oysters, crab, and roast duck of 1909 to a bus and a ham sandwich in the 1920s.[39]

But the greatest spectacle of the oil boom was the Teapot Dome scandal, which came to a head in the middle of an aberrant glut of oil, in the middle of massive speculation, and it became the touchstone of all concurrent investigations. Like the Red River hearings, the Teapot Dome hearings centered on speculation in contested oil leases, this time two prime pieces of western real estate: land in California and Wyoming that the government had set aside as naval reserves amid fears of future oil shortages. At the core of the matter lay the administration's exchange of leases on the naval reserves for contributions to both the Republican Party and former senator, now interior secretary, Albert Fall's New Mexico ranch.[40] At the core also lay notions of proper development and the role of the West in the nation.

Though the targeted participants were labeled the "Ohio Gang" in deference to President Harding's home state and the home base of his kingmaker, Attorney General Harry M. Daugherty, most of the action, protagonists, and targets were western: Fall; Doheny, who was accused of bribery and who had substantial interests in California and Mexico; and Harry Sinclair, who made his fortune as an independent speculator bucking big oil in the Oklahoma oil fields and by 1920 was opening fields in Venezuela and Colombia, operating in Mexico, Nicaragua, Costa Rica, Panama, and Angola, and reaching out for Russian oil, as well as for Teapot Dome. While Sinclair was in cahoots with the Rockefellers behind the scenes, he and Doheny forever posed as the unassuming little guys, the pioneers opening up the country. Most of the congressional investigating committee also represented western states and constituencies, including the reform senators Gerald Nye from North Dakota and George Norris, the Nebraska senator who, with Jeanette Rankin, had opposed U.S. entry into World War I, as well as the committee chairman, Thomas Walsh, like Fall a frontier lawyer and now a reform senator from Montana. Walsh and Fall tended to dress the part, sporting large mustaches and bits of western dress.[41]

This was a western showdown between the western incarnation of reform politics and those who literally capitalized on the western landscape. It was a western showdown that took place in a Washington DC courtroom, and the relationship between private investment and the West's public and Indian lands and resources was at stake, as well as the relation between speculation, law, corporate capital, and democracy. The western nature of the scandal also highlighted the increasing political power of the West, the divergent politics of westerners, and the centrality of western politics to the rest of the country and its state capacity. By 1928 both major party conventions would be held west of the Mississippi, and the victorious presidential candidate—Herbert Hoover, born in Iowa, raised in Oregon, and educated in California at Stanford University—was a westerner, as were both parties' vice presidential candidates.[42]

When Harding chose his friend and mentor, Albert Fall, as secretary of the interior, he gained a larger-than-life, quick-tempered, dramatic, and forceful cabinet member who was prone to pound the table and roar with laughter at the ceiling when facing opposition. Having sat next to Fall in the Senate and socialized extensively with him, Harding must have known. Fall had arrived in the New Mexico Territory in 1886, not long after the railroad. Like other men on the make in that era, he had first prospected and then acquired mine holdings on both sides of the New Mexico–Mexico border. He built, in addition, bank holdings and a law practice that included Colonel William C. Greene, the owner of a vast empire of timber, mines, railroads, and ranchlands in northern Mexico. In 1904 Fall moved to a sprawling ranch in southern New Mexico, opened a law office in Las Cruces, and two years later became a Republican, the dominant party of the region, moving into politics and landing in the Senate in 1912 as New Mexico became a state. Conservationist Gifford Pinchot commented, regarding Fall's appointment, "He has been with [the] exploitation gang, but not a leader," and concluded, "On the record, it would have been possible to pick a worse man for Secretary of Interior, but not altogether easy."[43]

Fall immediately moved to gratify western ideals of access to government lands and justify Pinchot's fears. As part of a general executive branch reorganization, he proposed centralizing control of the vast lumber, coal, and oil resources of Alaska in the president's hands (and, by extension, his own) to ease their development and found sympathetic congressmen to introduce his proposals; he proposed transferring the Forest Service to the Interior Department to reduce conflict between would-be homesteaders and the forest administration; he admitted he wanted to control what he called "the business end of timber sales" but not the daily forest management and got Senator William H. King of Utah to introduce such a bill. When oil was found on Navajo reservation land, Fall shifted millions of acres from the reservation to the public domain, easing the way for oil companies and redirecting any proceeds to the states and the federal government instead of the Navajo Nation. Fall also exceeded his quota of sheep grazing in the Alamo National Forest threefold, fenced land in the public domain, and threatened that the Forest Service would "rue the day" it came after him. And by sleight of hand and under the radar he managed to get the naval coal reserve in Alaska and the naval oil reserves in California and Wyoming (including Teapot Dome) transferred to his domain with the intent of opening them to private leasing.[44]

Despite the lack of clear knowledge about what went on behind the scenes, Fall's behavior left his opponents spoiling for a fight. One wrote that "an open fight on the whole conservation business would be an excellent thing. With the . . . present administration . . . out and out for big business, there is bound to be a lot of damage done secretly anyway; why not," he concluded in classic western parlance, "have a show-down." It was not just oil that was at stake. The Forest Service, too, had hopped on the development wagon and by 1922, according to historian Nancy Langston, was making such extensive concessions and had a prospectus "so enthusiastic, it almost sounded as if they were trying to sell patent medicine, not government timber."[45]

When conservationist opponents looked for allies, however, they found even progressive Republicans unsympathetic. Even the Democrat Walsh had advocated leasing the oil reserves. Progressive reformer and future presidential candidate Senator Robert LaFollette of Wisconsin managed to get a unanimous resolution through the Senate in April 1922, calling for an investigation, but it took him another year and a half to generate any action. The Senate's Committee on Public Lands and Surveys, which would oversee the investigation, had thirteen members. Only one of them, Senator Irvine L. Lenroot of Wisconsin, represented a state east of the Mississippi River. Both of New Mexico's senators and both of Montana's senators served on the committee, in addition to senators from Nebraska, Washington, North and South Dakota, Oregon, Nevada, and Wyoming. Walsh found these westerners less than enthusiastic about the work. All the western congressmen, including Walsh, as well as the targets of their investigation, favored opening public lands to private development—Walsh was upset by corruption, not by leasing.[46]

There was a case to be made for leasing Teapot Dome. Not only was oil leaking out of the dome, but adjacent property owners were already drilling. Fall argued that to ensure the oil remained in federal government hands, it had to be stored above ground, that is, it had to be drilled and harvested. But he had given the lease to Sinclair without opening competitive bidding—urgency demanded quick action, he argued. The committee was not convinced. Fall's property ambitions in New Mexico had left him deeply in debt. The committee saw Doheny's $100,000 cash loan to Fall just before gaining the lease on Teapot Dome in 1922 as a bribe, as it did Sinclair's purchase of a third interest in Fall's ranch for $233,000.[47]

The investigation gained traction in the fall of 1923, touching more and more members of Harding's cabinet: the secretary of the navy, who had given Fall the power over the reserves; the secretary of the treasury, Andrew Mellon, who had invested several hundred thousand dollars in the questionable leases; and perhaps the rest of the cabinet. The *Santa Fe New Mexican* reported that the nation was "getting a delightful picture of what a business government really is and exactly what Mr. Harding had in mind when he declared a return to 'normalcy.'" Under the stress and spotlight, committee members and their targets alike began to suffer nervous breakdowns. Many key witnesses were found to be on extended vacations, hunting in Africa or cruising the world's waters.[48]

The case played out differently for its public and its private defendants. For many of its most high profile political participants, the scandal had a lasting effect. Fall, convicted of accepting a bribe from Doheny, served his sentence in a New Mexico state prison near Santa Fe because of his chronic tuberculosis; he then lost his ranch when Doheny's oil company foreclosed. Evicted from Three Rivers, the Falls moved to their El Paso home, where Mrs. Fall supported them operating a restaurant and canning fruits and vegetables. Ironically, William McAdoo, the 1924 Democratic presidential hopeful, had moved from New York to California to distance himself from the notorious Tammany political machine. But long before the scandal broke, he had become Edward Doheny's general counsel. His connection with Doheny was among the many factors that doomed his 1924 candidacy, in which the visibility of Teapot Dome should have ensured a Democratic victory. (Eleanor Roosevelt and her friend who also happened to be Walsh's romantic interest drove through the country in a campaign car with a large teapot perched on top.)[49]

The private speculators fared better. Sinclair's resources vastly outclassed those of his federal prosecutors. There was a seductiveness to these speculators that could prove fatal to federal investigations. The federal agent sent to investigate C. C. Julian swallowed his story hook, line, and sinker and then went to work for him. Sinclair, who had perhaps hoped to have the whole Republican Party in his pocket, certainly had the Wyoming judge who presided over his first Teapot Dome trial in 1925. Everyone loved a big-spending speculator, particularly in oil-dependent, Republican Wyoming. There both jobs and politics depended on crude, and Sinclair and his allies controlled the largest fields and behaved like congenial barons. According to Teapot Dome historian Laton McCartney, Sinclair "would come into a bar in Cheyenne's Cherokee Strip and buy rounds for everyone in the place until closing time." Before the trial, Sinclair courted presiding judge T. Blake Kennedy's "closest friend," taking him and his wife on a Caribbean cruise and artfully losing large sums to him at poker, as much as $40,000 in one game. The judge had headed the Wyoming Republican delegation that nominated Harding. Harding, in turn, had appointed Kennedy to the bench. It is perhaps not surprising that Kennedy upheld the legitimacy of Sinclair's Teapot Dome lease.[50]

On appeal, once out of Wyoming's oil dominion, Sinclair fared less well, and in 1927 at the U.S. Supreme Court, both Doheny and Sinclair lost their leases and the money they had spent developing them. But that is all they lost. None of Sinclair's behavior in Wyoming and none of Doheny's behavior in taking the leases were condemned. It was only Fall's actions, including accepting a bribe, that invalidated their leases. Sinclair did ultimately serve a brief sentence, but it was for his contempt of the Senate committee and his jury tampering in a connected case. He emerged from jail unscathed and unrepentant, his fortune and corporation intact. Doheny never even did jail time. Senator George W. Norris had claimed that "it was impossible to convict a hundred million dollars in the United States," and Doheny's case seemed to prove it.[51]

There had been times, en route to Teapot Dome, when it seemed the state itself was a speculator—in the Indian agents who leased

Kiowa lands in the Red River where, despite advice to the contrary, the government receiver drilled wells of his own; in Forest Service leases to companies that regularly defaulted on junk bonds; and in Albert Fall's actions. Harvesting lumber in national forests required enormous capital outlay for the building of railroad lines and mills; in one case, local residents accused Forest Service employees of "colluding in fraud" by offering the successful bidding company low prices on a contract the company never intended to meet. What the courts seem to set out, though, and the people in the succeeding elections seemed to validate was that the state's job was to construct a speculator citizen and arena, not to be a speculator. Thus, newly elected Hoover, himself a product of the trans-Mississippi West, promised in 1929 that the government would no longer trade in oil leases.[52]

Making a "Modern" West: Indian Oil and Indian Citizenship

Once it became clear that anyone and everyone in the United States—citizens, lawyers, doctors, congressmen, widows, widowers, and everyone else—could be lured into unwise and fraudulent speculations and consumption, the notion that Indians were somehow especially vulnerable and required special protections was harder to sustain.[53] Notions of blood quantum and racial thinking linking certain populations to market savvy cracked around the edges, and progressive congressmen had difficulty maintaining consistent arguments. They tried to balance the drive to develop the region and notions of personal liberty with their responsibility over their Indian wards and in the face of mass consumption, youth cultures, and rampant, if not rugged, individualism.

In part the problem was the paucity of easy answers and the plethora of competing parties. Unlike the Five Civilized Tribes, the Osage held their subsurface rights collectively, as a tribe. They shared collectively in the income from oil leases, production, and rentals. That income was disbursed in shares to officially enrolled members of the tribe. Disturbed by the degree to which these increasingly and newly rich Indians had accrued debt, leading to land loss and endangering their future solvency, in 1921 Congress passed legislation withholding all but $4,000 a year from each enrolled member of the Osage tribe and entrusted the Bureau of Indian Affairs to invest the remainder in trust (often in Liberty bonds), negotiate debt reduction on the often questionable discriminatory and extortionate sums outstanding, and shift the terms by which credit could be extended. While this law meant that the income for an Osage family of four still exceeded that of most U.S. families—a continual sore point to their congressional interlocutors—it cut the Osage disposable annual income by about half, leading to many unhappy Osage members.[54]

But there was a work-around: an Osage deemed incompetent to manage his own affairs was appointed a guardian under Oklahoma's county courts. Once under county court supervision, the Indians passed out of the jurisdiction of the federal government. A flood of would-be guardians, speculating in Indians instead of oil, promised their future wards greater access to their funds and, by collaborating with local merchants and bankers, could and often did soak their wards, completely free of federal supervision. Even more alarmingly and not infrequently, they married very young Osage girls (something officials and witnesses labeled "a natural tendency of the white people" "since the Osage Indians are receiving a considerable amount of money"), and not infrequently they murdered their wards for their rights to the oil. Estimates of the number murdered vary from the BIA's official estimate of twenty-four to scholars and investigators, reaching behind evidence of cover-up, who believe the number lies in "scores if not the hundreds" or perhaps even the thousands.[55]

When the BIA moved to exert more authority and supervise the guardians, however, its unrestrained paternalism (and its channeling of "surplus" funds to northern Baptist philanthropies on the reservation) evoked its own resistance among the wounded white Oklahoma bankers, lawyers, merchants, and car dealers whose trade suffered and who insisted the money should be spent locally rather than on federal bonds. One such wounded guardian wrote his senator, tying together the disparate threads of oil, western development, race, and Teapot Dome: "It strikes us that any man with good judgment would know that this is a white man's country and progress and civilization depends upon the white man and the white civilization. . . . There is much danger in piling up large amounts of money where Doheny, Sinclair, Daugherty, McAdoo,

Fall, and the balance of the high-ups may make a raid thereon; better far the money be placed in the hands of the common guardian under the legal supervision of the State courts supplemented by the agency supervision and not discretionary power."[56]

Struggling to be heard above the din were the Indians themselves. Often they had different notions of virtue, property and ethics, kin and philanthropy, a different vision of the "modern" West. It fell to the House Committee on Indian Affairs to sort out the snarl. The committee's chairman, Homer P. Snyder of New York, whose background was in banking and who would later introduce the measure that granted all Indians, even those on reservations, citizenship, the issue was liberty. "What greater liberty can a man have who has the control of the expenditure of all of his funds?" he asked.[57] This definition of liberty was perfectly consonant with the 1920s' direct economic democracy.

Yet there was no sentiment in Congress simply to hand over control of the funds to those who owned them, the Osage. The federal government had already, by the early 1920s, separated political from economic citizenship. The Supreme Court had upheld the notion that conferring citizenship on Indians in no way disturbed their status as wards of the government. It did not confer full property rights. Most framed the issue as continued responsibility for Indians' well-being in a rapacious world. As one committee member put it, "Now they are rich, but they may be poor, sometime."[58] In preparation for that rainy day, admittedly some generations hence, BIA commissioner Charles Burke wanted to ensure that the Indians had sufficient funds in reserve and sufficient habits of thrift and industry that they would not depend on government largesse.

But the issue went beyond avoiding future government expense. Economic citizenship had to be earned. Indians had to demonstrate thrift and industry. And congressmen gave them a severely limited arena in which to do so. The training was not for speculator citizenship. It was for farming. That the Osage were heading to town, buying cars, and retiring to California was not seen as evidence of assimilation to modern America. Indians, it seemed, were not destined to be part of modern America in the view of the 1920s Congresses. It did not even matter that whites were also fleeing the farm, that farm consolidation occurred in Oklahoma along with most of the rest of the United States, or that the Osage land was not even suited to farming. Farming, to these senators and congressmen with rural roots, was still the location of virtue, and in an age where theories of evolution spectacularly defeated creationism, "primitive" Indians could not leap over the stage of farming directly to modern America with its easy living and $9,000 Pierce-Arrow automobiles. Congressman Everette Howard of Oklahoma wanted "to call attention to the fact that it has been the policy of the Government, as far back as I know, that the first thing they ever did for the Indians was to hire farmers to teach them farming; and even if they lose a little money on farming, it is a good thing."[59]

Many observers, indeed, seemed deeply invested in the notion that high living was unnatural for Indians. When itinerant Creek laborer Jackson Barnett became "the world's richest Indian," at first nothing in his life changed. Despite the oil flowing from his allotment, he continued to house and socialize with African American tenants, conduct savvy trades in ponies and livestock, and eat and stay with his mother's kin. Eventually he came to the attention of a twice-married independent and attractive white woman two decades his junior. What followed was a tug-of-war between Anna Laura Lowe (age thirty-nine; Barnett was sixty-four) and the Bureau of Indian Affairs over Barnett's fortune and his person, with both sides kidnapping and cajoling Barnett, calling forth contradictory witnesses to testify to his mental acuity and desires, claiming to be best able to look to his well-being, and embroiling the estate in a Dickensian mire of litigation.

While the presiding judge expressed skepticism that the implicitly primitive Barnett would want to live in a mansion or ride in a chauffeured limousine, Barnett testified to his pride in having a home with electric lights, a bathtub, a radio, a piano, a phonograph, and an oil paint portrait of himself. He called Lowe "a good wife." "Indians get married like other people," he claimed. "Why don't you let us alone?"[60]

All this is not to say that there were not differences in values between many of the "traditional" Indians and the 1920s individualist consumer binge. Barnett and others like him behaved in ways around consumption that their white observers found wasteful and irrational. One Osage Indian repeatedly bought good horses and furniture, only to give them away.[61] Another bought cars for his children, finding it difficult to deny them anything. If they had enough money, they did not haggle over the price of what they desired. Whites viewed such behavior as evidence of mental deficiency. But what seemed to whites evidence of incompetence, waste, foolishness, and degradation better fit with traditional Indian communal values, kinship exchange, and clan loyalties.

Indians walked a tricky line asserting their own views from a position of dramatic disempowerment, even when wealthy. There were plenty of people and groups ready to speak for them. Indians rarely testified themselves. When Osage farmer John Abbott testified at the hearings on Osage restrictions, he began, "It is very seldom an Indian has anything to say to such a distinguished gathering." Abbott had no guardian; he came as part of a seventy-seven-member delegation pleading for justice, supervision of guardians, and more judicious dispersal of funds to those without guardians. Abbott and other Osage who testified resented being badgered about whether they "worked" and the degree of their holdings; they asserted their property rights, they asserted their rights to greater federal accountability for their funds, and they often displayed a business ability that the committee admitted equaled its own. One of the Osage concluded, "At this time the Government keeps my money waiting for rainy days. I might die before rain would come."[62]

So why did the Osage make little headway in gaining control over their own funds? Not everyone was comfortable with the speculator state and its pioneer speculator heroes such as Sinclair, Doheny, and the claimants at the Red River. Already, artists and cultural rebels disillusioned by the technology and carnage of World War I had turned to what they invented as the premodern in Africa and the United States. They looked to those traditional Indian values as a counterweight. This interest in Indians became broader and its target more focused in 1922, when Congress considered the Bursum bill, which would have legitimated the property titles of non-Pueblo squatters on Pueblo land (see the next chapter). The General Federation of Women's Clubs led the charge with their two million members and powerful publicity, headed by the chair of its Indian welfare committee, Californian Stella Atwood, and her researcher, John Collier, who would go on to head the Bureau of Indian Affairs under Franklin Roosevelt. Albert Fall called it government by propaganda and accused the organization of being funded by Moscow—that nonspeculator state. Atwood, Collier, and their allies, including Mary Austin, Charles Lummis, and other artists and writers, argued that the United States needed to preserve the Pueblos for the spiritual salvation of the United States. Nothing better illustrates the juxtapositions the case highlights than when the Pueblo Indian delegation, en route to testify before Congress, toured the New York Stock Exchange in January 1923.[63] They were the perfect foil to the speculator state—they and not the radical direct democracy of the 1910s. Instead, a Pueblo nation characterized by communal values, an island in a sea of self-interest, was essential to retain. And unlike the radical mass movements, it could, indeed had to, be retained apart from the main event. And so in the 1920s the West epitomized both the terrain of speculation and the terrain of its exception.

8

Land

On January 15, 1923, seventeen Pueblo Indians, exhausted, missing their families, and worried about how their struggling farms were faring in their absence, testified before the U.S. House of Representatives Committee on Indian Affairs. They had traveled across the country, scraping together money, one Pueblo lending to another, to testify against a bill they saw as threatening their very existence. They had stopped in Chicago and visited New York. These were the chosen delegates of the Pueblo peoples, who, faced with a crisis, had held the first all-Pueblo conference. They, in turn, chose Pablo A'Beyta as their spokesman. He had better English than the others. He was joined in testimony before the Senate subcommittee of the Committee on Public Lands and Surveys by a chief who spoke through an interpreter. None of the others were called to testify. They counted, in addition, on their lawyer, Francis Wilson, and a priest, Father Schuster, to argue their case. They wanted to go home. They left Washington before they could testify at the House hearings, where John Collier and General Federation of Women's Clubs member Stella Atwood would speak on their behalf.[1]

What brought the Pueblos to such arousal locally and sent them to Washington was a set of bills generated by declining beef and agricultural prices, water and land disputes, and the desire of those in office to reap a profit from the land and enable others to do likewise. The bills' proponents wanted to develop, in short, the land of the West in much the same fashion that they hoped to develop the oil—through both speculation and capital-intensive production, large-scale and small, facilitated with government funds in the name of modernity and opportunity for the nation's citizenry.

Oil had little place in originary U.S. myth, but land certainly did. The promise of self-sufficiency and the virtues of the yeoman farmer warred with the lure of profits and the promise of participation in modern consumer life. The contestants were many—Pueblos, Japanese produce farmers, Akimel O'odham, Apaches, World War I veterans, Hispanos, ranchers, and others—aiming to determine the nature, function, and ownership of western land, the society that produced and was produced by it, and what it meant for the nation.

Federal agricultural and land policy in the 1920s grew out of this contest, as well as from the horrors of food shortages during the First World War, the spectacle of the starving Belgians in particular, whose salvation had made Herbert Hoover an international humanitarian hero. Not all contestants had a level field. The agricultural West—less the tenants than the landowners and investors and the merchants who served them—enjoyed anomalous national political power in the 1920s. Rural districts were overrepresented in the House of Representatives because of the era's rapid population shift to urban areas as yet unaccounted for in redistricting, and the West was overrepresented in the Senate relative to its population. New coalitions began targeting Congress rather than the presidency with the idea that they could make congressmen accountable to a farm bloc and create a bipartisan agricultural bloc in Congress that could get legislation—including irrigation, natural reserves, and anti-Japanese measures—enacted.[2] They did not, however, speak with one voice. Hearings in Washington DC and disputes on the ground bore witness to the continuing tension between fostering the merging of agriculture and business models and the distaste for such mergers and between the speculator citizen on the investing side and the desire to stabilize markets for producers.[3] The result not only materially altered the western landscape but also produced an agricultural system of capital and labor that lasted into the twenty-first century. This chapter turns first to the Pueblos and their allies, then to federal irrigation projects and farm labor, and finally to alternative models in order to understand the landscape of opportunity that federal farm policy, farmers, and workers created in the 1920s.

Alternative Western Visions: Native Lands, Native Rights, Native Allies

Those 1923 hearings had their origins in the postwar depression. As with agriculture, the beef industry had experienced record prices during World War I's food shortages only to have prices plummet afterward, falling to less than half the wartime price of $14.50 per hundredweight of beef. New Mexico senator Holm O. Bursum of Socorro County was among the suffering cattlemen. His compatriot, former New Mexico senator and now secretary of the interior Albert Fall, urged Bursum to introduce a bill to the Senate opening disputed Pueblo lands to developers by quieting title. Both men were land speculators, as well as cattlemen, and both saw the issue as keeping capital flowing into New Mexico.[4] In some ways, the bill was just another piece of Fall's land grab from Indian territories, but this grab included water rights, and it mobilized a powerful opposing coalition that blindsided its proponents.

Even undisputed Anglo settlement had threatened Pueblo water supplies by appropriating water that legally belonged to downstream users with prior water rights. Bursum's bill would require Pueblos to apply for purchase of additional water rights on the same terms as other New Mexicans even on land the Pueblos already owned but hadn't cultivated, land they needed as their population grew. The Pueblos already ran short of water. In the summer of 1922, Tesuque had not a single day of irrigation water. The Pueblos' attorney wanted such bills to include provision of water for the Pueblos if they would lose water under the bill. Money as a substitute would not work. The Pueblos needed to be able to "build additional ditches . . . so they can get water to put on their land." "They are not individual Indians that own land in severalty," their attorney, Wilson, explained. "They own the grants together."[5]

To the Pueblos, the bill not only jeopardized their economic future but also abrogated their right to self-determination. The Pueblo governors gathered, consulted, and published "An Appeal to the People of the United States" in the nation's newspapers and sent a copy to Congress. Their advocate, John Collier, investigator for the General Federation of Women's Clubs (GFWC) and its Indian welfare committee, wrote in *Sunset Magazine,* "It is too late for the Indians to save themselves by ferocity. They can not vote;

they have no status under the law; if there is no fair play and no imagination in the American people, when confronted by facts such as are stated here then the Indian can do one thing only—disperse, or die."[6]

Their attorney admitted that such provision of water for the Pueblos might interfere in a small way with the waters for the federally developed Elephant Butte Reservoir and its irrigating customers, which would require some negotiations between the BIA and the Reclamation Service. At particular issue were irrigable lands adjacent to the Rio Grande in northern New Mexico.[7] One set of communal irrigators—defined as "traditional" and therefore inefficient and undercapitalized—would come up against the other, the capital-intensive "modern" government showpiece.

With varying degrees of gentility, the congressional hearings resembled a mud-slinging fest in which the unfortunately and unintentionally prescient commissioner of Indian Affairs declared that if the charges leveled by Collier and the other publicists were true, then the officials involved, including New Mexican citizen, former judge, three-time senator, and now secretary of the interior Albert Fall, should be impeached. Some members of the House committee, notably William J. Sears from Florida, who had been trying to interest his constituents for years in the plight of the Seminoles, and Elmer O. Leatherwood from Utah, tended to be sympathetic, but the louder voices, including Olger B. Burtness (North Dakota) and the chairman, as hard-working committeemen, were livid that Collier accused them of breaking faith with Indians and being in league with "certain land-grabbing interests." They were particularly outraged not by Collier's *Sunset Magazine* article but by bulletin 81 of the National Popular Government League. The article claimed, "Land grabbing has long been the outdoor sport of the master leaders of the white race. . . . If in the grabbing you have to shoot, starve, break the hearts of or annihilate a few thousand red men, more or less, corrupt your own Government, smash treaties, hamstring your beneficent bureaus, make national honor a joke, and canting hypocrites of us all—it is unfortunate, but can not be helped." The bulletin claimed that the GFWC's Stella Atwood "branded the whole policy of the Indian Bureau as 'inhumane, expensive to the taxpayer, and largely fruitless of good results to the Indian,' and asked for 'a policy of economic and business common sense.'" Charles H. Burke, commissioner of Indian Affairs, called the article and its ilk libel. Secretary of Interior Fall, with some extravagance, claimed, "Such propaganda as this, if allowed to go entirely unchecked, will eventually break down this democratic Government of ours." Together, they accused Collier of being a self-interested con man.[8]

Committee chairman Homer Snyder of New York seemed particularly steamed at the intrusion of the GFWC (which had funded Collier's investigation) into affairs of state. Stella Atwood spearheaded the intrusion. She had grown up in St. Cloud, Minnesota, in the late nineteenth century, when Dakotas still gathered nearby. Her parents had witnessed Indian massacres, and her physician father's reaction had been to enlist her help in studying Native religion and society. By 1917, when she simultaneously founded the first local and the first district GFWC-affiliated Indian welfare committee, she had lived in Riverside, California, for over twenty years. There she had devoted herself as a clubwoman to education and settlement work with troubled youth. Then in 1916, while attending the annual convention of the Southern California District of the California Federation of Women's Clubs, she had heard Dr. Horace Porter speak passionately on the state lawsuit threatening the Soboba Indians, whose reservation lay near Riverside and who had been "the very Indians among whom Mrs. Jackson lived while writing Ramona," the wildly popular late nineteenth-century romance that brought the plight of Indians to national attention. It was his suggestion that each women's club establish an Indian welfare committee so that "Helen Hunt Jackson's dying plea [to save the Indians] be not forgotten."[9]

Atwood had first focused on the problems of the nearby reservations of the Morongos, the Cahuillas, and the Sobobas. When the United States established the military draft that year, Riverside city officials placed her on the draft board to deal with the Indians, exempted as noncitizens. As she listened to the stories of the Indians who came before the board, she heard of arbitrary arrests and federal control. She learned that their citizenship status made them ineligible for various legal protections and representative government, and she began investigating past legal cases and attending meetings with federal Indian agents. She had become an Indian advocate.[10]

In 1918 the California Federation of Women's Clubs (CFWC) established a state-level Indian welfare committee, headed by Atwood's close friend, and by 1919 the CFWC was urging its California affiliates to form local committees to investigate local Indian conditions, particularly using their influence against widespread county practices of refusing aged and indigent Indians admission to county hospitals and planning to lobby Congress for legislation "towards redeeming our long neglected promises to the 'landless Indians.'" In 1921, after Atwood petitioned the national executive board of the GFWC, that body formed a standing committee on Indian welfare, electing Atwood to chair it. Soon after, a high-ranking California clubwoman introduced Atwood to her friend John Collier, and within weeks Atwood had secured the financial support to hire Collier as an investigator of Indian conditions and pending legislation at state and national levels. According to Atwood, the GFWC hoped "to cooperate with the government in a sustained effort toward keeping for the Indians the land which they still possess and getting back for them the land of which they have been illegally dispossessed, and toward fostering the Indian arts and crafts" as a way to improve Indians' economic conditions. Collier credited the California clubwomen with his commitment to Indian reform. Collier concluded, "If one desired to make out a case for feminism . . . he could not find a better foundation for it than to contrast the action of American women toward the Indian with that of the American man." Collier and the clubwomen agreed that cultural preservation, assimilation, and greater Indian autonomy could coexist.[11] The dispute, in short, brought into question the entire structure and rationale of U.S. Indian policy in the West.

With the national enfranchisement of women only two years old in 1922, Collier repeatedly invoked the power of the GFWC's two million voters, who expected remedial action on the matter. The House committee members in turn testily and repeatedly asked how many members the GFWC really had, whom they claimed to represent, "whether they are here actually representing a great number of people as it is supposed that they are or whether they are just here on account of the salary they are paid for attempting to defeat legislation." They implicitly impugned the integrity of Stella Atwood, who received no salary, regarding the use of moneys raised. Snyder snarled, "I doubt the Indians will ever get a greater percentage of the money you raise than the $400 they've gotten of the $8800 you've raised so far." Committee member Alice Robertson, a Republican congresswoman from Oklahoma (and an antisuffragist), yielded to no person in her knowledge of Indian affairs; outraged at the accusations and depiction of the Pueblos, she challenged the quality of Atwood's research and her nerve. When Atwood explained that her committee had hired Collier because Atwood felt "I could not go out and go from place to place like a man could, perhaps, Miss Robertson," Robertson shot back, "I have done it," to which Atwood could only reply, "But you are a very unusual woman, you know." Committee members badgered Atwood and refused to let her ask a question.[12]

Instead of focusing on the evidence of conditions among the Pueblos, the committee became obsessed with the governance structure of the GFWC. Regardless of Robertson's presence on the committee, and despite the earlier suffrage victories in the West, it was as though the clubwomen were out of place, had overstepped the proper bounds of their sphere in challenging congressional action. Burke admitted, "I have thought it a great many times, that there is not a Pueblo Indian in New Mexico, or a woman in the State of California who could be of much assistance in working out a bill to deal with this intricate and complicated question involving the titles of the Pueblos in New Mexico." In this way Burke linked Indians of both sexes and women of all races as people who had no place in such congressional debates, as incapable of understanding, though Indians, at least, were direct parties to the issue.[13]

Since multiple parties had attacked the Bursum bill in and out of Congress, and even the committee chair confessed, "I do not understand that anybody is here justifying the Bursum bill," the issue was the new intrusion of a female voting bloc into waters that had nothing directly to do, unlike legislation on female citizenship and the Children's Bureau, with what the dominant suffrage crusaders had identified as municipal housekeeping and women's sphere. It is not surprising that this first intrusion's spearhead came from the West, where women had had the vote for longer than their eastern sisters. And the congressmen could not know that there would be no avalanche of female-sponsored reform legislation on every issue under the sun to follow. They did know, and they were not wrong, that this particular crusade threatened, as future Secretary of the Interior Harold Ickes later judged it had, to change "the course of Indian history, and Indian policy." Collier himself characterized the 1934 Indian Reorganization Act as "the culmination of that which Mrs. Atwood, and many others had struggled for."[14]

Those others, of course, included Indians. This was far from the first attempt by the Pueblos to defend their lands and titles, a project stretching back four centuries. Most recently they had waged the Tesuque war. According to a witness testifying before the congressional committee, in early 1922 a man named Newman had bought land at Tesuque, part of which had title dating back eighty to one hundred years and part only fifteen to twenty years. He claimed three thousand acres, all but sixty-two of which were heavily disputed. Newman let the Indians at Tesuque know he planned to fence the three thousand acres. The Indians, alarmed, "came out in a crowd, with their axes and shovels and hammers . . . and tore down the fence. . . . And, not satisfied with that work, they passed on to the land of a man named Healy, . . . an ex-marine." According to his own testimony, Healy "became angry and told them if they didn't get off at once I would shoot the hell out of them, and, being angry, my voice carried quite a ways and I had a reply all up and down the skirmish line, 'You go to hell.'" Healy told them to stay put until he fetched guns and ammunition. Healy hopped in his flivver, headed the six miles into Santa Fe, and rounded up "a couple of bandoliers of ammunition and with a couple of repeating rifles, determined to protect his own land." It was only the speedy action of Francis Wilson that convinced the Indians to go home about five minutes before Healy returned. Conflict was similarly narrowly avoided at Taos.[15]

Despite the fracas, Pueblo advocates insisted the Pueblos had no interest in disputing titles in the local towns, including Taos, or in dispossessing non-Pueblos with legitimate title. They simply wanted justice. Meanwhile, hundreds of non-Pueblo claimants, including a great many of those referred to in the hearings as "Mexican," were threatened with eviction.[16]

At issue, in part, was the doctrine of adverse possession: a person could claim legitimate title simply by inhabiting a piece of land for a set number of years, as few as ten years, if no one had contested that title. But what constituted contestation? If Pueblos had tried repeatedly to contest such claims and been rebuffed or refused their day in court or been delayed beyond the statute of limitations, did that matter? Sympathetic committee member Sears compared the Pueblo situation to that of his state's Seminole Indians, who, when faced with squatters, found none to litigate for them. In New Mexico a respected state historian claimed he never found a case where Indians obtained justice in New Mexico's state or territorial courts. Half a dozen Hispano witnesses would appear against three or four Indian ones; since Indians had no right to vote for anyone except the mayordomo of the irrigation ditch, the courts proved more responsive to the Hispanos, who, at that point, still controlled New Mexico's politics.[17]

The congressmen and the witnesses from the Bureau of Indian Affairs repeatedly pointed to their own good faith and the efficacy of their efforts and those of the Bureau of Indian Affairs within the constraints of federal budgets. They referred to recent committee visits to investigate conditions on myriad reservations, to the reversal of the long decline in Indian populations, to the hospitals and schools, and to the financial investment in agriculture, stock raising, wells, and irrigation that the federal government had made in the tribes and on the reservations. They pointed to funds that the federal government had spent that were unreimbursed by the tribes in kind or cash. They pointed out that "Indians are bank presidents, judges, public officials, lawyers, teachers, doctors, actors, storekeepers, manufacturers, clerks, salesmen, trained nurses, artists, authors; in short, they are successfully making their way in all the commercial and professional branches." Arizona representative Carl Hayden defended the earnestness and dedication of the universally low-paid employees of the Indian Service and its commissioner, responsible for over two hundred thousand members of over one hundred different tribes widely spread across the country, managing for them close to $1 billion worth of property.[18]

The committee's opponents contested none of their numbers. Despite this consensus on statistics, there remained no consensus at all on the impact of these efforts and the condition of daily life on the reservations. The congressional view of the positive promise of federal policy dominated in 1920, but by the end of the decade, the increasing attention drawn to Indian affairs by groups like the GFWC culminated in the federally commissioned 1928 Meriam Report, whose judgment would be grim. In the meantime, opposing groups would dispute the grounds of judgment and fault and the ultimate appropriate goals of federal-Indian relations. The situation of the Pueblos—lacking water or having other diminishing resources, scrambling to find other sources of income, increasingly sending men off reservation for wage work where they faced job and wage discrimination, leasing lands for grazing, marketing traditional crafts or practices and transforming them by doing so—was pervasive among Indians in the American West. By the early 1920s it was clear that a policy based on the idea that Indians would simply disappear was inadequate to a situation in which Indian populations were, in fact, growing.[19]

To Collier and many of the pueblos' residents, failure to provide additional land and water would mean more migration for work, and "the absence of the young men and women for periods of years will mean the break-up of the moral and spiritual life of the communities." While many in and out of the government supported that outcome, to Collier, the issue was one of choice. Give the Indians enough land that they could choose whether to stay on the land or "readjust their economic life. . . . [L]et them choose. . . . There is no reason on earth why the Pueblo should not take in the essential modern aspects and still keep their old customs." "In the delegation that came to Washington the other day," he continued, "there were Indian representatives who spoke perfect English and have refused to wear blankets but there were perfectly good Indians who still had long hair and wore blankets."[20]

In these hearings on the Bursum and related bills, the congressional conversation turned on the worthiness of the Pueblos themselves and not only on the worthiness of the Pueblos' defenders and their rights claims. To Representative Hayden, everything that counted for success came from whites—even irrigation, ignoring centuries-old practices. Who owned the land in the West became entangled with who *should* own the land. As with contests over oil resources and the creation of the citizen speculator, the issue was in part the nature of progress and modernity, of the future of the nation itself.

Those defending Anglo possession of part of Tesuque's grant complained, "When we hear so much about the excellent qualities of these people I say that facts disprove it in many instances." That not all of the 2,500 irrigable acres of the grant were irrigated "is the result of the slothfulness of somebody, and I think the slothfulness of the Indians themselves."[21]

The connection between access to land and water and cultural preservation lay at the heart of the hearings. When the Indian Office built a dam at Zuni, the Zunis quadrupled the land they had under cultivation. The issue was not laziness. What was sloth to the government was to the Pueblos avoiding what had already proven elsewhere to be a treacherous slide into largely commercial agriculture, relatively capital intensive on marginal land. The Pueblos had little capital and less desire to enter an individualistic market economy. Collier understood that the protection of Pueblo communalism and semisubsistence agriculture and the autonomy of Pueblo culture and their existence as a people was all of a piece—their economic decisions were bound up in their culture, including their dances and their religious and secret sacred practices. Even when those practices seemed obscene to outsiders, protecting them was "American," to Collier. "We have religious liberty," he insisted, "and these Pueblo religions are older than Christianity."[22] To Collier, the connection between access to water and freedom of religion was obvious. Removal of water mirrored the nineteenth-century removal of buffalo in an attempt to force buffalo-hunting tribes to conform to Anglo cultural models not only of production and consumption but also of family formation and, inescapably, religious practices that were not cordoned off for either Anglos or Indians into some separate compartment but deeply implicated throughout their mode of living.

By contrast, Burke, as head of the Bureau of Indian Affairs, saw assimilation as essential, bringing primitive peoples into the modern era, making possible their existence independent of the U.S. government. As the tourist industry began to exploit and exoticize Indian dances and ceremonies, Burke attempted to close them down. To Burke, that popular attention—even if lucrative—damaged the long-term assimilation of the Indians. Like Collier, he recognized that religious practices permeated every aspect of Indian life, and he repeatedly urged his superintendents to restrict or even repress Indian dances the BIA found indecent, to forbid children under five years of age from participating or even watching traditional dances, and to get the Indians to stop giving away their possessions. When deemed necessary, the BIA used armed force, including against the Hopis, in an attempt to end their religious practices.[23]

The congressional committees, like most of the country, including even Indian advocacy groups and the GFWC, were riven on the issue of assimilation versus autonomy. Most, though not all, on the committee remained convinced of the virtue of their own practices. The Indians' unwillingness to adopt capital-intensive, market-oriented farming worked against their claim to water and land. But the question went beyond agricultural practices. Legitimate land and water claims seemed to rest on other virtues. Woven into the debate were Indian health practices (did they shun reservation doctors?), Indian pursuit of wage labor, Indian complaints relative to the purported stoicism of desperate southern white cotton farmers whom the boll weevil had landed "in practically the same state of affairs that you have described the Indians to be in," and Indian patriotism. "How many of these young men went into the war?" asked Miss Robertson, a question that, even more than the medical questions, seemed to have little direct bearing on the issue of land titles.[24]

Representative Hayden claimed that his constituents represented "the civilizing spirit of America and to whom the lack of progress among Indians is an abomination." Indians, in this view, contributed little or nothing to progress; in fact, they burdened those who did contribute by withholding resources. It was "the white people of the West who are bearing the burden of State building." Congress owed it to them, "in all fairness," to provide funds "for road construction, irrigation projects, and every other form of development in the Indian country."[25]

As had become clear in the disputes over oil resources and the land that went with them, one source of contention was whether the United States resided on land taken from Indians, with Indians retaining small bits of what had been their larger domain, or whether Indians resided on land generously set aside for them by the U.S. government. Indians, understandably, favored the former view. John Abbott (Osage) testified, "No man can convince me that the Government ever gave the Osage Indians a piece of land. You gave us a piece of paper. That is all you gave us. The land belongs to us; handed down from our ancestors."[26]

The question was tied up in notions of sovereignty and citizenship. From at least the era of the contentious 1850s, when ideas of citizenship had become entangled in the rights or lack thereof of enslaved people, the question of whether Indians were citizens or subjects of the United States had come before Congress. Were they, in the words of Caleb Cushing, U.S. attorney general in 1856, "constituent members of the political sovereignty," or were they akin to people in an occupied land? The 1866 Civil Rights Act had excluded "Indians not taxed" from birthright citizenship, but the Fourteenth Amendment, after furious debate, had omitted the phrase, with the understanding that Indians with whom the United States made treaties were neither subjects nor citizens. Five years later, in 1871, Congress decided to end treaty-making with Indians, that "no Indian nation or tribe within the territory of the United States shall be acknowledged or recognized as an independent nation, tribe, or power with whom the United States may contract by treaty" but that existing treaties were still enforceable. As late as 1884, John Elk, who had severed all tribal relations and lived among whites, was denied the right to vote in local elections in Omaha, Nebraska, when the Supreme Court ruled against Indians' birthright citizenship. Three years later came the Dawes Severalty Act, bestowing citizenship on Indians who accepted the break-up of their communally held reservations into individually held parcels. Teddy Roosevelt in 1901 had called this allotment policy the "mighty pulverizing engine to break up the tribal mass."[27]

And, indeed, by 1901 some sixty thousand Indians had become citizens of the United States under its provisions. Additional provisions continued to chip away at tribal identity and shift Indians to U.S. citizenship, including the abolition of Indian Territory in forming the state of Oklahoma in 1907, which made all Indians in the former Indian Territory U.S. citizens; the grant of citizenship status to children of white citizen fathers; the 1919 congressional offer of citizenship to honorably discharged Indian veterans of the Great War; and in 1921 the extension of citizenship to all members of the Osage Tribe. By the early 1920s, some two-thirds of Indians in the United States were U.S. citizens. At the same time as these debates over Pueblo lands and water rights, Congress began to consider bills submitted by the Office of Indian Affairs to grant citizenship to the rest, regardless of their tribal status, their place of residence, or the nature of their land tenure.[28]

Just what would citizenship offer? Citizenship for the region's Mexican descendants had been guaranteed by the Treaty of Guadalupe Hidalgo. Yet citizenship had proven no protection against dispossession. Having lost the vastly greater part of their holdings to Anglos already, in the 1920s many of the contests over land titles occurred not between Anglos and Pueblos but between Spanish- or Mexican-descent farmers and their Pueblo neighbors. Witnesses and congressmen constantly posed "the Mexicans and the Americans" as landowners in the contest with the Indians, and when they referred instead only to "white" men, it was clear that Mexicans fell on the "white" side of the line. But the waters were muddy. The blurry lines resolved inconsistently to place the "Spanish Americans" or "Mexicans" into the same camp as the "Americans." When it turned out that their agricultural practices partook of communal elements and shied away from market dependency, they could wind up exiled from both the "progressive" Americans and the "Pueblos."[29]

In northern New Mexico, Hispanos, too, held land communally and largely steered clear of capital-intensive market dependence. But there was, as yet, little popular affection for them.[30] The irony of a bill meant to foster Anglo, capital-intensive development by pitting two communally oriented semisubsistence sets of farmers against one another was lost on all participants. In this contest, the Pueblos would come out marginally ahead, and the Hispanos would suffer further loss of land on their land base, already decimated by decades of Anglo encroachment.

Amid these discussions about progress, land, and rights, the United States reversed course and granted citizenship to all Native

Americans, no longer requiring them to give up tribal affiliation and take up individual landholding. The extension of citizenship to all Indians in 1924 seems at first glance oddly out of step with the times, given the passage that year of the harshly restrictive immigration acts that embedded concepts of race and racial inferiority into national policy to foster the eugenic shaping of the polity, denying immigrant status altogether to Asians and dramatically reducing the possibilities for eastern and southern Europeans. Assistant Secretary of Labor Edward J. Henning recognized the development as a pivot: "We have been accustomed, as far as I can read the literature of immigration, to regard the problem of immigration as a problem of wage earners rather than as a question of who shall be the citizens of this country now, to-morrow, or a century from now. I think there is a clear line of cleavage between the purely economic question of how to get a sufficient supply of wage earners and the question of who shall inhabit the land of our fathers."[31] The line of argument about citizenship and immigration had shifted from economics to eugenics.

But Native Americans were already here, and two-thirds of them were already citizens. For those two-thirds, becoming citizens had often not played out exactly as federal administrators had imagined. Becoming citizens under previous acts, they had used their independence to host traditional tribal dances and sustain their tribal language and religion, all things forbidden for reservation Indians. Lakota veterans, given citizenship for their military service, held give-away dances to fund their effort to get back the Black Hills. When the superintendent of one reservation attempted to jail participants in give-away dances, he reported to Burke that citizen Indians knew their rights; they knew about habeas corpus and knew their imprisonment was illegal. Burke was less than thrilled with veterans who had learned unintended lessons from their education in Americanization and viewed citizenship as legitimizing their choices to retain traditions and regain lands.[32]

Unlike the earlier extensions of citizenship to Indians, the 1924 Indian Citizenship Act endowing reservation Indians with citizenship promised in no way to alter Native relations to the tribe, the land, or the government. This act allowed Indians to be citizens and remain on reservations. It also allowed the government to continue its control over those reservations of citizens and over the citizens themselves. On the reservation, the government could still insist that citizenship meant speaking English, going to church, dancing the fox trot, and accumulating individual wealth. Like the other citizenship measures of that year, it enforced a particular assimilative and racially hierarchical vision of the nation.[33]

Even when the Indian Citizenship Act became law in June 1924, it did not enfranchise Indians in New Mexico and many other states. It clarified their citizenship status only on the federal level. States retained the right to determine who could vote, and they proved singularly recalcitrant. In New Mexico, Idaho, and Washington an Indian had to be a taxpayer; in North Dakota and Minnesota an Indian had to live like a white man, speak English, and be a Christian or at least attend a Christian church. In 1936 Colorado's attorney general insisted that while Indians might be citizens of the United States, they were not citizens of Colorado. In 1938 at least seven states denied the franchise to Indians.[34]

Federal Irrigation and the People's Money

Not long after Congress weighed competing claims to land and water on Pueblo lands, it confronted its own dismal record on irrigation. On federal projects launched with the Newlands legislation in 1902, borrowers had repaid only 10 percent of the no-interest loans, and 60 percent of the irrigators were in default. Over the course of ten days in May 1924, members of a special advisory committee of six, appointed by the secretary of the interior, sat in the House of Representatives hearing rooms and tried to explain to the members of the Committee on Irrigation and Reclamation, which was contemplating a bill to extend repayments on the projects, why the irrigation schemes the country had built across the West from Canada to Mexico over the past twenty years—begun with such promise, with such fervent belief in the ability of technology to work miracles and to reclaim the West as a land of opportunity for the small investor, the returning war veteran, at a cost of nearly $150 million of the people's money—had largely failed or were failing, literally underwater, waterlogged, or barren wastes of alkali.[35]

Of the government's total investment, it was already clear that over $18 million would never be recovered, and President Calvin Coolidge projected an additional loss of nearly $9 million spent constructing reservoirs and canals for lands proven unproductive. Over thirty thousand water users were trapped in this spiral. The advisory committee's report noted that three projects had been abandoned and several more would be if nothing were done to prevent it. The nation had "over 500,000 acres of land in the projects supplied with water but not being cultivated," which meant, on the basis of forty-acre farms, that the government sought "over 11,000 farmers to cultivate this land and pay water charges."[36]

The troubles seem to have begun at the outset. The congressional irrigation law had mandated expenditures in fifteen western states in proportion to the sales of public lands in those states, leading to intense pressure for immediate project selections in each state. Within four years of the law's passage, the federal government had selected twenty-four projects. With over twenty projects simultaneously in construction, as with oil booms, little experience was accrued. The committee's report pointed to "irremediable errors in the original locations," multiplying construction costs, which costs became those of the naive settlers. Buoyed by its faith in technology to triumph over nature, the government had selected as settlers those similarly unburdened by an understanding of farming, those "without capital or experience." In turn, "federal water users were tempted, as were other farmers, by the financial riot at the time of high prices during and immediately after the Great War; and they have been caught, with farmers everywhere, by the agricultural depression of the last few years."[37]

While the congressional committee, most of whose members hailed from west of the Mississippi and whose chair represented Idaho, was well aware that these farmers on irrigation projects were simply an extreme example of the general state of farming, most of them felt a particular responsibility for having inadvertently duped venturesome, ambitious settlers onto inadequately planned government projects. By 1924 the federal government had realized that it should have had agricultural and not just engineering specialists when it designed its western irrigation projects. Unfortunately, there was no correlation between the cost of a project and the value of water to the farmer.[38] The law mandated a payment schedule based on the former, and scores of farmers unable to make a living, let alone an irrigation payment, abandoned their farms, adding to the general flight from the land and the costs borne by those left behind.

Not every project failed. In the Salt River Valley, Arizona, roughly 90 percent of the settlers had farming experience. In a valley averaging only eight inches of rainfall per year, irrigation permitted crops to grow 289 days of the year, largely alfalfa, wheat, and cotton, and farmers successfully operated dairies and raised hogs and poultry. The project had cost the nation's taxpayers about $10 million, and since beginning repayment in 1917, ten years after water became available, the project's farmers had made every payment but two, enjoying reduced payments by special arrangement when prices plummeted. They were on track to pay off the whole debt by 1936. While adjoining unirrigated land would fetch under $10 per acre, the irrigated land had a worth of $250 to $300 per acre. In an area previously desert, the project held sixty public schools, sixty-five churches, twenty banks, and eighty thousand people in towns and on the five thousand farms. Even better, they had purchased over $11 million in war savings stamps and Liberty bonds. "If the books had been balanced at that time," averred Representative Hayden, "they owed the Government $10,000,000 and the Government owed them $11,000,000."[39]

Even the Salt River Valley farmers, however, despite the proximity of Phoenix as a market and good rail connections, had to forgo payments during the worst of the postwar recession. The deck was certainly stacked against other projects' would-be farmers. Even those projects that hung on were dramatically reduced. The Newlands project in Nevada, for example, originally embraced 350,000 acres; now it had 86,000.[40]

Having exposed the government's sins of optimism and inexperience, the advisory committee chose its heroes and villains. It created opposing categories of "the poor farmer, with honest courage but little or no capital," who merited better information and credit, versus "the greedy owner of private lands, ready to trade upon the natural desire of vigorous, hard-working men, for independent homes," who "should and could have been squelched." But as with oil, there was mixed sentiment regarding the speculator.

Explaining turnover on the projects, Ottamar Hamele, chief counsel of the U.S. Reclamation Service, claimed, "The usual reason he wants to sell out is because he wants to speculate. That is what we want to avoid. He is supposed to go on this land to make a home there."[41] On Idaho's Minidoka project "great numbers of farmers" had taken a plunge, and "in 1919, they sold their lands at a great profit" to farmers who could not now pay their charges. The chairman asked, quite reasonably, what if he doesn't want to make a home? What if the original farmer invested sweat equity and then sold to settlers who had not wanted to go through those hardships? Hamele responded, "You are commending speculation, Mr. Chairman. I think it is one of the worst things we have on Federal irrigation projects." Short-term speculation in farming had high costs in the long run. But even farmers who intended to pass their land down through the generations could find that the high costs of irrigation projects forced them, according to one expert, "to sacrifice the fertility of their soil in an endeavor to raise the highest possible money crop." According to Hamele, this speculative behavior was widespread in the Northwest and the Southwest.[42]

The federal involvement in high-stakes speculation on irrigated agriculture had sought to create in the West a landscape of small yeoman farmers less involved in the dominant 1920s speculating ethos and content to remain on the family farm that so many fled. But in the 1920s on the plains, everyone was a speculator—teachers, clerks, and small businessmen bought acreage outside of town and hit the road on weekends to reap every bushel they could from the land before they flipped it. The success of some large-scale farmers in the second half of the decade encouraged them, just as the oil kings encouraged small-scale speculators in oil. Hickman Price made a fortune farming fifty-four square miles around Plainview, Texas; J. H. Gruver did so in Oklahoma; and Ida Watkins farmed two thousand acres to become the "wheat queen" of Haskell County, Kansas, with a profit of $75,000 in 1926.[43]

When they were not speculators, settlers could still fall into other troubled categories. These were not rugged individualist farmers. In phrases that echoed simultaneous discussions of Native American policy, the committee's report deprecated the "dependence on Federal paternalism" that "settled down upon nearly all the projects" to the point that "the water users have come to look upon themselves as wards of the Government, a specially favored class with special claims upon governmental bounty." The report admitted that "the old pioneer settlement with its primitive farming is impossible under present conditions. Capital, technical knowledge, credit, and technical advice are all needed to make farming profitable under these costly projects." Not only did farmers need the feds, but they needed each other: "The good farmer, with small business capacity, should have been given the assistance of cooperative organizations for buying and selling."[44]

The spectacle of failed federal and individual speculation in irrigation in no way turned the advisory committee or the federal government from its belief both in the family farm and in costly, high-technology irrigation. On the contrary, the destiny of the nation required more of the same. The president wrote, "The probable loss and temporary difficulties of some of the settlers on projects does not mean that reclamation is a failure. The sum of beneficial results has been large in the building up of towns and agricultural communities and is adding tremendously to the agricultural production wealth of the country." Similarly, setting aside that in the twenty or so years since its inception only roughly 10 percent of the government's expenditures had been repaid, the special advisory committee concluded, "Thousands of happy families are growing up in the open country under influences that have always fashioned men and women of strength. Moreover, these projects have helped in the conquest, for human good, of the more difficult places of our country, and thereby have shown the great value of the arid and semiarid region, as part of the domain, which, in the providence of God, has been given to our country." The hapless farmers trapped on or deserting irrigation projects were "true Americans," which meant that they asked "not alms, but that the requirements made of them be proportional to their power to win means from the soil."[45]

Many if not all the irrigation projects had given preference to veterans of the Great War. Like the Civil War era Homestead Act, these projects aimed at once to compensate veterans, to relieve urban poverty, to forestall the return of massive unrest, and to secure the future of the republic by enabling the Jeffersonian vision of the yeoman farmer as backbone of democracy to survive on the dwindling fertile land of the public domain. Only by 1924 it was no longer clear whether virtue inhered in doing farmwork or flipping farm real estate; whether participating in building up the nation required either a substantial nest egg or substantial subsidies; and finally, whether the ideal farmer was a loner, rugged, manual-laboring risk-taker, which seemed to be seen by many committee members as an atavistic vision, or a member of a cooperative.[46]

Recognition of the benefits of cooperation together with the growth of irrigation projects both private and public and their woes fostered the invention of a new unit of government, the conservancy district. Seventeen western states passed a variety of enabling laws, which state supreme courts upheld. Conservancy districts could start as attempts at pluralist collaborative self-government. For example, seeking to ameliorate their water fluctuations, silting, and flooding, Pueblo, Anglo, and Hispano farmers along a 150-mile stretch of the Rio Grande Valley in New Mexico created the Middle Rio Grande Conservancy District in 1925. Not all the farmers totally depended on a market economy, but most if not all partly did so. The very expansion of commercial markets, including the growth of the railroad, timber, and cattle industries in northern New Mexico, had generated the environmental problems that had destroyed Hispano and Pueblo irrigation ditches and drove this unlikely alliance. In turn, paying for the irrigation infrastructure it sought would require a greater market commitment. While capital-intensive farming is usually associated with westering Anglos or eastering Japanese, it was three Spanish-surnamed state senators who had introduced the bill to establish the district. All three of the groups in New Mexico, according to historian Kenneth Orona, understood this action as an assertion of citizenship. The state's Conservancy Act (1923) would enable a self-governing political entity with the power to issue bonds and tax members.[47]

This was not previously vacant land newly brought into production by a federal irrigation project. This was land long farmed by semisubsistence farmers who wanted to hold on to their land. But the federal project brought instability. The district quickly fell afoul of competing interests. Landowners, businessmen, and

Albuquerque city officials wanted to levy taxes and issue bonds to finance the building of levees, dams, and canals. Hispano farmers realized that plan would increase taxes beyond their ability to pay, risking dispossession, and it would also require massive expropriation of farmland and change the ways they managed water and land. United, they presented their own counterpetition representing the majority of farmers in the region (as opposed to town dwellers) to block the project, gathering over three thousand signatures, 94 percent of them with Spanish surnames, at churches, post offices, and community meetings.[48]

Proponents framed the debate in the usual duality of "primitive" and "wasteful" methods of Hispana/o and Native American farmers as opposed to "a period of development and growth beyond the average dream." They promised, "The valley up and down the river near Albuquerque will become in spring time checkerboards of green." The presiding judge in the dispute resided and owned property in the area most likely to benefit and claimed that "business will hum and a sturdy look of complacency will settle on the faces of valley residents. There will be money in the pocket and a grin in the soul." He ruled against the Hispano petitioners in December 1925.[49]

When the taxes first came due in 1929, Hispano farmers mobilized again. The assessments covered not only land currently cultivated but also land that could be cultivated. They sought an injunction against the sale of the district's conservancy bonds. The judicial court once again upheld the district's powers. Undeterred, the Hispanos pursued the case to the U.S. Supreme Court, where, in early 1931, they also lost.[50]

Meanwhile, the Pueblos in the vicinity of the district had their own qualms. In September 1927 the council of All Indian Pueblos in New Mexico formally recognized the importance of flood control and drainage but, like the Hispanos, rejected the destruction of villages and property and the taxes, as well as basing payments on potential rather than actual benefits. Once again, Collier acted as a spokesman at the request of the Pueblos. Because the Pueblos were Indians, unlike in the case of the Hispanos, the federal government became involved, and Collier negotiated a compromise bill that limited the liability of the Pueblos and would not include acres the Pueblos had traditionally irrigated. Things changed on the House floor. Despite Pueblos' and Collier's opposition and publicity campaign, the bill that was signed into law more than doubled the debt new Pueblo farmlands would incur ($149.66 per acre), an impossibility to farmers who, like the Hispanos, raised crops for subsistence, as well as for market. Herbert Hagerman, the special commissioner for Indian Affairs, recognized that the Pueblo ditches, used for hundreds of years, still worked well. But powerful congressmen refused to exempt the Pueblo acres already under the ditch, and the Indian Office went along rather than have no flood remediation at all.[51] The conservancy district had promised a particular kind of economic citizenship, but it seemed it also required a particular kind of economic citizen.

It was clear in the 1920s that an enormous proportion of the nation's farmers were in deep trouble. Agricultural economics seemed not to favor the small farmer of almost any background, irrigator or not, government or private. The route to salvation was less clear. Congress remained bound to a particular vision of the farm but opposed extending payments on irrigation projects. At the same time, under tremendous pressure by farmers, by middecade many congressmen vowed not to end their session without passing a farm bill. In 1927 they did pass one of Oregon senator Charles L. McNary's bills to address the farm crisis not by extending loans but by buying and storing wheat, selling it abroad when necessary and storing it until prices rose. Coolidge vetoed it.[52] Neither the government's nor other farmers would get relief.

Labor and the American Farmer

Unwilling or unable to aid the farmer by easing credit terms or entering the commodities market directly, Congress turned to the labor side of the equation. The grain belt had largely solved the farmers' labor problem by mechanization. What seasonal workers they still needed often consisted of farmers' sons or college students. Irrigated farming, however, was both labor- and capital-intensive. It had taken some experimenting to find the right crops. In Utah, by substituting celery for other crops, farmers raised their yield from $30 to $300 per acre; on the Salt River in Arizona, in some areas they succeeded with orange trees, in others with less high yield lettuce, cantaloupes, alfalfa, wheat, and barley; in Texas, paper-shell pecans yielded a greater revenue than alfalfa or cotton but required considerable capital investment up front. California's irrigated land could not compete with the Midwest's vast spreads in producing grain crops. Only perishable crops would pay the price of irrigation. Many if not most of these higher-yield crops required enormous amounts of field labor. By 1928, in yet another set of hearings, C. S. Brown of the State Farm Bureau of Arizona and the Water Users' Association of Mesa, Arizona, was blunt in his allocation of responsibility for the predicament of western farmers: "We of the West are in the making. . . . [W]e have started projects that we can not carry without assistance, and you people helped us to start them—you loaned us the money to start them, and unless we have some kind of labor we will have our foundation digged from under us and our homes." Such farming required, as California's senator Hiram Johnson admitted, what "we used to call . . . 'squatting occupations'" with a circulating labor force in his state alone of possibly eighty thousand Mexicans.[53]

During the postwar recession, the federal government had reinstated the head tax and literacy test for Western Hemisphere immigrants. Coupled with declining European immigration under the 1921 quota laws, the reinstatement had led to panic among irrigators and other farmers. Though many Mexican migrants now stayed in the United States rather than returning seasonally and facing the tax repeatedly, that shift failed to calm the panic. If Mexicans stayed year-round, they could be as likely to flee the farm as anyone else and, indeed, already showed up as smelter workers in El Paso, meatpackers across the Midwest, steelworkers in Pennsylvania, and miners everywhere. In short, permanent immigrants did not solve the need for permanent migrant farm labor.[54]

West Coast farmers had already seen this pattern in regard to Asian immigrants. In the 1920s citrus growers employed Mexican, Japanese, and Sikh workers, each in their own residential camps in an effort to prevent labor solidarity. But Sikh and Japanese workers ultimately often became tenants and landowners. In 1912 Japanese farmers owned 12,276 acres in California; in 1920 they owned 361,276 acres and produced crops worth $67 million.[55]

The issue was not only disappearing farm labor. The issue was who constituted the American farmer. While Japanese-owned acreage comprised less than 2 percent of the twenty-eight million acres farmed in California that year, the rapid growth had led to fears that California could become a colony of Japan. In July 1919, pointing to the rising number of U.S.-born children of Japanese immigrants, California senator James Phelan had warned of "increasing the horde of nonassimilable aliens who are crowding the white men and women off the land. If this is not checked now . . . it means the end of the white race in California . . . and the end of our Western civilization." Moved by such sentiment, in February 1920 the U.S. government gave the last passports to picture brides, and the 128 who landed in San Francisco in April were among the last to come. In 1920 Arizona, California, Oregon, and Washington all had legislation prohibiting Japanese from owning land in those states.[56]

Phelan's apocalyptic language had helped ensure the passage of restrictive land laws across the West but not the disappearance of Japanese farmers. By 1925, a year after the United States enacted legislation prohibiting all Asian immigration, almost half of all Japanese in the United States with any employment worked in farming. Japanese immigrants entered farming both individually and collectively. By 1920 one immigrant man, Abiko Kyutaro, had founded three incorporated Christian Japanese farming colonies. The corporation owned the land; the farmers owned shares in the corporation. Such colonies provided a refuge for farm families excluded from landownership and forbidden even from leases of more than three years by California laws. Instead of pulling up stakes and cultivating new land every few years, they could own property and put down roots, literally and figuratively.[57] With intensive agriculture, the small plots they could purchase sufficed.

At the same time as the Cortez Colony's Japanese settlers arrived in the San Joaquin Valley, new anti-Japanese associations formed in the valley's Merced County. But the terrain of anti-Japanese activism in the West was more complicated than that juxtaposition would indicate. Albert Johnson, who headed the House Committee on Immigration and Naturalization in the 1920s, had long crusaded against Asian immigrants, using his newspaper and supporting the 1907 riot at Bellingham, Washington, that pushed South Asians literally into the sea. Johnson brought immigration hearings in 1920 to Washington State. While some Washington newspapers spewed anti-Japanese vitriol on a daily basis, charging Japanese with violating white women and stealing white women from their husbands, the hotel business from white merchants, and restaurant swill from virtuous white hog farmers, other newspapers were more balanced, and the Japanese themselves were not silent. Anti-Japanese sentiment was always within easy reach, but by the 1920s even organized labor on the West Coast had largely abandoned its virulent anti-Japanese stance. According to Representative Johnson, chairing the committee, labor in Seattle "had ceased to object to the admission of the Japanese on the ground that he had ceased to become a competitor of labor itself and was a competitor of the small business man." The testimony of Japanese immigrants and Japanese Americans gave other reasons. Mr. D. Matsumi, general manager of an import-export firm and president of the United North American Japanese Association, provided statistical evidence of Japanese assimilation regarding birth rates and evidence of Japanese as model farmers whose hard work explained why they outperformed others in the same industry. He also presented second-generation Japanese American witnesses as "living proof" of their assimilability.[58]

In many ways, the Japanese farmers differed little from other farmers. Like other farmers in California's San Joaquin Valley, they struggled with the bleak, sandstorm-scoured landscape and voracious jackrabbits. Their often quickly erected, drafty houses lacked electricity and running water. The lack of electricity and running water was particularly hard on the women, as it multiplied the difficulty of key domestic chores, including baking and laundry. And like many other struggling small farmers, everyone in the family worked the land and dug the irrigation ditches. Also like other farmers, they formed growers' associations for cooperative buying of supplies and equipment.[59]

Both the desire of local Anglo farmers for Japanese farmworkers and the economic integration of existing Japanese colonies and farmers into the economic and social fabric of local communities limited the impact of the resurgent anti-Japanese activism. Exclusion became the law of the land, and vigilantes ran Japanese workers out of town, but the Cortez Colony continued to grow, farmers in nearby Turlock (also known as Melon City) continued to hire Japanese farmworkers at wages lower than white farmworkers, and white youth gave a surprise midnight feast of ice cream and cake to a returning Japanese American Mills College girl and her sister at the Yamato Colony. Local papers began to distinguish between "the Japanese" and "our Japanese."[60]

Meanwhile, the U.S.-born children of Japanese immigrants, or Nisei, learned unintended lessons from the Americanization curriculum that saturated their public schools. As had Native Americans, the lessons the Nisei had in the "rights, duties, and dignity of American citizenship" could fly in the face of the discrimination they faced in practice. Japanese and Japanese Americans had fended off San Francisco's threat to force them into segregated schools early in the century, but in 1921 California's state legislature allowed an amendment to the state's education code permitting school districts to create separate elementary schools for "Indians, Chinese, Japanese or Mongolian children." Only agricultural communities in Sacramento County followed through and created "oriental" schools. Charles Shishida heard the school principal declare, after breaking up a fight between a Chinese and a Japanese student at the Walnut Grove Oriental School, "You're no Chink and you're no Jap! You're 100 percent American, so I don't want you to ever call names, you understand that?!" Shishida demanded of the principal, "If we're 100 percent American, why aren't we in the other school up there?" The flustered principal, unable to explain why they could not attend the all-white school half a mile away, responded, "None of your business! Give that boy an 'F' in deportment. That's just how it is, and it's going to stay that way."[61]

The schools remained segregated until after World War II, but Japanese parents had some success mobilizing the citizenship of their children in court cases to hold on to their land. In case after case between 1915 and 1925, Japanese immigrants watched the land their children held be taken away by the state under alien land laws in California and Washington. Fighting back in court against the erosion of their rights, they insisted that their children, as citizens, had the right to own land, and they, as parents, had the right to act for them as parents under the Fourteenth Amendment's protections. In 1922 the California Supreme Court decided that Tetsubumi Yano, though two years old, had the rights of a citizen to own her fourteen acres, cared for by her parents, and that being an alien ineligible for citizenship did not mean that her father, Hayao Yano, had forfeited his guardianship rights as a parent. In contrast, the Washington Supreme Court in 1925 stripped Japanese families of their landownership in the White River Gardens, Inc., whose shares Japanese immigrants had transferred to their citizen children when Washington made immigrant ownership of them illegal. The court allowed them to continue to work the land only as lessees. Despite the hostility, in the 1920s Japanese immigrants continued to settle and farm, and they founded their own churches and schools. By 1930 in Los Angeles County, 90 percent of locally consumed produce came from Japanese farms.[62]

At the myriad federal government hearings on immigration in the 1920s witnesses warned that the Japanese were taking over agriculture on the West Coast, that Mexicans were taking jobs from union members in the Midwest and as far east as Pennsylvania, that the wrong kind of immigrants were supplanting native citizens on the nation's small farms, and that these populations (despite the evidence of diverse wartime battalions in the Great War) would never become "Americans." They would destroy the quality of the nation's people and drag its government into revolution or despotism or disaster. Various groups agitated for the suspension of immigration altogether. They demanded ever narrower restrictions on ever more would-be immigrants, and they argued for restricting immigration from the Western Hemisphere instead of just everywhere else.[63]

There was little consensus on exactly what groups should be restricted under what conditions, but over and over in government hearings on immigration throughout the 1920s, the connection between the government's irrigation projects and the demand for low-cost labor came to the fore. In 1928 E. J. Walker, representing Arizona cotton growers on one of the few successful irrigation projects, insisted that many reclamation projects, even with the current supply of labor, could not repay construction charges. Alfred P. Thom, general counsel of the Association of Railway Executives, used the example of a North Dakota farmer with a large family. When the children left, he "was not able to produce enough upon his farm to pay the taxes. That process is going on all around us. . . . [I]t presents . . . the great question of what you are going to do to give the American people the necessary supply of common labor . . . essential to the welfare of our people." Irrigation determined the crops, and the crops demanded labor. J. C. Baily, vice president of the Holly Sugar Company, put it bluntly: restricting Mexicans would "seriously cripple these reclamation projects."[64]

Since sugar beets, now grown on thirteen federal reclamation projects from North Dakota southward, and other high-priced crops had replaced wheat or hay, financial conditions had improved; abandoned farms were being taken up, and farmers were paying their obligations to the government in full and on time. Farmers plowed up hay meadows producing less than $8 an acre to produce sugar beets yielding as much as $97 per acre. Mexican labor made growing sugar beets possible. When farmers switched from sugar beets to even more lucrative vegetables, fruits, and citrus in Brownsville, Texas, settlers from Wisconsin, Minnesota, Illinois, Iowa, New York, and elsewhere flocked to its "winter garden" district, soon to rival California, to partake of its lucrative possibilities, but it was Mexican laborers who cleared the land of mesquite and made the cultivation possible and Mexican laborers who worked the crops. Ninety-eight percent of the labor in South Texas, according to testimony from R. H. Smith, representing the South Texas Chamber of Commerce, was Mexican. California's farms, valued at $400 million, also depended on Mexican labor to cultivate, harvest, and ship their produce. Success required Mexican labor. Irrigation farmers as far north as Montana, Utah, and Idaho had tried Indian laborers from local reservations and dropped them in favor of the more experienced Mexicans.[65]

Mexican workers, it seemed, directly or indirectly undergirded every aspect of western development. The agricultural industry relied on railroads to transport their goods to market, and the western railroads, too, relied heavily on migrant Mexican workers to maintain their tracks. On many western lines Mexicans made up over half the maintenance-of-way workers and on some lines 90 percent of extra gangs, the floating groups of workers who lived in railroad cars and went wherever major repairs were needed. In the 1920s the lack of Western Hemisphere restrictions had allowed increased recruitment of Mexican labor. Higher Mexican labor costs would raise costs for farmers at a moment when all voices in and out of Congress recognized that agriculture needed relief.[66]

As they had in the 1920 hearings, in these later hearings, those demanding low-cost labor depicted Mexicans as uniquely suited for it. Mexicans were secured as farm laborers in various centers far from the U.S.-Mexico border, including, among others, St. Paul, Minnesota; Topeka, Kansas; Hastings, Nebraska; and Chicago, Illinois. Former congressman Carlos Bee from Texas claimed that neither whites nor blacks would grub raw land for cultivation, "but the Mexican is adapted for that special character of labor; whether in the providence of God he has been so constituted I won't say." Similarly, they argued that the climate made picking cotton impossible for anyone but "Mexicans" and Blacks. As for railroad maintenance, work that required as many as sixty thousand men, the work was highly seasonal; it required workers who could migrate and then disappear below the border or onto farms for equally seasonal labor. One witness declared that the Mexican "is a migratory being." Even better, a survey of sugar beet companies found that "the consensus of opinion is that they are agricultural workers pure and simple and that they prefer to remain in the country rather than go to the city."[67]

The twisted logic of the hearings manifested in the imagined racial formation of the future West. With a declining immigrant population and immigrant flight from farms equaling or even surpassing that of native-born Black and white migration to the cities, the price of labor rose even as the price of commodities fell. Farms were already under pressure from an increasing difference in living standards between rural and urban dwellers, so the added economic pressure meant that across the country the number of abandoned farms grew. Though a large number of witnesses and the congressmen themselves had grown up on and then left farms, they seemed wedded to the virtues of farm life in building a strong citizenry. Exempting those citizen farmers from farm labor seemed one way to anchor them to the land. Witnesses proposed admitting white immigrants as small farmers to replace the dwindling rural population. They would create colonies of small farms. But in the imagined West, they would not do farmwork, being racially unsuited to it. Former large landholders would build and run processing plants, providing factory jobs for white men, and Mexicans would toil in the dirt.[68]

As the 1920s wore on, recession returned with a vengeance in 1927. Two years before the stock market crash, the Florida hurricane collapsed the state's real estate bubble, the Mississippi River flooded, and Ford shut down for a year because of a saturated automobile market. As a result, in 1928, the same moment farmers laid claim to federal help in securing low-wage farm labor, the United States faced an employment crisis, with the figure of four million unemployed men frequently cited.

Congressional hearings became a litmus test of patriotic racism. Witness after witness was asked in 1928 whether they supported restricting Mexican immigration. Those who favored restriction contended that Mexicans were unassimilable. Edward Dowell, representing the California State Federation of Labor, complained, "You are going to fill up the great West of our country with Mexicans . . . and if we do not remain on guard it is not going to be our country; it is going to be somebody else's country. . . . Do you want the kind of people that sit in this Capitol, or that you have in the north or middle west, or do you want a mongrel population consisting largely of Mexicans and orientals?" Senator Hiram Johnson of California, who chaired the Senate Committee on Immigration and stood behind much of the restrictionist movement, aimed to protect "the life blood of the Nation" and, having felt he succeeded with the 1924 legislation in protecting the East, wanted to add restrictions to Mexican immigration to protect the West.[69]

Countering such prose, witnesses such as John Nance Garner, congressman from Texas, pointed to the long history of Mexicans in the United States: "I know Mexican families who are living on the same land their forbears owned 200 years ago. . . . Some of the Mexican people in our country are substantial citizens—Mexican descendants—as you will find anywhere in this country," and while current immigrants might not, as one of the senators asked, "average up to that statement," the implication was that ultimately they would assimilate. R. H. Smith, representing the South Texas Chamber of Commerce, complained that Congressman John Box, also from Texas, "has not even got a Mexican in his district, not even a Mexican in his county. . . . And yet he is vociferous in his desire to cut them off." Another witness who claimed that in New Mexico and Arizona metal mines, Mexicans comprised ten thousand of an estimated seventeen thousand miners, found them "a very satisfactory and an essential part of the labor supply in the Southwest regions." "The Mexican," one witness exclaimed, "needs above all things a press agent that will put him in the right light."[70]

As it had been at the start of the decade, a persistent thread was the contention by southerners that Mexican immigration promised to replicate what they saw as the ineradicable race problems of the South. These southern claims cannot be separated from what southerners framed as unfair competition from the West's cotton, with its low-wage immigrant labor, at a time when the South lost Black workers to the North in the Great Migration. But westerners opposing restriction focused instead on contrasting Mexicans with stereotypes about African Americans. They contrasted Mexican assimilability with the permanent "difference" of blacks and portrayed the unthreatening sexual nature of Mexicans. Stock grower Fred Bixby put it most plainly: "I have a family—three of them are girls. Ever since they were that high . . . I have had them on that range, riding the range with Mexicans, and they have been just as safe as if they had been with me. . . . Do you suppose we would send them out with a bunch of negroes? We would never think of such a thing." In a statement that would have shocked those fearing Mexican revolutionaries ten years earlier, Senator John B. Kendrick (Wyoming) claimed the Mexicans had "never proved in a single way a menace to any social order into which he has come." In this way, westerners could present themselves as racial loyalists, as participants in a broader consensus of racist patriotism, but as better informed than those opposing Mexican immigration.[71]

Those demanding unrestricted immigration had an ace in the hole. There was another problem with curtailing Mexican immigration that echoed the problem of responding to earlier white western demands regarding the Japanese: diplomacy and international trade. After years of revolutionary upheaval in Mexico and threats to the substantial U.S. interests there—put at approximately $1.25 billion in investments in 1928—relations between the two countries had finally started to improve. But Secretary of State Frank B. Kellogg warned that all could be undone by restriction and already was endangered by the intemperate and "far removed from complimentary" language used in congressional speeches.[72]

But the clincher was the argument that permanently migrant Mexican labor was essential to fulfill the promise of federal investment. Kendrick insisted, "We of the West . . . are today waging the mightiest contest of the century. We are making every consistent effort to subdue the desert." Investigators in the Arkansas Valley of Colorado found that "it is believed that a cheap labor supply is necessary for this industry . . . and that the Spanish-American or Mexican is the one to furnish it."[73] Only low-wage Mexican migrant farm labor would make possible the success of these development efforts. Only low-wage Mexican migrant farm labor would make possible industrial jobs for white residents and profits and modern life for the white farmer.

The argument's tacit success came not only in the continued exclusion of the Western Hemisphere from immigration quotas but also in the form of Border Patrol collaborations with California and Texas farmers. In 1925, for example, the Border Patrol hired more agents and started detaining Mexican immigrants in the Imperial Valley. The farmers who hired the immigrants called it harassment and petitioned Congress to stop. The Imperial Valley Chamber of Commerce and the local Border Patrol chief set up a labor bureau the next year, agreeing to let undocumented Mexicans pay the $18 immigration fee in four installments at local banks and then take the literacy test. They registered three thousand people in two months and over six thousand the following year, despite the lack of a labor shortage.[74] The Border Patrol, a federal agency, in this way supplied the growers with extremely vulnerable workers.

Mexican Americans and Japanese Americans pushed back against these increasingly confining definitions of citizenship, rights, and belonging both in and out of the courts. They protested against discrimination in shops and battled dispossession. In 1929 those "substantial citizens" in Texas created the League of United Latin American Citizens, and Nisei Californians created the Japanese American Citizens League. By their very organizational names, they countered the erasure of their existence evident in the hearings, and they asserted that American citizenship did not require, in turn, the erasure of their heritage. Farmworkers, both immigrant and citizen, similarly refused the docile parts designed for them. Beet workers in northern Colorado pooled their resources to buy cars during the season. Their employers were convinced that predatory car salesmen took advantage of the beet workers, accepting a down payment for a car the salesmen knew they would repossess within months, and some did, but the employers' greater grievance was the new automobility of workers. Migrants who owned cars could move at will. They could refuse a contract or bad conditions for a better one in the next county or even the next state.[75] The migrants refused, in short, to play their assigned roles.

"Real Farmers"?

An alternative to the capital-intensive, low-wage labor model existed in the small, intensive, often part-time farming that grew in the 1920s West. The line between farmers and townspeople blurred. California raisin growers were also often bankers and businessmen, doctors and lawyers. When Japanese families moved onto their land in agricultural colonies, often the married women continued their urban wage work, usually domestic service, in nearby towns. The California government's Durham irrigation project was close enough to town that its settlers could support themselves with wage work while waiting for their few acres of farmland to start producing. When the U.S. Bureau of Reclamation's Elwood Mead wanted to cement the picture of success at the Durham project, he concluded of one former tenant farmer, "He has taken a part in the life, he has a Ford, and is meeting his payments to the State and everybody else."[76] To Congressman John E. Raker (California), those were not farms:

> The Durham settlement is more like part of a town than it is a farm. They . . . have a street-car line; they have a railroad and bus lines that take them in 15 minutes to Chico and other towns; . . . they can go anywhere they want in a few minutes; and they can work in town and live on those places. Even a doctor or a lawyer can live there and do his business in Chico. . . . [It] would be a curse to

this country, in having those town settlements and communities instead of having real farmers, like we have in America, living in individual homes.[77]

In some ways, the senators and representatives caught themselves in an impossible loop. They objected to the Japanese, as Ralph H. Taylor, executive secretary of the Agricultural Legislative Committee of California, put it at a 1928 Senate hearing, "because of the fact that the Japanese very quickly, almost immediately, reached the point where they did not want to work for others but wanted to acquire landed properties of their own. He immediately became a supplanter rather than a 'supplementer.'" But, countered Senator Frank Willis of Ohio, "Do you think we ought to adopt here a class of people who have no ambition to become home owners or landowners? Do you want here a peasant class that does not want to own land or does not want to own a home?" Senator James Reed (Missouri) responded to this complaint by referencing Italian immigrants who aspired to landownership but not in the United States.[78] That Italian example made clear the desire in the United States not for immigrants lacking ambition but for permanently excludable, permanently migrant workers who could, perhaps, fulfill their dreams elsewhere or not at all.

Conclusion: Saving Western Farming and the American Dream

Throughout the 1920s, the federal government and the states struggled over the best way to ensure the survival of a particular version of the western farmer. Thirty-eight states adopted laws that permitted agricultural cooperatives to engage in monopoly, control growers through iron-clad contracts, and assert industry-wide control over marketing.[79] Cooperation itself, however, proved inadequate to save farming.

When the federal government decided to throw good money after bad to salvage the irrigation projects, it made an implicit promise to provide low-wage workers to the irrigation farmers and their dry-farming peers. The government and the farmers made a commitment to an ambiguous, marginalized incorporation of migrants and their growing and increasingly stable urban settlements. Throughout the decade the white West struggled to draw boundaries between those it fully incorporated, those who signified "the West," and "others" essential to the West's survival. Those "others" had their own visions of their place, and their presence sometimes predated "the West" itself.

The whiteness of irrigation projects mattered. In cataloging the success of the Salt River Valley project, a special report on the project to the House Committee on Indian Affairs included as significant information "nationality of settlers, American born predominate; foreign born, negligible." Mead claimed that the Durham project had particular value because "the white man will do any kind of farm work, because we know they are supplying the vegetables for the Chico markets to-day and before they went there the Chinese gardeners did it all."[80]

In arguing before Congress for what would eventually become Coolidge Dam, on the San Carlos Apache Indian Reservation, the first effort had emphasized the exclusive benefits to white farmers. The BIA, striving to protect the interests of its constituents, made the case for splitting the resultant water with the Akimel O'odham, who had been irrigation farmers for over three hundred years. What made the six thousand Akimel O'odham worthy was their historic relation to white people: they "have never killed a white man, have always been true and faithful to the United States Government." The Apaches, whose sacred burial ground would have to be swamped for the dam and who were not farmers, provided a convenient foil. Edgar B. Meritt, assistant commissioner of Indian Affairs, testified, "While the Apaches were killing the white man and the Government was spending millions of dollars to keep the Apaches on the reservation, the Pimas [Akimel O'odham] were not costing the Government a dollar, but helped the white man in every way possible."[81]

What did the Apaches think? Malcolm McDowell, secretary of the Board of Commissioners, maintained that even the Apaches favored the dam, though it was on their land and they were not farmers. They were sought after as "builders" and stood to earn $5 per day working on the dam. When committee chair Homer Snyder of New York objected, "They were very much opposed to it when we were down in that country," McDowell responded dismissively, "That is because of some little patches of their lands contiguous to the agency grounds were affected by being flooded by the reservoir." Those "little patches" turned out to be cemeteries, and according to Snyder, "they were particularly opposed to the moving of their dead Indians, to the removal of the cemeteries."[82]

The cavalier treatment of the Apaches' hostility to moving their dead, the wishful thinking that their opposition would be overcome by the promise of wage work, and the hope that the Akimel O'odham would be only too happy to sell their "surplus" land to pay for the dam, since it promised to restore some of the water taken illegally from them by white farmers, demonstrate the limits of the Bureau of Indian Affairs' concern with Indian welfare on Indian terms. Time and again the benefits to whites intruded on the committee's discussion. Or it may have been that the committee simply assumed that Congress would find the project more palatable if it enabled white development, saved white small farmers, and was paid for by opening more Indian land to white settlement.[83]

The swirling debate over immigration, migration and belonging, mobility and sovereignty and security shaped and was shaped by contests over land: Who was entitled to what piece of the American Dream and promise and on what literal grounds? The various contestants posed the higher end for the human race as what justified exclusions. In this debate, the Pacific Northwest of North America was endangered by Asian migrants; the Southwest was a lost cause because of its proximity to and encompassing of large Mexican populations; and the ultimate "America," untouched by eastern political scandal and immigrant machines and western Mexicans and Asians, was the heartland, and Kansas, which repeatedly appeared in the hearings, became the stand-in for the average American.[84]

Simultaneously, the 1924 immigration legislation, with its commitment to racialized categories, defined Chinese, Japanese, and South Asian immigrants as illegal, but no one could, by looking, distinguish between a Chinese immigrant and a Chinese American citizen. Just as all people of Mexican descent became, in popular parlance and often in official behavior, "Mexicans" rather than Americans, no matter what their citizenship, so, too, did Asians become permanent outsiders or what historian Mae Ngai calls "impossible subjects."[85] These "others," so essential, were not "outside" the boundaries of the United States; whether they were citizens defined as "nonwhite" or immigrants—permanent or temporary—they had a necessary place *within* the system of capital-intensive farming and the speculator state that helped create and finance it.

Whatever discomfort congressmen had with the spectacle of the small farmer as exploiter of low-paid labor rather than as virtuous, self-sufficient husbandman, they faced farmer demands and diplomatic imperatives. Those forces overwhelmed the restrictionists and secured farmers a continued supply of Western Hemisphere immigrant workers. In this way a diverse set of threads came together to weave a modern agricultural system. First, the federal government played the part of speculator, building high-cost irrigation projects in the name of both developing the West and ensuring the continuation of widespread landownership and the political stability it promised. Second, the speculator citizen buyer was created as the ideal citizen. Third, the small speculator, for whom speculation was the entry to full citizenship and the nation's promise of opportunity for all, would take the risk on the property with its levies, hoping to repay irrigation construction costs. And, finally, the same state simultaneously created those excluded from full citizenship—the Indian, the Mexican, the migrant worker, who was deemed as perpetually premodern, as incapable of speculation (equated, again, with modernity)—to enable those farmers to make ends meet.[86] In this way, federal agricultural policy and western farmers maintained the promise of the region as a "white man's West" and the identity of the true American, the real farmer, the full citizen as white. This modern agricultural system of capital and labor would generate World War II's guest worker bracero program, which outlasted the war by decades, and its successor, special farmworker visas still operative into the twenty-first century.

9

Speculating on the West Imagined

On October 2, 1924, day laborer Jesus Lajun lay ill in his home not far from the Los Angeles River. His fifteen-year-old daughter suffered too from a headache, a sore throat, and a fever. When the daughter, Francisca Concha Lajun, died on the way to the hospital two days later, the officials listed the cause as double pneumonia. City Health Department doctors visited the Lajuns and other patients in the neighborhood as more and more residents fell ill with similar symptoms and the death toll grew. Investigators tried to determine the cause: Was it meningitis, influenza, pneumonia, or typhus? Finally at the end of the month came the answer: bubonic plague.[1]

The way Los Angeles responded to the outbreak highlighted the shifting terrain of Mexican life in the city founded by Mexicans but newly invented and promoted by Anglos. The Mexican population of the city and county had continued to grow in the late nineteenth and early twentieth centuries along with that of Japanese, Sikh, and Chinese immigrants. After the advent of the railroad, however, as it had with so many southwestern cities, the deluge of Anglo migrants and European immigrants overwhelmed everyone else.

Los Angeles remained in many ways a northern frontier for Mexico, but it now became not only the western frontier for Anglos but also the future. The frontier was both temporal and spatial. Boosters with a heavy and highly speculative investment in the town's real estate celebrated a romanticized Spanish colonial heritage of conquistadores, minimized the role of Mexico in the years between Mexican independence and U.S. conquest, and as much as possible rendered their Mexican inhabitants as some holdover of the past, as invisible in the present, and with no role as harbingers of marvels to come. In this context, plague became not just a health disaster but also a public relations one.

The struggle over the West imagined, including controlling the narrative of the region and shaping its meaning and future, was by no means limited to Los Angeles. Nor was it new. Westerners had never been shy about promoting a western fantasy. William "Buffalo Bill" Cody had shepherded tourists through buffalo country in the 1870s and taken the Wild West show on the road in the 1880s. The West such entrepreneurs marketed was carefully curated. The people who profited from the color were rarely the people who provided it. These latter people could get in on the action by playing "Indians," "cowboys," and "Mexicans" in ways and on stages prepared for them by others, but they rarely ran the show. Indian dancers, for example, struggled with a federal bureaucracy that wanted to foster their financial independence but not their cultural autonomy.[2]

In the 1920s new dynamics, including, at the core, the decade's defining commitment to speculation and new technologies (including cars), joined old techniques of exploiting the "West" imagined. This chapter begins by returning to plague-ridden Los Angeles and the shape of the region's urban development; then moves to tourism, the national parks, and highways; and ends with Prohibition, cross-border vice tourism, and the burgeoning film industry.

Shaping Western Cities

Los Angeles Mexicans and Anglos differed in their imagined West. Anglos greeted with anxiety the growing presence of Mexicans in southern California. They counted and recounted and found that by 1920 women constituted 43 percent of the Mexican-born population in the United States. Rather than the presence of women (and churches and schools) serving as a reassuring signifier of stable family formation, it unleashed a fresh onslaught of anxiety. Mexicans were not a fleeting presence, people who docilely disappeared below the border each winter. Mexicans were having children in the United States, and those children would be citizens. In rural Los Angeles County the majority of babies were white; but Mexican and Japanese infants, referred together in one county health report as the "yellow peril," shared the remaining 40 percent almost equally. Mexicans took up their position alongside the Japanese as disrupters of the region's heavily promoted promise, reserved for westering whites. Well before the outbreak of the plague, officials and the mainstream press had conceived of the dominant threat to the region's well-being as racial.[3]

The plague began in a Mexican neighborhood and traveled relentlessly along lines of kin and community—neighbors who came to help others in distress, mothers, sisters, cousins, boarders, friends, a priest, a nurse, an ambulance driver. It killed almost forty people, 90 percent of whom were Mexican. Health officials had long spread the image of the neighborhood as disease prone; rates of infant and maternal mortality far outpaced those of more prosperous Anglo neighborhoods. The high disease rates came from city policies. While Americanization programs emphasized hygiene, cities did not fund adequate water and sewer systems to Mexican neighborhoods, allowed poorly maintained rental properties, and provided a segregated and dramatically uneven set of public health clinics. Instead of linking the difference in health outcomes to resources and services, however, authorities and press linked it to "nationality" and cultural practices. Mexicans, in their eyes, were disease prone. The connection was perhaps nowhere more dramatic than in the testing for syphilis, begun in 1924 only for Mexican women. Despite the fact that only 2 percent of those tested had positive results, health officials advocated testing all pregnant Mexican women and requiring treatment.[4]

To Los Angeles boosters, Mexicans endangered the city's health, endangered the body politic, endangered the city's future. As Los Angeles strove to market itself as the capital of sunshine, health, and well-being, its boosters saw Mexicans as almost literally the fly in the ointment. The plague cemented the connection in the popular Anglo imagination. Two years after the outbreak, a University of California zoology professor referred to "the Mexicans, with their various diseases . . . their tendencies to huddle together," as being "the means of spreading various epidemics throughout our population, and in general, deteriorating the physical welfare of the people."[5]

These ideas shaped the city's response to the plague. At midnight on October 31, the city health department began a quarantine of a seventeen-block zone around Lujan's house, encompassing about two thousand residents. The department hired 450 men, who, with the city police, roped off the neighborhood and patrolled its borders twenty-four hours a day. For two weeks they prohibited gatherings of any size and nature. Trolleys drove by without stopping. Los Angeles County Charities staff delivered food and milk to each house; physicians and nurses stood on the street and called into houses to enumerate the sick and dying. Visitors to the neighborhood caught in the quarantine slept in the Baptist Mission church. As the days passed, officials targeted more Mexican areas, apartment houses, and even "two isolated homes" in one district. In only two of the areas had the plague been verified. In the others, the only verifiable suspicious element was the presence of Mexican inhabitants.[6]

The guards shivered in the cool fall evenings and showed little compunction at tearing boards off houses to burn for warmth. Sometimes they justified the destruction as part of plague eradication. Their goal was to raise the houses high enough off the ground that dogs and cats could kill rats underneath them, so anything at foundation level was fair game. They burned old furniture, clothing, bedding, and whole shacks. They pumped poisonous gas and scattered rat poison everywhere. Afterward the district looked like a cyclone had rammed through it. While some residents succeeded in getting compensated for damaged property, officials often instead declared the structures public nuisances. By the end of the year, over a thousand Mexican dwellings had been destroyed. While one report noted that rat eradication had to occur "even in residence districts occupied by native Americans," it advocated particular focus on "the foreign quarter . . . in the Mexican, Russian [Jews], Chinese, and Japanese quarters by the destruction of all structures not worth rat proofing." Los Angeles health officials targeted these groups as "foreign" regardless of birthplace and threatened to eradicate their neighborhoods and not just the rats.[7]

Even as four new cases among the city's Mexican inhabitants appeared, the *Los Angeles Times* declared "no spread of disease." Historian Natalia Molina concludes, "For as long as the disease's effects were limited to Mexicans, who lived on both the geographical and the social margins of Los Angeles, the plague would continue to be considered under control." But rendering Mexicans immobile and invisible was tricky. During the plague, Mexican industrial laborers were permitted to leave the quarantined area daily to report to work. At the same time, Mexicans were unwelcome in downtown tourist venues. The Biltmore Hotel unceremoniously fired its 150 Mexican workers without regard to their residence. When a delegation of Mexican government officials and journalists protested, they met with Clarence Matson, who represented the Chamber of Commerce and whose view of the city's future was epitomized in his November 1924 article, "The Los Angeles of Tomorrow," in which he wrote, "Anglo Saxon civilization must climax in the generations to come. . . . The Los Angeles of Tomorrow will be the center of this climax."[8]

As plague deaths dwindled toward the end of the year and public health officials declared the outbreak over, the city's movers and shakers turned to damage control—not in terms of human health but in terms of economic health. By December 1924, as they watched property values drop precipitately, bankruptcies rise, and people flee, the Los Angeles Chamber of Commerce put out articles deploring hysterical reporting on the plague. The eastern press proved skeptical, and *The Nation* condemned the Los Angeles Chamber of Commerce for suppressing reporting on the plague and other disease outbreaks.[9]

The pressure to suppress came at least in part from those participating in the rampant speculation that would characterize the greater Los Angeles real estate market throughout the decade. In 1923 alone California issued over twenty-seven thousand real estate sales licenses. Rapid population growth combined with laws upholding zoning restrictions. Private property owners—though not government entities—could forbid sales to people of certain racial and ethnic groups. An ever-larger number of racist utopian developments blanketed the region.[10] Los Angeles boosters joined the image of the city as the pinnacle of Anglo-Saxon civilization to the promise of safe and entirely white neighborhoods.

The complicity of realtors ensured that mixed neighborhoods, those with Japanese, Mexican, African American, and white residents, were seen as unstable, vulnerable, and bad investments.

That line of thought heightened white property owners' fears in Los Angeles as it did across the nation when nonwhites moved into or even looked at property in a neighborhood. A white man in the West Jefferson area of Los Angeles, favoring organizing to restrict sales, argued, "We neighbors must really stand together . . . for it is clear that if the man next door sold his house to a Negro or a Japanese my property would immediately become worth a thousand dollars less."[11]

The speculative nature of real estate heightened the stakes. Small investors, property-owning families, aspirant social climbers risked their all and were often willing to go to violent measures to secure what they perceived as the greatest threat to their investment, inseparably in property and in whiteness. Lower-middle-class white families often invested in homes they could ill afford and faced refinancing them every five years; refinancing, in turn, was impossible if banks perceived the value of the property as having fallen.[12] Over the course of the decade through this combination of factors, Los Angeles developers, their realtors, and their customers turned the greater urban area into a highly segregated landscape.

Property speculation and its accompanying segregation were not unique to the U.S. West, but the extraordinary population growth of many western cities, along with the whiteness of the imagined future West, made them particularly acute. City growth in the West for the most part far exceeded the rate of urban growth in the country as a whole. Houston, thanks to the port improvements, war, and oil, grew by 111 percent to 292,352 people. Tulsa's explosive growth of the previous decade tapered off but still reached 96 percent, while Oklahoma City more than doubled its growth rate and ended the decade with 185,389. San Diego came close to doubling with a growth rate of 99 percent and a population of nearly 150,000. Los Angeles grew faster than any major city in the United States, reaching over 500,000 by 1920 and 1.2 million by 1930. Suburbs sprang up within the county—over 1,400 new subdivisions in only two years—and harbored another 1 million residents. The Los Angeles Chamber of Commerce declared in 1924, "For centuries, the Anglo-Saxon race has been marching westward. . . . The apex of this movement is Los Angeles County."[13]

As Hollywood moguls joined oil magnates in building Beverly

Hills mansions, and as the coincidence of cheap local gasoline and empty lots led to a sprawling metropolis, Los Angeles surpassed San Francisco in population. Before the 1920s the Los Angeles housing market had been relatively open. The open shop policies that dominated the city and destroyed the unions had paradoxically opened job opportunities for African American and Japanese workers excluded from so many AFL unions. In 1910 over a third of Black Angelenos owned their own homes, a national high, and more than one had occupied a seat on the Los Angeles Chamber of Commerce. The 1920s saw the steady foreclosure of those opportunities. White residents formed "protective" associations to, as the Hollywood Protective Association put it in 1923, "Keep Hollywood White." Ku Klux Klan membership surged in Los Angeles as elsewhere, swelled by government officials and police officers who seemed untroubled by threats of lynching those sympathetic to open housing. Residents saw themselves as part of a national effort to keep open housing or, the reverse, to keep homeownership white, making reference to Tulsa's riot of 1921 and similar struggles in Detroit.[14]

Cars made it possible for the wealthy to move farther from streetcars on what had been African American small ranches and chicken farms in Bel Air and Beverly Hills. Developers focused on producing a middle-class version of that dream on the flatlands west of the city. They constructed wide paved parkways with grassy medians and lush landscaping and installed electric lighting, and they priced the homes they built along those parkways under $10,000. Developer Walter Leimert teamed up with home furnishings companies to capitalize on the decade's ever-increasing fascination with the region's mythic Spanish past, offering Spanish mission–inspired houses with a package of similarly styled furniture, wall hangings, and dishes. By 1923 builders had erected almost a million buildings in mission style, promising a peaceful idyll in an orderly racial landscape to potential residents.[15]

The image promised peace, but the housing market fluctuated wildly. Large-scale developers such as Leimert struggled to stabilize it in the face of rampant speculation that by the decade's disastrous end would yield thousands of vacant lots. They relied on the restrictive covenants that covered not only who could inhabit these homes but also the size, style, and cost of the housing.[16] Not everyone played along. In older neighborhoods, residents disagreed on which restrictions, if any, were most essential. Even in newer neighborhoods, residents disagreed.

Migrants of modest means had joined the stream of over a million newcomers arriving in Los Angeles County in the 1920s, drawn from across the urbanizing nation by the well-advertised promise of cheap lots on which they could build their own homes with their own hands, raise a few chickens, rabbits, and even goats, and both market and eat the produce from a backyard garden. Such practices would decrease their dependence on wage labor, notoriously uncertain in the 1920s, when unions were besieged and unemployment insurance and social security did not exist. These migrants arrived with their goods on the back of a truck, built a garage, and then lived in it while they accumulated the cash or scavenged the lumber to build the rest of the house.

These settlers equated homeownership with full citizenship and success. They may have wanted city water and sewers, but they did not want expensive parks and streetlights or sometimes even paved streets that would drive up their taxes and endanger their ability to stay in their homes, and they resisted uniform setbacks, styles, and minimum house prices. Many agreed on the desirability of exclusively white subdivisions, but even in that case, costs could trump exclusivity. Faced with a choice between a costly annexation and an integrated, multiethnic existing high school, for example, the majority of the residents of the largely white suburb known as Home Gardens opted for the latter, and though some parents supported the KKK's effort to take over politics in increasingly Black neighboring Watts at middecade, their children experienced peaceful intermingling among Jordan High School's white, Black, Asian, and Latinx students in extracurricular activities.[17] Elsewhere, as in Compton, small populations of Japanese Americans and Mexican Americans lived alongside Anglos; they were not, like Blacks, excluded altogether. Segregation still played a role in daily life, though. Light-skinned Mexican Americans with unaccented English could pass as white, but their darker-skinned family members and friends had to use the local movie theater's side entrance and sit in designated sections.[18]

In new subdivisions, by contrast, private developers from Los Angeles to Tucson wrote restrictions into each property deed and proudly advertised the impregnable whiteness of their elite, middle-class, and working-class residential developments.[19] The Mexican-descent workers who built the houses and prepared the land found themselves cordoned off into their own tract when owners began to move into the newly finished houses. In Los Angeles a permanent Mexican community arose between elite Rancho Santa Fe and coastal Solana Beach, ultimately called Eden Gardens. Here, the residents built their own houses, and their children attended the segregated school that opened in 1928. They worked in the orange groves, the homes in Rancho Santa Fe, barbershops, and movie theaters.[20]

The cars that made the subdivision developments possible also complicated their survival economically and socially. The rate of car ownership grew astronomically in Los Angeles from 1910 forward. By 1920 the county had one car for every 3.6 residents; by 1925 one of every two Angelenos owned a car. The national average that year was one in six, and most cities had lower rates. Unlike in older industrial settlements in the eastern part of the United States, even in working-class subdivisions hosting both residents and industries, most earners worked elsewhere. There was no consonance of workplace and neighborhood. Promoters of working-class subdivisions, eager to lure factories, touted the residents as "100 per cent American," nonunion whites. The promoters succeeded, and Los Angeles by 1924 ranked eighth in the nation in manufacturing, climbing to fifth by 1935, the fastest rate of industrial growth in the country. Yet no union locals' picnics cluttered the calendar. Residents hopped on streetcars, drove in their cars, or hitchhiked to hit the beach, attend movies and clubs, or even shop. Local merchants, rooted in the subdivision, struggled against the tide to imbue their customers with loyalty.[21]

When homeownership meant legitimacy, full citizenship, autonomy, and success and was the only factor linking neighbor to neighbor, whites could turn violent in defense of their investments. The response when shoe store owner Mitsuhiko Shimuzu moved into Belvedere, undeterred by anti-Japanese white agitators, differed dramatically from some of the California valley towns. Once his family moved in, threatening signs sprang up around their house, and on February 28, 1923, when the family was away, neighbors set fire to the house, leaving behind coal tar, feathers, and a rope. A year later, a group of white men and women dragged Japanese tenant Mokichi Kawamoto, a manager at a Little Tokyo auto dealership, out of his house and beat him, vowing to kill him if he did not move out of the neighborhood. Local authorities, who included a past president of the Anti-Asiatic Association, blamed Kawamoto and did nothing.[22]

As did the Japanese landholders, African Americans fought throughout the decade for their property rights and most often lost. In 1926 the Southwest Chamber of Commerce organized to drive out Black Nationalist Mentis Carrere, who had moved into the Green Meadows neighborhood during the 1920s boom. As mobs nightly threw bricks at the house, Carrere and his supporters armed themselves. When the heirs of white Lulu Letteau discovered she had placed racial restrictive covenants on three lots near the Dunbar Hotel, despite the fact that the lots were owned by African Americans, the heirs sued to recover the land and won. As the Home Protection League broadened the eviction effort, the African American owners fought for their homes (although they then lost them) until a court of appeals ruled in April 1932 against the Letteau heirs, and the state supreme court denied the appeal. Racially restrictive covenants were legally enforceable, but not after a completed transaction.[23]

Westering African Americans had hardly been immune to the lure of utopian creations and real estate speculations. The Black town of Boley, Oklahoma, and its myriad counterparts had, after all, just such genesis at the beginning of the century. Greenwood, the Black section of Tulsa, Oklahoma, had epitomized the promise, with its swank hotels, prosperous businesses, schools, professionals, and homeowners, until the monumental backlash of white supremacists burned it down in 1921. As western states made it harder for Japanese immigrants to create agricultural colonies in the name of their children and eradicated Black towns' political heft through gerrymandering and restrictive voting laws, such geographical fantasies were increasingly for whites only. In late 1925 Wilbur C. Gordon purchased a 213-acre barley field just outside southwest Los

Angeles. He aimed to create Gordon Manor, a subdivision where his fellow African Americans could enjoy the same sort of carefully monitored middle-class landscape as their white counterparts. It was not to be. By April 1926 white developers and their allies had succeeded in getting the Los Angeles County Board of Supervisors to take Gordon's property through eminent domain. To that parcel the board added a one-hundred-acre tract inhabited by Japanese tenants who would be evicted so that the whole could become a regional park. The board's mission of eradicating Black and Japanese settlers having been accomplished, however, local residents and municipalities refused to fund the park, and it remained a large patch of weeds. Black and Japanese Angelenos would reside instead in the Eastside's older mixed communities of Little Tokyo and Central Avenue, with the area's working-class and industrial enclaves.[24]

Those mixed communities produced both creativity and conflict. The area west of Central Avenue was full of Jewish migrants and European, Mexican, and Asian immigrants, but it also contained what historian Lonnie Bunch called "a miniature Harlem," with jazz clubs and the Dunbar Hotel. The adjacent Little Tokyo catered to a diverse array of the area's migrant workers; Blacks, Germans, and Japanese got into fights on its streets, and in 1927 one-third of its thirty hotels and boardinghouses were for whites only. Yet Japanese and Black singers joined together in a choir for which "Tiny" Brantley played, and drummer Hideo Kawano performed with African American Johnny Otis and Mexican American Don Tosti. Across the river from Little Tokyo, Boyle Heights housed refugees from the Mexican Revolution and upwardly mobile Japanese, African American, and Jewish families. In 1930 African American homeownership in Los Angeles, at approximately one-third, approached that of the city's overall rate and continued to outpace that of Detroit, Chicago, and New York by two to six times. In short, while speculation and dreams of white exclusivity literally shaped the landscape of substantial districts of western cities, pockets of unrestricted housing remained.[25]

Tourism: Performing the West in Plays and Fiestas

In the midst of all this jockeying for physical space, the jockeying for imagined space, the image of the West in the popular imagination reached a crescendo. As it was in Los Angeles, across the Southwest the contest was inseparably tied to real estate speculation, development, and tourist dollars.

The region's marketing strategies had already made several shifts before the 1920s. From the arrival of the railroad in the 1880s, the region had marketed itself as the land of sunshine. It had promised to restore the health of those debilitated by the pace of industrial society or the scourge of the era, tuberculosis. In the 1910s, just as the Mexican Revolution and various cross-border incursions in both directions made the region seem less than restful and restorative, boosters revised their appeal from health to history. In so doing, they could promise a piece of Europe in the United States to lure tourists away from war-torn Europe and position the United States as the natural heir to a fatigued set of European conquerors, taking over from the genteel if decaying Spanish golden age. This vision paralleled its contemporary romanticized vision of the Old South, an orderly place where white men were in charge, women were charming and unthreatening, and workers were happy to be enslaved. In this vision of Spanish rule, selfless missionaries worked for the uplift of their grateful, cultureless charges, teaching them orderliness, chastity, and the meaning of hard work. In the context of a prolonged Mexican Revolution, it is not surprising that the Mexican era from 1821 to 1846, when mentioned at all, appeared as a dark age rather than as heir to Spain's empire. The dilapidated state of the mission ruins, seen as an organic decay, at the same time naturalized the end of Spanish rule and its replacement by the United States.[26]

At least two of the premier purveyors of this message lasted into the 1920s, but not without alteration. In southern California, *The Mission Play*, an extravaganza first staged on the grounds of the San Gabriel Mission with a cast of over one hundred in 1912, focused on the arrival of missionaries in the eighteenth century as bringing light to what were posed as incredibly primitive Indians. Missionaries, not soldiers, were the heroes of the play. Anglos, not Mexicans, were their heirs. Anglos arrived to rescue the region from the chaos that resulted, in the play, from Mexico's secularization of the missions. It is no accident that a major backer of the incredibly popular if not always financially successful *Mission Play* was antiunion *Los Angeles Times* publisher Harry Chandler, whose reporter John Steven McGroarty wrote the play. Breaking American theater records, with a run of 127 shows over ten weeks, the moral of the story (or "sermon," as one Catholic journal termed it) trumped its lack of verisimilitude. The heroic endeavor was bringing order out of chaos, including creating docile, industrious workers, "shouldering the white man's burden . . . so stoutly."

Keenly aware of the connection between the play and development, when the play faltered financially in the mid-1920s, the Los Angeles Chamber of Commerce stepped in, creating a corporation "to make the Mission Play safe and preserve it for future generations." Railroad magnates, oil and land barons, Harry Chandler, and other members of the local merchant elite bought in.[27]

In *The Mission Play* the priests are heroic the conquistadores are feckless, all too willing to abandon their Native charges.[28] In Santa Fe, New Mexico, by contrast, the heroes of the far earlier Spanish arrival were the conquistadores. In a three-day festival, deliberately aiming to rival *The Mission Play*, the first day celebrated the original inhabitants and still-present Pueblo Indians, whose own rapidly rising star as a tourist attraction was evident not only in the tourist Mecca of the Grand Canyon, where they performed their identity for visitors drawn by the spectacular scenery, but also in expositions from Chicago, to St. Louis, to San Diego. The second day featured the conquering and reconquering Spaniards, at first played by those who claimed descent from those early arrivals. The third day featured the arrival of the Anglos and the surrender of the territory to Brigadier General Stephen Watts Kearny in 1846.

As they were in the California play, more troubling elements were omitted from the festival, including Mexican independence and the bloody resistance to U.S. conquest. And while the fiesta's three days relegated both Pueblos and Hispanos to the past, the theme was multicultural harmony. Participants such as the Honorable George Washington Armijo, who in 1911 played Diego de Vargas (captain general and governor of New Mexico in the seventeenth century), had served as Rough Riders with Teddy Roosevelt in the Spanish-American War. They formed the perfect bridge from illustrious Spanish past to loyal U.S. present. Newspaper coverage in 1919 and 1920 focused on the multiculturalism: "Where else than in Santa Fe do Pueblo Indians, descendants of the cave and cliff dwellers, descendants of Spaniards and Moors, the Anglo-Saxon and all the other nationalities that have come to America from foreign shores, mingle so freely and so picturesquely?" Amid the hyperpatriotism of the post–World War I red scare, a Santa Fe newspaper headline clarified the import of this version of history: "Santa Fe Will Show It's American to the Core." Mexican independence featured only once, in 1921 at its centenary, and then disappeared. The Kearny pageant, by contrast, lasted until 1927. With the pageant, Santa Fe shouldered aside the English colonial East Coast to claim an older spot in the national story. Santa Fe was settled before colonial New England and was rooted in Pueblo tradition; one booster called the city's architecture "strictly American." The distinctiveness that had delayed New Mexico statehood for so long now became a positive attribute.[29]

As pageantry declined and spectacle (and the rise of Hollywood) replaced it, the contest over these self-presentations intensified. Pueblo architecture, having appeared in popular attractions at U.S. world's fairs since the 1890s, was legible to a wide audience. It featured prominently in San Diego's 1915 Panama-California Exposition. The ten-acre Painted Desert exhibit included nearly three hundred Native peoples of the region; its San Ildefonso Indians built low adobe structures and beehive ovens. It proved the fair's leading commercial attraction.

Edgar Lee Hewett, director of the joint Museum of New Mexico and School of American Archaeology, and his allies had overseen the exhibit's New Mexico building. It housed exhibits on natural resources and staged Indian ceremonial dances. It had little information on the state's contemporary Hispanos and nothing on Hispano history and culture. Hewett carried their success back to Santa Fe. Tourists, he concluded, wanted to see Indians, not Hispanos, and they wanted to see them safely exhibited by Anglos, not "Mexicans." By the end of the 1920s, as Pueblo Indians became ever more visible, including in congressional testimony, and Hispanos became a minority population in the state and legislature, what had been called "Spanish-Pueblo style" became simply "Pueblo style."[30]

Santa Fe's fiesta became contested ground. The Vargas pageant of 1911 and 1912, held on July 4, had been staged by Hispanos. When Hewett revived it in 1919, creating the three-day version, he put it in Anglo hands, seeing "Mexicans" as a peril to "the health of the race in its onward march."[31] As local interest in the fiesta waned, taking a leaf from California, Anglo organizers began to hire nonlocal professionals and moved the venue from the streets to a stage—removing it spatially and temporally from the still Hispano-dominated town.[32]

Precisely because the town still had a Hispano majority, those organizers had no monopoly on the presentation of the state's history. Hispano legislators had brought Hewett's Archaeological Institute of America to Santa Fe in 1909, but they had already resisted his vision in the restoration of the Palace of the Governors.[33] In the early 1920s they found allies in the state's growing colony of leftist artists, who saw the changing nature of the fiesta as at odds with the sense of preindustrial, communally centered villages they came to Santa Fe to find. Moreover, the price of admission proved too steep for many local residents.

Activist Dolly Sloan and poet Witter Bynner, both New York transplants, allied with Hispano elites to offer instead the Pasatiempo, a communal street festival, beginning in 1924, and the Hysterical Pageant, a satirical version of the now cordoned-off and sacralized official pageant, this one rife with painted sheep and giant puppets. The artists claimed the terrain of authenticity, that theirs was an organic expression of the community without the imported talent. In the Pasatiempo, when participants needed "costumes," they used their grandparents' clothes. The Pasatiempo included community singing, street dancing on the plaza, band concerts, and a children's animal show, as well as the Hysterical Pageant. People called it "the grand carnival."

The fiesta's pageants featured male heroes—missionaries and conquistadores. The Pasatiempo had festival queens and both women and men marketing their wares. The Pasatiempo highlighted Hispano village crafts, not Indian ones, and promoted them as equally deserving of preservation. They created a "native market," where Spanish-speaking village farmers sold their chiles, apples, and arts. The Old Santa Fe Association, which wanted to guide Santa Fe's growth and hold off Anglicization, supported the

Pasatiempo and allied with two less elite groups: La Unión Protectiva, a mutual aid society with about three hundred members, and El Centro de Cultura, a new middle-class Hispano literary and musical society. They, too, invented traditions; they just had different notions of the community they expressed.[34]

Commodifying Hispano identity and turning it into a tourist attraction, even if a less enticing one than that of the Pueblo Indians, itself signified the decline of Hispanos' actual power in the territory. California's native Spanish/Mexicans had already lost power by the 1920s, but in New Mexico and southern Arizona the 1920s witnessed their final displacement. The role of the Hispano elite in these developments was complicated. Despite the Hispano majority in Santa Fe, as early as 1912 the city planning board was led by a tightly bound set of Anglos and only two Hispanos, one the former governor, Miguel Otero. While most Hispanos continued, in Spanish, to identify as "Mexicano/a," elites increasingly turned to "Spanish-American" in English in order to recognize their own claims to Spanish descent and to distance themselves from those "Mexicans" the U.S. conquerors so visibly scorned. In the Anglo world, where "Mexican" conjured up a racial, political, and economic threat, "Spanish" conjured up a European heritage, tired perhaps, but white. In turn, the Spanish-language press's use of "Anglo-Americano," drifted more prominently into English, labeling the relative newcomers as "Anglo" rather than "American." The shift rendered Anglos one of the triad of Anglo-Pueblo-Spanish rather than the monopolizers of the default, normative, dominant "American."[35]

Ownership over history and regional identity could not be divorced from contests over land. Amid the national focus on Pueblos, with whom Hispanos were often contestants for land, and Hewett's crowd preferring Pueblos as well, New Mexico's Hispano educated elite struggled to maintain a place at the table. To some elite Hispanos, the Pueblo focus was a slap in the face. Adelina (Nina) Otero-Warren complained that it mocked "the twelve thousand 'people of Spanish blood' living within the boundaries of old Pueblo land grants, the ancestors of whom once 'assumed "the White Man's burden" in the Southwest' amid 'the crushing burdens of civilization.'" Federal protection of Indian interests stood in stark contrast, for many Hispanos, to the undiminished assault on Hispano landholding and Mexican land grants. In this context, they could become competitive boosters of their own legacy.[36]

The contest came to a head one day in the fall of 1927, when future president Harry S. Truman, then a judge, came to Santa Fe to present a statue titled *Pioneer Mother* or *Madonna of the Trail,* a ten-foot-tall, warm pink concrete celebration of the Anglo conquest of the West along the trail that began in Truman's Missouri and ended in Santa Fe. The National Old Trails Association, a Missouri group of boosters, patriots, and businessmen, had jumped on the highways bandwagon and aimed to commemorate the Santa Fe Trail. Truman had become its president in 1924 and enjoyed increasing national stature. The Daughters of the American Revolution (DAR) was a major mover of the effort to link Maryland to California via the Cumberland Gap, the Santa Fe Trail, and the Old Spanish Trail as a testimony to the triumph of the project of national expansion and unity. The DAR had chosen the "pioneer woman" image, intending to place identical copies of the statue in each of twelve states along the "Pioneer Memorial Highway." In Santa Fe they hit, as historian Jeffrey C. Sanders put it, an adobe wall.

It was not that New Mexico didn't appreciate the automobile and the benefits of good roads well traveled by tourists. But in 1927 the guardians of Santa Fe's Hispano pioneer past ran into the guardians of a different version of U.S. history. Mary Austin wrote in the *Santa Fe New Mexican,* "The pioneers of New Mexico are not the pioneers of the D.A.R.; they should have been consulted and . . . I considered it profoundly discourteous for the D.A.R. to think of setting up one of their monuments in the city of Santa Fe without widely expressed approbation of the New Mexico Pioneers." Truman and his DAR patrons packed up and headed instead for the more hospitable Albuquerque.[37]

In many ways the styling of Santa Fe succeeded. The tribute to "Spanish" culture drew tourists. The Pasatiempo's popularity led to changes in the fiesta. In 1927, the same year Truman's statue lost out in Santa Fe, the fiesta council added a fiesta queen, chosen from among the city's young Spanish-speaking women. In 1929 the council surrendered entirely to the Pasatiempo, putting

El Mercado at the center and having an all-Hispano cast reenact the Vargas entrada, a Catholic processional, and singing and dancing in the streets. Anglo critics of the statue incident complained that Santa Fe's Anglo past and its early Anglo homes were "being thrust out of the way without passing thought." But the decade was more complex. The city's population had doubled during the 1920s. Meanwhile, property and economic and political clout continued to pass from Hispano to Anglo hands.[38]

In Tucson, Arizona, which marketed itself as the gateway to "old" Mexico, the boosters developed what historian Lydia Otero labels an "Anglo Fantasy Heritage" to put alongside what Carey McWilliams derisively coined the "Spanish Fantasy Heritage" of New Mexico and California. While the population of Mexican descent in Tucson doubled between 1900 and 1920, Anglo arrivals overwhelmed them, reaching roughly 63 percent of Tucson's 20,300 inhabitants. As Anglo residents had done in Santa Fe, they brought with them different architectural styles: clapboard Victorians and bungalows. Tucson saw some Spanish colonial revival in the late 1920s aimed at the most prosperous new arrivals.[39] But instead of focusing on a history of Spanish dons and Franciscan friars, officials and boosters allowed the local mission churches to fall into decay. In the 1920s they brought polo to Tucson, golf and country clubs, and, finally, Rodeo Day to set next to the older rodeos of Cheyenne, Wyoming, and Pendleton, Oregon. Rodeo Days had Indian Days with "dances performed by 'real Indians'"; it had cowboy and cowgirl contests; it had a half-day parade. Local schools and government offices closed for the duration. It was a tremendous success. Motorcades and airplanes flooded the city with spectators, who exceeded the lodging capacity.[40]

Although almost everything about ranching and cowboys had come to the United States from Mexico, including the terminology of "lasso," "chaps," and so on, and many Tucsonenses and their ancestors had been ranchers and cowboys, Tucson sold the cowboy as distinctly American.[41] There was none of the sentimental masculinity performed in the Spanish Fantasy Heritage that linked conquest and religion. In the 1920s Tucson's Rodeo Day parades included Indian fighters, as well as Indians, including in one year, in a move almost inconceivable decades later, an Anglo participant lauded as a "hero" of the "battle" at Wounded Knee.

As Tucson, like Santa Fe, struggled to distinguish itself from California (and Phoenix), its boosters settled on the story of Anglo triumph over a hostile climate and hostile natives. Recognizing Mexican pioneers would have interfered with that narrative. The number of dude ranches around Tucson skyrocketed. Tourists anxious to play cowboy could have visited two in 1923 but over forty fifteen years later. Tucson became the "Dude Ranch Capital of the World."[42]

Speculators built their investments in the future on a controlled narrative of the western past and then had it literally enacted in fiestas, pageants, and rodeos. They aimed with these stories to draw a particular audience to create a particular western future, self-reinforcing. The effort to create such narratives, however, exposed both fissures and fantasies.

Tourism: Highways and National Parks

Speculators and boosters created a distinctive regional style and fantasy heritages to draw tourists, investors, and settlers. Their success came inseparably with other key developments. National parks, highways, and automobile tourism all came of age together in the 1920s. Mass tourism became another eastern use for the West, and as seen above, it was one heartily exploited by a West plagued with speculators and opportunists, impoverished farmers and indebted farm-town merchants.

Established in 1916, by 1919 the National Park Service "aimed to become a premier tourist-service agency."[43] The parks had largely forbidden automobile traffic, but the burgeoning number of car owners clamored for access and won. In 1920 there had been eight million cars registered to owners in the United States; in 1930 there were twenty-three million.[44] The open spaces of the West beckoned to adventurous and war-weary drivers.

It seemed unlikely to many that cars would ever replace trains. For example, more than one hundred thousand people visited the Grand Canyon each year in the early 1920s, the overwhelming majority by train. The terrible roads meant the journey took literally days from Flagstaff instead of hours. But then the Park Service created a two-lane, two-thousand-mile paved loop linking the Grand Canyon to Glacier National Park in Montana and the Rockies to Yosemite in California. By 1926 car traffic outpaced railroad traffic to the Grand Canyon.[45]

Federal fostering of car culture was not limited to the parks. In November 1926 the federal government formally established U.S. Route 66, which ran from Chicago through Missouri, Kansas, Oklahoma, Texas, New Mexico, and Arizona, ending in Los Angeles 2,448 miles later. On the state level, highway promoters used vehicle registration and license fees to develop a statewide highway system. Just as the railroads had transformed the corridors through which they ran, these roads transformed the surrounding countryside, encouraging towns to lure and serve tourists and speculators to invest in land along the route.[46]

In 1912 only about a dozen Americans drove across the country. In 1921 about twenty thousand did. By the mid-1920s ten to twenty million auto campers hit the road each season, or between a tenth and a sixth of the country's population. As automobile tourism outpaced railroad tourism, towns vied for the routing of interstate highways and even major local arteries the way they had fought in the previous century for railroads. A highway loop linking his properties to scenic attractions had formed part of Secretary of the Interior Albert Fall's failed schemes. More successfully, California clubwomen lobbied to build El Camino Real, the highway connecting the state's Spanish missions. The sale of $74 million worth of public bonds resulted in its construction in 1919. Other clubwomen lobbied for the Old Spanish Trail, stretching from Florida to San Diego, and celebrated its completion in 1929.[47]

Eager to cash in on through traffic and to corral pesky motorists away from their penchant to park in farmers' fields, help themselves to the produce, and leave behind their garbage, western towns created free municipal automobile campgrounds. The campgrounds soon sprouted central buildings with showers, washing facilities, electric lights, and fireplaces as rival municipalities vied to lure the traveler (and potential settler). By the early 1920s, Kansas had over 200 municipal auto campgrounds, and Colorado had 247. Denver's Overland Park was called the Manhattan of auto camps. It accommodated over two thousand auto campers at a time on the banks of the Platte River. Auto campers could find similar municipal accommodations in Seattle and Omaha. Even a small-town campsite on a main road hosted fifty to sixty cars a day.[48] In 1920 Cheyenne, Wyoming, hosted 2,540 auto campers from thirty-one states in a single day.

Tourists wanted to see the "real" West—the cowboys and farmers, the Grand Canyon and the deserts, and Hollywood, too. Emily Post complained of Cheyenne, Wyoming's eastern pretensions. What were neoclassical architecture and movie theaters doing in Wyoming? "It was the WEST, the great free, open West we had come to see," she griped. "Ranches, cowboys, Indians, not little cities like sample New Yorks."[49] Authenticity was meant to be part of the tourist experience, but its definition was far from clear.

By the late 1920s the over sixty Hispano villages upriver from Santa Fe and the Hispano village crafts on display in Santa Fe itself had shouldered their way into a share of the tourist spotlight alongside the Pueblos. When the Fred Harvey Company, which managed tourist facilities for the Santa Fe Railway, began its Indian Detours in 1926, car tours occasionally added the picturesque mountain villages of Chimayo and Truchas to the standard Indian destinations. The 1926 promotional brochure for these three-day "motor" outings promised that they traveled "through the storied heart of the Indo-Spanish Southwest." Promotional material referred to the villages as "medieval," frozen in time.[50]

It took some work to turn a blind eye to the high-heeled, modern-dressed young women in the villages, to the radios and sewing machines bought with wages that village families' migrant men brought back into the villages. But the villagers were indeed desperately poor. To Anglos for whom the Hispano villages offered a foil, a refuge from the failures of war-torn industrial society, the answer to the economic plight of the villages was less integration into that industrial world than marketing their history and handicrafts to it. In 1925 these Anglos, with some local elites, including Nina Otero-Warren, created the Spanish Colonial Arts Society. They used prizes, exhibits, and marketing, aiming, as writer Mary Austin put it, "to rescue from oblivion all talent and inherited craft stored up in our Spanish people." Under their aegis, Celso Gallegos, an elderly, infirm *santero* (maker of *santos*, or saints' images) from Agua Fria, himself a grandson of a *santero*, won a $60 prize in 1926. Tinsmiths, weavers, and woodcarvers also benefited. Prices rose, and as with Pueblo crafts, cheap copies proliferated.[51]

Villagers undoubtedly benefited from the marketing, but aesthetic control remained a contest. Anglo experts provided authorized "authentic" designs. Anglos similarly took control of the renovations of Chimayo's famous church and shrine to prevent the selling off of relics and protect it from locals who had installed modern towers and a low-maintenance tin roof. Crafts people knew they participated in these fairs and markets as performers. Historian Hal Rothman describes such compromises as the "devil's bargain" locals made with tourists. In order to support themselves, locals made themselves appear to fit visitors' fantasies.[52]

As in Los Angeles, Santa Fe, and Tucson, constructing the western landscape as a tourist attraction meant rearranging the population of the present, as well as the story of the past. At the Grand Canyon, under threat of seizure by eminent domain, Anglo pioneers had sold their land to the government and often moved away from the canyon entirely. The pattern of Indian life at the Grand Canyon tourist spots was already well established. As they had been doing since early in the century, the Hopis, who did not live as near the canyon as other Native peoples, performed "Hopiness," dressing in marked regalia and making crafts (marketed in park shops). These Hopis were joined by other Hopis working as laborers and bellhops and in other service jobs who were not performing Hopiness, who dressed like other laborers, and whose Indian identity was invisible to visitors. The performers and other workers gathered in the second-floor Hopi House apartment, which belonged to Jane Nichols, a Hopi woman from a trading family on Second Mesa. Their diet mixed Hopi and non-Hopi styles, and though they had access to tribal healers, many also or instead visited the railroad physician.[53]

Meanwhile, the locals, the Havasupais, farmed in the canyon and traveled to the rim to earn cash working, often in construction jobs, for the park and the railroad. By the 1920s they were bringing their families. They were not part of the park exhibit, and they became visible to the tourists in a very different way. Seeing their time on the rim as temporary, the Havasupais scavenged the Grand Canyon dump for scrap lumber, packing material, tin, and whatever else they could use to build shelters. They had, of course, no running water or other amenities. As automobile tourism rose, first more well-housed park personnel and then tourists found themselves driving by "unsightly box-cars and shacks." The Park Service had turned the Grand Canyon Village into a costly showcase; the shacks were an embarrassment.[54]

At Glacier National Park, the Blackfeet peoples similarly ran afoul of the performative landscape. They had been managing the hunt for deer and elk since the mid-nineteenth century. An 1896 treaty provided them with the right to hunt on their ceded lands as long as they remained "public lands of the United States" and in "accordance with the game laws of the state of Montana." These ceded lands now lay in Glacier National Park, and the Indians continued to hunt the elk and deer there, as well as on reservation lands. The deer and elk, important to the park's identity, ignored the park's boundaries. Park officials strove to keep the Native American hunters out of the park and the beasts in the park. To keep the park authentically "natural," officials provided the "wild" animals with hay in the winter. The tension was not new in the 1920s. But the relationship between the Blackfeet and the park had changed. In the early 1910s Indians were part of the marketing strategy for Glacier National Park promoted by the Great Northern Railway. The railroad planted stories about the Blackfeet in national magazines and newspapers, printed brochures highlighting their images, and arranged for groups of Blackfeet to visit major cities, setting up tepee camps on the roofs of downtown buildings. Presenting them as living unrestricted in the park, the publicity urged visitors to see "specimens of a Great Race soon to disappear." Nonetheless, already in 1913 one park promoter took care to remind his readers that the Blackfeet may have "hunted in the mountains and fished in the lakes [but these] are now yours as an American citizen." The Blackfeet, having not disappeared, filed suit in 1925 to maintain their access. Though now by the terms of the Indian Citizenship Act they were also "American" citizens, the Blackfeet lost. The courts decided that placing those lands in the National Park System meant they were no longer "public lands" and so no longer bound by the terms of the treaty.[55] The Blackfeet were no longer part of the park's picture.

At Spokane, Washington, the search for authenticity took a different turn. Spokane boosters partnered with the Northern Pacific Railway (eager to compete with the Santa Fe) to host the Northwest Indian Congress in 1925. They aimed to identify Spokane with "Indians," "advertising the Northwest and attracting eastern people." Unlike the Rodeo Days in Arizona, *The Mission Play* in California, or the festival in Santa Fe, however, this was not an event obsessed with reenactment, even while its text implied Indian consent in their own displacement.[56]

Spokane's use of Indian imagery in its marketing was not new. New in 1925 was the participation of actual Indians as partners in the campaign. Indians attending the congress listened to papers and held parades, performances, and contests for babies and for Indian princess costumes, while visiting tourists strolled through the tepee encampments and enjoyed the spectacle. Some Indians objected to exhibiting their people for the entertainment of tourists, but the city seemed as interested in convincing local Indians that Spokane wanted their business as it did in using those "authentic" Indians to draw tourists to a place newly labeled "the Pacific Northwest."[57]

A major player in the event was Asahel Curtis, brother of the more famous Edward S. Curtis, whose reputation rested on his multivolume, sepia-toned, nostalgic, and highly costumed and posed portraits of "the vanishing race." Asahel's photos, by contrast, showed Indians wearing eagle-feather headdresses with modern trousers who were vital and clearly participating in their contemporary surroundings. Both brothers commodified Indian identity, but Asahel included Indians as contemporary participants with a future in the city, whereas Edward, like those who could not imagine the Osages as participating in a speculative economy, depicted "Indians as outside the market and modernity."[58]

In this 1920s tourism, a diverse array of narratives served both local and national audiences. They offered different roles to would-be participants, as at Glacier and Spokane, and not all had equal access to shaping the narrative or the future West it imagined. Among the many things western marketers sold in the 1920s, as Frederick Jackson Turner had claimed it would since 1893, was the promise to regenerate democracy. The widely popular, middle-class *Saturday Evening Post* in 1920 emphasized the cross section of the country—by geography and even class, though never race—found in campsites and the lack of pretension, as well as the sharing of facilities, advice, and aid on the road.[59]

There was a limit to this type of democracy. As people farther and farther down the economic scale had access to cars in the 1920s, they too used the free campsites. Migrant farmworkers stayed at them between worksites and seasons. They were joined by farmers who lost their farms and others whose "tourism" was involuntary. These were not the people boosters and land speculators sought to attract with municipal funds. They had no money to spend in town. Towns began to impose limits on how long campers could stay. Some municipal sites began to charge a fee as early as 1923, and others began to close in favor of private sites that charged a fee. Los Angeles had thirty private camps in 1925. In Colorado only nine of sixty-four camps had been privately run in 1925; by 1928 sixty-five were private, and only twenty were public.[60]

As highways and cars proliferated, so did the routes of western tourism and speculative investment. Freed from the constraints of iron rails and empowered by low-priced cars, tourism was democratized. Vast numbers of middle-class people could join elites in their visits to carefully curated and staged wilderness. But not all were welcome at the performance.

Vice Tourism: Prohibition and Borders

For those seeking more adventurous travel yet, a wilder remnant of the "Wild West," there was a burgeoning vice tourism. States along the southern border had gone dry before national Prohibition, and the incentive of acquiring a military base had far outweighed the benefits of legal red-light districts during the war. Meanwhile, the 1914 Harrison Act had required federal registration of manufactured drug transactions, sales taxes, and medical prescriptions, and a series of court rulings had resulted in virtual prohibition of narcotics by 1922. As historian Gabriela Recio put it, "Traffickers replaced physicians." Newly criminalized "vice" was driven underground or across the border.[61]

National Prohibition in the United States at the end of the Great War nationalized the audience for tourism across borders. With state Prohibition in California, New Mexico, Arizona, and Texas, Anglo merchants had simply packed up their businesses and opened them on the other side of the border, sometimes with Mexican partners. Soldiers and students, along with more affluent locals on the border, had taken day trips to visit brothels, bars, and race tracks from Tijuana to Nogales to Ciudad Juárez. Despite efforts by the Mexican government, Mexican towns on the U.S. border already did a thriving trade in gambling, prostitution, and liquor. Now these Mexican towns no longer served only borderlands clientele. Both smuggling and legitimate business on the Mexican side of the border dramatically expanded.[62]

Not everyone jumped at the new business opportunity. San Diego was filled with midwestern Protestant prohibitionist migrants and a naval base. It lay a mere sixteen miles and a seventy-five-cent to one-dollar round-trip ticket north of Tijuana, Mexico. Tijuana was particularly notorious. "Tijuana has become one of the most infamous vice resorts on the western continent," complained the navy chairman of the Interdepartmental Social Hygiene Board in 1924, and he requested the secretary of state to use "every resource at your disposal for the protection of the Naval Forces." Angry locals concerned with soldier and youth morals in San Diego added their voices to his. Against the protests of merchants with holdings on both sides of the border, they successfully lobbied the federal government to close border crossings at 9:00 p.m. The move allegedly cut the industry proceeds by half.[63]

Prohibition was popular in the United States. Twenty-seven states had gone dry by 1917. As late as 1928 the new U.S. Congress had the largest dry majority in U.S. history. That popularity, however, did not seem to mean that U.S. citizens wanted to forgo alcohol. They just did not want to drink legally at home. Visitors to the Southwest wanted to dip their toe in another country and send a postcard home. In California they had glamorous company. Hollywood stars and movie moguls frequented Mexican resorts where they could not only swim, play golf, and dine in luxury but also gamble at the table or the U.S.-owned track and drink. In 1922 special trains left Los Angeles filled with over 1,500 additional passengers bound for the Tijuana Classic. In most U.S. border towns, businessmen realized the benefit of their status as a safe gateway to the raunchier other side. Often, as they were in Tijuana, the Mexican vice districts were really U.S.-run and U.S.-owned enterprises catering to U.S. citizens.[64]

While vice tourism was the general driver of the commerce, not all border towns focused on their X-rated attractions. In Ciudad Juárez, for example, many of the small restaurants and tourist spots were jointly owned by Mexicans and U.S. citizens. The West Texas Chamber of Commerce and the Chamber of Commerce of Ciudad Juárez were clear that the "interests of El Paso and Juarez are one." Unlike many border city pairs, El Paso, Texas, with its multiple transcontinental and other rail lines, had a population that vastly outnumbered, by about four times, its Mexican counterpart, Ciudad Juárez. Besides its watering holes, Ciudad Juárez had a skating rink, swimming pool, stocked fishing pond, and gymnasium. The two towns jointly hosted concerts, parades, and sporting events. Aiming to surpass California and Florida as tourist and convention destinations, they built casinos and luxury hotels across the international bridge. Despite reports of crime and victimized U.S. citizens, El Paso displayed none of the ambivalence of San Diego. An El Paso newspaper advertisement promised that amid the tumult of Mexican revolutionary politics, Ciudad Juárez extended "the heartiest welcome to Americans," and "they shall not be molested in any way." Even the distillers who dominated the Ciudad Juárez Chamber of Commerce saw the benefit of maintaining an aura of respectability for the town. As the decade went on, railroad companies advertised ten-day stopovers in El Paso for travelers en route to California. From El Paso, Ciudad Juárez was a mere sixteen-cent streetcar ride away. The resulting tourist demand outstripped supply, though the streetcars ran every five minutes and held over a hundred people; as many as twelve thousand people migrated back and forth daily between the cities; and in 1929 a new international bridge eased the crossing. Ciudad Juárez's population quadrupled over the course of the decade, reaching forty thousand in 1931.[65]

These tourists' demands helped shift production in Mexico. U.S. whiskey makers relocated to Mexico, and Mexican beer production blossomed. Two and a half months after Prohibition became the law of the United States, the first brewery opened in Ciudad Juárez. In the absence of U.S. competition, Mexican breweries became the second most important industry in the country by 1923, most but not all of the beer produced for a domestic market, at least purportedly.[66] Grupo Modelo was founded in 1922, its Corona and Modelo Especial brands introduced in 1925, and Negro Modelo appeared in 1926.

Mexicans had established smuggling routes during the revolution, bringing arms across the border. Now they brought liquor and added new forms of transport. One hundred cases of bourbon bought for $25 in Ciudad Juárez sold for over $6,000 in St. Louis, Kansas City, Denver, or Dallas. In 1922 a plane tracked by enforcers for months as it made regular runs between border cities was finally captured with 120 bottles of tequila bound for San Antonio. Pitched battles between smugglers and law officers occurred in El Paso's tenement section, and deadly gun battles occurred elsewhere along the border between smugglers and Border Patrol officers, killing twelve of the latter between 1924 and 1929.[67]

While Canadians took equal part in liquor smuggling, the U.S. press never painted them with the same brush they did Mexicans. Regular rum routes ran along both the Atlantic and Pacific coasts, as well as through the Great Lakes. One of the largest ships to ply the trade out of Vancouver was the five-masted schooner *Malahat*, which had begun its life in 1917 as a lumber ship. It ran liquor for the whole span of Prohibition, carrying up to one hundred thousand bottles or sixty thousand cases of illegal liquor in a single run to a safe distance off the California coast, from which smaller ships distributed it. But in contrast to news stories about Mexicans, U.S. press stories about Canadians rarely involved immigration or alcohol. Instead they focused on athletics or treaties between Canada and the United States. They rarely if ever called for U.S. intervention in Canada as they did in Mexico. While from time to time Mexican government officials promised reform, the Canadian government explicitly refused to enforce U.S. laws. Most smuggling from Mexico was in small lots. By contrast, Canadians Sam and

Harry Bronfman created the Seagram's brand and earned about $391,000 per month running it to the States. Yet the lack of Canadian cooperation seldom if ever led to the sorts of tensions that routinely plagued U.S.-Mexico government relations. In the Canadian West by 1921, Manitoba, Alberta, and Saskatchewan were dry provinces, leaving British Columbia as the main source of western traffic other than what flowed through Detroit and Chicago, down the Mississippi, and overland. And plenty flowed into Seattle. Nearly one hundred bootleggers and rumrunners held an open convention at a Seattle hotel in 1922 in a state that had gone bone dry in 1917. Together they set fair prices and established a code of business ethics.[68]

Mexican participation in liquor and drug smuggling was seen as further proof of an innate tendency to decadence and disorder. One result of this view was that Anglos in the Southwest assumed anyone of Mexican descent had cross-border smuggling connections. They approached the Mexicans they knew with impunity, and the cash-strapped among those Mexicans found ways to get the goods even if they had no previous connections.[69]

Of course, in the 1920s locals in the West and elsewhere hardly needed to cross borders to find lower-quality alcohol. A steady drumbeat of arrests and convictions appeared in local papers. Not all of them involved smuggling. With low barriers to entry and rural residents suffering from a prolonged farm depression, many westerners, including large numbers of women, produced moonshine. Often bootleggers were the only residents with cash. They used their proceeds not only to support their families but also to invest in their farms. One northern New Mexico villager used capital from moonshining to buy a baler.[70]

In more urban western settings, women cooked liquor on the kitchen stove. They sold their product to both local bars and individuals. With their husbands they opened "blind pigs" and speakeasies in their homes to compete with the numerous soda shops that mysteriously sprang up in the same spot and under the same ownership as the saloons that preceded them. According to historian Mary Murphy, the judges and juries who tried to enforce Prohibition in the 1920s were stunned by the "grey-haired mothers appearing in their courts on bootlegging charges." Unable to believe the guardians of hearth and home, the bastions of domestic virtue, were masterminding the liquor trade, they insisted instead that the sons or husbands were the "real culprit." But widows and wives supplemented their income with home brew. Eighty-year-old Mrs. Lavinia Gilman of Butte, Montana, operated a three-hundred-gallon still, and the widow Gallagher used the proceeds from her kitchen still to outfit her five children for Easter. Enterprising Slavic women sold their wine to boarders. Children collected empty bottles and sold them to moonshiners. Italians who had always made wine for the family went commercial.[71]

Coinciding with the high tide of the feminist movement, Prohibition in the West as elsewhere revolutionized women's proper place. Wage-earning girls had flocked to dance halls in the 1910s, but respectable young women had stayed away. Many states, including Montana, had banned women from saloons altogether, even the separate women's rooms and entrances. Now in the speakeasies, which were too expensive for many lower-income women but private enough for their more prosperous sisters, young women joined their beaux for drinks. In the roadhouses and the nightclubs that opened later in the decade, teachers and shop clerks partied with their male peers, dancing and drinking into the small hours of the morning without endangering their reputation.[72]

In the mining towns, border towns, and other locales where the majority of residents had opposed Prohibition, federal enforcers faced an uphill battle. Many southwestern border towns on the U.S. side had been unenthusiastic about Prohibition to begin with, their own opposition votes swept aside by upstate denizens who opposed local option. In the mining town of Butte, Montana, a former police chief ran the Cyrus Noble saloon, enjoying the patronage of both uniformed and plainclothes detectives. Confiscated stills and liquor failed to convince local juries of guilt. When Montana repealed its state Prohibition statute in 1926, the federal officers were on their own.[73]

The drug trade also flourished. The Mexican and U.S. governments had collaborated to eradicate the trade in opium since 1912. While Mexico signed the International Opium Convention in 1916, the U.S. Treasury Department reported that Mexicans continued to import opium through Ensenada in Baja California, convert it to the smoking variety, and export it to the United States. Baja's governor, Esteban Cantú Jiménez (1915–20), was deeply implicated in the trade. He seized the prohibited imported goods and resold them to the original owners at a substantial markup. Cantú and his compatriots were hardly alone in the trade. According to Recio, opium traffic "also involved U.S. citizens, Chinese, Rumanians, Palestinians, Spaniards, French, Greeks and Japanese." As Mexico and the United States hardened their enforcement on imports in the 1920s, Mexican traffickers began to plant opium in Sonora, Sinaloa, Nayarit, Chihuahua, and Durango, and Mexico's Northwest became the center of distribution, with the United States as the primary market.[74]

Both governments began to turn their attention to a wider array of drugs they saw as contributing to vice. While marijuana was still legal in most states west of the Mississippi, the Mexican government made its production and marketing illegal in 1920. In the United States, California led the way in 1907, and Wyoming and Texas included marijuana in their poison laws in the 1910s; Iowa, Nevada, Oregon, Washington, Arkansas, and Nebraska did so as well in the 1920s. Most states exempted medical marijuana. In some states the marijuana issue became conflated with that of Mexican migrant labor in a tightening labor market and amid tensions between large growers employing low-wage Mexican labor and small farmers having difficulty competing. Mexicans, they alleged, brought marijuana, used it, and spread the habit. In Arizona, on the other hand, a strong lobby developed in defense of recuperating veterans and their need for easy and inexpensive access to the drug.[75]

While both alcohol and drug abuse occurred in the United States, the source of contagion was envisioned as across the border. In San Diego's 1915 Panama-California Exposition, the Isthmus had offered visitors, for ten cents, entrance to a Chinese opium parlor, from which they could "take a slumming trip through the underworld with competent guides, who will explain in detail the life of the underworld showing opium and gambling dens in full operation, torture and white slave dens." Outside the exposition, the California press populated Tijuana and other Mexican border cities with the same scene: opium dens and captured young innocents, mingling Chinese and Mexican villains in a direct descent from sensationalized journalism of the late nineteenth century. A *Los Angeles Times* story bore headlines screaming, "BACK FROM TIA JUANA HELL-PIT." Two teenage girls, it seems, fell victim to promises of cabaret singing jobs in a Tijuana tavern. Imprisoned in an opium den, guarded by a "Chinaman, who spoke the Mexican language fluently," the opium-drugged girls escaped the Mexican-owned establishment by running into the street, where passing U.S. tourists rescued them. But the victims were not only young girls. The border depravity threatened the heart-blood of American prosperity. In March 1925 the *Los Angeles Times* reported the death by overdose of an engineer for the Arizona State Highway Department; he had been found in an Agua Prieta opium den.[76]

Whereas the U.S. West was supposed to be a melting pot that tempered selected nationalities into an American success story, the Mexican side of the border presented the flip side of the picture. Despite Mexican laws and policies by 1923 that barred "members of the Negro race" from entering Mexico and in Sonora banned marriage between Mexicans and people of Chinese heritage, the picture in the U.S. press was of mixture run amok, from which degradation followed. One story described the opium den as "a dive of the lowest order where addicts of all nationalities gather, . . . filled with men and women in various stages of dress and undress." Police had "forced Chinese who were operating the place to open the doors," where they learned a "negress," Myrtle Montes, administered morphine to the clients. In charge of the cleanup at Agua Prieta, on Mexican soil, was not the Mexican state but a Douglas, Arizona, police officer who oversaw the Mexican police roundup of "Chinese and others suspected of being connected with the Agua Prieta narcotic ring."[77]

Marketing this wilder West involved speculating on both sides of the border. It involved promoting U.S. border towns as safe gateways to adventure in a foreign land. It meant investing, literally, in increasing the distinction between the United States and Mexico. Despite the fact that many Mexican borderlands vice districts were largely homes to U.S.-financed and U.S.-run enterprises, success relied on promoting the dichotomy of U.S. virtue and Mexican vice, U.S. control and Mexican lawlessness. The marketing became entangled in the material reality as tourists enjoyed their holidays of forbidden pleasures and law officers engaged in fatal gun battles, ultimately targeting any Mexican as potentially criminal.

Hollywood

It turned out, however, that the United States had a western "hell pit" of its own, one that drew innocent young women in droves in the 1920s only to despoil them on the couches of the wealthy: Hollywood. The town of Hollywood itself had begun in 1887 as a temperance town trying to attract retiring midwesterners. In 1904 its biggest concerns were limiting the number of horses, cattle, sheep, and hogs that could be driven through town. But moviemakers were about to discover California. In 1907 Francis Boggs, a director of the Selig Polyscope Company, passed through California. He came back to stay two years later. While other towns in Texas, Colorado, and Oklahoma, as well as Chicago, vied for the industry before 1920, as early as 1910 every major film company had sent moviemakers to Los Angeles and established studios in the area. By 1912 the center of motion picture production had shifted from New York to California. Moviemakers were seduced by weather perfect for shooting film year-round, by the wide variety of scenery, and by the lack of unions. Wages were a fifth to a third below the prevailing rates of San Francisco (a union town) and about half the rates in New York. The capital stayed east, but the creative talent moved west.[78]

The whole industry, among the largest in the state, was highly speculative. No one knew what made a star, and thousands came to California believing they could be the next big thing. Fraud was rife, but the riches could be real. Mary Pickford was the first to realize the benefits of star power, doubling her salary in 1915 and getting half the profits from her films. In 1916 Charlie Chaplin made $10,000 a week and got a $150,000 bonus for signing on with Mutual Company. He was extraordinary, but leading men averaged $1,000 per week at a time when $2,500 per year made you the upper crust in midwestern towns. Supporting actors made $600. Adding to the glamor were the movie palaces—the places where ordinary viewers across the country saw Hollywood films. With marbled bathrooms and crystal chandeliers, velvet draperies and a phalanx of uniformed ushers, they transported viewers into another world. Sometimes they went further in creating a fantasy world—Grauman's Egyptian temple (1922), Houston's Majestic Italian garden (1923), and Grauman's Chinese in 1927.[79]

Movie-struck girls flocked to Los Angeles. Even Chicago was only a day's train ride away. Authors of advice books told them they needed at least $2,000, that people working as movie extras had to supply their own clothes, and that they would have to survive for at least a year without earning a cent. Yet movies did give more opportunities to women than most industries, and more than they ever would again. Many leading scenario writers were women, including Anita Loos; others directed films in the 1920s; and some held executive positions in production companies.

Most women who got a break, however, got it because a relative owed them a favor, or there had been a payoff in some other manner. In the mid-1920s manuals for these hopefuls claimed that about five thousand people, mainly innocent young women, were disappearing every year from Hollywood. Some turned up in brothels and opium dens and in Mexico, like the two would-be cabaret singers in Tijuana. Still others went home with fatal diseases.[80] In an early effort to improve its morals, Universal City elected Laura Oakley as police chief. Only the previous November she had starred in *Cowgirl Cinderella.* A former comedian, she played her new role straight, ensuring her fellow Universal employees, "There is only one thing to do to keep up the standard of morality, and that is to enforce the laws. I want to impress on you that I have taken the office of chief of police with the one aim of doing my duty, and I assure you that I will carry out the law to the letter."[81]

Meanwhile, the actors who made it lived it up. Together with the earlier-arriving oil nouveau riche, they were their own society. A new breed, "gossip writers," arose. Spectacular deaths occurred in mysterious circumstances, for example, that of Virginia Rappe, whose lifeless body was discovered after a multiday party hosted by film star Fatty Arbuckle. "Exposés," frank talk of divorces, and frank disapproval by the surrounding community led the industry moguls to fend off draconian legislation by creating an association and hiring Will Hays, the former chairman of the Republican National Committee, a Presbyterian elder from Indiana, and the current postmaster general of the United States. In 1922 they paid him $150,000 to act as a moral arbiter. Despite Hays's later implication in the Teapot Dome scandal, he proved an effective lobbyist. He halted progress on censorship bills pending in thirty states by promising that the industry would abide by the new Hays Code.[82]

Stars could get away with these hijinks because studios believed stars made or broke the success of films. Leading men and women commanded tremendous salaries and creative control. Pickford's 1916 contract called for the creation of the Pickford Film Corporation. Others followed suit, particularly the women. The ratio of female to male stars was about fifty-fifty—unlike the highest echelons of any other industry. As the industry grew and investors wanted in, they found a field where the most powerful individual was Mary Pickford. When Pickford and her peers turned to directing and producing they did so from a position of deep familiarity with a wide variety of aspects. Many had started as scriptwriters, editors, and production assistants in an era when lines between tasks blurred. Some had managed their own traveling troupes. Now they wanted more control. They wanted better production values than the cheaper studio output, which relied on their star power to succeed.[83]

Better production values meant more expense. After the smashing success of D. W. Griffith's racist masterpiece, *The Birth of a Nation*, in 1915, there was no turning back. Costs quickly skyrocketed, from a few thousand dollars for a two-reel film to between $20,000 and $40,000 for a feature in 1917.[84] The higher costs meant higher investment risk and more dependence on stars.

But then Cecil B. DeMille, eager to prove the importance of the director over the arrogant stars, promised he could make a successful film for producer Adolph Zukor without big stars. Starting in 1918 with farces that included *Old Wives for New*, he produced films that cost $40,000 to $70,000 and raked in $350,000 to $380,000. Other directors did even better. George Loane Tucker produced *The Miracle Man* (1919) for $120,000. The star earned only $125 per week; the film earned $3 million. Few stars could retain their creative perks. Women lost their most promising route to the top. Directing became a men's club, instantiated in Directors Associations and performed by Erich von Stroheim's brutality and Cecil

DeMille's trophy-head-studded office, filled with guns, swords, and cannons. The remaining women directors, such as Loos, were confined to increasingly rigidly defined genres of "women's" films.[85]

Even directors, though, ultimately lost control to the studios' new centralization. The studios kept costs down by overseeing scripts, casts, locations, and costumes. They also wanted to control distribution, struggling with theater owners who wanted to control output. Producers bought theaters to get access to the best houses; exhibitors bought production companies to ensure a good supply. Producer Samuel Goldwyn had acquired interest in about thirty theaters by 1921, only to have Loew's Inc., owner of the largest chain of luxury theaters in New York and having already purchased the Metro production company in 1920, buy Goldwyn Pictures in 1924, along with Louis B. Mayer's independent production company. The resulting new company was Metro-Goldwyn-Mayer. By the late 1920s there were only five major studios, each owning a chain of first-run theaters. Over twenty thousand movie theaters graced the nation's towns and cities. Many of these theaters changed films daily, and together they took in over fifty million paid admissions per year. To feed this demand, studios produced seven hundred commercial feature films annually, the largest portion of them westerns.[86]

Hollywood and the West that housed it had a twin relationship. Hollywood itself typified the American West in its rapid, speculative development, and Hollywood produced movies meant to preserve, recall, and call upon the American West as an archetypical American experience. Westerns enjoyed enormous and enduring popularity. From 1900 to 1960 at least a third of films in the United States were westerns. As early as 1903 short films, including the industry's first "blockbuster," *The Great Train Robbery* (twelve minutes, shot in New Jersey), had built on elements established in Wild West shows and dime novels. *The Great Train Robbery* pioneered innovative camera techniques, fast-paced nonstop action, and seamless scene changes. It laid the foundation for the hundreds of westerns produced in the 1910s, including two feature-length films by Cecil B. DeMille.[87]

As Hollywood films replaced other entertaining spectacles, the Indians and cowboys who once would have performed in Wild West shows turned to movies. In the 1910s film companies made deals with Wild West shows and their associated ranches to supply hundreds of extras, as well as oxen, bison, horses, covered wagons, and stagecoaches. By the 1920s five hundred cowboys a year came to Hollywood from ranches going broke in Arizona and Colorado. Like the Indians who joined Wild West shows to play "Indians," the cowboys were playing "cowboys," not necessarily themselves. Bill Tilghman, among the last of the great western marshals, made a number of films, interrupting shooting during one movie to round up bank robbers.[88]

Such actors enhanced the films' claim to authenticity, as they had for the Wild West shows. Filmmakers called them "original participants" and shot them on location. Some went to great lengths to evoke a documentary-style realism. Director James Cruz shot *The Covered Wagon* (1923) on location in Nevada and California. He employed 1,100 extras from the region, including 750 Indians, as well as 127 actors; reconstructed Fort Bridger; and lit a nine-square-mile prairie fire. His wagon train stretched five hundred wagons long. A single scene featured a thousand horses and oxen, two hundred mules, and a large herd of buffalo, some of whom were actually shot in the hunt scene. At $782,000, the film cost three times the average for a big-budget film, but it brought in $3.8 million at the box office. President Harding loved it. Similar films followed, including John Ford's *Iron Horse* (1924).[89]

But pictorial realism was not why audiences flocked to westerns. The plots were sentimental, not realistic. *The Covered Wagon* featured a love triangle, as well as menacing Indians, bad guys, and other hazards. Like popular melodramas and like the favorite scenes in Wild West shows, as well as Zane Grey's novels (best sellers well into the 1920s), westerns often featured the rescue of a beleaguered "white woman" by a mysterious stranger. But in the films even villains often had an underlying chivalry.[90] The cowboy as austere romantic archetype had been around since at least the dime novels of the mid-nineteenth century. The image had been perfected in the decades surrounding the turn of the twentieth century by the trifecta of Owen Wister, the Philadelphian whose 1902 novel, *The Virginian,* went through one silent and two talking film adaptations; Frederic Remington, the popular New York painter;

and Theodore Roosevelt. *The Covered Wagon* in 1923 was dedicated to Roosevelt's memory.[91] This was a white hero who sutured perfectly with the dominant narrative of the U.S. West: omnicompetent, effortlessly and benevolently masterful, whether over land, women, or people in general.

There was some irony in having decadent Hollywood manufacture virtue and the heroic common man. This was an older story, mass marketed in cheap fiction and Wild West shows in the nineteenth century and now, as befitted the modern West, with appropriate speculative investment, adapted to a new technology and a new decade. With vivid scenes and special effects and twenty thousand theaters, it reached into towns large and small and sold its version of western history across the country.

Conclusion

All of these ventures in speculative fiction—tourism, movies, real estate development—facilitated and legitimated the reshaping of the western landscape. The players had their roles. The West was not "the West" without its Indians, the "Southwest" without its Mexicans, but Indians and Mexicans had to disappear as autonomous, modern beings.[92] They had to be cordoned off into particular enclaves. Part of the contest in the speculative West was over who would profit from their imagined presence and what would be the connection between the imagined and the material.

In the 1920s Indians, Hispanos, Japanese, African Americans, and white women did not cede their share of the profits easily. And sometimes and for some time, they made good on their claims. Pueblo dancers negotiated better wages, white women produced movies, Black and Japanese landowners won their lawsuits. Mexicans constructed their own communities. But they did not, in the end, control the most enduring image, the dominant narrative, crafted in the era, the enduring "story" of the West. It was a story inscribed on urban landscapes and on every tourist highway, with a pink Madonna in every state.

The stories those dominating the West and the nation told, like the world's fairs at the start of the century, made a particular sense of the region's hierarchies and aspirations. In the Southwest, the appropriation of Spanish mission architecture covered, sometimes literally, the erasure of Mexican-descent people. When an earthquake destroyed much of Santa Barbara's downtown in 1925, the city fathers saw an opportunity. They created the nation's first architectural review board to ensure that "all new structures . . . [would] conform legally to the city's Spanish theme as even mailboxes and public trash receptacles were given a 'Spanish' design." They reviewed more than two thousand construction proposals in 1926, and they succeeded. What historian Phoebe Kropp calls "the Spanish mode" did not need to be consistent. It differed in New Mexico, California, Arizona, and Texas. In all those places, however, it provided "a malleable language for articulating both order and difference and arbitrating between past and present, primitive and modern, East and West, and Anglos and others."[93]

In 1924 Los Angeles had battled the plague and the public relations nightmare that came with it. It chose to do so in part by cordoning off Mexican neighborhoods and Mexicans themselves. Los Angeles promotional literature showed lots of missions and ancient Indians but very few pictures of young Mexican workers. They could be the past, but Anglos represented the future. In 1928 Harry Chandler, publisher of the *Los Angeles Times,* allied with Christine Sterling, a San Francisco transplant, in a plan to rejuvenate the site of Los Angeles's founding. Over the next few years, with the city leadership on board and $30,000 donated, she launched the Plaza Beautiful campaign for the area surrounding the Avila House, the oldest standing structure in the city, which had been scheduled for demolition. At the same time that actual Mexicans were increasingly being deported, pushed not only out of the neighborhood but also out of the country, she and her allies hoped to make the plaza a tourist attraction, featuring Olvera Street as a "picturesque Mexican market place."[94]

With the engines of Hollywood, the built environment, restrictive covenants, and federal policies, this version of the West imagined would prove remarkably durable. As Otero explains regarding Tucson, "The mythical landscapes and accompanying narratives of the Anglo fantasy heritage . . . in time, morphed into 'truth' narratives. They became powerful forces with dire consequences for the city's people, its economy, and the neighborhoods downtown when booster organizations acted to make the imagined a reality."[95] In this way, the speculations of the 1920s and their narratives made the power dynamics inscribed on the western land and in immigration and citizenship policies seem natural and inevitable, an uncontested "progress," and an organic result of an enterprising people.

Part 4

Mobilizing, 1928–40

When the national love affair with speculation came to a devastating breakup in October 1929, it may have looked novel to denizens of Wall Street, but to the inhabitants of Main Street in the western grain belt it looked all too familiar. The readers of Iowa's *Des Moines Register* only had to cast their minds back to the burst World War I commodities bubble, from which they had never fully recovered. For many farmers, the 1920s were not all they were cracked up to be. Except for those few halcyon years in the lingering glow of World War I, times were hard and debt was deep. When the stock market crash came in late 1929, the *Register* ran a cartoon by Ding Darling that showed the small speculator dwarfed by the looming dark seated figure of the stock market. Hand raised, the speculator promised "Never Again" as a parade of shadowy figures labeled "War Price Speculation," "Get Rich Quick Oil Stock," and "Florida Land Boom" claimed, "That's Just What He Told Me" and marched off the page.[1] For several years, from Iowa to the Dakotas, the Great Depression looked more like continuity than change.

The West suffered in greater degree from the Depression than the rest of the nation. According to historian Richard White, real income fell farther; seven of the ten states with the greatest decline were in the West. The region's economic activity dropped by half between 1929 and 1933; the population declined in the Southwest, Great Plains, and Rocky Mountain states. By 1931, despite years of bad harvests, declining consumer spending nationally meant that every section of the West had a commodity surplus. It wasn't only the grain farmers who suffered. Cattle prices fell by 66 percent from 1928 to 1931. Mining output declined throughout the 1920s. The lumber industry, which provided the base of the economy in the Pacific Northwest, had similarly declined starting with the post–

World War I recession and then suffered from the decline in construction from 1927 forward. The oil industry, despite attempts at coordination, continued its disastrous overproduction, with the exception of state government action in Texas and Oklahoma. As the price of oil fell from $1.30 a barrel for high-grade crude in 1930 to under $0.10 a barrel by the end of 1931, Governor Ross S. Sterling of Texas, a former oil company owner who was desperate to protect state revenues, used the state militia to shut down all oil wells in the East Texas field and got the legislature to give him the authority to do so. Facing state bankruptcy, Oklahoma governor William H. Murray also used the state militia to shut down production under the Oklahoma Conservation Act, upheld by the Supreme Court in 1932.[2]

The system perfected in the previous decades—the promise of economic democracy and economic citizenship built on speculation and low-wage excludable labor—collapsed on an unprecedented scale. People lured by the promise and stunned by the reality struggled to overcome the devastation. But those who had abandoned insurgent democracy had not forgotten it. They remembered the alternatives and would demand a different mix of possibilities. Ultimately, they would change the government, and the government would respond in kind. But their first mobilizations would be involuntary, forced by the state or by desperation.

The three chapters in this section trace the evolution of responses to the economic disaster. Chapter 10 covers the Depression's early years, from 1928 to the end of the Hoover administration in early 1933, focusing particularly on the mass expulsion of Mexicans and Mexican Americans, the redefining of the U.S. southern borderlands, the Bonus Army, and the Farmers' Holiday Association. Chapter 11 examines the first two years of Franklin Delano Roosevelt's New Deal, which generated unexpected results. Successful agricultural strikes, general strikes that shut down Minneapolis and the entire West Coast, Francis Townsend's Old Age Revolving Pension Fund, and Upton Sinclair's gubernatorial campaign in California helped pull federal government policies toward economic democracy. Chapter 12 follows the impact of New Deal policies that attempted to restore stability to the region from 1934 forward. With mammoth dams and sweeping legislation, large-

and small-scale planning, centralized and decentralized control, the administration attempted to restore not just the landscape and the economy but also the imagined West—at once the most modern manifestation of the nation and the most traditional promise of individual landed opportunity.

10

Demobilizing

The speculations of the 1920s had constructed a particular western landscape—oil rigs, irrigation schemes, fully exploited fields and forests, tourist traps, and restrictive covenants. The economic collapse blew it to bits. The signs of imminent collapse appeared before the stock market dove. The year 1927 had been a bad one, except for Lucky Lindbergh and the stock market. Charles Lindbergh, his rivals having crashed and burned, won the prize for the first to fly a heavier-than-air craft from the New World to the Old. The stock market continued its climb, seemingly detached from the economy that supposedly undergirded it. Few on the ground fared so well. Housing starts dwindled and foreclosures rose. Drought had plagued farmers throughout the 1920s; then in the summer of 1928 a hailstorm damaged much of North Dakota's wheat, followed by bank failures that autumn when the farmers had no harvest profits to deposit and land values plummeted. Banks failed in Arizona, too, as between 1929 and 1932 Arizona's annual agricultural revenues fell with the amount of rain from $41.8 million to $13.8 million, and cattle ranching revenues were cut nearly in half. Other sectors fared no better, with copper prices plummeting to less than a third of their 1929 value. Fruit and vegetable prices fell 30 percent from August 1930 to August 1931. Fifty thousand Arizonans simply left the state, whose population fell by 12 percent. In North and South Dakota, Wyoming, and Idaho farm income fell by over half. By early 1933 over half of mortgage holders in the Rocky Mountain states faced foreclosure.[1]

Caught in the storm, policy-makers on every level flailed, and citizens and migrants knew that the status quo could not hold. This chapter begins with one of the earliest and most draconian responses to the crash: the mass expulsion of Mexican-descent people and the reimagining of the southern borderlands. It moves next to the West's World War I veterans who traveled any way they could to besiege Congress and the president, demanding the bonuses promised them in return for their wartime sacrifice. Finally, it turns to midwestern dairy farmers who, in Iowa, Nebraska, and elsewhere, mobilized to create a different set of economic relations.

Reconstructing the Border

Years before dust, foreclosures, and evictions would blow farmers and tenants to California, long trails of Mexicans "repatriated" to Mexico. Their numbers peaked in 1932, when as many as four hundred thousand Mexicans and their citizen-born children moved south of the border. Some went by choice in the face of bleak prospects, many moved with the encouragement and subsidies of local municipalities, and others left by coercion. These deportees were earlier and their skin was often darker, but in crucial ways they were not different from the iconic "Okies" and "Arkies" who moved middecade. They were mobilized by the same agricultural ecology. Those displaced by repatriations, dust, foreclosure, and ultimately New Deal subsidies to landowners were really the same stream.

The same landscape created by commercial industrialized agriculture on both sides of the U.S.-Mexico border since the 1880s had set bodies in motion. In the 1930s even the wealthy in the United States could no longer ignore that this was an ecosystem that mobilized human labor as part of its technology of growing food. It mobilized laboring people not as the idealized farmer but as a moving part in the machinery. The deportees and the Okies and their ilk were part of the same agricultural ecology, a particular mechanistic, profit-maximizing way of viewing the land, of organizing agricultural production and its inputs. They were parts of the same ecosystem. It was not that laboring people were apart from "nature" in this ecological mode of production but that workers were part of the nature mobilized by capital in agribusiness in the same way that agribusiness farm owners mobilized seeds and fertilizer. The industrialized agricultural production had required an industrialized labor force. The ebbs and flows of agricultural demand and production and markets had heightened the appeal of a perpetually reserve labor force, one easily excluded from any community benefits when not needed and employed at will—a truly commodified labor force. No longer needed, the indispensable Mexicans who had saved western commercial farming (according to its proponents in Congress in the 1920s) and who as a result remained excluded from immigration quotas were recast as dispensable.[2]

The same capital that had mobilized Mexicans to move north to work on commercial farms now demobilized them as though some vast fight, some war to force the land to produce more profit, was now in abeyance.[3] In the 1920s nativists had succeeded in formally excluding ever-increasing numbers of those deemed perpetually un-American, in part a legacy of the demarcations constructed in the early years of the century. By 1924 the United States had excluded "Orientals" from legitimate immigration and dramatically reduced the number of southern and eastern Europeans who could enter the country. As the economy headed into a tailspin late in the 1920s, nothing would reverse that exclusionary trend. With four million unemployed, various and sundry citizens called for a check or even reversal of Mexican immigration. The call was not new. Even in the early 1920s various citizens had called for extending quotas to Western Hemisphere, particularly Mexican, immigrants. The call was simply more urgent.[4]

Farm owners struggled to wring every cent from their land and the labor that worked it. Their costs remained steady or increased, while their crops fetched less and less. They planted more acres and further glutted the market. As the value of California farm products fell by two-thirds from 1929 to 1932 and wages fell from thirty-five cents an hour in 1928 to fourteen cents an hour in 1933, not only Mexican nationals but also Mexican American citizens found themselves cast as outsiders, pressured to depart. The expulsion of Mexicans derived from and cemented their status as perpetual outsiders. It was mirrored by Mexico's own increasing hostility to immigrant workers. Mexico barred many immigrants from entry starting in the late 1920s, and Sonoran municipalities expelled Chinese immigrants in 1932.[5]

Despite the deportations, Mexicans and other Americans remained exempt from U.S. quota laws. The same 1924 legislation that had instituted the quotas, however, also created the Border Patrol. It provided $1 million for 472 men to patrol the nation's land borders. That number was almost 400 more than the largest force that had previously policed immigration at the borders. By 1939 the force would number 916.[6]

These heirs to the roving "Chinese inspectors" soon had a vastly increased mandate. Not only could they deny admissibility, they could detain any "alien" they suspected of smuggling anything, including themselves, across the border. At first, Prohibition offered Border Patrol officers along the Texas border more dramatic arrests than evasive agricultural workers. Funding for federal enforcement of narcotics prohibition alone, admittedly inadequate, was ten times that of the Border Patrol. Border Patrol agents were fond of telling stories where, at real personal peril, they foiled wily armed Mexican liquor smugglers on the borderlands' back roads. Even before the Depression, any Mexican in the vicinity of the border had become suspect, and Mexicans became the focus of U.S. immigration officers.[7]

From its start, the Border Patrol in the Texas districts drew boys who had grown up in the borderlands. They had grown up replaying the Texas Revolution at recess, fighting "Mexicans." Some descended from the original party of Anglos (non-Mexican-descent people) brought by empresario Stephen Austin in the early nineteenth century.[8]

Though "the Immigration Act of 1924 stated that any unauthorized migrants that entered the nation before 1925 without leaving would not be liable for prosecution or deportation," that's not always how things played out during the Depression. Espiridión de León had lived in the United States since 1916 and had married a Texas-born citizen in 1927. Long-term employed and law-abiding, León found himself grabbed by the collar one day in 1931 while peacefully walking down the street of his hometown, Mercedes, Texas, and threatened with a gun by immigration officers. Under duress he "confessed" that he had entered the United States after 1925, and the officers deported him to Río Rico, Tamaulipas, where he was isolated from his wife and their three children and unable to find a job. The notarized statement he had acquired in 1929 that testified to his continuous residence proved of no avail.[9]

South Texas, where León lived, had bucked the agricultural

trend of the rest of the country and experienced a boom in the 1920s. Anglos had flocked to newly irrigated fields and had relied, as did other beneficiaries of such development, on low-cost migrant labor to make those fields pay. As they had in California's Imperial Valley, these Anglo growers had arrived at a modus vivendi, a collaboration and mutual respect, with Border Patrol agents. The Border Patrol, including a small number of Mexican-descent agents, ensured worker registration, the payment of fees, and labor control. Workers who refused jobs at set wages were arrested as vagrants and subject to deportation as potential charges on the public purse. One resident revealed that without the Border Patrol, "migrant workers would 'leave to go where wages were higher.'"[10]

That cozy relationship was about to end. Restrictionist legislators had lost their battle in 1926 and 1928, but their efforts had spurred the executive branch to action. Faced with a worsening economy, rising unemployment, and farm labor activism, it ramped up border enforcement. In 1928 and 1929 the Immigration Service and Department of Labor ran large-scale deportation operations in Texas, spreading to California in 1930 and rapidly across the Southwest and as far north as Montana.[11]

The commissioner general of immigration had long supported inclusion of Mexicans in quota laws; now his agency, in the words of one historian, used their reports "fabricating a crime wave" to justify and create support for deportations, targeting South Texas as home to the largest number of Mexican immigrants. Local grower protests, joined by Representative John Nance Garner of Texas, proved fruitless. Immigration fell; deportations rose. In 1929 the United States recorded the entry of over forty thousand immigrants across the Mexican border, down from over sixty thousand the year before. The same year, 1929, agents deported almost twenty thousand Mexicans from the Rio Grande Valley in Texas alone. Protesting growers called it terrorism and un-American.[12]

After the stock market crash in October 1929, the raids grew ferocious, justified by the need, as Arizona's governor, George W. P. Hunt, would put it, for "protection" that would give preference to "local citizens, regardless of their race or color . . . in what little work is available." Raids reached beyond neighborhoods and workplaces to target health clinics and schools. In one 1931 case, agents detained more than five hundred El Paso schoolchildren. New immigration laws enhanced the criminality of illegal entry. By mid-1930 hundreds of Spanish-surnamed immigrants in California and Texas were spending as much as a year in jail prior to deportation. People deported who attempted to reenter faced felony charges. Mexican consuls in Texas found county jails "packed beyond capacity." By 1932 the commissioner general of immigration reported only 2,058 Mexicans entering the United States.[13]

Some in the United States resisted the enhanced enforcement. In California some citrus growers protected their Mexican workers from deportation, offering year-round employment or hiding them from repatriation agents. In Del Rio, Texas, Mexican American parents questioned neither deportation nor segregation per se, but in the context of dragnets that captured them along with immigrants and segregated them along with Black citizens suppressed by Jim Crow, they did insist on their rights as "white" citizens. They sued the school district for segregating their children from what they called "other white races." And they succeeded.[14]

In 1930 the Department of Labor, spurred by complaints, launched an investigation of corruption and violence in the Border Patrol and in 1933 reorganized the Border Patrol's parent agency into the joint Immigration and Naturalization Service. They hoped to cut out the informal practices, cozy relations, and gun-happy officers within the Border Patrol by firing all the officers and rehiring them on temporary contracts. Little seemed to change. Men who came of age in the Texas-Mexico borderlands held over 85 percent of Border Patrol supervisory positions; Kelly Lytle Hernández points out that "although they were federal officers enforcing national laws along an international boundary, Border Patrol officers in the 1920s and 1930s were entrenched in the local realities of race, labor, migration, masculinity, and violence that structured their lives as working-class men in the Texas-Mexico borderlands. They used the monopoly on violence granted them as immigration law enforcement officers to both maintain and manipulate the world in which they lived."[15]

For Mexican Americans, citizenship acquired new salience. It had not been an issue before—not in getting work and not in serving in the U.S. military in World War I. Now Mexican American children ran when they saw the Border Patrol; their parents started carrying their birth certificates. In these districts where as many as half the residents were U.S. citizens of Mexican descent, at times even a birth certificate was not enough. When nineteen-year-old José Hernández produced his in 1936 in Esperanza, Texas, the officer swore at him, denied its validity, and detained him. The indicator of suspicious behavior in the borderlands was looking Mexican. In 1930, for the first (and only) time, the United States declared "Mexican" a race and not a nationality for the purposes of that year's federal census. The conflation of "American" and "white" could be translated by census takers, as it was in San Antonio, as marking one Esperanza Alvarez, born in Texas, as "alien" under her naturalization status.[16]

It wasn't only the federal agents who drew such lines. In the early 1930s Los Angeles, Denver, and myriad communities in the Southwest sent their local and state officials after residents they believed to be Mexicans. Sometimes they offered them voluntary repatriation, subsidizing the costs. Other times they denied them relief, starving them out. Officials could strike at random, swearing at or slapping those they stopped, detaining them without warrants, going door to door, terrorizing whole communities. Women wept in the streets, unable to find their husbands after sweeps. Children who had been left behind had to fend for themselves. At times, officials denied Mexicans' humanity altogether. They rounded up men, women, and children from their refuges in public parks, forced them onto boxcars, and sent them across the border. Officials repatriated whole *colonias* (Mexican settlements), leaving only ghost towns. Los Angeles County's Welfare Department claimed to have repatriated fifty thousand Mexican nationals and their children, about one-third of the city's Mexican population, in one five-month period of 1931 alone. Those deported included wrongly deported U.S. citizens of Mexican descent who landed in Mexican border towns without funds or friends.

The shopkeepers who had served these people faced ruin. They had to sell their businesses—movie theaters, grocery shops, furniture stores, barbershops, and so on—in a hostile market, fetching pennies on the dollar. Out of options and fearing forcible deportation, many of these shopkeepers and others "voluntarily" accepted offers of half-fare transportation "home." Altogether, by force or choice, as many as one million Mexican nationals and their children left the United States for Mexico.[17]

Counties, municipalities, and even states were flailing about, swamped by an ever-rising tide of misery, striking out at any way to stem the tide. Tax delinquency rose as the Depression continued, and dwindling state and municipal revenues meant that, as elsewhere in the nation, local welfare resources were quickly overwhelmed. Departing Mexicans were replaced by transient Anglos who hopped freight trains and begged for food; one Eagle Pass, Texas, paper complained of a "steady stream of back-door moochers." In early 1931 hard-hit Los Angeles voters passed a bond issue of $5 million for a work relief program. The unsympathetic *Los Angeles Times* claimed it would benefit "mostly vagrants profiting from the public purse."[18] Even that amount, however, proved inadequate.

Los Angeles had at first thought that its peculiar industries—Hollywood, oil, food production—and its mild climate would insulate it from the Depression. Word got out that the Imperial Valley remained prosperous, and per capita income in the state boasted 40 percent more than the national average in the early 1930s. Migrants poured into the state. But prosperity was relative. After a decade of record profits in the state's agriculture, its farm income dove. In 1932 it was less than half what it had been in 1929. The migrants contributed to a glut of farm labor, and farm wages had also fallen by more than 50 percent. By mid-1932 Los Angeles was home to almost half the approximately seven hundred thousand unemployed in California. By August 1932 half of the city's building trade workers were unemployed. In Los Angeles, welfare rolls had ballooned from 3,500 individual recipients in 1930 to 35,000 families in 1931. Unemployment rose from 10 percent to 20 percent over the course of 1930; by 1933 the rate had peaked at 41.6 percent. Meanwhile, for those still employed, wages fell 38 percent in Los Angeles from 1926 to 1932.[19]

Anglos made up ever larger proportions of the city and county relief rolls. Pressure mounted to exclude "Mexicans" from jobs and relief. In 1931 the federal government and several western state governments, including California, required companies doing business with the government to hire only citizens. Los Angeles followed suit on the municipal level. Private businesses in Los Angeles replaced Mexican workers with Anglos. Though by 1934 only 10 percent of the approximately 126,000 families on relief in Los Angeles County were Mexican, many county residents continued to fantasize that eliminating Mexicans would eliminate the Depression.[20]

When Mexicans received any relief, they often received less than the basic grants Anglo families received. In Los Angeles Mexicans received $20 per month versus $30. And while many Anglos believed all "Mexicans" were "aliens," most "Mexicans" receiving relief in Los Angeles County had lived in the county for at least ten years, and 31 percent had lived there all their life. Baffled by the continued presence of those who labor importers had promised would disappear when unwanted, Colorado's Weld County Board of Commissioners complained to the commissioner general of immigration, "It was agreed and understood that these people were to remain in Mexico."[21]

In rural areas the peak of the deportations occurred as agricultural workers organized to better their conditions. Forging an alliance among these groups was not easy. Growers had turned increasingly to Filipino migrant workers after 1924. Because of their status as U.S. colonials, they were unaffected by the laws excluding Asian immigrants, and while Mexican migrant workers increasingly came as families, Filipinos overwhelmingly migrated as single men. Growers felt little need to provide them with any but the most rudimentary shelter.[22]

Tensions ran in multiple directions. Mexicans and Filipinos distrusted each other for undercutting wages in field work. White owners of small orchards resented Filipinos for taking the seasonal wage work in larger orchards they needed to make ends meet; they considered these orchard jobs "white" work as opposed to the "stoop labor" in field crops. Japanese farm owners and renters, like white farm owners and renters, hired Mexican and Filipino workers and defined themselves racially in juxtaposition to those groups. Violent anti-Filipino riots broke out in central California in 1930. They centered on taxi dance halls where Filipino men paid to dance with Mexican and white women.[23]

But farmworker wages had fallen to fourteen cents per hour as farm prices collapsed. Up against the wall, workers joined forces. In 1928 the Federation of Mexican Societies of Southern California created La Confederación de Uniones Mexicanos, with twenty-two locals and three thousand workers. Harsh reprisals, including deportations, led to its swift collapse, but not the end of organizing efforts. In 1930 the Agricultural Workers Industrial League, created by Communist organizers and Filipino and Mexican field hands, allied with white packing-shed workers in a sympathy strike that brought nine hundred field workers out. Local police invaded homes and arrested union members; they hired gunmen from Texas and Arizona to guard the area. They charged the workers with attempting to overthrow the U.S. government, and the jury agreed. In 1931 and 1932 a successor union, the Cannery and Agricultural Workers Industrial Union (CAWIU), led strikes that joined Mexican, Filipino, and Japanese lettuce workers in the Imperial Valley. The response to CAWIU organizing was similarly draconian. As historian John Laslett relates, "Charging criminal conspiracy, a motley crew of sheriff's deputies, hired gunmen, and vigilantes descended on rural communities such as Brawley and El Centro" using illegal methods when necessary. They targeted the protestors as Communists. Meanwhile, in Colorado, sugar beet workers had threatened to strike for years. In May 1932 eighteen thousand beet workers finally did in response to massive wage cuts. That same month Colorado's deportations hit their peak. Deputies patrolled the fields, arresting strikers and accusing the leaders of being outside agitators and Communists, though those they jailed proved to have local roots. Fourteen days after the strike had begun, the fields were quiet, the beet tenders were back at work, and none of their aims had been achieved.[24]

At the same time Mexican workers in the United States faced ever-increasing pressure to depart, Mexican revolutionary artists David Alfaro Siqueiros and Diego Rivera were completing commissioned murals in Los Angeles and Detroit, respectively. In Los Angeles the mural's patrons meant it to form part of their reconstruction of the Mexican barrio as a tourist attraction. Siqueiros dedicated *América Tropical*, his mural at Olvera Street, to the local Mexican community. It depicted "a Native American impaled on a crucifix with a screaming American eagle hovering on top." Rivera's mural at the Detroit Institute of the Arts depicted the benefits and drawbacks of the industrial age. Despite calls for its eradication, Ford kept the mural in Detroit, but the outcry led F. K. Ferenz of the Plaza Art Center on Olvera Street, who had commissioned the mural, to paint over *América Tropical*.[25] Apparently, this was not the message the masterminds of the Olvera Street Market development had in mind.

As it had in Texas, the deportation regime produced tales of terror, leading to a federally appointed commission. It reported in 1932 that "the apprehension and examination of supposed aliens are often characterized by methods [that are] unconstitutional, tyrannic, and oppressive." A Los Angeles County Bar Association investigation titled its report "Lawless Enforcement of the Law." The Mexican press proposed reprisals, including the confiscation of property held by U.S. citizens, a boycott of U.S. goods, and the deportation of seven thousand U.S. citizens doing business in Mexico. In the run-up to the 1932 Olympic Games, hosted by Los Angeles, the Chamber of Commerce and the Automobile Club of Southern California, among other civic leaders, strove to strike a more conciliatory note with their southern neighbor. The city's mass deportation raids ended. In November 1932 Representative John Nance Garner, who had opposed restriction, was elected vice president. While states would continue to erect barriers, and Colorado illegally called out the National Guard to close its border with New Mexico in 1935 and 1936, federal mass deportations ended.[26]

The mass deportations had strained the Mexican government. The mass of refugees, approximately one million by late 1932, according to the U.S. Department of Labor, overwhelmed the Mexican government at the border. Few had returned prosperous. Most had not returned by choice. They and their village neighbors and extended family had relied on U.S. wages, sometimes for decades. American-born children often spoke little Spanish. Some arrived without documentation, rendering them basically stateless. Many arrived starving and ill. As many as 25 percent arrived in Mexico penniless. Every day some died in border repatriation centers. Food and water supplies vanished. The cost of shelter skyrocketed. In Ciudad Juárez, across the U.S. border from El Paso, two thousand *repatriados* camped in a large corral in early January 1931, awaiting transportation to the interior.[27]

The Mexican government responded with colonization schemes much like those of the United States in the 1920s and with nationalism. In a nation only recently emerging from a violent and chaotic revolution, the campaign offered an opportunity to foster a sense of identity that was national ("Mexican"), not local ("Sonoran") or transnational and migratory. The *repatriados* were welcomed home to the *patria*, to which they belonged as Mexicans. At the same time as the massive campaign welcoming home the migrants, Mexico's anti-Chinese policies reached a high point. The conjunction was no accident. By settling *repatriados* strategically, the Mexican government hoped to "Mexicanize" areas of the country that had large foreign populations, particularly if those foreign populations were Chinese and Japanese, as they were in Valle Mexicali, Baja California, for example. Mexico also imposed barriers to Black immigration. Repatriation, managed properly, could bolster racial nationalism and keep Mexican water, property, and profits in Mexico, out of U.S. hands.[28]

Colonization efforts proved deeply flawed, as had the U.S. efforts the previous decade. Colonists arrived to find "nothing, bare land, no living quarters, no running water, no electricity" at Mexicali in Baja. The government had run out of irrigation-ready land in Chihuahua by the end of 1931. Farm machinery, tools, equipment, and mules never arrived. Where irrigation had long been practiced, as happened in U.S. projects, it lowered the water table and turned the soil too alkaline for intensive farming. Money ran out. Irrigation works were cancelled. By the end of 1933, of five hundred original settlers at the project in Oaxaca, only eight remained. The overwhelming majority of *repatriados* headed for the towns of their relatives and friends. In turn, Mexican communities complained of the additional burden caused by destitute repatriates.[29]

Repatriados demanded instead the promised communal lands. In late 1932 they formed La Unión de Repatriados Mexicanos and put pressure on the Mexican government "to halt repatriation efforts until the promises they made to the returnees were fulfilled." In April 1933 they asked the Los Angeles newspaper *La*

Opinión to publish stories about their dire straits as a way to discourage further repatriation. This plea was only the most recent in a string of reports going back as far as November 1931 of abandonment, lack of opportunities, and lack of resources. Mexican consulates pulled back their support of repatriation, one of the reasons the movement from north to south dramatically slowed.[30]

The repatriations and nationalisms and the regimes that supported them changed the border and the borderlands. People and capital had flowed across national borders for a century. U.S. capitalists still had holdings in Mexico, and Mexicans continued to reside in the United States, but they lived in a dramatically different community. One-third of their neighbors were gone. What had been a rapidly growing community often had the hallmarks of a ghost town. Those who had left early, repatriating by choice, had been among the most prosperous and the most skilled, including office and sales clerks. They were the ones who returned in caravans loaded with consumer goods, tools, and capital. Those who returned voluntarily after deportation began in earnest had usually been those with the fewest ties to their neighborhoods in the United States. They were single men. They were young families, recently arrived. They had always intended to return. Those who remained tended to be those still employed or with roots in the community for over a decade. Often, they owned property. The ratio of immigrants to U.S.-born in these communities flipped—from over 90 percent immigrants to over 50 percent U.S.-born. The rise of residential restrictions in the 1920s meant by the 1930s that these heavily U.S.-born families lived in largely Mexican ethnic neighborhoods, increasingly invisible to the Anglo communities nearby.[31]

The Bonus Army

As states, municipalities, and the federal government strived to expel Mexicans, countless U.S. residents, mostly citizens, hit the road, their ties to the land severed by economic disaster. By 1932 two million boys and men, in addition to twenty-five thousand families and untold numbers of single women and girls, drifted across the United States, living on the road. Daily, 1,500 men and boys passed through Kansas City. Hundreds of thousands hopped on empty freight cars, though such freeloading ran counter to federal law and created nightmares for the railroads. The Southern Pacific Railroad alone arrested or threw off its trains as many as 683,000 would-be freeloaders a year.[32]

When they hit the West Coast, they had nowhere else to go. Long host to a large population of seasonal workers and with a legacy of radical democratic organizing, westerners generated their own particular responses and took them back across the nation.

One such response came from Walter W. Waters. Waters grew up in Idaho and Oregon. In 1916, at the age of eighteen, Waters was called up with the National Guard to give chase to Pancho Villa. Having switched from Idaho's to Oregon's National Guard, he headed for France a year later with the 146th Field Artillery. He was honorably discharged a sergeant in mid-1919 after serving with the army of occupation. It took him awhile to find his feet. He ran through a host of occupations—garage mechanic, car salesman, farmhand—and then joined the roving fruit pickers in Washington State. By the decade's end he worked as a superintendent in a cannery and had married a coworker. The cannery foundered in the Depression, as did a second one, and early 1932 found him jobless in Portland, sharing a two-room apartment with his wife on "the wrong side of the tracks."[33]

In March 1932 Waters began talking to veterans' meetings about heading to Washington DC together, hopping freight trains, to shake their promised veterans' bonus out of the government. He had noticed that industrial lobbyists for "special interests" succeeded in getting goods and wanted to follow suit. His first speech was a flop; succeeding speeches fared little better. But with 4,500 jobless veterans in Portland and the city's relief dwindling to $4 per week for a family of five, Waters's crowds began to grow. In mid-May about 280 veterans waited in the Union Pacific freight yards and forced the hand of reluctant train officials, who offered them empty stock cars for the first leg of the journey.[34]

Unmoored by jobs and unable to support families or even themselves, veterans of World War I headed for Washington DC to demand the bonuses enacted by law over presidential veto in 1924 and scheduled for payment, with interest, in 1945. Men who qualified to receive $400 (the average) in 1925 now held government-issued filigreed banknote certificates that read $1,000 redeemable twenty years later.[35]

The effort for an earlier payout had started in 1928 in the same state as the deportations. Wright Patman, himself a veteran who had enlisted fresh out of law school in 1917, ran for Congress as "an agrarian progressive" from a Texas district "so poor that fewer than 2,000 of his 255,452 constituents made enough to pay income taxes." Patman claimed to have paid for law school by working as a tenant farmer and had earned the regular soldier's pay of $1 per day when shipyard workers on the home front made $20 a day. Corporations and profiteers, he claimed, had been paid in full with bonuses for their wartime participation. Patman won and two months after taking office introduced a House bill for immediate payment of the bonus. The Senate version also came from a westerner: Smith Wildman Brookhart, "an Iowa Republican and a self-styled 'cowhide radical.'" The joint bill never made it out of committee.[36]

A third westerner had been invested as president in the same election: Herbert Hoover, who hated the impoverished Iowa farm life of his boyhood, studied engineering at Stanford, married rich, and became an internationally known mining engineer, a millionaire whose direction of food relief in Belgium during the war marked him as compassionate and whose endorsement by organized labor enhanced his progressive credentials. He firmly opposed early payment of the bonus, as it would have required raising taxes, and promised a veto if it passed in Congress.[37]

Still, with the deepening depression, the measure proved ever more popular, and yet another westerner, South Dakota Republican Royal C. Johnson, who had taken leave from Congress to enlist in the war as an infantry private and who had been promoted and highly decorated by the war's end, now chaired the House Committee on World War Veterans' Legislation. With three other Republicans, he drafted a bill allowing veterans to borrow on the certificates; in early 1931 it passed both houses with large majorities, and Hoover signed it.[38] Patman was not satisfied.

Neither the idea of a veterans' march on Washington nor hungry citizens descending en masse on the capital were new. Communist organizers had gathered three thousand participants to come to Washington DC in December 1931. A month earlier, about forty Portland veterans had hopped on the freights, met with Oregon congressmen in the nation's capital, and had the pleasure of a passenger train return trip, thanks to the generosity of Oregon's senator Frederick Steiwer, himself a former U.S. Army lieutenant in France.[39] Now this group in May 1932, calling itself the Bonus Expeditionary Force, a play on the title of U.S. troops sent to France in World War I, came by fits and starts, with inadequate provisions and funds, relying on the generosity of communities and the intimidated rail companies and their often sympathetic local officials (often veterans).

The Bonus Force came in orderly fashion. After all, these were military men with military discipline. They formed in forty-men companies, each with an elected captain, lieutenant, bugler, and first-aid squad. They staged parades, they drilled, they collected and distributed donations, and they followed Waters's rules: "no panhandling, no liquor, no radical talk."[40]

In Wyoming and Iowa residents organized parades; the American Legion gave cigarettes or food; the police sometimes negotiated with the railroads; and in Council Bluffs, Iowa, the mayor gave them the key to the city. Many in the crowds would have joined them if they could.[41] Other such vagabonds may have been seen as detritus; these men were received as heroes.

Until they reached the capital. There thousands of other veterans from east, south, and west joined the Oregonians. They had their sympathizers in Congress, including Farmer-Labor Party congressman Paul J. Kvale of Minnesota, but even their sympathizers were alarmed by the specter of thousands of military men encamped, desperate, in the nation's capital.[42] Waters continued to lead the group, and the group remained orderly.

It also remained racially integrated, unlike the American Expeditionary Force. In segregated Washington DC, the absence of Jim Crow was as scary to officials as the march itself. To military intelligence officials, among others, it was one more sign of the radicalism of the marchers. General Douglas MacArthur warned a commencement audience in Pittsburgh in June 1932 of Communism's omnipresence; at the same moment elsewhere in the city, Mrs. William Perrotta, the "Joan of Arc of the West," and her husband led a contingent of 350 California veterans to Washington. Not Communists, like other veterans they still "were tarred with the red brush." Waters did everything in his power, including trying veterans and sentencing them to fifteen lashes if determined as Communists, to distance his marchers from the accusation.[43]

In mid-June, after the House passed the Bonus Bill, six thousand veterans occupied Capitol Hill to await the verdict in the Senate; thirteen thousand more from the Bonus Army encampments prepared to join them. Even western sympathizers in Congress found the occupation ominous. Democrat senator Elmer Thomas of Oklahoma, who voted for the bonus bill, said that, regardless of the verdict, the Bonus Army would immediately plan to evacuate Washington. Senator Hiram Johnson, a progressive Republican from California, wrote his son, "If the farmers of this Nation who are suffering united, as these men have united, and with the same abandon, started a march upon the Capitol, and joined ranks with those of the city whose souls have been seared with misery during the past few years, it would not be difficult for a real revolution to start in this country."[44]

The bill failed in the Senate. Immediate uproar was averted by singing "America" to the accompaniment of the Army Band, but though Congress appropriated $100,000 in early July to try to get the veterans to leave town, veterans continued to arrive, and demonstrations continued. Congress adjourned, and Hoover wanted the Bonus Army gone, too. Eviction began July 22.[45]

By July 27 eviction had devolved into a pitched and extremely unequal battle between resistant veterans and General MacArthur's troops. Men with fixed bayonets rode through peaceful encampments and set them on fire. Reporters across the Washington Channel looking at the encampment at Anacostia saw "a blaze so big that it lighted the whole sky . . . a nightmare come to life." MacArthur called the Bonus Force marchers "insurrectionists" and claimed that not one in ten was actually a veteran. Hoover followed suit, claiming in a public statement on July 29, "A challenge to the authority of the United States Government has been met, swiftly and firmly."[46]

At least for now, the westerners who had come east would have to look elsewhere for relief and the fulfilment of promises it seemed their region no longer held. A month later, Mexican president Pascual Ortiz Rubio found himself sending a personal telegram in response to Doak E. Carter, leader of a group of twenty-nine thousand World War I veterans who had asked permission to colonize in Mexico. President Rubio, now at the height of repatriation, let Doak know he could not allow foreigners to colonize when he had not enough land for the Mexican nationals the United States was repatriating.[47]

The Farmers' Holiday

Those who did not or could not return to Mexico or head for Washington DC responded to the crisis in other ways. Some, like the Bonus Force marchers, asserted their rights. In March 1930 five hundred protesters, most of them Black women and men, marched on Houston's city hall, demanding unemployment relief and an end to racist legislation. In Dallas, Texas, the Trade Union Unity League and Unemployed Councils schooled residents in rights and recourses; in February 1931 organizers included demands for gainful employment or compensation equivalent to a living wage, aid for the unemployed, banning eviction for failure to pay rent, and free utilities for the poor and unemployed. In Phoenix the next year, the Afro-American League and the International Labor Defense sponsored a march on the state capitol, demanding relief and an end to discrimination.[48]

Others, including ethnic communities across the nation, turned to family networks and to self-help despite desperately dwindling resources. In 1931 Mrs. María Olazábal with a few other women in her Los Angeles neighborhood founded the Cooperative Society of Unemployed Mexican Ladies. In "total cleanliness," they "made and sold tamales at cost to the barrio's unemployed."[49]

On the northern plains, farmers similarly dug deeper into community networks. They restricted the networks to those they deemed worthy, whose efforts to make a living were visible. They excluded Native Americans on reservations and those they labeled "drifters." But when there was no harvest, the harvest could not be shared. These farmers had hardly lived in the lap of luxury in the best of times. Only 10 percent of farm households in South Dakota had running water in 1930. Pumps, buckets, and outhouses were part of their daily routine. Like Mexican migrant workers, however, they were modernizers. They bought automobiles and farm machinery at rates greater than the national average. But the men made the decisions. While 80 percent of farm wives in 1932 put running water as their highest priority, it was clear their husbands did not agree.[50]

In the nation's heartland, conditions had gone from bad to worse. Crops and livestock fetched less than they cost to produce. In 1932 farmers on the northern plains raised "two dollar wheat" that sold for only fifty cents in Minneapolis and less at some local elevators. Middlemen could not sell it for more than the shipping cost. Farmers harvested a bumper crop and had no buyers. While word spread of hunger, even starvation, in U.S. cities, farmers had to watch their wheat rot in piles on the farm.[51]

As conditions worsened, farm women struggled to make up the difference. A government report had shown that almost 90 percent of midwestern women kept chickens (on average, 102 of them), and over 90 percent participated in dairy production. They produced 70 percent of what their families consumed, from food to clothing, toys to toothpaste. Now they expanded their gardens, raised more chickens, sold more eggs (and milk and butter where they could), and pieced together the less worn parts of their husbands' clothes and flour sacks and whatever other bits of cloth they could lay their hands on, turning them into trousers and shirts for their children. They returned to preindustrial ways of making cleansers and cloth, methods they and their mothers had not used in forty years. They produced at least half of farm cash income in the 1930s, despite their ever-greater isolation, as they could no longer afford gas or even cars to take them to town or to bring the doctor.[52]

Like the veterans, these men and women farmers decided to take matters into their own hands. They came from a long tradition of mass uprising. The men and women of the farm belt had not only participated enthusiastically in the radical democracy movements of the 1910s. They had voted Populists into office in South Dakota in the 1890s. They had voted the Nonpartisan League into office in North Dakota in the 1910s. They had founded the Farmers Union in 1902, whose rapid growth and spread as a lobbying group for dirt farmers (those who did their own labor) had led

Theodore Roosevelt to appoint its president, Charles S. Barrett, to his Country Life Commission and Woodrow Wilson to appoint him as an agricultural advisor at the Versailles Peace Conference. In January 1931 three hundred farmers descended on the rural town of England, Arkansas, about twenty miles from Little Rock. Tired of watching their families starve after the worst drought year on record and plummeting agricultural prices, they demanded food. Threatened with looting, the merchants, themselves suffering economically, handed out $1,500 in staples. The story went viral. Will Rogers recalled, "Paul Revere just woke up Concord. . . . These birds woke up America."[53]

In Iowa the state's Farmers Union convention in September 1931 passed a resolution asking for a "farmers buying, selling, and taxpaying strike" until Congress passed sufficient agricultural legislation. The next May at the state fair, the farmers followed up by organizing the national Farmers' Holiday Association (FHA). Milo Reno, born on an Iowa farm in January 1866, the seventh son and twelfth child of a farmer, trained as a minister and long a Farmers Union activist, now at the age of sixty-six became the leader of the FHA. Reno declared that after all the failed policies and promises, the farmer, now "discouraged, broken-hearted and bankrupt, has come to realize . . . that if his rights as an American citizen and an independent owner and operator of a farm are restored, it will be by his own efforts." Farmers in eight other midwestern states joined Iowa in the new movement.[54]

The FHA's members determined to raise commodity prices and stop foreclosures. Hoover, like Coolidge, had vetoed the farmers' favored legislation to support prices, the McNary-Haugen Bill. Instead he had signed the Agricultural Marketing Act of 1929, which created the Federal Farm Board to establish large farm cooperative marketing associations with the idea that, in line with Hoover's voluntarist managed capitalism, the associations would stabilize farm prices and create markets. It proved inadequate.[55] Farmers demanded more effective relief.

Things came to a head in 1932 for a reason. Prices continued to plummet. In that single year the return for hogs per head fell by almost half, an unprecedented drop. Foreclosures continued to mount. In 1932 the cost of producing a bushel of corn was ninety-two cents; prevailing prices that June were ten cents. Hogs cost eleven cents per pound to produce and fetched only three cents; butterfat cost sixty-two cents per pound to produce and earned eighteen cents. Still, prices continued to drop.[56]

The FHA argued that farmers should take a holiday until the conditions improved. It was a mode of self-help. One organizer drove more than ten thousand miles recruiting members in the summer of 1932. Another worked through Farmers Union locals in North Dakota and claimed fifty thousand members in the state. The FHA had a broad base of support, numbering bankers and businessmen on FHA steering committees. Proposals included tax relief for farmers, tax increases for corporations, railroad regulation, increasing the currency supply, and keeping commodities off the market when market prices fell below the cost of production. The proposals included a subsidized domestic price, as farmers had proposed in the 1920s.[57]

They looked not for mere subsistence but, as they had in the 1920s, for participation in what they saw as the modern consumer marketplace, something they deserved as worthy producers. The goods they claimed they were entitled to consume ranged widely, including higher education, hospitalization during childbirth, dental care, and recreation.[58]

There was a tendency to see the issue in regional terms—western producers and eastern bankers. As one Oklahoma rancher testified to Congress, "We will march eastward, and we will cut the East off. We will cut the East off from the West. We have got the granaries; we have the hogs, the cattle, the corn, and the East has nothing but mortgages on our places."[59] But it was where markets were local, in dairy farming, that farm activism had its greatest victories. While milk prices had dropped steadily after World War I, dairy farmers had remained more prosperous than grain farmers. Less affected by global markets, they experienced the Depression as a more sudden shock. Butter prices fell by half between 1927 and 1932. Suddenly, foreclosures skyrocketed. In 1932 banks foreclosed on 6,400 Iowa farm mortgages. In 1933 Iowa had the highest foreclosure rate in the nation, and Iowa's dairy districts had the state's highest foreclosure rates.

Because milk spoils readily, distributors, to whom dairy farmers sold their milk, tended to be few in number, like their suppliers, and to have relatively local catchment areas—twenty to thirty miles around urban centers. The largest distributor around Sioux City, Iowa, the J. R. Roberts Dairy Company, had expanded its catchment area to ensure a steady surplus, allowing it to dictate prices: the company paid farmers two cents a quart and charged consumers eight cents. In response, dairy farmers formed the Producers' Cooperative Association in May 1932; nine hundred members had signed up by August. The company's owner refused to negotiate, boasting of having broken co-ops in the past.

The dairy farmers framed their demands as a matter of justice and equity: "The milk distributors at the present time are not giving the producers a just and equitable share of the consumer's money." The co-op members voted to join the FHA strike, withholding from J. R. Roberts but providing free milk distribution (donations welcome) to ensure public sympathy. Co-op members halted fifteen milk trucks west of Sioux City on August 11; they took the milk from two of them and dumped it on the road. The next evening they patrolled all roads leading into the city from the east and north. By August 14 they had 1,500 dairy farmers covering five highways, stopping virtually all shipments.

Though officials recruited one hundred deputies to keep the roads open, the deputies declined to interfere with the persuasive dairy farmer activists. The Iowa governor promised that law and order would be maintained but determinedly left the maintaining in local hands. Many truckers, most farmers, and organized labor in the state sided with the strikers. Sioux City usually saw six hundred trucks enter each day; now it received twelve. Distributors turned to the railroads and brought milk in from Nebraska, but at prohibitive cost. The strategy was unsustainable. By August 18 the strikers had cut J. R. Roberts's receipts in half. South Dakota and Nebraska farmers joined in, blocking access to the north and south. Sioux City provided just one of the over three hundred such protests in August and September. After ten days, distributors in Sioux City compromised on a new price; a week later, the parties signed an agreement in the offices of the Chamber of Commerce.[60]

Grain farmers went on strike in Iowa, Minnesota, and the Dakotas. It was, perhaps, unrealistic to try such a massive action on such short notice. There was little central coordination. In some areas farmers began to withhold goods in August, while others started in October. Some farmers sold their grain as soon as prices rose slightly. Other women and men farmers blockaded roads, uncoupled livestock cars, and got arrested. The leaders of the movement, including Milo Reno, did not endorse violence, but as one historian put it, "Where desperate men met desperate men," myriad instances of violence followed. Picketers smashed truck windows. Trucks rammed picketing vehicles. One sheriff downed three picketers with his fists. Sheriffs' men gassed crowds that included farm men and women and their children. Sheriffs arrested picketers. Crowds of hundreds of farmer sympathizers threatened to storm the jails where picketers were held, in one case, despite facing a perimeter of machine guns. A sheriff, a banker, and a former police officer joined with six others in two cars, firing on picketers and hurling gas bombs.

As tensions rose among the farmers, Milo Reno, former Farmers' Alliance and Populist activist, president of the Iowa Farmers Union and now the FHA, called off the strike pending a conference of midwestern governors meeting in Sioux City on September 9. To the disappointment of the FHA, the governors, as Governor Warren Green of South Dakota announced, "most emphatically do not favor any embargo on farm products," though they hoped to work out a plan for a "voluntary holding movement." Reno, in turn, announced the resumption of the strike. Each branch went its own way, some more successfully than others.[61]

It would be easy to write off the farm strike as a failure—an effort locally to affect prices set by global markets. But the action had distinct successes. During the strike, direct action by farmers halted at least 140 foreclosure sales. FHA actions against farm evictions and foreclosures continued after the strike. When mediation failed, the FHA mobilized its members, sometimes hundreds of women and men, to intimidate sheriffs out of evicting or to halt auction bids at a penny per item. Such "penny sales" allowed the evicted farm family to recoup their goods. Sympathetic telephone operators enabled the FHA, as a farmer claimed, to "rouse the whole countryside in fifteen minutes." At one penny sale in Milbank, South Dakota, the auctioneer reaped only $6.30, but the FHA paid twice that for its out-of-town members' lunch. At another, women stripped the pants off the auctioneer and locked him in the barn.[62] These activist women and men successfully laid claim to a different economic order than that of the bankers, one with broad community support, one that retained the promise of landownership that had brought so many of them west in the first place.

There were also electoral successes. Success in the electoral sphere could shift the state in the direction of the farmers' vision of the modern West. In 1932 the FHA and the Farmers Union elected members to the South Dakota state legislature. In North Dakota, Governor William "Wild Bill" Langer not only supported penny sales by ordering sheriffs not to evict but declared a foreclosure moratorium, authorizing the National Guard to prevent foreclosure on any farm or small business property. "Shoot the banker if he comes on your farm," he had declared when running for office. "Treat him like a chicken thief." In rural counties the vote for Langer was almost unanimous.[63]

Across the northern border, in Canada, prairie farmers suffered like their U.S. counterparts, and they responded in similar ways. By 1932 two-thirds of Saskatchewan families received relief. Leftist groups, United Farmers members from Alberta, Independent Labour Party members from Manitoba, and Saskatchewan's Farmer-Labor Party members gathered in Calgary on July 31, 1932. As the U.S. FHA gained momentum, these Canadians formed the Co-operative Commonwealth Federation (CCF), Canada's first socialist party. At its head was James Shaver Woodsworth, a member of Parliament and former Methodist minister.

These were democratic socialists, not revolutionary Communists, but they did lay the economic ills of the era at the feet of the system, not the individual. When hundreds of Canadians from across the country met at Regina, Saskatchewan, in 1933 to articulate the CCF's goals and structure, they included farmers, workers, preachers, socialists, lawyers, poets, and academics. They voted for universal pensions, health and welfare insurance, unemployment insurance, a minimum wage, and farm security, and this party platform became known as the Regina Manifesto. By 1935 the party had five members in Parliament, one of whom would become premier in 1944.[64]

From Canada to Mexico, Americans called on each other's support to weather the economic hard times. When they formalized their organizations, whether in the FHA or the CCF, they built on a long western tradition. Rather than seeing mutual aid and cooperation as at odds with self-help, they saw them as natural outgrowths, as self-governance, as assertions of Americans' democratic rights inseparable from their vision of a just economy. When they entered politics, their organizations built on the past but looked to the future.

Conclusion

The dislocations wrought by the collapse of the 1920s economic system—the expelled Mexicans, displaced veterans, and farmers, all demobilized from the speculative economy—bore testimony to the fragility of that system. The collapse shook the foundations of the promised "white man's country." The misfit between exploitive labor relations and the imagined self-supporting virtue of the American farmer had required some fancy footwork. It had led to whitened depictions of farmers and farming, scenes of crops that grew themselves in a bucolic countryside. When they had to be visible at all, as during World War I, Mexicans had appeared as temporary, aiding patriotic hard-pressed white family farmers.[65] The pervasive collapse exposed the sleight of hand. The mass deportations made the rootedness and scale of Mexican family migrant labor in the United States highly visible.

Meanwhile, the white farmers resisting eviction and refusing demobilization held on to the promised status even as the system undergirding it collapsed. As millions hit the road and thousands joined in protest in Mexico and in the U.S. and Canadian Wests, governments struggled to contain the disaster. The mobilizations at the start of the downturn had been largely involuntary. The mobilizations on the eve of the New Deal, though spurred by desperation, were not.

The federal government's response to the West's misery, according to historian Richard White, pitted two western traditions against each other: "a self-conceived rugged individualism and the historical reality of dependence on federal aid." Absent from that dyad is the third western tradition: mass mobilization and a more collective vision of modernity. The Farmers' Holiday Association demonstrated that continuity and its power to reshape the landscape of rules and power that governed life in the region.

In the face of this upheaval, Edward P. Costigan, junior senator from Colorado, proposed direct relief from the federal government. Costigan had cut his teeth on Colorado's labor wars and had served as counsel for the United Mine Workers defendants after the Ludlow strike. He understood the moment's peril and desperation, as well as its promise. President Hoover at first opposed him. With three million unemployed in the West alone, however, and with the election looming, Hoover did, in the end, sign Costigan's Emergency Relief and Construction Act of 1932. Because the Reconstruction Finance Corporation that administered it, though authorized to give $300 million in loans to businesses, gave only about $30 million, it had little impact.[66] Not surprisingly, Hoover lost the 1932 election to Franklin Roosevelt and his New Deal. Roosevelt carried every state west of the Mississippi.

11
Mobilizing the New Deal

When Roosevelt's New Deal arrived in the West, unrest came to a climax. Buoyed by hope that Roosevelt would prove more responsive than Hoover and faced with still-deteriorating conditions, protests grew. Desperation forged new partnerships. New legal protections for workers' organizing came out of the famous first one hundred days of the new federal administration. Organizations formed and re-formed. Workers across the West on farms and in mines and cities joined forces and demanded a better life, decent living conditions, and more than starvation wages. They walked out of cotton fields; they stopped shelling pecans and sewing garments; they stopped driving trucks and unloading ships; and, ultimately, they shut down San Francisco and Minneapolis with general strikes. Their members struck with increasing confidence, regardless of the letter of the law, that the federal government had their back.

Joining across class lines, they also launched a national movement for old-age pensions and the California gubernatorial candidacy of the socialist turned Democrat Upton Sinclair. Roosevelt's administration found itself pushed and pulled by the assertions of people on the ground. Those people twisted and reshaped programs launched by the administration, pushing the programs into the mold of their own vision of political economy and of a modern West and its opportunities.[1] They demanded and sometimes won the fruits of resurgent democratic movements.

This chapter focuses particularly on three of the many dramatic uprisings in the early New Deal: California's cotton strike, the San Francisco and Minneapolis general strikes, and Upton Sinclair's campaign for governor. These three were among the largest of the movements in these years and the most revealing of how the strands present in preceding years of the West wove together and the power they had not only to redefine the workplace but to reshape politics.

Coalitions

Setting people in motion had set ideas in motion. Those demobilized people carried ideas with them. Exiled Japanese communists mingled with veterans of Mexico's revolutions on Los Angeles street corners. Filipino workers continued to organize in the fields of California as they had since the turn of the century alongside Mexican workers, and now they organized in the canneries of Alaska as well. Veterans of the 1910s democratic insurgencies in the United States gathered again in coal-mining towns in Colorado and New Mexico and on the docks of San Pedro, Seattle, and San Francisco.

As conditions worsened, the number of unemployed and underemployed reached 30 percent or more of the population, and evictions skyrocketed both from city apartments and houses and from rural farms and tenancies. Communist Party organizers seemed to many the only voices arguing for the rights of the dispossessed. Few joined the party, but many responded to the efforts of Communist organizers who mobilized neighbors to halt evictions, organized the unemployed to demand relief, and helped farmworkers create unions. Critics accused the Communist Party of using the dispossessed and disenfranchised as pawns. Faced with such criticism, Pettis Perry, a transplant from Alabama seeking to escape the ubiquitous spectacle of African Americans beaten and lynched, saw about fifty Black faces in a sea of whites at a Los Angeles rally in support of the Scottsboro boys, Black teenagers framed for rape in Alabama; he watched as officers beat whites at the rally and concluded, "If they're willing to get shot, willing to go to jail, willing to get beaten up, willing to pick a Negro for Vice President [as the party had on its ticket in 1932], just to get me into the party, then that's the bait for me." He joined the Communist Party–affiliated International Labor Defense in 1932.[2]

The efforts to demarcate, divide, and segregate had never been complete. The segregated neighborhoods created by real estate speculation sat beside neighborhoods so diverse that no single group dominated, whether in West Fresno, parts of East and West

Los Angeles, San Francisco's Tenderloin and South of Market, Seattle's Central District, Denver's Curtis Park, or others. In Los Angeles, Japanese, Russian Jews, Italians, Mexicans, African Americans, and Anglos mixed along Central Avenue. Around that city's old Mexican Plaza about 60 percent of the population in 1920 had remained Mexican, but 20 percent were Italian and another 20 percent a little of everything. In the *Los Angeles Times*, Harry Chandler called Los Angeles the "white spot of America," but it was spotty indeed.[3]

In urban gathering places, on speakers' corners and docks, in rural fields and migrant camps, in struggling political movements that persisted despite violence and repression, people had continued to gather across lines of color and national descent. In Los Angeles, despite official efforts during the 1910s free speech fights and after, the Plaza remained the core of a vibrant popular politics. On Sunday afternoons during the Great Depression, Russian Jews, Japanese, Filipinos, African Americans, Mexicans, and Anglos spoke and listened. They brought their histories with the IWW, the Socialist Party, the Communist Party, and others. They spoke in defense of the Scottsboro boys; they spoke about Imperial Valley farmworkers, about Nazi Germany, and about unemployment.[4]

Coalitions could be intimate. During one such demonstration in 1932, Elaine Black, the daughter of Russian Jewish immigrants and an officer in the International Labor Defense arm of the Communist Party, met her future husband, Karl Yoneda, the son of Japanese immigrants and a member of the International Longshoremen's Association. Yoneda owed his membership to his adoption by his African American friend Len Greer in front of the membership committee, which otherwise would have excluded him due to race. He worked as a labor organizer of longshoremen, cannery, and other workers on the West Coast. Yoneda and Black married in Washington State to avoid California's laws against interracial marriage.[5]

Lines between urban and rural blurred. Dispossessed farmers and off-season migrant farm labor met on the same street corners with the urban unemployed. Together they created a critique of the system that brought them there. Together they marched through the city streets to the halls of power.[6]

The forces arrayed against these mobilizations also swelled. Los Angeles had already created an anti-Communist "red squad." Its treatment of a Communist-led hunger march in the spring of 1930 was, according to a federal commission, "an eight hour clubbing party." Private employers paid the squad's overtime and provided supplies, sending them to wreak havoc on major agricultural strikes in the Los Angeles hinterland. There were other methods in growers' arsenals. Local officials in Colorado and elsewhere timed the 1932 deportations to coincide with strikes, threatening the fragile coalition of U.S. citizens and Mexican immigrants. Labor contractors, too, took violent exception to workers organizing.[7]

On the eve of the New Deal, after three years of economic depression, the generosity that had fueled early relief efforts and passed bonds to fund them had given way to fear and self-preservation. Eligibility for and equity in relief became major issues in rural areas, in cities, and in mining and other towns. People condemned working wives as stealing jobs from would-be breadwinning men. People demanded relief come with a rising tide of requirements, including labor and citizenship. Mexican and Black farmworkers in particular frequently met a hostile reception when it came to getting relief. The secretary of the Texas Citrus League complained to the Texas relief director, "We fail to see why the welfare of unskilled Mexican field labor should be promoted at the expense of American growers and tax-payers." Particularly after the deportations, of course, most "Mexican" field workers were tax-paying U.S. citizens, as the editor of the *Hidalgo County News* made clear when he argued, in contrast, that tax-paying Mexican American U.S. citizens should be free to choose between starvation farm wages and higher-paying federal work projects.[8]

Then, in 1933, the New Deal's National Industrial Recovery Act (NIRA) included section 7a, which acknowledged labor's right to organize independent of employers, and set up the National Recovery Administration (NRA) to enforce the act. With that federal promise and the New Deal's relief measures pumping much-needed capital into the economy, even areas where organizing had flagged awoke to new possibilities. A wave of strike activity swept the region in virtually every sector. Not only farmworkers, dockworkers, coal miners, and timber workers struck, but so did waitresses and store clerks. The Communist Party USA continued to sponsor new unions, and the American Federation of Labor (AFL) continued to expand its efforts. At times, the Communist Party USA and the AFL battled each other, sacrificing the interests of the workers. But on the whole, unskilled workers in particular saw a vast expansion of their ability to organize effectively in their own interests.

In 1917 a strike in Gallup, New Mexico, had pitted Mexican-heritage U.S. citizens against Mexicans imported to break the strike. In 1933 Mexican nationals and Mexican-heritage U.S. citizens again dominated Gallup's workforce, and as they did in Texas, Mexican-heritage residents faced discrimination in relief even when eligible. By 1933 half of Gallup's miners had little or no work. Those with jobs often worked only part-time, but that part-time work rendered them ineligible for relief. Leftist Unemployed Councils led marches demanding milk and shoes for children, and Hispano organizations demanded equal rights for all *citizens*. They seemed poised to repeat the friction of 1917. Instead, they joined forces across lines of citizenship.

Leaning on section 7a, Gallup's workers rejected both a company union and the United Mine Workers (Anglo dominated), opting overwhelmingly for the Communist-affiliated National Miners Union (NMU). Unlike the other unions, the NMU emphasized both militant action and cross-racial and cross-ethnic organizing independent of citizenship. In late August 1933 Gallup's miners walked out. They demanded union recognition. They shut down the mines.

Despite the peaceful nature of the strike, after only a day the governor called out the National Guard and put the county under martial law. He did so at the behest not only of the mine owners and local officials but also of the rival UMW. The government banned NMU meetings, and five hundred state militiamen escorted strikebreakers around the thousand or so strikers and sympathizers, who maintained a twenty-four-hour picket line. The town of Gallup depended on the mining company for water and electricity. It would not oppose the company.

The miners mobilized their own networks. Locally, miners' families included smallholders in the region, as they had at Ludlow in

1914, who provided the strikers with produce from their gardens and their livestock. Regionally, the Farmers' Holiday Association recognized a common cause and mobilized farmers in Colorado, Nebraska, and Wyoming who collected food and brought it to the strikers. The New Mexico Federation of Labor, pressured by its Spanish-speaking members and despite its hostility to the NMU, supported the strike.

In crucial ways, the solidarity of these mine workers and their farmer allies threatened to upend the status quo. Who would control the workplace, and what level of autonomy would wages provide? Their struggle resonated with the Farmers' Holiday Association, which saw in it a demand for the western promise of access to an independent livelihood, pushing against the dominance of large-scale corporations. The threat was as clear to New Mexico's mine owners and the armed forces that protected them as it was to California farm owners and their armed allies. In the face of the New Mexico standoff, and with the National Guard costing the state $500 per day, in October the leader of the U.S. troops at Gallup arrested the entire leadership of the NMU. He charged them with inciting insurrection against New Mexico. He threatened to deport the two Mexican nationals among the leaders.

The move failed to quell the "insurrection." The rank and file simply added the release of its leaders to its strike demands, and about four hundred strikers and sympathizers, largely women and children, defied martial law and picketed the stockyards where the Mexican leaders awaited deportation. It was only the governor's unexpected death that broke the logjam. The lieutenant governor stepped into office, determined to settle the strike. The negotiated settlement included releasing the jailed leaders, rehiring strikers, and adopting the NRA code for bituminous coal. The NMU had more fundamental changes in mind. It organized workers on federal relief and the unemployed (often former miners) and ran candidates in state elections.[9]

Cotton

Between April, when NIRA became law, and December 1933 fifty thousand of California's agricultural workers went on strike. In twenty-nine of those strikes, led by the Cannery and Agricultural

Workers Industrial Union (CAWIU), workers won better wages and conditions. Farm ownership was overwhelmingly white in California (over 88 percent), and agricultural labor, including 368,000 Mexicans, overwhelmingly not. Moreover, ownership was highly concentrated in the hands of a relatively small percentage of farmers who participated in networks of land corporations, processing, and marketing organizations. Specializing in one or two crops, the large-scale farms operated as mechanized plantations—except at certain seasons when the needs of particular crops demanded fifty or more times the number of year-round employees to prune or thin or harvest by hand. Looking after the needs of these powerful constituents, the collective might of southern and western senators had excluded farm labor from the benefits of the NIRA's section 7a, but farmworkers refused to acknowledge the exclusion. With the help of some California officials' creative interpretation of the law, they forced the hand of the federal government.[10]

The strikes began in Santa Clara Valley fruit orchards and traveled with the migrants to berry, sugar beet, apricot, pear, peach, lettuce, and grape harvests. In May six thousand Mexicans went on strike in the El Monte berry fields. The scale of the strike and its economic threat helped California's NRA and National Labor Relations Board administrators, despite section 7a's exclusion, to claim jurisdiction over "industrial disputes in agriculture."[11]

Flushed with success after NRA mediation, workers vowed to carry the strike to cotton. Cotton proved the climax of the thirty-seven agricultural worker strikes in California that year. Its extraordinary scale, covering over one hundred miles and four counties and lasting twenty-seven days, made the cotton strike, according to historian Devra Weber, "the largest, longest, and most bitter agricultural conflict to that date." Wages ate up about a third of the crop's total value, and farmers worked hard to control them. In response to short and well-timed local strikes, farmers had organized the Agricultural Labor Bureau (ALB) in 1926 to centralize recruitment and distribution of workers and control wages. The ALB standardized wages industry-wide in a conference with ginners, large growers, and investors—but not workers. It hindered growers wanting to pay more by making their loans contingent on approved farmworker wages. Wages dropped from $1.65 per one hundred pounds picked in 1925 to $1.25 in 1926. When workers protested, striking in 1926, the ALB brought in Mexicans from Los Angeles to break the strike.[12]

Growers took other steps to discourage strikes. Migrants often bought cars by pooling their wages. The cars made it easier for them to move from crop to crop and, when conditions and wages warranted it, from employer to employer. Employers characterized such workers as lazy, shiftless, and rootless, blaming the automobile for their "lack of stability."[13] Unable to deny them cars, however, growers improved housing for workers, encouraging the overwhelmingly Mexican workers (75 percent of the cotton workforce—90 percent on larger ranches) to stay year-round. As many as 280 families lived in a single such labor camp. As they did with company towns in other industries, the growers set up schools and arranged for goods either brought in by wagon or sold in company stores. The company housing and company stores, as usual in company towns, however, meant that growers could evict workers at will and could manipulate wages and prices to ensure perpetual indebtedness.[14]

Cotton workers, like other migrant workers, were far from homogeneous. California's cotton growers, looking for experienced labor, had started recruiting southern Black workers in the 1910s. These workers spread across the valley and numbered among the inhabitants of the valley's Black utopian community, Allensworth, founded in 1908. The Mexican-descent workers, who vastly outnumbered the Black workers, had previously worked not only in agriculture but also in mines, on railroads, and as artisans, steel workers, packing-house workers, or small shopkeepers in Mexico and in Kansas, Colorado, and Arizona and across the U.S. West. They carried with them memories of the Mexican Revolution and told its stories and sang its songs around campfires in the labor camps. They carried their experience of strikes at Cananea and other mines. They migrated in groups and increasingly as families. By 1925, 90 percent of Mexican cotton pickers worked alongside their families. And with families they built social networks. Edward Bañales remembered "when he fought with his contractor and walked out in disgust it was 'families and friends [who] would quit with you.'"[15]

For a moment in 1933, after the peak of the deportations and before the mass dislocations caused by the dust storms and the unintended consequences of the Agricultural Adjustment Act (AAA), when large landowners took land out of production by evicting tenants and sharecroppers, agricultural workers had some leverage. With the Depression, cotton prices had plummeted. A pound of cotton fetched twenty cents in 1927 and six cents in 1932. Small farmers lost their land, and cotton-chopping and cotton-picking wages fell to less than half the 1928 level. In such dire circumstances, it would seem desperate workers would accept any wages. But the mass deportations meant that workers available had also diminished, and the crop still had to be tended. Labor contractor Francisco Palomares had a contract to import a thousand workers from El Monte's berry fields to the cotton fields of the San Joaquin Valley in 1933. Afraid of importing the strike with the workers, he cancelled the contract. The Los Angeles Chamber of Commerce fell back on a strategy of threatening deportation to keep the workers quiet.[16] It wasn't enough.

The Tagus ranch was both the San Joaquin Valley's largest peach grower and a major cotton producer. In August a small group of Tagus workers had organized a union. A CAWIU organizer arrived to encourage them; they joined CAWIU and led seven hundred Tagus workers on strike. They demanded a forty-hour week, an increase in pay, union recognition, and an end to forced buying from the company store. By mid-August four thousand workers on the peach crop had joined the strike. Panicky growers began to raise wages, pressuring Tagus to follow suit. Despite the agricultural worker exclusion from section 7a, the NRA mediated between the parties as it had in El Monte. When Tagus capitulated, the Agricultural Labor Bureau raised wages industry-wide. CAWIU quickly established nineteen locals, blanketing the valley, and Tagus workers moved to cotton.[17]

The strikes would have happened even without the CAWIU; the Tagus workers had organized before CAWIU arrived, and organizers recalled that "strikes were breaking out all over." Farmworkers had experience in the smaller-scale strikes and fleeting organizations of the 1920s.[18] CAWIU facilitated coordination. In mid-September seventy-eight cotton worker delegates met at CAWIU headquarters to agree on their demands. They wanted an end to the contract-labor system, "no recrimination against strikers[,] . . . hiring only through the union," and $1 for picking a hundred pounds of cotton.

Two days later the growers and ginners convened at the ALB. The New Deal's AAA policies, including price supports, had boosted cotton prices in California by 75 percent over the previous year, and while they needed workers, growers had little desire to share that boost with the workers or to strengthen the CAWIU. They offered sixty cents per hundred pounds picked, a twenty-cent raise over the previous year. In response, two to three thousand workers immediately walked out of the fields, and under pressure from the workers, the union called a strike on October 4. Over eighteen thousand cotton pickers went out on strike.[19]

Mexican strikers carried signs in Spanish declaring support of the NRA. The growers evicted the strikers from the labor camps. They started at the Peterson ranch near Corcoran, where 150 families were on strike. With armed guards, seventy-five growers loaded the families' belongings onto trucks and dumped them onto the highway. Within days, growers had evicted over 3,500 workers in the vicinity, an action replicated throughout the valley.

The evicted strikers formed refugee camps, with hundreds of workers in each camp, and they converted local barrio homes, pool halls, and bars into strike headquarters. A small farmer on the outskirts of Corcoran allowed strikers to use four acres for what became the largest refugee camp, with about 3,500 workers, dwarfing the size of Corcoran itself. They slept in makeshift tents of their own devising, cooked over fires, and fed the ubiquitous dogs and occasional goat or chickens. They put up a barbed-wire fence for protection and guarded the entrance. They set up a water and latrine system, and they ate rabbits and fish they caught and greens they foraged, supplemented with food donated or purchased. They set up a community kitchen and temporary schools, and a circus, the Circo Azteca, which had occupied the land before the strike, entertained them nightly along with strikers who played guitar and sang and told stories. In caravans of cars they headed for hot spots where strikebreakers picked cotton along the one hundred miles and two thousand ranches of the strike. They intercepted pickers and set up picket lines and called out to pickers to join them.

Shocked by the strikers' strength and persistence, the growers tried to import four thousand unemployed Mexicans from Los Angeles; fewer than five hundred came, and few of those stayed to pick. By October 9 approximately twelve thousand farmworkers were on strike in Tulare, Kings, and Kern Counties alone.

The small farmer who provided land for the strikers was unusual but not alone in supporting the workers. In addition, small merchants, often Japanese, Mexican, Portuguese, or Russian Jewish, extended credit to strikers and donated food and clothes. The merchants' customer base was the workers, not the owners.

The forces of law and order, on the other hand, weighed in on the side of the growers. The district attorney of one of the strike counties confessed, "The growers were really more trouble and danger than the strikers were. We could control the strikers because they didn't amount to anything and couldn't even vote, but the growers were well known and had lots of influence and we were much more afraid we couldn't control them." An undersheriff was less half-hearted in his allegiance. He claimed, "We protect our farmers here in Kern County. They are our best people. They are always with us. They keep the county going. They put us in here and they can put us out again, so we serve them. But the Mexicans are trash. . . . We herd them like pigs." In the pocket of the growers, these local law officers arrested picketers on any charges they could muster, including once "for addressing the audience in Spanish." They beefed up their arms and added dozens of new deputies, including ranchers and their managers. Strikers, too, began to arm, though few had guns. There was a lot of tinder awaiting a spark.

On October 10 Mexican and Anglo strikers had gathered in the open air in the small town of Pixley to listen to a CAWIU organizer when a caravan of ten cars filled with growers drove up. As the workers headed toward shelter at the union hall, a grower took aim. Dolores Hernández, a fifty-year-old striker, pushed aside the gun, "was knocked down by one grower," and as he lay in the dirt street "was shot to death by another." Crouching behind their cars, the growers opened fire on the crowd and the union hall. By the time the shooting stopped, the growers had killed a Mexican honorary consular representative from Tulare and a Mexican farmworker from the Tagus ranch and had wounded eight others. The attack seemed to be part of a general offensive by the growers. At the same time, at the Frick ranch thirty armed growers confronted 250 strikers, barring them from access to the pickers in the field; after five hours of verbal jousting, a grower shot and instantly killed a Mexican striker. Some growers joined in wounding other strikers, and other growers attacked strikers around the valley.

At first, law officers made no attempt to arrest the shooters. After all, it was a newly appointed sheriff's deputy who reportedly led the Pixley attack, and highway patrolmen and sheriffs had witnessed the attack firsthand and not interfered. But in an age before smart phones, images could still go viral. Across the United States, newspapers printed photographs of the attack on the unarmed strikers and Mexican consular representative. The images and story evoked, according to Weber, "a flood of protests that brought state and federal mediators, the Mexican government," reporters, and supporters. In response, local officials arrested eleven local growers for the Pixley killings; they also arrested a union leader and sixteen strikers and charged them with disturbing the peace.[20]

The murders outraged workers. They strengthened the workers' resolve and brought new allies. Even the local newspaper, usually supporting the growers, condemned the killings. Public pressure at every level from local to international mounted, demanding investigation of the killings and resolution of the strike. Reluctantly, California governor James Rolph agreed to meet with a delegation of strikers. They asked for relief, protection for strikers, and prosecution of the growers responsible for the killings. Boards of supervisors in two of the affected counties had refused relief to strikers, hoping to force them back to work. Rolph now agreed to provide the strikers with necessities, trucked in milk and food to distribute, and assured the strikers that accepting the relief would not lead to deportation for those immigrants among them.[21]

The federal government saw the official and vigilante violence as threatening workers' confidence in the New Deal and hindering economic recovery. The federal government knew that both workers and growers depended on New Deal programs. Workers depended on relief and jobs programs. Growers relied on price supports. Rabbi Irving Reichart, director of mediation and adjustment for the NRA in California, warned growers that their benefits depended on "a fair deal to those who labor in the industry" and their "willingness to deal with labor representatives . . . duly elected spokesmen for their group." Federal officials similarly warned workers that relief depended on accepting federal arbitration. To the frustration of workers and despite the reference to "duly elected spokesmen," George Creel, the regional administrator of the NRA and member of the National Labor Relations Board, refused to recognize the CAWIU as the workers' bargaining agent. Creel, who had directed the U.S. propaganda machine in World War I, remained true to his progressive roots. At Creel's direction the governor appointed a fact-finding commission "to investigate the strike and suggest a settlement." The commission had neither a laborer nor a grower; it had a labor historian, a San Francisco Catholic archbishop, and a college president. It was a perfect demonstration of the progressive idea—the foundation of many New Dealers, as it was with Creel—that professionals stood, disinterested, above the fray.[22]

The commission issued its report in November. It found that strikers' civil rights had been violated and that seventy-five cents, the rate the commission recommended, was the most farmers could afford to pay. Growers balked. Creel threatened to withhold crop loans and AAA payments. Facing also the threat of a crop rotting in the fields, growers capitulated on the wages. Strikers, on the other hand, wanted eighty cents, union recognition, release of imprisoned strikers, and no discrimination in rehiring. Creel withdrew relief and mobilized a thousand workers through the U.S. Farm Labor Service in Los Angeles to pick the crop. The strikers capitulated, voting to accept seventy-five cents and end the strike.[23]

Despite the government's refusal to recognize the CAWIU as the workers' bargaining agent, the role of the NRA in mediating the strike left the cotton pickers still convinced that the federal government had guaranteed their right to a union and collective bargaining. They carried that expectation with them throughout the 1933–34 season, as 1,500 cotton pickers went out on strike in Arizona in November and 5,000 Mexican farmworkers went on strike in California's Imperial Valley in January.[24]

Upton Sinclair and EPIC

The building expectations and frustrations engendered even larger labor and political movements. While not realizing instant success, they pushed the New Deal into creating increased financial security for most Americans and the possibility of workers having a larger share in creating their own destiny. Among the most significant of these movements, the Townsend Old Age Revolving Pensions movement, the general strikes of San Francisco and Minneapolis, and Upton Sinclair's End Poverty in California (EPIC) emerged west of the Mississippi from the seeds of radical democracy sown in the 1910s.

Sinclair had a long history with radical and reform politics even before he moved to southern California. With Jack London he had created the national Intercollegiate Socialist Society to teach college students about socialism; he first published his novel *The Jungle* as a serial in the socialist paper *Appeal to Reason*, having announced to the meatpackers union, "Hello! I'm Upton Sinclair! . . . And I've come to write the *Uncle Tom's Cabin* of the Labor Movement!" (In the 1913 film version of *The Jungle*, Sinclair played labor leader and socialist presidential candidate Eugene V. Debs.) Sinclair marched in the enormous 1912 New York woman suffrage parade and numbered among his friends feminist Charlotte Perkins Gilman and Jane Addams. When he moved to Pasadena, California, in 1915 he was writing a novel on the Ludlow strike and massacre.[25]

In Pasadena, a small town populated "mostly by retired millionaires and those who served" them, according to Sinclair's wife, he joined the local chapter of the Socialist Party. He became chair and helped found the Workers Cooperative Association of Pasadena, where workers exchanged magazines, books, clothing, shoes, coal, wood fuel, oil, and food. He made friends with King Gillette, founder of the razor fortune and a utopian socialist, and Kate Crane Gartz, daughter of the Chicago plumbing fixture magnate who used her fortune to defend workers' rights and civil liberties. He also made friends with Henry Ford, hardly a socialist sympathizer, although Sinclair kept thinking he could win Ford over. He continued to publish leftist fiction and nonfiction and to rally for workers' rights of free speech and against wrongful imprisonment and educational and newspaper corruption.[26]

Of course, not everyone was a fan. He garnered the enduring enmity of the powerful and rabidly antiunion *Los Angeles Times*. In 1916 *Times* publisher Harrison Gray Otis wrote, "He is an effeminate young man with a fatuous smile, a weak chin and a sloping forehead, talking in a false treble. Never before an audience of red-blooded men could Upton Sinclair have voiced his weak, pernicious, vicious, doctrines."[27] In this diatribe, Otis both denigrated newly enfranchised California women's political acumen and policed the gender of their male allies, placing both outside the bounds of proper citizenship.

Though he did not mobilize gender politics, the San Pedro police chief was also not a fan. During the 1923 San Pedro general strike of the IWW, strikers, denied a public place to meet, met on a private hill offered by its tenant. They dubbed it Liberty Hill, and two thousand strikers rallied atop it, all of them singing as they were arrested, singing through the streets, singing with the strikers already jailed. Sinclair decided to bring his prominent friends to challenge the attack on free speech and began reciting the First Amendment, at which point the San Pedro police dragged him off to jail. Sinclair dropped his civil suit for false arrest, and as a quid pro quo, the police chief lost his job. With his own funds and those of Charlie Chaplin and others, Sinclair launched the southern California branch of the ACLU.[28] Sinclair also continued writing investigative fiction, covering prison conditions, the oil industry (the Literary Guild named *Oil* [1926] a major selection; it came out two months before the collapse of the Julian Petroleum Corporation [see chapter 7]), the liquor industry, and the movie industry (which would come back to bite him).[29]

By the fall of 1933 Sinclair had established himself as a popular leftist figure and social critic with a circle of well-heeled, influential friends. Discouraged by Socialist Party candidate Norman Thomas's dismal showing in the 1932 presidential election, Sinclair allowed a group of Democrats in Santa Monica to persuade him to run for governor as a Democrat against the unpopular incumbent, Frank Merriam. In September Sinclair changed his party registration from socialist to Democrat, published his vision in the pamphlet *I, Governor of California and How I Ended Poverty: A True Story of the Future*, and entered the fray.[30]

Poverty was, understandably, a popular topic during the Depression. In the same month that Sinclair changed his party and published his pamphlet, retired Dr. Francis Everett Townsend published a letter in the *Long Beach Press Telegram.* Townsend proposed that all fifteen to twenty million U.S. citizens over the age of sixty receive and be required to spend each month $150. The stipend would simultaneously remove a large number of workers from the oversaturated labor market and stimulate the economy to the tune of $2 billion to $3 billion per month. Townsend proposed to raise the necessary funds by a sales tax. He expanded on the proposal in five more letters over the course of the next three months.[31]

The idea was an instant success locally. In Long Beach a third of the 150,000 residents would qualify. They had been part of the mass exodus of retirees to California in more prosperous days, when people could actually imagine retiring. Like the elderly across the country, many had lost their savings in the Depression, and the children who might have supported them had lost their jobs. Townsend himself was sixty-seven. While his own situation was dire, he credited his brainstorm of Old Age Revolving Pensions instead to seeing from his window three elderly women rummaging in a garbage can, leading him, he claimed, to "bellow with wild hatred I had for things as they were." He and a thirty-nine-year-old partner incorporated Old Age Revolving Pensions, Limited, on January 1, 1934, and by the next January the organization's Townsend Clubs had five hundred thousand members sending nearly $1 million in dues and donations to the headquarters in Los Angeles.[32]

Sinclair's pamphlet also sold well: 150,000 copies in four months at twenty cents each, becoming the best-selling book in the history of California. The pamphlet's EPIC plan engendered over eight hundred EPIC clubs. In the pamphlet, candidate Sinclair implements a twelve-point legislative and administrative program. It begins with a public California Authority for Land, which uses idle land and land sold for taxes to establish agricultural colonies with dormitories, kitchens, cafeterias, common spaces, and commonly held agricultural machinery; in these colonies the unemployed settle and produce enough food to feed themselves and engage in limited exchange. Similarly, the California Authority for Production uses idle industrial plants, putting them into production with unemployed workers and having the workers exchange the manufactured goods with the agricultural communes using scrip. Alongside these developments, the state legislature repeals the sales tax (a regressive tax) in favor of progressive, graduated income, property, and inheritance taxes. Those in need over the age of sixty and with at least three years' residence in California qualify for a monthly pension similarly available to those unable to support themselves and to widowed women with dependent children. In an era before the existence of Social Security and at the very beginning of the New Deal's public works programs, when not much of a dent had been put in the unemployed status of seven hundred thousand Californians, these ideas appealed to many and appalled others.[33]

Sinclair had taken inspiration from the network of self-help cooperatives and barter clubs blooming across the Los Angeles Basin in 1932 and 1933. They had their origins in the working-class suburb of Compton, where army veterans collaborated with nearby Japanese American farmers to work as harvesters in return for a share of the surplus produce. Other farmers and then trucking companies joined in, and then members began growing their own produce and organizing bakeries, barber shops, and construction and repair units and making clothing. Some property owners let them use empty storefronts or warehouses. By June 1933 twenty-three thousand members in 115 such clubs operated in Los Angeles County. Overall in southern California, at its peak the self-help co-ops involved over 120,000 people. In turn, using ideas from the pamphlet, a small group of women in Berkeley started the Unemployed Exchange Association, operating a handloom. It grew to thousands of unemployed workers who exchanged labor and food they could not sell on the market for all kinds of services. Sinclair supporters began publishing the weekly *Epic News* at five cents per copy. The circulation hit over one million. Sinclair won more votes in the Democratic primary the following August than all six of his opponents combined.[34]

Powerful Republicans panicked—former president Herbert Hoover, Bank of America's A. P. Giannini, Irving Thalberg of Hollywood, and Harry Chandler, publisher and owner of the *Los Angeles Times*, among others. These were men of action. A San Francisco group titled California League Against Sinclairism hired Campaigns Inc., an organization with a proven record of manipulating small influential weeklies. In southern California, Chandler called a meeting with the Chamber of Commerce, and they hired an advertising firm, Lord and Thomas, to create a media blitz that would destroy Sinclair.[35]

It was the first major use of professional advertising in politics. It was incredibly successful. The firm placed copy on the front page of newspapers as though it were news and printed quotes out of context from Sinclair's novels as though they were part of his platform, revealing his "hostility toward organized religion, his fascination with health fads, his controversial views on sex and marriage, and sympathetic statements he had once made about the Soviet Union." They spent $200,000 erecting billboards and created fake organizations, front groups, to circulate six million pamphlets proving Sinclair was a revolutionary Communist free-love atheist. To round out the project, the *Los Angeles Times* sent its political writer, Kyle Palmer, to collaborate with Will Hays, the president of the Motion Picture Producers and Distributors of America, to organize a campaign among the studios against Sinclair. MGM's Louie B. Mayer, ardent Republican, was only too happy to oblige. MGM created fake newsreels showing actors posing as Russian immigrant revolutionaries supporting Sinclair. They funded the newsreels by docking employees' pay a day's wages and disseminated the newsreels across the state. They threatened to withhold feature films from theater owners unless they showed the newsreels.[36]

Protests by major stars, including Jean Harlow, James Cagney, and Fredric March, had little impact. The newsreels blanketed California. While the U.S. Communist Party condemned Sinclair for joining the Democratic Party, megachurch evangelist Aimee Semple McPherson, rumored to face foreclosure on her temple, accepted money to join an anti-Sinclair rally just before election day. Called "America! Awake! The Enemy Is at Your Gates!," the rally featured lowering the U.S. flag and raising the Russian flag.[37]

EPIC supporters threatened the status quo in an even more fundamental way than the striking miners and cotton hands. They built on and fostered a system outside of and parallel to that of the state's dominant capitalist one. They carried the upending into the political realm. And on both sides they mobilized powerful new and old media of mass communication.

San Francisco: War on the Docks

While California's gubernatorial race heated up, so did San Francisco's docks. Dockworkers had a long history of combining unpredictable work with cosmopolitan interactions. Merchant seamen who wanted more stability moved from ships to port cities and became dockworkers. Occupational boundaries blurred. Pacific Northwest loggers, steeped in IWW ideas, floated downstream with the trees they had cut and became dockworkers loading those trees onto schooners.[38]

The work was labor-intensive—heavy lifting—and a culture of masculinity on the docks encompassed both strength and autonomy. Like the timber workers and agricultural workers, many of these workers had a history of involvement with the IWW. Because the work was unsteady, depending on the arrival of ships to unload, dockworkers had to live near the docks, creating whole communities, heavily male, of workers from radically diverse backgrounds who had traveled the globe. Ideas traveled with workers, whether migrant farmworkers or waterfront workers. Daily life on the docks in the 1930s became, as one historian put it, "a constant state of guerilla warfare."[39]

Too transient to be closely tied to family, church, ethnic, or other institutions, waterfront workers and seamen formed their ideas of politics with each other in the context of national and global migrations and global politics around empire, rights, and working conditions. Harry Bridges, who would lead the dockworkers in San Francisco, left his comfortably middle-class roots and clerk's position in Australia at the age of fifteen. He later recalled, "I took a trip that gave me a look at India and another at Suez, and what I saw there didn't seem to line up with what my father had told me about the dear old British. Then I got 'home' and saw London. It was the filthiest, most unhealthy place I had ever seen. . . . So this, I say, is British democracy. . . . I kept traveling around, and the more I saw the more I knew there was something wrong with the system."[40]

Even if maritime workers had no wider view than bars and brothels, their travel and work put them in close contact with a variety of races and nationalities that encouraged them to draw boundaries differently from those who drew bright lines around the nation's borders. Many of the most active had forsaken the more nationalist American Federation of Labor for the Industrial Workers of the World in the 1910s and then joined the Communists in the early 1930s. They were no more likely to bow to Communist Party dictates than to those of the AFL. Their commitment to self-direction converged with a robust U.S. western tradition of radical democratic activism seen so clearly in the upheavals of the 1910s and with older roots that ranged from small farmer Populists to Knights of Labor proponents of economic democracy.[41]

Dockworkers worked in conditions on the docks that had never recovered from the post–World War I slump. When shipowners broke a massive 1919 longshoremen's strike, they created a company union—a union the employers controlled—and required any would-be dockworker to show evidence of membership, a blue book, before he could be hired. Any self-assertion or questioning of employer authority meant blacklisting—the refusal of work by any employer on the waterfront. By 1933 dockworkers in the Los Angeles port of San Pedro averaged $10.45 per week, too little to survive without charitable relief. On the ships, workers toiled for twelve-hour days, slept in cramped bug-infested quarters, and ate foully.[42] Off the ships, dockworkers faced the humiliating shape-up, where far too many men crowded around bosses for far too few jobs paying far too little for far too many hours.

Other forces also kept workers from making effective common cause. Employers used the racism of maritime workers against them, bringing in Black workers to substitute for strikers. Black workers could seldom get such jobs any other way. Then there were the competing unions with their competing visions—craft unions, industrial unions, AFL affiliates, and unions influenced by the Communist Party. And, perhaps most significant, there were the coalitions of waterfront employers. They did not stop at controlling hiring. They had joined in two regional organizations that relentlessly struck at any attempt to organize dockworkers or seamen. One, the Industrial Association of San Francisco, established in 1921, enrolled about a thousand members by the 1930s, including Southern Pacific Railroad, Standard Oil of California, Pacific Gas and Electric, and California and Hawaiian Sugar. By the 1930s they had already spent millions fending off union organizing.[43]

The passage of 1933's NIRA, section 7a, which gave workers "the right to organize and bargain collectively through representatives of their own choosing," breathed fire into the waterfront workers, as it had into the farmworkers.[44] When the dockworkers and seamen struck in 1934, it was with unprecedented unity and ferocity. On May 9 workers from ship to shore downed tools and stopped work on the Pacific coast from Bellingham, Washington, to San Diego, California. A major demand was to place control of hiring in the hands of an independent union.[45]

The great achievement of the strike organizers was to take competing unions with varying philosophies—waterfront and shipboard workers, former craftsmen wedded to the AFL and former IWW members, the International Longshoremen's Association (ILA), the International Seamen's Union (ISU), the Marine Workers Industrial Union (MWIU), and both Communists and anti-Communists—and get them to act together. They were greatly aided by the miserable conditions of the trade and the hope unleashed by section 7a. In March 1934, defeating their own conservative union leadership, longshoremen in San Francisco voted to make three major demands: an independent, union-controlled hiring hall; a coast-wide agreement on wages and conditions; and a workers' waterfront federation, a counterpart to the shipowners' associations, that could develop a unified response to shipowners in the event of a strike. When the referendum went to a coast-wide vote, the margin was nearly ten to one. Over six thousand longshoremen favored a strike to achieve these demands, and fewer than seven hundred opposed it.[46]

Not everyone joined the strike. Many seamen remained outside the strike, sometimes because their shipowners refused to let them disembark. Others faced overwhelming opposition. At San Pedro, the port of Los Angeles, employers paid $145,000 to maintain an army of local police, who deployed approximately seven hundred officers to the harbor, amplified by hundreds of special deputies and private security guards. Over the course of the strike, police arrested five hundred men in San Pedro in what the *Los Angeles*

Daily News called a "campaign of brutality and terrorism." Lone strikers, unarmed, were beaten until their bones broke. Despite the brutality, the number of pickets on the docks in Los Angeles harbor increased from 300 to 1,800. And though the harbor was open, Los Angeles harbor commissioners announced in late May that the strike had cost the port $60,000 a month in lost wharf and dock charges, that the number of ship arrivals had fallen from 117 per week to 78, and that lumber shipments had fallen from over four million board feet to zero.[47]

Los Angeles harbor was virtually alone in remaining open. Within days of the longshoremen's coast-wide walkout on May 9, teamsters and other workers refused to handle cargo, and the impact was clear. In San Francisco, shipowners brought in nearly a thousand white-collar workers and college students, including much of the University of California football team, along with several hundred Black men (who, while no longer excluded from the union, had not been recruited either) to replace the striking workers. It was to no avail. A white San Francisco union leader and a Black union member went down to the pier employing most of the Black longshoremen and called on them to join the strike; within a day they did so, saying, "We didn't know that you wanted us."[48]

The new union built new coalitions. It brought Black members into the strike committee and hired Brotherhood of Sleeping Car Porters union organizer C. L. Dellums. Its May 13 parade featured Black members prominently among the leadership, followed by wives and children and supporters, Chinese and Filipino seamen, and members of sympathetic unions. They worked with Unemployed Councils to discourage even the desperate from replacing them on the docks. In keeping with a western tradition of small farmers and nonfarmworkers making common cause, whether formalized in the Farmer-Labor Party or not, farmers kept strikers provided with plentiful food donations.[49]

Up and down the coast, strikers and scabs and police joined in pitched battles. In Oakland four hundred strikers "drove police before them and staged a hand to hand battle with 72 strike breakers" on the municipal pier. In Portland another four hundred striking longshoremen attacked a ship housing scabs, throwing one policeman in the water and beating others. In Seattle six hundred

Tacoma longshoremen and several hundred strikers from Everett, the scene of a dramatic attack on the IWW just a decade and a half earlier, stormed the docks. Joined by locals, their combined force of two thousand men swept the police aside and stopped work on eleven ships that had been loading cargo. This flying squad then headed to other cities, and within days, according to one shipowner spokesman, "all work at Pacific Northwest ports had to cease. . . . The strikers took over entire control of the waterfront."[50]

While the secretary of state contemplated sending the army to end what seemed to be an insurrection and not just a strike, Secretary of Labor Frances Perkins insisted Roosevelt not start his administration by "shooting it out with working people." She won, and the federal government rushed its assistant secretary of labor to San Francisco, hoping to negotiate a compromise.[51]

The strikers, bucking the AFL leadership, emphatically rejected the agreements. San Francisco shipowners responded. On July 3 they brought in seven hundred police to move the cargo right through the picket lines. In the words of one paper, the waterfront became "a vast tangle of fighting men." By July 5 the *San Francisco Chronicle* declared "War in San Francisco!" One witness described as a "small investor" reported: "Struggling knots of longshoremen, closely pressed by officers mounted and on foot, swarmed everywhere. The air was filled with blinding gas. The howl of the sirens. The low boom of the gas guns. The crack of pistol-fire. The whine of bullets. . . . As the police moved from one group to the next, men lay bloody, unconscious, or in convulsions—in the gutters, on the sidewalks, in the streets." To this witness, the strikers displayed "insane courage." "In the face of bullets, gas, clubs, horses' hoofs, death; against fast patrol cars and the radio, they fought back with rocks and bolts till the street was a mass of debris. . . . They were fighting desperately for something that seemed to be life for them."[52]

In the face of three successive police assaults, guns blazing and tear gas spewing, the strikers held. At the end of the day at least two men, a striker and a strike sympathizer, lay dead as the National Guard troops erected barbed-wire fortifications on the waterfront and the shipowners used armored personnel carriers to bring in replacement workers.[53]

With the power of the government behind them, it seemed the shipowners had won, but on July 9 the workers held a massive funeral procession for the two dead men the length of Market Street, "those careworn weary faces determined in their fight for justice," as witnesses recalled, "an oncoming sea," "a river of men flowing . . . like cooling lava." The crowd and the marchers alike, silent; as one marcher recalled, "The *silence*—you could hear it—not a placard, not a slogan, complete and utter silence." Convinced by the power of their own numbers and in the face of sacrifices already made, the workers renewed their commitment to unite and fight. While the established leaders of the San Francisco unions opposed it, the members voted for it, and on July 16 in Oakland and San Francisco, workers of every stripe shut down the city with a general strike.[54]

By one estimate over one hundred thousand workers in San Francisco, Oakland, and Alameda County participated in the general strike. The sense of empowerment and of self-respect on the part of the workers was palpable. They walked the streets in their Sunday clothes with their union buttons adorning their lapels. The streetcar workers, who had already received a wage hike, shut down the trolleys and then reopened the mass transit system under their own control "as a mass transportation system for working people." Faced with this seizure of company property, East Bay businessmen saw revolution. Secretary of Labor Perkins saw union leadership as impelled by the rank and file, workers who had suffered inhumane treatment by both union bosses and employers and who took matters into their own hands.[55]

Harry Bridges, the Australian disillusioned by his youthful visit to London, became the unlikely leader of the strike in San Francisco. Unprepossessing, thin, small, haggard, and with a worn overcoat, his only remarkable feature being his long nose, Bridges had a deep knowledge of conditions and a gift for articulating the sensibilities of the other workers. He delivered speeches with a cold logic, a clean, clear, rapid-fire brilliance that persuaded even hostile audiences from Portland, Oregon, to the union's national board.[56]

Employers and the press saw Communist revolution. Their constant red-baiting forced workers themselves to confront the issue. There were certainly Communist Party members among the strikers, even loud Communist Party members, but they did not direct the strike or cause the strike, and Bridges himself denied he had ever been a party member.[57] The issue was more of a problem for union leadership than for the rank and file, most of whom came to see red-baiting as just another antiunion tactic. The leadership of rival unions could feud, but the rank-and-file members prevailed. The experiences during the strike drew the men together. In San Francisco an angry mob stormed the office of a union official who had tried to prevent unity between the AFL and the Communist affiliates. Most workers in the Communist-affiliated union, the MWIU, were not, in fact, Communists, and as one MWIU member put it, "Up to this very minute no one has crammed a communist license down my throat nor have I been forced to change my religion or politics. The main issue is the strike; the main point is solidarity and a continuous picket line."[58]

Still, the employers, media, and government officials framed the issue as a war on Communism. On July 17 National Guardsmen "with machine guns mounted on trucks cordoned off an entire block. Police then entered the [MWIU] hall, arrested 85 people, and systematically destroyed everything in sight." Newspapers applauded the actions. Vigilantes joined in. The terror spread to surrounding small towns and agricultural communities. The Finnish workers witnessed their hall "reduced to kindling, while the helpless workers watched their thousand-dollar library, their theater with its two grand pianos, all their equipment that spelled years of sacrifice, reduced to rubble."[59]

The more conservative leaders of the AFL maneuvered to channel the strike into what they saw as safer waters. George Kidwell of the teamsters in particular wanted both employers and unions to accept arbitration. Under his leadership, the teamsters voted to return to work unconditionally, leaving the maritime workers without their most effective allies. Up and down the coast, faced with this reality, the longshoremen voted to accept arbitration. The seamen were harder to convince. They feared they would make no gains on their key demands regarding hiring practices. Bridges urged collective action, even on ending the strike: "We must go back together and on good terms. If the longshoremen go back and the sailors stay out that will break the unity of the whole thing.

That is the best thing we have in our hands. Unity!" A day later, the seamen held a bonfire and defiantly burned the hiring books of the company union. But then they, too, went back to work with the promise of arbitration a few days later.

The coastal strike had lasted eighty-three days. The workers would not achieve all their aims through arbitration, but neither would the shipowners regain the level of control over hiring they had before the strike. The experience and practice of the strike enabled the workers to establish union control of hiring through militant action, and Bridges would be elected year after year to the presidency of a new, independent longshoremen's union.[60] While union members had reluctantly accepted federal arbitration, the New Deal had allowed them to shift the balance of power closer to their vision of economic democracy.

Revolution in the Heartland

The teamsters played a vital supporting role in the San Francisco general strike; they would play a starring role in three successive strikes in Minneapolis. A wildly successful if brief strike in February 1934 gained little, though it shut down the city.[61] Another strike followed in May that spread through the city, just as the Pacific coast strike got under way, and finally, in July, the culminating strike took place.

As with the dockworkers' strikes, the Minneapolis strikes had been long in building. Minneapolis had prospered as a regional hub, a central location for railroads crossing the country, a gathering point for the wheat, lumber, and iron of its hinterland. After World War I, as with so much of the West, the prosperity faltered. The Pacific Northwest displaced Minnesota's central role in the lumber industry. The Panama Canal formed a rival route for its railroad freight. And farming, as with the rest of the country, never fully recovered. With auto manufacturing in a tailspin by the late 1920s, the demand for steel, and hence Minnesota's iron, dwindled. When the Depression hit, many farmers joined the Farmers' Holiday Association, and the people of Minnesota elected Floyd Olson governor on the Farmer-Labor Party ticket.[62]

Like the dockworkers and seamen on the Pacific coast, many truckers had transient histories; many had belonged to the IWW.

They had worked as lumbermen and even been to sea before they settled down and joined the International Brotherhood of Teamsters union. They had experience in the IWW strongholds of the Mesabi Iron Range in the northern part of the state and in the wheat fields to the west. They more often had wives and children than did the dockworkers and seamen, but they suffered the same levels of unemployment and falling wages. As with the Pacific coast strike, myriad influences combined to form the thinking of the truckers, including the Nonpartisan League and its heir, the Farmer-Labor Party, the IWW and the AFL, Trotskyites and Stalinists, wages and conditions, and their own past organizing experience in Minneapolis.[63]

As the Depression wore on and truckers' wages dropped under the NRA code, the truckers began organizing from the bottom up, ignoring the conservative leadership of their AFL union.[64] But the truly radicalizing experience was the state's deployment of violence to protect the employers. When deputized amateurs shot unarmed, massed picketers, truckers' thoughts turned to revolution. And as it had in San Francisco, it proved difficult to put the genie back into the bottle.

The women the truckers married had their own histories of organizing. Like the men, they often came from Scandinavian backgrounds with a history of social democracy. Like the men, too, while many women came with families, they had often migrated to the city before marriage. Indeed, between 1910 and 1930 nearly twice as many women age twenty to twenty-four migrated to the city as did men. They had vibrant neighborhood lives in Scandinavian churches, Finnish workers' organizations, the Jewish Workmen's Circle, the Black Phyllis Wheatley House and Urban League, and other ethnically based groups. They were joined by Native Americans from nearby reservations seeking work. Nor were unions new to the women of Minneapolis. In November 1918, under the leadership of Myrtle Cain, women had staged a successful telephone operators strike. They had continued to organize afterward in textiles and consumer cooperatives, electing a machinist for mayor from 1916 to 1918 and Myrtle Cain to the state legislature in 1922. They drew people into the Working People's Nonpartisan League of Minnesota before the wartime victories of the labor-socialist coalition faded away. The 1930s found many of these women unemployed and with even less public support than unemployed men. The city had no shelters in 1930 for unemployed women workers, so the Minneapolis mayor housed them in the city jail.[65]

In short, by 1934 women in Minneapolis had their own consciousness as workers and family members and their own organizing experience. Many truckers' wives and daughters worked or had worked in the garment and textile industries or at the telephone exchange. They understood the efficacy of organizing and the importance of family solidarity and the possibilities of workplace democracy. By the end of the 1930s the number of unionized women in the garment and textile industry would rival that of men in General Drivers' Local 574. They were active in the neighborhood Unemployed Councils, which fought evictions and insisted on better welfare provisions. In 1934 they organized a women's auxiliary to the drivers' local that proved vital, providing support services from medical care and food distribution to picket duty. Despite the increasingly desperate conditions, they provided a united front.[66]

In May 1934, their numbers multiplied several times over by the success of the February action, the truckers struck again to gain the benefits denied them after the February strike. The issue in May was not delivery of coal, as it had been in February, but produce, and the City Market became the literal battleground. Strikers turned back farm delivery trucks, guarding fifty entry points to the city, and similarly stymied transport within the city.

When the mayor authorized five hundred new police to break the strike, both the American Legion and the Veterans of Foreign Wars refused the invitation to join. Instead, the mayor found his collaborators among the salesmen, clerks, and elites of the city, 1,500 of them. Arrests of strikers rose from 18 in the first two days to 150 on the next. Four hundred twenty-five of the newly deputized headed for battle at the City Market, where produce distributors feared their wares would rot. From the resulting fray, sixteen workers and four police landed in the hospital. Then a skillfully constructed ambush by the employers' Citizens' Alliance ended in the beating of men and women workers until blood ran and limbs broke.

Spurred by the violence, the ranks of each side ballooned. Thirty-five thousand members of the city's building trades declared a sympathetic general strike. Other unions' members went "on holiday."[67]

Tuesday morning, May 22, twenty to thirty thousand workers occupied the City Market. The police organized a total force of 1,500 to 2,000, including newly deputized citizens. While it is not clear exactly what happened next, it is completely clear that the market quickly became, in the words of one witness, "a free for all." Reluctant to use their guns, the police could not match the strikers. The strikers reserved special animus for the new deputies. When a prounion woman laid out a female deputy, all hell broke loose. As the strikers and sympathizers surged into the streets, the deputies fled, abandoning their badges as they ran, their trucks surrounded by violently disposed strikers. Two deputies died in the battle, one of them C. Arthur Lyman, long the attorney for the Citizens' Alliance, a father of four, and a pillar of the community. The strikers remained in control of the area for the remainder of the strike.[68]

The Battle of Deputies Run, as the May 22 clash came to be called, landed the Minneapolis strike on front pages nationally alongside the Pacific coast maritime strike. It had been just over a year since the Roosevelt administration had come to Washington DC, and the lines of struggle in the West over whose vision of modernity and democracy would prevail seemed ever more clearly drawn and the proximity to insurrection easier to imagine. The governor called a truce, and with a show of strength on all sides—five thousand strikers at a rally and National Guardsmen on alert—the union and the employers agreed to negotiate through the New Deal's Regional Labor Board. The resulting agreement promised to reinstate all workers "not guilty of a crime," and the workers withdrew the demand for a closed shop while achieving provisions "that established *de facto* recognition of the Union."[69]

As with the February strike, though the union victory was far from complete, the show of strength resulted in a flood of new union members. The General Drivers' Union membership reached seven thousand by the summer. The union also broadened its alliances. As it had in New Mexico, the union turned to organizing the unemployed. In Minneapolis it organized a union of the unemployed five thousand strong. The union negotiated with the Famers' Holiday Association, the National Farm Bureau, and the Market Gardeners Association to avoid future City Market battles.[70]

The Citizens' Alliance, too, regrouped. It raised $50,000 to use in future labor disputes and countered the union's new newspaper by flooding the airwaves and newspapers with paid advertisements condemning the union leadership as Communist agitators who aimed to make, in all capitals, "MINNEAPOLIS THE BIRTHPLACE OF A NEW SOVIET REPUBLIC." With the governor's help, they narrowed the workers covered by the negotiated agreement.[71]

Early July saw mass rallies and meetings by the union, answering red-baiting with fiery rhetoric about wealth inequality and exploitation. When the local met, the membership voted unanimously to strike beginning on the following Monday. Over 2,500 trade unionists affirmed the decision. Round three of the teamsters' struggle with Minneapolis's 166 trucking firms was on.[72]

Both sides prepared for violence but held back. Olson mobilized the National Guard at a Minneapolis armory. Strikers picketed without weapons. Employers threatened striking workers with dismissal. The police chief let it be known the department had two hundred shotguns and would soon have three hundred more. Meanwhile, they negotiated; Father Francis J. Haas, a federal mediator, arrived from Washington.

As negotiations fizzled in Minneapolis, Minneapolis citizens read in newspaper headlines that San Francisco's strike had reached a climax; sentries with fixed bayonets and machine guns patrolled San Francisco's Embarcadero. The heat did not help calm the population at home. The thermometer hit 98 degrees Fahrenheit, and the humidity reached similar levels.[73]

At this moment, the National Guard commander sprung a trap. He told strike leaders the police planned to move a truck in the Market District, and they would be well armed. The union dispatched a force of about five thousand. They met a foot patrol of fifty armed police. When the truck pulled up, it came with one hundred police in squad cars, their gun barrels poking out of the car windows like "quills on a porcupine." The men on the truck loaded a few cartons and began pulling away, only to be blocked by an open-bed truck with about a dozen strikers standing on the back. Immediately and without warning, the police opened fire on the strikers. As the strikers fell from the truck, the police sprayed those rushing to their aid with buckshot. A later inquiry concluded, "Police took direct aim at the pickets and fired to kill; physical safety of police was at no time endangered; no weapons were in the possession of pickets in the truck; at no time did pickets attack the police, and it was obvious that pickets came unprepared for such an attack; the truck movement in question was not a serious attempt to move merchandise, but a 'plant' arranged by the police."[74] While two policemen were hospitalized, one by friendly fire, sixteen strike supporters were treated at the hospital and arrested, although the charges were later dropped. Forty-seven injured picketers, fearing arrest at the hospital, were treated by the twenty-five volunteer registered nurses at Local 574's strike headquarters.

Forty-nine-year-old Henry B. Ness, father of four, like the Citizens' Alliance member killed in the earlier strike, died as the result of the thirty-eight bullets that ripped into his torso that day. A veteran of World War I, Ness had belonged to the local for sixteen years. More than forty thousand men, women, and children trailed his hearse as it moved from strike headquarters. Traffic came to a standstill, and police stayed away from the funeral route. He was buried with full military honors, and a squad of soldiers from nearby Fort Snelling fired the last volley over the coffin. Highlighting his status as a war veteran undermined Citizens' Alliance claims to have a monopoly on what constituted loyal citizenship and a patriotic vision of the nation's political economy.

Governor Olson had had enough. Increasingly frustrated with the employers' Citizens' Alliance, he kept the National Guard on hand, but "he refused to countenance 'the shooting of unarmed citizens of Minneapolis, strikers and bystanders alike, in their backs, in order to carry out the wishes of the Citizens' Alliance.'" He also let it be known that "he disagreed with employers responding to the 'plea for a living wage by a family man receiving only $12 a week' by 'calling that man a communist.'" When the Citizens' Alliance refused the negotiated settlement, Olson gave the alliance full blame and declared martial law on July 26. With the militia in control of the streets, monitoring trucks permitted and not permitted to move, workers held mass meetings and pulled in their belts. Employer solidarity began to crack, and a new federal mediator arrived in mid-August, fresh from settling the longshoremen's strike in San Francisco.

Roosevelt made it clear to his negotiator, P. A. Donoghue, that he wanted the strike long settled before the November elections. Within a week, Donoghue brought peace to Minneapolis. The 167 pickets held in the military stockade were released. Both sides ratified the agreement. By the time the dust settled in the formerly notoriously open shop town of Minneapolis, the truckers had union recognition, better wages, and better conditions. As one historian put it, "Rank-and-file democracy prevailed." In November they extended their victory to the polls, ousting the Republican mayor and replacing him with Farmer-Laborite Thomas E. Latimer. At the state level, the Farmer-Labor Party succeeded in abolishing labor injunctions, passing a moratorium on farm mortgages, and instituting significant tax reform.[75]

Crossing Borders

As they had in the 1910s, politics and people flowed across borders. Historian Benny J. Andrés Jr. calls the Imperial Valley "a corridor of radicalism." While Mexican veterans of the revolution strengthened the cotton farm labor strikes, Mexican repatriates demanded ejidos (communally held land) in Baja California. Lázaro Cárdenas, elected president of Mexico in 1934, began negotiating with the monopolistic U.S.-held Colorado River Land Company to sell the repatriates small farms on long-term loans. The repatriates, however, frustrated by the terms and the pace of official efforts, starting seizing the land. In doing so, they often ousted existing tenants, including Chinese and Japanese colonists. In response, within three years Cárdenas expropriated the company's land, negotiated with the repatriates, protected existing Mexican but not Asian colonists, and established forty-four ejidos, settling 4,730 families onto the communal farms.[76]

In Canada's Manitoba and Saskatchewan Provinces, five of the fifteen rural legislators elected on the Co-operative Commonwealth Federation (CCF; see chapter 10) ticket between 1934 and 1938 hailed from the United States. They came from the Midwest, brought up there on Populism and already organizers of cooperatives, wheat pools, and churches. Capital tended to flow in the opposite direction. When Alberta elected the related Social Credit government in August 1935, several U.S. firms transferred their liquid assets out of the province.[77]

Meanwhile, EPIC and the CCF seemed to converge in Washington State. Washington's self-help and barter organizations, similar to those in California, joined together in the Unemployed Citizens League (UCL) in 1931. The next spring, Washington's UCLs created the United Producers of Washington, and by that fall the Seattle UCL alone had twelve thousand members. They created the Central Federation of UCLs amid jostling by competing factions from the IWW, the Socialist Party, the Communist Party, the Farmer-Labor Party, Seattle general strike veterans, Democrats, and others. At the head they placed a retired contractor carpenter and former state secretary of the Minnesota Knights of Labor. They entered the political fray, endorsing candidates in the Democratic primaries who swept into office on FDR's 1932 coattails. In 1934 they joined forces with EPIC in both Oregon and Washington. In Washington they won offices at the state and congressional levels, and the Washington Commonwealth Federation became a formal caucus within the state Democratic Party. The movement pulled the Democratic Party to the left and made the state a leader in social and labor legislation, moving the western heritage of economic democracy into the structure of government.[78]

In California in November, even with the virtually universal media campaign against him, Sinclair won twice the number of votes any previous Democratic candidate had won in that state. Still, it was not enough to elect him. Incumbent Frank Merriam had only stepped into the governorship three months earlier when his predecessor had a heart attack amid the San Francisco general strike. Merriam had called out the National Guard to control the waterfront, ensuring the loyalty of the state's Republican apparatus. He retained his office, 1 million votes to Sinclair's 879,537. On the other hand, forty-one EPIC-backed candidates won seats in the California legislature, and nine won seats in Congress. By 1936 Democrats controlled the state assembly and held the majority of the congressional delegation. And, as in Washington, the Democratic state party had been pulled permanently leftward. Democrat Culbert Olson, who had won a state senate seat with EPIC backing in 1934, four years later would triumph, beating Merriam for governor by over two hundred thousand votes. Moreover, Sinclair's running mate in 1934 won the California senate race in 1936. And John Steven McGroarty, editorial writer for the *Los Angeles Times*, creator of *The Mission Play* (see chapter 9), and named California poet laureate in 1933, won election to Congress, where in 1935 he introduced a resolution calling for the implementation of the Townsend Plan. Nine months later Congress gave birth to the Social Security Act.[79]

Conclusion

In the first years of the New Deal, struggles over its meaning often grew violent. Just what sort of deal was this, and for whom? Section 7a of the National Industrial Recovery Act was not supposed to cover agricultural workers, but farmworkers in the West defied that decision. They succeeded by acting as if 7a included them, and they benefited as though it had included them. They mobilized the New Deal and forced its hand. Federal officials mediated. On the other hand, section 7a *was* supposed to cover the workers who organized the Pacific coast and Minneapolis, but everything lay in how the law was carried out, and the workers again mobilized the New Deal to back their vision of economic democracy and western opportunity.

The peculiarly western heritage of these workers played a crucial role in their mobilizing and their victories. They were veterans of the 1910s insurgent democracies just over a decade earlier. Those movements had included a vision of radically inclusive democracy. They had been generated in a world of shifting land tenure, consolidation, and revolution. Dramatically suppressed in the 1920s and channeled into other realms of participation when the dreams of inclusion via the market exploded, the older visions remained. Teamsters had been longshoremen and IWW lumbermen; agricultural workers had been Mexican revolutionaries and Filipino insurgents. They all shared a western imaginary that promised opportunity and a share in the wealth of the country.

In the 1930s their vision of western democracy encompassed not only wage workers but also smallholders. Many if not most of these workers would have grown up on farms. Their vision wedded the IWW to the Nonpartisan League and produced, for example, the Farmers' Holiday Association, which supported not only agrarian assertions but also coal-mining and trucking strikes. These movements adamantly crossed the line into electoral politics and transformed not only governorships and legislatures but also major parties. Their ideas grew out of profoundly local conditions and experiences, as well as transnational roots and routes. These activists redefined participatory democracy. They linked workplace and political democracy.

Filipinos' leadership in these efforts led, ironically, to independence for the Philippines. The United States had ruled the islands since the Spanish-American War, successfully opposing a bloody war for independence immediately thereafter. As a result, Filipinos had the status of U.S. nationals and, unlike others from Asian countries, could enter the United States at will. Whether it was their experience in anticolonial movements or labor conditions in the United States or both, they played a major part in organizing efforts wherever they worked. Grower efforts to encourage what they called a "race war" between Mexicans and Filipinos in the fields failed. To exclude the Filipino organizers, the United States took the only path available. In 1934 Congress passed the Tydings-McDuffie Act, giving autonomy to the Philippines and in the same breath rendering Filipinos deportable and limiting the numbers for legal entry to fifty per year.[80]

Ferocious strikes would continue for the rest of the decade. The results would be mixed. In San Francisco Chinese women would blockade the harbor, preventing the loading of scrap iron for Japan, and they would convince the longshoremen's union to join their campaign. Women garment workers would win in San Antonio, and farmworkers would lose in California's fields. The New Deal's incentives to reduce acreage with the AAA in 1933, coupled with the desperation of small farmers and tenants pushed off the land by acreage reduction, meant California growers would miss Mexican workers less. Corporate growers reaped a harvest of desperation as approximately 350,000 people fleeing other states entered California in the 1930s.[81] But the dramatic mobilizations in the West from 1932 to 1934 had altered local, state, and even national politics.

12

Moving People and Animals to Save the People and the Land

From the vantage point of Washington DC, the New Deal administration watched swirling clouds of discontent. They saw unprecedented numbers of people moving—thrown out or marching across the West. They saw desperation and determination, and they aimed for stability. They would replace chaos with planning.

The New Deal's efforts toward a planned economy ranged beyond the West, but they had a particular relationship to the region. On the campaign trail in September 1932, Franklin Delano Roosevelt had declared to the Commonwealth Club of San Francisco that "as long as we had free land . . . society chose to give the ambitious man free play." But by 1900, he continued, sounding much like Frederick Jackson Turner in 1893, "we were reaching our last frontier; there was no more free land and our industrial combinations had become great uncontrolled and irresponsible units of power within the state." The time had come, he insisted, for "enlightened administration."[1]

Because the federal government owned a larger portion of the land west of the Mississippi than in any other region, because the federal government maintained oversight of the nation's Native American reservations, and because of the general devastation of the region, the federal planners could dream big on that western landscape. They could revive the imagined West as a blank slate on which they could draw plans for a modern economy. At the same time, those plans hewed to an older vision of western opportunity, the function of the region for the nation. They attempted to reimagine a landscape that maximized both central and local control, both large-scale enterprises and individual opportunity for those deemed worthy.

The Roosevelt administration would use the 1933 legislation of the administration's first one hundred days, and they would forge new legislation to carry out their New Deal plans. They would resettle the people and the land. They would save the dream of Jeffersonian democracy, the promise of opportunity and belonging. They would readjust the human ecology of the West, literally redrawing the landscape. They would use large-scale planning and projects to enable small, self-sufficient farms. By doing so, they would cement again the image of the West as at once the ultimate past of the nation whose imagined origins lay in opportunity for the common man and the future of the modern, technologically advanced, planned nation. At least, so they thought.

Planners ran into pusillanimous players on the ground with their own visions and competing interests. They ran into contentious congressmen and ambivalent administrators. They ran into determined ranchers and farmers and Native Americans convinced of different truths about their land and its future. As they pushed through the Indian Reorganization Act, the Taylor Grazing Act, and the various incarnations of resettlement, as they addressed environmental degradation and modern consumer dreams, they treated the West as a vast chessboard, moving people, animals, and water. They faced opponents at least as skilled and just as determined to realize a different vision of a modern West.

The outcome of this chess game changed the literal landscape of the region, reassigning land and its uses, building enormous dams, and redirecting water and other resources. It created new structures of governance and changed the distribution of risk and reward, though not always as intended. The chapter begins with the largest, most centralized efforts of the federal government and moves through efforts of more mixed federal and local control to end with the small farmers, their tenants, and the land they sought to shape.

Big Dams, Big Dreams

Many of the most impressive and enduring of New Deal projects took years if not decades to complete. The monumental dams, in particular, served as massive jobs programs in the West during the middle years of the 1930s and began producing electricity and distributing water toward the decade's end, just as the United States geared up for war and had other uses for labor.

Dams had been a hard sell during the late 1920s unless as flood remediation. There was little demand for the power they would generate in rural areas and little incentive to produce more irrigation when agricultural surpluses already plagued farmers. This view changed dramatically with the New Deal.[2]

Four years into the Depression, big dams became a kind of all-purpose miracle. Not only could they employ massive numbers of workers, but, as had been promised by so many schemes for so many decades, dams would open up the West for modern development. To those who insisted that the small farm remained the moral compass of the nation, modernization would, in turn, stave off a flood of desperate Communist fodder headed to vulnerable depressed cities. People would no longer flee their farms when dams gave farm households access to modern conveniences. In 1935 only 2.3 percent of farms in North Dakota had electricity, 3.4 percent of those in South Dakota, and less than 6 percent in Nebraska. Dams would redeem the countryside and spread the consumer revolution. They would deliver electricity to every farm, and every farm wife could enjoy the benefits of an electric iron, lights, and other modern purchased conveniences, stimulating production everywhere. Hydroelectric dams would restore the urban/rural balance.[3] With dams the federal government could write the nation's future on the western landscape and provide opportunity for all.

That miracle found support on both sides of the aisle. Journalists and politicians blanketed the dams in superlatives. In 1933 Stuart Chase in *Fortune* claimed electric power would create a new civilization with better commodities, better humans, and better connections, creating more harmony; Richard Neuberger, later U.S. senator from Oregon, in *Harper's* called the Grand Coulee Dam "The Biggest Thing on Earth" in 1937. In the same year, a Boulder City, Nevada, promotional brochure called Boulder Dam a "world wonder" that had "thrown this impregnable fortress against the forces of a devastating river which for centuries had wastefully spent its power." Once again, the United States sent "frontiersmen" to subdue nature.[4]

Their massiveness and the superlative claims were part of the point. The dams were monuments to planning, to collective endeavor, and to humanity's ability to triumph amid a devastating economic depression where individual triumph was scarce. Over 700 feet high and over 600 feet thick, the 1,244-foot-long Boulder Dam, later renamed Hoover Dam, had begun before the Depression hit. Authorized in 1928 as a private initiative, it promised to regulate the unruly Colorado River, create the world's largest artificial lake (Lake Mead), and irrigate California's Imperial Valley. Completed in 1935 with federal Public Works Administration funding, it would take another fifty years for the electricity the dam generated to pay off the dam's costs, but the dam did enable the irrigation of 2.5 million acres in five states.[5]

The string of enormous dam projects that followed included in 1933 the Bonneville Dam, near Portland, Oregon, on the Columbia River, completed in 1938 at a cost of $75 million, producing six hundred thousand kilowatts of electricity and 180 miles of navigable seaway inland from the Pacific. In 1934 came the Fort Peck project, resulting by 1939 in one of the largest earthen dams in the world, and the Grand Coulee Dam, ninety-two miles northwest of Spokane, Washington, completed in 1941 and soon after powering the region's war industries. In 1935 came Parker Dam, 150 miles south of Boulder Dam in Arizona; and in 1937 Congress authorized the Big Thompson project in Colorado, including a thirteen-mile tunnel, five power plants, a chain of reservoirs, and the movement of about three hundred thousand acre-feet of the Colorado River a year. It took almost twenty years to build. In the same year, the Bureau of Reclamation collaborated with California on the Central Valley project, a series of dams, including the huge Shasta Dam, power plants, canals, and transmission lines, some of which began operating in 1947. Altogether, the Bureau of Reclamation spent $279,220,973 generating electricity, managing rivers, and producing irrigation in the West.[6]

The costs and rewards of this modernizing project were not evenly distributed. These massive dams transformed the landscape of the West in the name of a utopian vision of universal access to modern living and small farming. The percentage of rural families with electricity doubled and even tripled in some western states.

But as in the 1920s, not everyone was deemed equally worthy of participating in that envisioned future. The Fort Peck Dam, for example, had required the removal of Native peoples, including the Lakotas, from traditional lands. The Boulder Dam siphoned water away from the Navajos and Hopis. While some of them would secure wage work building the dams, which employed tens of thousands of workers, few of them would benefit from the electricity and water the dams channeled.[7]

The larger benefits tended to go to larger entities. The Central Valley project benefited mainly the giant corporate farms that already dominated California's agricultural industry. And even before the dams were finished, their construction nurtured a consortium called the Six Companies, including future giant Bechtel-Kaiser of San Francisco. Joining together allowed the companies to raise more capital, underbid competitors for Boulder Dam, and get what was the largest labor contract the federal government had ever awarded, netting them $10 million in profits. The Six Companies followed up that success by winning contracts for the Bonneville and Grand Coulee Dams and many smaller projects. When the Japanese bombed the U.S. Pacific fleet in Pearl Harbor on December 7, 1941, the federal government would turn to these large corporations. They had the proven track records and the ability to operate on the necessary scale rapidly to coordinate the production of supplies and labor to construct ships and other war matériel, and they would grow larger still.[8]

The dams had laid the foundations in both corporate and physical infrastructure for the region's even more massive buildup during World War II. In this sense, the dams fulfilled Interior Secretary Harold Ickes's vision, by coordinated planning encompassing mining, industry, and agriculture in the West, to shift the region away from its status as a colony with "its resources dumped out of it and . . . later left stranded" and toward modern prosperity.[9] This version of the modern West could disturb these older patterns, but it would replicate others.

The Indian Reorganization Act

The big dams intruded on Native American life, land, and resources. They took land, provided jobs, and redirected power and water.

They also ran headlong into a massive reimagining of federal Indian policy.

In an ideal world, the Indian New Deal section of this book would start with a split screen. That format would best express both the dramatic disagreements among historians as to the benefits and drawbacks of Roosevelt administration changes in Indian policy and the widely divergent impact of the policies on the ground. On one side would be Bert Hills Close to Lodge coming to see the Indian agent on the Pine Ridge Reservation in South Dakota. "I want to get permission to have a dance tonight for our group in the village," he said. It was 1933, and twenty-five-year-old Ben Reifel (Brulé Lakota) had only recently arrived in Oglala as a farm agent. Reifel recalled, "I had just received a copy of a telegram signed by John Collier, Commissioner of Indian Affairs. It said, 'If the Indian people want to have dances, dances all night, all week, that is their business.' So I read it to him. Bert sat there, stroked his braids, looked off in the distance, and he said in Lakota, 'Well, I'll be damned.'"[10]

This is the more traditional story. This story sees John Collier as a hero. President Roosevelt appointed Collier as commissioner of Indian Affairs in early 1933. Collier had already achieved notoriety for his role in the 1920s Pueblo struggle for autonomy against the federal and state governments and for exposing conditions on the reservations that helped lead to the 1928 Meriam Report. As former secretary of the Indian Defense Association and vigorous congressional lobbyist he had succeeded in getting $150,000 for the relief of Navajos (Diné) whose herds had been decimated by the harsh winter of 1931–32.[11] In this version, Collier and the 1934 Indian Reorganization Act overturned a century of genocidal (human and cultural) policy to endow Indians with self-governance, cultural autonomy, enlarged reservations, and federal support.

On the other side is the memory of Susan Begay (Diné), who watched government men ride up to her home near Kayenta and kill the sheep and goats she had carefully tended her whole life, the source of her wealth and authority and sustenance and her legacy for her children. "They did it right before my eyes," she recalled forty years later. "I was there with my husband. They took so many," including sheep belonging to her mother and older sister. "'That is enough; it is enough,' I tried to say," but the men herded the goats behind the bluff, beat them with clubs, and shot them. Many of the women wept. The same Collier who sent the telegram on dancing gave the Navajos no choice on stock reduction, arguing that he operated in their best interest.[12]

In this version, the New Deal's stock reduction policy, aimed at restoring the overgrazed range, stands in for New Deal progressives' attachment to what they viewed as enlightened paternalism coupled with cultural obtuseness. It sees their blindness to a tendency to read their own cultural assumptions as objective science and their vision of only one form of democracy as torpedoing the promise of betterment for reservation Indians. It merely transposed one regime of draconian Washington dominance for another.

The distinction is about more than the difference between the Lakotas and the Navajos, whose social, economic, and political organizations differed dramatically even before contact. The Indian New Deal as it worked out in the U.S. West in some ways is emblematic of the whole New Deal in the region, its vaulting ambition, its myriad experiments, its contending constituents and architects, its attempt both to enhance and broaden participatory democracy and to implement centralized planning and large-scale projects.

When government men showed up to destroy Susan Begay's sheep and goats, they believed themselves to be part of a forward-looking policy to save both the Navajos and the pastureland from decades of overgrazing. Before the dust began to swirl on the Great Plains, years of drought had withered grasses in Arizona and New Mexico. By the 1930s much of the West had fallen into an ecological disaster as great as—and connected to—the economic one. It emerged from a convergence of climate forces and development practices and beliefs, and the New Deal scrambled to enact solutions not only on the Navajo reservation but with the Taylor Grazing Act (1934) and various resettlement experiments.[13]

Even before that first memo in 1933 and through his twelve-year run as commissioner of Indian Affairs, Collier fought with Congress and later mobilized the Roosevelt administration with the strong backing of Interior Secretary Harold Ickes to increase Native autonomy and funding and to improve reservation conditions.[14] He repeatedly visited dozens of reservations, seeking opinions among their residents. At the same time, he drastically underestimated the variety of Native American beliefs, practices, and interests and the level of factionalism. And he had to compromise with the even more vociferous and powerful opposition in Congress.

Collier's vision for improving conditions for Indians included self-government through majority rule and elections at the tribal level, restoration of communal assets, economic incorporation that allowed tribes to negotiate for services and launch cooperative economic enterprises, and restoration of some of the ninety million acres lost to them since the 1887 Dawes Severalty Act. At Collier's initiative, Congress passed a series of acts, beginning in May 1933 with the Pueblo Relief Act, to provide increased funds, work programs, schools, wells, livestock, and land for Indians. But the centerpiece of the program was the Indian Reorganization Act, or Wheeler-Howard Act, of 1934, which Collier workshopped at meetings with Native Americans in six western states plus Wisconsin that spring.[15]

Reception was decidedly mixed. In some communities, Collier reaped what he had sowed in his anti-BIA activism of the previous decade when he had stoked the fires of Native distrust. But there were other objections. Creek Indian Joseph Bruner denounced Collier as a Communist and an atheist. Others feared the loss of mineral rights, herds, and autonomy. The Crows had more faith in the rights embedded in their treaties with the U.S. government and the political stability of their current council than in what they saw as "the dictatorship" of the commissioner's office under the proposed law. The Sioux wanted the proposed exchange of individual lands for rights in common holdings to be voluntary. The Tohono O'odham "had no tradition of tribal unity. Their language had no word equivalents for 'representative' and 'budget.'" Nonetheless, at the end of the day, Collier told Congress that "polls taken at the ten meetings revealed that fifty-four tribes . . . approved the bill, while only twelve tribes . . . opposed the measure."[16]

Meanwhile, criticism in Congress was stiff. Non-Natives often deplored pulling back the support of Christianization. Many non-Natives equally deplored the withdrawal of Native resources (water, minerals, oil, and land) from easy access by non-Natives. Collier agreed to thirty amendments, most of them the invention of congressmen, some of whom would have preferred total inaction. He faced sentiments like that of Arizona senator Carl Hayden, that struggling Indians "must do just like the white farmers have done in all the history of this country. When the farms will not support them they must move to town. They must engage in industry and they must learn other occupations."[17] Among non-Native opponents, there was little recognition of Indians' rights to their lands as a space apart from the non-Native United States, little concept of Indian sovereignty or autonomy.

To counter such opposition, Collier persuaded President Roosevelt to muscle Democratic congressmen into supporting the bill, which passed into law in June 1934. But the bill showed battle scars. It dropped from fifty pages to six, with similarly reduced benefits and protections. The final version eradicated the provision for a tribal court system with right of appeal to federal appellate courts and the Supreme Court and erased the provisions for tribal power "to compel" the removal of any federal employee on grounds of inefficiency or "other causes." Also missing from the final version was "a training program to prepare Indians to take over and administer community services, including courses of study in Indian history and culture," and, finally, "an orderly procedure for transferring services and functions from the Bureau to an organized Indian community."[18] In short, the act did much less to hand over substantive power and control to organized Native Americans.

Despite that, this was the first major piece of legislation dealing with Indian affairs taken to the tribes for open discussion, and despite Collier's aim to empower the tribes, the watered-down nature of the bill and its retention of BIA supervision did little to dampen tribal distrust. In the end, only 181 tribes or bands of 258 possible signed on to the promises of the Indian Reorganization Act, only 93 ratified tribal constitutions, and only 73 set up charters of incorporation allowing them to borrow from the revolving credit fund. Those who did not sign on often defeated the measure by narrow margins, as did the Navajos, resentful over unrelated measures of stock reduction; and some refused for reasons that mixed rivalries within tribes, resentment over policies, and affinity for traditional consensual governance structures that made majority rule seem arbitrary and disrespectful.[19]

Yet what the act did was not trivial. It made dramatic changes in landholding, governance, and economics. It reversed over four hundred years of indigenous land loss by repealing the allotment laws and providing funds for the purchase of additional lands, restoring four million of the ninety million lost acres. It authorized $250,000 annually for organizing tribal governments and corporations. Tribal councils could now hire legal counsel. Their lawyers could not only defend the tribe regarding the sale or lease of tribal lands but also negotiate with the federal or state government for services and appropriations. Tribal corporations could borrow from a $10 million revolving credit fund to develop reservation resources and business enterprises. Finally, the act created $250,000 per year in scholarships for Native American students and a hiring policy that gave preference to Native Americans in the Bureau of Indian Affairs' civil service positions. These provisions gave Native Americans a far greater degree of power over political, cultural, and economic affairs than they had enjoyed since the reservation system originated. The act changed the federal conversation about who directed Native affairs and brought new resources to the reservations and new powers of property ownership.[20] It changed, in part, the terms of the contest.

The contestants, however, remained and even multiplied. Collier's adherence to the principle of cultural autonomy and religious freedom led to new scandals that split even old alliances. His plans for expanding reservations ran into even more resistance.[21] The imagined blank slate of the West was crowded, as it had always been, with prior claimants.

Native Policy in Practice

The Navajo case in particular illuminates the trickiness of shared governance even where the federal government held most of the cards. Amid competing notions of what constituted knowledge and expertise and divergent notions of what constituted the modern West, even with the best will in the world to solve the problems and save the land and the people, the outcomes, unlike the construction of the dams, would not follow anyone's exact blueprints.

Multiple claims rendered parts of the arid Navajo region officially a "checkerboard." None of it flourished. New Deal scientists looked at the barren earth and rising levels of sand and soil swept downstream in rivers flowing through the Navajo (Diné) lands. To them it seemed obvious that the vastly increased herds of sheep and goats (between 1 million and 1.37 million) on which Navajo self-sufficiency depended had destroyed the forage and loosened the soil. The damage to the land threatened both Navajo survival and the long-term success of the Boulder Dam, the immense public works project then under construction south of Las Vegas.[22]

To the New Dealers, the answer seemed equally obvious: reduce the livestock to the carrying capacity of the land and tether the remaining stock to specific parcels whose carrying capacity the experts had determined.[23]

Navajo analysis differed. Many Diné did not recognize the incremental climate and environmental shifts of the past three decades that literally changed the ground under their feet. But they knew that, contrary to policy makers' assumptions, the land had no prior golden age of lush fields. They knew that there were cycles of drought. They blamed the barren earth on lack of rainfall rather than overstocking. And they blamed competition from Anglo and Hispano ranchers who did not acknowledge Diné prior land claims and depleted their land and resources, reducing their range and water, forcing their stock onto smaller parcels, and making it harder to move their stock seasonally. They knew that to survive, livestock had to migrate seasonally across vast distances and with great flexibility. They knew that trenching by streams had lowered the water table and made farming impossible on many parts of the reservation. They knew, too, that the number of sheep and goats, despite increasing, had actually not risen proportionately to the human population; the Navajos had held roughly a million sheep and goats in the 1880s, a number that had fallen with drought periodically and recovered but that had not reached the one hundred combined sheep, goats, and cattle a household needed to survive. Finally, they knew that the livestock were not evenly divided among Navajos and that 2,500 families had no stock. But they also knew that the large holders, the five large family groups that controlled 10 percent of the reservation, redistributed their wealth, gifting the poor relations with food and aid, and that if those large holders had fewer animals, the poor would suffer.[24]

The Navajos had tried to exclude competing stock growers, expand their range, and develop their water resources, as well as evoke ceremonial practices to restore balance. They had flocked to the Senate hearings in 1931 to explain the need for more land and water. More than sixty of them, men and women, in suits and in jeans, blankets and calico dresses, testified in the face of senators convinced the solution lay in greater market orientation, ridding the tribe of goats and horses with little market value, and abandoning poor land.[25]

Many Diné agreed that they needed to reduce the herds. But when their initial compliance failed to reduce the numbers to New Dealers' specifications, the resulting policy practices—aimed at reducing the livestock by half and then more—appalled them in their lack of consultation and respect for Navajo knowledge and practices and in their brutality. These practices provoked resistance. After government riders herded three thousand goats and sheep into a corral and shot them in Kayenta, for example, the Diné hid their sheep, goats, and horses. They burned their permits and went to jail for refusing to comply with the legal limits. In short, they defied the U.S. government. They knew that tethering animals to specific parcels spelled disaster. They knew that women's ability to ensure the survival of the people relied on women's ability to sell their sheep and lambs, weave and market wool blankets and rugs, and, if need be, eat the goats. They watched the policies undermine the authority of women and the self-sufficiency of the tribe.[26]

While Collier was more concerned about Navajo survival than he was about Boulder Dam, the Diné also knew that federal concern for the dam drove the reductions, and they resented what they saw as the Navajos paying for white development of Los Angeles. The Diné were not necessarily wrong. Historian Andrew Needham concludes that "the choice to route energy and water toward metropolitan consumers" not only "furthered the development of Los Angeles at the expense of the Salt River Valley and Navajo Reservation," it created a new region linking the three entities and epitomized the "metropolitan preferences" embedded in much of the era's policies. And, indeed, though stock reduction had been mooted about and attempted in smaller ways for decades, it was the conclusion of the federal government that the "Navajo Reservation is practically 'Public Enemy No. 1' in causing the Colorado Silt Problem," which spurred the more draconian, uncompromising policy.[27]

This metropolitan preference had arisen at a moment of dramatic urban population growth in the 1920s, and the policies were Janus-faced. They tried to provide incentives for rural people to stay put and to resettle displaced rural people on the land and even some urban people on the land in the name of self-sufficiency and health. At the same time, they addressed the urbanizing trend under way for decades and the declaration in the 1920 census (so like the declaration of the end of the frontier in the 1890 census) that the United States was now an "urban" nation, with most of the U.S. population living in towns of at least 2,500 people.

The West as a region had both the most rapidly growing urban areas and the most vast and troubled rural ones. But while there was a determination to bring electricity and modern conveniences to white rural populations, as well as urban ones, there seemed little such determination to bring them to Indian reservations, revealing a continuing vision that differentiated spaces and peoples as modern and not modern. It was typical of the New Deal, with its myriad experiments and decentralized bureaucracy, that policies would contradict each other in action.

Many New Dealers saw the resistance to stock reduction as pathological and were slow to reevaluate even when results failed to match expectations. They called the Diné response a "stock reduction complex" caused by "ignorance, blindness, laziness and dishonesty" and spurred on by "creators of misunderstanding" and "impassioned demagogs [*sic*]." And yet even these draconian moves failed to halt the rangeland from turning into desert. Families now without either sheep or goats found their only income in leasing their land to Anglo stockmen, who, in turn, overran the range.[28]

The New Dealers should have known better. A frequent Navajo joke in the 1920s and 1930s ran "a typical Diné homestead includes two parents, three children, a grandmother, and an anthropologist." Indeed, with Collier, anthropologists replaced missionaries as the dominant influence on the Indian Bureau. But anthropologists could actually lead policy makers astray or, if not astray, in the direction of their own tendencies to trust in university-generated scientific expertise and their own experience. Anthropologist W. W. Hill claimed that agriculture, not stock-raising, lay at the foundation of Navajo culture. He knew that agriculture predated sheep in the region by hundreds of years. And not all Navajos herded sheep, but almost all of them farmed. With that in view, it seemed reasonable to policy makers to diminish the role of sheep for the tribe and move them to agriculture. But Hill ignored Navajo oral tradition that bound the creation of the sheep with the origins of the people.[29]

Sheep underlay the very foundation of social organization on the reservation. They mostly belonged to women, providing the material basis for the tribe's matrilineal culture. Women passed the herds to their daughters. But anthropologists and federal officials mostly talked to men, and by the 1930s, things had gotten more complicated on the reservation. Most Navajos still lived in families centered around a woman and included a woman, her husband, her daughters, her sons-in-law, and her grandchildren. But many Navajo families had started to live differently, driven by subsistence needs, including moving to town for work. Anthropologists saw the diversity in family formation and leaned on the men to interpret its significance, since few Navajo women spoke English. Even when they understood it, federal bureaucracy seemed incapable of accommodating such diversity. In census records, for example, they reverted to their own prevailing norms, listing the husband as head of family and owner of herds.[30] Few federal officials seemed to recognize that such misunderstandings, willful or not, could lead to policy disaster.

It was a forester, not an anthropologist, who tried to stem the tide. Future Wilderness Society founder Robert Marshall, the man Collier appointed head of the BIA's forestry division in 1933, warned Collier against trying to mix "cultural freedom and cultural dictatorship" and argued, "We have insisted dozens of times in the past on some principle in spite of the objections of the Indians[,] who subsequently proved to be right after all." He advocated for limiting federal intervention to advice attached to resources, for "Indian initiative with white advice instead of white initiative with Indian advice."[31]

In making changes, the federal government looked to the Navajo council as their local, democratically elected partner. But that partnership came rooted in a history of inequality and a present of competing visions. The BIA had created the council in the previous decade as an appointed body of three Navajo men to ease the mineral leasing of tribal lands to non-Native commercial entities. Collier had called that council a "rubber stamp." Collier wanted the council instead to function as a legitimate representative body that could offer meaningful assent to federal plans, but the Navajos still saw it as an arm of the federal government. Although councilmen often tried vigorously to dissuade the government from ill-conceived programs, when they failed, they dutifully voted for them at the council.[32]

Both "traditionalists" and "progressives" understood women's place in the tribe better than the federal government did. Despite having only council*men*, the council's actions showed the deeply imbricated nature of men's and women's roles and women's authority among the Navajos. Having watched their neighbors, particularly the women, lose their livelihood and sustenance, having gone from self-sufficiency to dependence, in 1938 the Navajos prepared for their first popular election of the tribal council. Long after women had earned equal suffrage in the United States, federal officials raised woman suffrage as a question. It was not a question to the Navajos. "The right of women to vote was so self-evident," according to historian Marsha Weisiger, "that the leadership of the existing, appointed council saw no point in even discussing the issue. Robert Curley pointed out that women had 'just as much right as men' to vote; why would it be otherwise? Without another word, the men passed the measure unanimously."[33] That the BIA had posed it as a question demonstrated the gulf between Navajo and administration understanding that had troubled New Deal policies from the start.

These profound misapprehensions by policy makers that colored assumptions about Native property ownership, market involvement, and the importance of Native methods of conservation applied far beyond the Navajos and with similar results. When balancing the interests of competing parties in the West—Canada versus the United States, states versus the federal government, market versus subsistence, indigenous versus European American—the federal government rarely invited Native peoples to the table. When it included Native interests at all, despite Collier's explicit efforts, it most often left unchallenged the long-standing belief that federal officials could adequately represent them. As a result, at the same time federal policy strove to enhance the economic sustainability of Native peoples, such negotiations often undermined successful practices.[34]

Collier imagined that other income sources would substitute for such losses. He launched an employment service to help reservation Indians find off-reservation employment and expanded the employment of Indians at the Office of Indian Affairs. He promised that Diné wages from New Deal jobs programs, in particular the Emergency Conservation Work (ECW), would triple Navajo income. It never came close, and it excluded entirely the aged tribal members who had depended on their goats for food and clothing. But dependency on wages did rise. In 1930 the Navajos had already depended on wages for approximately 30 percent of their income; by 1937 wages accounted for almost 40 percent of Navajos' $128 per capita annual income.[35]

Both men and women earned wages, but the increasing reliance on a wage economy shifted power dynamics among the Navajos. During the New Deal, new opportunities came largely only to the men. Young Navajo men flocked to the programs and "drilled wells, erected windmills, built check dams in arroyos, constructed reservoirs, poisoned prairie dogs and weeds." Most continued to see their wage work as in the service of sustaining their herding, their hogans, and their matrilineal households. They dropped the wage work and returned home when the sheep demanded it. This was what they saw as the "living" they were making by their wage work. But wage work and the declining numbers of women's sheep and goats shifted dynamics in the family and tribe. In smallholder families, men brought in an increasing share of the household income independent of the family and created new patterns of social status.[36]

As did members of other tribes, Navajos responded to these new threats and opportunities creatively. Beginning in the 1920s and increasingly in the 1930s, for example, the Diné—often with coal-mining experience in Gallup, New Mexico's, mines—opened small coal mines on their land, worked largely by extended family members seasonally. They sold the coal to kin, locals, and the Navajo BIA agency. In this enterprise they joined similar efforts by Mexican American and Anglo men in Colorado and New Mexico, but they operated the mines in the Navajo way, including performing rituals to restore their harmony with the earth. And they used their proceeds to help sustain their sheep. There was a lot of coal on the reservation, and it offered some men the chance to steer clear of the wage market and migration off-reservation. By 1936 there were thirty-four coal mines operated by seventy-two Navajos on the northern Navajo reservation in New Mexico alone, producing 3,300 tons of coal each year.[37]

As the BIA became increasingly aware of the expanding mining enterprise, mining became another arena of contest over knowledge, methods, and aims. Navajo methods varied; some used surface mining, and some dug tunnels and used timbers. To keep costs down and prices competitive, they tended to take out only the lumps of coal. That practice left behind highly explosive but less profitable slack. F. W. Calhoun, a U.S. Geological Survey mining engineer, found Navajos' methods wasteful and unsafe and recommended they surrender control to the BIA, that the mines be centralized, and that the Navajos shift from being operators to wage workers. In 1937 the tribal council compromised. They left the Navajos as operators but placed the BIA officer in charge of ensuring that the mines ran "in accordance with regulations" and laws to promote safety and economy.[38] In short, here too the Navajos resisted the BIA demand for centralized control and planning.

As did many Native Americans, the Navajos came out of the Great Depression with enhanced autonomy, more resources, and a more democratically elected and accountable council. Their ability to do so rested not simply on federal policy but on their insistence that their own ideas about governance, reflecting their own knowledge, cultural practices, and understanding of power dynamics, including the power of women, also undergird the new structures. But older and often contradictory patterns of federal governance persisted as well. Where Native Americans and the federal government were not the only players, as with Akimel O'odham struggles over water rights and Navajo grazing rights, Native Americans often found themselves excluded from negotiations. They also found their departures from federal prescriptions pathologized. And despite Native American attempts to realize their own vision of modernity and market involvement, federal policies often marginalized them economically, diverting the benefits of massive dams, for example, and, despite the revolving credit fund, pushing wage work over ownership.

Home on the Range

It no doubt would have surprised them to make the connection, but whatever their background, ranchers affected by the 1934 Taylor Grazing Act found themselves in almost exactly the same position as the Navajos under the stock reduction program. Ranchers large and small had constructed their holdings around their grazing rights on public land, creating often a patchwork of private and public holdings, the private unsustainable (and without value) minus access to the federal public lands. Concern about carrying capacity hit those lands in the same way it hit the Navajo range. With drought, overstocking, and invasive Russian thistle, also known as tumbleweed, the cattle that ran the range had little food. Less than 10 percent of privately held shortgrass range was in decent condition. To address the issue, the federal government sought to create the same sort of federal partnership as they had with the Navajo council. It aimed to expand democratic participation in governing land use and economics and with the same ultimate federal control—an uneasy perpetual set of negotiations that was always threatening to blow up and was riddled with unintended consequences.[39]

The free range that enabled ranchers' prosperity was, according to Teddy Roosevelt, ephemeral, like the "wild" Indian, doomed to disappear with the ongoing march of agricultural settlement. But despite the Unlawful Enclosures Act of 1885 and the range wars of the 1890s, both the public domain and its illegal fencing had survived into the 1930s. Battles over grazing permits and fees charged by the Forest Service to protect the public's interest similarly persisted, as did claims that the fees drove out small ranchers and turned ranchers into government tenants. State governments, ranchers large and small, irrigation farmers, local grazing boards, stock growers' associations, and federal government agencies had struggled through the 1920s over water and land rights.[40]

In Nevada state laws recognized the arid realities of the Great Basin. In the early twentieth century, the state legislature had created a legal regime that granted water rights by two criteria: prior use ("first in time, first in right") and beneficial use (meaning the benefit to the greater good). Granting long-term water rights in arid regions provided the assurance that only those "improving" the water source through pumps and/or wells benefited from the investment, and controlling the water resources in effect controlled access to the range. A modest homestead, enough land to grow the hay necessary to winter over, and water rights sufficient to grow it enabled monopoly use of hundreds of acres of range. Such water rights could be lost only through disuse for five consecutive years.[41]

Even these measures could not save ranchers from the economic free fall. Like western farmers, ranchers had seen only dire days after World War I, with declining prices and the onset of drought through much of the northern plains. Homesteaders who had entered claims under the terms of the 1916 Stock-Raising Homestead Act, taking advantage of the glory days of peak prices during World War I, were particularly hard hit.[42] They wanted more local and state control over the public domain.

Nevada presented perhaps the most extreme example of the dilemma, as the federal government owned over 80 percent of the state's land. The denial of vesting full property rights in the states or individuals, to such frustrated advocates, denied full citizenship, full sovereignty, to the state's residents.[43]

In 1934, the same year the New Deal turned to draconian stock reduction measures on the Navajo reservation and the Indian Reorganization Act became law, the Taylor Grazing Act joined the panoply of New Deal legislation. The Senate debated the bill as Great Plains dust began to sift across the nation's capital. In that literally darkened atmosphere, measures to regulate grazing on the public domain that had been considered and rejected over the prior three decades became law.[44]

According to historian Karen Merill, the act marked the closing of the frontier far more thoroughly than Turner's 1893 statement had. While some historians have seen the act as a victory for organized ranchers, and other historians have seen it as "quashing any initiative ranchers might have to improve the public land they used," Merill instead sees the act "as a political instrument to adjudicate existing property relations and rights."[45]

To adjudicate those rights, the act called for the federal government to cooperate with local associations in setting policy. As they had with the Diné, the local associations, in this case ranchers' associations, predated the Depression. Their elected advisory boards would set the policy. Because New Dealers recognized these ranchers in a way they did not recognize the Diné, as people with local knowledge of the myriad grazing environments and capacities, the associations gained new power, and the participating stock growers strengthened the connection between their property and public lands and federal planning power.

As it had been with the Navajo council, it was not always clear just whom these elected boards represented. Secretary of the Interior Harold Ickes expressed concern that the public interest, the government interest, and the small stock holder were not being protected by the associations, often dominated, as were other New Deal boards, by the larger enterprises.[46] It was, at best, a delicate balancing act between the imagined "little man," the big ranchers, and the public interest. At worst, it was large-scale ranchers' capture of public lands.

Like the Navajos and the ranchers around the reservation, ranchers affected by the Taylor Grazing Act had long relied on gluing public lands to their private ones. Some could only access the property they owned by crossing the public land they used; some could only accrue sufficient land to graze cattle by wedding their forest reserve permits to the land they owned.

The Taylor Grazing Act threatened this property regime by limiting access to the open range, regardless of rights in watering holes. Of the 173 million acres the act authorized the president to withdraw from the public domain, the secretary of the interior designated 80 million acres for grazing districts. In those districts, the secretary could establish regulations over range use, as on the Navajo reservation, to protect and rehabilitate the land. Preferences in issuing permits would go to ranch owners, occupants, settlers, or owners of water or water rights, including those currently permitted only if they complied with regulations.[47]

Any federal attempt to replace worn-out but conveniently located lands with "equivalent" lands or to consolidate small, isolated parcels of public land surrounded by private land into a district that could more easily be managed ran into a particularly western nightmare. Ranchers considered their access to public lands, their permits, as property rights, and banks lent them money based on those permits. The ranchers and their representatives spoke, as did Senator Pat McCarran of Nevada in early 1939, of "the right of the commons, as that incorporeal hereditament was known."[48]

New Dealers sought to appease the ranchers. They engineered price supports for beef. Authorized by Congress, in June 1934 the federal government began, as it did for the Navajos, to buy cattle and distribute the meat to the unemployed. In less than a year, the government bought over eight million head, often in far less than prime condition, three-quarters of them from the plains and one-quarter of them from Texas alone, netting the cattlemen $111.7 million. The ranchers, like the Navajos when they had the choice, sold those in worst shape. Almost a fifth of those purchased in Oklahoma could not have survived a train trip to market. The federal government supplemented the program with feed loans, payments for changing range management by deferring grazing on depleted pastures, better managing water, and stabilizing herds. With this help, work relief, government-delivered surplus commodities, credit from the grocer, backyard chickens, a milk cow, and a yearly sow, ranchers and their hands could stay put, and commercial packing plants could keep operating. Numbers of cattle fell and beef prices rose by about 50 percent between 1933 and 1939.[49]

But those were not the only measures. Though the federal government technically controlled the public domain, it had less power over these ranchers than it did over disenfranchised reservation residents. Unlike many Navajos even after the 1924 Indian Citizenship Law, ranchers enjoyed the power of voting for senators and representatives. In response to ranchers' complaints about loss of access, a 1936 act enlarged the 80-million-acre initial limit to 142 million acres of a total of 163 million acres of U.S. unreserved and unallocated public lands.[50] The New Deal administration would not sell the land to the ranchers or hand it over to the states, but this measure ceded much control over the public domain to the ranchers.

Ranchers had more power vis-à-vis the federal administration than the Navajos did. When their interests collided, what emerged was a messy and perpetually renegotiated compromise. On the local level and in the associations, the power and resources of the smallholder seldom equaled those of large ranching enterprises, which, like NRA boards in other industries, were able to set policies in their own interests. For all their desire to demonstrate the imagined modern state capable of imposing sustainability and order in collaboration with local democratic control, the central planners ran into the realities of existing inequalities, and in the context of massive unrest, they proved more interested in nurturing stability than redistributing power.

Dust and Dreams

These New Deal measures to conserve the range were part of the broader New Deal response to the growing ecological disaster that was the American West. The rampant speculative practices of the "frontier," which reached new heights in the 1920s, had come home to roost. The remediating task now largely fell to the interior secretary and the agriculture secretary. They disagreed over the degree to which planning should be centralized, but the policies they oversaw, whether on the Navajo reservation or with the stock growers or in the succession of New Deal agencies that built new communities of "resettled" farmers, partook of the same agrarian vision: a single-class civic republicanism, a modernized countryside, an economic democracy of consumers and producers, and a federal responsibility for conserving even privately owned land.[51] New Dealers struggled over how to make that vision concrete amid the highly visible desperation of the region's farmers.

The drought had started long before the dust began to blow. In 1931 on the northern plains, farm ponds dried up and trees lost their leaves. While the plains had little more rain than the Sonoran Desert, they did not suffer alone. Between 1930 and 1936 only two states in the United States escaped drought: Maine and Vermont. Rain continued scarce until 1941. The drought came with intense heat, 118 degrees in Nebraska in the summer of 1934, 115 in Iowa. Grasshoppers ate what survived the drought—wheat, corn, and even fence posts and clothes drying on the line. According to historian Donald Worster, "By 1936, farm losses . . . reached $25 million a day, and more than 2 million farmers were drawing relief checks."[52]

The scale and the dramatic visual representation of the drought and dust struck the American public like a tsunami, the grand finale of the ecological disaster. The intense, speculative development of the 1920s had ripped the native shortgrass off the plains in favor of wheat wherever it was remotely possible to plant it. During World War I's peak prices, farmers bought machinery and expanded their planting. Teachers and townspeople bought a few acres and farmed them on weekends or hired someone to do it. These people, in particular, had no long-term interest in the land and often little experience with farming.

When the drought came, no deep roots held the soil in place. When the winds came, they snatched the topsoil from the plains like an avenging angel and carried it east to Georgia, New York, and Chicago. The worst came in May 1934, when one storm sifted twelve million tons of dust over Chicago, four pounds per person in the city, and the next day darkened Buffalo and, moving one hundred miles an hour, smothered Boston, New York, Washington DC, and Atlanta before moving out to sea. Seven times in the spring of 1935, dust storms cut the visibility in Amarillo, Texas, to zero, once for eleven hours. It was impossible to ignore the dust storms. After that May, the worst storms stayed on the southern plains—parts of Kansas, Colorado, Texas, New Mexico, and Oklahoma, peaking at seventy-two storms in 1937.

Cattle suffocated. An affliction called "dust pneumonia" ran rampant. In one Kansas county in one month, thirty-three patients died of acute respiratory distress. Dust coated rivers, killing the fish. Dust sandblasted house exteriors, collapsed roofs, destroyed motors, and sifted through the cracks to coat church pews. With every brief, tantalizing break in the drought, farmers planted, only to witness the return of the devastating drought and dust storms.

One storm in March 1939 darkened one hundred thousand acres, carrying enough dirt to cover five million acres a foot deep. Druggists sold out of sedatives. Photographs of the wreckage saturated newsreels, magazines, and newspapers across the country.

Some farmers witnessed decades and even generations of success evaporate in a few years. They had borrowed to buy machinery, and they bought machinery to prove they were modern enough to be worthy of borrowing. In counties where only half the farmers had indoor water, only one in four had electric lights, fewer had refrigerators or washing machines, and none had indoor toilets, almost every farmer had a car and a tractor and half kept a truck. They borrowed against everything—their crops, their homes, their equipment, their future crops—when state law allowed. Like the rest of the country, they collapsed under the weight of the debt when borrowing became impossible. Irrigation districts, almost always overcapitalized in any case, with declining revenue due to declining prices and tax delinquency, defaulted on bonds. Many farmers declared bankruptcy; some simply left without a trace. Cimarron County, Oklahoma, lost 40 percent of its rural population, most of them small farmers.[53]

Their land, by and large, went to the wealthier who remained, continuing the consolidation of the previous decades. Those remaining tended to own large acreage and ran highly mechanized operations, as did the Collingwood Corporation on its hundreds of quarter sections in southwestern Kansas. Others lived in town, where they ran local businesses. They followed the logic of the speculative 1920s. They were not "husbandmen." Their interest in the land was not to build a home for themselves and their heirs in perpetuity. The land was an interchangeable part of their diversified portfolio, a way to make cash to support their lives elsewhere.[54]

The devastation left the administration facing two areas of extraordinary poverty on the plains, even by the standards of the decade. One covered most of the Dakotas and the neighboring counties; the other was the southern plains' dust bowl. Finding little relief under Hoover, who called the $45 million seed-and-feed loan fund created by Congress "a raid on the public treasury," the plains went heavily for Roosevelt in 1932.[55]

In many ways, the problems of the plains farmers were not much different from those of the ranchers and of the Navajos: degradation of the land, competing claims on the land, and competing visions of remediation. The larger difference was the degree of federal control or lack of it. For most of the Great Plains, the federal government did not own the land, as it did the public grazing grounds of the ranchers. Nor did it have the legal control over the local governments that it did with the Navajos and other Indians. There was little it could mandate. What the locals, firmly convinced that the disaster was a temporary aberration, wanted was the federal government to tide them over until the drought ended, to make it possible to stay on the land. What they most resisted was exactly what the federal government had been able to enforce on the ranchers and the Navajos: relocation.[56]

The administration set up a program to buy the worst-hit lands to be held in federal hands in perpetuity, hoping to turn up to 180,000 acres of dunes into stabilized grassland. Desperate, many owners sold out. Some resettled, enticed by the promise of available water. By the end of 1936, the Resettlement Administration had purchased over nine million acres.[57]

But those nine million acres were a small piece of the puzzle. Absent the power the public domain and the structure of Indian oversight gave it, the administration turned to appeasement. In previous periods of drought and disaster on the high plains (e.g., in the 1890s), the federal government had done little more than allow the soldiers in local forts to hand out blankets. Settlers had starved, frozen, and departed. In the 1930s, with the specter of Communist revolution, the government had more incentive to keep people rooted to the land. In June 1933 the New Deal launched the Farm Credit Administration; over three years it loaned $600 million, disproportionately to the plains farmers unable to get other loans, and organized committees to adjust farm debts to payable levels. And in mid-1934 Roosevelt asked Congress for $525 million in drought relief, and Congress promptly granted it. These funds provided $275 million for cattlemen; $125 million to employ farmers on public works; and other funds for relocation, seed loans, work camps for youths, and a shelterbelt program.[58]

Ironically, New Deal programs intended to stabilize the population kept one segment in place but facilitated the further dispossession of another. For example, it paid farmers to plant less land in crops judged to have a market glut (renting their acreage), engendering at times the spectacle of paying farmers not to plant where nothing would grow in any case. Though the deal required farmers to share their parity and rental checks with their tenants and sharecroppers and keep their tenants and sharecroppers on the land, one farmer owner said of his tenants, "I let 'em all go. . . . In '34 had I reckon four renters and I didn't make anything. I bought tractors on the money the government give me and get shet o' my renters. You'll find it everywhere all over the country thataway." Over the course of the 1930s, tenant farms in Texas fell in number by 32 percent, even more—42 percent—in the Blackland Prairie region. The number of tractors in Texas, on the other hand, rose from thirty-seven thousand to ninety-nine thousand. Texas cotton acreage had fallen by more than half, and Texas farmers in 1939 received nearly $50 million from the federal government not to grow cotton, the bulk of it paid to large landowners. Large-scale mechanized farms that had few or no tenants or croppers and that used a reduced number of wage workers dominated the industry.[59]

The prevalent images of the Depression in the U.S. West show a long trail of broken-down vehicles piled high with the residue of desperate lives, driven out by dust and despair from the nation's heartland. These images come in large part courtesy of the small group of intellectuals who saw the connection between the ecological disaster and market practices.[60] But their images told only part of the story. Even before the 1930s, people on the plains had been on the move. Mechanization had displaced tenants and sharecroppers and shattered the rungs of the agricultural ladder that was supposed to lead from landlessness to landownership. This shattering had led to mass migration, almost as much in the 1920s as in the 1930s. Mechanization of wheat farming on the plains had cut the labor needs of production in half. Between 1910 and 1930 the number of farmers and agricultural workers in the Southwest declined by 341,000. During each of the first decades of the twentieth century, the turnover rate in Haskell County, Kansas, was over 50 percent. Not everyone on the move went to California, but between 1920 and 1930 more than 2.5 million migrants did. It was proportionately the largest peace-time migration in U.S. history. Some were pushed by mechanization, but others were pulled by the promise of new cotton acreage at good rents in California.[61]

In the 1930s the migration would be as it had been in the mid-nineteenth century: east to west along lines of latitude. The Pacific Northwest's 460,000 new settlers came along the Lincoln Highway. Only 14 percent came from the southern plains. The millions who came to California did so along the well-paved and already famous Route 66.[62] They moved rural to rural and urban to urban.

More pushed than pulled and usually poorer than in the previous decade, migrants still had to have the resources to move. Those without the resources to get to California moved less far. While nine million acres of high plains farmland was abandoned during the 1930s and ten thousand houses sat empty, only two states in the United States ended the decade with dramatically lower population than in 1930: Oklahoma, which lost 18.4 percent of its 1930 population, and Kansas, whose net loss was 12 percent, or 227,000 people. It was not that the dust bowl residents stayed put. Unless oil and gas boomed in their counties, the tenants, often with shallow roots to any particular piece of land, left the vicinity, but they didn't go far. Some West Texans went to western New Mexico. Other families moved to Colorado's western slope.[63]

Those who made it to California were most often neither destitute nor farmers. A few hailed from the wheat belt of the dust bowl, but more came from the Oklahoma / North Texas cotton belt or the family farms of the Arkansas and Missouri Ozarks. Many had served the farmers as merchants until the farmers had no cash to spend.[64] They tended to fare better in the cities of California than in the Central Valley, where they joined the harsh conditions of exploited farm labor.[65]

What kind of refuge was California? Was this a partly voluntary resettlement that would resolve the environmental disaster? California agriculture was just as speculative and just as mired in high fixed costs (irrigation and taxes). And where massive co-ops like Sunkist operated like large corporations, they were just as "cutthroat" as elsewhere in the United States and just as unstable. Crop after crop suffered from periodic overproduction. The only control growers had was over wages. Many of the operations were large. In 1939 *Fortune* magazine reported that one-tenth of the state's farms grew over half of the state's crops, and California held a third of all the U.S. farms that produced $30,000 or more in crop value. Journalist Carey McWilliams called them "factories in the field." *Fortune* connected the dots and concluded that profit-maximizing factory farming had led to the abuse of the land and the people who worked it.[66]

In the 1930s California agriculture boomed. The New Deal made the state's recovery rapid. Cotton prices rebounded, and California farms yielded three to four times per acre what the Southwest did. In the San Joaquin Valley alone, cotton acreage grew by almost five hundred thousand acres between 1932 and 1936, and cotton-picking wages for a time rose alongside. Having "repatriated" Mexican workers, agriculture faced a short-lived labor shortage, and California farmers paid 20–50 percent more than the southern plains for picking cotton. As word got out, Oklahoma cotton farmers headed for California. Those who could, farmed, and those who could not farm, picked.[67]

The San Joaquin Valley towns they entered had barely come into existence. Cotton had only come to the valley in the 1920s. The valley's farm towns—Arvin, McFarland, Buttonwillow, and others—sprouted with the cotton. Ten years later, the new towns found themselves inundated with dust bowl migrants and displaced tenants. In the heart of the valley's cotton area, Kern County's population grew by 64 percent in the 1930s.

Few of the migrants—only 2 percent—came with enough resources to become farm owners in the valley or even tenants or managers by 1940. Particularly in the rural areas, their mobility was not only westward but also downward. White-collar workers became blue-collar workers, and industrial workers became farm laborers. By 1940 non-Hispanic whites made up 76 percent of the farmworkers in the San Joaquin Valley, more than a third of them from the Southwest. Mexicans would not regain the majority until the 1950s.[68]

The labor shortage quickly evaporated, and with it, successful union organizing by farmworkers. By middecade two to three migrants vied for each of the 175,000 peak season picking jobs.

They would earn only half of what it took to survive. Those who failed to get employment camped by the side of the road, used water from the irrigation ditch, and tried to keep their children alive for the year it took to qualify for relief. Half of these new agricultural workers refused to migrate at all, and another quarter migrated for a year and then parked themselves next to filling stations and grocery stores. At the peak, in 1937, thousands lived in squatter villages. They lacked gasoline for their cars and food for their children. They lived in tents on damp ground, and the children stayed home from school (when there was a school), being too weak, or sick, or inadequately clothed and shod. Nationally, with John Steinbeck and Paul Taylor writing on their plight and Dorothea Lange documenting it in photographs, they gained a sympathy Mexican and Mexican American migrants never had.[69]

To the locals, on the other hand, they looked dirty and unkempt—and costly. In a single valley county, school expenditures rose 172 percent, health and sanitation costs doubled, and hospitalization costs for indigents rose almost three times. Inhabitants of the five southern San Joaquin Valley counties saw their taxes rise 100 percent in five years. More than half of the relief recipients had lived in California less than five years. The locals saw the migrants' failure on the plains as biological, not environmental, and "Okie" came to be a pejorative term for the migrants. Signs in San Joaquin Valley and elsewhere warned them to stay in their place, as did one theater sign, "Negroes and Okies upstairs."[70]

The migrants resisted the lesson, as historian Neil Foley put it, that "not all whites . . . were possessed of equal degrees of whiteness." They held on to their notion of themselves not as what they now were—migrant labor—but as what they had been or aspired to be—respectable farmers. In California they would elect a Democrat for governor in 1938, perhaps as much driven by the party's historic allegiance to white supremacy in their home states as by its proworker stand in California, but they would not join with other farmworkers in a union.[71]

The Family Farm?

If California was not the panacea, it was not always clear what the alternative was. The Mennonites in Kansas remained committed to a simpler world, privileging self-sufficiency yet highly communal, diversifying their farms, and, though they bought tractors and cars, rarely speculating in wheat. They had allowed the 1920s whirlwind of mass consumption to pass them by, and few of them now faced forced removal. They were the exceptions, a model for some, including some New Deal planners, but a curiosity for most. Few farmers waxed nostalgic about the days of self-sufficiency, endless hours, and backbreaking work. Most farmers, whether in California, Oklahoma, or elsewhere, wanted radios, cars, high school for their children, and other emblems of modern life.[72]

New Dealers looked for a middle ground. The New Deal administration invested in massive projects—Boulder, Bonneville, and Grand Coulee Dams, among others—that sustained corporate agriculture, but it also created utopian agricultural projects whose target was the small family farmer with diversified income. The administration had many examples on which to draw, including those veterans' colonization efforts in Durham and Delhi, California, accused of socialism in the 1920s hearings; the Mormon village of Richmond, Utah, settled for a generation with small lots that allowed families subsistence gardens and livestock and wage work in the settlement's sugar beet factory; and Japanese Americans surviving on one or two acres. The notion of industrial workers living in a pastoral environment with fresh milk and vegetables for the children and a backstop against factory slowdowns held enormous appeal.[73]

A $25 million rider to the National Industrial Recovery Act gave the president free rein in creating subsistence homesteads. It framed the enactment as "aiding the redistribution of the overbalance of population in industrial centers," which were rife with unrest. The administration promised to avoid cash crops to dampen criticism from beleaguered full-time farmers. It envisioned the funds as loans whose repayment would constitute a revolving fund for the same purpose. These communities would perpetuate indefinitely a Jeffersonian smallholder democratic ballast for a national ship that seemed increasingly invested in large-scale corporate enterprises.[74]

While the New Deal introduced centralized planning, market stabilization, and agrarian experimentation on an unprecedented scale, it did little to question faith in the family farm. Even the more holistic experiments—the homesteads and planned communities, not limited to the West but partaking of a peculiarly western ethos and imaginary—held on to basic premises about the nuclear family farm, sustainability, and the market that were not supported by the world around them. The contradictions were glaringly evident to many critics at the time. For icons of 1920s success, including Charles Lindbergh, Henry Ford, and Herbert Hoover, "success" had required fleeing the farm. Critics believed that New Deal policies to provide loans to desperate farmers and would-be farmers, including displaced tenants and sharecroppers, made no sense. Moreover, those policies ran at cross-purposes with other New Deal policies. Senator Huey Long explained, "We have two agencies of farm relief, one to hire a man not to raise, and the other to hire him to buy land on which to raise. Where in the hell are we going?"[75]

The contradiction emerged not only from the deep Jeffersonianism of many New Dealers but also from the Roosevelt administration's efforts to counter twin threats: first, a political threat from Louisiana senator and governor Huey Long, whose Share the Wealth clubs proved popular in both Arkansas and Louisiana, and second, sharecropper and tenant unrest, spreading, ever more Left-leaning, in Arkansas and garnering national publicity for the brutality with which landowners tried to suppress it. Those restive farmers of England, Arkansas (see chapter 10), were not alone. New Deal policies had swelled their numbers by what one historian called the "extraordinarily landlord-minded" policies of the Agricultural Adjustment Administration (AAA).[76]

When farm owners refused to share their parity and rental checks with their tenants and sharecroppers and dismissed them with impunity, the federal government refused to be a recourse. With the same mindset that made the federal government complicit in racist relief policies, the administration saw such interference as inimical to local rule and as endangering the essential support of powerful Democrats in Congress. Instead, the enforcement of regulations lay in the hands of local committees staffed by farm owners. When one AAA official (ultimately fired for his protenant views) "asked a county gent why no sharecroppers or tenants sat on county committees . . . [t]he agent replied, 'Hell! You wouldn't put a chicken on a poultry board, would you?'"[77]

Things came to a head in 1934. An absentee landlord from St. Louis allegedly took the tenants' share of AAA parity payments for his 4,500-acre Arkansas plantation. The tenants sought the help of two sympathetic local businessmen, H. L. Mitchell, a former sharecropper who owned a small dry-cleaning shop, and Henry Clay East, who operated the service station next door. The two men formed the core of the local socialist group, and together they organized the Unemployed League, garnered more federal financial aid from the Civil Works Administration, and brought perpetual socialist presidential candidate Norman Thomas to speak at Tyronza, Arkansas's high school auditorium. After viewing local conditions, Thomas concluded that the AAA was a "cruel and lunatic order of society" and privately told Mitchell they needed a sharecroppers union. Not long after, on one hot July evening, eleven white and seven Black sharecroppers met in Tyronza's dilapidated schoolhouse and formed what became the Southern Tenant Farmers Union (STFU). It was an odd group for the time and place. Some of the white men had been KKK members, and one of the older Black men had belonged to the union so brutally broken up in the wake of the 1919 Elaine, Arkansas, massacre.[78]

Landlords were less than thrilled with this development, and the Roosevelt administration, needing the support of large farmers, tried to avoid explicit social reform. As the STFU grew (organizing 328 locals and more than sixteen thousand sharecroppers in Arkansas) and word spread about conditions, STFU members received death threats. One young Federal Emergency Relief Administration employee, a Methodist minister and STFU organizer, told the gathered tenants and sharecroppers at Marked Tree, Arkansas, in early 1935, "Well, that is a game two can play. . . . If necessary I could lead the sharecroppers to lynch every planter in Poinsett County." The county prosecuting attorney arrested him as he left the speakers' platform, charging and ultimately winning a conviction of anarchy and attempting to overthrow and usurp the state government.[79]

Farm owners and their allies beat and jailed union members and shot into and burned homes and churches where they met. When Norman Thomas returned, a group of riding bosses dragged him from the platform and beat his companions; "We don't need no

Gawddamn Yankee bastard to tell us what to do with our n[——]s," they claimed.[80]

As it did so often during the New Deal, the unrest helped shape a policy that tried to appease all parties. Secretary of Agriculture Henry Wallace would later insist that the government was helping to stabilize rather than to disrupt the farm labor supply. In 1935 he testified to Congress:

> The present conditions, particularly in the South . . . provide soil for Communist and Socialist agitators. . . . I realize that the cure is not violence or oppressive legislation to curb these activities but rather to give these dispossessed people a stake in the social system. The American way to preserve the traditional order is to provide these refugees of the economic system with an opportunity to build and develop their own homes and to live on the land which they may call their own and on which they can make a modest living year after year.[81]

The New Deal focused its early resettlement efforts almost entirely on Arkansas at the height of the unrest. It scrambled to create the Plum Bayou project near England, Arkansas, resettling 180 white families on forty-two acres each, and Lakeview near the Elaine Massacre, for eighty Black families.[82]

Meanwhile, the STFU continued to organize, and Arkansas landlords evicted families for union activity in the dead of winter, circulating lists of union members to other farm owners. In the late spring of 1936, the STFU organized a cotton croppers' strike, joined by five thousand sharecroppers in eastern Arkansas. The newsreel *March of Time* covered the strike, in which strikers faced beatings and arrests on vagrancy charges and were forced at gunpoint to work in the fields. *Time* magazine covered the flogging of a union organizer. Readers seemingly unmoved by similar conditions for Mexican and Black field workers were outraged to find white cotton pickers reminiscent of "Chinese coolies" in conditions worse than "backward sections of Europe . . . and part of Africa." With his state facing a federal grand jury investigation on possible violation of peonage laws, the Arkansas governor announced in August 1936 that he would appoint a special commission of impartial citizens to investigate tenancy and recommend solutions.

The STFU shouldered itself onto the commission, showing up to the first meeting uninvited. The governor acceded, and the commission, named for its chairman, Texarkana newspaper publisher Clyde E. Palmer, found the STFU president, J. R. Butler, and another union representative taking their seats among the businessmen, planters, professionals, and government officials in mid-September 1936.

The union view of how to solve the agrarian crisis differed from that of most commission members. The STFU argued against New Deal measures such as the proposed Bankhead-Jones Act, which would settle workers or resettle farmers displaced from marginal land or through tenant evictions caused, in part, by other New Deal policies on small plots of better land with a view to eventual ownership. Such small farms, the STFU claimed, would turn them into a "subsidized peasantry." Instead, some union members favored large cooperative farms. Others favored consolidated fields where farmers could share high-cost equipment. In short, they favored a mode of farming more like the large agribusiness units that had better weathered the farming crisis of the 1920s, one more capital intensive and industrialized, more in harmony with what in other sectors would have been called "modern."

In contrast, the commission's conclusion sounded much like the New Deal plans first in the Subsistence Homestead Administration; then in the Resettlement Administration, which absorbed it and focused on resettling families displaced when the administration purchased their submarginal lands; and finally, in the Farm Security Administration, which absorbed both. Committed to the Jeffersonian idea of owning a small farm home as the source of social stability and patriotism, the commission's report endorsed legislation to "discourage the ownership of farm lands in large tracts necessitating cultivation through tenancy or day labor" and promised that the actions it recommended would "end all danger from socialist and communist activities in rural sections."[83]

Most Arkansans seemed to agree with the commission's report and sentiment. A Gallup poll taken in December 1936 showed that 89 percent of respondents favored government loans that would allow farmers to buy their own farms. In Texas, too, white tenants wanted their own farms. Even before the Palmer Commission released its report, speaking at Omaha, Nebraska, after touring the drought-stricken plains, FDR had declared the "ultimate object of every farm family owning its own farm." He insisted on "the fundamental belief that the American farmer, living on his own land, remains our ideal of self-reliance and of spiritual balance—the source from which the reservoirs of the Nation's strength are constantly renewed." And even STFU members when polled in 1935 had strongly favored farm ownership or long-term leases over cooperative farming.[84]

New Deal developments would try to balance cooperative features that took advantage of economies of scale with individual homes and acreage. The architects of the New Deal community projects aiming to realize this vision had grown up in the rural United States, had benefited from education in agricultural colleges and midwestern state universities, and had joined a cadre of new experts with a critique of dominant practices. They and their ilk shifted the view from man's unilateral domination over nature in the name of ever-more market production to a more interdependent vision that required human adaptation in tandem with a managed landscape.[85]

Between 1933 and 1935 the Division of Subsistence Homesteads created thirty-four communities in seventeen states. Applications poured in. Applicants came from a wide range of previous farming experience and widely varying degrees of previous prosperity. The homes, though stripped of all unnecessary decoration, with their three to five bedrooms, a kitchen with a built-in sink (but not indoor plumbing), and a screened porch, without question were better than tenant and cropper shacks. A storeroom stood ready to become a modern bathroom should the resident ever save enough to afford it. Co-ops included stores, community buildings, tools, heavy machinery, and medical care. For some project residents, the homes, which at times were far from ready when they arrived, marked a step down; the neighbors were confiningly close, and the supervision was irksome at best. For others, formerly isolated from neighborly contact, the proximity of other farmers and community activities was transformative.[86]

Even this compromise had a hard time salvaging the family farm. Though the vetting process for admission screened for health, farming experience, and a proven track record of a hearty work ethic, unlike those in the 1910s and 1920s projects, many of the project residents still foundered for many of the same reasons they had foundered over the past decade and more: droughts, floods, and a saturated agricultural market. In addition, few settlers understood the actual costs they had incurred. They knew what the government had paid for the land but did not learn what the government improvements to the property had cost until they were fully committed and in some cases had already been living for several months and even years on the land. Just as with the 1920s irrigation projects, many of the 1930s projects were overcapitalized. Government project managers exacerbated the problem when they encouraged farmers to invest in equipment to bring the land to full productivity more quickly, further raising the level of debt and the vulnerability to bad weather. In Plum Bayou the average per-family investment was $8,052.80; settlers struggled to repay, on average, even $4,214.12.[87]

Farmers who had battled failing farms and submarginal land in the 1920s and 1930s had arrived at the projects with high hopes and a commitment to hard work. They put up with less than adequate housing when they arrived, living in dilapidated outbuildings until their homes were finished. They worked twelve-hour and even twenty-four-hour cycles irrigating land, and they adapted to new crops and new conditions. After all that, when threatened with foreclosure, the farmers protested. They blamed the overly rosy projections of the project managers who recruited them, and they hired lawyers, including the high-profile Robert LaFollette, who helped them successfully resist what they saw as a bait and switch and forestalled the evictions.[88]

The farmers often had to learn completely new ways to farm. Dry farmers, initially thrilled at the guarantee of water that came with irrigation projects, were shocked that it took roughly ten times the labor of dry farming, pulling farm wives into the fields on a regular basis. Irrigated farming required new crops, which in turn required learning new cultivation techniques. Different soil required different tillage, shallow, not deep, and even different plows. Farmers who had learned to maximize profits by focusing on a single crop now learned diversified farming, a shift that seemed insane. "Imagine on such a small acreage trying to grow six or seven crops!" exclaimed one resident at Milk River Farms, Montana.[89]

And then there was the issue of democratic governance. Farmers objected strongly to the level of federal supervision. Federal agents insisted on monitoring production and consumption of their indebted farm families, criticizing the amount spent for coffee, the number of haircuts, and whether money could be spent on school clothes. One farm woman insisted, "I didn't think it was any of their damned business." The men complained of being treated like "a bunch of paupers [who] have no head of their own." Funds could not be withdrawn without the project manager's approval.[90] White farmers framed their objections in the language of endangered whiteness, and indeed, the economic measures precisely mirrored the wardship to which Indians had objected in the 1920s.[91]

Revolts by Arkansas settlers in early projects who felt misled financially and disenfranchised politically by the intense federal supervision led to changes that helped smooth the way for the later projects. In the context of the Depression (as opposed to the 1920s) and then the coming war, the government seemed more willing to forgive the debt to save the ideal of the small family farmer as the backbone of democracy. In many ways, that was exactly how the farmers saw themselves. Their protests forced the government to compromise on the mix of centralized planning and local democratic control.[92]

Projects with part-time farmers proved more consistently financially successful even if their relationship to the agrarian vision was more attenuated. These New Deal subsistence homesteads carefully screened for settlers who had part-time work and so could repay housing loans, had experience in farming suited to the region, and were relatively homogeneous. Each family had a milk cow and chickens. Settlers canned berries and vegetables so assiduously that they ran out of storage space. They gained health, self-esteem, and confidence and cut their grocery bills by as much as half. In the first ten years, few departed. Subsistence homestead communities garnered both success and media attention and became tourist attractions. Unlike the earlier Arkansas projects, these communities' construction came in under budget, and most never missed paying an installment to the government.[93]

While these New Deal small-scale resettlement projects could keep alive a particular vision of the West as a land of opportunity for the smallholder, their impact on the landscape as a whole was relatively slight compared to the major reclamation projects. Most farmers did not want to move. And the federal administration could not or would not move them. The resulting administrative differences between federal policy toward farmers, Indians, and ranchers are instructive. To Secretary of the Interior Harold Ickes, a proposed costly dam in the Oklahoma panhandle smacked of throwing good money after bad. "We'll have to move them out of there," he concluded, "and turn the land back to the public domain." Locals called him ignorant, and when a few years later the creation of the Resettlement Administration stoked rumors of forced evacuation, a farmer in New Mexico warned, "They'll have to take a shotgun to move us out of here. We're going to stay here just as long as we damn please." And so the Resettlement Administration became the Farm Security Administration, aiming to secure for the small farm owner his or her hold on the land, stimulate the economy by putting money in farmers' hands, and avoid turning farm towns into ghost towns. Between payments for not planting wheat, payments for starving cattle and sheep, summer fallow, spring crop, and feed loans, farmers in Cimarron County, Oklahoma, for example, received $923,387 in 1934. By 1937 federal farm programs had bestowed an average of $4,000 per farm in that county. The farmers paid down their debts to John Deere and other equipment manufacturers, kicked off their tenants, and hunkered down.[94]

Conclusion

The Great Depression had provided the federal administration with an unprecedented opportunity to remake the West. The scale of man-made and environmental disaster had led Congress to provide vastly enlarged resources, and the New Deal spent them disproportionately in the West.[95] The resources allowed the government to create new bureaucracies and expand old ones in order to restore order to the region, its resources, and its inhabitants and to foster both central planning and its counterpart, local participatory democracy.

There were many ironies that attended this expansion. Mass protests and mass migrations resulted *from*, as well as resulted *in*, New Deal plans for an orderly march to the future. And Huey Long was right. New Dealers often operated from competing visions. Their plans, in addition, bore battle scars from encounters with combative congressmen, corporate farmers, and large-scale ranchers, as well as independent-minded tribal members and smallholders. Not always receptive to local knowledge and with perhaps at times excessive faith in the current state of scientific expertise and the ability to overcome constraints of environment and market, some New Deal projects foundered in a morass of unintended consequences. Moreover, in struggling to balance a need for order with a commitment to democratic process, the New Deal created and fostered locally elected bodies that, in turn, amplified resistance to New Deal plans and in some cases entrenched existing inequalities.

The administration wanted to treat the U.S. West like an enormous chessboard on which it could move people, animals, and water. It seemed to assume that if it could just move the people, move and adjust the number of cattle and sheep and the production of crops, and drill enough wells, it could save not just market agriculture and family farmers but also hope and faith in the American dream, realized in the West, for the long term.

That model worked well for the massive dam projects. Those projects had their complexities, both technical and diplomatic, with states and nations competing for water. But in the end, once the project was approved, the federal government held all the cards. The dams enormously enhanced the capacity of the federal government to plan and implement massive projects, and the dams did indeed change the contours of the chessboard.

New Deal legislation also finally granted farmers the ever-normal granary they had sought since the nineteenth century. Federal incentives to reduce production and care for the land helped reduce the risk and smooth the vagaries of farming and ranching. That they also fostered the rising power of larger-scale entities was seen as unavoidable.

Not all attempts to redesign the chessboard worked so well. The government planted 220 million trees on thirty thousand farms to try to tame the winds that hurtled over the land with such destructive power. The shelterbelt of trees did cut the velocity of winds in their vicinity; they reduced evaporation of scarce water, and planting them employed many desperate men. On the other hand, few shelterbelts stood in the dust bowl. They cost far more than the value of the land, and they did not stop the dust storms.[96]

The government's new agricultural methods—terracing and contour plowing, for example—met with more success. Twenty-two million acres on the southern plains got the new treatment from eager progressive entrepreneurial farmers.[97] They epitomized federal commitments to the West as a showcase of modernity, a malleable landscape.

Part of the modernity, as always, remained the contest over who is fit for modernity, as well as what is "modern." This particular imagined modernity was composed of small machine-invested operators, a Jeffersonian democracy for the twentieth century. "Democracy" expanded to include local direction of the economy in elected irrigation, grazing, and soil conservation boards. It did not, in the end, include tenants and farmworkers. It included in strictly limited ways Native Americans on reservations. And it included a perpetually colliding, diverse set of interests, the hallmark of democracy, and the frustration of New Deal planners blindsided by the hostility their programs engendered. Finally, though it mitigated risk, this imagined modernity included an ineluctable commitment to risk. As one farmer put it in 1936, "We know how to farm better than we do farm. We simply take chances, winning in good season, and losing when it fails to rain, or if the wind blows out our crops." Another concluded, "It's not in our blood to play a safe game."[98]

Because and in spite of the New Deal, high-risk, capital-intensive, monoculture agriculture survived, but so, too, did the New Deal vision of local economic democracy. Like the grazing districts fostered by the Taylor Grazing Act and the irrigation districts of the 1920s, the Soil Conservation Service (SCS) districts long outlasted the decade. By putting innovation in local hands and democratic units, the SCS hoped to appease suspicious and reluctant farmers. In the spring of 1936 the SCS published a template of an enabling law for states to adopt if they wished. It "would allow local people to set up, through petition and referendum, their own district, with self-determined boundaries, and to make binding regulations for a five-year period." Similarly, though shorter-lived, the idea of county planning committees made up of local farmers who would manage and coordinate agricultural production and New Deal resources on the ground spread far beyond the community projects. Across the country in the late 1930s and early 1940s, two-thirds of all counties had such planning committees, and according to historian Jess Gilbert, over two hundred thousand "farm men and women served on community and county committees that adapted and coordinated New Deal programs throughout rural America." Gilbert calls it "participatory modernization."[99]

New Deal efforts to manage the land performed continual balancing acts. The New Deal balanced inclusion and exclusion, sacrificing farmworkers and tenants and doing nothing to halt the permanent racialized exclusion of "Mexicans" in the course of saving not only many small farms but also the promise of the small farm for those included in the imagined nation. It moved, if not mountains, then rivers by building vast dams, encouraged large-scale agribusiness, and, at the same time, built models of smallholder communities and participatory democracy. It saved the imagined West as both the home of opportunity and the showcase of the modern nation.

Conclusion

Making a Modern West

Had he still been alive in 1940, Teddy Roosevelt would have looked out over the expanse of U.S. territory west of the Mississippi and been pleased. In 1898 New Mexico, Arizona, and Oklahoma had yet to become states. There was still an Indian Territory. It was still possible for white and Black men west of the Mississippi to fantasize about finding "savages" in the local "wilderness," as Booker T. Washington and Alfred Kroeber did. Except for customs officers and "Chinese inspectors," land borders were unpoliced. Laws barred most Chinese immigrants, but courts could declare Japanese immigrants "white," and they could hold land anywhere. Native Americans joined Wild West shows, but they also hunted in what would become national parks. And men and women of every background tried their hand at homesteading.

Teddy Roosevelt had worried about "race suicide" among whites. He had worried that, lacking a physically demanding arena in which to prove themselves, the country's white men were becoming effeminate, unfit to rule. He wanted the United States to take its place among the new nation-based empires of the world. And, finally, he believed that men could mobilize science to conquer nature while preserving places of wilderness to restore modern men from the overwhelming stresses of daily life.

Four decades later the Border Patrol had joined the customs office in policing the national borders. New definitions of citizenship and race curated the region's population. Using the latest technology, enormous dams channeled the power of great rivers, expanding irrigation and generating electricity. National parks dotted remote areas from which Native Americans were excluded. Wartime necessity had endowed the region with new bases and modern ports, and in the name of building up the country and offering opportunity to white men, federal policies ensured dependence on and made perpetually vulnerable a Mexican migrant agricultural workforce. And despite and because of all these changes, the old myths had endured, including the love affair with the idea of the self-sufficient yeoman farmer and the U.S. West as the terrain on which he could best flourish.

The West was a land of contradictions. Boley, Oklahoma, and Yoncalla, Oregon, with their origins in dreams of opportunity for Black and white settlers, respectively, both survived in 1940. They each held less than a thousand inhabitants in a rapidly urbanizing West where Los Angeles reached a population of a million and a half.[1] Myriad newcomers each decade, lured by the promise of opportunity, mingled with the persistent pioneers. Every town in the West had its "pioneers," even if the town fathers usually excluded from that category the seventh-generation Spanish-speaking farmers in northern New Mexico and southern Colorado, the Chinese shopkeepers and service workers, and the Native Americans who against all odds held on to notions of peoplehood and sovereignty and often territory, negotiating with their new neighbors and their perpetual would-be conquerors. When the pioneers prospered, though the master narrative was about independence and self-sufficiency, it was often the result of collective activity—cooperatives, for example—and state and federal intervention.

Between 1898 and 1940 westerners and policy makers constructed the "modern West" out of contests over the meaning of that phrase. The contests encompassed the meaning of democracy and the nature of belonging—who was in and who was out. In many ways contests over participation in western history were the same as they had been from the start of European conquest. Federal government activism in the West was not new, but it took on new tasks and dimensions. From the start of this period at the very turn of the century it played a key part in encoding demarcations into the law and the landscape.

To become a nation able to make claims in a contest among empires, the federal government participated in creating and policing new categories of race and sexuality, wilderness and development, citizen and subject. Roosevelt and his peers in the federal government saw the U.S. West as a fitting arena to address many of these concerns. The Newlands Reclamation Act launched the federal government's foray into reengineering the western landscape. The Gentlemen's Agreement with Japan led to the first monitoring of land-based immigration. Treaties with Native Americans were unilaterally abrogated; Indian Territory became part of the new state of Oklahoma. And Roosevelt created one hundred national forests west of the Mississippi River.

Those carefully demarcated boundaries were often more fictive than material. Whatever barriers white westerners and their government erected, the West was never an isolated region with impervious edges. Colliding diasporas filled the territory with rival claimants asserting their rights to a piece of the dream and asserting their identity as constituent members of the region. Mexican revolutionaries, Filipino and Sikh anti-imperialists, and African American activists rubbed shoulders on picket lines and in jail cells during each of these decades. They found both allies and antagonists among the widely diverse Asian and European immigrants and white migrants.

Local inhabitants proved to have their own definitions of modernity, progress, and development and of the bounds of democracy itself. Copper and coal miners, timber workers and farmworkers demanded a democracy that encompassed the workplace and a notion of the region's opportunity that included them. Native Americans, who numbered among all those occupations and others, held fast to their claims to sovereignty and resisted the dismantling of their lands. In these efforts, women and men mobilized together, and people and ideas crossed national boundaries, as did the capital that spurred the large-scale economic development from Alberta to Sonora.

In the century's first decade, the swirling movement of workers and ideas collided with spectacular violence in the Pacific Northwest. Irishmen and Englishmen recruited other European-descent workers and, demanding the privileges of their whiteness, battled Sikh and Japanese immigrants. Mexican Americans clashed with Black federal troops stationed in border towns. In the second decade, the 1910s, in contrast, more often workers of every stripe joined together. Anticolonial Sikhs, leftist Japanese, revolutionary Mexicans, and dissident European-descent workers mobilized together. Diverse coalitions changed the conditions on the northern plains via the Nonpartisan League, elected women to national office, battled coal and copper corporations both North and South, and asserted their rights even in the context of war.

The success of these movements was dramatically curtailed by the U.S. entrance into the Great War. The necessity of war production and mobilization of troops made clear legibility of borders and peoples seem a requirement for survival. The demands of World War I on the domestic front facilitated the massive repression of such agitation both in official action by legislatures and municipalities and in vigilante action, which reached new depths of violence.

The people who emerged from that agitation and repression and from the sharp recession that followed the war often looked to other means to secure their participation in the modern West and the fulfillment of their dreams. Individual fabulous successes, wheat queens and oil kings, lured would-be imitators in the context of a lackluster economy for much of the region. People speculated in crops, mechanizing beyond their means; people speculated in oil; and people speculated on the very idea of the West. Federal and state governments fostered this shift from political to economic participation by their regulatory policies, as well as their Liberty bonds. But not all westerners were welcomed into that speculative arena. Farmer owners and agricultural corporations demanded low-cost labor to sustain their farms, often created with federal support. Pacific coast states passed laws preventing Asian immigrants from owning land. Realtors fostered racially segregated "modern" cities. And Hollywood went corporate but continued to create a narrative of western history (and so the history of the United States) that cast white men as the heroes, conquering the West and its peoples, and white women as the damsels in distress. These structures seemed to tie citizenship and belonging to whiteness and a particular version of economic participation.

These decades were the glory days of the white man's West. In the 1930s, with the spectacle of degraded white farmers in the national news, the language of the white man's West faded even as the exclusions that engendered it continued apace. "Mexican" became a federal census racial category in 1930 rather than a nationality. When Coloradans complained about the "aliens" and in the same breath the "Mexicans" on the state's relief rolls, they weren't particular about citizenship.[2] The interracial organizing of the Southern Tenant Farmers Union ran into the stumbling block of agrarian racial class formation in Texas. Newly displaced white tenants refused to join hands with black and Mexican sharecroppers and laborers.[3] They were fighting to maintain a vision of the West being redrawn under their feet.

Those desperate westerners on all sides drew the federal government into the fray. Striking cotton pickers early in the decade, teamsters and longshoremen at the midpoint, and farmers throughout demanded a rearrangement of the region's economy. Another Roosevelt, Franklin Delano Roosevelt, dealt a New Deal in the 1930s. The threads came together—the insurgent vision of inclusive democracy that extended to the workplace and the economy, the centralized planning that enabled grand projects to transform the landscape, and the balance of individualism and cooperation apparent in each decade.

The West suffered more from the Great Depression than other regions, and it disproportionately benefited from the New Deal. In the United States as a whole, the New Deal spent $399 per person, but in the Rocky Mountain states the figure was $716, in the West Coast states $536, and in the Great Plains $424. In Nevada the federal government spent $1,499 per person.[4]

Future president Lyndon Baines Johnson built his career on bringing these pieces together in the Texas Hill Country to the west of Austin and San Antonio. Having grown up among the eroded hills and struggling farmers, having watched his father, one of those drawn to farming in the aftermath of World War I, perpetually in debt and finally lose his farm altogether, Johnson concluded, "It was a family tragedy I never want to see duplicated." The region's farms lacked running water and electricity; life for the women was an endless round of drudgery, hauling water, boiling clothes, canning fruits and vegetables, and tending chickens. In 1931, back from his teens in California, Johnson was teaching high school when he got a job as a legislative secretary with the new U.S. congressman from the district and headed for Washington DC. Once there, Johnson, pointing to the overwhelming constituent mail, successfully pressured his reluctant boss to vote for the Agricultural Adjustment Act, and Johnson spent hours going from one county agent to the next, farmer to farmer, making sure that his district's farmers benefited. When the congressman from his home district died unexpectedly, Johnson was ready to step in. His predecessor had already been hard at work getting a dam and a conservation district, succeeding in late 1934 with the Lower Colorado River Authority (LCRA) Bill, and had then worked to ensure that Interior Secretary Harold Ickes would approve funding despite the opposition of Texas Power and Light, which sued to forestall the four dams that would generate power. In May 1935 Roosevelt approved $20 million for the LCRA, the third largest amount after the Hoover Dam ($38 million) and Grand Coulee ($23 million). Once in office, Johnson brought his constituents not only New Deal largesse but also a vision of rural development—small modern farms, conservation and reformed farming and financial systems, and controlled rivers. He also worked for the legislation and appropriations that could make the vision material reality—the planning, the power-generating dams, the agricultural extension work, and the loan programs.[5]

These programs and the movements that helped generate them were rarely as committed to equity as they were to order and economic opportunity for whites. Jobs programs and relief programs discriminated against Mexican Americans and African Americans in the West as elsewhere. But the West was not just an echo of a racist South in this regard. With its repeated invocations of "a white man's country," the West played a key role in establishing and maintaining a particular national racial formation that depended on the West for maintenance and legitimacy. Though that formation was perpetually contested by those it excluded, the West in that formation provided to a nation full of immigrants and racial diversity an avowedly white man's country. With all its inherent contradictions, this was the modern West in 1940.

NOTES

Introduction

1. Hansen, *Encounter on the Great Plains*, 100: "Nationally, 60 percent of the two million homesteaders who filed an initial claim failed to prove up." Hurt, *The Big Empty*, 1–8, offers the following numbers on homesteading: between 1900 and World War I, 100,000 people settled west of the Missouri River in South Dakota, and between 1898 and 1915, 250,000 people claimed land in North Dakota; in northeastern Colorado almost 75 percent of settlers filed their claims after 1900, and homesteading peaked in 1910. When the federal government opened unallotted Indian lands through lottery in West River Country, South Dakota, more than 100,000 men and women registered starting in July 1904; in 1908 six trains arrived daily in Pierre, South Dakota, bringing as many as 800 passengers a day seeking homesteads on the Rosebud Reservation. Texas retained control over its public lands when it entered the United States and created its own homesteading rules, creating just as much activity as elsewhere. The population of the Texas panhandle jumped 400 percent between 1900 and 1910, reaching over 89,000. Though women remained a minority of homesteaders (e.g., 20 percent of homesteaders in North Dakota), they tended to prove up (succeed in gaining title to the land) at the same rate as men. Except in Texas, women claiming homesteads, like men, had to be heads of household; Texas prohibited single women from filing claims. "By 1910," according to Hurt, "settlers had claimed all but the most arid portion of the Great Plains" (8).

2. On the significance of property, see Correia, *Properties of Violence*, 7. Hurt, *The Big Empty*, 6, in addition, points to the distinctiveness of the western landscape yielding "a sense of place," a theme less central to this volume. And on land as "a foundational form of wealth, a source of power," see Chang, *The Color of the Land*, 1.

3. Many other historians have made this point, including White, "Race Relations in the American West"; Smith, "'We Are Equal,'" 82; Taylor, *In Search of the Racial Frontier*, 17–18; and my own earlier work, Deutsch, "Landscape of Enclaves"; Deutsch, "Coming Together and Coming Apart"; and with Sanchez and Okihiro, "Contemporary Peoples / Contested Places."

4. Welke, *Law and the Borders*, 37–38. Welke also argues, as I will in the next chapters, that "while the particulars have differed over time and place, borders of belonging have been integral to the modern liberal order."

5. Rydell, *All the World's a Fair*, 106–209. On the analogous relationship between empire and nation-state in the British case, see Burton, "Who Needs the Nation?" (see p. 238 for patrolling the borders of the state, citing Appadurai [1993]; and throughout, colonialism as what "provided the opportunity for Britons of all classes to conceive of the nation and to experience themselves as members of a 'national culture'"). On giving an "impression of coherence," see Layoun, "The Female Body," 65. See Peavy and Smith, "'Leav[ing] the White[s],'" for one such particularly acute example at the Louisiana Purchase Exhibition in St. Louis in 1904, where, under the aegis of contesting schools of anthropology (like history, in the process of professionalizing as an academic subject and focused on physical human bodies), globally collected "natives" participated (when willing) in athletic contests for which they had no training in sports they had never seen and often never heard of largely to prove the superiority of the white race. The one glitch was the unquestioned superiority of the Fort Shaw women's basketball team, which in exhibition games at the fair and in the region helped popularize the new sport, bringing large audiences to witness their total dominance of the game. And on how people labeled "different" were exiled within the nation, see Bhabha, "DissemiNation," 300. For an exploration of these trends globally, see Lake and Reynolds, *Drawing the Global Colour Line.*

6. Rydell, *All the World's a Fair*, 106–209, quotation on 160.

7. Glassberg, *American Historical Pageantry*, 140; Rydell, *All the World's a Fair*, 106–209.

8. Welke, *Law and the Borders*, 45.

9. See Bederman, *Manliness and Civilization*; Hoganson, *Fighting for Manhood*; and Kaplan and Pease, *Cultures of U.S. Imperialism.* Roosevelt (*The Rough Riders*) also chronicled his experience in the Spanish-American War. Book review as quoted in Lake and Reynolds, *Drawing the Global Colour Line*, 101.

10. Quoted in Campney, *This Is Not Dixie*, 157.

11. Koshy, "Morphing Race into Ethnicity," 166, 169. On the trickiness of categorizing by race nationally, particularly where groups failed to fall into neat preexisting categories, see Gross, *What Blood Won't Tell.* Lim, *Porous Borders*, 2–5, points out this complexity in both the United States and Mexico along with the state's desire to create a legible population and police the racial borderlands; when Lim turns to the census, she points to the 1930 instructions that eliminated the category of "mulatto" and determined that all persons born in Mexico or with Mexican-born parents who were not definitely white, Negro, Indian, Chinese, or Japanese "should be returned as Mexican." Lim concludes, "By 1930, all suggestions of race mixing were officially erased" (5).

12. There are many fine works on the twentieth-century West with a variety of definitions concerning the landmass covered, one by the extraordinary

Earl Spencer Pomeroy and completed by his student, Etulain, *The American Far West,* which excludes the states on the western border of the Mississippi River, including Alaska and Hawai'i, and omits Texas as more southern than western. Pomeroy focused on rapid population growth, high immigration rates, and new technologies of agriculture, mining, and manufacturing and their "implications for laborers, capitalists, government and the inhabitants of farms and towns" (xxiii). He, too, found that his "governing theme . . . concerns the ways in which people in the West have become—and have not become—westerners and members of their western communities, not merely establishing their economic opportunities, but also redefining their relations with each other and the nation" (xxiv). The book, however, pays little attention to borders, the Mexican Revolution, and woman suffrage. A similarly fine book is Wrobel, *America's West.* It similarly omits those states bordering the Mississippi River and attends less to Alaska and Hawai'i; Wrobel attends more to the subregional differences in the West. He frames the key shift from nineteenth to twentieth century as "America developed its West in the nineteenth century, but the West, to no small degree, developed America in the first half of the twentieth" (1, 4). The book also takes a national rather than a more transnational bent but does more to cover electoral politics and cultural production.

13. These paragraphs and the following largely appeared in Cole and Parker, "Being American in Boley." I am reproducing the citations here. For examples of Indian cattle ranchers, see Iverson, *When Indians Became Cowboys*; and Green, *The Creek People,* 78. On market savvy, see U.S. Cong., S., Committee on Indian Affairs, *Report of the Select Committee* (1907), particularly vol. 1, J. Coody Johnson on Creek freedmen (441) and Dana H. Kelsey (589); and vol. 2, David Hodge (1299), Legus Perryman (1304–5), Mrs. Lila D. Lindsay (1311), and S. W. Brown (1312). And on how lease money went to enrich "men who are really white men and not Indians," see 55 Cong. Rec. 5552–53, 1917. On the women's basketball team, see Peavy and Smith, "'Leav[ing] the White[s],'" 238–57; and Bauer, *We Were All Like Migrant Workers Here,* 137–38. See also Deloria, *Playing Indian* and *Indians in Unexpected Places,* who reaches similar conclusions.

14. Theories about the U.S. West have long had a particularly intimate relationship with popular culture. In the 1990s, nationally, there was a renaissance of frontier imagery, including Black westerns, and a celebration of the centenary of Frederick Jackson Turner's seminal essay, "The Significance of the Frontier in American History." Turner's narrative of western history—popular in dime novels long before his professional talk and definitely popular with Theodore Roosevelt and Woodrow Wilson—is also a great national story, a sort of bible of exodus into the wilderness and redemption. And its seductiveness lies in the fact that anyone could test himself or herself by its terms. Many historians quietly and not-so-quietly suggested, as many had since the essay first appeared, that there had to

be a different story line. After all, it was not just wilderness that westering European Americans hoped to subdue, it was peoples and cultures. That Turner could exclude that part of the story and why he achieved a place in the historiography never equaled by Herbert Eugene Bolton was a statement about dynamics and power relations in the 1890s, a period of sustained mass migration globally, massive labor unrest, and the rise of modern European empires, Jim Crow, and a global color line. Turner's essay's enduring power, as well as its challenge, was a statement about power relations in the 1990s, about the United States' relation to the rest of the world, and about relations within U.S. borders. In the 1990s in the popular press, that enduring power was still evident—*Life Magazine*'s special April issue in 1993 presented it in its virgin glory. There are no Native American authors in the issue, though there is a story on a Native American healer, no Mexican Americans, no Asians, no features on those groups. This was not a "borderlands" concept of the frontier—no transnationalism here. By 2000 the challenge mounted to that dominant narrative had made more headway in the mass media. The film *Smoke Signals* enjoyed a modest popular success with its depiction of Indians. More mainstream, *Time Magazine*'s July 2002 coverage of the Lewis and Clark bicentennial had Indians alive and kicking and wearing modern dress; their identity was less essentialized: contemporary Indian women were depicted as having mixed ethnic heritage and different tribal affiliations. Mexicans were still invisible. Indians remained associated with the frontier and Mexicans with borders.

In the academy, that challenge to the Turnerian model coalesced into the new borderlands theory, emerging from cultural anthropology, geography, literary studies, postcolonial studies, and Latinx studies and drawing strength from a rising discourse of transnationalism. That change is reflected in early twenty-first-century "westerns" appearing on various media platforms—almost universally darker, as well as often culturally diverse and more sensitive to power dynamics, capital, and issues around borders.

15. Herbert Eugene Bolton is the iconic founder of the borderlands school; he had been Turner's student. His major book is *The Spanish Borderlands* (1921). Unlike contemporary borderlands scholars, he focused almost entirely on the Spanish imperial role, not the Mexican. See Montoya, *Translating Property*.

16. Bhabha, "DissemiNation," 291–322; Soja, *Thirdspace*; Bodnar, *The Transplanted*; and compare Welchman and Avalos, *Rethinking Borders*, 198: "There is, of course, no (unitary) *border*, just as there is (say) no singular *vision*; rather there are borders (and visions) whose constitution is the product of specific institutions and discourses." Quoted by Tatum, "On the Border," 96; and see Anzaldúa, *Borderlands / La Frontera*; Pérez, *The Decolonial Imaginary*. See also Layoun, "The Female Body," 65. Regarding Canada, see the contests over the admission of Sikhs; for example, Lake and Reynolds, *Drawing the Global Colour Line*; Saldivar, *Border Matters*, 79–80. See also Barber and Barber, *Nature's Northwest*, xii, 46.

17. According to Bhabha, "DissemiNation," moving margins to the center "disturbs the rationale for discrimination," it doesn't just change the object of analysis; and migrants are particularly problematic because, uncontainable within the boundary of a national culture, they are "themselves the marks of a shifting boundary that alienates the frontiers of the modern nation" (312, 315). Moraga, *Loving in the War Years*; Sandoval, *Methodology of the Oppressed*. This is a dilemma by no means localizable to the physical border or to Mexicans and Mexican Americans, as Peck, *Reinventing Free Labor*, testifies. We now can see these borderlands as places where nations struggled to produce modernity. See Stoler, "Tense and Tender Ties," 848–49. See Pérez, *Decolonial Imaginary*; and Shah, *Stranger Intimacy*.

18. See, for example, Reséndez, *Changing National Identities*; Leiker, *Racial Borders*; and Lim, *Porous Borders*, 11–14. Lim, along with Hernández in *Migra!*, sees the national border in a constant state of flux. To claim that this is a book about the "West" is already to start with a point of view, literally, and a particular historical narrative; others have pointed out that the U.S. "West" is Mexico's North and Asia's East.

19. Anzaldúa, *Borderlands / La Frontera*. See also recent work on the early twentieth century by Leyva, Stern, and Shah and on citizenship and immigration by Gardner and Gutiérrez, as well as Fregoso's interdisciplinary work on the border and transnational citizenship. And on violence and transnational capital on the border, see Soto, "A Run for the Border."

20. On Canada only offering homesteads to men, see Cavanaugh and Warne, introduction to *Telling Tales*, 11, 14.

21. For a few of the copious examples, see Goldman's older book, *Gold Diggers and Silver Miners*; on missionaries and boardinghouse keepers and the literature on picture brides, see Deutsch, *No Separate Refuge*.

22. See beet workers' demands for garden irrigation in Deutsch, *No Separate Refuge*; Jameson, *All That Glitters*; Murphy, *Mining Cultures*; Gordon, *The Great Arizona Orphan Abduction*. There is a subliterature on religious figures that can cross over into social justice figures, for example, the women of the Azusa Street Revival in the southwestern United States and Teresa Urrea. Like the stories of the occasionally prominent revolutionary women, these are not figures that organized women as women and for women's rights. On Urrea, see, for example, Perales, "Teresa Urrea"; Galarza, *Barrio Boy*, 15–16. Galarza's father, a Lutheran bookkeeper and supervisor on a hacienda, gave his Catholic mother a sewing machine for a wedding present. When they agreed to divorce by an exchange of letters, she sent her relatives to negotiate—she got the ring, Ernesto (1905–84), and the Ajax sewing machine to support them.

23. You could see women missionary "rescue" of various groups, including Chinese women and Japanese women in the United States in these terms; see Pascoe, *Relations of Rescue*; and on Issei Christian activism in northern California, Yasutake, *Transnational Women's Activism*, 122–25. Compare Stoler, "Carnal Knowledge," 52, 54, 62, 72. See, for example, Long, *The Great Southern Babylon*,

208–9. Compare Kramer, *The Blood of Government.* Pascoe, *What Comes Naturally,* 6, 8–9, 62–63, 118–19, and throughout. The lists of banned groups could be long. Arizona's 1931 law included five designated groups ("Negroes, Hindus, Mongolians, members of the Malay race, or Indians, and their descendants"), and Oklahoma (1907) and Arkansas (1911) adopted the "one-drop standards of racial purity." The five western states without such laws were Washington, New Mexico, Kansas, Iowa, and Minnesota.

24. See Shah, *Contagious Divides*; and Molina, *Fit to Be Citizens?*

25. Regarding performance of the state on the border, see Nevins, *Operation Gatekeeper,* particularly the introduction; but also Adams, *The Spectacular State.*

26. See, in this regard, Campomanes, "1898 and the Nature of the New Empire," quoting Oscar Wilde (1893): "The youth of America is their oldest tradition. It has been going on for 300 years" (134). And Campomanes: "It was to be oldest because it was eternal Nature all over again but also the youngest precisely because it was defined as a new beginning; and to be 'a land without history,' therefore, was ultimately to recapitulate nothing less than human History ('Civilization') itself, to keep it perpetually *renewable*" (134).

1. Man and Nature

1. *Genoa Weekly Courier* (Gardnerville NV), January 25, 1901. For an edited version of the address given during the Columbian Exposition in Chicago, see http://nationalhumanitiescenter.org/pds/gilded/empire/textl/turner.pdf.

2. Hurt, *The Big Empty,* 10. George H. Maxwell, "Nature's Storage Reservoirs," *Forester* 5 (August 1899): 185, quoted in Pisani, *To Reclaim a Divided West,* 286. The big jump in California irrigation came between 1900 and 1910. According to Henderson, *California and the Fictions of Capital,* 53, it was "a near-even exchange with decreasing grain acreage." See also his table (15), which includes Tulare County, California, which went from 86,854 irrigated acres in 1899 to 265,404 irrigated acres in 1909. Much of this development was financed by Californians' accumulated capital from mining and earlier agricultural enterprises. Thomas F. Walsh, "Humanitarian Aspect of National Irrigation," *Forestry and Irrigation* 8 (December 1902): 506, quoted in Pisani, *To Reclaim a Divided West,* 91–292; see also Bennett, "'Nature's Garden and a Possible Utopia,'" 233.

3. The exception was Utah, which Pisani, *To Reclaim a Divided West,* 293, calls "an irrigation commonwealth." In Utah 90 percent of farmers owned their land. On coal, see Smith, *Rocky Mountain Heartland,* 57. On Oregon and Idaho, cattle, sheep, and timber, consult Langston, *Forest Dreams,* 75–76; and among many others on the Southwest's land grants, see Warren, *The Hunter's Game,* 10–13, 71–75.

4. Wister, *The Virginian*; Lamar, *The New Encyclopedia of the American West,* 577–79; Mercer, *The Banditti of the Plains*; see also the film *Heaven's Gate*; and Slotkin, *Gunfighter Nation,* 172–74. Pisani, *To Reclaim a Divided West,* 245–46.

Pisani mentions the Union Pacific, Wyoming's largest corporation, providing the special railroad cars to carry the twenty-two hired gunmen and their associates from Cheyenne to Caspar. The Warren Livestock Company owned only about one-third of the roughly 285,000 acres it controlled and fenced a large swath eleven miles wide and twenty-five miles long, including much in the public domain. Carey remained active in the Wyoming Livestock Association. A failed irrigation development project—the largest in Wyoming—in which he had partnered in the mid-1880s, building one hundred miles of main canals and then unable to secure title to the public lands the canals would serve, led him to author the Carey Act (252). Underwood in 57 Cong. Rec. 6672, 1919, quoted in Pisani, *To Reclaim a Divided West*, 294–95. On an investigation of northwestern New Mexico in 1904 that found the whole area, Navajo and non-Navajo, overgrazed, with the worst area surrounding Gallup, outside the reservation, see Weiseger, *Dreaming of Sheep*, 128, 130. And on drought and overgrazing in the first years of the twentieth century, see White, *Roots of Dependency*, 219–20, 231.

5. Pisani, *To Reclaim a Divided West*, 294–98.

6. An Indian Territory socialist in 1901 quoted in Green, *Grass-Roots Socialism*, 27; and on the Farmers Union in Oklahoma, Indian Territory, and Texas and its alliance of small farmers and tenants, see Green, *Grass-Roots Socialism*, 54. Tucker, "Populism Up-to-Date," 198–201. See also Hurt, *The Big Empty*, 8–19, who argues that the approximately seventy thousand members in Oklahoma became a significant voting bloc, many drifting to the Socialist Party by 1908 because they found neither Democrats nor Republicans responsive, and the Socialist Party had come to recognize tenants as among the working class. Pisani, *To Reclaim a Divided West*, 292. On the northern Midwest of the United States experiencing a 1910 drought just as the Canadian Pacific Railway opened land for homesteading in Alberta and Saskatchewan, see Hansen, *Encounter on the Great Plains*, 100. And Jameson and Mouat, "Telling Differences," 187, 205–7, point out that an earlier southward migration had brought Canadian Populist leaders to settle in the United States.

7. Meeks, *Border Citizens*, 21; Pisani, *To Reclaim a Divided West*, 43, 49, 50. Pisani points out that Utah was exceptional in using its water law to discourage outside capital and limit settlement. On Tohono O'odham cultivating beans in the Sonoran Desert, see Worster, *Rivers of Empire*, 33. On the lack of water storage in these systems, see Jackson, *Building the Ultimate Dam*, 34.

8. Robbins and Barber, *Nature's Northwest*, 46, identify the low point of the North American Indian population at about 1900, while the rest of the population grew swiftly. Excerpt from the text of the Reclamation Act / Newlands Act of 1902; and Romero, "Ditches," 171.

9. Green, *Nevada*, 183, 192; Romero, "Ditches," 171, 173, quoted in Bennett, "'Nature's Garden,'" 228. Dewey, *Pesos and Dollars*, 60. Wimberly et al. point out that the booster literature presented Mexicans as a feature of the land "who could be legitimately exploited in the same way as the other fea-

tures of the area, like the plants, animals, land, and water" ("Peons and Progressives," 441).

10. Deutsch, *No Separate Refuge*, 38–39. Land and resources outside the market were widely posed as "waste" and "inefficient"; see, for example, Andrés, *Power and Control*, 3; Langston, *Forest Dreams*, 98, on the failure to put all things to commercial use as both a moral and an economic failure; and Tyrrell, *Crisis of the Wasteful Nation*, who puts the development of this discourse in global context.

11. Warren discusses the conversion of a "patchwork of local commons regimes that dominated the western landscape" to "a system of natural resources administration in which centralized powers play a large often dominant role" (*The Hunter's Game*, 10). *Report of the Special Committee of the United States Senate on the Irrigation and Reclamation of Arid Lands* (Washington DC, 1890), serial 2707, vol. 2, p. 148, quoted in Pisani, *To Reclaim a Divided West*, 43, as one reason the United States was unlikely to borrow Hispanic laws on water use. On the other hand, as Hundley points out in *The Great Thirst*, 135–37, 139, U.S. courts could make selective use of what they saw as Mexican precedent; in Los Angeles, if areas did not allow themselves to be annexed, they would not have access to water.

12. Fiege, *Irrigated Eden*, 42, 53, 71–72, 136–38.

13. Pisani, *To Reclaim a Divided West*, 75–76, 104.

14. Montejano, *Anglos and Mexicans*, 104, 109; Dewey, *Pesos and Dollars*, 57–59, 62.

15. Pisani, *To Reclaim a Divided West*, 37, 98, 104 (Fortier quote), 169. See also Dewey, *Pesos and Dollars*, 61. Even in South Texas the private projects, undercapitalized and relying on outside capital, frequently failed, with most land only selling in the 1920s.

16. Pisani, *To Reclaim a Divided West*, 287–90. On Newlands, who married a Comstock lode heiress, favoring irrigation as a social pacifier, see also Worster, *Rivers of Empire*, 160–62, 166–68.

17. *Idaho Republican* (Blackfoot), February 11, 1907; *Twin Falls News*, December 2, 1904; and D. W. Ross, *Biennial Report of the State Engineer to the Governor of Idaho for the Years 1899–1900* (Boise: Capital Printing Office, n.d.), 7, all cited in Fiege, *Irrigated Eden*, 11.

18. Pisani, *To Reclaim a Divided West*, 72, 73; Worster, *Rivers of Empire*, 116–24, 143–56, 165–68; Hundley, *The Great Thirst*, 116.

19. Definitions are from Lamar, *The New Encyclopedia of the American West*, 164, 784. Pisani, *To Reclaim a Divided West*, 252–53, on the Carey Act: each state with land defined as desert in the earlier Desert Land Act could select up to one million acres for reclamation; once individual tracts had been irrigated and occupied by settlers, the state received patents to the land. The states could construct their own hydraulic works or contract with private companies at a price per acre fixed by the state. Any money over what the state paid to the private contractor had to be used for further reclamation. Construc-

tion and settlement had to be completed within ten years of the act's date (1894–1904). No one could acquire more than 160 acres; the land could not be leased, and at least 20 of the 160 acres had to be cultivated by settlers. This act was part of the antimonopoly fervor in ranching states that still had lots of unclaimed water, for example, Wyoming, Montana, and Idaho. Settlers had to apply for water rights when they filed for land. See pp. 300–325 on the myriad, diverse local interests that had to be accommodated in the act.

20. Pisani, *To Reclaim a Divided West*, 273–74, 280. He succeeded where Wyoming senator Francis Warren had failed with a filibuster in 1899 (283–84).

21. Pisani, *To Reclaim a Divided West*, 254–59. The quotation about Cody's future is from *Cheyenne Daily Sun-Leader*, February 23, 1900; the other from W. F. Cody, *An Autobiography of Buffalo Bill* (New York, 1927), 327, both quoted in Pisani, *To Reclaim a Divided West*, 259. See also Bonner, *William Cody's Wyoming Empire*, for example, 49ff., particularly 55–56, 66, 137–38, 180–81, 203–5. On the amendment to the Newlands Act, see Bridges, *Morning Glories*, 39.

22. Andrés, *Power and Control*, 19–27.

23. State projects included the Twin Falls Land and Water Company, which opened its irrigation project in 1905, supplanting myriad family and village canals and ditches that diverted Snake River water for the benefit of farms. Fiege, *Irrigated Eden*, 12, 21, 23, citing *Twin Falls News*, December 2, 1904, 42, citing *Idaho First* 5 (September 1914): 3–6, re: Jessie Warrington (the publicist), "The Wonderful Redemption of a Desert: A Story of the Past, Present, and Future of the Famous Twin Falls Country" (94).

24. Fiege, *Irrigated Eden*, 30–31, for example, and 85; Pisani, *To Reclaim a Divided West*, 63–64, 67. By 1907 Idaho, Utah, Nevada, Montana, the Dakotas, Oregon, and Oklahoma each had a state engineer.

25. Fiege, *Irrigated Eden*, 98.

26. Jackson, *Building the Ultimate Dam*, 2, 5, 59–75; of Eastwood's seventeen dams, sixteen were built with private capital. Harris, "The Developers," 7–12.

27. Under these terms, the projects found few takers, and so the projects themselves needed to find alternative sources of income. In 1911 Congress allowed the projects to sell waters to farmers outside the projects and in 1914 extended the repayment period from ten years (which none of the projects met) to twenty years of graduated payments. Worster, *Rivers*, 175–78. On Idaho under the Carey Act, see Moore, "Idaho Elects a Jewish Governor."

28. Pisani, *To Reclaim a Divided West*, 322–23; Worster, *Rivers of Empire*, 170–76. The 1902 act led to the creation of a new division within the Geological Survey in the Department of the Interior called the Reclamation Service. In 1907 it became an independent agency and in 1923 was renamed the Bureau of Reclamation. Gerald Nash cites the Uncompahgre Project in southwestern Colorado as the first success of the Newlands Act, leading to increasing crops of lettuce, onions, beets, and apples by the engineering feet of tunneling below the Continental Divide to bring water from the Gunnison River, but the success was purely relative, according to Dudley, "The First Five."

Benton-Cohen, *Borderline Americans*, 35–36. On the legalities of water rights in Arizona, see Reich, "The 'Hispanic' Roots."

29. Benton-Cohen, *Borderline Americans*, 149–52, 156–59. See, for example, Deutsch, *No Separate Refuge*, 14, 21, 184; and Wimberly et al., "Peons and Progressives," 443, on Tejano subsistence ranchers. Montejano, *Anglos and Mexicans*, 104–5, also argues that it was not the introduction of commercial agriculture itself that spurred displacement for Mexican and even small Anglo *rancheros* but the introduction of "ready-made farm communities, transplanted societies from the Midwest and the North." It replaced paternalistic work arrangements with "contract wage labor and business rationality." The new communities ruptured cultural agreement on mutual obligation and respect that had tied the *ranchero* communities together. The displacement took on the character of a racial struggle as the Texas border regions were redrawn into new county and property-owning configurations.

30. Fiege, *Irrigated Eden*, 122–23, 125–27 (the list is a quote).

31. Montejano, *Anglos and Mexicans*, 143–44. It would take another decade before the white primary was thoroughly established, disenfranchising Mexican Americans in local elections.

32. Smith, *The Magnificent Experiment*, x, 4, 6, 9.

33. Smith, *The Magnificent Experiment*, 16–17, 26–29. Fowler moved in 1889 and Heard in 1895.

34. Smith, *The Magnificent Experiment*, 29, 40–41, 45–46, 52, 54–55, 57, 59, 65. Part of the difficulty was the number of users with prior rights to upstream water who did not join the project, particularly in Tempe. The company in question had demanded $200,000 for the site but settled for $40,000.

35. Smith, *The Magnificent Experiment*.

36. Smith, *The Magnificent Experiment*, 61, 65, 70, 72, 76, 78.

37. Smith, *The Magnificent Experiment*, 81, 89, 92, 94–95, 96. The Reclamation Service accepted a construction bid in February 1905 from the Denver company that built the Galveston seawall and proposed a two-year build for $1,147,600. Worster, *Rivers*, 172–73, on the dam height, also mentions the Apache, local Mexican, and Anglo hobo workers.

38. Smith, *The Magnificent Experiment*, 106, 109. The average crop value per farm on the Salt River was the highest of all Reclamation Service projects at $1,699, but with the cost of $45 per acre to repay, the farmer would still have little left at the end of the year. See also White, *Land Use*, 113, 115, 117, regarding similar dynamics around forests. And on foresters' "overreliance on universal scientific theories that made it increasingly difficult for them to value complexity, inefficiency, uncertainty, and redundancy—all the hallmarks of old growth," see Langston, *Forest Dreams*, 99.

39. Smith, *Rocky Mountain Heartland*, 23; Hurt, *The Big Empty*, 3. Hurt points out that women homesteaders, who made up 20 percent of North Dakota homesteaders, proved up as often as men. And see Wrobel, *America's West*, 38–39: western states, already growing rapidly in the 1890s, increased their

rate of growth from 1900 to 1910, with the exception of Kansas and Nebraska. Smith, *The Magnificent Experiment*, 157–58. Cotton in 1916 returned $125 per acre, and citrus returned similar amounts.

40. Burke, *A Land Apart*, 116; Robbins and Barber, *Nature's Northwest*, 47. U.S. Supreme Court, Winters v. United States, 207 U.S. 564 (1908) upheld treaty guarantees to reserved water rights, but often, as they did with the Umatilla River, non-Indian farmers continued to pump water "as if it were exclusively their own."

41. Hundley, *The Great Thirst*, 139–40.

42. Hundley, *The Great Thirst*, 141, 143–44, 146.

43. Hundley, *The Great Thirst*, 144–59.

44. Smith, *Pacific Visions*, 151–52.

45. Smith, *Pacific Visions*, 144–46.

46. Smith, *Pacific Visions*, 153–54.

47. Smith, *Pacific Visions*, 159, 160–63.

48. Smith, *Pacific Visions*, 161–64, quoting Muir in *Harper's Weekly*, June 6, 1898 (163) and citing John Ise, *The United States Forest Policy* (New Haven CT: Yale University Press, 1920), 135, 140–41, and Gifford Pinchot, *Breaking New Ground* (New York: Harcourt, Brace, 1947), 115. Correia, *Properties of Violence*, 76.

49. Nash, *The American West*, 31. See also Childers, *The Size of the Risk*, 16: the Forest Service, established in 1906, "supported primarily timber protection and harvest as a dominant use" whereas other land, including national parks, remained open to virtually anything that could lead to economic benefit, including grazing, wildlife management, and recreation, and all purposes were subordinate to settlement "under various land disposal laws" in keeping with the U.S. tradition of favoring private property.

50. Langston, *Forest Dreams*, 82–84, 87–88, 97, 110.

51. Smith, *Pacific Visions*, 174–75. See Hundley, *The Great Thirst*, 176–77. Denver had a similar water monopoly, the Denver Union Water Company, consolidating water delivery to the city beginning in 1894, according to Crifasi, *A Land Made from Water*, 276.

52. Smith, *Pacific Visions*, 175–76; Hundley, *The Great Thirst*, 115.

53. Smith, *Pacific Visions*, 166–70. The California Federation of Women's Clubs was formed in 1900, for example. Stern, *Eugenic Nation*, 23–124, on the coalition of scientists and female reformers who organized the Sempervirens Club to save the redwood groves on the Santa Cruz Mountains and the purchase in 1902 with the aid of the Native Sons and Native Daughters of California of almost four thousand acres in the Big Basin to create the state's first redwood park.

54. Smith, *Pacific Visions*, 171.

55. John Muir, "Hetch Hetchy Valley," *Sierra Club Bulletin* 6 (January 1908): 211, 220; Muir, *The Yosemite* (New York: Century, 1912), 261–62; and Muir, *My First Summer in the Sierra* (Boston: Houghton Mifflin Co., 1911), 205, 354, quoted in Hundley, *The Great Thirst*, 180. The intimacy of camping trips as recruitment

vehicles seems to have appealed to both groups, as when Muir camped with Roosevelt in Yosemite and when opponents Carrie Stevens Walter and photographer Andrew P. Hill included the largest shareholder in the Big Basin Lumber Company along with eight other men and two women in a three-day excursion in Big Basin as part of their campaign. Smith, *Pacific Visions*, 168.

56. Smith, *Pacific Visions*, 178–80; "Men of Science Oppose Hetch Hetchy Water Project," *Independent* (Berkeley), November 16, 1907 (178).

57. Nash, *The American West*, 165, quoting Muir, "The Tuolumne Yosemite in Danger," *Outlook* 87 (1907): 489; and Robert Underwood Johnson, now editor of *Century*, in "A High Price to Pay for Water," *Century* 86 (1908): 633.

58. Smith, *Pacific Visions*, 178 (quoting Manson to G. W. Woodruff, April 6, 1910, Manson Papers, Bancroft Library), 182–84. And see Rome, "'Political Hermaphrodites,'" who argues that this use of gender had "enduring consequences," making environmentalist men less willing to work with women (443) and pushing them toward a less sentimental (450) language of environmental reform. See Douglas, *The Feminization of American Culture.*

59. Nash, *The American West*, 171–81. Kent later authored the bill that created the National Park Service. Ironically, Hetch Hetchy's dam did not hinder the power of Pacific Gas and Electric, as it alone had the facilities to deliver the utilities to San Francisco. Hundley, *The Great Thirst*, 190–91; Smith, *Pacific Visions*, 172–73, 184–85.

60. Spence, *Dispossessing the Wilderness*, 101.

61. Spence, *Dispossessing the Wilderness*, 109, quoting Helen Hunt Jackson, *Bits of Travel at Home* (Boston: Roberts Brothers, 1878), 107, and John Muir, *The Mountains of California* (New York: Century, 1894), 93, on 110–11. See Bauer, *Work*, 106–56. The Indians were furious but gave way after initial resistance. See also Green, *Nevada*, 199, on the impact on Western Shoshones of the 2.1 million acres set aside for the Toiyabe National Forest and the new fees and limits that hurt their ability to continue using the land for grazing.

62. Rothman, *Devil's Bargains*, 71–73. In the 1890s it became common for Yosemite women (particularly Miwok and Paiute) to make baskets to sell to tourists, developing a lively trade that drew dealers from thousands of miles away.

63. J. Smeaton Chase, *Yosemite Trails: Camp and Pack-Train in the Yosemite Region of the Sierra Nevada* (Boston: Houghton Mifflin, 1911), 32–33, quoted in Spence, *Dispossessing the Wilderness*, 107–8. See Bauer, *Work*, 146; they also had to obey state game laws and purchase expensive hunting licenses, even for hunting on the reservation. See Jacoby, *Crimes against Nature*, 174–91, for similar patterns at the Grand Canyon. See Troutman, *Indian Blues*, 33, 35, 37, 44.

64. Spence, *Dispossessing the Wilderness*, 62–69, including Justice Edward Douglas White's opinion for the majority in Ward v. Race Horse, 163 U.S. 504 (1896), reprinted in the *Annual Report of the Commissioner of Indian Affairs, 1896*, 60–66. On the fate of the children, see Warren, *Hunter's Game*, 3, who also details (71–93) the difficulty New Mexico faced in shutting down Indian

hunting on their traditional territories now within private land grants owned by national and transnational elites, as well as the territory's official encouragement of killing Indians found hunting in the hopes of attracting federal attention and enforcement. According to Jacoby, *Crimes against Nature*, 129–39, white working-class poachers posed a similar annoyance. Local communities sympathized with poachers who hunted to feed their families or for their neighbors in hard times but not with commercial poachers.

65. Reid, *The Sea Is My Country*, 190–95, 228–29.

66. Dorsey, *The Dawn of Conservation Diplomacy*, 20–21, 33, 51, 63, 65–70, 72–75, 77, 112, 143. Reid, *The Sea Is My Country*, 211, points out that the legislative view saw the sea as a "highly regulated commons that favored non-Natives over indigenous people," privileging white commercial and sports fishing. And see White, *The Organic Machine*, 45–46.

67. Dorsey, *The Dawn of Conservation Diplomacy*, 105, 106, 134, 138–39, 143, 145, 148, 153, 157, 159.

68. Reid, *The Sea Is My Country*, 229. On the Lummis, see Robbins and Barber, *Nature's Northwest*, 49. On the Salish, who because of the erosion of fishing rights, being "cut off by law from centuries-old fishing grounds," and the allotment of their catch to white commercial fishers were forced onto the reservation and into a heavier dependence on wage labor over the first decade of the twentieth century, see White, *Land Use*, 71–73.

69. Warren, *The Hunter's Game*, 18.

70. See Stern, *Eugenic Nation*, for example: "The affinity between eugenic and environmentalist ideas about the purity and preservation of nature" had an origin in the Save the Redwoods League, supported "generously" by Charles M. Goethe, a Sacramento businessman who launched the Eugenics Society of Northern California (7). David Starr Jordan, president of Stanford University, cofounded the Sierra Club in 1900 and believed some species needed protection and preservation and others should be eliminated or excluded (22, 120); he also played a pivotal role in establishing the Eugenics Record Office in 1910. Madison Grant and John Muir both saw the redwoods as representing "the 'great race'" or "the noblest of a noble race," according to Stern, a "metaphor for defending race purity and ensuring the survival of white America" (124). Roosevelt's activism led to a 1907 amendment by an Oregon senator forbidding the president to set aside any additional land in the six northwestern states; before the measure could go into effect, Roosevelt set aside an additional 16 million acres, claiming to protect them from "land grabbers and . . . the representatives of the great special interests at the expense of the public interest." Altogether Roosevelt enlarged the national forests from 43 million acres to 194 million acres. Roosevelt, *An Autobiography*, 444; Scott, "The President and the National Parks."

71. Spiro, *Defending*, 63–64.

72. Spiro, *Defending*, 96–99, 143–293.

73. Romero, "Ditches," 188.

2. The Changing Meaning of Crossing Lines

1. Hundley, *The Great Thirst*, 206–9; Smith, *The Magnificent Experiment*, 153–54.

2. Montoya, *Translating Property*, 114–15, 125–27. On Montana, see Milner and O'Connor, *As Big as the West*; and Delaney's excellent dissertation on the younger Stuart brother, "'My Destiny to Wander.'" Hart, *Empire and Revolution*, 260. See also St. John, "Divided Ranges," 127.

3. Hart, *Empire and Revolution*, 193 on Greeley; 196, 211 on Doukhobors; 229 on debt peons; 236 on small businesses by 1902 investing $511,465,166; 239 on Mormons.

4. Truett, *Fugitive Landscapes*, 83–103. Things did not always run so smoothly. Like the squatters and homesteaders on the Maxwell Land Grant in the United States, some of the heirs on one grant Greene tried to purchase, though they owned just 6 percent of the grant, would not sell their rights and so retained control over the entire grant, resisting CCCC efforts at every turn. The state recognized their right to do so, and the CCCC could not afford to ignore what the state recognized.

5. Evans, *Bound in Twine*. Dramatic early twentieth-century expansion of wheat farming on the plains (Saskatchewan province alone went from just over thirteen thousand farms in 1900 to fifty-six thousand in 1906, producing 4.3 million bales in 1900 to 50 million in 1906) required baling, and baling required twine. Hart, *Empire and Revolution*: eastern capital developed the trans-Mississippi West (91); southwestern capital invested in Mexico (including particularly California, New Orleans, Texas, and Arkansas) but also the Northwest (92–94). In Portland, Oregon, four leading businessmen formed the Mexican Rubber Culture Company in 1902 (192). See, for example, Robbins, *Colony and Empire*, 35, on the huge land grants to groups financing and building the railroad concessions.

6. Evans, *Bound in Twine*, 41–45. See Gordon, *The Great Arizona Orphan Abduction*, 48–49. Under Díaz, 1 percent of rural families came to own 85 percent of the land, leaving 96 percent of Mexicans landless. See Hart, *Empire and Revolution*, 262: over 90 percent of municipal common land in Mexico, which had made up about 25 percent of Mexico's surface area, went into the hands of individual Mexican local and national elites in this period through privatization laws.

7. Deutsch, *No Separate Refuge*, 20.

8. Deutsch, *No Separate Refuge*, 23.

9. For example, see Montejano, *Anglos and Mexicans*; Lozano, *An American Language*, 39, 87, 91, 125; and see below on Arizona.

10. See Bederman, *Manliness and Civilization*; Hoganson, *Fighting for Manhood*; and Kaplan and Pease, *Cultures of U.S. Imperialism*. On the role of Mexico in this reformulation, see Stern, "Buildings, Boundaries, and Blood"; Jacobson, *Whiteness of a Different Color*; and Mount, "Nuevo Mexicanos." Thanks to Ernesto Chavez and John Nieto-Phillips. Lozano, *An American Language*, 39, 91.

11. Cantrell, "'Our Very Pronounced Theory.'" See also Bridges, *Morning Glories*, 66. The Texas poll tax disenfranchised almost two-thirds of the electorate, and Houston enacted its own city poll tax. Similar measures were enacted elsewhere: Albuquerque, New Mexico, had "faulty" registration lists; and both California and Arizona had literacy tests and registration requirements put in place by reformers with ties to eastern capital and Washington DC. See Noel, "'I Am an American,'" 433, on the new territories as a spur.

12. Myriad pageants and "world's" fairs were at pains to demonstrate the continuity. See Glassberg, *American Historical Pageantry*; and Rydell, *All the World's a Fair*. On citizenship, see Smith, *Civic Ideals*, 410–69. See Welke, *Law and the Borders*, 37–39: the new island territories were declared by the U.S. Supreme Court to be analogous to "domestic dependent nations" that "both protected the borders of belonging by rendering the racialized other . . . subject to, even dependent upon, white protection and tutelage, and firmly outside the rights that came with citizenship"; that language of protection and the denial of full citizenship mirrored discourses about U.S. women, feminizing the male and female inhabitants of the new possessions. See Nieto-Phillips, *The Language of Blood*, 82–83, for example, on petitioning for statehood.

13. 56 Cong. Rec. 33, 1711 (1900), quoted in Smith, *Civic Ideals*, 431; U.S. Congress, House, Industrial Commission on Immigration, *Reports*, ix. In other words, in James C. Scott's terms (*Seeing Like a State*) the United States now, officially, saw through the lens of "race."

14. Stern, "Buildings, Boundaries, and Blood," 78–79; Jacobson, *Whiteness of a Different Color*, 229.

15. Johnston, "The Spanish-American War," 16–17, quoting *Arizona Daily Star*, April 28, 1898, 2, and May 11, 1898, 2.

16. *Daily Optic* (Las Vegas NM), July 2, 1898, 2. The vision of the United States not as a republic, like Mexico, but as an imperialist power, like Spain, was anathema in U.S. territorial newspapers early in the war. See Johnston, "The Spanish-American War," 14–16.

17. *Daily Optic*, October 13, 1898. See the wonderful account of the land grant from pre-Spanish to the present in Correia, *Properties of Violence*, 76. And see Reich, "Western Courts," 81, 83. *La Voz del Pueblo*, March 20, 1897. And see Lozano, *An American Language*, 109. The paper also regularly reprinted news from elsewhere, particularly Texas, on the mistreatment of Mexicans in the United States, for example, *La Voz del Pueblo*, February 12, 1898, March 5, 1898, 2. The accusation had come from the major Republican territorial newspaper, the *New Mexican*, and was leveled at the Union Party of Populists and Democrats.

18. *La Voz del Pueblo*, April 2, 1898, 2, July 2, 1898. The Spanish-American War started on April 26, 1898.

19. *Daily Optic*, April 23, 1898, 2, April 15, 1898; *Daily Star* (Tucson), April 30, 1898, 1. The *Daily Optic*, in an article titled "New Mexicans' Loyalty," date-

line Santa Fe, April 29, reported that "telegrams from Santa Fe, Las Vegas, and other points in the territory have been sent to the President, imploring him to place New Mexico under martial law, as the petitioners fear an immense uprising among the overwhelming Spanish-speaking population against the Americans. Such telegrams are entirely uncalled for."

20. *Daily Optic,* May 16, 1898. See also Montgomery, *The Spanish Redemption,* 77.

21. *La Voz del Pueblo,* July 9, July 16, 1898. And see Noel, "'I Am an American,'" 433. That population figure was set by the 1787 Northwest Ordinance; in 1900 Arizona had 122,000 and New Mexico 195,000 residents; of the New Mexico population, at least 90,000 had Mexican heritage (437). *Daily Optic,* July 2, 1898. And see *Daily Optic,* October 10, 1898.

22. Leiker, *Racial Borders,* 127–28, citing E. E. Neal, an attorney, in his letter to federal investigators over an 1899 fracas between the U.S. troops stationed at Fort Ringgold.

23. *La Voz del Pueblo,* July 16, 1898, August 13, 1898, November 19, 1898, 1. On New Mexico's statehood battle, see also Holtby, *Forty-Seventh Star.*

24. *Daily Optic,* August 9, 1898, 2; see also August 10, 1898, 2, October 17, 1898. The sixty thousand were all non-Spanish American "races." On October 12, 1898, the *Daily Optic* claimed the vote ran five to one in favor of the "Spanish-Americans." See September 15, 1898, 2, for the quotation, italics added, and October 19, 1898, 2. Moreover, the paper condemned the "present governor of New Mexico in discriminating against the natives of this Territory in his appointment of military officers."

25. *Daily Optic,* October 31, 1898.

26. Lamar, *The Far Southwest,* 198–99. Also see the *Daily Optic,* April 26, 1898, 2. Conversation with Howard Lamar, June 2000. See Johnston, "The Spanish-American War," 12. In a similar vein, the *Arizona Daily Star,* May 13, 1898, 2, ran an article titled "The Anglo-Saxon," in which it claimed that an American was by definition an Anglo-Saxon. Simply being fluent in Spanish was enough to make a person suspect. *Arizona Daily Star,* May 18, 1898.

27. U.S. Congress, House, Industrial Commission on Immigration, *Reports,* 749–52 for statistics; 753 on mining. In regard to racial classifications, see, for example, Pascoe, *What Comes Naturally.*

28. U.S. Congress, House, Industrial Commission on Immigration, *Reports,* 759, 800, see Exhibit L, "Affidavit of Mr. Fred W. Wadham, Respecting Alien Labor and Asiatic Immigration." On Mexicans appearing in the *Monthly Catalog of U.S. Government Publications,* see February 1895, cases decided in the Court of Claims; April 1895, a case involving the Homestead entry of Francisco Mirabel; and July 1895, Superior Court cases.

29. U.S. Congress, Senate, Committee on Immigration, *Reports,* 255–56, 682–91, 256, 279, 280; Clark, "Mexican Labor."

30. Noel, "'I Am an American,'" 441, 447. On his relationship with McKinley, see Otero, *My Nine Years as Governor,* 28–35, and his later frustration with

Roosevelt (26, 217, 314). Nieto-Phillips, *The Language of Blood,* 8. And see Lipsitz, "How History Happens," 410.

31. Noel, "'I Am an American,'" 438, 445–46, on teacher and future governor Octaviano A. Larrazolo. Nieto-Phillips, *The Language of Blood,* 19, 126, 140–41, 145–51, 166; Lummis successfully replaced the "black legend" of Spanish colonial horrors with what Nieto-Phillips calls a "white legend," a Spanish colonial pastoral. Montgomery, *The Spanish Redemption,* 89–90. Rothman, *Devil's Bargains,* 85, on the rising status of archaeology leading Congress in 1906 to pass the Antiquities Act and establish Mesa Verde National Park.

32. Noel, "'I Am an American,'" 434; Nieto-Phillips, *The Language of Blood,* 85–89, 442–43; and see Montgomery, *The Spanish Redemption,* 76. See also Lozano, *An American Language,* 113, 119–34. On a more theoretical level, see Bhabha, "DissemiNation," 296, on rhetorical strategies of hybridity, masking, and inversion.

33. Noel, "'I Am an American,'" 444.

34. Nieto-Phillips, *The Language of Blood,* 13. Nellie Snyder as quoted from a local weekly, *The Review,* 14, 16. On women missionaries in Neomexicano villages, see Deutsch, *No Separate Refuge,* 63–86. A similar incident happened in Los Angeles in 1902 when clubwoman Caroline Severance, former abolitionist, outraged "Spanish American" women of the city who threatened to withdraw from that year's La Fiesta de los Flores; see Deverell, *Whitewashed Adobe,* 88.

35. Noel, "'I Am an American,'" 455; Nieto-Phillips, *The Language of Blood,* 89 (quotation), 91; Montgomery, *The Spanish Redemption,* 93. The proposed joint state was to be named Montezuma.

36. Noel, "'I Am an American,'" 435, 449–50, 459. Ironically, according to Burke, *A Land Apart,* 36, organized labor in Arizona wanted statehood in the hopes of getting prolabor legislation regarding hours, corporate taxes, and safety.

37. Rothman, *Devil's Bargains,* 70–71. See Gordon, *The Great Arizona Orphan Abduction,* 166–67, 192, 202 on the questionable character of some of the "Anglo" women, including a saloonkeeper's wife and a woman who performed in a hotel bar; 223–25 on the strike becoming identified as "Mexican" and the "white" workers, wooed by the company, dropping out.

38. Mariano Martinez, "'Arizona Americans': A Citizen of Mexican Descent Discusses Some of His Neighbors," *New York Times,* October 31, 1904, 8. Martinez's dateline was October 22, 1904. And see relevant press coverage in Weber, *Foreigners in Their Native Land,* 191–95, including from the *Tucson Citizen.*

39. Welke, *Law and the Borders,* 80.

40. Noel, "'I Am an American,'" 460–61, 463, 465; Nieto-Phillips, *The Language of Blood,* 92. On Jácome, see Sheridan, *Los Tucsonenses,* 96. According to Burke, *A Land Apart,* 37, the language provision disenfranchised ethnic Mexicans, as well as southern and eastern Europeans; almost half the precincts in the heavily Mexican-descent border county of Cochise could not hold primary elections because of voting restrictions.

41. Nieto-Phillips, *The Language of Blood*, 135–37.

42. Deutsch, *No Separate Refuge*, 88, according to Colorado Fuel and Iron in 1902. Emmons, *The Butte Irish*, 13.

43. Lipsitz, "How History Happens," 406. And see Hernández, *Migra!*, 25, 71.

44. Lim, *Porous Borders*, 2; Lew-Williams, "'Chinamen' and 'Delinquent Girls'"; and see Shah, *Stranger Intimacy*.

45. Emmons, *The Butte Irish*, 103–19; Thistlethwaite, "Migration from Europe."

46. Robbins and Barber, *Nature's Northwest*, 46. Hernández, *City of Inmates*, 119: the Mexican workers refused to join the AFL because it excluded Japanese workers. Haywood quoted in Andrews, *Killing for Coal*, 240. Brundage, *The Making of Western Labor Radicalism*, 155–56.

47. Jameson, *All That Glitters*, 161, 176–80, 201, 208, 209, 211, 212, 216–17, 220, 246. See also Andrews, *Killing for Coal*, 241–42; Brundage, *The Making of Western Labor Radicalism*, 138ff.; and Reitman, "The Politics," 215–16, on the different response of Colorado's 1901 governor, who sided with the miners. Hernández, *City of Inmates*, 102.

48. Gordon, *The Great Arizona Orphan Abduction*, 210, 51: "By 1910, three-quarters of active Mexican mines were U.S.-owned."

49. Smith, *Rocky Mountain Heartland*, 36; Gordon, *The Great Arizona Orphan Abduction*, 216–17, 219. See also Emmons, *The Butte Irish*, 148.

50. Robbins and Barber, *Nature's Northwest*, 45; Emmons, *The Butte Irish*, 23–24. See Smith, *Rocky Mountain Heartland*, 37, on the popularity of the Socialist Party in the Rockies; the Western Federation of Miners endorsed socialism, and Montana copper towns elected socialist mayors. Gordon, *The Great Arizona Orphan Abduction*, 214.

51. Gordon, *The Great Arizona Orphan Abduction*, 57–59, quoting Morris J. Elsing, "Mining Methods Employed at Cananea, Mexico," *Engineering and Mining Journal-Press*, November 5, 1910, 914–17. The coal mines of southern Colorado had similarly high rates of turnover (see Deutsch, *No Separate Refuge*).

52. Gordon, *The Great Arizona Orphan Abduction*, 62–63, 214, 219. In Mexico copper miners earned $1.50 at best.

53. Gordon, *The Great Arizona Orphan Abduction*, 220.

54. Benton-Cohen, *Borderline Americans*, 81–82, quoting Clarence King, *The United States Mining Laws and Regulations Thereunder, and State and Territorial Mining Laws, to Which Are Appended Local Mining Rules and Regulations* (Washington DC, 1885), 254, 267 on 85, 96, 99, 100. See also Emmons, *The Butte Irish*, 256–58, on immigrants from the Austro-Hungarian Empire and a 1910 series, "The Bohunk Invasion," in the *Butte Evening News*. One article called them "European Chinamen" and credited them with destroying two Colorado mining towns, Leadville and Cripple Creek, by driving out the Irish.

55. Deutsch, "Coming Together," 58–61. See Benton-Cohen, *Borderline Americans*, 85–86, on the Dillingham Commission's conclusion that "only racial discrimination can explain the great differences . . . between the wages

of these Mexican surface laborers and those of native-born and north European employees engaged in other kinds of common labor."

56. The following account of the strike relies heavily on Gordon, *The Great Arizona Orphan Abduction*, 221–33, 235–36, quoting Rynning, *Gun Notches.*

57. Gordon, *The Great Arizona Orphan Abduction*, 238–40. The townspeople blamed the company for the flood and asked for $100,000 in estimated damages. The company ultimately paid $10,000.

58. Gordon, *The Great Arizona Orphan Abduction*, 223, 225, 230; Truett, *Fugitive Landscapes*, 138.

59. Graybill, *Policing*, 117–18, 167–200.

60. Graybill, *Policing*, 194; Gordon, *The Great Arizona Orphan Abduction*, 225.

61. See, for example, Peck, *Reinventing Free Labor.* Peck argues for a connection between transience and being cast as nonwhite (166), so that Greeks and Italians, who often came in as contracted labor, were not included in the term "white" when contemporaries listed groups but instead were often listed with Mexicans, Chinese, and "Negroes." That instability became part of the instability of racial categories at the time (see, e.g., 168–69).

62. Chang, "Circulating Race and Empire," 155–56, on Haywood's announcement.

63. Benton-Cohen, *Borderline Americans*, 93. On the role of Irish immigrants in the nineteenth-century anti-Chinese movement, see Saxton, *Indispensable Enemy.*

64. Chang, "Circulating Race and Empire," 683–84, 693–96, quoting *B.C. Saturday Sunset* (Vancouver), July 16, 1907. Lake and Reynolds, *Drawing the Global Colour Line*, 164. Canada had disallowed British Columbia's attempt to prevent Japanese immigration on the grounds that it violated imperial interests. Chang, "Circulating Race and Empire," 700. Chang calls these "imperial circuits of knowledge production" (681). See also Jensen, *Passage from India*, x, 3.

65. Chang, "Circulating Race and Empire," 687–89. The name change came in December 2007. The Asiatic Exclusion League established at least nine branches in Washington and British Columbia. See also Chang, "Enforcing Transnational White Solidarity," 29–33.

66. Chang, "Circulating Race and Empire," 689–90; Chang, "Enforcing Transnational White Solidarity," 683; Lake and Reynolds, *Drawing the Global Colour Line*, 181–82.

67. Chang, "Enforcing Transnational White Solidarity," 684. The Canadian agreement was called the Hayashi-Lemieux Agreement. The agreements went into effect in 1908. Lake and Reynolds, *Drawing the Global Colour Line*, 179–80, on the poll tax and the Colonial Office noninterference. Thompson, *Forging the Prairie West*, 73. See Geiger, "Caught in the Gap," 202–3, on Britain repeatedly disallowing British Columbia's efforts to pass exclusionary laws that echoed those of Natal against Japanese immigrants. See also Lee, *At America's Gates*, esp. chap. 5.

68. Chang, "Enforcing Transnational White Solidarity," 681, 686; and Chang, "Circulating Race and Empire," 687. Lake and Reynolds, *Drawing the Global Colour Line,* 191, on Roosevelt; see also 173–77. And see the *Vancouver Saturday Sunset* 1907 cartoon "THE SAME ACT WHICH EXCLUDES ORIENTALS SHOULD OPEN WIDE THE PORTALS OF BRITISH COLUMBIA TO WHITE IMMIGRATION," depicting a mass of disembarking shipboard arrivals coming toward two gates, "Oriental Exclusion," which remained closed, and "White Immigration," with a welcoming Britannia holding the gate wide open (courtesy of Tamara Extian-Babiuk).

69. Chang, "Circulating Race and Empire," 688, 691. On collaborative policing of smuggling rings trafficking in Chinese workers across the United States, see also Lim, *Porous Borders,* 114ff. Chang, "Enforcing Transnational White Solidarity," 682, 684–85. U.S. Immigration Bureau inspector-at-large Marcus Braun wanted as many officers (sixty) on the Washington–British Columbia border as patrolled the 1,900-mile U.S.-Mexico border. By 1910 they had fifty officers and a string of substations placed in most U.S.-Canada border towns. See Lee, *At America's Gates,* 178–79, on the trajectory of Canada's efforts to exclude Asians, culminating in prohibition of all people of Chinese origin or descent, with few exceptions, in 1923, and on the rockier collaboration between the United States and Mexico (180–84).

70. This quotation appears in both Chang, "Circulating Race and Empire," 685, and Chang, "Enforcing Transnational White Solidarity," 683; he cites Everett Crawford's piece republished in the *Everett (WA) Labor Journal,* May 6, 1910.

71. Lake and Reynolds, *Drawing the Global Colour Line,* quoted on 241–42; Stern, *Eugenic Nation,* 34–35.

72. *Montreal Daily Star* and *Vancouver Daily Post* 1908 courtesy of Tamara Extian-Babiuk. And see Thompson, *Forging the Prairie West,* 74–75; Jensen, *Passage from India,* 42; Lee, *At America's Gates,* 4, 68, 81, 125.

73. Sadowski-Smith, "Unskilled Labor Migration," 788. See Geiger, "Caught in the Gap," 210, on Mexico and Japanese migrants.

74. Hart, *Empire and Revolution,* 261.

75. Hernández, *City of Inmates,* 104–5.

76. Truett, *Fugitive Landscapes,* 144–45.

77. Truett, *Fugitive Landscapes,* 139, 145–46.

78. Truett, *Fugitive Landscapes,* 146–48.

79. Truett, *Fugitive Landscapes,* 149. It was, however, Greene's swan song. He soon lost control of the company, and in the financial Panic of 1907, mining officials closed Cananea, opening a completely overhauled company in mid-1908 (149–50). Young, "Deconstructing *La Raza,*" 247–53.

80. Hernández, *City of Inmates,* 106–9, 111.

81. Hernández, *City of Inmates,* 118–20.

82. Evans, *Bound in Twine,* 69, 73. The colony in Tucson is still the largest Yaqui enclave in the United States. Burke, *A Land Apart,* 95, points out

that the lack of a reservation in the United States made the Yaquis particularly vulnerable.

83. Evans, *Bound in Twine*, 70–81.

84. Truett, *Fugitive Landscapes*, 142. See Peck, *Reinventing Free Labor*, 94–95, 100–104, 110–12. On the Canadian Agreement of 1901 and 1903 expanding collaboration between U.S. officials and Canadian transportation companies and, as on immigration, the rockier relationship with the Mexican government, see 94–95. Evans, *Bound in Twine*, 70–81.

85. Delgado, "Border Control and Sexual Policing," 165.

86. See Young, *Catarino Garza's Revolution*, on both the antifederal and anti-*federale* sentiment on both sides of the border and Garza and his followers, as well as their legacy. Leiker, *Racial Borders*, 13, 119, 122. On Cortez, see the classic analysis by Paredes, *With a Pistol in His Hand.* See Young, "Deconstructing *La Raza*," 238, 242, 245–46. Border elites were divided over Díaz. In Laredo, Tucson, and elsewhere, elite pro- and anti-Díaz activists took refuge. See also Sheridan, *Los Tucsonenses*, 93, 106, 166; Leiker, *Racial Borders*, 119, 122.

87. Leiker, *Racial Borders*, 124–28, citing McKibbin to AG, December 4, 1899, Adjutant General's Office, file 296983, RG 94, National Archives, Washington DC. And see p. 133 (quote) and p. 137 on Brownsville's police, who, according to witnesses, were "eager and overzealous to do their duty, especially with the soldiers," whom they arrested for minor infractions, in contrast to civilians, even before 1906. See Mckiernan-González, *Fevered Measures*, 40ff., for Brownsville's earlier tensions with federal authority over quarantine enforcement.

88. Leiker, *Racial Borders*, 129, 130. According to Leiker, there were four hundred Black merchants and professionals in El Paso. See p. 118 for an 1899 Laredo incident. The guides misled the U.S. soldiers and refused to track at night even in bright moonlight. The commander complained, "I was therefore compelled to camp within a few miles of the outlaws." Hedekin to Post Adj., December 30, 1892, in Garza Revolution Papers, Records of the U.S. Army, RG 393, National Archives, Washington DC, 2, quoted in Young, *Catarino Garza's Revolution*, 214, 230. And see Taylor, *In Search of the Racial Frontier*, 176–78, on tensions in Brownsville.

89. Leiker, *Racial Borders*, 131–33.

90. Leiker, *Racial Borders*, 135, 137, quoting Blocksom testimony, in U.S. Congress, Senate, *Report on the Brownsville Affray*, 430. According to Leiker, on August 10, three days before the violence, two enterprising soldiers opened a "Negro beer joint."

91. Leiker, *Racial Borders*, 135–36, 138–39.

92. Leiker, *Racial Borders*, 138–39; Gerstle, *American Crucible*, 33–38. See Lake and Reynolds, *Drawing the Global Colour Line*, 112, on Roosevelt.

93. Leiker, *Racial Borders*, 139, 140–41, 142.

94. Perales, "Teresa Urrea." See also, on religion, Espinosa, "'Your Daughters Shall Prophesy,'" 25–28, on the Azusa Street Revival, 1906–9.

95. Weisiger, *Dreaming of Sheep*, 100: by the 1890s "weaving had become a form of wage labor" but also "a spiritual process." On Canadian women, see Jameson and McManus, introduction to *One Step*, xxii.

96. The law was part of Oregon's blend of Populism and Progressivism, which also led to initiative and referendum in 1902 and direct primary in 1904. See Haarsager, *Organized Womanhood*, 248–49. See also Robbins and Barber, *Nature's Northwest*, 50–51; Deutsch, *No Separate Refuge*, 93.

97. Gardner, *The Qualities of a Citizen*, 73, 78–79. On the Gentlemen's Agreement and the Immigration Act of 1903, which "mandated the deportation of all immigrants who became public charges within two years of entering the United States" and "excluded prostitutes, procurers, and anyone who tried to bring a woman to the United States for purposes of prostitution" (pregnant women were particularly suspect of becoming public charges), see Luibhéid, *Entry Denied*, 9, 11, 55, 58–60. The 1907 act added the new provision mandating the deportation of any woman who began practicing prostitution within three years of entering the United States, even if she had never previously practiced prostitution; Japanese women entering under the Gentlemen's Agreement had to be married. See also Delgado, "Border Control and Sexual Policing," 160, 162. The Page Act of 1875 had only excluded sex workers from Asia; the prohibition of alien women and girls from prostitution for three years after arrival was a provision initially part of the 1902 International Agreement for the Suppression of the White Slave Traffic, an accord the United States had not ratified at the time but did in 1908.

98. Delgado, "Border Control and Sexual Policing," 164, 172. Despite U.S. efforts, Delgado makes clear there was a robust traffic in prostitutes back and forth across the border (e.g., 167, 173). Regarding the northern border, see Barman, "Writing Women," esp. 117. Gardner, *The Qualities of a Citizen*, 87–89, 97–99.

99. Anderson, "The Idea of Chinatown." And see Wong, "The 1903 Boston Chinatown Raid." Shah, *Stranger Intimacy*.

100. Greenlee, "Due to Her Tender Age," 14–15. See Delgado, "Border Control and Sexual Policing," 168, on Galveston's red-light districts in 1909; in Arizona and New Mexico Territories, according to Delgado, prostitution "was neither socially encouraged nor explicitly criminalized." In New Mexico an ordinance required prostitutes to pay a monthly vagrancy fee of $5 and submit to regular medical examinations (170). Long, *The Great Southern Babylon*, 181–82, 209. Boyd, *Wide Open Town*, 42. In Los Angeles the 1902 amendments to the city charter outlawed gambling and prostitution within the city limits instead of, as previously, limiting those activities to a segregated zone; see Woods, "A Penchant for Probity," 105.

101. See, for example, Pascoe, *Relations of Rescue*; and Deutsch, *Women and the City*.

102. From *The Hieroglyphics of Love: Stories of Sonoratown and Old Mexico* (1906) quoted in Lewthwaite, *Race, Place, and Reform*, 1.

103. Brundage, *The Making of Western Labor Radicalism*, 157; Streeby, *Radical Sensations*, 4. Regarding contemporary investigators, see Emma F. Langdon, *A History of the Industrial Wars in Colorado, 1903–4–5* (1905) as quoted and cited in Slotkin, *Gunfighter Nation*, 157.

3. Being American in Boley, Oklahoma

1. Wickett, *Contested Territory*, 109. By 1900 most wealthy Native Americans had white farmers on their estates; the Creek chief Pleasant Porter employed over one hundred white men on his four-thousand-acre ranch. African American farm ownership rates surpassed those of white farmers in both Indian and Oklahoma Territories in 1900; over 75 percent of Black farmers owned their farms, and only 46 percent of the much larger number of white farmers did. And see Chang, *The Color of the Land*, 81, 91–92, 158; Massachusetts senator Orville Platt, member of the Dawes Commission, speaking to whites in the Choctaw Nation, "lamented that in Indian Territory 'the white man' was reduced to the status of a 'ward of the Indian, and a neglected ward at that'" (81). Platt would go on to offer the Platt Amendment in 1903, extending U.S. control over Cuban foreign relations, fiscal affairs, and, ultimately, government. Warde, *George Washington Grayson*, 175; Thompson, *Closing the Frontier*, 77–79, 83. In response to the demands of poor, disenfranchised whites in Indian Territory, the Populists lobbied for joint statehood of Indian and Oklahoma Territories. May, *African Americans and Native Americans*, 229: by 1900 Indian Territory held twenty-three all-Black communities; most were built on freedmen allotments in the Creek Nation; only five were ever founded in Oklahoma Territory.

2. Chang, *The Color of the Land*, 53–54, 58–61. Often, but not always, these were operated by whites who leased Creek land, but "in 1887 the U.S. commissioner of Indian Affairs estimated that 61 Creek citizens controlled 1,072,251 acres, almost one-third of the Creek lands" (59).

3. Quoted in Chang, *The Color of the Land*, 74.

4. On the failure of allotment when tried by other tribes, see U.S. Congress, Senate, Committee on Indian Affairs, *Report*, 1:623. And see Warde, *George Washington Grayson*, 186–208. On the ratification, see Saunt, *Black, White, and Indian*, 179. See Chang, *The Color of the Land*, 89, on the negotiations from 1898 to 1899, when a referendum provided a narrow victory for allotment. A 1902 supplementary amendment abrogated all Creek Nation laws of descent. May, *African Americans and Native Americans*, 115; May places the uprising in 1902. This late allotment was not unique to the Five Civilized Tribes; in 1901 U.S. Indian inspector James McLaughlin negotiated an agreement with the Spirit Lake Dakotas to allot their "surplus" reservation land; Congress dragged its feet and only passed relevant legislation in 1904, when the surrounding Scandinavian and Yankee communities greeted the measure with a "hail of joy," as quoted in Hansen, *Encounter on the Great Plains*, 94–95. See Harmon, *Rich Indians*, 3–4, 164, 168, on the contradictory attitudes of policy makers toward wealthy whites and wealthy Indians.

5. Wickett, *Contested Territory*, 52, quotes Chitto Harjo, who would lead the resistance to allotment: "I hear that the Government is cutting up my land and is giving it away to black people. . . . These black people, who are they? They are negroes who came here as slaves. They have no right to this land. It was never given to them. It was given to me and my people and we paid for it with our land back in Alabama." McIntosh, "Chitto Harjo," 121; U.S. Congress, Senate, Committee on Indian Affairs, *Report*, 2:1252.

6. May, "Collision and Collusion," 315–16, 320; U.S. Congress, Senate, Committee on Indian Affairs, *Report*, 1:440–41 (statement of J. Coody Johnson). Johnson held that few Creek freedmen spoke English and that two-thirds had been induced to sell their lands "for a very inadequate consideration." See also 1:v, 620–21 (Pleasant Porter); and 1263–64, 1267, 1271 (Mr. M. L. Motte). Chang, *The Color of Land*, 117–18. In 1901 Congress had required allottees to set aside 40 acres of their 160-acre allotment as a "homestead," inalienable and not subject to taxes; the "surplus" 120 acres could not be sold for five years. But in 1904, bowing to pressure from would-be land buyers, "Congress injected racial difference into the previously race-blind restriction laws" (117). Black Creeks who had selected allotments where they lived held among the richest lands in Oklahoma, along the Arkansas River. In 1904 Congress removed all restrictions on "surplus lands" of adult allottees "not of Indian blood" (i.e., Black Creeks), making 549,480 acres available for purchase. It also made the lands taxable with statehood. In 1908 Congress lifted restrictions on the homesteads. In contrast, the 1906 law placed more restrictions on "full-blood" land for the Five Tribes, disallowing sale or encumbering the land for twenty-five years. See Washington, "Boley," 31; and see Saunt, *Black, White, and Indian*, 161–62.

7. According to www.native-language.org/oklahoma.htm (accessed June 20, 2019), the Creeks would have moved onto the territory at the intersection of the Wichita to the south, Caddo to the southeast, Osage to the northeast, and Kiowa and Kiowa Apache to the northwest. See www.theamericanindiancenter.org/oklahomatribal-history (accessed June 20, 2019) on how most of these tribes had headed into the territory after European contact; the United States resettled them on reservations in Kansas and Nebraska when the government removed the Five Civilized Tribes to Indian Territory.

8. Washington, "Boley," 31.

9. Washington, "Boley," 28; Crockett, *The Black Towns*, 35. See also Taylor, *In Search of the Racial Frontier*, 149–51. Taylor cites historian Kenneth Hamilton's figure of forty-six Black towns in five western states and territories in the late nineteenth and early twentieth centuries; according to Taylor, it was two white entrepreneurs, William Boley and Lake Moore, who hired African American Tom Haynes to promote the Black town. By 1907, according to Taylor, the town had a thousand residents and another thousand in the surrounding area.

10. Washington, "Boley," 28.

11. Washington, "Boley," 29.

12. Washington, "Boley," 29.

13. Washington, "Boley," 30, 29. The "vanishing race" trope is extensive, and the intersection with the perils of intermarriage was common. One pertinent example is the 1908 novel *The Man of Yesterday: A Romance of a Vanishing Race*, a potboiler by Mary Holland Kinkaid about a Chickasaw woman torn between the love of an Indian and a white man; when the white lover betrays her, the Indian lover kills him in revenge. Washington Grayson picked up the novel in 1914; see Saunt, *Black, White, and Indian*, 178.

14. Washington, "Boley," 30–31. Chang finds about twenty all-Black towns founded in this era in Oklahoma and Indian Territory, with Langston in Oklahoma and Boley in Indian Territory the largest. Zellar, *African Creeks*, 238, finds thirty-two all-Black towns in Oklahoma by 1907, all but a handful in Creek country, many emerging from African Creek settlements. Both Boley and Clearview were established on African Creek allotments. Hahn, *A Nation under Our Feet*, 454–55, claims "more than 20 in Oklahoma" such towns and even more in the Deep South. He sees them as part of a "separatist impulse" and Oklahoma's as part of the migration of about one hundred thousand African Americans to Oklahoma between 1890 and 1910, including many from Arkansas, as well as other parts east and south.

15. Chang, *The Color of the Land*, 152.

16. Pascoe, *What Comes Naturally*, 98. They included Washington, Nevada, Idaho, Arizona, and Oregon. Oklahoma Constitution, article 23, section 11; Reese, *Women of Oklahoma*, 61; U.S. Congress, Senate, Committee on Indian Affairs, *Report*, 1:697 (Miss Alice Robertson). On the meaning of "Oklahoma," see Chang, *The Color of the Land*, 1.

17. Martin, *Sacred Revolt*, 72–73, citing Eugene Current-Garcia and Dorothy B. Hatfield, eds., *Shem Ham & Japheth: The Papers of W O Tuggle Comprising His Indian Diary Sketches & Observations, Myths and Washington Journals in the Territory & at the Capital, 1879–1882* (Athens: University of Georgia Press, 1973), 37. Africans had come to the Creek Nation in the East as traders, escaped slaves, and enslaved people well versed in European American technology. Because Creeks at that time did not organize themselves by color or ethnicity, even slaves could travel freely, own property, and marry into the owner's family; often the children of the enslaved were free. See also Littlefield and Petty-Hunter, *The Fus Fixico Letters*, 56n2. And see Chang, *The Color of the Land*, 21, 24. See Warde, *George Washington Grayson*, 200–201, regarding Legus Perryman, Grayson, and Pleasant Porter, though the latter in 1904 joined a Cherokee man trying to organize a political party limited to "Indians by blood," which "explicitly excluded blacks"—probably freedmen rather than Afro-Creeks, who would, by matrilineal descent, have been "Indians by blood" rather than Indians by grant of citizenship after the Civil War. U.S. Congress, Senate, Committee on Indian Affairs, *Report*, 1:1973: J. George Wright, U.S. Indian inspector, provided a table listing those enrolled by the Dawes

Commission as 6,692 "full-blood," 3,371 "mixed-blood," and 5,636 freedmen, with 1,017 Indian children and 569 freedmen's children, for a total of 17,285 Creeks. Newer literature on the Five Civilized Tribes in this era has focused on the racial complexity with more nuance. See, for example, Saunt, *Black, White, and Indian*; May, *African Americans and Native Americans*, xv, who writes, "so-called freedmen among the Creeks and Cherokees had often been free relatives of the Indians bound only by tribal customs"; Wickett, *Contested Territory*; Schreier, "Indian or Freedman?"; Chang, *The Color of the Land*; Zellar, *African Creeks*; Miles, *Ties That Bind*; and Naylor, *African Cherokees*.

18. Chang, *The Color of the Land*, 10, 40, 44 (quotation), 55, 67–68, 82–83, 102–4. The creation of towns was "a long-established way of incorporating new peoples into the nation, following the practice and logic of the old Muskogee confederacy." In this case it both "kept the bulk of black Creeks outside the other Creek towns" and "gave black Creeks seats in both houses of the National Council" (55). Chang sees this redefinition of membership as the most significant break with tradition and as evident in the Four Mothers Nation movement, intertribal (Creeks, Cherokees, Chickasaws, Choctaws) only for "full-bloods." Chang concludes, "Making property and codifying race were two inseparable parts of the American attempt at unmaking the Creek Nation and remaking its people" (104). In a symbolic final blow to the place-based nature of Creek identity, in 1902 the United States rented the Creek Council House as a courthouse.

19. For an example of a positive statement, see U.S. Congress, Senate, Committee on Indian Affairs, *Report*, 1:440–41 (statement of J. Coody Johnson); and see 648, 697–98; Pleasant Porter (reputedly himself having some African descent), wealthy cattle rancher and Creek chief, used derogatory language to refer to Creek freedmen and the increase in their numbers. Debo, *The Road to Disappearance*, 290, 331–33; Wickett, *Contested Territory*, 52–53, 179, on the Guthrie paper complaining in the 1890s that Republicans imported destitute Kansas "negroes" to vote; and see Savage, "Lynching, Race, and the Law," 11, for Black Kansas railroad workers in Colorado—the paper covered ten reported lynchings of Black men in Colorado in those years and pointed out that the difference with the South was less the alleged crimes of the lynched than the split response of the general Colorado population; and see Campney, *This Is Not Dixie*, 156, on rising racial violence in that state between 1903 and 1906. May, *African Americans and Native Americans*, 224, 230. On Porter, see Zellar, *African Creeks*, 227. Chang, *The Color of the Land*, 26–30, 33–34, 36, 40, 95, on the splits between elite, slave-owning Cherokees versus the smallholders who may also have practiced a less restrictive form of slavery; the two factions at times had different councils, as well as different views on "what it meant to be a Creek nation." Chang also points out that the Confederacy promised to defend Indian lands. Some Creeks on the Union side hoped freedmen's votes would allow them to outvote Confederate Creeks, who tended to have different notions of property, wealth, and the commons.

The former Confederate Creeks, on the other hand, opposed such an alliance and complained that the Creek freedmen towns illegally granted citizenship to incoming non-Creek freedmen. Further complicating matters, many of these incoming Blacks had some Indian heritage, though not necessarily Creek, whose traditions their families had sustained despite enslavement.

20. Saunt, *Black, White, and Indian*, 188, 200–201.

21. As it had among the Cherokees, the U.S. Civil War had split the Creek Nation. Among the Creeks, however, the largest group joined the Union. After the war, unlike the Choctaws and the Chickasaws, the Creeks did not delay in granting citizenship to their freedmen. Perdue, "Indians in Southern History," 150–52. At the same time, Creek leaders often threatened to "curtail" freed people's rights by reducing allotments or denying them a share in the nation's treasury; see Saunt, *Black, White, and Indian*, 154. Chang, *The Color of the Land*, 65. Unlike the Cherokees, the Creeks also granted freedmen property rights in the nation. Statement of Mr. J. S. Murchison, referring to 1866 treaties and distinguishing between Creek and Cherokee relations with freedmen, U.S. Congress, Senate, Committee on Indian Affairs, *Report*, 1:308. And see Naylor, *African Cherokees*, 13: the 1827 New Echota Constitution of the Cherokee Nation limited the rights of the children of Cherokees and Black people, even when the parents were both free. See Schreier, "Indian or Freedman?," 460–61, 463, 466, 468, 471, 477–78, on preventing them even from applying for tribal citizenship. Foreman, *The Five Civilized Tribes*, 213, 216.

22. U.S. Congress, Senate, Committee on Indian Affairs, *Report*, 1:97 (statement of Redbird Smith); May, "Collision and Collusion," 239.

23. Crockett, *The Black Towns*, 76, using a quotation from Boley's newspaper in 1905. For example, *Boley Progress*, March 9, 1905, 1.

24. Washington, "Boley," 30. As quoted by Sigmund Sameth, "Creek Negroes: A Study of Race Relations" (master's thesis, University of Oklahoma, 1940), 56, found in Crockett, *The Black Towns*, 28n52, 39–40. And see Wickett, *Contested Territory*, 52–53, quoting a Cherokee freedman insisting in 1891 on his right as a tribal citizen: "You talk about adoption; we are not of that class of people; we never came here from Kansas, Missouri, or Texas to be adopted into this nation. We were born here; this is our birthplace and I think it would be a hard matter for the Cherokees to adopt of their own family." May, *African Americans and Native Americans*, 231, finds that both Indian and Black Creeks opposed the establishment of Boley. Chang, *The Color of the Land*, 30, 159, on such friction in Boley and the social distance between freedmen from the states and Creek freedmen; he argues that on large Creek plantations enslavement was as dehumanizing as elsewhere.

25. U.S. Congress, Senate, Committee on Indian Affairs, *Report*, 1:92. Schools were often a flash point of conflict on reservations; see Bauer, *We Were All Like Migrant Workers Here*, 139. May, *African Americans and Native Americans*, 234. Regarding schools, see Zellar, *African Creeks*, 246–49. And see Taylor, *In Search of the Racial Frontier*, 147, on Black participation in Oklahoma land runs

generating hostility from white cowboys and on the Cherokee Strip from Fox Indians whose land it was.

26. As quoted in Wickett, *Contested Territory*, 170. And see Mize, "Black, White, and Read," 223, 229, 232; Mize, "The Sequoyah Convention," 181, 183, 187. May, *African Americans and Native Americans*, 226. Mize, "Black, White, and Read," 233. The name "Sequoyah" was chosen to honor the Cherokee inventor of the Cherokee syllabary.

27. Wickett, *Contested Territory*, 170–72. Mize, "Black, White, and Read," 227–28, 230–31; the vote to ratify stood at 56,279 in favor and 9,073 against (235); Congressman Arthur Phillips Murphy of Missouri, an attorney for the Creek Nation, and Senator Porter James McCumber of North Dakota filed statehood bills for Sequoyah, but they were not considered. Roosevelt had signaled his preference for a single state during a visit to Muskogee. See Chang, *The Color of the Land*, 7, on white settler aspirations. See Zellar, *African Creeks*, 241, and Naylor, *African Cherokees*, 195–96, on the leadership and Murray. On the relationship of Blacks to the Sequoyah movement, see Swindler, *Sources and Documents*, 47; Gibson, *The American Indian*, 502; Warde, *George Washington Grayson*, 204.

28. Saunt, *Black, White, and Indian*, 161. See Wickett, *Contested Territory*, 102–3, 109, on the increasing inequality of wealth among the Five Civilized Tribes. And see May, *African Americans and Native Americans*, 146; Chang, *The Color of the Land*, 6.

29. Littlefield and Underhill, "The 'Crazy Snake Uprising,'" 309. See May, *African Americans and Native Americans*, 112–14. According to May, a better translation for "crazy" would be "courageous" (145). Chang, *The Color of Land*, 97, on the name translation; 99 on Snake actions against former ally Isparhecher, cutting a mile of his fence for renting to a non-Creek and threatening him "for flying the U.S. flag"; 100 on the arrest of 97 men and indicting 253 named Creeks for enforcing Snakes' laws; all pleaded guilty, and all were pardoned. Those arraigned included freedmen, and the widespread support of the rebellion becomes apparent in that those arraigned also included men from thirty-eight of the forty-four non-Black towns. Harjo was apparently willing to accept "the form of allotments" as long as "the practice of common ownership and town governance" continued. Zellar, *African Creeks*, 228.

30. Chang, *The Color of Land*, 94–95, 118. In 1906 Congress made the Dawes designations conclusive.

31. Wickett, *Contested Territory*, 111–12, 130–32, 137. And see Naylor, *African Creeks*, 194, quoting the *Indian Chieftain* newspaper: "Whitecappers are expelling negroes from the southern part of this territory. Not a colored resident remains in Norman," which was hostile to both tenants and landowners. Crockett, *The Black Towns*, 92. See Saunt, *Black, White, and Indian*, 186, who finds that segregation started in Oklahoma Territory and spread to Indian Territory; beginning in 1892, using violence, intimidation, and the law, whites expelled Blacks from a string of towns, including Norman (1896), Lawton (1902), and

Shawnee (1902). Henryetta's expulsion was in 1907; ironically, the town was named for Washington Grayson's old cattle business partner, Hugh Henry.

32. Wickett, *Contested Territory*, 175, 183–85; they seemed vindicated when a slate with no Black Republicans resulted in a Republican victory in Muskogee. Zellar, *African Creeks*, 249. Indian Territory African Americans called a Suffrage League Convention in Muskogee in September 1906 and "blasted" the lily-white Republicans' maneuvering.

33. November 20, 1906, as quoted in Wickett, *Contested Territory*, 181, 196. For the buttons, see Zellar, *African Creeks*, 250.

34. Wickett, *Contested Territory*, 192, 193, 195. And see Green, *Grass-Roots Socialism*, 58. Haskell was a Muskogee railroad promoter. See Naylor, *African Creeks*, 195, on the composition of the constitutional convention: fifty-five delegates each from Indian Territory and Oklahoma Territory and two from the Osage Nation. Reese, *Women of Oklahoma*, 76–77.

35. May, *African Americans and Native Americans*, 243, 246–47; *Pacific Reporter*, 220:876, Blake v. Sessions et al., 1923.

36. *Muscogee Cimeter*, January 24, 1908, quoted in May, *African Americans and Native Americans*, 244, 246. See Shepard, *Deemed Unsuitable*, on the doctor. Saskatchewan had also been created in 1905. On Canadian desires for whiteness, see Owen, "'Lighting the Pathways,'" who explains that the Canadians wanted to ensure that what he calls an Anglo-Celtic majority would settle the prairies so that, with this commitment to British heritage, Canada could become a leader of the British Empire (3).

37. May, *African Americans and Native Americans*, 91–92; Littlefield and Underhill, "The 'Crazy Snake Uprising,'" 322, 324; Crockett, *The Black Towns*, 94, 98; Thompson, *Closing the Frontier*, 134, notes that only four out of five hundred Blacks in Boley could vote; Franklin, *Journey toward Hope*, 39, 108–9; Reese, *Women of Oklahoma*, 179–80; U.S. Congress, Senate, Committee on Indian Affairs, *Report*, 1:681–82, 687, on the Creek candidates for the convention. And see Wickett, *Contested Territory*, 198–201, on gerrymandering and forcing Boley residents to vote at a precinct twelve miles away. See also Chang, *The Color of the Land*, 64, on how the U.S. Supreme Court threw out Oklahoma's grandfather clause in 1915, the first such law to be ruled unconstitutional.

38. Littlefield and Underhill, "The 'Crazy Snake Uprising,'" 311, on whites; Crockett, *The Black Towns*, on Blacks. And Chang, *The Color of Land*, 92, 102, on the complexity of Black Creek identifications.

39. Littlefield and Underhill, "The 'Crazy Snake Uprising,'" 311–12. According to May, *African Americans and Native Americans*, 156, there were anti-Harjo Creeks among the attackers.

40. Quoted in Littlefield and Underhill, "The 'Crazy Snake Uprising,'" 323–24. Kelsey quoted in McIntosh, "Chitto Harjo," 136. The troops never found Harjo, who had sought refuge among the Choctaw Snakes and died in 1911.

41. From April 2, 1909, quoted in Littlefield and Underhill, "The 'Crazy Snake Uprising,'" 316. Saunt, *Black, White, and Indian*, 174. The *Indian Journal*

had been chartered by the Creek Council as early as 1876. *Boley Progress*, April 18, 1909, 4 (editorial). Of course, this view was self-serving to those promoting to Black newcomers the ease of acquiring allotments of land from hospitable Creeks. See U.S. Congress, Senate, Committee on Indian Affairs, *Report*, 2:1255 (Cornelius Perryman), 1261 (Robert Johnson), 1308 (Legus Perryman).

42. Reese, *Women of Oklahoma*, 6, 16.

43. Littlefield and Underhill, "The 'Crazy Snake Uprising,'" 312, 317.

44. Posey, "Journal," 13–14; Debo, *The Road*, 305–6. Chang, *The Color of the Land*, 48, finds "male-led trading houses but also female-led farming" among small farmers and a continuity of "the much older Creek practice of female-directed agriculture." For examples, see *Pacific Reporter*, 230:753–54, Proctor et al. v. Foster et al., 1924; 220:881, Davis v. Reeder et al., 1924; and 215:792, Smith v. Lindsay et al., 1923. The law accepted that, among the Creeks, a man and a woman who lived together as husband and wife were considered married; when they separated, they were considered divorced. Compare Wall, "Gender and the 'Citizen Indian,'" 215–17. On other aspects of male-female relations such as education and games, see Posey, "Journal," 7; U.S. Congress, Senate, Committee on Indian Affairs, *Report*, 1:239 (Mr. D. F. Redd), 2:1311 (Mrs. Lila D. Lindsay). Note also that the constitution that emerged from the Sequoyah movement's convention in 1905 declared that the real and personal property of a femme covert acquired before or after marriage by any means, as long as she chose, remained her separate estate and property as if she were femme sole. Swindler, *Sources and Documents*, 71.

45. *Boley Progress*, August 4, 1905, 1, March 16, 1905, 1, May 10, 1906, 1; and Washington, "Boley," 28.

46. Crockett, *The Black Towns*, 63, 81–82; U.S. Congress, Senate, Committee on Indian Affairs, *Ho Tul Yaholla*, 2. See Brown, "Negotiating and Transforming," 107–46.

47. U.S. Congress, Senate, Committee on Indian Affairs, *Report*, 1:1989 (address to the Senatorial Committee of the Commercial Club of Muskogee, Indian Territory).

48. Field, "'Turn Our Faces to the West,'" 123 for a map of the towns; and 119–20 and 125n20 for aspirations for a Black state. Crockett, *The Black Towns*, 38. Littlefield and Underhill, "The 'Crazy Snake Uprising,'" 323.

49. Chang, *The Color of the Land*, 107, 154, citing the experience of a couple from Mississippi who came to Indian Territory when they became disillusioned with the promise of opportunity in Kansas. See Ruffin and Mack, introduction to *Freedom's Racial Frontier*, 6, for population figures from 1890 to 1940; according to the table, the proportion fell from just under 7 percent to just under 5 percent. Wickett, *Contested Territory*, 190–91. Seventy-three Democratic candidates for the convention had endorsed farmer-labor demands. Green, *Grass-Roots Socialism*, 57–58, 63–64.

4. Revolution and Revolutionaries

1. Starn, *Ishi's Brain*, 32–36, including the newspaper cites.

2. Starn, *Ishi's Brain*, 36–38, 40–41.

3. Starn, *Ishi's Brain*, 44, 143; Rydell, *All the World's a Fair.*

4. Starn, *Ishi's Brain*, 24–25, 30, 33–34, 115, 292–93. On the visit of the Konkow fruit picker, see Schneider, review of *Wild Men.*

5. Starn, *Ishi's Brain*, 36, 239–40.

6. Starn, *Ishi's Brain*, 43, 44, 148, 151; Vizenor, *Manifest Manners*, 128, 132, 133.

7. Hoxie, *A Final Promise*, 108–10, claims the rising speed was enabled by the increasing presence of western senators and the ceding of all things Indian to them by the rest of Congress; on dispossession, see 153–87. Kehoe, *North American Indians*, 588–89. See also Hansen, *Encounter on the Great Plains*, 193–94, on the SAI's work on citizenship and enfranchisement; and 195–96 on the ritual shooting of the "last arrow" spectacle that Commissioner of Indian Affairs Cato Sells started in 1916 to symbolize Indians giving up hunting to embrace the plow. See Bess, "The Price of Pima Cotton," 183, on an insurrection including Mexicans, Yaquis, and Pimas that resulted in seven deaths.

8. Horne, *Black and Brown*, 94–95, 147, 158, refers to a battle between the Buffalo Soldiers and the Yaquis from the United States and Mexico along the U.S.-Mexico border as late as 1918. On Yaquis with Villa, see Hart, *Empire and Revolution*, 326. Truett, *Fugitive Landscapes*, 118. On the 1905–6 Mexican anti-Yaqui campaign, see, for example, Evans, *Bound in Twine*, 67–89. For anecdotes of revolutionary Mexican women smuggling guns under their skirts across the U.S.-Mexico border, see Salas, *Soldaderas*, 56. Nelson C. Bledsoe, oral history, April 3, 1961, Arizona Historical Society, Tucson, quoted in St. John, *Line in the Sand*, 128, 122–23, particularly referring to Yaqui arms smugglers around Nogales. Meeks, *Border Citizens*, 56–58, 105–6. See also Bess, "The Price of Pima Cotton," 171–89. The loss of water rights was part of a pervasive pattern; see Hoxie, *A Final Promise*, 168–72, for examples in Wyoming and Utah.

9. See, for example, Nash, *The American West*, 29, on Weyerhauser, Guggenheim on Montana copper; Byrkit, *Forging the Copper Collar*; and Smith, *Jeannette Rankin.* According to Nash (31–32), the trans-Mississippi West held over 90 percent of all metal reserves in the United States, and in 1914 the region produced 90 percent of U.S. copper. Lansing, *Insurgent Democracy*, 48, reveals that by 1911 Minnesotans owned almost half the grain companies in Winnipeg, and the imbrication of Minneapolis and Winnipeg only grew from there.

10. Martínez, *Fragments*, 2, 67–68; Hart, *Empire and Revolution*, 264–65, 272.

11. Díaz, *Border Contraband*, 73–81; Sánchez's forebears ranked among Laredo's founding families. Martínez, *Fragments*, 1–10; Work, "Enforcing Neutrality," 181, 185.

12. Britton, *Revolution and Ideology*, 34, 35, 37, 38 (the Casa del Obrero Mundial).

13. Martínez, *Fragments*, 7–8, 213–15. The movement to overthrow Huerta aimed to restore constitutional government, led by Carranza, Villa, and Obregón. Villa and Carranza split, with Villa joining the more radical Emiliano Zapata from Morelos. Obregón stayed with Carranza and opposed Villa. In 1910 sixty thousand U.S. citizens lived in Mexico; in 1920 only twelve thousand did.

14. Hart, *Empire and Revolution*, 277, 278–82, 286–90, 299.

15. Harris and Sadler, *The Secret War in El Paso*, 24–26, 31, 86, 89, 111, 132.

16. Horne, *Black and Brown*, 130–31; Hart, *Empire and Revolution*, 154–60. U.S. demand had exploded since 1900, and U.S. production had declined. The British had a strong presence in Mexican oil production; by 1905 British investors controlled almost a million acres in oil leases or outright ownership, particularly around Veracruz. And see Sandos, *Rebellion*, 156, on the 20 percent of surface land.

17. Hart, *Empire and Revolution*, 162–63, 306–11, and see 331 on the close friendship between Wilson and Cleveland Dodge of Phelps Dodge. See also Alter, "From the Copper-Colored Sons," 85. St. John, *Line in the Sand*, 131. See also Sandos, *Rebellion*, 51. Hart, *Empire and Revolution*, 321.

18. Britton, *Revolution and Ideology*, 27, claims that denying arms delivery to Huerta was one reason Wilson ordered the invasion of Veracruz in the context of rivalry among the United States, Britain, and Germany to control Mexico's oil regions with global conflict on the horizon. See Martínez, *Fragments*, 7–8, 68, 137.

19. Work, "Enforcing Neutrality," 192–93; Hart, *Empire and Revolution*, 326.

20. Britton, *Revolution and Ideology*, 25–26. See Dewey, *Pesos and Dollars*, 64, on an irrigation project in Tamaulipas funded by the Texas Company facing resistance from the area's longtime residents who used the land for grazing and halted by the revolution, leading to bankruptcy for the project; Harris and Sadler, *The Texas Rangers*, 252.

21. Young, "Deconstructing *La Raza*," 255. El Primer Congreso Mexicanista, held in Laredo in 1911, included Mexican American representatives from throughout the state and Mexican consuls in Texas; see Díaz, *Border Contraband*, 78. For the quotation, see Foley, *The White Scourge*, 57. See also Vargas, *Crucible of Struggle*, 184, 186. On other forms of resistance, see Martinez, *The Injustice*, 9.

22. Horne, *Black and Brown*, 160, 162–65; thousands of Mexicans and Anglos fled the four counties involved. Leiker, *Racial Borders*, 159. The plan called for separate states for Blacks and Indians. Sandos, *Rebellion*, 88–89, 10, 105. See Martínez, *Fragments*, 138, 145–48, for the plan itself; see 165 regarding possible German complicity in the Plan de San Diego with the aim of keeping the United States out of the European conflict. The plan attacked U.S. whites but spared Germans and included Japanese among the conspirators.

23. Zamora, *The World of the Mexican Worker*, 82–83, 154–56, regarding reprisals against Mexican socialists in particular. And see Young, "Decon-

structing *La Raza*," 255, on lynchings in 1910 and 1911. Leiker, *Racial Borders*, 150, 160, puts the number of dead at over three hundred and attributes the term "getting rangered" to the Texas Rangers' practice of executing Mexicans and Mexican Americans without trial in this period. By June 1916 the U.S. Army had pulled fifty thousand troops from the Punitive Expedition in an attempt to restrain bloody white reprisals between Laredo and Brownsville. Sandos, *Rebellion*, 105, 110, maintains that Mexicans and Tejanos found soldiers more trustworthy than Rangers and civilians; nearly 40 percent of Tejanos and Mexicans left Cameron and Hidalgo Counties in September and October 1915. With so much tinder, the precise spark that lit the Plan de San Diego is a matter of dispute. Several historians have linked it to Carranza. Martínez, *Fragments*, 138–40, including quotation from *World's Work* (January 1917). Harris and Sadler, *The Texas Rangers*, 290–95, on Carranza's complicity. Samponaro and Vanderwood, *War Scare on the Rio Grande*, 77, citing Walter Prescott Webb, who estimated that between five hundred and five thousand Mexicans were killed in this period, as opposed to sixty-two U.S. civilians and sixty-four soldiers. The authors also claim (82) that Governor William P. Hobby used the Rangers to discourage Mexican voting and credit Canales's investigation in part to this move. See also Martinez, *The Injustice*, 7. Díaz, *Border Contraband*, 78, finds Laredo less subject to such violence and Tejanos more powerful than in the lower valley. In contrast, Weber, *From South Texas to the Nation*, 30–39, finds that the raids revived in the summer of 1916 around Laredo (38). Weber concludes that the Texas Rangers pursued "ethnic cleansing," attempting "to rid larger portions of South Texas of Mexicans through wholesale, anonymous murder" (38).

24. Martínez, *Fragments*, 140–41. The killing of the engineers was known as the Santa Isabel massacre, and anti-Mexican riots in El Paso and mobilizations in Juárez followed. Harris and Sadler, *The Secret War in El Paso*, 248; Hart, *Empire and Revolution*, 329, 271–72, 278, 290. By 1910 there were nine prosperous Mormon colonies in Mexico, several in Chihuahua and Sonora, with over four thousand farmers mostly from states with large Mormon populations: Colorado, Utah, and Idaho. By 1910 also the United States had outpaced Europe in its investments in Central America. According to Morgan, "From Brutal Ally to Humble Believer," before 1916 Mormon colonists found Villa an honorable partner and a reasonable leader who offered to pay for goods taken and kept his troops sober and under control. With Wilson's recognition of Carranza, however, Villa turned on the colonists.

25. Work, "Enforcing Neutrality," 188–90; Morgan, "The Centennial of Pancho Villa's Raid." Morgan points out that this history was at odds with the attempts by 1910 of the Columbus & Western New Mexico Townsite Company to create Columbus as a white family place incidentally on the border with the dubious claim that less than 5 percent of the population was Mexican descent.

26. *Albuquerque Morning Journal*, March 9, 1916. Hart, *Empire and Revolution*, 330, puts the number of U.S. residents of Columbus killed at eighteen.

27. *Albuquerque Morning Journal,* March 3, 1916. See Work, "Enforcing Neutrality," 185, 197: only after the Villa raid could the U.S. Army cross the border in pursuit; antibanditry was not the army's job, though enforcing neutrality laws was.

28. According to St. John, *Line in the Sand,* 131–35, "Wilson waffled between support for Villa and Carranza" (131). On the Pershing expedition, see Katz, *The Life and Times,* 567–71. According to Horne, *Black and Brown,* 146, they also succeeded in trying out new technologies of war: "It was the first campaign . . . to employ motorized devices like trucks, motorcycles, tanks and airplanes" and the first to be widely filmed for the public. On the film, see Alter, "From the Copper-Colored Sons," 98. See Leiker, *Racial Borders,* 167, for the number of troops. Martínez, *Fragments,* 140, puts the number of Pershing's troops at six thousand. Work, "Enforcing Neutrality," 181; Samponaro and Vanderwood, *War Scare on the Rio Grande,* 107.

29. Morgan, "From Brutal Ally to Humble Believer," 121–22. Alter, "From the Copper-Colored Sons," 99, notes that Villa had earlier "left the vast estates of Hearst, Harrison, and US Senator Fall intact in order not to provoke US intervention," unlike Zapata in Morales. On Fall, see Montgomery, *The Spanish Redemption,* 122–23. Britton, *Revolution and Ideology,* 6, 33. Hart, *Empire and Revolution,* 332.

30. Deutsch, *No Separate Refuge,* 110. And see Sandos, *Rebellion,* 84, 143, on the cosmopolitan nature of the Mexican population, including those drawn into the Plan de San Diego, with German, Japanese, and Italian participants "reminiscent of PLM-IWW joint ventures at Cananea" (84).

31. Green, *Grass-Roots Socialism,* 68, 71–72. See Chang, *The Color of Land,* 90, on those who "rushed to be enrolled," 109, 123, 128–30, 144. See Zellar, *African Creeks,* 213–17, 254–55, 306, 54n, on allotment and dispossession. The Indian Appropriations Act of 1908 removed all restrictions from freedmen, intermarried whites, and Indians with less than half "blood." It also gave Oklahoma's probate courts oversight for the estates of minors; the corruption that followed led to the act being known as "the Crime of 1908." Burbank, *When Farmers Voted Red,* 90–103. The Socialist Party had won 25–35 percent of the vote in southern Oklahoma in 1914. Like New Mexico, Oklahoma was full of lawyers drawn to a region with heavily disputed land claims. In New Mexico through their involvement in the ensuing legal contests, the lawyers accumulated acreage formerly owned by the state's Hispanos; in Oklahoma they gained acreage formerly owned by Indians. Such was William H. "Alfalfa Bill" Murray, who had borrowed the fare to move from Texas to Indian Territory, where he married the daughter of the elected Chickasaw chief and entered local politics, served as president of Oklahoma's constitutional convention, and served three terms in Congress.

32. Wrobel, *America's West,* 41.

33. Green, *Grass-Roots Socialism,* 24–25, 41, 72, 74. While the Socialist Party was popular in Texas, earlier disenfranchisement and the poll tax meant the

turnout of both Black and white poor farmers was lower than in Oklahoma. Chang, *The Color of the Land*, 178, finds the Farmers Union rather than the Populists the forerunner of the Socialist Party among whites in Indian Territory. Hurt, *The Big Empty*, 18–19, 78. Tucker, "Populism Up-to-Date," 198–208.

34. Johnston, "The Myth of the Harmonious City," 254–56; Wefald, *A Voice of Protest*, 59; Smith, *Rocky Mountain Heartland*, 26, 32, 37, 49. See also Keyssar, *The Right to Vote*; and Jameson, *All That Glitters*, 187–96.

35. Quoted in Beatty, *Age of Betrayal*, 167; thanks to Nora Hafez for the citation. See Wrobel, *America's West*, 64–73, on the various iterations of progressive legislation in the region.

36. Hurt, *The Big Empty*, 17, 30. Republicans carried five of eight Great Plains states in 1900; seven of eight in 1904; four went for Bryan, the Populist Democrat, the rest for the Republican, Taft, in 1908. Wrobel, *America's West*, 66, 68, 71. Arizona's first state governor, George W. P. Hunt, brought old-age pensions to the state and defended workers. See also Wefald, *A Voice of Protest*, 65–66, on South Dakota's Republican administration at the end of the decade. That legislative session (1919) approved state ownership of a coal mine and cement plant, state hail insurance, and a state bonding department. Brundage, *The Making of Western Labor Radicalism*, 163, also argues that this alliance "kept labor radicals in a minority position." Smith, *Rocky Mountain Heartland*, 49, 55. These measures included South Dakota's laws prohibiting corporations from making campaign or personal contributions for political purposes and direct primaries in 1907. In the same year Nebraska got direct primaries and five years later the direct democracy measures of initiative and referendum. Montana in 1913 got initiative, referendum, direct primaries, direct election of senators, and the Australian (secret) ballot. Kansas, whose governor's wife presided over the Equal Suffrage Association, won woman suffrage in 1912. Washington State sent progressive Miles Poindexter to the House in 1908 and the Senate in 1910. Robbins and Barber, *Nature's Northwest*, 50–54.

37. Wrobel, *America's West*, 72; Van Nuys, *Americanizing the West*, 39. And see Daniels, *The Politics of Prejudice*, 21, 47, 55, 57, on Roosevelt asking the aid of the Republican California machine to head off offenses to the Japanese in the wake of the Gentlemen's Agreement. See Kurashige, *The Shifting Grounds*, 21.

38. Sandos, *Rebellion*, 71–74, 83; Weber, *From South Texas to the Nation*, 79–80. The two counties were Maverick and Dimmit in the Winter Garden region, which formed from dissatisfaction with the "handling of the Mexican vote" (*Carrizo Springs Javelin* [Dimmit County] editorial, "The White Men's Primary," May 8, 1914, 79, series 3, carton 12, folder 27, Paul S. Taylor Collection, Bancroft Library, University of California at Berkeley).

39. Green, *Grass-Roots Socialism*, xv, 110–13, 123, 148–49, argues that white tenants identified more with industrial workers than with yeomen farmers. The Oklahoma Renters' Union in 1910 retained its whites-only policy. See Chang, *The Color of the Land*, 181, on how many white farmers blamed allotees for their plight (and had done so since the Populists agitated for the merger

of Indian Territory and Oklahoma Territory in the face of their disenfranchisement by Indians). Alter, "From the Copper-Colored Sons," 85, credits the work of "Mexican radicals such as J. A. Hernández and F. A. Hernández" with building the Socialist Party's Renters' Union beginning in 1913 with the transformed attitude toward Mexicans, Mexican Americans, and Tejanos as comrades. Land reform was a key feature; see p. 90 on an example of displacement with Black tenants. Foley, *The White Scourge*, 106, 145; on Hickey's transformation from race-baiter to race unifier, see 95–96, 98, 104–5; and on 108 the rhetorical transformation of nonunion Anglo tenant farmers into "satisfied peons" in contrast to the Mexican tenants with PLM ties; on the Taft ranch run as a set of company towns, see 118–19, 122, 124. The company's six one-thousand-acre cotton farms each employed more than 25 Mexican wage workers, 150–200 Mexican workers year-round, and about 25 white tenants; African Americans worked at the Taft Company's oil mill, cotton gins, machine shop, grain elevator, mixed-feed plant, and cottonseed oil refinery, as well as the cotton farms.

40. Green, *Grass-Roots Socialism*, 151–56. On Mexican politics, see Burbank, *When Farmers Voted Red*, 112; local socialists voiced support for the revolution, and local antisocialists threatened to lynch them.

41. Green, *Grass-Roots Socialism*, 176, 179–80; Alter, "From the Copper-Colored Sons," 90.

42. Alter, "From the Copper-Colored Sons," 83, 87, 100–101. The Magón brothers had set up briefly in Laredo before moving to San Antonio, starting their newspaper, *Regeneración* (1904), and then moving to St. Louis, Missouri, in 1905. Foley, *The White Scourge*, 116–17; Sandos, *Rebellion*, 17, 174–75. The PLM's paper, *Regeneración*, had subscribers not only in Mexico but also in Texas, Arizona, Cuba, and California, where it was printed. Johnson, *Revolution in Texas*; Zamora, *The World of the Mexican Worker*, 65. See, for example, Young, *Catarino Garza's Revolution*; Raat, *Revoltosos!*; Acuña, *Occupied America*, 150–51; Weber, *Dark Sweat, White Gold*, 85–86. In Streeby, *Radical Sensations*, see in particular the introduction on the connection between Flores Magón, the PLM, and U.S. radicals, including the Texan Lucy Parson (Lucía González de Parsons), labor battles in Mexico, and the IWW (founded in the same year as the PLM, 1905).

43. Kurashige, *The Shifting Grounds*, 13. U.S. Congress, House, Committee on Immigration and Naturalization, *Restriction of Immigration* (1916), 1108, 1112, 1119, 1125 (Raker); U.S. Congress, Senate, Committee on Immigration, *Selective Immigration Legislation*, 198, 207, 293, 298 (Furuseth's testimony).

44. See, for example, Leier, "Monopoly Capitalism," particularly 127 on Lucy Parsons's and Elizabeth Gurley Flynn's speaking tours of British Columbia; one IWW member complained that "all this anti-Japanese talk comes from the employing class. Which is better: to have the Japanese in the Union with you, or to force him to scab on the outside?" And see Putman, *Class and Gender Politics*. Gunther Peck, a pioneer in transnational labor history,

mentions Oxnard's inclusiveness, the threatened refusal of workers to join the AFL, versus the exclusiveness of workers in Bingham, Utah, in "Padrones and Protest." See Sohi, *Echoes of Mutiny*, 2–13, 28–30, on rising efforts to bar South Asian immigration to the United States (which finally succeeded with the Barred Zone of 1917), 34, 37–40, 45–47, 54, 57–59, 78–79, 83, 96, 108–9, 117, 120–24, 127, 133, 134, 143, 146–49, and on collaboration with the British imperial government in surveilling Indian activists in the United States, as well as the increasing identity as "Indian" of migrants (142ff.). Chang, "Mobilizing Revolutionary Manhood," 79, 84, 94, argues that "South Asian revolutionary activists exploited the issue of immigration restriction to build popular support for their cause" (79). South Asian and Chinese workers were particularly important in the Canadian IWW. See also Chang, *Pacific Connections*, 165.

45. Huginne, "A New Hero Comes to Town"; Sandos, *Rebellion.*

46. University of Washington, Civil Rights and Labor History Consortium, "IWW Strikes," gives citations for each strike, often from the labor press at the time but also from the classic histories of the IWW, Dubofsky, *We Shall Be All*, and Brissenden, *I.W.W.*

47. McWilliams, *Factories*, 155–56.

48. McWilliams, *Factories*, 156–57.

49. Clark, *Mill Town*, 200, on the meaning of the free speech fights for the IWW: "To Wobbly theoreticians, the free-speech fight was a revolutionary act."

50. University of Washington, Civil Rights and Labor History Consortium, "IWW Strikes." The strike won better wages and board for cantaloupe pickers and teamsters.

51. On Japanese agricultural mobilizing, see, for example, Chang, "Mobilizing Revolutionary Manhood," 88–89, in reference to the 1909 strike of Japanese sugar plantation workers who demanded the same wage as Portuguese and Puerto Rican workers, stayed out for three months, lost the strike, but soon gained the equal wage and the respect of the IWW on the mainland as they read updates in the *Industrial Worker*. And see McWilliams, *Factories*, 84, 86–87, 100, 106, on testimony at the 1911 House of Representatives Hardwick Committee that demanded Japanese labor, arguing, "American labor will not go into the fields" despite earlier testimony that no difficulty had been experienced getting white labor when the sugar factory paid American growers the price they demanded. There had been a farm laborers' union organized in 1903 at San Jose after two years of organizing, but it was short-lived. By 1909 thirty thousand Japanese worked in California as farm laborers.

52. The following accounts of the free speech fights at San Diego and the Wheatland strike, unless otherwise indicated, are taken from McWilliams, *Factories*, 152–67.

53. Clemens, *The People's Lobby*, 255, 257.

54. McWilliams, *Factories*, 164–65, 166, 169; University of Washington, Civil Rights and Labor History Consortium, "IWW Strikes."

55. For the most recent, elegant, and nuanced account of the strike, see Andrews, *Killing for Coal.*

56. The companies also encouraged workers to select check-weighmen, who determined how much coal a worker had mined. Wolff, *Industrializing the Rockies.*

57. Andrews, *Killing for Coal.*

58. Martelle, *Blood Passion,* 45, to Rockefeller.

59. See Weber, *From South Texas to the Nation,* 49–50, on similar claims by the Southwestern Land Company.

60. Andrews, *Killing for Coal.*

61. Martelle, *Blood Passion.*

62. See Pascoe, *Helen Ring Robinson,* 24–28 (on the Denver Women's Press Club), 44, 82, 84 (on her 1915 congressional testimony), 87–90.

63. *New York Times,* May 14, 1914. "The Wild Women of Colorado," reported Mrs. Alma V. Lafferty, former Colorado legislator, threatened to have five thousand suffragists march on the Colorado governor unless they got answers and action on their report regarding Ludlow. The *Times* saw this threat as a good reason not to let women into politics, posing it as irrational and asking who was looking after the children.

64. On Everett and the massacre, see Clark, *Mill Town,* 166, 180, 184, 197, 205, 210–11.

65. Martelle, *Blood Passion*; Mason, "Neither Friends nor Foes," 66, on how workman's compensation was one of a raft of measures that passed in 1911 when Hiram Johnson, unlike his predecessor, did not veto it. And see Swatt et al., *Game Changers,* 60, 67–75; Berman, *Radicalism in the Mountain West.*

66. Kropp, *California Vieja,* 56–59, 66, 103, 106, 111–12, 138, 150–53, 164–65; the fair led to the triumph of the Spanish colonial style in the region over the previous craftsman bungalow.

67. St. John, *Line in the Sand,* 124–26, and see the photo on 125. Martínez, *Fragments,* 68, "El Pasoans hit by stray bullets while watching the battle from the river bank and rooftops." Samponaro and Vanderwood, *War Scare on the Rio Grande,* 5–6, 46 (Neale quotation).

5. Women and Their Alliances

1. Deutsch, *Ballots to Breadlines,* 23. "Women of Yoncalla Capture All Offices," *Morning Oregonian,* November 6, 1920, 1, col. 4; and "Election Plan Kept Secret by Women," *Morning Oregonian,* November 10, 1920, 4. For local coverage of Yoncalla, see the *Morning Oregonian,* November 6, 1920, 1, col. 4, and November 10, 1920, 4.

2. Wallace, "Umatilla's 'Petticoat Government.'" According to the 1910 manuscript census, the Brownells (the ninety-second household), were fifty-seven and fifty-one, had been married for thirty-one years, and had six children, all living. She was from the Midwest. He was from Canada and in 1910 was a farmer who owned his own farm. For local coverage, see the *East Ore-*

gonian (Pendleton), December 6, 1916, 1, col. 2, December 11, 1916, 4, col. 1, January 10, 1917, 1, cols. 1 and 2, and December 22, 1916, 3, col. 5. See also Wrobel, *America's West,* 63, regarding Kanab, Utah, in 1912, which elected an all-female town council.

3. Louise McKinney quoted in Lansing, *Insurgent Democracy,* 42.

4. See, for example, Whaley, *Oregon and the Collapse of Illahee,* on racial formations and settler colonialism, particularly 225–26 regarding Native Americans.

5. See Gordon, *The Great Arizona Orphan Abduction,* 161–66; Moynihan, *Rebel for Rights*; Osselaer, *Winning Their Place,* 27–31. In this context it is significant that of the states west of the Mississippi, only New Mexico awaited the federal amendment's passage in 1920 to grant full woman suffrage. And see Perez, "Transterritorial Currents," 620, on the need to extend Patrick Wolfe's concept of "settler colonialism."

6. Pascoe, *What Comes Naturally,* 98, 118–19.

7. Bederman, *Manliness and Civilization,* for example; Kramer, *The Blood of Government.*

8. Chauncey, *Gay New York,* particularly the introduction. See also Mitchell, *Coyote Nation,* 38. Mitchell cites Polingaysi Quoyawayma, *No Turning Back: A True Account of a Hopi Indian Girl's Struggle to Bridge the Gap between the World of Her People and the World of the White Man* (Albuquerque: University of New Mexico Press, 1964), 24–25, 59, 106, regarding "grown Hopi men crying because white men had cut their hair." Similar tensions occurred with the Navajos and Zunis and at Taos Pueblo, as well as with the Lakotas and others (on the Lakotas, see Zitkala-Sa, *American Indian Stories*); according to Mitchell, *Coyote Nation,* 38, long hair on men was one of the traditions whites deemed "detrimental to progress" (citing Alice Devine at Taos Pueblo in 1902). The insistence on a particular practice of gender distinction also furthered Indian dispossession. Weiseger, *Dreaming of Sheep,* 145, notes that while the Bureau of Indian Affairs recognized that the wife was the head of the family among Navajos and allotted land to women, the General Land Office did not and as a result until 1920 rejected Navajo married women's applications for homesteads because they were not "heads of families."

9. Boag, *Same-Sex Affairs.*

10. Boag, *Same-Sex Affairs,* throughout but particularly 1–4, 6–7, 52, 58, 126, 136, 138, 157. Shortly after the 1912 story appeared in the press, many of the Portland implicated fled. Three were arrested in Vancouver, British Columbia; two in Fresno, California; one in Los Angeles; one in Salem, Oregon; one in Medford, Oregon; one in Vancouver, Washington; and four in Seattle. This anxiety about male sexuality mirrored the turn-of-the-century anxiety about female sexuality, termed "the girl problem," as adolescence emerged in the literature as a separate life stage (see, for example, 59–60) and as young women gained more autonomy in a working-class version of the "New Woman." Many of those young women who disappeared so sensationally in this period were not kidnapped and enslaved as prostitutes but

were trying to escape the confines of their parental homes. As fears regarding trafficking in women, whose label "white slavery" demonstrated that only white women were the objects of concern, reformers and their legislator allies increased their efforts to regulate prostitution. The first actions of many suffragists when they reached elected office were to enact legislation they saw as protecting young women. The literature on female delinquency is voluminous; see, for example, Odem, *Delinquent Daughters*; Shah, *Stranger Intimacy*. See Clark, *Deliver Us from Evil*, 103, on legislation to "abate" vice districts. Rosen, *Lost Sisterhood*, acknowledges that "white slavery *did* exist. People *did* buy and sell women for the purpose of forcing them into prostitution" but also contends that concern for it became a hysteria that peaked between 1911 and 1916 (15, 117, 123); on age of consent and minimum wage, see 27–28. Holt, "The First New Nations," xii, similarly claims, "Science (and pseudo-science) was only one of the tools of racial and national imagining, a language for its expression, but not its source."

11. The 1910 manuscript census shows, for example, a hotelkeeper born in Connecticut of Scottish parents who ran a rooming house for railroad workers and employed a Japanese cook next door to a Chinese rooming house whose nine residents arrived from 1873 to 1894. District 269 showed more Chinese residents.

12. Flexner, *Century of Struggle*, 263.

13. On the rise of socialism, see Green, *Grass-Roots Socialism*, xi, 90, who finds that the strongest support for Debs in the United States lay in Oklahoma, Texas, Louisiana, and Arkansas with a constituency of indebted homesteaders, tenant farmers, coal miners, railroad workers, lumberjacks, and others. Burbank, *When Farmers Voted Red*, 4, 6, 11, 56, argues that the dispossession of Indians in the opening decades of the twentieth century also hurt their white renters and lessees. Katz, "A Politics of Coalition," 249, argues that the ethnic makeup of the working class in southern California (as native born and Protestant) made it easier to achieve cross-class alliances than in northern California, where immigrants and their children formed a majority of workers; socialist women were prominent leaders of the woman suffrage movement and its constituent organizations in southern California. Among the three main county woman suffrage organizations there was the WCTU, which, like the others, had socialist women in leadership roles (256). See also Gullett, *Becoming Citizens*, 178–96, 204, on the cross-class coalitions among women created by work for a minimum wage and maximum-hours legislation. Dr. Marie Equi was a socialist suffrage leader in Oregon and involved in some of the disputes there; see, for example, Krieger, "Queen of the Bolsheviks." Abigail Scott Duniway, newspaper woman with a sometimes helpful and sometimes troublesome newspaper editor for her brother, long dominated the Oregon suffrage movement, which, like the one in Washington, had many factions with competing strategies. Duniway in particular fell out with the WCTU. See, for example, Moynihan, *Rebel for Rights*;

Kessler, "A Siege of the Citadels"; Kessler, "The Ideas of Woman Suffrage"; Nash, "Abigail versus Harvey"; and Armitage, "Tied to Other Lives," 5–15. Also on Duniway's hostility not only to prohibition but also to the WCTU, see Clark, *Deliver Us from Evil*, 105–6, quoting from Duniway's 1914 autobiography, *Path Breaking: An Autobiographical History of the Equal Suffrage Movement in Pacific Coast States*, where she claimed that the WCTU rank and file were not suffragists and never worked for the vote. On northern California, see Nickliss, "Phoebe Apperson Hearst's 'Great Reserve of Power,'" who argues that Hearst only came out publicly for woman suffrage in 1911 just before the vote, turning on Wilson because he would not send troops to protect her Mexican property, and her stature meant the endorsement had impact. See also Sewell, *Women and the Everyday City*, who argues that the daily accretion of women's autonomous presence as consumers and workers in the city laid the groundwork for their acceptance as political participants. Flexner, *Century of Struggle*, 265, shows that the margin of victory was minute in California: 1 vote per precinct, or 3,587 votes. At the onset of World War I, eleven western states and one territory and no states east of the Mississippi had woman suffrage. See Beeton, "How the West Was Won," 115; Mead, *How the Vote Was Won*, 4, 51–52.

14. Smith, *Jeannette Rankin*, 58, 83; Osselaer, *Winning Their Place*, 29.

15. Osselaer, *Winning Their Place*, 27–33, 98–99.

16. Smith, *Jeannette Rankin*, 33–34, 37–38, 43, 46, 48–49. Other sources on Rankin include Anderson, "Steps to Political Equality"; Schaffer, "Jeannette Rankin"; and Murphy, *Mining Cultures*, 24–26.

17. Smith, *Jeannette Rankin*, 51–55.

18. Smith, *Jeannette Rankin*, 38, 56, 58.

19. Smith, *Jeannette Rankin*, 58–89, 91–92, 96–97; Clemens, *The People's Lobby*, 70.

20. Smith, *Jeannette Rankin*, 38, 98. He was apparently unpopular in Montana, though he was close friends with political and other elites. People accused him of charging exorbitant fees, exploiting parolees, and overgrazing his ranches.

21. Morlan, *Political Prairie Fire*, 5–6, 8, shows that the North Dakota wheat crop in 1915 was approximately 140 million bushels. Lansing, *Insurgent Democracy*, 6, argues that the percentage of tenant-run farms rose from 6.9 to 14.3.

22. Tucker, "Populism Up-to-Date," 201; Morlan, *Political Prairie Fire*, 3, 5, 20; Lansing, *Insurgent Democracy*, 7, 8, 10, 11, 27, on the power of Minneapolis millers and railroad companies.

23. Morlan, *Political Prairie Fire*, 22–23.

24. *Fargo Forum*, January 24, 1916, 1, quoted in Morlan, *Political Prairie Fire*, 43; Lansing, *Insurgent Democracy*, 13, 25, 31. Farmers suspected the Socialist Party of being dominated by city folk, wanting to organize farm labor, and favoring collectivization of farming, but Minot city leader Arthur LeSueur instead called for state ownership of elevators, banks, and packinghouses

and state-sponsored insurance; the party also critiqued other farmer organizations, including the NPL, as not dealing with the right fundamental issues.

25. *Leader*, April 6, 1916, 6, quoted in Morlan, *Political Prairie Fire*, 54.

26. Morlan, *Political Prairie Fire*, 24, 29, 31, 39, 50, 52, 54–55, 59, 75, 87, 89.

27. Morlan, *Political Prairie Fire*, 101–6, 122–24; Lansing, *Insurgent Democracy*, 39, 84. The league controlled not only the House of Representatives and the governorship but also the state supreme court. Alter, "From the Copper-Colored Sons," 108.

28. Morlan, *Political Prairie Fire*, 125. The league had come to Canada, according to Morlan, with S. E. Haight, who worked for the league in North Dakota for several months and then returned to his farm in Saskatchewan and organized there. Canadian farmers had the same grievances as did U.S. farmers, and the league spread rapidly in Saskatchewan and Alberta, but Manitoba had more entrenched traditional parties and a more conservative Grain Growers' Association, and the league made little impression (79). See Lansing, *Insurgent Democracy*, 8–9, on the early spread of the Society of Equity to wheat-producing regions of Saskatchewan and Alberta and the cooperative associations that followed and successfully pushed their governments to support farmer-owned cooperatives directly. Millers and other corporations fought back. For one migrant family who moved from Oregon to southern Alberta in 1907, see Evans, "'We Just Lived It.'" On Black migrants, see Shepard, *Deemed Unsuitable*. On Canada's policy, see Owen, "'Lighting the Pathways'"; Canadians wanted to ensure that what he calls an Anglo-Celtic majority would settle the prairies so that, with this commitment to British heritage, Canada could become a leader of the British Empire. On Canadian women heading south to homestead, see Jameson and McManus, introduction to *One Step*, xxii. See Jameson and Mouat, "Telling Differences," 187, 205–7; Barman, "Writing Women," 117.

29. For the argument about southern Alberta U.S. immigrant voters, the NPL, and McKinney and Macadams, see Langford, "'All That Glitters,'" 78–81.

30. Quoted in Lansing, *Insurgent Democracy*, 42. Smith, *Jeannette Rankin*, 83, 86, 88, 99, 100, 102, 103. Because of redistricting and population growth, only in this election could each Montana citizen vote for two congressional representatives. Gutfeld, *Montana's Agony*, 93–94. From 1909 to 1916 were great years for wheat in Montana; the price doubled, harvests were high, and land values rose: the number of farms in the state more than doubled, and the number of acres almost tripled. Then came drought from 1917 until the mid-1920s.

31. Cramer, "Public and Political," 55, 57, 60; Cleverdon, *The Woman Suffrage Movement*, 57, 77, 89; Clark, *Deliver Us from Evil*, 108–28. Between 1914 and 1916 Seattle went from opposing Prohibition by 15,000 votes to supporting it by 20,000 votes; Spokane underwent an even more dramatic shift, from a margin of 1,500 opposed to a margin of 12,000 in favor. According to Sheehan, "'Women Helping Women,'" 396, "The WCTU in the west was quite a militant organization . . . advocating legal change and intervention in the

private affairs of individuals and government involvement in areas traditionally reserved for the private sector." See also Thompson, "'The Beginning of Our Regeneration.'" See also Little, "Claiming a Unique Place." Lansing, *Insurgent Democracy*, 81, points out that Canadian NPL cartoonists chose to use women to represent the league where the U.S. NPL used Uncle Sam; in the United States, "women appeared in League cartoons only as subordinate farm wives or as the more traditional stylized representations of democracy or the nation," but in Saskatchewan and Alberta they appeared as the NPL itself. For example, in an early 1917 cartoon on the back cover of a Saskatchewan NPL pamphlet, "an agrarian woman" chased "a greedy pig identified as 'big biz' away from the profits meant for farmers represented as babies." And see Lansing, *Insurgent Democracy*, 82, on the response to McKinney's success: "Non-Partisan League platform is the only place where the high-minded women of the Province can stand with dignity and clean feet."

32. Buhle, *Women and American Socialism*, 108, 111, 112, 115, 119, 230; the Omaha, Nebraska, Woman's Socialist Union, affiliated with the Socialist Party, intentionally imitated the WCTU standard meeting rituals. In Iowa a Socialist Party organizer was a WCTU veteran. See also Katz, "A Politics of Coalition." Of course, this Christian socialism was also prevalent among socialist men. See Burbank, *When Farmers Voted Red*, 15, 24; Clemens, *The People's Lobby*, 192; Cramer, "Public and Political," 62. One reason the WCTU is often given short shrift in U.S. woman suffrage histories is the dominance of the Stanton-Anthony narrative and their allies. See, for example, Armitage, "Tied to Other Lives"; Tyrell, *Woman's World / Woman's Empire*, 231–34.

33. Soden, "The Women's Christian Temperance Union." Sodden also claims that the WCTU became the strongest women's organization in the region, with chapters in almost every county of Oregon, Washington, and Idaho, working in elections, using billboard campaigns and automobile parades, brass bands, and youth torch-lit marches, and in Oregon working to establish a minimum wage for women and for a variety of other social issues. And see Tyrell, *Woman's World / Woman's Empire*, 224; Smith, *Jeannette Rankin*, 102, 132, 135–40.

34. Tyrell, *Woman's World / Woman's Empire*, 51, 71, 74, 85; Macías, *Against All Odds*, 65, 69–80; Pérez, *The Decolonial Imaginary*, 36–37, 40–41, 47–48, 61–62, 67; Soto, *Emergence of the Modern Mexican Woman*, 19–22. See also Mead, *How the Vote Was Won*, 51–52. Osten, "'Beautifying the Revolution,'" 72, repeats the frequent argument that Alvarado wanted to enfranchise women to expand his base and posits that a similar motive could have guided Vidal in Chiapas in 1925. The constitution of the Socialist Party of Chiapas in 1920 included an assertion of equal rights for women, invoking England and the United States as "the vanguard of civilization" (32). In Tabasco, radical socialist governor Francisco Mújica held the first Mexican Feminist Congress in 1915, but women only gained suffrage in Tabasco in 1931; they did so in the Yucatán in 1922, in San Luis Potosí in 1923, and in Chiapas in 1925. In Yucatán it was later withdrawn with the end of the socialist government, but not in Chiapas

(25–27). Both Alvarado and Chiapas's Socialist Party framed the necessity to enfranchise women as the need for their moral force to resolve the political dilemmas facing the state—a similar line to that of the WCTU and other women's reform organizations.

35. In Martínez, *Fragments*, 15–20; originally in Gamio, *The Mexican Immigrant*, 29–35.

36. *New York Times*, May 10, 1911, 2, in Soto, *Emergence of the Modern Mexican Woman*, 31–34. Salas, *Soldaderas*, 56, 60.

37. Shah, *Contagious Divides*, 3, 120–55; Stern, *Eugenic Nation*, 58. Stern sees medicalization and militarization working in tandem "to create a regime of eugenic gatekeeping on the U.S.-Mexican border that aimed to ensure the putative purity of the 'American' family-nation while generating long-lasting stereotypes of Mexicans as filthy, lousy, and prone to irresponsible breeding" (58–59). Mckiernan-González, *Fevered Measures*, 178.

38. Stern, *Eugenic Nation*, 59, 60. Mckiernan-González, *Fevered Measures*, 57–58, 172–75, 208–35, finds that in the early years of the revolution, the Mexican Central Railroad became a funnel, bringing refugees not only into Texas but also into the rest of the United States. That flow heightened the visibility of border politics.

39. Mckiernan-González, *Fevered Measures*, 229; and see Leiker, *Racial Borders*.

40. Mckiernan-González, *Fevered Measures*, 174–77. Inspector Morris Buttner died on February 27, 1916.

41. Mckiernan-González, *Fevered Measures*, 184–85.

42. Mckiernan-González, *Fevered Measures*, 178–79.

43. Quinn, *Original Sin*, 47–48, quoted in Mckiernan-González, *Fevered Measures*, 181.

44. Mckiernan-González, *Fevered Measures*, 183.

45. *New York Times*, January 29, 1917, 4; *El Paso Times*, January 29, 1917, 1; *San Antonio Express*, January 29, 1917, 1, all quoted in Mckiernan-González, *Fevered Measures*, 178–97, quotes from 184.

46. Rothbard, "World War I as Fulfillment"; Keire, *For Business & Pleasure*, 105–6. Newly appointed Secretary of War Newton D. Baker sent Raymond Fosdick, a former New York City commissioner, to investigate conditions among troops on the border. Fosdick found that "venereal disease rates were soaring," and red-light districts in Douglas, Arizona, El Paso, Texas, and Columbus, New Mexico, exceeded his worst expectations. Clark, *Deliver Us from Evil*, 128, shows that training officers often declared entire cities off limits to trainees until they eliminated brothels. Butler, *Daughters of Joy*. Rosen, *The Lost Sisterhood*, 16, 28–29, 33. In 1902 Minneapolis's mayor hired two physicians to give weekly checkups to all sex workers and issue them certificates of health; from March 1913 until May 1915 San Francisco regulated prostitution through its new Municipal Clinic for the Prevention of Venereal Disease. Voisey, "The 'Votes for Women' Movement," 167, provides an example of the level of "vice" commerce in western Canada and the United States;

downtown Winnipeg boasted sixty bars, fifty-one pool halls, fifty brothels, and "innumerable liquor retailers." Regina and Edmonton were similar. In Saskatoon "brothels specialized in Negroes and Orientals."

47. Rothbard, "World War I as Fulfillment." The government used naval troops to close Storyville in November 1917. Rothbard cites Allen Davis, *Spearheads of Reform: The Social Settlements and the Progressive Movement, 1890–1914* (New York: Oxford University Press, 1967); Paul Boyer, *Urban Masses and Moral Order in America, 1820–1920* (Cambridge MA: Harvard University Press, 1978), 201; Daniel R. Beaver, *Newton D. Baker and the American War Effort, 1917–1919* (Lincoln: University of Nebraska Press, 1966), 221–24; and C. H. Cramer, *Newton D. Baker: A Biography* (Cleveland: World Publishing Company, 1961), 99–102, among others. Keire, *For Business & Pleasure*, 107. While Rothbard asserts that the military closed the districts, Keire instead states, "From July 1917 to September 1918, over a hundred cities eliminated their tenderloins." See Horne, *Black and Brown*, 141–42, on the mushrooming of red-light districts on the Mexican side of the border. Some maintained a Black/white color line, but most had none.

48. According to Cleverdon, *The Woman Suffrage Movement*, about 90 percent of the woman suffrage news in the United Farmers' *Grain Growers Guide* in Manitoba came from the United States. Similarly, the *Manitoba Free Press*, the largest newspaper in the Prairies, got most of its suffrage news from the United States, and when Liberals in Manitoba endorsed woman suffrage in 1914, they used the example of the United States to justify their position (48). See Osselaer, *Winning Their Place*, 6, on the WCTU as the largest, with fifty thousand female members.

49. And, of course, the decade's democratic impulse was global. See Sohi, "Race, Surveillance, and Indian Anticolonialism"; and Jensen, *Passage from India*, 121–245.

50. Pascoe, *What Comes Naturally*, 168. The nonparticipating states were New Mexico, all the New England states, and New Jersey. See Long, *The Great Southern Babylon*, 208–9: in 1910 Louisiana increased the penalties for long-term interracial "concubinage," which it had first made illegal in 1908. And see Lee, *Fictive Kinship*. Boag, *Same-Sex Affairs*, 52, cites a headline near the end of 1912: "PREPARE FOR INFLUX OF ALIENS IN 1913"; Boag also notes the disproportionate arrest rate of foreigners in the city and even more of Greeks.

51. Some of the efforts of organized women aimed at reinforcing racial hierarchies, as with suffragist Bethenia Owens-Adair's 1917 campaign in Oregon for sterilization of the feebleminded in state institutions. Stern, *Eugenic Nation*, 23; Creese, "The Politics of Dependence," 373–74. And see Flamming, "African-Americans," 207, on how the Los Angeles Woman Suffrage League barred Black women, who then organized their own clubs. See Gullett, *Becoming Citizens*, 186, on the split record of the movement in California. Lansing, *Insurgent Democracy*, x. On Seattle cross-class women's radicalism, see the Wom-

en's Union Card and Label League, est. 1911, in Greenwald, "Working-Class Feminism," 105ff. On Seattle, see also Putman, *Class and Gender Politics*, 86, 112, 113, 128, 135, 142, 167. See Tyrell, *Woman's World / Woman's Empire*, 242–46; Sterrett, *Public Pensions*, 111, 113–18; Raftery, "Los Angeles Clubwomen," 154–55, 157; Langford, "'All That Glitters,'" 72. See Gullett, *Becoming Citizens*, 204, on the California legislature approving eleven of the seventeen bills put forward by the Women's Legislative Council of California in the wake of woman suffrage victory there.

52. See Clemens, *The People's Lobby*, 254. Clemens argues that while the measure increased the role of the government in the family, it removed aspects of women's second-class citizenship status that often found their basis in women's dependence on husbands and fathers. Such measures included minimum wage legislation, mothers' pension laws, eligibility for jury service, equal guardianship, and so on. Putman, *Class and Gender Politics*, 99, 102, 113.

6. Global Conflict and Local Strife

1. This is the conclusion of both Wrobel, *America's West*, 83, who refers to the region's large German and Austro-Hungarian populations and its tendency to see the war as "a capitalist conflict and the working classes as its primary victims," and Robbins and Barber, *Nature's Northwest*, 62, for similar reasons, adding the Irish and Scandinavian populations as also at best lukewarm toward Great Britain.

2. Van Nuys, *Americanizing the West*, 49–51, 57–58; Smith, *Rocky Mountain Heartland*, 79, on Montana's sedition law (modeled on the national law), which made it illegal to criticize the federal or state government or armed forces during wartime. Robbins and Barber, *Nature's Northwest*, 64, 65, state that Idaho enacted the first criminal syndicalism law in the United States in early 1917 and that Montana authorities brought about 130 sedition cases largely against farmers and workers.

3. Holtby, *Lest We Forget*, 39; North, *California at War*, 24–25. See Gutfeld, *Montana's Agony*, 62–65, on Montana's Council of Defense.

4. Holtby, *Lest We Forget*, 23–24, 39, 41. See Hyman, *Soldiers and Spruce*, 58–62, on Washington's struggles to control both the powerful business interests in lumber and agriculture and the AFL and more radical workers through the state and local councils. And Van Nuys, *Americanizing the West*, 45, 58, gives Anaconda Copper Mining Company and Washington lumber companies as examples of council capture by companies determined to stamp out radical labor agitation.

5. Berman, *Reformers*, 148, quoting a letter from Frances Munds to George Hunt, September 12, 1918, George Hunt Collection, Arizona Collection, Arizona State University, Tempe. Berman also cites the *New York Evening Post* investigative reporter Robert W. Bruere, who claimed that "all labor leaders, all strikers and all persons who sympathize or are suspected of sympathizing with strikers are lumped under the general designation of 'I.W.W.' or

'WOBBLY'" (Bruere, *Following the Trail of the IWW* [New York: New York Evening Post, 1918], 5).

6. Luebke, *Ethnicity on the Great Plains*, xi, xii. North Dakota's population was 42.7 percent foreign-born in 1890 and Minnesota's was 35.7 percent. See the table on xvi: in 1900 North Dakota was 35.4 percent foreign-born, South Dakota 22 percent, Nebraska 16.6 percent, Montana 27.6 percent, Wyoming 18.8 percent, and Colorado 16.9 percent; these numbers, of course, did not include the number of Mexican-descent citizens in the southwestern states, which had low percentages of foreign-born at the time but in southern Arizona and all of New Mexico a Mexican-descent majority. In south and south-central Texas by 1910, European and Mexican immigrants and their U.S.-born children comprised the majority of the population (xxi). In 1900 the percentage of the total population who were foreign-born whites and their U.S.-born children of German descent was 10.1 in North Dakota (22.6 percent were from Norway), 13.9 in South Dakota, 18 in Nebraska. Taken as a whole, the largest foreign-descent group on the northern plains was German. Van Nuys, *Americanizing the West*, 51.

7. Heatherton, "University of Radicalism," 559, 564, 566, 569, 571, citing Elizabeth Gurley Flynn's account. Smith, *Rocky Mountain Heartland*, 81.

8. Deutsch, *No Separate Refuge*, 110–11.

9. Deutsch, *No Separate Refuge*, 111. See Sandos, *Rebellion*, 79, on the number of Spanish-language papers. Van Nuys, *Americanizing the West*, 28–29.

10. Deutsch, *No Separate Refuge*, 113; Alter, "From the Copper-Colored Sons," 105; Lozano, *An American Language*, 157.

11. See Britten, *American Indians in World War I*, 20, 28, 38–44, 62–65, on myriad reasons for Indian enlistment, including economic opportunity, job security, excitement, and adventure, as with all Americans. For Indians in addition was the opportunity to escape reservation conditions and earn far better wages than were available at home, as well as the rare opportunity to qualify for admission to warrior societies.

12. Kennedy, *Over Here*, 162–63, explains that the differential rates nationally at which draft boards declared Blacks registering for the draft eligible to serve (36 percent, but only 25 percent of whites) resulted partly from a ban on accepting Black volunteers (white volunteers reduced the pool of eligible whites) and the job discrimination that left few Blacks able to claim industrial exemptions or even exemptions as husbands and fathers with economic dependents, since army pay with family allotment often increased Black family income. Blacks were 10 percent of the U.S. population but 13 percent of its draftees. Deutsch, *No Separate Refuge*, 112. While little boys in Hispano villages, as elsewhere, played soldier, approximately ten thousand of their older brothers, making up 65 percent of New Mexico's contingent, served in the war.

13. Britten, *American Indians in World War I*, 53–54.

14. Britten, *American Indians in World War I*, 51–58. The Dawes Severalty Act (1887) and the Burke Act (1906) both governed eligibility for citizenship.

15. *Albuquerque Morning Journal*, June 9, 1917, 1. Joseph H. Peck, *What Next, Doctor Peck?* (Englewood Cliffs NJ: Prentice-Hall, 1959), 189–91, excerpted in Bergon and Papanikolas, *Looking Far West*, 55–56.

16. Britten, *American Indians in World War I*, 67–69.

17. Britten, *American Indians in World War I*, 61, 70–71.

18. Deutsch, *No Separate Refuge*, 112–13. Kennedy, *Over Here*, 156–57, 165: about 337,000 dodged the draft. And see Horne, *Black and Brown*, 126–27, citing historian Daniel La Botz on the vast number of draft resisters nationwide, in addition to the 337,649 men who registered but did not report when called up or deserted afterward, for a total of nearly 4 million.

19. Green, *Grass-Roots Socialism*, 365–65, 367–68. Burbank, *When Farmers Voted Red*, 140, 143–45, also points to a mutual suspicion of town and country—the town convinced of a socialist conspiracy that would lead to revolution and loss of property and life, and the country convinced of a conspiracy of "bankers, merchants, and landlords" already robbing them of their livelihoods. Chang, *The Color of the Land*, 185–86, 186, notes that reports mentioned the participation of "Snake" Indians.

20. Green, *Grass-Roots Socialism*, 368, 370–71, quotation from *Tulsa Daily World*, November 12, 1917. See also Chang, *The Color of the Land*, 189–91, who points out that Tulsa was the headquarters of Phillips Petroleum "and home to thousands of oil workers, many of them former farmers from Oklahoma" and elsewhere. The bomb exploded on October 29, 1917, and the trial ended on November 9, 1917.

21. Deutsch, *No Separate Refuge*, 108.

22. Robbins and Barber, *Nature's Northwest*, 63; Smith, *Rocky Mountain Heartland*, 71; Holtby, *Lest We Forget*, 46.

23. Wrobel, *America's West*, 108–9; Britten, *American Indians in World War I*, 132, 145–46; Holtby, *Lest We Forget*, 45.

24. Robbins and Barber, *Nature's Northwest*, 61; North, *California at War*, 123–36.

25. North, *California at War*, 148.

26. North, *California at War*, 147, 149. Between 1916 and 1920 prices rose over 80 percent. Deutsch, *No Separate Refuge*, 114–15; Thompson, *Closing the Frontier*, 100–101.

27. Deutsch, *No Separate Refuge*, 112–14.

28. Adams, *Three Roads to Magdalena*, 85; McWilliams, *Factories*, 178–79.

29. Deutsch, *No Separate Refuge*, 108–9.

30. Deutsch, *No Separate Refuge*, 109. See also Hernández, *Migra!*, 191. The act also created the Asiatic Barred Zone, prohibiting entry by any immigrant of Asian descent; the new visa fee was $10, and the head tax was $8. Legal entry was limited to official ports of entry, and newly minted citizens could still be deported within five years.

31. Weber, *From South Texas to the Nation*, 105–6. The Immigration Act went into effect on May 5, 1917, and the exemptions were issued on May 23; they

expanded to railroads, mines, and construction in the border states in July 1918. The exemptions reduced pressure to reverse the exclusion of "Asiatic labor." A significant portion of wages were withheld to guarantee the voluntary repatriation of the immigrants. See also Deutsch, *No Separate Refuge*, 109–10.

32. Hyman, *Soldiers and Spruce*, 26.

33. Hyman, *Soldiers and Spruce*, 19–21. See Hart, *Empire and Revolution*, 341.

34. *Albuquerque Morning Journal*, June 29, July 2, 3, 4, 5, 7, 1917.

35. *Albuquerque Morning Journal*, July 11, 13, 1917. According to Berman, *Reformers*, 145, in May 1917 "less than one hundred Wobblies were able to convince some six thousand miners" to go on strike. Strikes followed in Globe, Miami, Clifton, Morenci, and Metcalf, as well as Bisbee. Benton-Cohen, *Borderline Americans*, 227.

36. Osselaer, *Winning Their Place*, 106–7. And see Benton-Cohen, *Borderline Americans*, 228. According to Berman, *Reformers*, 139, Hunt barely squeaked in for a third term as governor in 1916, winning by forty-three votes out of over fifty-five thousand only after a recount.

37. *Albuquerque Morning Journal*, July 7, 14, 15, 1917.

38. Alter, "From the Copper-Colored Sons," 106–7; Foley, *The White Scourge*, 114–15.

39. McWilliams, *Factories*, 169–72.

40. *Albuquerque Morning Journal*, July 15, 16, 1917.

41. *Albuquerque Morning Journal*, July 16, 17, 1917; Benton-Cohen, *Borderline Americans*, 227–28; St. John, *Line in the Sand*, 140–41. The number of troops swelled all along the border, quadrupling the population of Nogales, Arizona, for example. Horne, *Black and Brown*, 143, writes that the deportees outnumbered the regular residents of Columbus.

42. *Albuquerque Morning Journal*, July 15, 16, 1917.

43. Deutsch, *No Separate Refuge*, 110.

44. The strike had spread to telephone operators, carpenters, electricians, and streetcar operators. Smith, *Jeannette Rankin*, 127–29.

45. Smith, *Jeannette Rankin*, 129–30; Preston, *Aliens and Dissenters*, 93, 95, 103, 129–37.

46. Smith, *Jeannette Rankin*, 131–33, 137. She had the support of the Nonpartisan League, which some towns prohibited from holding meetings (136). When she lost the Republican nomination, Rankin decided to run on the National Party ticket (138), a coalition of socialists, progressives, Prohibitionists, and the Nonpartisan League. The Democratic candidate, former progressive Walsh, began to court conservatives and won the election (139–40). According to Morlan, *Political Prairie Fire*, 125, 134–36, 146–47, 184, 206–7, 211, 214, there was some effort to negotiate a deal between the IWW and Nonpartisan League members for harvest labor, which, though it failed, resulted in less upheaval during the 1917 harvest than elsewhere. Watkins, *Rural Democracy*, 1, 170–74. See Gutfeld, *Montana's Agony*, 95–100, for similar dynamics in Montana. Lansing, *Insurgent Democracy*, 176–77, credits the attempt by the

Commission on Public Safety to destroy the St. Paul streetcar union with not only leading to violence and martial law at the end of 1917 but also driving the labor movement from the Democrats to the NPL.

47. Putman, *Class and Gender Politics*, 186–87, 204. See also Preston, *Aliens and Dissenters*, 95, 103–5, 129; Clemens, *The People's Lobby*, 267. See Watkins, *Rural Democracy*, 167–68, 173–74, on Centralia, where the IWW was repeatedly run out of town from 1910 to 1918. Chang, *Pacific Connections*, 174–75.

48. Putman, *Class and Gender Politics*, 183–85, 192–95. The quotation appears in Anna Louise Strong to Mr. Kellog, February 26, 1918, folder 66, box 7B, Anna Louise Strong Papers, Special Collections, University of Washington Libraries, Seattle.

49. Putman, *Class and Gender Politics*, 191. See also Mickelson, "The Loyal Legion of Loggers and Lumbermen"; Preston, *Aliens and Dissenters*, 130, 131–33. Haywood, *The Autobiography*, 290–309, describes the strikes and raids of the era, starting with the iron miners' strikes in the Iron Range in Minnesota; Everett, Washington; Butte, Montana; and Jerome and Bisbee, Arizona; and the Preparedness Parade in San Francisco.

50. Preston, *Aliens and Dissenters*, 164, 173, 175, 178, 226. Few of those detained for deportation were actually deported.

51. Hyman, *Soldiers and Spruce*, 42–44.

52. Hyman, *Soldiers and Spruce*, 30, 46–47, 50–51, 109 (Brice P. Disque quote).

53. Hyman, *Soldiers and Spruce*, 50–52, 66, 76.

54. Hyman, *Soldiers and Spruce*, 78, 84, 95, 98, 107.

55. Hyman, *Soldiers and Spruce*, 112, 115, 121, 176–82, 245, 254, 285, 296, 305, 308, 325.

56. See Horne, *Black and Brown*, 92, on guarding Bisbee deportees. See also Benton-Cohen, *Borderline Americans*, 103. According to Benton-Cohen, the legislature passed a Jim Crow law in 1910. Few, if any, African Americans could get access to Bisbee's mining jobs. Leiker, *Racial Borders*, 143, 146–47, 151. Kennedy, *Over Here*, 171, on Pershing's Philippines service and appointment.

57. In Arizona the segregated schools emerged from the desires of Tucson's Black population, who were not being well served in the integrated schools. The city's Black school, due to its proximity to a military base that housed Black troops (Fort Huachuca), had a steady stream of Black writers, activists, and artists visiting. On prospering in the borderlands, see Horne, *Black and Brown*, 53–55.

58. Horne, *Black and Brown*, 57–58. Horne points out that the benefits were relative. Job restrictions were still many. Leiker, *Racial Borders*, 151, 168–69.

59. On the biracial union and its unsuccessful 1920–21 strike, when white workers succumbed to a threat to make the workforce entirely Black, see Abel, "Opening the Closed Shop," 185–218. Steptoe, *Houston Bound*, 35–36.

60. Pruitt, "'Beautiful People,'" 51–56.

61. Horne, *Black and Brown*, 79 on Galveston, citing a 1915 witness who claimed the town had "a class of Negroes more insolent and defiant than

any other place in Texas"; 80–81 on Columbus; and 87 on Austin losing over one-third of its Black population between 1915 and 1918 and El Paso more than doubling.

62. Reich, "Soldiers of Democracy," 1482–83; Alter, "From the Copper-Colored Sons," 97–98; Lentz-Smith, *Freedom Struggles*, 45–51, 61.

63. Horne, *Black and Brown*, 74, 164, 176–77. In 1918 sixty Blacks were lynched; in 1919 seventy-six. Andrés, *Power and Control*, 74, 104; Delgado, *Making the Chinese Mexican*, 121, 124, 131–32, 158–59, 157–58, 161; Lentz-Smith, *Freedom Struggles*, 61. On the connections African Americans drew between their own struggles, anticolonial struggles of Africans, the bravery of Black troops in France, and the propaganda, see, for example, Reich, "Soldiers of Democracy," 1479, 1482–83.

64. Lentz-Smith, *Freedom Struggles*, 62–69; Reich, "Soldiers of Democracy," 1485. The soldiers had been stationed at Camp Logan.

65. Lentz-Smith, *Freedom Struggles*, 70, 76, quoting Clara Threadgill-Dennis, writing during the court-martial for the San Antonio Black newspaper, *The Inquirer*.

66. Lentz-Smith, *Freedom Struggles*, 71, 73, 74, 78. See Wrobel, *Promised Lands*, 172–73, on Albert Fall discouraging Black settlement in New Mexico. Horne, *Black and Brown*, 72, 75, 111, 117, 118; Heatherton, "University of Radicalism," 571. See Steptoe, *Houston Bound*, 38: in 1918 the Houston NAACP sued the city of Houston over police brutality. See Kennedy, *Over Here*, 160–62, on how the U.S. government not only removed Black troops from Texas but also delayed initiating a draft for Black men in deference to outraged white Texans until September 22, 1917, and then maintained a two-to-one ratio of white to Black trainees at all integrated camps. Blacks were also excluded from wartime officer training camps until NAACP insistence led in July 1917 to the establishment of a Black officer training camp. It graduated its sole class (of 639 officers) in October at Fort Des Moines, Iowa. The officers were all assigned to the Ninety-Second, whose superior officers remained white.

67. Martínez, *Fragments*, 141; St. John, *Line in the Sand*, 119, 139–40.

68. St. John, *Line in the Sand*, 144–45. According to Horne, *Black and Brown*, 167, Black troopers factored among the twenty-nine U.S. enlisted men wounded in the battle, and the U.S. government blamed German agents for instigating the attack.

69. Deutsch, *No Separate Refuge*, 117–18. See Krugler, *1919*, 3; major riots in the U.S. West included those in Longview, Texas; Bisbee, Arizona; Omaha, Nebraska; Phillips County, Arkansas; and Bogalusa, Louisiana. Correia, *Properties of Violence*, 69–71.

70. Green, *Grass-Roots Socialism*, 393–94. The quotation seems to come from *Harlow's Weekly* (Oklahoma City), September 24 or October 8, 1919. Clemens, *The People's Lobby*, 285.

71. Clemens, *The People's Lobby*, 287. See also Putman, *Class and Gender Politics*, 202–3.

72. Preston, *Aliens and Dissenters*, 197–98; Putman, *Class and Gender Politics*, 205. Both authors credit the absence of more conservative Seattle labor leaders at a national labor gathering for the unanimity of the decision.

73. Preston, *Aliens and Dissenters*, 198, quoting U.S. Attorney Robert Saunders to the Attorney General, February 4, 1919, Department of Justice file 198783-4, RG 60, Department of Justice, National Archives, Washington DC; Clemens, *The People's Lobby*, 287–88, quoting Robert Whitaker, "Washington: The Dawn of a Tomorrow," *The Nation*, December 19, 1923, 709; Putman, *Class and Gender Politics*, 206. According to Blair, "The 1920 Anti-Japanese Crusade," Japanese workers in Seattle "maintained solidarity with organized labor" during the general strike despite being barred from almost all local unions.

74. Putman, *Class and Gender Politics*, 206–7.

75. Clemens, *The People's Lobby*, 288–89. Those attacked by the federal government and ejected from their organizations included the leader of the Washington State Grange. See also Putman, *Class and Gender Politics*, 207–9.

76. Putman, *Class and Gender Politics*, 207–9, 211–12, on how a short-lived Farmer-Labor Party managed to elect a couple of its candidates to the Washington legislature in the early 1920s. See Watkins, *Rural Democracy*, 166–68 on Centralia; 176–80 on the Grange-NPL-Labor alliance.

77. Mckiernan-González, *Fevered Measures*, 194–97.

78. Martínez, *Fragments*, 139, 207, 215. Fall included nearly three hundred witnesses hoping for a U.S. intervention in Mexico to safeguard U.S. holdings, including his own; and Britton, *Revolution and Ideology*, 41, claiming Bolshevism was spreading to the United States via Mexican consuls and diplomats. Fall and the Murray Hill group employed their own publicity agent "to furnish news releases to the national press" and to pressure Wilson to restrain Carranza. On Canales, see Alter, "From the Copper-Colored Sons," 86; and Martinez, *The Injustice*, 182–215.

79. Leiker, *Racial Borders*, 150, giving as an example a *Houston Chronicle* sketch of the Columbus raid. By the end of 1919 even Texas seemed aware of the problematic nature of Ranger activities, and the state legislature launched a series of investigations into charges of murder and incompetence in Ranger companies. Reich, "Soldiers of Democracy," 1498; quotation from Assistant Director and Chief, Bureau of Investigation, to R. W. Timothy, Waco, Texas, August 9, 1919, in *Federal Surveillance of Afro-Americans (1917–1925)*, ed. Theodore Kornweibel, reel 10, frames 22–23 (Frederick MD: University Publications of America, 1985); Krugler, *1919*, 58–64.

80. Reich, "Soldiers of Democracy," 1499–1501, citing "Race Riot propaganda" from Hobby to A. Mitchell Palmer, July 29, 1919, box 391, Record Group 301, Papers of the Governor, Texas State Library, Austin; and citing "sawed off pump shot guns" from *Federal Surveillance of Afro-Americans (1917–1925)*, ed. Kornweibel, reel 10, frame 28; by 1922 few branches remained in Texas. The NAACP had 7,700 Texas members in 1919 and fewer than 1,100 in 1921. Regarding women and the Texas white primary, see McArthur, "Min-

nie Fisher Cunningham's Back Door Lobby"; because Texas had a white primary, opponents of woman suffrage could not argue that it would open the door to Black women voting. Steptoe, *Houston Bound*, 35, 38–41.

81. Krugler, *1919*, 50–58, 145–63.

82. Reich, "Soldiers of Democracy," 1501; Krugler, *1919*, 165–74.

83. Deutsch, *No Separate Refuge*, 119–20.

84. Deutsch, *No Separate Refuge*, 109, 120.

85. Deutsch, *No Separate Refuge*, 120.

86. Deutsch, *No Separate Refuge*, 121.

87. Deutsch, *No Separate Refuge*, 119, for Larrazolo quote, 121; Nieto-Phillips, *The Language of Blood*, 201–2; Lozano, *An American Language*, 140.

88. Deutsch, *No Separate Refuge*, 121–22. And see Barkan, *From All Points*, 322, quoting Congressman James Slayden of Texas, who wrote in 1921 that "Mexican" is a race, not a citizenship, that one-fourth of Mexicans in Texas were born in Texas, but "they are 'Mexican' just as all blacks are Negroes though they may have five generations of American ancestry."

89. Deutsch, *No Separate Refuge*, 122.

90. Deutsch, *No Separate Refuge*, 122.

91. Deutsch, *No Separate Refuge*, 122–23.

92. Deutsch, *No Separate Refuge*, 123.

93. Deutsch, *No Separate Refuge*, 123–24.

94. Deutsch, *No Separate Refuge*, 124.

95. Deutsch, *No Separate Refuge*, 124. See also Zamora, *The World of the Mexican Worker*, 69, on how Mexicans in Texas facing repatriation established organizations such as the Unión Colonizadora Mexicana, which received money and logistical aid from the Mexican government and the AFL to transport Mexican families from Fort Worth, San Antonio, and Houston to the Mexican border.

96. Deutsch, *No Separate Refuge*, 125.

97. Kang, *The INS on the Line*, 45–48.

98. Deutsch, *No Separate Refuge*, 125.

99. Deutsch, *No Separate Refuge*, 116, 126; Weber, *From South Texas to the Nation*, 45–46, 58, 70, 87; Gutiérrez, *Walls and Mirrors*, 57, 63; Sánchez, *Becoming Mexican American*, 96.

100. Deutsch, *No Separate Refuge*, 116.

101. Benton-Cohen, *Borderline Americans*, 229–31, quotation from "Bisbee, the Most Southern Mile-High City in North America," *Arizona Labor Journal*, May 31, 1929, 27. When the postwar cutbacks came, white workers were protected.

102. Deutsch, *No Separate Refuge*, 126.

103. Hirsch, *Riot and Remembrance*, 13, 20, 30; May, *African-Americans*, 245. On the 1910s Oklahoma oil boom, Sinclair's rivalry with Standard Oil, and the "poor man's field," see Thompson, *Closing the Frontier*, 117–21. There are many additional excellent books on the Tulsa race riot. See, for example, Krehbiel, *Tulsa, 1921*; Ellsworth, *Death in a Promised Land*; and Brophy, *Reconstructing the Dreamland*.

104. Hirsch, *Riot and Remembrance*, 29–30, 38. The proportion of Blacks in 1910 Tulsa was 10.2 percent.

105. Hirsch, *Riot and Remembrance*, 38, quotes the April 12, 1912, lead story in the *Tulsa Democrat.* The headline ran, "Shall Tulsa Be Muskogeeized?" Muskogee lay on former Creek Territory and had a high concentration of people of color (41–42). The ordinance exempted live-in Black domestic servants working for white families.

106. Hirsch, *Riot and Remembrance*, 42–43, 47–50. The church cost $92,000.

107. Chang, *The Color of the Land*, 192–93, quote from C. W. Callarman, "South Central District," in "Annual Report of the Extension Division, Oklahoma Agricultural and Mechanical College, 1920–1921," by W. A. Conner, 42, T-881, reel 6, National Archives, Washington DC; see 194 on first referring to Seminole County, Oklahoma, then referring to Okfuskee County.

108. Hirsch, *Riot and Remembrance*, 77.

109. Hirsch, *Riot and Remembrance*, 78–79, 82.

110. Hirsch, *Riot and Remembrance*, 68–71, 78–82. The *Tribune* reportedly carried the plan, but no surviving copy of its editorial page for May 31, 1921, exists. It was removed before the paper was converted to microfilm.

111. Hirsch, *Riot and Remembrance*, 82, 83–85.

112. Hirsch, *Riot and Remembrance*, 82, 85–87, 89.

113. Hirsch, *Riot and Remembrance*, 89–93, 96ff.

114. Hirsch, *Riot and Remembrance*, 108–9.

115. Hirsch, *Riot and Remembrance*, 117–21, 124–28, 134–39, 141. After visiting Tulsa, Walter White wrote a scathing indictment of the riot: "The Eruption of Tulsa," *The Nation*, June 29, 1921, 909–10, http://historymatters.gmu.edu/d/5119. White put the death toll at 50 white men and 150–200 Black men, women, and children; he called the perpetrators "a mob of 100-per-cent Americans" and pointed to Tulsa's southern pioneers, "lethargic and unprogressive by nature," as well as resentful of the wealthy "Negroes making greater progress than they themselves are achieving."

116. Preston, *Aliens and Dissenters*, 230–33; Morgan, "The Centennial of Pancho Villa's Raid"; Buhle, *Women and American Socialism*, 215, 241; Green, *Grass-Roots Socialism*, 394. Chang, *The Color of the Land*, 182, points out that with commodity prices high in 1916, the Democrats in Oklahoma had trounced the socialists, the latter losing all their seats in the state house. "Dave Leip's Atlas of U.S. Presidential Elections," https://uselectionatlas.org. See Hirsch, *Riot and Remembrance*, 139, 148: when W. E. B. Du Bois visited Tulsa in 1926 he called it "the most astonishing case of Negro grit of which I ever heard."

117. Lansing, *Insurgent Democracy*, 183.

118. Morlan, *Political Prairie Fire*, 229–31, 264, 266–68, 289, 290–93. For the decision, see Green v. Frazier 253 U.S. 233 (1920); and Scott v. Frazier [Frazier was the governor of North Dakota], 253 U.S. 243 (1920); and for the justice's question, see "State Socialism Constitutional," *Literary Digest*, June 26, 1920, 20–21; and *Leader*, April 26, 1920, 4, May 17, 1920, 4, both quoted in Morlan,

Political Prairie Fire. See Watkins, *Rural Democracy*, 178–80, on the emergence of a Farmer-Labor Party in western Washington in 1920 and the continued strength of the Nonpartisan League in the eastern part of the state, which backed progressives; together they outperformed the Democrats but could not unseat the Republicans.

119. See following chapters on landownership restrictions, as well as Daniels, *The Politics of Prejudice*. See Welke, *Law and the Borders*, 144. These are the years when the United States decided court cases that further defined "the boundaries of whiteness under the Naturalization Act"; see *Ozawa v. U.S.* (1922) and *U.S. v. Thind* (1922). When the subjects argued for rights on the basis that they, too, were white, they "reinforced the legitimacy of limiting naturalization to those defined as white."

Part 3. Speculating, 1920–29

1. Holtby, *Lest We Forget*, 221. Based on federal census records, improved farm acreage for many western states, including North Dakota, Montana, South Dakota, Oklahoma, Colorado, Washington, and Idaho, fell during the first half of the decade; in all of them the trend reversed in the second half, particularly sharply in Montana, Wyoming, and Colorado and far more modestly in Washington, Utah, and Idaho. In Nevada the acreage rose in the first half of the decade and then steadily declined. Courtesy of Brad Wood. Hurt, *The Big Empty*, 79–80, 91, shows that rain was above average on the Great Plains in the 1920s and wheat paid more than cattle. See Thompson, *Closing the Frontier*, 173–77, on the evictions of tenants and the shift to cattle in some parts of the state and the wheat boom in others.

2. Robbins and Barber, *Nature's Northwest*, 70–71, 75, 77. On the decline of the 4L, see Hyman, *Soldiers and Spruce*, 332–38.

3. Smith, *Rocky Mountain Heartland*, 110–12, 123. And see Thompson, *Closing the Frontier*, 169–70, 172, on cotton and coal; in 1920 cotton cost a penny a pound more to produce than it fetched, and the surplus of coal miners and dropping prices meant coal miners worked fewer and fewer days per year, dipping to eighty days a year in the Henryetta fields until the mining company went bankrupt in 1924.

4. Criminal syndicalism laws continued to be enforced at the state level into the 1920s. See, for example, Thompson, *Closing the Frontier*, 196–97, on Arthur Berg being arrested for carrying an IWW union card, convicted in 1923, and given the maximum sentence. Homer Wear was arrested in June 1923 for distributing an article supporting Californians charged under California's Criminal Syndicalism Act; he got six years in prison and a fine of $750. Both men's sentences were reversed in 1925.

5. Ott, "'The Free and Open People's Market,'" 53, 64 for democratic capitalism and Soviet Union quotations; 65 for shareholder democracy; 60, 62 on direct economic democracy and modernity.

6. Canaday, *The Straight State*, 3, quoting Hugh Heclo, *Modern Social Politics in Britain and Sweden: From Relief to Income Maintenance* (New Haven CT: Yale University Press, 1974), 305.

7. I think about this as analogous to Margot Canaday's depiction of the process of inventing sexual categories by the state; for example, "after the Second World War, an increasingly powerful state wrote this new knowledge into federal policy, helping to produce the category of homosexuality through regulation" (*The Straight State*, 3–4). Canaday, in writing of sexuality, asserts that state identification of traits, behaviors, and so on "was a catalyst in the formation of homosexual identity. The state, in other words, did not merely implicate but also *constituted* homosexuality in the construction of a stratified citizenry" (3).

8. Lyon, *Prisons and Patriots*; Canaday, *The Straight State*, 8, citing Smith, *Civic Ideals*, on U.S. citizenship in the twentieth century not continually expanding but persistently being a "nexus of exclusion and inclusion"; Lyon also cites Ursula Vogel, "Marriage and the Boundaries of Citizenship," in *The Condition of Citizenship*, ed. Bart van Steenbergen (Thousand Oaks CA: Sage 1994), 77. Gutiérrez, "Antinomies of the Nation," argues that immigrants found ways to create proxy citizenship when excluded, redefining the boundaries and terms of citizenship by their actions.

9. Canaday, *The Straight State*, 10, cites Lisa J. Disch, review of *Being Political: Genealogies of Citizenship*, by Engin F. Isin, *Environment and Planning D: Society and Space* 21 (June 2003): 380–82, as above, and "otherness is immanent to citizenship."

7. Oil

1. U.S. Congress, House, Committee on the Public Lands, *Oil and Gas Lands*, 101, 224. This area of two to three thousand acres had started to be developed for oil in 1911, when the Texas Chief came in, beginning on the floodplain, and then onto the riverbed proper (43).

2. U.S. Congress, House, Committee on the Public Lands, *Oil and Gas Lands*, 28, 43, 96–101, 240–41, 133, 301, 307, 309–11, 320–21, 352 (July 6, 1922, letter from Mark Denson, Rocky Ford, Colorado, a civil engineer and deputy mineral surveyor who had charge of locating these claims, to Mr. Everett Owens of Denver, giving a record of events).

3. U.S. Congress, House, Committee on the Public Lands, *Oil and Gas Lands*, 28–29, 33, 312; U.S. Congress, Senate, Committee on Public Lands, *Red River Oil Lands*, 22, for mention that there were 160 claims filed on the disputed land.

4. Olien and Olien, *Easy Money*, x, point out that "speculative manias" were not new in the 1920s and had characterized western development in railroads, land, and canal shares; p. 25 refers to a boom also in Kentucky, the only nonwestern state; p. 37 cites Louisiana as maintaining fourth place, growing dramatically from over fifteen million barrels in 1919 to over ninety-

two million in 1939, followed by Kansas, which more than doubled output between 1919 and 1939, reaching over fifty-seven million barrels in that year. For 1919, 1929, and 1939, see U.S. Bureau of the Census, *Sixteenth Census,* 1:129, table 4; for 1909, U.S. Bureau of the Census, *Thirteenth Census,* 11:279, table 23. Thanks to Brad Wood.

5. Olien and Olien, *Easy Money,* for many examples; and Tygiel, *The Great Los Angeles Swindle,* 120, 163, 165.

6. U.S. Congress, House, Committee on the Public Lands, *Oil and Gas Lands.* The Committee on Public Lands included eleven westerners (Oregon, Kansas, Colorado, Idaho, California [2], Washington, Utah, Arizona, Arkansas, and Alaska), five members from the Southeast, and one from Indiana. Smith, *Rocky Mountain Heartland,* 93–94; Hurt, *The Big Empty,* 76–78. On the Farmer-Labor Reconstruction League, made up of wheat farmers and cotton tenants and labor and borrowing its platform from the 1906 Farmers Union and Socialist Party, see Thompson, *Closing the Frontier,* 11, 199, 208–11. On the percentages of the 1924 presidential vote, see Clemens, *The People's Lobby,* 299–301.

7. Canaday, *The Straight State,* makes a similar argument about homosexuality and the state (e.g., 2). Here I am looking particularly at the Department of the Interior, which had charge of public lands, including selling and marketing them, and Congress, which had oversight and legislative powers regarding the same.

8. Hawley, *The Great War,* 21–22, has wages rising just a little more than the 40 percent jump in the cost of living. According to Thompson, *Closing the Frontier,* 169, 172, cotton prices went from eight cents per pound in 1914 to thirty-nine cents a pound in 1919, only to fall to fifteen cents a pound thereafter; in June 1920 farmers received twenty-four cents a pound, but it cost twenty-five cents to produce, and by December the price had fallen to nine cents a pound. Olien and Olien, *Easy Money,* 4, 5, on wheat reaching $3.52 per bushel in futures in May 1917, a record high at the Chicago Board of Trade; cotton prices in 1919 were the highest in fifty-two years. Clark, *Deliver Us from Evil,* argues that the enactment of Prohibition limited their ability to spend it on drink. See Ott, "'The Free and Open People's Market,'" 44–71, particularly 44–45: a few hundred thousand Americans owned stock before World War I (about 3 percent of U.S. households); by 1929 an estimated eight million did (or roughly a quarter of households). The NYSE began actively to try to enlarge the number of shareholders in 1922, convinced that they would bolster the NYSE's fight against government regulation.

9. Hawley, *The Great War,* 57, on unemployment hitting 12 percent in 1921; by 1923 it was under 4 percent, but while most sectors experienced that rapid recovery, agriculture did not. See Olien and Olien, *Easy Money,* 10, 26, 51, on how the average price of crude oil rose from sixty-four cents per barrel before 1916.

10. Olien and Olien, *Easy Money,* 6, 27.

11. Hawley, *The Great War*, 71–72, claims that by 1929, 40 percent of U.S. families had radio receiving sets for nearly eight hundred broadcasting stations. Olien and Olien, *Easy Money*, 4, 26; in addition, navies had switched to fuel oil from coal just before World War I.

12. Thompson, *Closing the Frontier*, 117, 178: 1911 was already the second major oil boom in Oklahoma, and the United States produced 65 percent of the world's oil. Saunt, *Black, White, and Indian*, 163; Hawley, *The Great War*, 73; Olien and Olien, *Easy Money*, 36.

13. U.S. Congress, House, Committee on the Public Lands, *Oil and Gas Lands*, 261, 265; Olien and Olien, *Easy Money*, x, 36, on the cost of drilling.

14. Olien and Olien, *Easy Money*, x, 25; U.S. Congress, House, Committee on the Public Lands, *Oil and Gas Lands*, 255, 261–62.

15. U.S. Congress, House, Committee on the Public Lands, *Oil and Gas Lands*, 102, 168–69 (testimony of Mr. E. H. Wicks of Pittsburgh).

16. Olien and Olien, *Easy Money*, xi, 9–10, 56, 58, 64, 76, 78, 82–84, 90, 117.

17. Olien and Olien, *Easy Money*, 23, 92–130.

18. Olien and Olien, *Easy Money*, 55, define the blue-sky statutes as "aimed at barring sales of securities by companies whose assets amounted to no more than 'so many feet of blue sky.'" Tygiel, *The Great Los Angeles Swindle*, 60–62.

19. Olien and Olien, *Easy Money*, 22–23, 123–29, 130, 145, 146. See also Ott, "'The Free and Open People's Market,'" 44, on the efforts of the NYSE to fight off the possibility of regulation at the height of progressive activity in Congress, starting in 1913; see 48–49, 50, 51, on the growth of blue-sky laws after the Panic of 1907. Twenty-four states passed laws requiring securities brokers to be licensed in the wake of the panic "and established commissions to approve new securities issues."

20. U.S. Congress, House, Committee on the Public Lands, *Oil and Gas Lands*, 210, 272, 287.

21. U.S. Congress, House, Committee on the Public Lands, *Oil and Gas Lands*, 255, 261, 303–4, 305, 369. The term "pioneer" recurs frequently, used particularly by Roote (see, e.g., 180, 210).

22. U.S. Congress, House, Committee on the Public Lands, *Oil and Gas Lands*, 369, 370–74, 376–81.

23. U.S. Congress, House, Committee on the Public Lands, *Oil and Gas Lands*, 370–74.

24. U.S. Congress, House, Committee on the Public Lands, *Oil and Gas Lands*, 393, 396, and on sympathy, see 105–7, 147.

25. U.S. Congress, House, Committee on the Public Lands, *Oil and Gas Lands*, 411, 435–36. When the Supreme Court ruled in favor of the Texas claimants, returning to them thirteen-sixteenths of the total gross production of the wells they claimed, Dyar, "trying to protect the interests of the United States," attacked their claim to be pioneers.

26. U.S. Congress, House, Committee on the Public Lands, *Oil and Gas Lands*, 435–36, 438. Toward the end of the hearings, Dyar acknowledged his

error regarding Burk Divide, where the increased investment all came from the original investors. They had not bought into a lawsuit, and as it did with Mellish, the original locator remained. Because of the good-faith agreement, the United States paid back the proceeds of the oil, except for the standard royalty payment to the government for drilling on government land (445). U.S. Congress, Senate, Committee on Public Lands, *Red River Oil Lands*, 29. Dyar tried again before the Senate committee in 1924 to get the law of 1923 allowing permits and leasing on the southern half of the Red River repealed, but he failed.

27. U.S. Congress, House, Committee on the Public Lands, *Oil and Gas Lands*, 210. Roote is here arguing that the mining law was generally applicable except where it had been explicitly abrogated, as Congress had done for six states, not including Oklahoma (and see 2, 15, 38–39). In 1920 Congress had passed an act permitting the mining of coal, phosphate, oil, oil shale, gas, and sodium in the public domain, but the United States held that U.S. public domain in Oklahoma had been excepted. Oklahoma lands had been reserved under the homestead law to "actual settlers only." The land was presumed to be agricultural, not mining land. See also Iverson, *The Navajo Nation*, 19, on how an 1891 law allowed the exploitation of minerals on Indian land only where Indians had bought and paid for the land. Arizona congressman Carl Hayden and Senators Henry F. Ashurst (Arizona) and Albert Fall (New Mexico) introduced what became the Metalliferous Minerals Leasing Act in 1918, which allowed the secretary of the interior to lease Indian lands to mine valuable minerals; Indians would get a minimum 5 percent royalty, "but that money could be apportioned by Congress as it deemed proper." Allison, *Sovereignty for Survival*, 19–22, 31–32. See also White, *Roots of Dependency*, 232–33, on how oil was discovered on the reservation in 1922; in 1927, 25 percent of oil and gas revenues up to $1.2 million were set aside for land purchases to enlarge the reservation.

28. There was a single reservation shared by the Kiowas and Comanches. U.S. Congress, House, Committee on the Public Lands, *Oil and Gas Lands*, 223, 411, 421; Olien and Olien, *Easy Money*, 28.

29. Olien and Olien, *Easy Money*, 26. In 1920 alone thirty-four thousand wells were drilled, twice the number of 1915. Thompson, *Closing the Frontier*, 178–79. On national wage rates, see U.S. Bureau of Labor Statistics, *Union Scale of Wages*; wages that year were 9 percent higher on average than in 1922.

30. Hawley, *The Great War*, 73. See Chang, *The Color of the Land*, 193–94. The number of white farm owners in most eastern Oklahoma counties plunged between 1920 and 1925; in Creek County nonwhite owner-operators went from 145 to 206 between 1920 and 1925; in Okmulgee County from 228 to 274; and in Okfuskee County from 490 to 728. In Seminole County, on the other hand, they fell by 21 percent, almost as much as the drop among white farmers. Thompson, *Closing the Frontier*, 170. In the Oklahoma coal fields throughout the 1920s, the industry had a surplus of miners, and they worked only 124 to 150 days.

31. The KKK often but not always used violence to achieve its ends. For a useful overview of the copious literature on the 1920s KKK, see Lay, *The Invisible Empire*; and Moore, "Historical Interpretations."

32. Gordon, *The Second Coming*, 102, 105 on anti-IWW activities in Nebraska and the Pacific Northwest; 106 on the Oregon Klan's support of national railway workers striking in 1922, leading many strikers to join the Klan. Robbins and Barber, *Nature's Northwest*, 73–74. Wrobel, *America's West*, 115, shows how, certainly, the KKK also targeted Blacks, whipping a Black Dallas bellhop and branding his forehead; members also stripped, beat, tarred, and feathered a white woman "suspected of marital impropriety" (116); Hurt, *The Big Empty*, 47–55; Smith, *Rocky Mountain Heartland*, 99. And see Goldberg, "Denver," on the Klan's capture of first the Democratic and then the Republican Party and its ultimate ouster via anticorruption.

33. Chang, *The Color of the Land*, 198–99, 200. Chang refers to the beating of Charles Smith, a Black prisoner, in 1922 for insubordination to his jailers. See also Steptoe, *Houston Bound*, 41–43.

34. Chang, *The Color of the Land*, 196–97, 200. See Thompson, *Closing the Frontier*, 192–93; while seventy of the incidents took place in Tulsa County, it is worth noting that the Tulsa riot was not instigated by the Klan. Hirsch, *Riot and Remembrance*, 163, 165–67, puts the proportion at one of every ten white Protestant males in the state, making it among the strongest Klan territories in the country, with a membership larger than organized labor or even any political party. See Tygiel, *The Great Los Angeles Swindle*, 64; it was a decade saturated with the language of race—race consciousness so deeply entered the fiber of daily existence that everything from candy to behavior carried racial labels and connotations.

35. Chang, *The Color of the Land*, 201–2, 213–14. According to Chang, anti-Klan farmers adopted Working Class Union tactics, threatening "to burn the homes of tenants who rented from Klansmen." Thompson, *Closing the Frontier*, 213–14, who concludes, "For a brief period the Klan was perhaps the dominant political force in the State" (214); the Klan nonetheless collapsed within three years. Hirsch, *Riot and Remembrance*, 167.

36. Wrobel, *America's West*, 116–24; Stuckey, review of *Perseverance*.

37. Stratton, *Tempest over Teapot Dome*, 110, 112, 113, 214.

38. Olien and Olien, *Easy Money*, 19, 74, 130: for example, the Permian Basin in Texas and New Mexico and the Rocky Mountain Overthrust in Wyoming.

39. Olien and Olien, *Easy Money*, 19–23. See also Sabin, *Crude Politics*, 127.

40. For examples, see U.S. Congress, House, Committee on Indian Affairs, *Modifying Osage Fund Restrictions*, serial 1, 32, 72, 216. On the glut, see also Hawley, *The New Deal*: new "pools" that were opened between 1926 and 1931 led to excess capacity; the failure of voluntary restriction led "industry leaders and conservationists" to plead for federal controls "to check the fall in prices and to prevent the immense waste involved in competitive development" (27); Noggle, *Teapot Dome*, vii, 16: the Taft administration had set aside

two naval oil reserves on government land in California; the nine thousand acres that composed Teapot Dome (named for its geological feature) were set aside in 1915 for the exclusive use or benefit of the United States Navy, which had switched from coal to oil. McCartney, *The Teapot Dome Scandal*, 248, regarding the $100,000 Doheny gave Fall for his struggling New Mexico Three Rivers ranch.

41. McCartney, *The Teapot Dome Scandal*, 89–90, 148, on Sinclair, who had inherited his father's pharmacy after college but preferred gambling; and Stratton, *Tempest over Teapot Dome*, 299, on rags to riches. Nye replaced Ladd as senator of North Dakota and so was on the committee when Ladd died suddenly in June 1925.

42. The Harding administration came into an ongoing fight between Wilson's secretary of the interior, who wanted to lease the reserves, and his secretary of the navy, who did not. As of 1920 the navy had won, and congressional action gave the naval secretary full discretion over the use of the reserves. Noggle, *Teapot Dome*, 17 (*Lane v. Josephus Daniels*), 204. On Hoover, see Burner, *Herbert Hoover*; Leuchtenburg, *Herbert Hoover*; Whyte, *Hoover*; and Wilson, *Herbert Hoover*.

43. Noggle, *Teapot Dome*, 9–11, 13. On Greene, see Truett, *Fugitive Landscapes*, 83–103, 133–56. See Stratton, *Tempest over Teapot Dome*, 30–57, for Fall's path to electoral politics, starting with his challenges to the Santa Fe Ring and the cultivation of Hispano allies.

44. Noggle, *Teapot Dome*, 22–26, 33. Fall snatched the reserves from under the nose of the naval secretary, having an underling at the navy authorize the transfer; the naval secretary became aware of the transfer but took no action. McCartney, *The Teapot Dome Scandal*, 119–20, on the Navajos. Had it remained reservation land, the companies would have had to get tribal council approval and share royalties with the tribe. The Navajos benefited little from the oil on land that remained on the reservation because the agent appointed by Fall overthrew the tribal council and sold off land as quickly as possible, including one promising site to a friend for $1,000 who flipped it for $3 million to an oil company. Fall's dealings with the Navajos were not exposed until 1933. See Stratton, *Tempest over Teapot Dome*, 211 on the larger reorganization; and 224–25 on leases on Navajo and other reservations resulting from a June 1922 decision by Fall that classified all executive order reservation land as public lands, only temporarily placed in Indian hands, and so open to oil and gas exploration under the General Leasing Act of 1920.

45. Quoted in Noggle, *Teapot Dome*, 25, citing Frederick E. Olmsted to Gifford Pinchot, December 5, 1921, box 240, Gifford Pinchot Papers, Library of Congress, Washington DC. Langston, *Forest Dreams*, 177–79, quotation on 178.

46. Noggle, *Teapot Dome*, 34, 43–45, 66. See McCartney, *The Teapot Dome Scandal*, 110, 161, 169, on Fall's and Walsh's common approach to western development, Fall wanting to open the Navajo reservation and Walsh the Blackfoot and Flathead reservations to white settlement. See

also 161–63. Norris was the exception. See Stratton, *Tempest over Teapot Dome,* 222, on Fall having opposed Walsh's bill to dam the outlet of Lake Yellowstone. The list is from another hearing of 1923, U.S. Congress, Senate, Committee on Public Lands, *Pueblo Indian Lands.* The regional near monopoly masked certain party divisions. The committee had "party stalwarts" (including conservationist Reed Smoot of Utah) who were likely to uphold the administration but also Republican insurgents, including George W. Norris of Nebraska; it had Democrats, including Thomas J. Walsh of Montana and John B. Kendrick of Wyoming; and it had the Nonpartisan League's Edwin F. Ladd of North Dakota. Some would remain convinced that party politics motivated the battle, with Walsh, the Democrat, gunning for Fall and the Republican administration. See Noggle, *Teapot Dome,* 67, for example: as Walsh was about to abandon the investigation, Democratic National Committee chair Cordell Hull provided some much-needed aid.

47. Stratton, *Tempest over Teapot Dome,* 120–22, 149–54, 236–37, 252–76.

48. Noggle, *Teapot Dome,* quoted on 107, and see 120 on Lenroot, who had replaced Smoot as committee chair. Smoot resigned from the committee on March 11, 1924, recuperating from a nervous breakdown. Senator Ladd of North Dakota succeeded Lenroot as chair. And see McCartney, *The Teapot Dome Scandal,* 252, on how, during the Cheyenne trial, the president of the dummy Continental Trading company was big-game hunting in Africa; Standard Oil's Robert Stewart was also out of the country; others were in France. None of the principals in the creation of the Teapot deal could be brought to testify. Sinclair and Fall both took the Fifth.

49. Noggle, *Teapot Dome,* 100–102, 163, 202–4, 210–15. Walsh, so popular in 1924 when he presided over an unbelievably dysfunctional Democratic National Convention during which voices from the floor demanded that he himself become the candidate, utterly failed in a 1928 bid. In 1928 Walsh was Catholic and dry; Smith was Catholic and wet; Walsh withdrew on May 4. McCartney, *The Teapot Dome Scandal,* 248, writes that on July 1, after the sixth of what would be over one hundred ballots, the convention received the announcement that Fall, Sinclair, and Doheny and his son had been indicted due to Walsh's efforts.

50. McCartney, *The Teapot Dome Scandal,* 250–53. See 251 for Sinclair's fields (courtesy of Fall) as the largest reserve of light crude oil in the world, employing "a sizable percentage of the state's workforce."

51. Noggle, *Teapot Dome,* 182–84, 185, 211 (quoting Norris). Intent is crucial. Fall had taken a bribe, but in the eyes of the Supreme Court, Doheny hadn't intended for the money to be used that way (211–14). The Los Angeles District Court had convicted Doheny on the grounds that his $100,000 loan to Fall was a bribe that had induced Fall to grant Doheny a lease on the Elk Hills reserve in California, a ruling upheld by the U.S. Circuit Court of Appeals in San Francisco.

52. Quoted in Noggle, *Teapot Dome*, 209. Langston, *Forest Dreams*, 181–83: companies that won bids on these contracts funded them by selling "basically junk bonds issued on the expected future worth of the company" (182).

53. Harmon, *Rich Indians*, 175, 182, points out that the magazine and other writers "seldom missed a chance to show that the rich, especially the new rich, were prone to wildly impractical expenditures" (175), whether a white Oklahoma farmer or "Negro Oil Magnates," *Los Angeles Daily Times*, May 24, 1922, sec. 2, 7.

54. See U.S. Congress, House, Committee on Indian Affairs, *Modifying Osage Fund Restrictions*, 148, 302–3. Harmon, *Rich Indians*, 176: the Osage income had jumped dramatically in the late 1910s, from $384 annually per Osage allotment to $2,719 in 1917 and to $8,090 in 1920 at a time when the disposable per capita income in the United States was $635.

55. U.S. Congress, House, Committee on Indian Affairs, *Modifying Osage Fund Restrictions*, 33 on murders; 93 on Tall Chief; 250 on "natural tendency" (J. George Wright, superintendent of the Osage Agency). The guardianships did often result in greater access to credit for their wards, which led one Indian not under guardianship to comment that people with guardians seemed to have better standing in the community, that merchants liked them better. And see Harmon, *Rich Indians*, 197; Grann, *Killers of the Flower Moon*, 282–84.

56. U.S. Congress, House, Committee on Indian Affairs, *Modifying Osage Fund Restrictions*, 44 (L. Lafe Hubler to Senator J. W. Harreld).

57. U.S. Congress, House, Committee on Indian Affairs, *Modifying Osage Fund Restrictions*, 201. The chairman also declared: "The Osages have a great deal of money and we have to look at it with the idea in mind of individual American liberty. If a man is competent and can prove himself competent, if he has a certain amount of money, it should be turned over to him to do as he pleases with it" (65). The question was how to determine competence. See also Ott, "'The Free and Open People's Market,'" 50, on the public relations war beginning in 1913 to define proposed government regulation of the stock exchange as inhibiting the freedom of the small investor.

58. U.S. Congress, House, Committee on Indian Affairs, *Modifying Osage Fund Restrictions*, 151–52, chairman (201), and a point made by Pawhuska, Oklahoma, attorney T. J. Leahy (201), in response to Snyder's comment about liberty: "The Supreme court of the United States has held repeatedly that granting of citizenship to an Indian does not destroy the status of an Indian or supervisory control" (312, Roach). See Hoxie, *A Final Promise*, particularly 211–38. See also Stein, "The Indian Citizenship Act of 1924." In 1916 the U.S. Supreme Court held citizenship not incompatible with wardship, and the Citizenship Act contained a provision that it would not impair extant Indian property rights; that is, unlike the Dawes Act, it did not end the holding of land in common by the tribe. Congress had already granted the right to become a citizen to Indian veterans of World War I in January

1919. It was optional and had to be done by the courts; few used it. State suffrage qualifications were not affected by the 1924 Citizenship Act. In Oklahoma Indians had gotten citizenship by an act of Congress in 1901 and had voting rights; Indians in New Mexico and Arizona would not have voting rights until 1948.

59. U.S. Congress, House, Committee on Indian Affairs, *Modifying Osage Fund Restrictions*, 85, 89, 160, 237, 255; Jesse J. Worten, Pawhuska, Oklahoma, district judge, twenty-fourth district, regarding a committee discussion of the benefits of giving the Osages agricultural education, felt obliged to add, "But, you will realize that Osage County is practically a grazing county; there is not much farming." The congressmen kept asking Eves Tall Chief what he did as he described his farming operations (84–90); the congressmen seem skeptical that Indians "work." At one point, Tall Chief even says, "As far as our working and being industrious people, we are not as a rule, but they are very attentive to their families and their home life" (93). On loafer or farmer, see Osage County farm agent S. M. McCuiston (254).

60. Thorne, *The World's Richest Indian*, 179, 185, 188. Creeks, including Barnett, continued to confound the neatly drawn lines that made the population legible and orderly not just to the state but to mass media audiences. Barnett had Afro-Creek heritage; a federal judge annulled the marriage in 1934, two months before Barnett's death, skeptical that an attractive white woman, "one who would likely encounter many a prepossessing man of the white race who would become interested in her," would instead marry "an aging man, a black Indian" (188). But Lowe had the sympathy of the public; two hundred thousand people signed a petition to the U.S. attorney general to stay her eviction after Barnett's death as she struggled to meet the expenses of legal disputes in multiple jurisdictions. Each one required its own legal firm, for a total of fourteen legal firms between 1920, when she married Barnett, and 1938 (179–80, 186, 197).

61. U.S. Congress, House, Committee on Indian Affairs, *Modifying Osage Fund Restrictions*, 229–30. Barnett had supported Harjo and the Crazy Snake uprising. Harmon, *Rich Indians*, 189, saw the Osages as divided "into two subcultures—a division rooted in divergent economic ideologies."

62. U.S. Congress, House, Committee on Indian Affairs, *Modifying Osage Fund Restrictions*, 144–56, quote from 156.

63. Jacobs, *Engendered Encounters*, 103, for Mary Austin's version: "In New York City they took the Pueblo delegates to the stock exchange, which, according to Austin, 'unbent.' 'When the Indians stood up in the gallery and sang the Morning Song,' Austin marveled, 'the Exchange simply got up on its hind legs and howled.' Activists raised a hefty five hundred dollars a day from the stock exchange to fund the defense of the Pueblos." Citing 222n72, Austin to Mabel Dodge Luhan, January 27, February 1, [1923], Mabel Dodge Luhan Papers, Beinecke Rare Book Library, Yale University, New Haven CT.

8. Land

1. Huebner, "An Unexpected Alliance," 356–58. According to Huebner, that was the Bursum bill, and it died in committee. U.S. Congress, House, Committee on Indian Affairs, *Pueblo Indian Land Titles,* 245, 396: the all-Pueblo meeting was November 5, 1922. Collier admitted it would not have happened if he had not traveled from pueblo to pueblo, but the meeting was called by the Pueblo Indians themselves. See also 246–47, 396.

2. According to Clemens, *The People's Lobby,* 290–304, 311.

3. See Woeste, *The Farmer's Benevolent Trust,* 8–11, 132, 140, 153–57.

4. See Orona, "Muddy Water," chap. 3, 10–12. See Thompson, *Closing the Frontier,* 218.

5. Orona, "Muddy Water," chap. 3, 12–13. See also Troutman, *Indian Blues,* 25–26. On Fall's relationship with the Indians whose reservation abutted his ranch, see Stratton, *Tempest over Teapot Dome,* 113 on water rights disputes with the Mescalero Apaches as a "constant source of irritant"; 118 on his 1913 recalling to the Senate his 1880s arrival in New Mexico only to see "an American holding in his hand the bleeding scalp of a woman who had been killed" by an Apache within a mile of Silver City's courthouse; 121 on his opposition to Apache cattle ranching as rivaling his own. U.S. Congress, House, Committee on Indian Affairs, *Pueblo Indian Land Titles,* 49, 103.

6. Orona, "Muddy Water," chap. 3, 13, 19–22, 65–66. And see Huebner, "An Unexpected Alliance," 355. U.S. Congress, House, Committee on Indian Affairs, *Pueblo Indian Land Titles,* 412. This is in Fall's letter, where he asks that the House of Representatives appoint a select committee to investigate the issue (413). According to Jacobs, *Engendered Encounters,* 1, Stella Atwood quipped, "They used to use war clubs; now they use women's clubs."

7. U.S. Congress, House, Committee on Indian Affairs, *Pueblo Indian Land Titles,* 49; Huebner, "An Unexpected Alliance," 354.

8. U.S. Congress, House, Committee on Indian Affairs, *Pueblo Indian Land Titles,* 1, 2, quoting John Collier's article in *Sunset Magazine,* January 1923, including among those it listed as having financial interests in Pueblo lands Fall and Senator Bursum, among others (91, 99, 109, 397, 400–402). Virtually all Indian advocates who spoke for autonomy and against enforced assimilation were tarred as con artists. On Sears's sympathy, see 244, 310, 348 (Edgar B). According to Thompson, *Closing the Frontier,* 39–40, the Seminoles lost almost 90 percent of their restricted allotted land through fraud and theft. See 67 Cong. Rec. H2413 (daily ed. February 10, 1922) (Hayden); U.S. Congress, Senate, Committee on Public Lands, *Pueblo Indian Lands,* 181–82, 218, 255.

9. U.S. Congress, House, Committee on Indian Affairs, *Pueblo Indian Land Titles,* 399. Huebner, "An Unexpected Alliance," 344, 345n12, 346, 347, quotes from the CFWC Southern District, Minutes of the Convention in Redlands, November 15–16, 1916, 9–10, folder V.5, Riverside Women's Club Collection, Riverside Public Library, Riverside, California.

10. Huebner, "An Unexpected Alliance," 344, 347–48.

11. Huebner, "An Unexpected Alliance," 348–49, 350–51, quoting Atwood's 1922 *Survey* article, "The Case for the Indian," 57; 351–52 from *The Clubwoman*, June 1922; 17 from his speech at the twenty-first annual convention of the CFWC in Los Angeles, May 1922.

12. U.S. Congress, House, Committee on Indian Affairs, *Pueblo Indian Land Titles*, 10–11 on Snyder; 12 on interrogating Francis C. Wilson, an attorney from Santa Fe representing the GFWC Indian welfare committee, the Eastern Association on Indian Affairs in New York, the New Mexico Association on Indian Affairs of Santa Fe, and the Pueblo Indians of New Mexico, who designated him their representative at their general council in November; and 76, 78–80, 84, 86–88, 98–99, 105, 108, 112–14, 123, 210, 397–98; see also Huebner, "An Unexpected Alliance," 358–59. On Alice Robertson, see Chamberlin, *Minority of Members*; and Tolchin, *Women in Congress*.

13. U.S. Congress, House, Committee on Indian Affairs, *Pueblo Indian Land Titles*, 109, 243–44, 399. Clara True, like Robertson, had come to her experience with Indians through a missionary background. She was often frustrated by and critical of the BIA, particularly regarding her own lack of advancement there, but she remained loyal to its vision of assimilation and mobilized her connections among Pueblos against the Collier-Atwood allies in the early 1920s, creating scandalous friction and factions at the GFWC annual meetings, for example. See Jacobs, *Engendered Encounters*, 30, 59–60, 124–26.

14. U.S. Congress, House, Committee on Indian Affairs, *Pueblo Indian Land Titles*, 109. Atwood had vetted the bill with three lawyers in Pueblo country who universally opposed it (105). See also p. 404, November 27, 1922. See Huebner, "An Unexpected Alliance," 365, Harold Ickes to Harry Atwood, telegram, May 15, 1939, folder 12, box 1, series 1, part 2, Correspondence and Paper of Others, John Collier Papers, Yale University Library, New Haven CT, and Collier in unidentified periodical, June [*sic*—should be listed as July 12, 1939].

15. U.S. Congress, House, Committee on Indian Affairs, *Pueblo Indian Land Titles*, 306–8, 309.

16. U.S. Congress, House, Committee on Indian Affairs, *Pueblo Indian Land Titles*, 18, 21. Atwood uses the term on p. 85.

17. U.S. Congress, House, Committee on Indian Affairs, *Pueblo Indian Land Titles*, 23, 29, 46, 234–35, 312–13. For Wilson on adverse possession, see 46 and 300–301, for example, citing S.C. 129 U.S. 182: "Uninterrupted occupancy of land by a person who has in fact no title thereto, for the period of 10 years adversely to the true owner, operates to extinguish the title of the true owner, and vests the right to the premises absolutely in the occupier." See Huebner, "An Unexpected Alliance," 230, for similar problems the Navajos faced when Anglos overgrazed land on which Navajos depended and then could move their animals to winter ranges or truck in feed, which Navajos could not, nor could they afford the increased rates for leasing railroad lands.

18. U.S. Congress, House, Committee on Indian Affairs, *Pueblo Indian Land Titles*, 348–58, 399–400 (testimony by Edgar B. Meritt, assistant commissioner of Indian Affairs for the past decade, in the Indian Service for about eight years before that, and in government service for the decade before, for a total of twenty-eight years in government service, including time as the chief law officer of the Indian Bureau). 67 Cong. Rec. H2407, 2408, 2411 (daily ed. February 10, 1922) (Hayden). And see McDonald, *American Indians*, 13–14, on withholding rations from Indians who did not send their children to school and on Chief Runs the Enemy of the Teton Sioux, who sent his seven children to school; all of them contracted consumption and died.

19. U.S. Congress, House, Committee on Indian Affairs, *Pueblo Indian Land Titles*, 197, 205ff., on the Navajos, for example, as industrious, leasing land for their sheep, doing wage work, and farming more intensively in the new irrigation system that simultaneously was creating drainage problems and saturating the land with alkali; testimony indicated that the range had reached capacity in the West. Dr. Frederick L. Hoffman of Newark, New Jersey, a health statistician for Prudential Life Insurance Company, in an article in the *Journal of the American Medical Association*, August 14, 1920, that Collier read into the record, argued for transferring the Indian medical service from the Bureau of Indian Affairs to the United States Public Health Service, seeing it "not [as] a question of economy, but a question of life and death" (197). He referred in particular to the Navaho reservation, where tuberculosis accounted for 48 percent of causes of death and 25 percent of the population suffered from trachoma, where "the medical staff is not available." See also p. 232 on Pueblo health and the paucity of doctors, one for five pueblos covering 175 square miles, for example, "and the roads are bad." As for Indians acquiring lands by other means, see Childers, *The Size of the Risk*, 25; Schulze, *Are We Not Foreigners Here?*, 137–38.

20. U.S. Congress, House, Committee on Indian Affairs, *Pueblo Indian Land Titles*, 221–22, 229–30, 232–33, 240–41. San Juan was, next to Taos, the most well off regarding land and water of any pueblo north of Santa Fe except Taos.

21. U.S. Congress, House, Committee on Indian Affairs, *Pueblo Indian Land Titles*, 310–11, 348.

22. U.S. Congress, House, Committee on Indian Affairs, *Pueblo Indian Land Titles*, 235–36, 344.

23. Huebner, "An Unexpected Alliance," 359, for Burke's various circulars between 1921 and 1923; and see, for example, on kidnapping children to force them to Anglo schools, James, *The Hopi Indians*, 85. Also see McDonald, *American Indians*, 17.

24. For example, for the GFWC and Indian advocacy groups, see Huebner, "An Unexpected Alliance," 359–63. U.S. Congress, House, Committee on Indian Affairs, *Pueblo Indian Land Titles*, 190–200, 203–4, 224–25, 239; Robertson, along with others, also suspected that Indians made a killing on mar-

keting crafts and performing the much-contested dances. After all, Indian pottery was all the rage. Troutman, *Indian Blues*, 88.

25. 67 Cong. Rec. H2412–13 (daily ed. February 10, 1922) (Hayden). Although the connection is not made here, these seem to be the roads for oil speculators.

26. 67 Cong. Rec. H2407, 2411 (daily ed. February 10, 1922) (Hayden); U.S. Congress, House, Committee on Indian Affairs, *Modifying Osage Fund Restrictions*, serial 1, 94–95; note also, however, that he continues, "To-day we are talking about it—a very wealthy country we have got. We bought it from the Shawnees" (U.S. Congress, House, Committee on Indian Affairs, *Pueblo Indian Land Titles*, 244).

27. All quotations are from McCool, Olson, and Robinson, *Native Vote*, 2–5, 6, from the Dawes Act, a.k.a. the General Allotment Act of 1887. McDonald, *American Indians*, 9, 12, concludes that the U.S. Supreme Court in this case upheld Nebraska's decision to deny Indians the vote by declaring that Indians had no birthright citizenship.

28. McCool, Olson, and Robinson, *Native Vote*, 7. This provision for Indian veterans came with similar provision for immigrants who served in the U.S. military during World War I; see Welke, *Law and the Borders*, 35, on Congress granting the right to naturalize without first declaring intent or residing for five years in the United States to any "alien" who had served in World War I.

29. U.S. Congress, House, Committee on Indian Affairs, *Pueblo Indian Land Titles*, 216–19, 311, 403. When Renehan distinguished between legal traditions of the different regimes that held dominion over the area in defending Mexican land titles, he did so by essentializing "Anglo-Saxon people" and "the theory of the Spanish or Mexican . . . and the traditions and habits and customs of Spanish people" (311).

30. U.S. Congress, House, Committee on Indian Affairs, *Pueblo Indian Land Titles*, 344. Both examples on that page are of Mexican farmers. One takes advantage of a government decision to move a road that had been a boundary marker to build a fence to the new road, gaining one hundred acres; the other claimed to have a fifty-year-old deed signed by the Pueblo governors of the time. The chairman did not want Collier's examples put in the record because they relied on Indian testimony; Roach pointed out that Renehan's cases based on his statements were read into the record; there followed a discussion of what constituted "the standpoint of the Indian" rather than "the standpoint of some fellow who wrote up the standpoint of the Indian"; signatures were not seen as validating the testimony because of the use of an interpreter (344–45).

31. U.S. Congress, Senate, Committee on Immigration, *Selective Immigration Legislation*, 57.

32. Troutman, *Indian Blues*, 60. The United States was not alone in changing its citizenship laws in the 1920s. See Lyon, *Prisons and Patriots*, 18: in 1924 the Japanese government, which had previously automatically granted Japanese citizenship to Nisei, now required parents to register their children's births with a Japanese consulate within two weeks of birth in order to attain

Japanese citizenship for them. It also eased the renouncing of Japanese citizenship, previously forbidden for men of military age.

33. Troutman, *Indian Blues*, 70, argues that with rising numbers of citizen Indians, Office of Indian Affairs officials and missionaries wanted to reclaim and control their daily lives, including dancing, which they saw as a major manifestation of identity. U.S. Congress, House, Committee on Indian Affairs, *Alabama and Coushatta Indians of Texas*, 14, refers to Cramer v. United States, 325 U.S. 1 (1945), where the opinion held, "This duty of protection and power extends to individual Indians, even though they may have become citizens." Welke, *Law and the Borders*, 4, has argued that "the extension of citizenship could itself be or become an instrument of authority and subordination." And see Holtby, *Lest We Forget*, 240, on Bursum's work regarding Indian rights to pensions and his bitterness that New Mexico denied Indians the vote after 1924; see also Hoxie, *This Indian Country*, 273–75.

34. U.S. Congress, House, Committee on Indian Affairs, *Disposition of Unallotted Lands*, May 19, 1924, considered H.R. 6355, the Indian Citizenship Bill, with Homer Snyder presiding, long a championship of the measure. McCool, Olson, and Robinson, *Native Vote*, 1–18. And McDonald, *American Indians*, 18. It was a 1948 Pueblo lawsuit (challenged and upheld in 1975), brought by Miguel Trujillo from Isleta Pueblo, a World War II marine veteran and teacher at Laguna Pueblo, that successfully challenged the requirement that Indians had to pay property tax in order to be qualified to vote—a requirement imposed on no one else. An Akimel O'odham lawsuit in Arizona led to the abolition of many of these voting restrictions in 1948 for Indians under "guardianship," though other restrictions survived into the 1970s.

35. Orona, "Muddy Water," chap. 3, 1, citing Marc Reisner, *Cadillac Desert: The American West and Its Disappearing Water* (New York: Penguin Books, 1993), 30, 116. And see U.S. Congress, House, Committee on Irrigation and Reclamation, *Extension of the Time of Payment*, 1–4 and the table on 97, which demonstrates for most projects that the crop returns per acre were usually under or barely over the average construction cost per acre except for the boom years of 1919–22, as well as the minute amount repaid to the federal government on projects in Arizona, California, Colorado, Idaho, Montana, Nebraska, Nevada, New Mexico, North Dakota, Oregon, South Dakota, Utah, Washington, and Wyoming. See also Childers, *The Size of the Risk*, 23.

36. U.S. Congress, House, Committee on Irrigation and Reclamation, *Extension of the Time of Payment*, 1, 4, 224 (Mead).

37. U.S. Congress, House, Committee on Irrigation and Reclamation, *Extension of the Time of Payment*, 4–6. The original plan called for settlers to repay irrigation construction costs at the rate of 6 percent of construction costs per year rather than basing repayment on farm income; the suggested shift was to 5 percent of farm income.

38. U.S. Congress, House, Committee on Irrigation and Reclamation, *Extension of the Time of Payment*, 5, 15–16, 93, 111, 180–81. All but two of the fif-

teen committee members hailed from west of the Mississippi: Addison Smith, Idaho, chairman (R); Nicholas Sinnott, Oregon (R); Edward Little, Kansas (R); Elmer Leatherwood, Utah (R); Robert Simmons, Nebraska (R); Scott Leavitt, Montana (R); Charles Winter, Wyoming (R); Milton Garber, Oklahoma (R); Carl Hayden, Arizona (D); Claude Hudspeth, Texas (D); John Raker, California (D); William Lankford, Georgia (D); Charles Richards, Nevada (D); J. B. Reed, Arkansas (D); Miles Allgood, Alabama (D). Shale seems to have been a Wyoming project; the alkali example included a Yuma project in Arizona (191).

39. U.S. Congress, House, Committee on Indian Affairs, *Pima Indians*, 14, 22–23; for the year 1922, see 27. On December 1, 1923, the Salt River Valley Water Users' Association paid their reimbursement with a check for $609,000, the largest reimbursement the Reclamation Service had ever received.

40. U.S. Congress, House, Committee on Irrigation and Reclamation, *Extension of the Time of Payment*, 14, 32. The committee members could not agree on whether federal projects should require experience and a certain level of resources ($1,200 to $1,500) of its prospective settlers. Some believed such requirements flew in the face of the promise of opportunity and extraordinary effort; others saw lack of such requirements as a setup for failure (60–71, 76–77, 234–35, 237).

41. U.S. Congress, House, Committee on Irrigation and Reclamation, *Extension of the Time of Payment*, 5, 24, 69–71, 259.

42. U.S. Congress, House, Committee on Irrigation and Reclamation, *Extension of the Time of Payment*, 335–36, 343–44.

43. Worster, *Dust Bowl*, 92–93.

44. U.S. Congress, House, Committee on Irrigation and Reclamation, *Extension of the Time of Payment*, 5–6.

45. U.S. Congress, House, Committee on Irrigation and Reclamation, *Extension of the Time of Payment*, 6, 7. And see U.S. Congress, Senate, Committee on Immigration, *Restriction of Western Hemisphere Immigration*, 71 (testimony of Senator John B. Kendrick [Wyoming] on the altruistic aims of investors in sugar beet factories, which, he claimed, had never returned to stockholders a single penny but had "done all these things for the community and for the country").

46. U.S. Congress, House, Committee on Immigration and Naturalization, *Restriction of Immigration* (1924), 1076 (e.g., Congressman Raker, California).

47. U.S. Congress, House, Committee on Irrigation and Reclamation, *Extension of the Time of Payment*, 8, 39 (the seventeen states and the secretary of the interior's "full power and authority to deal with those districts"), 194 (the federal government had contracts with ten to twelve irrigation districts in South and North Dakota, Montana, Oregon, Washington, Texas, and New Mexico), 211 (variations and courts in Idaho and Washington—the irrigation district's promises to pay were general obligations against all district lands). Orona, "Muddy Water," ii, 9, 10–11, 25, 31; chap. 3, 3–4; between 1874

and 1919 the Rio Grande flooded the surrounding lands six times (18–19). See also U.S. Congress, House, Committee on Indian Affairs, *Pueblo Indian Land Titles*, 362–63.

48. Orona, "Muddy Water," chap. 4, 1, 3–4, 19–20. The petition to create the MRGCD was presented on September 17, 1923, with 119 signatures (100 were required); 31 percent of the signatories had Spanish surnames, and the signers included six women, all without Spanish surnames. Over half the signatories listed their residence as Albuquerque.

49. Orona, "Muddy Water," chap. 4, 5, 7–9, 10–11, 16, 21.

50. Orona, "Muddy Water," chap. 4, 17–20, 22, 24, 28–29, 30. See also Burke, *A Land Apart*, 199, 273, on the Mesilla Valley irrigation and its equation of whiteness and citizenship relating both to the Japanese and to Mexican-descent farmers; 70 percent of the irrigated farmland was waterlogged by 1917, and taxes were high because of the dam construction costs. By 1928, 90 percent of the irrigators in the Mesilla Valley grew cotton, and new Anglos replaced many Spanish-speaking farmers who had farmed a more diverse crop.

51. Orona, "Muddy Water," chap. 4, 24, 27–28, and chap. 5, 6, for Hagerman quote, Hagerman to E. B. Merritt, Assistant Commissioner of Indian Affairs, February 28, 1927, Herbert J. Hagerman Papers, Center for Southwest Research, University of New Mexico, Albuquerque. See also U.S. Congress, Senate, Committee on Indian Affairs, *The Middle Rio Grande Conservancy District*, 41–44, 48, 49, 53, 55. They attempted to deny John Collier the ability to testify at the hearing, but the committee chair, Nonpartisan Leaguer Lynn Frazier of North Dakota, forestalled them (48).

52. U.S. Congress, House, Committee on Irrigation and Reclamation, *Extension of the Time of Payment*, 247–48; Clemens, *The People's Lobby*, 304.

53. Hall, "Harvest Wobblies," 375–78, 444–52; now Hall, *Harvest Wobblies*; U.S. Congress, House, Committee on Irrigation and Reclamation, *Extension of the Time of Payment*, 95; U.S. Congress, Senate, Committee on Immigration, *Restriction of Western Hemisphere Immigration*, 59–61, 149–51.

54. For example, U.S. Congress, Senate, Committee on Immigration, *Selective Immigration Legislation*, 55, 57, 58–59, 62, 142, 163, 164; Senator Willis of Ohio claimed there were two thousand Mexicans in Gary, Indiana, alone (184); and see U.S. Congress, Senate, Committee on Immigration, *Restriction of Western Hemisphere Immigration*, 11 (Bixby), 30, 48; Perales, *Smeltertown*, 47ff.

55. Garcia, *A World of Its Own*, 51; Matsumoto, *Farming the Home Place*, 31. On Sikhs, see Leonard, *Making Ethnic Choices*; and Shah, *Stranger Intimacy*.

56. Lyon, *Prisons and Patriots*, 29; Matsumoto, *Farming the Home Place*, 25, 32; by 1920 approximately one-fifth of the 111,010 Japanese on the U.S. mainland were married women. U.S. Congress, House, Committee on Immigration and Naturalization, *Statement of Sidney L. Gulick*, 21. See *Seattle Star* clipping in Blair, "The 1920 Anti-Japanese Crusade," stating that "'picture brides' are swarming to the United States." U.S. Congress, Senate, Committee on Immigration, *Selective Immigration Legislation*, 63 (Henry H. Curran, the commis-

sioner of immigration, worried not only about picture brides but also about Ellis Island adoptions and made particular reference to Italian strategies in anticipation of the 1924 act).

57. Matsumoto, *Farming the Home Place*, 11–12, 17–18. See 25, 42, on a 1920 law that barred "aliens ineligible to citizenship" from most of the ways they used to work around restrictions, from leasing or acquiring land through corporations (a strategy used by some colonies) or in the names of their American-born (and thus citizen) children. But many had already done so, and the laws seem not always to have been enforced, particularly where farmers wanted Japanese tenants. Matsumoto focuses on the Cortez Colony, begun in 1919 by a handful of families and growing to about thirty families, each operating twenty-to-forty-acre farms. Washington may have been more strict; see, for example, Teiko Tomita, who helped her husband farm the land they leased on the Yakama Indian Reservation in the early 1920s until new legislation and significant local pressure forced the Department of the Interior to apply the state's 1921 and 1923 laws against leasing to Japanese immigrants (Nomura, "*Tsugiki*, a Grafting," 288).

58. Matsumoto, *Farming the Home Place*, 32; Blair, "The 1920 Anti-Japanese Crusade," 2–8. Blair points out that nationally favoring immigration restriction was a Republican stance, but on the West Coast, it was the purview of Democrats. It no doubt also helped that because they were excluded from most unions (though not the IWW), Japanese workers had formed their own, adopting the same pay scales and shop standards as white unions, and they refused to scab during Seattle's 1916 longshoremen's strike and the Seattle general strike in 1919. The United North American Japanese Association had branches in Montana and Alaska, and another union with the same name existed in Oregon and California. The second-generation witnesses were young, ages fourteen to twenty-three. And see Lee, *Claiming the Oriental Gateway.*

59. Matsumoto, *Farming the Home Place*, 25, 45, 46 for "rabbit drives"; and 48–51 for exclusionist Senator Phelan's inaccurate claim that "white women will not and no woman should work in the fields," seeing the Japanese practice as further evidence of the danger to Western civilization.

60. Matsumoto, *Farming the Home Place*, 32–34, 35, for "our Japanese." See also Tsu, *Garden of the World*, 139–65.

61. Lyon, *Prisons and Patriots*, 14–15, 39, 40. Oregon, Washington, and California all required citizenship training by law.

62. Lyon, *Prisons and Patriots*, 26, on the pattern of legal enactments as "the systematic erosion of Issei rights" from 1919 to 1923 (27, 29–34). See also Molina, *Fit to Be Citizens?*, 106. The pattern resembled that of South Asians in California; in 1919 Asian Indians occupied eighty-eight thousand acres in California, mostly in the Sacramento Valley, but including thirty-two thousand in the Imperial Valley. By 1924 about 60 percent of the Imperial Valley had absentee owners, and 88 percent of the land was tenant operated; see Jensen, *Passage from India*, 34, 37.

63. U.S. Congress, House, Committee on Immigration and Naturalization, *Statement of Sidney L. Gulick.* And see U.S. Congress, House, Committee on Immigration and Naturalization, *Restriction of Immigration* (1924), 972–76, 1160–61; U.S. Congress, Senate, Committee on Immigration, *Selective Immigration Legislation,* 184. See also U.S. Congress, Senate, Committee on Immigration, *Restriction of Western Hemisphere Immigration,* 1, 6 (California State Federation of Labor on Mexicans as relief burden); 7 on taking jobs in unskilled "public work"; and 9 on expense to community of cheap labor for the grower.

64. U.S. Congress, House, Committee on Immigration and Naturalization, *Restriction of Immigration* (1924), for example, 1081 (John Raker, California [D]: "The farmer has got to be paid more for his produce. Labor has to come down"). Raker opposed solving the problem with immigration. U.S. Congress, Senate, Committee on Immigration, *Restriction of Western Hemisphere Immigration,* 39, 88, 136; he claimed, "Not a single Government project relying upon the growth of beets has failed" (136).

65. U.S. Congress, Senate, Committee on Immigration, *Restriction of Western Hemisphere Immigration,* 113–15, 183–87, 128–92 (Harry A. Austin, secretary of the U.S. Beet Sugar Association), 118 (Shattuck, Denver Chamber of Commerce), 95 (Thom), 107. Sugar beets were the major crop on projects in Colorado, Idaho, Montana, Nebraska, Wyoming, and South Dakota. Sugar prices peaked in the mid-1920s; in the wake of the 1929 crash, the United States introduced tariffs on sugar; Hahamovitch, *No Man's Land,* 137.

66. U.S. Congress, Senate, Committee on Immigration, *Restriction of Western Hemisphere Immigration,* 43, 89, 93, 99, 100–105 (E. J. Walker), and see 104–5 (McInnis). Hernández, *Migra!,* 24–25. Kelly Lytle Hernández claims 98 percent of South Texas agricultural workers were Mexican. See also Charles C. Teague, "A Settlement on Mexican Immigration," *Saturday Evening Post,* March 10, 1928, reprinted in Balderrama and Rodríguez, *Decade of Betrayal,* 25–27, in response to claims that California spent too great a proportion of its charitable funds on Mexicans.

67. U.S. Congress, Senate, Committee on Immigration, *Restriction of Western Hemisphere Immigration,* 18, 22, 26–27, 31, and see 35–44 (E. J. Walker of the Arizona Cotton Growers' Association on the connection between irrigation and long-staple cotton, "successfully" grown only because of Mexican labor), 97, 124 (Thom), 116 (Smith, South Texas Chamber of Commerce), and 122–23, 131. A survey found 3–25 percent of the Mexican laborers "drifting" away from beet fields, with an average of 10 percent. U.S. Congress, House, Committee on Immigration and Naturalization, *Restriction of Immigration* (1924), 1078 (Fred Roberts, Corpus Christi, Texas).

68. U.S. Congress, House, Committee on Immigration and Naturalization, *Restriction of Immigration* (1924), 1078, 1081, 1085–86, 1091–92. And see U.S. Congress, Senate, Committee on Immigration, *Restriction of Western Hemisphere Immigration,* 127 (Austin citing Department of Agricultural estimates that in 1926 over two million people left the farms for the cities and only just

over one million moved to the farms; with increased immigration restriction from Europe, this pattern meant that "there has been little or no influx of agricultural labor to fill this gap"), and see 134–35 (E. F. Heckman, American Beet Sugar, on the connection between 1924 law, migration to cities, and shortage of agricultural labor, including due to the imposition of the head tax and visa fee for Western Hemisphere migrants). And see Andrés, *Power and Control*, 72, 84.

69. U.S. Congress, Senate, Committee on Immigration, *Restriction of Western Hemisphere Immigration*, 10, 11–20, 27–28, 50, 56, 147–48, 187–88.

70. U.S. Congress, Senate, Committee on Immigration, *Restriction of Western Hemisphere Immigration*, 21, 49, 55–59, 110–12, 132.

71. U.S. Congress, Senate, Committee on Immigration, *Restriction of Western Hemisphere Immigration*, 18, 20, 30, 59–60, 69–71, 73–74, 79, 137, 148. On cotton competition, as well as Mexican labor allowing white leisure and Mexicans as less threatening to the social order than Blacks, see, for example, Hernández, *Migra!*, 29–30, 54.

72. U.S. Congress, Senate, Committee on Immigration, *Restriction of Western Hemisphere Immigration*, 165, 169–70.

73. U.S. Congress, Senate, Committee on Immigration, *Restriction of Western Hemisphere Immigration*, 69. See also U.S. Congress, House, Committee on Immigration and Naturalization, *Seasonal Agricultural Laborers from Mexico*, 246; Brown et al., *Children Working*, 112. Mautner and Abbott, *Child Labor*, 155.

74. Andrés, *Power and Control*, 111; Hernández, *Migra!*, 89, 227; she estimates that as many as five hundred thousand Mexicans came to the United States outside of an entry port in the 1920s and finds that the Border Patrol in the 1920s recruited in the South but excluded African American applicants.

75. Daniels, *The Politics of Prejudice*; Lyon, *Prisons and Patriots*; García, *Mexican-Americans*; Garcia, *The Rise*; Orozco, *No Mexicans*. And see Deutsch, *No Separate Refuge*, 154–55, 188; by the end of the decade they were also, once again, organizing Colorado's coal miners, who worked seasonally in beets. They created the Spanish Speaking Workers Union in 1928 with the aid of the IWW. The membership stretched across the routes of migration, reaching into northern New Mexico villages (157, 173).

76. U.S. Congress, House, Committee on Irrigation and Reclamation, *Extension of the Time of Payment*, 72–73, 239; Worster, *Rivers of Empire*, 178–86. For the Japanese women, see Matsumoto, *Farming the Home Place*, 43, 45. See also Beda, "'We Want No Extravagance.'"

77. U.S. Congress, House, Committee on Irrigation and Reclamation, *Extension of the Time of Payment*, 75–76: Raker called this a "European method."

78. U.S. Congress, Senate, Committee on Immigration, *Restriction of Western Hemisphere Immigration*, 52, 73, 75, 77.

79. Woeste, *The Farmer's Benevolent Trust*, 9, 14, 138–39. See also Shover, "The Farmers' Holiday Association Strike."

80. U.S. Congress, House, Committee on Indian Affairs, *Pima Indians*, 23; U.S. Congress, House, Committee on Irrigation and Reclamation, *Extension of the Time of Payment*, 75.

81. U.S. Congress, House, Committee on Indian Affairs, *Pima Indians*, 4, 8, 13–15.

82. U.S. Congress, House, Committee on Indian Affairs, *Pima Indians*, 8.

83. U.S. Congress, House, Committee on Indian Affairs, *Pima Indians*, 8, 12, 15. The Coolidge Dam was built between 1924 and 1928, was dedicated in 1930, and began generating electricity in 1935.

84. U.S. Congress, House, Committee on Immigration and Naturalization, *Restriction of Immigration* (1924), 939, for example.

85. Welke, *Law and the Borders*, 71; Ngai, *Impossible Subjects*. And see U.S. Congress, Senate, Committee on Immigration, *Selective Immigration Legislation*, 137.

86. Welke, *Law and the Borders*, 7, 11, on the ways in which notions of ability shaped citizenship, with women as "too delicate," Blacks as "inferior," and, I would argue, Native Americans as too communal, not "owning" themselves (not the self-possessed liberal subject), because their "self" was owned by the tribe, the clan, the communal property title. Ability, race, and gender, Welke argues, were "deeply rooted not just in U.S. history, but in the political theory of liberalism and republicanism and the historical contexts in which they were articulated. Capitalism assumed the free, self-owning, rights-bearing sovereign individual, the 'liberal' self" (11).

9. Speculating on the West Imagined

1. Deverell, *Whitewashed Adobe*, 176–78.

2. Troutman, *Indian Blues*, 104–5.

3. Molina, *Fit to Be Citizens?*, points to a pattern of "reframing essentially economic issues as public health concerns," which then "legitimated practices that otherwise might have been challenged immediately as discriminatory" (31); for example, one slogan in support of the 1920 Land Act "urged, 'Keep California White'" (55); see also 75, 91, 107.

4. Deverell, *Whitewashed Adobe*, 182 (reference to Americanization programs). See Molina, *Fit to Be Citizens?*, 76–78, 80, 82–83, 84, 88, 90–91, 95, 114, on "Mexican clinics" and clinics for "whites only." A study the next year in two other clinics found only slight differences in Mexican and "American" rates. On similar tests in Colorado, see Deutsch, *No Separate Refuge*, 134.

5. Deverell, *Whitewashed Adobe*, 205, quoting Samuel Holmes, "An Argument against Mexican Immigration," *Transactions of the Commonwealth Club of California*, March 23, 1926, 23; on 310n74, Deverell points out that Vernon McCombs, Methodist minister and missionary, in *From over the Border* (New York: Council of Women for Home Missions and Missionary Education Movement of the United States and Canada, 1925), 36, instead blamed conditions created by the host community.

6. Deverell, *Whitewashed Adobe*, 183–85. See Molina, *Fit to Be Citizens?*, 84: the areas were around Clara Street and a six-block area in Belvedere where two cases appeared but no others.

7. Deverell, *Whitewashed Adobe*, out of 2,500 buildings destroyed, 186–88, 191, 193, quoting "L.A. Tenement Problem and the Bubonic-Pneumonic Plagues: Report of Survey by Representatives of Nine Leading Organizations," *Municipal League of Los Angeles* 7 (February 1925): 2–6. See also Molina, *Fit to Be Citizens?*, 78–79.

8. Molina, *Fit to Be Citizens?*, 85, 87–88; Deverell, *Whitewashed Adobe*, 172 quote: the Matson article appeared in *Southern California Business*, November 1924, 198–99, 308n55.

9. Deverell, *Whitewashed Adobe*, 195–97. *The Nation* articles, written by William Boardman Knox, former editor of the *Los Angeles Daily News*, came out in 1925 and 1926. See Montgomery, *The Spanish Redemption*, 105, on New Mexico's similar marketing, with the territory's Bureau of Immigration publishing *Land of Sunshine* to tout, in part, the healthy climate starting in 1904.

10. Olien and Olien, *Easy Money*, 19; Kurashige, *The Shifting Grounds*, 26–29, 34. And see Camarillo, "Navigating Segregated Life," 654. See Gibson, *El Norte*, 312–14, on the increasing segregation of Rio Grande Valley towns.

11. Quoted in Kurashige, *The Shifting Grounds*, 59; Stern, *Eugenic Nation*, 140–41.

12. Boyle, *Arc of Justice*. And Kurashige, *The Shifting Grounds*, for example, 33, on realtors.

13. Quoted in Kurashige, *The Shifting Grounds*, 14–15, 25. Population figures courtesy of Brad Wood based on U.S. Bureau of the Census, *Sixteenth Census*, vol. 1, *Number of Inhabitants*, https://www.census.gov/library/publications/1942/dec/population-vol-1.html; and Wrobel, *America's West*, 93, fig. 4.2, which in turn drew on Etulain, *Beyond the Missouri*, 306.

14. Hundley, *The Great Thirst*, 170–71; Kurashige, *The Shifting Grounds*, 17–18 on the 1903 Pacific electric railroad strike, Huntington, and the open shop; 19 on homeownership and the fortunes some Black Angelenos made in real estate; see also 23–24, 57.

15. Kurashige, *The Shifting Grounds*, 29–30. See Kropp, *California Vieja*, 159ff., on the elite suburb Rancho Santa Fe. See O'Connor, *A Sort of Utopia*; Montgomery, *The Spanish Redemption*, 104.

16. Kurashige, *The Shifting Grounds*, 31. And see Kropp, *California Vieja*, 177–79.

17. Nicolaides, *My Blue Heaven*, 11–13, 16–21, 29–30, 32–33, 43, 136–37 (on the difference between the "perfect town" of merchants and realtors and of laboring-class residents), 140, 142, 159–64. And see Sánchez, "The 'New Nationalism,'" 229–30. On such mingling elsewhere, see Steptoe, *Houston Bound*, 63–96, on Houston's complicated racial landscape, with its dispersed Black population, two "Mexican" wards (one Tejano, one Mexican immi-

grant), and the Creole population; and Lee, *Claiming the Oriental Gateway*, 5, 13, 63, 105, 116, 136 (on Seattle).

18. Camarillo, "Navigating Segregated Life," 645, recounting the experience of Rose López and her friends in 1925.

19. Kurashige, *The Shifting Grounds*, 32, 43, cites Becky M. Nicolaides on the whiteness of oil worker suburbs incorporated between 1917 and 1930 (in 1930 only 1,766 of 650,219 residents in these suburbs were Blacks)—the Oil Workers International Union was a whites-only union; for Phoenix, see Burke, *A Land Apart*, 189; and Needham, *Power Lines*, 93. On Tucson, see Spargur, "Contrasting Experiences"; Chiv, "Chinese in Tucson"; Poirier, "The Myths of Chinese." And see Kurashige, *The Shifting Grounds*, 68, 72; Kropp, *California Vieja*, 181, 190.

20. Kropp, *California Vieja*, 101; Garcia, *A World of Its Own*, 64–100. See Romo, *East Los Angeles*, 116; Sánchez, *Becoming Mexican American*, 231, on the AFL trying "half-heartedly" to organize "segregated locals" in the LA building trades of the mid-1920s; Monroy, "Like Swallows," 445–46; and Perry and Perry, *A History of the Los Angeles Labor Movement*, 197–202.

21. Nicolaides, *My Blue Heaven*, 22, 24–25, 48–49, 67, 69, 72–73, 78–79, 145, 148, on the 1930 triumph of the anti-improvement forces in local elections. See Sabin, *Crude Politics*, 160–65, on the continued reliance on streetcars in Los Angeles, San Diego, and San Francisco in the late 1920s despite the high per capita number of cars.

22. Kurashige, *The Shifting Grounds*, 53, 55–56.

23. Kurashige, *The Shifting Grounds*, 51, 57.

24. See Hirsch, *Riot and Remembrance*; Kurashige, *The Shifting Grounds*, 36–37, 40.

25. Kurashige, *The Shifting Grounds*, 40–42, 58, 62; Spargur, "Contrasting Experience." In Tucson's 1920s "Chinatown," as in most "Chinatowns," Chinese immigrants and shopkeepers lived next door to a variety of other non-Anglo residents, including Mexican-descent, Japanese, and African American families (based on census work around South Meyer Street in the 1920 census by Poirier, "The Myths of Chinese").

26. Kropp, *California Vieja*, 2–3, 5, 74–75, 80. For examples of the copious literature on the Spanish Fantasy Heritage, see Montgomery, *The Spanish Redemption*, 101, 103; Deverell, *Whitewashed Adobe*; Wilson, *The Myth of Santa Fe*. And see Otero, *La Calle*, 65, who cites David Weber's insights regarding the Mexican era as a dark age.

27. Deverell, *Whitewashed Adobe*, 84–89, 207, 229 (for Lummis quote), 208 (the play opened in April), 209–10, 211, 212 (on how the initial impetus came from a wealthy owner of the Spanish revival style Mission Inn, inspired by his attendance at Oberammergau's Passion Play in 1910), 216 (for *Times* quote on cast), 217 (for *Tidings* quote on "white man's burden" in response to a San Francisco critique on their neglect of local Mexican needs), 221, 222. On the finances, see 223–26, 231, 241; on the intervention of the Chamber of

Commerce, see 232–34. See also Wilson, *The Myth of Santa Fe,* 90, on mission style. See Montgomery, *The Spanish Redemption,* 98–99. See also Kropp, *California Vieja,* 36ff., on the earlier history of cashing in on the Ramona story.

28. Deverell, *Whitewashed Adobe,* 219–20.

29. Wilson, *The Myth of Santa Fe,* 8, 198 (for clipping from *Santa Fe New Mexican,* July 5, 1911, on Armijo—his son Theodore Roosevelt Armijo was by his side), 201, 204–5 (headline from April 30, 1920), 207. For histories that contest that narrative, see, for example, Reséndez, *Changing National Identities*; and Mora, *Border Dilemmas.* Montgomery, *The Spanish Redemption,* 128–29, 133, 140–41.

30. Wilson, *The Myth of Santa Fe,* 100–101, 113, 114, 128, 129, 137, 138, 141, 237, 242–44. According to Montgomery, *The Spanish Redemption,* 90, 107, 117, 119–20, the Santa Fe boosters had little choice but to focus on their past distinctiveness; with a thin tax base and impoverished population, architecture was a relatively inexpensive strategy. And Kropp, *California Vieja,* 140–41, 144.

31. Wilson, *The Myth of Santa Fe,* 134–35. Montgomery, *The Spanish Redemption,* 92, argues that despite the greater popularity of the Pueblos as a tourist attraction, "the political clout of Hispanos" made the chosen promoted vernacular style a blend of Spanish mission and Pueblo architecture; see 122 for the Hewett quote.

32. Wilson, *The Myth of Santa Fe,* 205–7; Montgomery, *The Spanish Redemption,* 138–40.

33. Montgomery, *The Spanish Redemption,* 114–15, and 116–17 on Hewett and the Panama-California Exposition of 1915 in San Diego.

34. Wilson, *The Myth of Santa Fe,* 211–13, 217, 243. And see Montgomery, *The Spanish Redemption,* 141–43, 146, 149, 154.

35. Wilson, *The Myth of Santa Fe,* 3, 122–23, 148–49, 193; see 158 on calling themselves "mexicanos" in Spanish and distinguishing between *surumatos* (immigrants) and *manitos* (northern New Mexican natives). And see Montgomery, *The Spanish Redemption,* 1–3, 16, 66–67 on the creation of "Little Texas" in eastern New Mexico and the retention of a Hispano majority in the northern and some western counties; 89 quoting the *Santa Fe New Mexican,* January 22, 1916 ("But for language, Old Mexico is as foreign a country to most of New Mexico's citizens as to those of Arkansas or Wisconsin"); 148 on Europeanness; and 153: in 1928 La Unión Protectiva and El Auxiliar Feminil helped Benigno Muñiz and 350 reenactors stage a comic version of Pancho Villa's Columbus raid. And see Otero, *La Calle,* 65.

36. Montgomery, *The Spanish Redemption,* 124–26, for claims of "completely American," and 140, quoting Otero-Warren during her time as federal inspector of Indian schools in the 1920s, when she also referred to Indians as "people 'whose heads and hearts are not like our own,' a people 'decreed' by the laws of civilization to disappear as a distinct race." See Troutman, *Indian Blues,* 80, 103, on marketing Santa Fe's annual Indian Market as American folk, a claim echoed by Indian dancers. See, for example, Aurelio M. Espi-

nosa in Wilson, *The Myth of Santa Fe,* 150–51, quoting a 1916 introduction to an article in the *Journal of American Folklore,* for which he served as associate editor; on ties to Anglo culture, see 152, including George W. Armijo's Anglo grandmother and Nina Otero-Warren's, Fabiola Cabeza de Baca Gilbert's, and Aurora Lucero-White Lea's Anglo husbands.

37. Sanders, "Public Art," 178–95, quotation on 190.

38. Montgomery, *The Spanish Redemption,* 129–30, 150–51, 155. And see Sanders, "Public Art," 191. On the Fiesta Queen, see also Wilson, *The Myth of Santa Fe,* 213. On power shifting to Anglos, see Nieto-Phillips, *The Language of Blood,* 174–76, and the displacement onto "culture."

39. Montgomery, *The Spanish Redemption,* 15. Kropp, *California Vieja,* 6, dates McWilliams's use to 1946. Otero, *La Calle,* 20, 47, 66; Vallance, "La Iglésia de San Agustín," 9–11.

40. Otero, *La Calle,* 76. On the Arizona Polo Association, see Ephemera file, Places–AZ–Tucson–Schools–University of Arizona–Polo, Arizona Historical Society, Tucson, as cited in Doucette, "Tucson's Love Affair." On the connection with the Rodeo Days, see Ephemera file, Places–AZ–Tucson–Celebrations–La Fiesta de los Vaqueros–General, Arizona Historical Society, Tucson, also cited in Doucette. For golf, see Wilkey, "The Rise of Exclusive Institutions."

41. Otero, *La Calle,* 76. See Barraclough, *Charros,* 12–16, on creating the "American" cowboy.

42. Otero, *La Calle,* 75; Burke, *A Land Apart,* 203–5. The phenomenon extended far beyond Tucson.

43. Rothman, *Devil's Bargains,* 68.

44. Rothman, *Devil's Bargains,* 146: there had been 458,000 in 1910; in that year fewer than 10 percent of rural roads were paved.

45. Burke, *A Land Apart,* 205; Hyde, *An American Vision,* 297–98.

46. Rothman, *Devil's Bargains,* 148–49; "Route 66," Wikipedia, https://en.wikipedia.org/wiki/U.S._Route_66 (accessed May 27, 2020). And see Kropp, *California Vieja,* 71, on the hotels and services along the Mission Road beginning in the 1910s with the start of construction and marking (72). On state highways, see Sabin, *Crude Politics,* 160–62.

47. Belasco, *Americans on the Road,* 72, 74; Kropp, *California Vieja,* 54–66, 67, 69–70; Gibson, *El Norte,* 317. On Fall, see Stratton, *Tempest over Teapot Dome,* 222–23.

48. Rothman, *Devil's Bargains,* 144; see Belasco, *Americans on the Road,* 4, 71–72, 74–75, 76–78.

49. Belasco, *Americans on the Road,* 26, quoting Emily Post, *By Motor to the Golden Gate* (New York: D. Appleton & Co., 1916), 88.

50. Montgomery, *The Spanish Redemption,* 161–64, 211. On Indian Detours and the brochures whose texts also included "the lure of the real Southwest beyond the pinched horizons of your train window," see Lockerby, "Owning the Intangible?," 47, quoting *Indian Detour* (New York: Rand McNally and Company, 1926), 4.

51. Montgomery, *The Spanish Redemption*, 172–74.

52. Montgomery, *The Spanish Redemption*, 167–68, 175, 188 (McCormick quote on incapacity for industrialization); Deutsch, *No Separate Refuge*, 190–93; Rothman, *Devil's Bargains*, 10–11, quoted in Otero, *La Calle*, 83. And see Kropp, *California Vieja*, 10, 12 on the celebration of "cultural differences, but largely as commodities available for Anglo possession"; and 147–48 on the famous potter María Martínez. Luis-Brown, *Waves of Decolonization*, 148–49, complicates the issue, arguing that movements organizing around these putatively primitive marginalized groups vied for greater visibility and rights and for self-determination but without the ability to seize state apparatus and that such movements across the globe provided a frame for nationalist groups to adopt and adapt.

53. Rothman, *Devil's Bargains*, 72–73, 78.

54. Rothman, *Devil's Bargains*, 75–77.

55. Warren, *The Hunter's Game*, 126–47; Spence, *Dispossessing the Wilderness*, 83–86: the promoter quoted is Edward Frank Allen, "The Greatness of Glacier National Park," *Travel* 20 (1913): 9–13.

56. Olson, "Heritage Schemes," 159, quoting Alexander Hood to Charles H. Burke, November 28, 1925, Bureau of Indian Affairs, Colville Agency, folder 157, RG 75, National Archives, Seattle, 167 on competition, 161, 173.

57. Morrissey, *Mental Territories*, 114–15, 164; Olson, "Heritage Schemes," 165, 172 (quoting "Comments on Indian Congress," *Kamiah [ID] Progress*, November 5, 1925), 173, and see 174: one topic of discussion at the congress was the Indian Citizenship Act of 1924, including opposition to it by attendees.

58. Olson, "Heritage Schemes," 159–78.

59. Belasco, *Americans on the Road*, 92, 96.

60. Belasco, *Americans on the Road*, 4, 106, 110, 122, 126.

61. On the other hand, see Kneller, "Barrio Libre." Recio, "U.S. Prohibition," 452–53; Woods, "A Penchant for Probity."

62. Recio, "U.S. Prohibition," 454; Lumsden, "The Effect," 8–9. See also, for example, Vanderwood, *Satan's Playground.* See Ponzo, "Disdain and Drink," on students in Nogales citing the *Arizona Daily Star*, January 13, 1923, and October 8, 1922, and citing *Customs Service Records, 1892–1977*, March 12, 1915, and December 1, 1923; Ponzo points out that enforcement also shifted from local to federal agents. See Horne, *Black and Brown*, on soldiers. See U.S. WCTU, *White Ribbon Bulletin*, July 1928, reporting Señorita Alvarado writing of a WCTU Fiesta in Mexico City, and the honorary president was President Calles's daughter, Mrs. Calles-Torreblanca; Mexico City boasted twenty WCTU chapters, with six additional chapters elsewhere in Mexico. At the same time, see Britton, *Revolution and Ideology*, 50–51, on cosmopolitan bohemian gatherings of intellectuals in Mexico City.

63. Jamiolkowski, "Feisty Locals," 2, 6, 8–11 (State Department memo quoted on 10). Besides her own excellent original and secondary published research, Jamiolkowski also used Edward L. Langston, "The Impact of Pro-

hibition on the Mexican–United States Border: The El Paso–Ciudad Juárez Case" (PhD diss., Texas Tech University, 1971), and Robin Robinson, "Vice and Tourism on the U.S.-Mexico Border: A Comparison of Three Communities in the Era of U.S. Prohibition" (PhD diss., Arizona State University, 2002).

64. Jamiolkowski, "Feisty Locals," 4, 5, 7.

65. Jamiolkowski, "Feisty Locals," 12, quoting *West Texas Today* (Stanford: Official Production of the West Texas Chamber of Commerce, October 1929), 13–14; Lumsden, "The Effect," 3, 6, 8, citing George Seldes, "10,000 Yanks a Day Go over the River to Drink," *Chicago Daily Tribune*, March 28, 1927, and "Repeal No Aid to Mexico," *New York Times*, May 19, 1930, on the five new bridges built across the Rio Grande during Prohibition, and 9–10, citing Tom Mahoney, "The City That Thirst Built," *Atlanta Journal-Constitution*, March 15, 1931.

66. Recio, "U.S. Prohibition," 454–55; and Lumsden, "The Effect," 9, citing Robin E. Robinson, "Vice and Tourism on the U.S.-Mexico Border: A Comparison of Three Communities in the Era of U.S. Prohibition" (PhD diss., Arizona State University, 2002), 20.

67. Lumsden, "The Effect," 8, citing W. H. Timmons, *El Paso: A Borderlands History* (El Paso: Western Texas Press, 2005), 271. Garrett, "Defying Prohibition," 7, citing "Plane Smuggling Liquor Captured," *San Jose Mercury Herald*, January 18, 1922, 4, and 8, citing "Bitter Fight Staged with Liquor Runners," *San Jose Mercury Herald*, September 9, 1922, 3. See also Hernández, *Migra!*, 58–59.

68. Garrett, "Defying Prohibition," 8, 17, referring to articles in San Jose, California, papers. Lumsden, "The Effect," 10, on demands for U.S. intervention pushing for dry Mexico, citing, for example, Jack Starr-Hunt, "Dry Fight On in Mexico: Methodist Church, Leading Battle, Bases Hope on Calles's Aid; Unions to Help," *Los Angeles Times*, December 7, 1924. And see Nevola, "Alcohol or Lack Thereof," 2, 3, 6, citing Ethan A. Nadelmann, *Cops across Borders: The Internationalization of U.S. Criminal Law Enforcement* (University Park: Pennsylvania State University Press, 1993), 96, and 7, 10, citing "4 Canadian Provinces Bone Dry after Feb. 1," *Chicago Daily Tribune*, January 1, 1921, and microfilm, 1959, microcopy no. 274, Henry L. Walsh, 1925, M7328, roll 29, National Archives and Records Service, Washington DC; Okrent, *Last Call*, 150; and "CANADA WON'T HELP TO STOP RUM RUNNING: Windsor Magistrate's Ruling Ends Co-operation to Prevent Liquor Crossing the Border," *New York Times*, August 13, 1921: "Magistrate Gund expressed the opinion that the United States was big enough to take care of its own laws," citing Robert Buffington, "Prohibition in the Borderlands: National Government-Border Community Relations," *Pacific Historical Review* 63, no. 1 (February 1994): 24. See also Clark, *The Dry Years*, 153; Robbins and Barber, *Nature's Northwest*, 103.

69. Nevola, "Alcohol or Lack Thereof," 5, quoting Henry L. Walsh in a report from the American consul in 1925. Kneller, "Barrio Libre," citing Eliazar Diaz Herreras, "Remembering Tucson," Oral History, Arizona Historical Society, Tucson.

70. Montgomery, *The Spanish Redemption,* 165; Deutsch, *No Separate Refuge,* 281n144.

71. Murphy, "Bootlegging Mothers," 175, 176–77, 184–86.

72. Murphy, "Bootlegging Mothers," 182, 187, 188; Montana banned women from saloons in 1907.

73. For example, Pima County voters had opposed Prohibition 2,230 to 1,799 when the state carried it in 1914. See Ware, "Alcohol, Temperance, and Prohibition"; and *Arizona Republican,* December 15, 1914, cited in Baridon, "Tucson's Refusal," 2, 5–6, 11. See also Jamiolkowski, "Feisty Locals," 16–18, on the weakness of the Protestant Progressive movement in El Paso relative to San Diego, including the *El Paso Times* denouncing the KKK and El Paso's exemption to early closing of the border. And see John R. Meers, "The California Wine and Grape Industry and Prohibition," *California Historical Society Quarterly* 46, no. 1 (March 1967): 20, cited in Garrett, "Defying Prohibition," 5–6; Murphy, "Bootlegging Mothers," 183.

74. Recio, "U.S. Prohibition," 455–56, 458; see also Jamiolkowski, "Feisty Locals," 3: one race track and casino alone generated a $15,000-per-month license fee. And see Garrett, "Defying Prohibition," 14–15, quoting a statement released by the Mexican Embassy to the effect that President de la Huerta intended to stop "the systematic exploitation of the immoral conditions" of Baja California ("Stop Gambling in Lower California," *San Jose Mercury Herald,* August 21, 1920, 1).

75. Recio, "U.S. Prohibition," 457. See the well-researched "Legal History of Cannabis in the United States," Wikipedia, https://en.wikipedia.org/wiki/Legal_history_of_cannabis_in_the_United_States (accessed November 20, 2020), citing *New York Times* articles. See also Johnson, *Grass Roots,* 17–42.

76. See Johnson, *Grass Roots,* 36–38, on the discourse shifting to a homegrown menace by the late 1920s. Kropp, *California Vieja,* 138. *Los Angeles Times,* April 26, 1915, 11, quoted in Brown-Pinsky, "Opium and Race," 13, and 14, quoting "Death Reveals Huge Drug Ring," *Los Angeles Times,* March 3, 1925, 9, dateline Douglas, Arizona.

77. Brown-Pinsky, "Opium and Race," 15–16, quoting "Death Reveals Huge Drug Ring," *Los Angeles Times,* March 3, 1925, 9, dateline Douglas, Arizona. On Mexico's laws and policies, see Lim, *Porous Borders,* 179, 184, 187.

78. Sklar, *Movie-Made America,* 67–68; Slotkin, *Gunfighter Nation,* 235, on other film center contenders, including Tulsa, Oklahoma. See also Cooper, *Universal Women,* xvi, on how rivals for LA included Chicago, Philadelphia, Fort Lee, New Jersey, and Jacksonville, Florida.

79. Sklar, *Movie-Made America,* 69, 71, 74. On fraud, see Olien and Olien, *Easy Money,* 11, on the Vigilance Committee of the National Association of the Motion Picture Industry testimony that investors put approximately $50 million into fraudulent motion picture ventures. Mahar, "Women, Filmmaking, and the Gendering," 289, 323–24.

80. Sklar, *Movie-Made America*, 74–76. On women in Hollywood, particularly at Universal Studios, see Cooper, *Universal Women*, xiv, xvii, xxix, 6–7, 8, and see 23 on the distinguishing of genres as new, 47–48, 61, and 86 on the girl detective / cowgirl subgenre, 87 on reframing women directors as replacements for war-bound men, 104, 128 on the end of 1917 seeing the replacement of shorts by the feature film, strengthening "central coordination" and the division of labor, and 185 on the dispersal of the studios' women directors.

81. Cooper, *Universal Women*, 59, 61.

82. Sklar, *Movie-Made America*, 77–79, 82–83, 132. And see Mahar, "Women, Filmmaking, and the Gendering," 260–61.

83. Mahar, "Women, Filmmaking, and the Gendering," 290, 291, 293, 294, 298, 299–307.

84. Mahar, "Women, Filmmaking, and the Gendering," 295.

85. Mahar, "Women, Filmmaking, and the Gendering," 209, 308, 316–17, 318, 356. And see Cooper, *Universal Women*.

86. Mahar, "Women, Filmmaking, and the Gendering," 295, 319–21, 325–26, 328; Sklar, *Movie-Made America*, 146, 149–51; Cooper, *Universal Women*, xv, xvi, 14, 16. Etulain, *Re-imagining the Modern American West*, argues that the 1920s saw a shift in fiction, film, and art from frontier themes to the distinctiveness of the West as a region or set of subregions.

87. Aquila, *The Sagebrush Trail*, 15–18, 20–21; Slotkin, *Gunfighter Nation*, 231; Reiner, "Kings of the Wild Frontier," 20. Wrobel, *Promised Lands*, 108, on declining interest in the "Wild West" in the early twentieth century.

88. Aquila, *The Sagebrush Trail*, 34–39; Slotkin, *Gunfighter Nation*, 235–36; Cooper, *Universal Women*, 32.

89. Slotkin, *Gunfighter Nation*, 212–17, 241; Aquila, *The Sagebrush Trail*, 54–57.

90. Smith, *Rocky Mountain Heartland*, 115. Slotkin, *Gunfighter Nation*, 212–17, 241, 243–44, 247–52; Zane Grey's most popular book, *Riders of the Purple Sage*, sold over a million copies in hardcover. And see Sklar, *Movie-Made America*, 30. There were exceptions to this pattern; see Aquila, *The Sagebrush Trail*, 45–49, 51, and see 60 on the various iterations of *Squaw Man*. There were occasional Indian stars, the hero Braveheart in 1925, and all-Black westerns with Bill Pickett and others.

91. Reiner, "Kings of the Wild Frontier," 21–23. See also Aquila, *The Sagebrush Trail*, 59, on Mix.

92. Deverell, *Whitewashed Adobe*, 129, quoting Karl De Schweinitz, "Social Work with Families in Los Angeles," chap. 4 in *Family Case Work: A Manual for Social Case Workers in Los Angeles County California*, by Erle Fiske Young (Los Angeles: Western Educational Services, 1927), typescript.

93. Kropp, *California Vieja*, 7, 156; Sagarena, *Aztlán and Arcadia*, 120–21.

94. Wrobel, *Promised Lands*, 176; Sánchez, *Becoming Mexican American*, 225–26.

95. For a helpful conceptualization of the dynamics involved, see Sandoval, *Methodology of the Oppressed*, 98–100, on the ways in which the "fabri-

cated quality of colonialism" disappears through "occupation, exploitation, incorporation, and hegemonic domination of meaning." It is in this sense that Pérez, *The Decolonial Imaginary*, refers to decolonization, an emancipation of consciousness by the refusal to "learn" the hegemonic narrative and adopt its meaning. Otero, *La Calle*, 59, 62, points out that, unlike Tucson, Phoenix had no Mexican or Spanish past and that Anglos had run the town since its founding in 1868; by 1920 it had passed Tucson in population and industry and "came to represent the boomtown model of growth, industry, and modernity in Arizona" (62). Despite Tucson being on the main railroad line and getting, like Albuquerque, the university instead of the capital, its growth pattern was more like that of Santa Fe, and Hispanos retained more, though dwindling, power than in Phoenix.

Part 4. Mobilizing, 1928–40

1. November 8, 1929. Courtesy of Ding Darling Foundation (1999).

2. White, *"It's Your Misfortune,"* 463–24, 469–70. Controlling these two huge producers helped raise the price of oil to about a dollar a barrel by 1934. See also Wrobel, *America's West*, 130.

10. Demobilizing

1. Stock, *Main Street in Crisis*, 18. Ann Marie Low wrote in her diary after the stock market crash in October 1929, "There seems to be quite a furor in the country over a big stock market crash that wiped a lot of people out. We are ahead of them. The hailstorm in July of 1928 and bank failures that fall wiped out a lot of people locally." Dewey, *Pesos and Dollars*, 203, on plummeting land values between 1930 and 1933 in Texas's Rio Grande Valley: in Cameron County from $27.8 million to $18.2 million and in Hidalgo from $39.8 million to $26.8 million; it continued to drop, to $16.179 million in 1935. Thompson, *Closing the Frontier*, 216: 1925–30 were the driest years on record in Oklahoma, and yields plummeted. Needham, *Power Lines*, 60, 203; Wrobel, *America's West*, 130; Smith, *Rocky Mountain Heartland*, 123.

2. Deutsch, *No Separate Refuge*, 120, 136. See Peck, "The Nature of Labor," on class relations, structures of capital, environmental change, and geographies of labor.

3. Lipsitz, "How History Happens," 406, argues that Sánchez's book "revealed how the history of the Mexican working class in Los Angeles was also the history of US capital disrupting and transforming the social and spatial organization of Mexican society." And see Hernández, *Migra!*, 25 on Díaz's modernization, releasing five million from debt peonage, then free to lay tens of thousands of miles of track; and 71 on "U.S.-based agribusiness companies operating in Mexico's Mexicali Valley . . . building enormous cotton farms with Asian workers." The Colorado River Land Company "actively recruited Chinese laborers . . . so as not to interrupt the flow of Mexican migrants to the United States."

4. Stock, *Main Street in Crisis*, 19; see Garcia, *A World of Its Own*, 90–93, 106, on Hoover's administration blocking the Harris Bill in 1930, which aimed at curbing Mexican immigration, "on the grounds that the law's prejudicial language would damage diplomatic relations with Mexico."

5. Sánchez, *Becoming Mexican American*, 210–11, for the statistics. St. John, *Line in the Sand*, 192–95. In 1934 Mexico instituted a $10 registration fee for immigrants and established a Border Defense force. In 1927 Mexico had suspended admissions of immigrant workers of Syrian, Lebanese, Armenian, Palestinian, and Turkish origin. Anti-Chinese activity had run high during the 1920s in Mexico. With the Depression, Sonora denied jobs to Chinese. In 1931 members of the Chinese community in Sonora began to sell off their property, announcing their plans to leave Mexico; many fled to the United States but faced deportation there. See also Hernández, *Migra!*, 77–80. In at least one case, in March 1932, the literal legal limbo of the Chinese immigrants resulted in Mexican and U.S. officials pushing Chinese immigrants back and forth across the border. The number of Chinese affected may have run into the thousands, and the fraction apprehended by U.S. authorities made up as many as half the cases at the border in 1932. See also Cadava, *Standing on Common Ground*, 44, on Sonoran expulsions of hundreds of Chinese and the appropriation of their businesses from 1900 through the 1930s with the support of state leaders.

6. St. John, *Line in the Sand*, 175, describing the case of a seventy-three-year-old U.S. male citizen who objected to the detention and treatment of "respectable Mexican women" in 1925, 179 on passport requirements, 184, 186. They were subject to head taxes, visa fees, fumigations, and passport requirements that created incentives to find a way around border checkpoints.

7. St. John, *Line in the Sand*, 186; Hernández, *Migra!*, 26, 33–35, 45, 47, 51, 55–65, for examples of a bootlegging story; citizen or not, the suspects and defendants were also described as "Mexican"; "American" and "white" were synonyms in the Border Patrol lexicon.

8. Hernández, *Migra!*, 17–21, 45, and see 73–74 on the more eclectic members of the California district. Like the rest of the state's population, they were often immigrants and had often tried their hand at a number of occupations, including farming.

9. Weber, "Homing Pigeons," 167–68.

10. Weber, "Homing Pigeons," 168; St. John, *Line in the Sand*, 187, 190. Hernández, *Migra!*, 27, 46, 51, 54–55, 81, and see 72–75 on the California district, which in its first years, similarly, did not focus on Mexican workers, instead recording apprehending Swiss, Germans, Chinese, "Hindu," and Italians, as well as a few Mexican smuggled workers. Apprehensions in the two Texas-based districts reached a high of 25,164 in 1929 at a time when an estimated 300,000 migrant workers harvested the fields; "each year Border Patrol officers apprehended less than 3 percent of the number of persons they reported having questioned, examined, or investigated during the year" (53). See pp. 27, 92 on the public charge provision.

11. Hernández, *Migra!*, 76–77; Weber, "Homing Pigeons," 169. On Montana, see Overmyer-Velázquez, *Beyond la Frontera*, 56.

12. St. John, *Line in the Sand*, 187, 189; Weber, "Homing Pigeons," 182–83.

13. Weber, "Homing Pigeons," 184; Lim, *Porous Borders*, 172; Hernández, *Migra!*, 92–93; St. John, *Line in the Sand*, 188–89.

14. Garcia, *A World of Its Own*, 108–9; Foley, "Straddling the Color Line," 344–45, 350.

15. Hernández, *Migra!*, 64, 68. There had been earlier attempts. In 1927 Clifford Perkins, head of the Border Patrol, had tried to bring Laredo into line. The town was almost entirely populated by people of Mexican descent. Only the chief of police was Anglo.

16. St. John, *Line in the Sand*, 190; Otero, "Refusing to Be Undocumented"; Balderrama and Rodríguez, *Decade of Betrayal*, 103; Hernández, *Migra!*, 49–50, 53–54. The owner of the store where the arrest occurred, Mr. G. E. Spinnler, registered a protest. The Border Patrol recorded questioning and investigating ten times the number of adult males of Mexican descent. Johnson, "Women in San Antonio," 11, citing 1930 census, San Antonio, Bexar, Texas, 10B, enumeration district 0018.

17. St. John, *Line in the Sand*, 191. According to St. John, in the February 1931 raid of Los Angeles's plaza in the barrio, officials detained over four hundred people but only took seventeen into custody. See also Hoffman, *Unwanted Americans*; Balderrama and Rodríguez, *Decade of Betrayal*, 67–82, and see 73–74 for the La Placita raid in Los Angeles involving agents from as far away as Nogales, as well as Los Angeles police and county officers—this raid, on February 26, 1931, netted thirty Mexicans, five Chinese, and one Japanese national detainee, 126–27, 134–35 (sometimes these women, within a few years, were utterly destitute, having no choice but to accept repatriation), 127 (on "whole *colonias*"), 128 (on the LA repatriation figure), 136–37 (on the shopkeepers), 150–51, 208–9 (on farmers). On p. 82 Balderrama and Rodríguez claim that only fifty thousand were actually deported. Elsewhere they cite a total number of one million repatriates. And see Sánchez, *Becoming Mexican American*, 214: the La Placita raid came in the context of a publicity campaign designed to frighten Mexicans into leaving. Sánchez writes that "fewer than 300 Mexican aliens were actually deported by federal authorities during this entire campaign," but the scare successfully drove many more from the city. And see Dewey, *Pesos and Dollars*, 208, 292n66.

18. White, *"It's Your Misfortune,"* 467. State legislatures proved reluctant to raise taxes in this situation. White gives examples from Texas, North Dakota, and Oklahoma; in the latter case, Governor Murray "donated part of his own salary to feed the hungry." At the same time, he "called out the national guard to enforce segregation in Oklahoma City." Dewey, *Pesos and Dollars*, 208, quoted in Laslett, *Sunshine Was Never Enough*, 110.

19. Tsu, *Garden of the World*, 169; Andrés, *Power and Control*, 117; Laslett, *Sunshine Was Never Enough*, 108; Balderrama and Rodríguez, *Decade of Betrayal*, 94; Sánchez, *Becoming Mexican American*, 210.

20. Sánchez, *Becoming Mexican American*, 211, 212; Balderrama and Rodríguez, *Decade of Betrayal*, 94. In California it was the Alien Labor Act of 1931.

21. Balderrama and Rodríguez, *Decade of Betrayal*, 90, 94, 95. And see Sánchez, *Becoming Mexican American*, 212, on the Catholic Welfare Bureau, almost entirely funded by public money, cutting "American" family food allowances by 10 percent and "Mexican" by 25 percent in 1931. Deutsch, *No Separate Refuge*, 165.

22. Tsu, *Garden of the World*, 171, 174.

23. Tsu, *Garden of the World*, 177, 179–80, 184–85, 189; Andrés, *Power and Control*, 128, 133–42.

24. Laslett, *Sunshine Was Never Enough*, 111; Deutsch, *No Separate Refuge*, 165, 171–72.

25. Balderrama and Rodríguez, *Decade of Betrayal*, 161. According to Overmyer-Velázquez, *Beyond la Frontera*, 57, Diego Rivera funded a train for repatriates from Detroit. On the Siqueiros mural, see Goldman, "Siqueiros," 321–27 (picture of mural on 323).

26. Quoted from the Wickersham Commission report in Balderrama and Rodríguez, *Decade of Betrayal*, 67: the INS denied any wrongdoing; 70, 75–76, 81, 82. Deutsch, *No Separate Refuge*, 165–67.

27. Balderrama and Rodríguez, *Decade of Betrayal*, 140–43, 150–51, 195, 243–45, 247, on the 25 percent estimated by Mexican authorities. *El Universal* gave the figures 1.6 million for 1931 and 400,000 in the first three months of 1932, attributing the figures to the U.S. Department of Labor on August 22, 1932; other estimates were lower, including estimates by the Mexican government. The authors conclude that one million is a "conservative middle ground." And see Sánchez, *Becoming Mexican American*, 217–18.

28. Overmyer-Velázquez, *Beyond la Frontera*, 67–69 on Mexicanizing; chap. 3, 51–79 throughout on national identity. See also Lim, *Porous Borders*, 158–59, 163, 166, 185–89.

29. Overmyer-Velázquez, *Beyond la Frontera*: 80 percent went to the towns and only 5 percent went to cities (60), and as of 1934 fewer than 5 percent were placed in irrigation projects (67). Balderrama and Rodríguez, *Decade of Betrayal*, 176–77, 195, 197–98, and see 215, 219 on Mexican government planning for agricultural policies for repatriates.

30. Sánchez, *Becoming Mexican American*, 219–21. Los Angeles County had been sending trainloads of repatriates every two months until April 1933, with an average of 908 people each for the past two years; but by early August 1933 county officials sent only 453, and in December, despite additional inducements, including the promise of a stipend on arrival in Mexico, they sent even fewer. Overmyer-Velázquez, *Beyond la Frontera*, 60–61, 64.

31. Sánchez, *Becoming Mexican American*, 212–13, 216, 221.

32. Dickson and Allen, *The Bonus Army*, 61, 64.

33. Dickson and Allen, *The Bonus Army*, 56–58. On the Bonus Army, see also Tuccille, *The War against the Vets*.

34. Dickson and Allen, *The Bonus Army*, 58, 60–62. The company had arranged to have trains pass too fast for the veterans to hop on, so the veterans spent the night in the yards and blocked the tracks. They then scrambled to the top of the cars and, though it was suicide, given the low overpasses, threatened to stay there unless they were given cars.

35. Dickson and Allen, *The Bonus Army*, 18, 21, 26, 28.

36. Dickson and Allen, *The Bonus Army*, 30–31.

37. Dickson and Allen, *The Bonus Army*, 31–34; on Hoover as progressive, see Wilson, *Herbert Hoover*.

38. Dickson and Allen, *The Bonus Army*, 37–38, 48.

39. Dickson and Allen, *The Bonus Army*, 45, 58–59.

40. Dickson and Allen, *The Bonus Army*, 63–64, 65–66, 90.

41. Dickson and Allen, *The Bonus Army*, 6, 64–65.

42. Dickson and Allen, *The Bonus Army*, 76–77, and see 87–88 for some of the locations that sent contingents, including Salt Lake City (two hundred), New Orleans, Minneapolis (two hundred), Texas (five hundred), Little Rock (three hundred), Great Falls, Montana, and others from Alabama, New Jersey, South Carolina, and so on.

43. Dickson and Allen, *The Bonus Army*, 7, 118, 120–21, 122, 125.

44. Quoted in Dickson and Allen, *The Bonus Army*, 127–29.

45. As Waters began to flirt with fascism, General MacArthur planned a violent end to the movement. Dickson and Allen, *The Bonus Army*, 130, 135, 139 (on Major George S. Patton Jr. agreeing with MacArthur on the red menace), 143–45. One contingent left California with 2,600 people, ran out of gas, and left 1,500 stranded in Tucson; only 450 arrived in Washington, on July 12. Secret intelligence reports warned of Communist hopes for violence in Washington's streets (152).

46. Dickson and Allen, *The Bonus Army*, 169, 173ff., 181 (quoting Reporter Bess Furman), 182, 187. The Bonus Army remustered in early 1933, again with contingents from across the United States, often mobilized from encampments set up in the wake of the 1932 evictions. Near San Antonio, Texas, Camp Diga (Agricultural and Industrial Democracy spelled backward), the brainchild of "former first lieutenant and future congressman Maury Maverick," was set up in an abandoned oil plant and ran as a cooperative, with 160 men, women, and children living in boxcars donated by Missouri Pacific Lines and cooking on army field stoves "salvaged from the trash at Fort Sam Houston" (203). Roosevelt, too, opposed the bonus for a variety of reasons (223). It would pass over Roosevelt's veto (253). By July 31, 1936, about six months after passage, payments totaled just under $1.1 billion (254), giving a typical veteran's family an overnight 30 percent increase in income (262–

63) and the United States a cash infusion equal to nearly 1 percent of GNP (262). "The promised boost to local economies was huge" (262).

47. Balderrama and Rodríguez, *Decade of Betrayal*, 206.

48. Balderrama and Rodríguez, *Decade of Betrayal*, 103–4; Taylor, *In Search of the Racial Frontier*, 231.

49. Sánchez, *Becoming Mexican American*, 129–30, 209.

50. Stock, *Main Street in Crisis*, 75, 90, 114.

51. Stock, *Main Street in Crisis*, 19.

52. Stock, *Main Street in Crisis*, 149, 152, 159.

53. Tucker, "Populism Up-to-Date," esp. 199–200. Barrett, from Georgia, presided over the Farmers Union for more than two decades, but the union had been founded in Texas, and by the 1910s the growth and strength had shifted definitively to the Midwest and Northwest. In 1919 the most substantial membership lay in Kansas, Nebraska, and Iowa (Milo Reno's organization, founded in 1914, according to its current website). It ran its strongest cooperatives in 1920 in Kansas, Nebraska, Colorado, Oregon, Washington, Idaho, Iowa, and South Dakota, in that order. It marketed livestock with a union-sponsored firm at terminals in Omaha and South St. Paul starting in 1917. The union limited its membership to farmers, rural laborers, teachers, ministers, country doctors, and sympathetic country editors and from time to time purged the nonfarmer element. By the 1920s the National Farmers Union had a strong contingent of Nonpartisan League veterans, including M. W. Thatcher, who led the successful Northwest Organizing Committee from 1927 to 1930. Will Rogers, *The Autobiography of Will Rogers*, ed. Donald Day (Boston: Houghton Mifflin, 1949), 237, as quoted in Holley, *Uncle Sam's Farmers*, 4, and for the protest, see 3–4.

54. As quoted in Tucker, "Populism Up-to-Date," 205. See also Ford, "Women on Holiday," 289: by January 1934 women made up about 20 percent of delegates pictured at the FHA convention; Taylor, "Femininity as Strategy," 253ff.; Stock, *Main Street in Crisis*, 130–32; Shover, "The Farmers' Holiday Association Strike," 197. See Dileva, "Iowa Farm Price Revolt," 186–87, on Reno, and 188, quote from the *Des Moines Register*, August 25, 1932, 9.

55. Stock, *Main Street in Crisis*, 128; White, *"It's Your Misfortune,"* 469. The federal government "also offered cattlemen feed loans in 1931," but at the cost of a government lien on the cattle. Most western cattle was already heavily mortgaged, and so ranchers were ineligible for this aid. See also Taylor, "Femininity as Strategy," 254.

56. Shover, "The Farmers' Holiday Association Strike," 196. The National Farmers Union defeated Reno's call for a farm strike at its 1931 convention because it would have jeopardized their members' investments in cooperative facilities. Reno succeeded on the state level in Iowa at the convention there and, after substantially cultivating Farmers Unions in Wisconsin, South Dakota, and Minnesota, gathered two thousand farmers in Des Moines on May 3 to launch the Farmers' Holiday Association, naming Reno president

and resolving to begin withholding crops from market on July 4. Taylor, "Femininity as Strategy," 255.

57. Stock, *Main Street in Crisis*, 132–35. Emil Loriks, a South Dakota Farmers Union official, was the hard-driving organizer. And see Tucker, "Populism Up-to-Date," 203. By 1928 Nebraska, North Dakota, Kansas, Oklahoma, Iowa, South Dakota, Montana, and Colorado had the strongest Farmers Unions; in 1927 North Dakota's charter covered ten thousand members; a year later the number doubled, placing North Dakota with Nebraska as the strongest states. See also Dileva, "Iowa Farm Price Revolt," 186, who cites the first use of "Holiday" for the strike in February 1932 when 1,500 Boone County farmers in the Farmers Union pledged their support for moving toward one.

58. Stock, *Main Street in Crisis*, 135.

59. As quoted in White, *"It's Your Misfortune,"* 472.

60. Shover, "The Farmers' Holiday Association Strike," 199–200. Shover argues that the strike method appealed most to corn-hog and dairy farmers and spread largely in those areas of Nebraska, South Dakota, and Minnesota, while its greatest support remained in Iowa and Wisconsin. It's not clear from Shover how widespread the settlement was. At the end of August, for example, deputies and pickets fought a three-night battle outside Omaha over livestock shipments; deputies arrested eighty-seven people. Reno and state FHA leaders called a truce on September 1, 1932. Dileva, "Iowa Farm Price Revolt," 172, 173, 174–75, 177, and see 180–83 on negotiations, 184 on foreclosures (3,700 were foreclosed in 1933, and despite a state moratorium law, insurance companies foreclosed "two-thirds of the mortgaged farm land in the state by 1934"), 195–96 on labor unions, 199 on the governor, 201. See Taylor, "Femininity as Strategy," 255, on hog prices and the foreclosure rate, which had doubled from 1930 to 1931 and nearly again in 1932.

61. Stock, *Main Street in Crisis*, 136–37; Tucker, "Populism Up-to-Date," 205. See also Shover, "The Farmers' Holiday Association Strike," 197, on the tensions between Farmers Union members who favored cooperatives as a solution and those who favored cost-of-production legislation (e.g., livestock raisers). Reno had been arguing for cost-of-production since at least 1927 (198, 202). And see Dileva, "Iowa Farm Price Revolt," 174, 191–92, 193–98, 201, 202. See Ford, "Women on Holiday," 291ff., on women's participation in direct action. And see Taylor, "Femininity as Strategy," 258–62, 265; Hurt, *The Big Empty*, 81, on Omaha farmers fighting deputies to keep Omaha milk from reaching Iowa.

62. Shover, "The Farmers' Holiday Association Strike," 196. See Ford, "Women on Holiday," 290–93. Hurt, *The Big Empty*, 27–28, claims the first penny sale was in Nebraska. Stock, *Main Street in Crisis*, 137–39. Such actions continued until 1936. Taylor, "Femininity as Strategy," 257–58, 276.

63. Quoted in Stock, *Main Street in Crisis*, 139–40, and see 141: Langer proclaimed a "wheat embargo" in the fall of 1933, halting all sales of wheat

within state borders; it remained in force for three months, raising the price only slightly, before it was ruled unconstitutional.

64. Canadian Broadcasting Corporation, "Co-operative Commonwealth Federation." See also Horn, "Frank Underhill's Early Drafts"; and Young, *The Anatomy of a Party.*

65. Holmes, "Farmer's Market," 33, 34, 36.

66. White, *"It's Your Misfortune,"* 468.

11. Mobilizing the New Deal

1. The idea that workers shaped the New Deal by their actions and expectations is not new. Cohen pioneered the idea in her book, *Making a New Deal.*

2. Quoted in Wild, *Street Meeting*, 194: by 1939 Perry chaired the Communist Party of Los Angeles. Fisk University graduate James W. Ford ran as the Communist Party USA candidate for vice president in 1932, 1936, and 1940.

3. Wild, *Street Meeting*, 2, 9, 22, quote on 38–39.

4. Steptoe, *Houston Bound*, depicts the simultaneous separation and convergence of Mexican Americans, Mexican nationals, Creoles, and African Americans in Houston. Wild, *Street Meeting*, 151, 179–83. Such efforts to marginalize popular political speech, including the expansion of the "no-speech zone," did have some success—by the mid-1920s Brooklyn Avenue in Boyle Heights had replaced some of the popular downtown sites, and in these outlying parks and neighborhoods such meetings suffered less surveillance (174, 178).

5. Wild, *Street Meeting*, 1–2, 194: they married in 1935. The ILA had a tradition that permitted the automatic induction of the children of union members. In 1942 Yoneda and Black wound up in a Japanese internment camp.

6. Gregory, *American Exodus*, 58, shows that the largest number of farmworkers in California in 1930 were native-born whites (43 percent). Only about one-fifth were Mexicans (21 percent), with 17 percent European whites, 8 percent Filipinos, and 7 percent Japanese. But the native-born whites were the least mobile: they tended to get year-round work, usually in tree crops, which required the use of ladders, and not in stoop labor, which was so despised.

7. Escobar, *Race, Police*, 81, 83. On Alaska, see Fresco, "Cannery Workers."

8. Mullins, *The Depression*, 4, for his term "cooperative individualism," which he finds characterizes popular thinking about relief, and see 90 and throughout. Foley, *The White Scourge*, 179, quoting and citing Irene Ledesma, "New Deal Works Programs and Mexican-Americans in McAllen, Texas, 1933–1936" (master's thesis, University of Texas at Edinburg, 1977), 66.

9. Deutsch, "Labor, Land, and Protest," 276–78, drawing heavily on Zaragosa Vargas, *Labor Rights Are Civil Rights: Mexican American Workers in Twentieth-Century America* (Princeton NJ: Princeton University Press, 2005), 99. One of the key organizers was Juan Ochoa, born in Hillsborough, New Mexico. Companies violated the NRA code, and in early 1935 the NMU and UMW joined in a successful walkout.

10. Starr, *Endangered Dreams*, 62–63, 67–71, on the founding of the CAWIU in 1930 by the Trade Union Unity League and its pre-1933 strike efforts (all of which met with draconian grower and state action and failed), including a lettuce pickers' strike that included not only eight thousand Mexican workers but also Filipino, Chinese, Japanese, and Sikh workers. In 1935 the CAWIU "disestablished itself in favor of the . . . CIO." The top 2 percent of California's farmers held 25 percent of the state's total acreage and produced 32 percent of the value of its crops. A peach orchard could operate with thirty full-time year-round employees but need two thousand harvest workers; a twenty-acre hop ranch could employ twelve staff year-round and five hundred at harvest, for example. See Weber, *Dark Sweat, White Gold*, 80; according to Weber, the exclusion came under the Re-employment Agreement of the executive branch, and see 105 on California officials who were convinced that agricultural labor either was included or would be soon. McWilliams, *Factories*, 212–19.

11. Weber, *Dark Sweat, White Gold*, 80. See Guerin-Gonzales, *Mexican Workers & American Dreams*, 116–20, on the berry pickers' strike. Growers brought Filipinos, Anglos, Mexicans, and Los Angeles schoolchildren to replace strikers, but ultimately the Japanese growers and the Mexican union Confederación de Uniones de Campesinos y Obreros Mexicanos (CUCOM) settled the strike, recognizing the union as the workers' bargaining agent, giving preference to union members in hiring, and discharging strikebreakers, as well as paying higher wages. When growers failed to live up to the agreement, the union sued. Over half the workers were first- or second-generation U.S. citizens. At least one member of the Los Angeles Chamber of Commerce favored getting "some of these people going back, American citizens or otherwise" (118). See also Tsu, *Garden of the World*, 189–90.

12. Weber, *Dark Sweat, White Gold*, 38–42, and see 79 on how the strikes affected 65 percent of the state's crops. See Starr, *Endangered Dreams*, 66–67, 79, on efforts in 1927 and 1928 for Mexican workers to organize, including with the aid of the Mexican consul general in Calexico. The growers used a red scare and police power to destroy the union in the Imperial Valley; the strikes affected 65 percent of the state's crops.

13. Deutsch, *No Separate Refuge*, 188; and Weber, *Dark Sweat, White Gold*, 43.

14. In 1933 California had only four inspectors to cover five thousand labor camps that housed nearly two hundred thousand migrant workers. Weber, *Dark Sweat, White Gold*, 43–45, 48; Andrés, *Power and Control*, 122.

15. Weber, *Dark Sweat, White Gold*, 53, 64, 72. See Starr, *Endangered Dreams*, 64–65, on the difference between Filipino workers, who tended to be men traveling alone, and Mexicans traveling as families and the mutual aid societies they created. On Black workers, see Rivera, "Solidarity," 13, 15–16, 59–60, 65, 69, 71.

16. Weber, *Dark Sweat, White Gold*, 80, 89, points out that federal relief had begun, and urban employment had simultaneously risen slightly; wages fell from one dollar per one hundred pounds to forty cents.

17. Weber, *Dark Sweat, White Gold,* 81–82.

18. Weber, *Dark Sweat, White Gold,* 82 (quoting Pat Chambers and Caroline Decker), 84–85 (CUOM claimed three thousand members in twenty-two southern California locals in 1928; having faltered, it was revived in 1933 as the Confederación de Uniones de Campesinos y Obreros Mexicanos, which received funds from and by 1933 was affiliated with the Mexican union, the Confederación Regional Obrera Mexicana), 86–87 (on the IWW), and 88 (on the 1928 and 1930 strikes, led by Mexicans and the TUUL in the Imperial Valley; in 1931 the TUUL had "spawned the CAWIU"). According to Weber, "Veterans of earlier strikes formed the core of this leadership" for the 1933 strike wave (93).

19. Weber, *Dark Sweat, White Gold,* 79, 82 led by CAWIU. The following account of the strike relies heavily on Weber; for other accounts, see Starr, *Endangered Dreams,* 61–83, and an extensive bibliography on 364–66. And see Andrés, *Power and Control,* 117–24.

20. Weber, *Dark Sweat, White Gold,* 82–83, 88–91, 93, 97–101. Growers found a sympathetic, anti-Communist, elite Mexican consul, Enrique Bravo, who tried to create a separate, all-Mexican union, but he could not lure the workers away from the CAWIU (101–2). Growers would try the same thing with more success in the Imperial Valley with Joaquín Terrazas. See Andrés, *Power and Control,* 142ff.

21. Weber, *Dark Sweat, White Gold,* 102, 104, on how NRA regulations stipulated that only strikers involved in arbitration were eligible for relief; being on relief had been a criterion for deportation (becoming a "public charge").

22. Weber, *Dark Sweat, White Gold,* 103 (quoting the director of mediation and adjustment for the NRA in California, Rabbi Irving Reichart), 105–6 (quoting George Creel). The NRA and NLB had already helped in the El Monte and Tagus strikes and others. The federal government had just mediated a cotton strike in Arizona (*Madera Tribune,* September 30, 1933), with the union claiming 2,500 members plus 500 nonmembers on strike "in the various fields, particularly at Yuma." State officials claimed there were thirteen thousand pickers in Arizona.

23. Weber, *Dark Sweat, White Gold,* 108, 109.

24. Weber, *Dark Sweat, White Gold,* 110. The picture varied across the West. In Texas cotton-picking rates similarly plunged with the onset of the Depression until rates hit a nadir of thirty cents per hundred pounds picked in 1932. Yet Texas experienced little of the coordinated labor resistance California and Arizona did. Only in spinach in 1930 at Crystal City and onions in 1933 at Laredo did workers launch large-scale movements to increase their wages and improve their conditions. No strikes occurred in cotton, though Texas growers had not created the employer associations California cotton growers had. Texas cotton grew in a mix of small farms in the eastern and central parts of the state and larger ranches in the western and south-central parts. Wages varied. When workers organized, they did so locally and usually briefly,

as they had in California earlier. See Weber, *From South Texas to the Nation,* 133, 155–57; and Foley, *The White Scourge,* 184–86ff. California saw 140 strikes with 127,176 farmworkers from 1930 to 1939; Texas saw 6 strikes with 4,057 farmworkers in that time, and none on a cotton ranch. Foley also points out that California produced only 3 percent of U.S. cotton but had 47 percent of the nation's large-scale industrialized farms (198). Foley cites historian Emilio Zamora, who claimed the ranch owners had "more effective methods of control" (*The World of the Mexican Worker,* 199) and more isolated workers.

25. Coodley, *Upton Sinclair,* 35, 40–42, 55, 64, 67. Sinclair had organized protests in the aftermath of the tent fire at Ludlow, first in New York City at Rockefeller's Broadway office and then at Rockefeller's estate in Tarrytown. Dray, *There Is Power in a Union,* 345–47.

26. Coodley, *Upton Sinclair,* 69–73, 79, 85, 89, 90.

27. Quoted in Coodley, *Upton Sinclair,* 69.

28. Coodley, *Upton Sinclair,* 90–93, quotes on 92.

29. Coodley, *Upton Sinclair,* 94, 96, 97–98, 107, 112–16. Coodley attributes Sinclair's strong dry stance to being "the feminist son of an alcoholic"; his exposé of the film industry focused on Fox, leading Fox to forbid its employees from reading the book.

30. Coodley, *Upton Sinclair,* 116–17; Gregory, "Upton Sinclair's 1934 EPIC Campaign," 53–54, 59. Merriam had only come into the governorship six months earlier when his predecessor died.

31. Starr, *Endangered Dreams,* 133. Sinclair's pamphlet was published on September 30, 1933.

32. Starr, *Endangered Dreams,* 133–35. Half of elderly Americans needed outside help. By the end of 1936 there were about 2.2 million members, and the *Townsend National Weekly* brought in another $250,000 per year in advertising. Ultimately the pension figure was raised to $200, financed by a national transaction sales tax of 2 percent, creating a revolving fund of $18-$24 billion. Starr describes Townsend as lean to the point of sepulchral and in ill health, though he lived to the age of ninety-three. See Brinkley, *Voices of Protest,* 222: Townsend's medical practice in the Black Hills of South Dakota began in 1903; he moved to California in 1920. Brinkley points out that such plans had been advocated by others, including Seattle dentist Stuart McCord, but without the success in publicizing them (223).

33. Starr, *Endangered Dreams,* 131–32. And see Gregory, "Upton Sinclair's 1934 EPIC Campaign," 54, 56. Sinclair estimated that by the end of the campaign California boasted close to two thousand EPIC clubs.

34. Gregory, "Upton Sinclair's 1934 EPIC Campaign," 55, 57, 59, 72–73. Sinclair also spoke often on the radio in purchased time slots. George Creel, who had run Washington's propaganda campaign during World War I, was the most serious Democratic contender; now he headed the NRA on the West Coast. As the New Deal kicked in, co-ops focused more on getting relief and

less on cooperative exchange, and the economic aspects began to fall apart. Laslett, *Sunshine Was Never Enough,* 116; Coodley, *Upton Sinclair,* 117–18, 120.

35. Coodley, *Upton Sinclair,* 119.

36. Coodley, *Upton Sinclair,* 122–23; Gregory, "Upton Sinclair's 1934 EPIC Campaign," 60—the quote is from Gregory. It wasn't just Chandler. William Randolph Hearst, "Democratic Party kingmaker," also threw the weight of his media empire, "five of the largest-circulation newspapers in the state," against Sinclair and for Merriam.

37. Coodley, *Upton Sinclair,* 123–24. See Swatt et al., *Game Changers,* 82–86, on how part of the impetus to use media to reach voters came from the realization that direct democracy decreased the power of political parties, and at the same time, papers struggled financially in the Depression; paid political copy was a great boon. These campaigns also used radio, including a twice-weekly show, *The Unmasking of Upton Sinclair.*

38. Johnson, *How Many Machine Guns,* 70.

39. Nelson, *Workers on the Waterfront,* 1 (quote), 2, 9.

40. Nelson, *Workers on the Waterfront,* 25–26, on the dwindling significance of ethnic boardinghouses for maritime workers on the West Coast; quote from 27.

41. Nelson, *Workers on the Waterfront,* 28–29, 133, on Black dockworkers. The unions struggled with myriad other lines of division—the International Seamen's Union was itself a federation of sixteen "relatively autonomous divisions," including those based on geography. There were also divisions based on race and nationality between Scandinavians, Irish, Chinese, and Filipinos. The ISU called for "Asiatic exclusion" (31–32); only lumber schooners on the Pacific coast "required a high level of cooperation" (33). Johnson, *How Many Machine Guns,* 7–9, 24–26, 75.

42. Johnson, *How Many Machine Guns,* 72; Nelson, *Workers on the Waterfront,* 72. Nelson says that even in the booming late 1920s the seamen made $25 to $27 less than during the war and its immediate aftermath (104).

43. Nelson, *Workers on the Waterfront,* 71. And see Johnson, *How Many Machine Guns,* 72, on how the Pacific coast International Longshoremen's Association had barred "colored people" from its mid-nineteenth-century founding; in 1919 organized employers hired African American strikebreakers, but few were kept permanently, and they were not allowed into the Blue Book union.

44. Nelson, *Workers on the Waterfront,* quoted on 118 and 71.

45. Nelson, *Workers on the Waterfront,* 3, 100, 105, 106, 113, and 71–72, on San Francisco's shift from closed shop for 90 percent of the city's manual workers to open shop over the course of three years, culminating in 1923, thanks to the efforts of the Industrial Association. See Selvin, *A Terrible Anger,* 44–45 on Jack Bryan, a longshoreman who ran the association with an iron hand; and 47–51 on attempts to revive an independent union.

46. Nelson, *Workers on the Waterfront,* 114, 121, 125, 128, for example, but throughout the book.

47. Johnson, *How Many Machine Guns*, 87, 128, 130–32.

48. Nelson, *Workers on the Waterfront*, 133, on strikebreakers: in early 1934 one estimate placed the number of Black workers on the San Francisco waterfront at only fifty, and see p. 134 on Henry Schmidt's recruitment of the Black workers. See Selvin, *A Terrible Anger*, 90–93, on the nature of the strikebreakers, characterized by Theodore Durein in the *Reader's Digest*, drawing from his own experience, as "mostly pasty-faced clerks, house-to-house salesmen, college students, and a motley array of unemployed who had never shouldered anything heavier than a BVD strap before in their lives" (90). One football player's father snatched him off the docks and contributed $100 to the strike fund.

49. Johnson, *How Many Machine Guns*, 82–85; by characterizing racial division as an employer tactic, the union could encourage inclusivity without directly attacking or eliminating racism.

50. Nelson, *Workers on the Waterfront*, 129. See Johnson, *How Many Machine Guns*, 85, on Portland featuring particularly ferocious battles; when Senator Wagner toured waterfront Portland, police shot at his car.

51. Johnson, *How Many Machine Guns*, 100–101.

52. Nelson, *Workers on the Waterfront*, 128–30, from Donald Mackenzie Brown, "Dividends and Stevedores," *Scribner's* 97 (January 1935): 52–56.

53. Nelson, *Workers on the Waterfront*, 128, 132.

54. Nelson, *Workers on the Waterfront*, 128, 132–33, 147, quotations on 132–33 from the *San Francisco Chronicle*, July 10, 1934, 1, and other sources, including interviews and memoirs housed in the ILWU Archives; see 300n11.

55. Nelson, *Workers on the Waterfront*, 137–39; Johnson, *How Many Machine Guns*, 100–101.

56. Nelson, *Workers on the Waterfront*, 139–40. The following descriptors were used by his contemporaries: cold, clean, clear, rapid-fire, precise, like the blow of a hammer, brilliance.

57. Nelson, *Workers on the Waterfront*, 144–45; Selvin, *A Terrible Anger*, 64–65; Selvin, "An Exercise in Hysteria."

58. Nelson, *Workers on the Waterfront*, 79–82, 145–46, quoting *Foc'sle Head*, June 28, 1934, 2.

59. Nelson, *Workers on the Waterfront*, 147–48.

60. Nelson, *Workers on the Waterfront*, 149–52, 154–55 (only Everett, Washington, voted against by the margin of a single vote), 164–65. See also Palmer, *Revolutionary Teamsters*, 18, and they won the understanding that six hours constituted a full day's work and thirty hours a week's work, averaged monthly. Selvin, *A Terrible Anger*, 235–40, on the settlement and the power gained by the workers. See also Kagel, "The General Strike," 216–17; Johnson, *How Many Machine Guns*, 103. To achieve a more democratic organization, workers formed the International Longshoremen's and Warehousemen's Union, which affiliated with the CIO in 1937, and continuously elected Harry Bridges as president.

61. Palmer, *Revolutionary Teamsters*, 3, 5–60, 216, and 219, on the February strike.

62. Palmer, *Revolutionary Teamsters*, 38, on the impact of the Panama Canal and Pacific lumber. Palmer argues that the prosperity had enabled the open-shop. And see p. 34 on how Floyd Bjørnstjerne Olson, age thirty-eight, was elected on the Farmer-Labor ticket in 1930; while claiming in that campaign that he was "not a 'bitter radical and theorist, but a well-balanced progressive,'" by 1934 he declared, "I am what I want to be—a radical." On the alliance with the Farmers' Holiday Association, see p. 70. And see Faue, *Community of Suffering*, 58, on the hinterland that encompassed the agricultural areas of Iowa, the Dakotas, and Minnesota where farms and banks failed: the "rural crisis fueled the deteriorating urban conditions."

63. Palmer, *Revolutionary Teamsters*, 5: James Cannon, for example, born in Rosedale, Kansas, had agitated for the IWW and struggled to build a Leninist Communist Party in the United States; he was, according to Palmer, "American Trotskyism's founding figure." On p. 34 Palmer points out that "tens of thousands of migratory timber-workers and field-hands" passed through Minneapolis in the early twentieth century, and see 44–49 on leadership. See Faue, *Community of Suffering*, 51, 111, on the Farmer-Labor Party as the heir to the Nonpartisan League.

64. Palmer, *Revolutionary Teamsters*, 52.

65. Faue, *Community of Suffering*, 23, 27, 31–32, 50, 62, 111–13. On Cain, see 47, 53. Their strike headquarters were in the Nonpartisan League campaign office; Cain worked in the Working People's Nonpartisan League, the WTUL, and the Woman's Party, as well as labor unions. See p. 55 on the crumbling of the coalition under the strain of fractures in the Socialist Party, the Communist Party, and the Populists and the attacks of the Citizens' Alliance and open-shop campaign. Compare Creese, "The Politics of Dependence," 378, on the total ineligibility of single women in Vancouver to receive relief until early 1933, and even then on draconian terms. Palmer, *Revolutionary Teamsters*, 31, citing Faue, *Community of Suffering*, 80, quoting Cannon in May, and 61 on a Chippewa trucker and reservation women coming to Minneapolis in 1930 seeking work.

66. Faue, *Community of Suffering*, 64–65, 66, 106, 96, 101. The garment industry employed nearly five thousand workers in Minneapolis, three-quarters of them women, and women presided over the local. And see p. 115: the Ladies' Auxiliary of General Drivers' 574 had three hundred members, who not only worked in the commissary and staffed a hospital but also distributed strike newspapers, raised funds, and occupied part of city hall during union negotiations to meet the mayor.

67. Palmer, *Revolutionary Teamsters*, 86–99.

68. Palmer, *Revolutionary Teamsters*, 99–100, 101, 102.

69. Palmer, *Revolutionary Teamsters*, 106, 107, 112 (also on the front pages was a mass strike in Toledo, Ohio), 128 (on how the strike ended officially on May 26).

70. Palmer, *Revolutionary Teamsters*, 110, 130, 131. Faue, *Community of Suffering*, 116, points out that women, active in organizing the unemployed around relief and consumer issues, brought marginalized families into the union movement.

71. Palmer, *Revolutionary Teamsters*, 128 (from the *Minneapolis Tribune*), 129, 130. The women's auxiliary of Local 547 had begun to put out a four-page paper, *The Organizer*, issued in runs of five thousand copies. Faue, *Community of Suffering*, 111.

72. Palmer, *Revolutionary Teamsters*, 141 (the demands, more specifically, were that Local 547 represented—and had the right to represent—all workers in the trucking sector, including those who loaded trucks inside companies; that the entire union membership should receive higher wages backdated to the end of the May strike; and that the employers should sign a contract with the General Drivers' Union), 145, 151 (on the number of firms), 152.

73. The following account of the strike relies on Palmer, *Revolutionary Teamsters*, 154–55, 160, 161, 163, 165–66, 172, 174, 176, 179, 194, 202, 210.

74. Palmer, *Revolutionary Teamsters*, 161, 163.

75. Palmer, *Revolutionary Teamsters*, 213, 224, 226; Faue, *Community of Suffering*, 111.

76. Andrés, *Power and Control*, 127, 153–55. The move was part of the government's attempt to Mexicanize Baja and resulted in the repatriation of Chinese colonists and the departure of Japanese ones.

77. Thompson and Seager, *Canada*, 230–44, 275. Because of the way representation worked in the provinces, though liberals in Vancouver got 42 percent of the vote and the CCF got 31 percent, liberals gained thirty-four seats, and the CCF only gained seven. In Saskatchewan Farmer-Labour, with one-quarter of the vote, got five seats. In 1935 the CCF had twice the national popular vote of Social Credit but half as many MPs, and in British Columbia the CCF had a plurality (ninety-seven thousand votes) but got two fewer seats than did the Conservative Party, with seventy-one thousand.

78. University of Washington, "Upton Sinclair's End Poverty in California Campaign"; Gregory, "Upton Sinclair's 1934 EPIC Campaign," 76. See Acena, "The Washington Commonwealth Federation": among the leaders was Reverend Frank Shorter, an Australian-born social gospel Congregational minister who became chairman of his local Seattle Socialist Party in 1933 and got kicked out of his congregation in 1934 for allowing the church to be used by radical groups. Western Washington, with per capita income down by a third, was harder hit than the eastern part of the state, making Seattle a hub for the movement, which was enabled also by locals with experience in the IWW and other leftist movements. In November Washingtonians elected Commonwealth Builder candidates to the U.S. Senate, the state senate (eight), and the state lower house (twenty-seven). Those victorious in 1934 included Mary U. Farquharson, a socialist who, like Sinclair, left the Socialist Party and ran as a Democrat and whose husband was among the founders of the Com-

monwealth Builders, Inc. (19). Oregon's trajectory was a bit different. See Robbins, *A Man for All Seasons*, 37–50. The political economy ideas of Monroe Sweetland, who was friendly with some of the key players in Washington's Commonwealth movement, had already come out of the Minnesota Farmer-Labor Progressive movement and the CCF in Canada. The Oregon Commonwealth Federation and others defeated the incumbent in the Democratic primary, but the result was to throw the election to the Republican gubernatorial candidate in 1938, and almost all the other OCF candidates lost as well.

79. Coodley, *Upton Sinclair*, 128; Gregory, *American Exodus*, 89ff., 92, 93, 97. Amid local hostility toward California's new residents, dust bowl refugees registered to vote in record numbers; voter registration rose about 7 percent statewide in 1938 but just under 20 percent in the San Joaquin Valley. Olson won his largest leads in the southern San Joaquin Valley, up to 71 percent of the vote where migrants from the Southwest clustered. But see Gregory, "Upton Sinclair's 1934 EPIC Campaign," 60ff., on who voted for Sinclair—largely white urban industrial workers, particularly in Los Angeles. Sinclair did little campaigning outside the city and its environs and certainly failed to get agribusiness leaders. Gregory doesn't mention this, but it is likely that many agricultural workers were too transient to be able to register to vote. One of the EPIC state assembly candidates, African American Augustus Hawkins, age twenty-seven, a real estate broker, won, "becoming the first African American Democrat elected to the legislature," where he served for twenty-eight years before heading to Congress for another twenty-eight. Gregory argues that California, Washington, and Oregon all had been strongly if not monopolistically Republican for decades, which had weakened the Democratic infrastructure and leadership and made it possible for an outsider to take over the party. See Swatt et al., *Game Changers*, 77, 81; Starr, *Endangered Dreams*, 136. Nothing seemed to daunt Townsend's popularity, including the revelation that he and his partner pocketed about $2,000 per week from the *Townsend Weekly*. The movement drew members across racial lines.

80. Garcia, *A World of Its Own*, 109; Immerwahr, *How to Hide*, 161 (the act granted independence in ten years if the Filipinos met the benchmarks but immediately made Filipinos "foreign" and subject to immigration law); Tsu, *Garden of the World*, 195. In the 1935 Filipino Repatriation Act the federal government would bear the costs of transport if the Filipinos forfeited their right to reenter the United States. The government expected that up to fifteen thousand Filipinos would take the offer; only just over two thousand did so between 1936 and 1941.

81. Hernández, *Migra!*, 80. According to Garcia, *A World of Its Own*, 118, the 1936 citrus strike was brutally suppressed in Orange County, the farmers having organized an Associated Farmers vigilante group in 1934 to battle what they saw as Communist-dominated unions. Andrés, *Power and Control*, 122–23, 148–53, claims that the Associated Farmers had few actual farmers; it had railroads, utilities, grocery stores, banks, canneries, sugar refineries,

insurance and investment companies, and other corporations and represented agribusiness. Its powerful lobby led to cuts in relief that particularly affected Spanish-surnamed and Native American workers and to the elimination of the Federal Transient Service, which had fed seventy-seven thousand indigent migrants a month, as well as to the federal government ignoring the findings of its own appointed mediator. See Starr, *Endangered Dreams*, 82; and see McWilliams, *Factories*, 230–63 (on the dismal record and brutal retaliation against strikers after 1933), 266 (on the value of farm products in California from 1928 to 1937—bookended at over $620 million, with a nadir of $372 million in 1932, $421 million in 1933, and $501 million in 1934). See also Yung, *Unbound Feet*, 241–43.

12. Moving People and Animals

1. Quoted in Wrobel, *America's West*, 129. Wrobel argues that FDR's view was that the frontier's end "explained the need for the New Deal," replacing open land as a safety valve with state programs (129, 131). But FDR also retained the love affair with the yeoman farmer (see below).

2. Phillips, *This Land*, 24, 30, 44, 47, 80.

3. White, *The Organic Machine*, 53–60, 67–69. The 1920 Federal Water Power Act enabled the projects; most western waterpower sites on nonnavigable rivers lay on federal land, and since the federal government controlled interstate commerce, it also controlled navigable river sites, meaning that even if the dams were developed by private or municipal concerns, the federal government could regulate rates. Wrobel, *America's West*, 142.

4. White, *The Organic Machine*, 58; Arrigo, *Imaging Hoover Dam*, 90. Not everyone was so thrilled. When a decade's negotiations among the relevant state governments finally allowed the signing of a dam contract in 1931, the *Chicago Tribune* complained that eastern taxpayers were paying for western development. Wiley and Gottlieb, *Empires in the Sun*, 5–6.

5. Nash, *The Federal Landscape*, 24–25; Wrobel, *America's West*, 139.

6. Nash, *The Federal Landscape*, 24–27; Carriker, *Urban Farming in the West*, 164. Carriker contrasts the sum with the $693,497 spent by the Department of Subsistence Homesteads, which built 225 modest homes. See also Smith, *Rocky Mountain Heartland*, 133–35. Wrobel, *America's West*, 142, points out that in Idaho the number of farms without electricity fell from 70 percent to 46 percent; in Montana the number with electricity grew from 1,758 in 1935 to 6,000 in 1939; in Wyoming 527 ranches and farms had electricity in 1935 and 3,300 did in 1939, for example.

7. Nash, *The Federal Landscape*, 24–27; Arrigo, *Imaging Hoover Dam*, 73, on employment figures. Smith, *Rocky Mountain Heartland*, 133–37. Fort Peck Dam employed about eleven thousand workers at its seasonal peak.

8. Carriker, *Urban Farming*, 164; Needham, *Power Lines*; Worster, *Under Western Skies*, 73–75; White, *"It's Your Misfortune,"* 488–89. The other companies were MacDonald & Kahn, which, like Bechtel-Kaiser, was from San Fran-

cisco; Morrison-Knudson Corporation of Boise; Utah Construction Company of Salt Lake City; and J. F. Shea and the Pacific Bridge Corporation of Portland. Wiley and Gottlieb, *Empires in the Sun*, 2–29.

9. Harold Ickes, in U.S. Congress, Senate, Subcommittee of the Committee on Public Lands and Surveys, *Hearings Pursuant to Senate Resolution #53*, 77th Cong., 1st sess. (Washington DC: Government Printing Office, 1942), as quoted in Nash, *The Federal Landscape*, 22.

10. Ben Reifel remarks in Philp, "Indian Self Rule," 394; McNickle (Salish-Kutenai), "The Indian New Deal," 411.

11. White, *Roots of Dependency*, 254.

12. Sarah Begay, interview, June 20, 1974, 8–9, in *Navajo Stock Reduction Interviews*, ed. Dean Sundberg and Fern Charley, microfilm, Oral History Program, California State University, Fullerton, quoted in Weisiger, *Dreaming of Sheep*, 18. See also 175–76 on how the reduction practices varied regionally on the reservation, with some Diné even nostalgic about the goat reduction because of the amount of meat available; in other areas, however, the reduction wiped out smallholders and left carcasses of thousands of animals to rot and be scavenged. See also Philp, *John Collier's Crusade*, 188–89.

13. See, in this light, Roosevelt's 1934 statement: "Men and Nature must walk hand in hand. The throwing out of balance of the resources of nature throws out of balance the lives of men. We think of our land and water and human resources not as a static and sterile possession but as life-giving assets to be directed by wise provision for the future days. We seek to use our natural resources not as a thing apart but as something that is interwoven with industry, labor, finance, taxation, agriculture, homes, recreation, good citizenship. The . . . results of this process will have a greater influence on the future American standard of living than all the rest of our economies together," in 74 Cong. Rec. 865–66 (January 24, 1935), as quoted in Richard Lowitt, *The New Deal and the West* (Bloomington: Indiana University Press, 1984), 205, and requoted by Nash, *The Federal Landscape*, 22.

14. Weisiger, *Dreaming of Sheep*, 163; Philp, *John Collier's Crusade*, 115. Harold Ickes and his wife, Anna, who spoke Navajo and wrote on Indian life in the Southwest, were among the first members of the Indian Defense Association in 1923. McNickle, "The Indian New Deal," 411.

15. Philp, *John Collier's Crusade*, 118: in return for the additional $761,958, the Pueblos agreed to drop ejection suits against non-Indians. The funds had to be used for permanent economic advantages, such as land and water rights. See Olson and Wilson, *Native Americans*, 110–16, 120–21, for the Pueblo Relief Act and for the states: South Dakota, Oregon, Arizona, New Mexico, California, Oklahoma. Other programs and acts included the Indian Emergency Conservation Work program ($5.9 million for seventy-two camps on thirty-three reservations building dams, wells, fences, roads, and fire controls and employing over eighty-five thousand Indians between 1933 and 1942) to supplement Indian participation in the Civilian Conservation Corps; a

program to purchase purebred cattle in collaboration with the Agriculture Department; a debt cancellation program; a school construction program that built one hundred day schools serving also as community centers and teaching tribal languages and anthropology, as well as more traditional subjects; the Indian Arts and Crafts Board to improve the quality and marketing of Native American arts and crafts; the Johnson-O'Malley Act to provide public schools with extra funding in support of their Native American students (funds that instead often went to general school maintenance and fell afoul of state versus federal tensions, except in Minnesota, where collaboration flourished). In addition, in 1936 Congress passed acts specific to Oklahoma and Alaska Natives endowing them with the provisions of the Indian Reorganization Act, from which they had been excluded, Alaska by oversight and Oklahoma by opposition of Oklahoma congressmen. At issue in Oklahoma were state taxes, rates of assimilation, conflict between those labeled "full-blood" and "mixed-blood," and the myriad special interests created by decades of corruption and predatory land practices.

16. McNickle, "The Indian New Deal," 411; Olson and Wilson, *Native Americans,* 107–28. Bruner would later serve as president of the American Indian Federation. Olson and Wilson describe him as a "full-blood." The Hopis, similarly, owed allegiance to their mesas, not to the "tribe." Hoxie, *This Indian Country,* 303–5, 315. And see Rupert Costo (Cahuilla) in Philp, "Indian Self Rule," 390, on the benefits of allotments. For other examples, see Philp, *John Collier's Crusade,* 161–78; and Hurt, *The Big Empty,* 120–21.

17. Olson and Wilson, *Native Americans,* 118–19. And see White, *Roots of Dependency,* 253. Hayden quoted in Iverson, *The Navajo Nation,* 26, 40–41.

18. Olson and Wilson, *Native Americans,* 118–19; McNickle, "The Indian New Deal," 411–12.

19. These numbers are from Philp, *John Collier's Crusade,* 163; other sources give different numbers. Olson and Wilson, *Native Americans,* 122–23; the Navajo vote was 8,197 to 7,679 in June 1935. McNickle, "The Indian New Deal," 412, says that 77 of 258 voted against. Hoxie, *This Indian Country,* 307, explains that of the 258 referendums on the IRA, two-thirds voted to accept it, but the larger tribes, including the Navajos and the Sioux, tilted the total votes to 40 percent against. And see Iverson, *The Navajo Nation,* 20–21, 24, on the rarity of close council votes given the dominance of a consensus model. Weisiger, *Dreaming of Sheep,* 178–79, 203, 206–7: from 1936 to 1941 Navajo protests against the range policy grew as the policy began to have an impact on the richest owners and on horses; the Diné in the eastern checkerboard had voted overwhelmingly against the act and brought the whole measure to a narrow defeat. As the largest tribe, it was a profound rebuke. Interviews in Philp, "Indian Self Rule," make clear the diverse array of opinions about the act at the time and after, in the long and in the short term, though most agreed it clarified relations with the federal government (90) and increased the power of the tribes in that relationship. See also Robbins and Barber, *Nature's Northwest,* 113.

20. Olson and Wilson, *Native Americans*, 118–19, 125, 127. Some projects included California Pomos' dairy and farming business, Chippewa tourist cabins in Wisconsin, and the Swinomish Reservation in Washington oyster-fishing project. See also Philp, *John Collier's Crusade*, 182–83; McNickle, "The Indian New Deal," 411–12.

21. While conflict over Indian dances seemed to disappear in the 1930s, conflict over peyote flourished; the dispute hit the national media, leading to Senate hearings in Santa Fe. Olson and Wilson, *Native Americans*, 125–26. See also Iverson, *The Navajo Nation*, 26, 32, 39. Weisiger, *Dreaming of Sheep*, 185–88, on the needs of approximately 36 Anglo and Hispano commercial growers against 9,700 Navajos who were dependent on their current range in the district. See also Nash, *The Federal Landscape*, 37–38: in 1934 Collier had acquired 425,000 acres formerly in Spanish land grants through a land retirement program of the Bureau of Agricultural Economics using AAA funds. Chavez gained control of the lands and arranged their transfer to the Resettlement Administration, hoping the recipients would be Hispano villagers and not Navajos, and Chavez won.

22. Sheep numbers had steadily risen since the early part of the century, encouraged partly by a Bureau of Indian Affairs policy forbidding the sale of female lambs and breeding ewes. After declining precipitously in the nineteenth century, the Diné population, like many Native peoples, began climbing in the twentieth. Since their move back to their homeland in 1868, their population had grown from eight thousand to approximately thirty-nine thousand, and their herds had multiplied by a factor of fifteen. Weisiger, *Dreaming of Sheep*, 58.

23. Cronon, "Foreword," x; Weisiger, *Dreaming of Sheep*, 50–52, 58, 140–42, 147, 155–58. And see O'Neill, *Working the Navajo Way*, 23–24. See also White, *Roots of Dependency*, 216 (on how the federal government expanded the reservation by executive order six separate times between 1876 and 1901, tripling the size of the reservation, but many Navajos still lived or grazed off-reservation, and even the expanded reservation was smaller than the old homeland), 220 (on the numbers of sheep and goats). See Iverson, *The Navajo Nation*, 23–24, on 1920s policies.

24. White, *Roots of Dependency*, 215, 219, 222, 226–27, 230, 254, 286–87, on cycles of "aggradation and cutting" occurring for centuries resulting from the area's geology, and it, rather than grazing, was a prime reason for the area's erosion. Weisiger, *Dreaming of Sheep*, 6–8, 10, 20.

25. Weisiger, *Dreaming of Sheep*, 159–64, 198–99, on the 1931 hearings, including Collier's role. Lynn Frazier (North Dakota) chaired the committee, and Burton Wheeler (Montana) dominated the proceedings. Also serving were Elmer Thomas (Oklahoma), Sam Bratton (New Mexico), and Henry Ashurst (Arizona), the latter as ex officio. They held the hearings at multiple sites on the reservation. Two women and over sixty men testified. And see Iverson, *The Navajo Nation*, 27.

26. Weisiger, *Dreaming of Sheep*, 6, 8–9, 18, 25; O'Neill, *Working the Navajo Way*, 24.

27. Cronon, "Foreword," xii; Weisiger, *Dreaming of Sheep*, xv–xvii, 8–9, 11, 22–24, 26, 28–29, 58, 80–82, 85, 90–92, 97, 158–59, 165, 167, 170, 172, 175, 210–12, 214, 216–17 (on resistance); O'Neill, *Working the Navajo Way*, 21; White, *Roots of Dependency*, 217, 230–31, 251, 253, 255, 266, 273, 286, quotation is on 251; Needham, *Power Lines*, 31.

28. W. G. McGinnies, senior soil conservationist, and Superintendent E. R. Fryer quoted in Iverson, *The Navajo Nation*, 29. See Weisiger, *Dreaming of Sheep*, 176–78; White, *Roots of Dependency*, 290, 295–98, 303–7.

29. Philp, *John Collier's Crusade*, 161. And see McNickle, "The Indian New Deal," 415, on congressional hindering of the BIA "spending money on something called anthropology." Hill published in the *Journal of Anthropology*. Weisiger, *Dreaming of Sheep*, 69–78, 90, 158; White, *Roots of Dependency*, 223.

30. O'Neill, *Working the Navajo Way*, 9, 25; Weisiger, *Dreaming of Sheep*, 91, 94, 95–98, 131, 202, 209.

31. Quoted in Weisiger, *Dreaming of Sheep*, 181–85, 196–97, 202.

32. Iverson, *The Navajo Nation*, 30–31; White, *Roots of Dependency*, 257, 260 (quotation), 262; Philp, *John Collier's Crusade*, 109; McNickle, "The Indian New Deal," 414.

33. Weisiger, *Dreaming of Sheep*, 101–2; Iverson, *The Navajo Nation*, 31; Needham, *Power Lines*, 50.

34. Reid, *The Sea Is My Country*, 241, 251–57. Like the Arizona and New Mexico complaints about the costs to the states of road maintenance, in the mid-1930s Washington's Game Department director saw the issue as one of state's rights and pointed to the taxes whites paid to maintain the fisheries department. In 1940 the Makahs brought suit. Burke, *A Land Apart*, 117, points out that the BIA encouraged the Akimel O'odham to prepare their land for irrigated cotton, but the IRA did not include access for water advocacy, nor did Congress grant the Pimas and Maricopas the right to attend hearings about water rights in court; silting meant they got less water than expected.

35. LaPier and Beck, "A 'One-Man Relocation Team,'" 18 (paraphrasing Cathleen D. Cahill, *Federal Fathers & Mothers: A Social History of the United States Indian Service, 1869–1933* [Chapel Hill: University of North Carolina Press, 2011] on 1912 employment), 21–22, 23, 35. Long the primary employer of white-collar and professional Native workers, the Office of Indian Affairs had employed approximately two thousand Indians as early as 1912, accounting for one-third of its personnel. Collier worked with Roosevelt to adjust personnel hiring rules and create Native preferences for qualified applicants in hiring and promotion. In 1934 Indians had still filled one-third of OIA positions; by 1939 they filled over half. At the same time, the OIA tried to increase the quality of the jobs Indians could get outside the OIA. O'Neill, *Working the Navajo Way*, 3; White, *Roots of Dependency*, 269, 282. See Burke, *A Land Apart*, 174, on the revival of the Indian Fair from 1936 to 1938 in Santa Fe successfully selling Pueblo crafts.

36. Weisiger, *Dreaming of Sheep*, 92, 101, 165, 172, 184–94. And see White, *Roots of Dependency*, 244, 256, 259, 274, 296–97, 400n19, on the $800,000 the CCC and Soil Conservation Service provided to Navajos in wages at its peak; dramatic cuts in the CCC and SCS came just at the moment of the 1938 stock reductions, reducing the wages by approximately $750,000. And see Nash, *The Federal Landscape*, 35: about seventy-seven thousand Native Americans worked on CCC projects. Iverson, *The Navajo Nation*, 27, on the SCS's first project. See also O'Neill, *Working the Navajo Way*, 10, 13, 70, 74–75, 79. The Fruitland settlement, established by the BIA in 1933 as a soil conservation experiment, began with twenty-acre plots of newly irrigated land assigned to each "male head" of 191 Navajo families, often new to the area and "disconnected from their matrilineal networks"; within four years, the BIA had reduced the plots to ten acres and required the residents to surrender their livestock for the land, forcing the residents into wage work to survive.

37. O'Neill, *Working the Navajo Way*, 30–34, 36 (quotation), 39.

38. O'Neill, *Working the Navajo Way*, 40, 42, 44–49, 50–52. They also imposed a royalty to the tribe on coal that Navajo operators sold, just as was required of non-Indians with mineral leases on reservation land; the agency had taken coal from the reservation without payment or royalty for its own operations, seeing this practice as payment in kind for BIA services on the reservation, and it resisted changing that system despite the agency's head counsel insisting that this was "the sort of thing [for] which past administrations have been severely, and I think justly, criticized" (48–49).

39. Merill, *Public Lands*, 29, on the quilt-like pattern. Worster, *Dust Bowl*, 113.

40. Merill, *Public Lands*, 16–17, 23, 27, 48, 61, 63, 104–17.

41. Childers, *The Size of the Risk*, 23–24, 33, 35–36. Nevada continued to legislate on ranching in the 1920s, including a law providing a means for the state to collect property tax, charged per head of livestock—an essential tax in a state where 90 percent of the state's acreage lay in the public domain and so was not taxable.

42. Merill, *Public Lands*, 137–38. Childers, *The Size of the Risk*, 31–32, shows that livestock prices had begun to climb again between 1925 and 1929, only to be battered by the Depression and a devastating drought. Worster, *Under Western Skies*, 48.

43. Quoted in Merill, *Public Lands*, 127–29.

44. Childers, *The Size of the Risk*, 20–22, 33.

45. Merill, *Public Lands*, 135–36.

46. Merill, *Public Lands*, 151, 153, 174, 179 for Carrington quote. In 1938 Ickes would force Carrington to resign; in 1939 Congress passed a law giving these advisory boards legal status, making it impossible for the secretary of the interior to eliminate them and giving them greater power over the allocation of the range. Childers, *The Size of the Risk*, 29, 35, on Farrington Carpenter. Childers argues that Nevada ranchers, unlike those who Merill argues favored state and not federal control, feared that state control would privi-

lege larger operators who had come into the northern part of the territory before the smaller-propertied white settlers.

47. Merill, *Public Lands*, 141, 181, 186. The act set the grazing rates at five cents per animal unit per month for cattle and one cent for sheep, a rate half to a twelfth of what stockowners paid for grazing on railroad or private range; in addition, as on reservation land, the federal government improved the range by drilling new wells, building fences, and so on. According to Worster, *Dust Bowl*, 190, the act closed eighty million acres to further settlement—the designation of grazing resource was to be permanent. Wrobel, *America's West*, 146, points out that the withdrawal made the land ineligible for the Homestead Act.

48. Merill, *Public Lands*, 149–61, quote on 179, 182. The Nevada public domain, according to Merill, was one-third of the total public domain of the continental United States.

49. Worster, *Dust Bowl*, 110–14, 115, 130–31; the price went from $4.14 per hundredweight to $7.76. According to Worster, the typical southern plains ranch was over 6,300 acres.

50. McCool, Olson, and Robinson, *Native Vote*, 1–18; McDonald, *American Indians*, 18. Until 1975 New Mexico required Indians and only Indians to pay property taxes in order to be qualified to vote, and reservation land was not taxable. Indians in Arizona faced similar barriers also into the 1970s. Childers, *The Size of the Risk*, 15–16, 38, 38–41. Langston, *Forest Dreams*, 202–12, 224, points out how little was understood about what damaged the grazing lands, leading to ineffective New Deal remedies. Ranchers' loyalties to their local associations made them effective lobbyists to their congressmen and senators, creating enormous pressure on local Forest Service officials.

51. Worster, *Dust Bowl*, 186. Phillips, *This Land*, argues that the New Deal's conservation policy had Keynesian impulses—that fostering the farmer's consumer capacity aimed not just to make the farm more attractive but also to stimulate the broader economy. See particularly pp. 3 and 4 on equalizing rural and urban incomes.

52. The following account of the impact of the dust storms draws on Worster, *Dust Bowl*, 11–15 (text quote from 12), 29, 31–34, 93.

53. Worster, *Dust Bowl*, 121, 123, 125–26. Foreclosure sales peaked in 1933, with $3 billion worth of property, or 5 percent of farms across the United States. Forty-five out of a thousand farms in Oklahoma, about the average for the ten Great Plains states, went up for sale, as well as fifty-three in Kansas and seventy-nine in South Dakota, about three times the rate of 1929. See Gilbert, "Agrarian Intellectuals." And see Dewey, *Pesos and Dollars*, 209, on the consolidation of farms in the Lower Rio Grande Valley in Texas, where she finds the average size of farms rising throughout the region in the Depression years, almost doubling in three counties (from 46 in 1930 to 98.3 in 1940 in Cameron County, 87 to 111.1 in Hidalgo County, and 732 to 1,404 in Dimmit County). And see p. 224, where she points out that where ranchers had

to own land rather than rely on the public domain, they lost heavily in bankruptcy court and often could not begin again; and on 210 and 212 she argues that the high rate of bankruptcy in the Depression reflected a sense that "quitting, not insolvency, was becoming the mark of the loser." And see 202, 206, 207, 215–16, on bankruptcies; related legislation included that sponsored by North Dakota's Nonpartisan League senator and his congressional counterpart.

54. Worster, *Dust Bowl*, 152, 159. In 1940, 50 percent of Haskell County, Kansas, resident farm operators were tenants; a few who remained, usually in town, and had a little cash and invested in the bankrupt farms became wealthy when the rains returned (122).

55. Worster, *Dust Bowl*, 35, 38.

56. Worster, *Dust Bowl*, 41.

57. Worster, *Dust Bowl*, 124, 190; Phillips, *This Land*, 121, 125.

58. Worster, *Dust Bowl*, 39–40, 124. Hurt, *Problems of Plenty*, argues that these programs continued a rising trend dating back to the 1910s in which farmers became increasingly dependent on the federal government, which acted in response to farmers' demands.

59. Worster, *Dust Bowl*, 58 (quote citing various Paul Taylor articles), 183. Taylor claimed that the number of tractors on Oklahoma farms rose by 25 percent between 1929 and 1936. Mechanization, in addition, exacerbated the surplus in wheat, reducing the need for animal feed—tractors had led to a reduction by ten million of the horse and mule population, whose feed had required thirty million acres of cropland. See Hurt, *The Big Empty*, 94–95, on migration patterns. And see Foley, *The White Scourge*, 178. From 1930 to 1936 "about one-third of the farmers in Lynn County [Texas] had been evicted and rehired as day laborers" (187).

60. Worster, *Dust Bowl*, 44–47. Such luminaries as John Steinbeck, Dorothea Lange, Woody Guthrie, and Archibald MacLeish were neither silent nor marginalized. Some worked for the various New Deal arts agencies, others wrote in popular publications. Their skepticism that the West remained capable of fulfilling the American dream for the rest of the nation matched that, according to a *Fortune* opinion poll, of 40 percent of the United States. But the dream of the homesteading yeoman farmer proved remarkably resilient and had its proponents in agrarians.

61. Worster, *Dust Bowl*, 91–92, 146; the plains were perfectly suited to mechanized farming. By the end of the 1920s, "more than three-fourths of the farmers in the winter wheat section owned" a combine. "Instead of hiring ten or twenty bindlestiffs—seasonal harvest laborers coming in on the railroad—who drank heavily, frightened the children, required the wife to feed them, and sometimes demanded higher wages," the farmer bought a combine he could manage with one or two others and could harvest five hundred acres in two weeks. Gregory, *American Exodus*, 7–8.

62. Gregory, *American Exodus*, 27, 32, 39 (urban migrants tended to head for cities [79 percent] and rural to rural). See Worster, *Dust Bowl*, 50: two-

fifths of the migrants crossing state lines in the United States in the 1930s headed for California, which gained a net 1.1 million people from migration.

63. Worster, *Dust Bowl,* 48–50. Oklahoma lost 440,000 people. In some states the losses were localized: "Of 32 Texas panhandle counties, 23 lost population and only nine gained—and the latter were all oil and gas counties." In southwestern Kansas, a single county's population (Morton) fell 47 percent. According to Worster, in the large swath of Oklahoma that sent most of the "refugees," tenants operated 61.2 percent of the farms in 1935, and 28 percent of the farm population, that is, 275,000 people, moved to a new farm each year (60). And see pp. 146–47 for Haskell County, Kansas, where in 1935, 200 of the 461 farm operators had arrived within the past five years; the county's population dropped in the 1930s by 25 percent, which was a lesser loss than in the 1890s and less turnover than the 1920s, when 28 percent left, only to be replaced with even more newcomers. While Worster and Gregory see this as rootlessness, the fact that people usually didn't move far seems to me instead to show an attachment to an area smaller than a region, a community in which there were perhaps kin, just as most migrants to California went along routes already traveled by kin. See Gregory, *American Exodus,* 30, on shallow roots.

64. Gregory, *American Exodus,* 10, 15, 17. In 1939 the Bureau of Agricultural Economics found that only 43 percent had been in agriculture just before migrating, and the 1940 census revealed that only 36 percent of southwestern migrants to California had lived on farms in 1935. According to Gregory, fewer than sixteen thousand came to California from the dust bowl, about 6 percent of the total migration to California from the southwestern states. Many fled drought (not all drought produced dust) or the boll weevil. Increasing numbers of those working the land were tenant farmers or share renters, until by 1930 they made up over 60 percent of the farmers in Oklahoma, Arkansas, and Texas and 35 percent in Missouri. Owners could and did use federal money to mechanize, replacing tenants with machines, reducing the tenant population of the region by 24 percent by 1940 (11–13). According to Worster, *Dust Bowl,* 61, "of Oklahoma's total net migration loss of 500,000, perhaps only 2 to 3 per cent were from the westernmost part of the state, where the black blizzards were." Worster points to Woody Guthrie, born in Okemah, Oklahoma, in 1912, moving to the Texas panhandle in 1929 and staying through the dust storms until hitching to California in 1937; in between he "rambled around until cotton, oil, wheat, corn, and white faced steers were all mixed into his songs, as they were mixed into the lives of his people" (61).

65. This sense of migration is drawn from Gregory, *American Exodus,* 28, 29.

66. Worster, *Dust Bowl,* 56.

67. Gregory, *American Exodus,* 23–25.

68. Gregory, *American Exodus,* 58–62, 83. California's population grew 21 percent, and Los Angeles County's population grew 26 percent. The valley as a whole grew by 39 percent; in Kern County that meant fifty-two thousand new people, over half of whom hailed from the Southwest.

69. Worster, *Dust Bowl,* 53. See Gregory, *American Exodus,* 48, 63–70, 72, 81, regarding Taylor, who had written on the 1933 cotton workers' strike and returned in the summer of 1935 to write for *Survey Graphic*: "Long had he labored to publicize the plight of California's farm labor force. Now he discovered the empathetic value of white skin." According to Tsu, *Garden of the World,* 200–201, Steinbeck saw the Mexicans and Filipino labor as disappearing via deportation and so felt he could focus on those he called "'resourceful and intelligent Americans' of 'English, German and Scandinavian descent,'" finding it particularly a "shame for white Americans of 'good stock' to be living so shabbily." And see Wrobel, *America's West,* 178–83, on Lange and the Farm Security Administration photographers. According to Wrobel, it was not until over forty years later that it was revealed that the subject of Lange's iconic migrant mother photograph, Florence Owens Thompson, was Cherokee.

70. Gregory, *American Exodus,* 85; Worster, *Dust Bowl,* 52–53.

71. Foley, *The White Scourge,* 180–81.

72. Worster, *Dust Bowl,* 58, 165–68, 173–76, 165–68; and Deutsch, *No Separate Refuge,* 123, 140–42.

73. Carriker, *Urban Farming in the West,* 14–16, 40–41, 46. Wilson also advised the Soviet government on experimental farming as a USDA employee and ultimately managed twenty experimental farms. There were also concerns that the subsistence homesteads amounted to a subsidy for private industry.

74. Carriker, *Urban Farming in the West,* 17, 19; Wrobel, *America's West,* 176.

75. 74 Cong. Rec. 6137, 9939 (April 1935), quoted in Holley, *Uncle Sam's Farmers,* 88.

76. Holley, *Uncle Sam's Farmers,* 65–66, 86–89, 359, 84, quoting Russell Lord, *The Wallaces of Iowa* (Boston: Houghton Mifflin, 1947).

77. Foley, *The White Scourge,* 166–67 (quote is on 167), 172, 177; Hurt, *Problems of Plenty,* 87. Landlords already had much to dislike in New Deal agricultural legislation, including the loan provision, which meant tenants and sharecroppers no longer relied on landlords for credit.

78. Holley, *Uncle Sam's Farmers,* 82–83, including the Thomas quote from Norman Thomas, *The Choice before Us: Mankind at the Crossroads* (New York: Macmillan, 1934), 7.

79. Holley, *Uncle Sam's Farmers,* 84–85, quoting Ward Rogers from Howard Kester, *Revolt among the Sharecroppers* (New York: Oovici, Fried, 1936), 68. See Foley, *White Scourge,* 187, for numbers. Despite the large number of evictions in Texas, few STFU locals organized there (eight, with fewer than five hundred members), and mostly in West Texas in the area of large ranches, with the exception of a small town in central Texas where Black sharecroppers organized (187). Unlike Arkansas, Texas maintained segregated STFU locals (188), and STFU organizers usually spoke no Spanish; the structure of the 1930s farm economy in Texas mandated that successful organizing would need to include both farmworkers (often non-English-speaking Mexican) and sharecroppers and tenants, who often hired farmworkers and whose interests

were often at odds. There were attempts to bring these disparate parties into one organization, and a meeting with "the three races" occurred in a Black church. Some Mexicans from Texas and perhaps from Mexico attended the STFU conference in Muskogee, Oklahoma, in January 1937 (188–90), but Texas had no paid STFU organizer, despite the state having "one of the highest percentages of tenancy in the South and producing more than one-third of the nation's cotton" (191); it did have an energetic Black teacher and minister in Littig, Texas (J. E. Clayton), who had founded a school for Black children there and who urged the organization of Mexican sharecroppers and day laborers, organized a Black local, and locally contributed to the funds of striking pecan shellers in San Antonio, a group largely comprised of Mexican women (190).

80. Holley, *Uncle Sam's Farmers*, 86, quoting the *New York Times*, April 6, 1935, or Abner Sage and Howard Kester (80–81), though it could be John Herling, "Field Notes from Arkansas," *The Nation*, April 10, 1935, 419–20, or H. L. Mitchell and J. R. Butler, "The Cropper Learns His Fate," *The Nation*, September 18, 1935, 328–29.

81. Holley, *Uncle Sam's Farmers*, 178, 187, 191–92, quoting Wallace in U.S. Congress, Senate, Committee on Agriculture and Forestry, *Hearings on the Bill to Create a Farm Tenant Homes Corporation*, 74th Cong., 1st sess., 1935, which he found in Sidney Baldwin, *Poverty and Politics: The Rise and Decline of the Farm Security Administration* (Chapel Hill: University of North Carolina Press, 1968), 135.

82. The following account of subsistence homesteads relies on Holley, *Uncle Sam's Farmers*, 109, on Plum Bayou and Lakeview. The Black farmers held the land, their homes, the community buildings, and the equipment collectively, unlike the white farmers at Plum Bayou; they received weekly wages for their labor and shared in the profits annually, when there were profits (110–11, 114). In Louisiana in 1937 one white community resettlement project displaced Black sharecroppers, who were then resettled (145 Black families) on a different project also in Louisiana (Mounds) (112–13). Arkansas had the best record on the proportion of Black farmers served by the FSA, but it was still lower than the percentage of Black farmers. Thirty-two percent of the spaces in its colonies went to Black farmers, but the proportion of Black farmers who could qualify for such places was lower than for white farmers because of a history of discrimination in wages, credit, and opportunities. Black farmers benefited most from the tenant purchase and rehabilitation loans (180–82). Moreover, the FSA was concerned with the survival of the program and wanted to ensure as little conflict and as great a credit track record as possible; it only pursued the creation of Black resettlement colonies where the local white majority supported it: "Every adjoining landowner had to request the project." Perhaps that caution made sense to them because of the history of white violence toward Black landowners (182–83). "Tugwell ordered the personnel department to accept Negro job applica-

tions on the same basis as whites" both in the settlement as colonists and managers and in the office, but the numbers remained low, and Black personnel never supervised whites (184). See 92–93, quoting various journalistic accounts, and 94–96.

83. Holley, *Uncle Sam's Farmers*, 95–96. According to Worster, *Dust Bowl*, 155, "an overwhelming majority of the country's 6 million farms were still family operations." See Cannon, *Remaking the Agrarian Dream*, 1–3, 5. By 1943 the agencies had created twelve resettlement projects for full-time farmers in the Mountain West, encompassing 760 households. The largest was near the Canadian border in Montana, Milk River Farms, with 163 farmers over 150 miles. There were two other projects in Montana; three in New Mexico, including the tiny Dona Ana Farms for five Mexican American families on 207 acres of irrigated land near Las Cruces; two in Colorado; one each in Idaho and Arizona; and two scattered settlement projects in Utah.

84. Holley, *Uncle Sam's Farmers*, 95–96, 97 (FDR quote), 106. Ironically, Rexford Tugwell, who ran the Resettlement Administration, was not a Jeffersonian, seeing small farm ownership because of the economic commitments and market structure as potentially even more tenuous than tenancy. He agreed with those, including the STFU, who saw the small family farm as anachronistic and favored large community projects with mechanized farming and cooperative organization (105–6). The FSA had two hundred resettlement projects, only about a tenth of which operated collectively (107). FDR's Committee on Farm Tenancy endorsed the Jeffersonian vision, employing the term "farm security" and leading to the replacement of the temporary Resettlement Administration with the more permanent Farm Security Administration in 1937 (99–100). Foley, *White Scourge*, 184–201; this aspiration helps to explain their poor showing in the STFU—if they could not rise to ownership, they headed out of the Texas countryside altogether. The STFU tried to organize whites, Blacks, and Mexicans in West Texas and Blacks in central Texas and ultimately farmworkers and farm tenants (who often hired farmworkers) into the same union but with little success.

85. Gilbert, "Agrarian Intellectuals," 217, 222; Carriker, *Urban Farming in the West*, 13. Cannon, *Remaking the Agrarian Dream*, 9–11, finds that the post–World War I agricultural depression engendered criticism of what he calls "the nation's jerrybuilt land-use patterns." The Bureau of Agricultural Economics agreed, and agricultural economists, planners, and engineers created in 1927 the Committee on the Bases of a Sound Land Policy. By 1930 even local counties (e.g., the Commercial Club of Phillips County, Montana) had underwritten a draft plan for resettling dryland farmers on irrigated tracts in the Milk River Valley. On the recommendation of a 1931 Land Utilization Conference in Chicago, the secretary of agriculture appointed a National Land Use Planning Committee, which eventually joined the New Deal's National Resources Board, surveying rural land use and necessary adjustments. The survey concluded that one hundred thousand households would require federal help to

relocate. The AAA began a land purchase program to follow the recommendations. It seemed everyone was eager to cooperate—ranchers wanting to enlarge their range, farmers wanting to dump their land, townspeople wanting an economic boost, and politicians wanting to appease constituents all proffered lands for sale to the government (11, 15–19). As far as possible, the government relied on experts to make the choices, but some choices seemed inescapably political, defying common sense and local knowledge and setting the projects up for ultimate failure. Phillips, *This Land*, 42–43, reveals that Wilson and a partner went into farming using USDA crop data, landing on flax as the most profitable, sunk their own and borrowed funds into the venture, only to find the weather wreaking havoc with the scheme. In the 1920s Wilson and his former economics instructor and now Bureau of Agricultural Economics boss started a new corporation composed of seven farms, Fairway Farms, to demonstrate that with enough credit and guidance tenants could become owners; Fairway lost money but showed that "enormous farms, with maximum machine power and very little human labor, could compete in the depressed world market," not the lesson Wilson had hoped to learn. According to Carriker, "Farming on the northern Great Plains had become a circus, [Wilson] said, as land seekers whose former occupations had been teacher, miner, and dance hall girl rushed to grab property pell-mell without any education in, or understanding of soil management. Moreover, a lot of the claimants were just speculators, called 'plungers,' who would never use the land" (14). Worster, *Dust Bowl*, 199–201, 204, 206–9.

86. Carriker, *Urban Farming in the West*, 37, 39. There were five subsistence homestead projects in Texas (44), one in Arizona, one in Washington, and two in California. Community projects were homogeneous, mixture being seen as too great a burden on the development of community collaboration. There was only one homestead project developed for African Americans (near Newport News, Virginia) (48), and there was a proposal for one in Pueblo for Spanish speakers (48–49, 60, 61, 69). Projects for Native Americans were handed over to Collier. White, *Roots of Dependency*, 283–85; quotation is from Gilbert, "Agrarian Intellectuals," 231; and "civic republicanism" may be Gilbert's phrase (217); "participatory modernizations" on 235; committees were vulnerable to being dominated by larger or wealthier farmers or experts (235–36). Holley, *Uncle Sam's Farmers*, 127, 130–33. See Cannon, *Remaking the Agrarian Dream*, 2–3, 5, 20–21, 26, 32, 35, 57–60, 67–68. Casa Grande Valley Farms in Arizona was the only fully cooperative farm government project in the Mountain West; called by some in the region "Little Russia," it lay between Florence and Coolidge, fifty miles southeast of Phoenix. Its five thousand acres benefited from the San Carlos irrigation system, with each of its sixty adobe homes on two-acre lots and sharing a central community building. And see Glanz, "Federal Land Use Policy," which focuses on the eight Nebraska projects. Altogether, the Division of Subsistence Home-

steads, FERA resettlement, and the Resettlement Administration created forty-eight communities west of the Mississippi River.

87. Holley, *Uncle Sam's Farmers,* 134, 137, 140, 141, 143, 150, 151, 155. Settlers fared better at Terrebonne, Louisiana, where the good soil allowed them to sell truck vegetables to make the project pay. Even there, while settlers were paid a daily wage, the anticipated year-end dividend never materialized (163–68). Cannon, *Remaking the Agrarian Dream,* 73–88, points out that these farmers had been undercapitalized before they moved onto the projects; the project managers encouraged them to invest in machinery to bring the land into production faster, but that raised their debt levels and made them particularly vulnerable to bad harvests. When they could not repay their loans, they tended to blame the bad advice they'd been given, and when threatened with eviction, they called on lawyers, outraged that, having been persuaded to leave the farms they had owned to embark on this new project, those who had enticed them there could take away everything.

88. See Cannon, *Remaking the Agrarian Dream,* 25–26, 29, 30, 34–35, 57–58, 75–76ff., 83, 87–88, 121–22. Only one of the sixty-five farmers moving onto the San Luis Valley Farms in 1937–38, for example, arrived without debt.

89. Cannon, *Remaking the Agrarian Dream,* 60–72, quotation on 66, ten times the labor on 69.

90. Cannon, *Remaking the Agrarian Dream,* 83–85, quote on 83.

91. Holley, *Uncle Sam's Farmers,* 214.

92. Holley, *Uncle Sam's Farmers,* 203–7, 209–12, 214, 230, 237–38. And see Cannon, *Remaking the Agrarian Dream,* 73–85, 123, 125. Some farmers simply left the projects when they realized they faced long-term indebtedness, while others complained of high prices for marginal land and misleading promises. See his table on p. 135 on persistence and land purchase for relocated farmers demonstrating the correlation between farm size and income and purchase rates, and on 144 for "Continual Ownership of Project Lands by FSA Clients of Their Descendants," which was often over 50 percent as late as 1955.

93. Carriker, *Urban Farming in the West,* 84–111, 117, 141–51. See Cannon, *Remaking the Agrarian Dream,* 98–113, on critics of the projects who exaggerated the out-migration and blamed a lack of community spirit evidenced by low turnout (roughly 30 percent) for community clubs and classes; Cannon finds, in contrast, that out-migration was low relative to other communities and that even where resettlement project residents hailed from diverse states and even countries, they actively joined in community social and political events at twice or more the rate at which they attended classes. Even on projects notorious for factionalism, as at Casa Grande, where there was some friction between some of the residents who had come from more urban areas with modern conveniences and access to education and those they scorned as having never seen an inside toilet, the contestants were few and the premium on solidarity was high (102, 104).

94. Worster, *Dust Bowl*, 42, 127. Overall, the western states received more than $300 per capita between 1933 and 1939.

95. Nash, *The Federal Landscape*, 39. In the United States as a whole, the New Deal spent $399 per person, but the figure was $716 in the Rocky Mountain states, $536 in the coastal states, and $424 in the Great Plains. In Nevada the federal government spent $1,499 per person. See also on disproportionate per capita spending Wrobel, *America's West*, 145 (CCC), 157 (WPA), 158 (PWA).

96. Worster, *Dust Bowl*, 220–21.

97. Worster, *Dust Bowl*, 224.

98. As quoted in Worster, *Dust Bowl*, 228. Worster notes (210–15) the conflict between the land-use planners who held that profit maximizing endangered the long-term viability of the land and favored returning some of the Great Plains to grass and the SCS agronomists who were "dedicated to helping private citizens manage their soils for greater productivity," with increasing distance between the two after 1935. In 1936 the Soil Conservation and Domestic Allotment Act created a two-year program to pay farm operators to stop planting "soil depleting crops," including wheat, and substitute "soil conserving" grasses or legumes, a program that failed to entice participants in the face of rising wheat prices (217). They had more success in getting farmers to adopt contour plowing (following the lay of the land) and ridges on the contour about every one hundred feet to dam the runoff (218). See Nash, *The Federal Landscape*, 30, on the creation of the Soil Conservation Service by the USDA in 1935; Hugh Bennett, the soil scientist in charge, estimated that 322 million acres had been eroded by winds, with another 50 million at risk. According to Worster (158, 163), the New Deal did not aim to alter fundamentally the American economic culture. And when the rains returned, so did the surpluses. In 1938 wheat harvests were the second largest ever for the United States, and prices dropped. Farmers, at 25 percent of the U.S. population, garnered only 8 percent of the national income—less with each succeeding year. Despite its costs to the land and the people who lived on it, in the main, "the system of non-resident tenure, factory-like monoculture, and market speculation" survived (163).

99. Worster, *Dust Bowl*, 192, 219–20. By the summer of 1940 a fifth of the dust bowl was covered by such districts. Gilbert, "Agrarian Intellectuals," 235. It would last only as long as the New Deal, after which pressure from the Farm Bureau, dominated by larger commercial farmers, and the experts at land-grant colleges and extension services dissolved the committees in favor of their own efforts.

Conclusion

1. U.S. Bureau of the Census, *Sixteenth Census*, vol. 1. For data on Oklahoma, see https://www2.census.gov/library/publications/decennial/1940/population-volume-1/33973538v1ch08.pdf.

2. Deutsch, *No Separate Refuge*, 165–66, 174–76.

3. Foley, *The White Scourge*, 190–93, 196–99.

4. Nash, *The Federal Landscape*, 39.

5. Phillips, *This Land*, 149, 153–56, 160–62, 164, 168–69, 174–86 (on rural electrification, etc.).

BIBLIOGRAPHY

Abel, Joseph. "Opening the Closed Shop: The Galveston Longshoremen's Strike of 1920–1921." In *Texas Labor History*, edited by Bruce A. Glasrud and James C. Maroney, 185–218. College Station: Texas A&M University Press, 2013.

Acena, Albert Anthony. "The Washington Commonwealth Federation: Reform Politics and the Popular Front." PhD diss., University of Washington, 1975. ProQuest (7617378).

Ackerman, Lillian A. "Gender Equality on the Colville Indian Reservation in Traditional and Contemporary Contexts." In *Women in Pacific Northwest History*, rev. ed., edited by Karen Blair, 237–57. Seattle: University of Washington Press, 2001.

Acuña, Rudolfo. *Occupied America: A History of Chicanos*. 3rd ed. New York: Harper and Row Publishers, 1988.

Adams, David Wallace. *Three Roads to Magdalena: Coming of Age in a Southwest Borderland, 1890–1990*. Lawrence: University Press of Kansas, 2016.

Adams, David Wallace, and Crista DeLuzio, eds. *On the Borders of Love and Power: Families and Kinship in the Intercultural American Southwest*. Berkeley: University of California Press, 2012.

Adams, Laura. *The Spectacular State: Culture and National Identity in Uzbekistan*. Durham NC: Duke University Press, 2010.

Adilman, Tamara. "A Preliminary Sketch of Chinese Women and Work in British Columbia, 1858–1950." In *British Columbia Reconsidered: Essays on Women*, edited by Gillian Laura Creese and Veronica Jane Strong-Boag, 303–39. Vancouver: Press Gang Publishers, 1992.

Allison, James Robert, III. *Sovereignty for Survival: American Energy Development and Indian Self-Determination*. New Haven CT: Yale University Press, 2015.

Alter, Thomas. "From the Copper-Colored Sons of Montezuma to Comrade Pancho Villa: The Radicalizing Effect of Mexican Revolutionaries on the Texas Socialist Party, 1910–1917." *Labor: Studies in Working-Class History of the Americas* 12, no. 4 (December 2015): 83–109.

Anderson, Karen. *Changing Woman: A History of Racial Ethnic Women in Modern America*. New York: Oxford University Press, 1996.

Anderson, Kathryn. "Steps to Political Equality: Woman Suffrage and Electoral Politics in the Lives of Emily Newell Blair, Anne Henrietta Martin, and Jeannette Rankin." *Frontiers: A Journal of Women Studies* 18, no. 1 (1997): 101–21.

Anderson, Kay J. "The Idea of Chinatown: The Power of Place and Institutional Practice in the Making of a Racial Category." *Annals of the Association of American Geographers* 77, no. 4 (1987): 580–98.

Andrés, Benny J., Jr. *Power and Control in the Imperial Valley: Nature, Agribusiness, and Workers on the California Borderland, 1900–1940.* College Station: Texas A&M University Press, 2015.

Andrews, Tom. *Killing for Coal: America's Deadliest Labor War.* Cambridge MA: Harvard University Press, 2008.

Anzaldúa, Gloria. *Borderlands / La Frontera: The New Mestiza.* San Francisco: Aunt Lute Books, 1987.

Aquila, Richard. *The Sagebrush Trail: Western Movies and Twentieth-Century America.* Tucson: University of Arizona Press, 2015.

Arat-Koç, Sedef. "From 'Mothers of the Nation' to Migrant Workers: Immigration Policies and Domestic Workers in Canadian History." In *Rethinking Canada: The Promise of Women's History,* 5th ed., edited by Mona Gleason and Adele Perry, 195–209. Don Mills ON: Oxford University Press, 2006.

Armitage, Susan. "Tied to Other Lives: Women in Pacific Northwest History." In *Women in Pacific Northwest History,* rev. ed., edited by Karen Blair, 5–24. Seattle: University of Washington Press, 2001.

Arrigo, Anthony F. *Imaging Hoover Dam: The Making of a Cultural Icon.* Reno: University of Nevada Press, 2014.

Arrington, Leonard. "The New Deal in the West: A Preliminary Statistical Inquiry." *Pacific Historical Review* 38, no. 3 (August 1969): 311–16. http://www.jstor.org/stable/3636102.

———. "The Sagebrush Resurrection: New Deal Expenditures in the Western States, 1933–1939." *Pacific Historical Review* 52, no. 1 (February 1983): 1–16. http://www.jstor.org/stable/3639452.

Avery, Donald. "Ethnic and Class Relations in Western Canada during the First World War: A Case Study of European Immigrants and Anglo-Canadian Nativism." In *Canada and the First World War: Essays in Honour of Robert Craig Brown,* edited by David Mackenzie, 272–99. Toronto: University of Toronto Press, 2005.

Ayukawa, Michiko Midge. "Good Wives and Wise Mothers: Japanese Picture Brides in Early Twentieth Century British Columbia." In *Rethinking Canada: The Promise of Women's History,* 4th ed., edited by Veronica Strong-Boas, Mona Gleason, and Adele Perry, 174–86. Don Mills ON: Oxford University Press, 2002.

Baillargeon, Denyse. "Indispensable but Not a Citizen: The Housewife in the Great Depression." In *Rethinking Canada: The Promise of Women's History,* 5th ed., edited by Mona Gleason and Adele Perry, 179–94. Don Mills ON: Oxford University Press, 2006.

———. "Working for Pay and Managing the Household Finances." In *Labouring Canada: Class, Gender, and Race in Canadian Working-Class History*, edited by Bryan D. Palmer and Joan Sangster, 223–39. Don Mills ON: Oxford University Press, 2008.

Balderrama, Francisco E., and Raymond Rodríguez. *Decade of Betrayal: Mexican Repatriation in the 1930s.* Rev. ed. Albuquerque: University of New Mexico Press, 2006.

Baridon, Jason. "Tucson's Refusal to Accept Statewide Prohibition in Arizona: A Synthesis of Racial, Religious, Political, and Economic Factors." Term paper, University of Arizona, n.d. In the author's possession.

Barkan, Elliott Robert. *From All Points: America's Immigrant West, 1870s–1952.* Bloomington: Indiana University Press, 2007.

Barman, Jean. "Writing Women into the History of the North American Wests, One Woman at a Time." In *One Step over the Line: Toward a History of Women in the North American Wests,* edited by Elizabeth Jameson and Sheila McManus, 99–128. Edmonton: University of Alberta Press, 2008.

Barraclough, Laura R. *Charros: How Mexican Cowboys Are Remapping Race and American Identity.* Berkeley: University of California Press, 2019.

Barry, Eidlin. "'Upon This (Foundering) Rock': Minneapolis Teamsters and the Transformation of US Business Unionism, 1934–1941." *Labor History* 50, no. 3 (August 2009): 249–67.

Bauer, William J., Jr. *We Were All Like Migrant Workers Here: Work, Community, and Memory on California's Round Valley Reservation, 1850–1941.* Chapel Hill: University of North Carolina Press, 2009.

———. *Work, Community, and Memory on California's Round Valley Reservation, 1850–1941.* Chapel Hill: University of North Carolina Press, 2009.

Beda, Steven C. "'We Want No Extravagance': Paternalism, Working-Class Community and Nature in the Northwest's Timber Towns, 1917–1929." Paper presented at the Organization of American Historians annual conference, Milwaukee WI, April 2012.

Bederman, Gail. *Manliness and Civilization: A Cultural History of Gender and Race in the United States, 1880–1917.* Chicago: University of Chicago Press, 1995.

Beeton, Beverly. "How the West Was Won for Woman Suffrage." In *One Woman, One Vote: Rediscovering the Woman Suffrage Movement,* edited by Marjorie Wheeler Spruill, 99–116. Troutdale OR: NewSage Press, 1995.

Belasco, Warren James. *Americans on the Road: From Autocamp to Motel, 1910–1945.* Cambridge MA: MIT Press, 1979.

Bennett, Jason Patrick. "'Nature's Garden and a Possible Utopia': Farming for Fruit and Industrious Men in the Transboundary Pacific Northwest, 1895–1914." In *The Borderlands of the American and Canadian Wests: Essays on the Regional History of the Forty-Ninth Parallel,* edited by Sterling Evans, 222–40. Lincoln: University of Nebraska Press, 2006.

Benton-Cohen, Katherine. *Borderline Americans: Racial Division and Labor War in the Arizona Borderlands.* Cambridge MA: Harvard University Press, 2009.

———. "Other Immigrants: Mexicans and the Dillingham Commission of 1907–1911." *Journal of American Ethnic History* 30, no. 2 (Winter 2011): 33–57.

Bergon, Frank, and Zeese Papanikolas, eds. *Looking Far West: The Search for the American West in History, Myth, and Literature.* New York: New American Library, 1978.

Berman, David R. *Radicalism in the Mountain West, 1890–1920: Socialists, Populists, Miners and Wobblies.* Boulder: University of Colorado Press, 2007.

———. *Reformers, Corporations, and the Electorate: An Analysis of Arizona's Age of Reform.* Niwot: University of Colorado Press, 1992.

Bernard, Elaine. "Last Back: Folklore and the Telephone Operators in the 1919 Vancouver General Strike." In *Not Just Pin Money: Selected Essays on the History of Women's Work in British Columbia,* edited by Barbara K. Latham and Roberta J. Pazdro, 279–86. Victoria BC: Camosun College, 1984.

Bess, Jennifer. "The Price of Pima Cotton: The Cooperative Testing and Demonstration Farm at Sacaton, Arizona, and the Decline of the Pima Agricultural Economy, 1907–1920." *Western Historical Quarterly* 46 (Summer 2015): 171–89.

Bessenden, Paul. *I.W.W.: A Study of American Syndicalism.* New York: Russell and Russell, 1957.

Bhabha, Homi K. "DissemiNation: Time, Narrative, and the Margins of the Modern Nation." In *Nation and Narration,* edited by Homi Bhabha, 291–322. London: Routledge, 1990.

Blackwelder, Julia Kirk. *Women of the Depression: Caste and Culture in San Antonio, 1929–1939.* College Station: Texas A&M University Press, 1984.

Blair, Doug. "The 1920 Anti-Japanese Crusade and Congressional Hearings." Seattle Civil Rights & Labor History Project, University of Washington, 2006. http://depts.washington.edu/civlr/Japanese_restriction.htm.

Blair, Karen J. "The Seattle Ladies Music Club, 1890–1930." In *Women in Pacific Northwest History,* rev. ed., edited by Karen Blair, 267–83. Seattle: University of Washington Press, 2001.

———, ed. *Women in Pacific Northwest History.* Rev. ed. Seattle: University of Washington Press, 2001.

Blanton, Carlos Kevin. *George I. Sánchez: The Long Fight for Mexican American Integration.* New Haven CT: Yale University Press, 2014.

Boag, Peter. *Same-Sex Affairs: Constructing and Controlling Homosexuality in the Pacific Northwest.* Berkeley: University of California Press, 2003.

Bodnar, John. *The Transplanted: A History of Immigrants in Urban America.* Bloomington: Indiana University Press, 1985.

Bonner, Robert. *William F. Cody's Wyoming Empire: The Buffalo Bill Nobody Knows.* Norman: University of Oklahoma Press, 2007.

Bonnifield, Paul. *The Dust Bowl: Men, Dirt & Depression.* Albuquerque: University of New Mexico Press, 1979.

Boris, Eileen. *Home to Work: Motherhood and the Politics of Industrial Homework in the United States.* Cambridge: Cambridge University Press, 1994.

Borokov, Matthew F. *The San Diego World's Fairs and Southwestern Memory, 1880–1940.* Albuquerque: University of New Mexico Press, 2005.

Boyd, Nan Alamilla. *Wide Open Town: A History of Queer San Francisco.* Berkeley: University of California Press, 2003.

Boyle, Kevin. *Arc of Justice: A Saga of Race, Civil Rights, and Murder in the Jazz Age.* New York: Henry Holt and Company, 2004.

Braudy, Leo. *The Hollywood Sign: Fantasy and Reality of an American Icon.* New Haven CT: Yale University Press, 2011.

Brégent-Heald, Dominique. "Projecting the In-Between: Cinematic Representations of Borderlands and Borders in North America, 1908–1940." In *Bridging National Borders in North America: Transnational and Comparative Histories,* edited by Benjamin Johnson and Andrew R. Graybill, 249–74. Durham NC: Duke University Press, 2010.

Bridges, Amy. *Morning Glories: Municipal Reform in the Southwest.* Princeton NJ: Princeton University Press, 1997.

Briggs, Laura, Gladys McCormick, and J. T. Way. "Transnationalism: A Category of Analysis." *American Quarterly* 60, no. 3 (September 2008): 625–48.

Brinkley, Alan. *Voices of Protest: Huey Long, Father Coughlin, and the Great Depression.* New York: Vintage Books, 1983.

Britten, Thomas A. *American Indians in World War I: At Home and at War.* Albuquerque: University of New Mexico Press, 1997.

Britton, John A. *Revolution and Ideology: Images of the Mexican Revolution in the United States.* Lexington: University Press of Kentucky, 1995.

Brophy, Alfred L. *Reconstructing the Dreamland: The Tulsa Riot of 1921; Race, Reparations and Reconciliation.* New York: Oxford University Press, 2002.

Brown, Elsa Barkley. "Negotiating and Transforming the Public Sphere: African American Political Life in the Transition from Slavery to Freedom." *Public Culture* 7 (1994): 107–46.

Brown, Sara, et al. *Children Working the Sugar Beet Fields of Certain Districts of the South Platte Valley, Colorado.* New York: National Child Labor Committee, 1925.

Brownell, Susan, ed. *The 1904 Anthropology Days and Olympic Games.* Lincoln: University of Nebraska Press, 2008.

Brown-Pinsky, Asher. "Opium and Race in Southern California 1881–1925." Term paper, n.d. In the author's possession.

Brundage, David. *The Making of Western Labor Radicalism: Denver's Organized Workers, 1878–1905.* Urbana: University of Illinois Press, 1994.

Buford, Kate. *Native American Son: The Life and Sporting Legend of Jim Thorpe.* New York: Alfred A. Knopf, 2010.

Buhle, Mari Jo. *Women and American Socialism.* Urbana: University of Illinois Press, 1981.

Burbank, Garin. *When Farmers Voted Red: The Gospel of Socialism in the Oklahoma Countryside, 1910–1924*. Westwood CT: Greenwood Press, 1976.

Burke, Flannery. *A Land Apart: The Southwest and the Nation in the Twentieth Century*. Tucson: University of Arizona Press, 2017.

Burner, David. *Herbert Hoover The Public Life*. New York: Knopf Doubleday, 1979.

Burnett, Kristin. "Aboriginal and White Women in the Publications of John Maclean, Egerton Ryerson Young, and John McDougall." In *Unsettled Pasts: Reconceiving the West through Women's History*, edited by Sarah Carter, Lesley Erickson, Patricia Roome, and Char Smith, 101–22. Calgary: University of Calgary Press, 2005.

Burton, Antoinette. "Who Needs the Nation? Interrogating 'British' History." *Journal of Historical Sociology* 10, no. 3 (September 1997): 227–48.

Butler, Anne M. *Daughters of Joy, Sisters of Misery: Prostitution in the American West, 1865–1890*. Urbana: University of Illinois Press, 1985.

Bye, Christine Georgina. "'I Think So Much of Edward': Family, Favouritism, and Gender on a Prairie Farm in the 1930s." In *Unsettled Pasts: Reconceiving the West through Women's History*, edited by Sarah Carter, Lesley Erickson, Patricia Roome, and Char Smith, 205–37. Calgary: University of Calgary Press, 2005.

Cadava, Gerald L. *Standing on Common Ground: The Making of a Sunbelt Borderland*. Cambridge MA: Harvard University Press, 2013.

Calderón, Roberto R. *Mexican Coal Mining Labor in Texas and Coahuila, 1880–1930*. College Station: Texas A&M University Press, 2000.

Camarillo, Albert M. "Navigating Segregated Life in America's Racial Borderhoods, 1910s–1950s." *Journal of American History* 100, no. 3 (December 2013): 645–62.

Campney, Brent M. S. *This Is Not Dixie: Racist Violence in Kansas 1861–1927*. Urbana: University of Illinois Press, 2015.

Campomanes, Oscar. "1898 and the Nature of the New Empire." *Radical Historical Review* 73 (January 1999): 130–46.

Campos, Isaac. *Home Grown: Marijuana and the Origins of Mexico's War on Drugs*. Chapel Hill: University of North Carolina Press, 2012.

Canaday, Margot. *The Straight State: Sexuality and Citizenship in Twentieth-Century America*. Princeton NJ: Princeton University Press, 2009.

Canadian Broadcasting Corporation. "Co-operative Commonwealth Federation." *Canada: A People's History*. www.cbc.ca/history/EPISCONTENTSE1EP13CH3PA1LE.html. Accessed May 13, 2011.

Cannon, Brian Q. *Remaking the Agrarian Dream: New Deal Rural Resettlement in the Mountain West*. Albuquerque: University of New Mexico Press, 1996.

Cantrell, Gregg. "'Our Very Pronounced Theory of Equal Rights to All': Race, Citizenship, and Populism in the South Texas Borderlands." *Journal of American History* 100, no. 3 (December 2013): 663–90.

Carriker, Robert M. *Urban Farming in the West: A New Deal Experiment in Subsistence Homesteads*. Tucson: University of Arizona Press, 2010.

Carter, Connie, and Eileen Daoust. "From Home to House: Women in the BC Legislature." In *Not Just Pin Money: Selected Essays on the History of Women's Work in British Columbia*, edited by Barbara K. Latham and Roberta J. Pazdro, 389–405. Victoria BC: Camosun College, 1984.

Carter, Sarah. "'Complicated and Clouded': The Federal Administration of Marriage and Divorce among the First Nations of Western Canada, 1887–1906." In *Unsettled Pasts: Reconceiving the West through Women's History*, edited by Sarah Carter, Lesley Erickson, Patricia Roome, and Char Smith, 151–78. Calgary: University of Calgary Press, 2005.

———. "First Nations Women and Colonization on the Canadian Prairies, 1870s–1920s." In *Rethinking Canada: The Promise of Women's History*, 4th ed., edited by Veronica Strong-Boas, Mona Gleason, and Adele Perry, 135–363. Don Mills ON: Oxford University Press, 2002.

———. *The Importance of Being Monogamous: Marriage and Nation Building in Western Canada to 1915*. Edmonton: University of Alberta Press, 2008.

Carter, Sarah, Lesley Erickson, Patricia Roome, and Char Smith, eds. *Unsettled Pasts: Reconceiving the West through Women's History*. Calgary: University of Calgary Press, 2005.

Cavanaugh, Catherine. "Irene Marryat Parlby: An 'Imperial Daughter' in the Canadian West, 1896–1934." In *Telling Tales: Essays in Western Women's History*, edited by Catherine A. Cavanaugh and Randi R. Warne, 100–122. Vancouver: University of British Columbia Press, 2000.

Cavanaugh, Catherine A., and Randi R. Warne, eds. *Standing on New Ground: Women in Alberta*. Edmonton: University of Alberta Press, 1993.

———, eds. *Telling Tales: Essays in Western Women's History*. Vancouver: University of British Columbia Press, 2000.

Chacón, Justin Akers. *Radicals in the Barrio: Magonistas, Socialists, Wobblies, and Communists in the Mexican American Working Class*. Chicago: Haymarket Books, 2018.

Chacón, Ramón D. "Labor Unrest and Industrialized Agriculture in California: The Case of the 1933 San Joaquin Valley Cotton Strike." *Social Science Quarterly* 65, no. 2 (June 1984): 336–53.

Chamberlin, Hope. *Minority of Members: Women in the U.S. Congress*. New York: Praeger, 1973.

Chang, David. *The Color of the Land: Race, Nation, and the Politics of Landownership in Oklahoma, 1832–1929*. Chapel Hill: University of North Carolina Press, 2010.

Chang, Kornel. "Circulating Race and Empire: Transnational Labor Activism and the Politics of Anti-Asian Agitation in the Anglo-American Pacific World, 1880–1910." *Journal of American History* 96, no. 3 (December 2009): 678–701.

———. "Enforcing Transnational White Solidarity: Asian Migration and the Formation of the U.S.-Canadian Boundary." *American Quarterly* 60, no. 3 (September 2008): 671–96.

———. "Mobilizing Revolutionary Manhood: Race, Gender, and Resistance in the Pacific Northwest Borderlands." In *The Rising Tide of Color: Race, State Violence, and Radical Movements across the Pacific*, edited by Moon-Ho Jung, 72–101. Seattle: University of Washington Press, 2014.

———. *Pacific Connections: The Making of the U.S.-Canadian Borderlands.* Berkeley: University of California Press, 2012.

Chauncey, George. *Gay New York: Gender, Urban Culture, and the Making of the Gay Male World.* New York: Basic Books, 1995.

Childers, Leisl Carr. *The Size of the Risk: Histories of Multiple Use in the Great Basin.* Norman: University of Oklahoma Press, 2015.

Chiv, Steven. "Chinese in Tucson." Term paper, University of Arizona, May 2000. In the author's possession.

Clark, Norman H. *Deliver Us from Evil: An Interpretation of American Prohibition.* New York: W. W. Norton & Company, 1976.

———. *The Dry Years: Prohibition and Social Change in Washington.* Seattle: University of Washington Press, 1988.

———. *Mill Town: A Social History of Everett, Washington, from Its Earliest Beginnings on the Shores of Puget Sound to the Tragic and Infamous Event Known as the Everett Massacre.* Seattle: University of Washington Press, 1970.

Clark, Victor S. "Mexican Labor in the United States." *Bulletin of the U.S. Bureau of Labor* 78 (September 1908): 466–522.

Clemens, Elisabeth S. *The People's Lobby: Organizational Innovation and the Rise of Interest Group Politics in the United States, 1890–1915.* Chicago: University of Chicago Press, 1997.

Cleverdon, Catharine L. *The Woman Suffrage Movement in Canada.* 2nd ed. Toronto: University of Toronto Press, 1974. First published in 1950 by the University of Toronto Press.

Cochran, Robert. *Louise Pound: Scholar, Athlete, Feminist Pioneer.* Lincoln: University of Nebraska Press, 2009.

Cocks, Catherine. "The Welcoming Voice of the Southland: American Tourism across the U.S.-Mexico Border, 1880–1940." In *Bridging National Borders in North America: Transnational and Comparative Histories,* edited by Benjamin Johnson and Andrew R. Graybill, 225–48. Durham NC: Duke University Press, 2010.

Cocoltchos, Christopher N. "The Invisible Empire and the Search for the Orderly Community: The Ku Klux Klan in Anaheim, California." In *The Invisible Empire in the West: Toward a New Historical Appraisal of the Ku Klux Klan of the 1920s,* edited by Shawn Lay, 97–120. Urbana: University of Illinois Press, 1992.

Cohen, Lizabeth. *Making a New Deal: Industrial Workers in Chicago, 1919–1939.* Cambridge: Cambridge University Press, 1990.

Cole, Catherine C., and Ann Milovic. "Education, Community Service, and Social Life: The Alberta Women's Institutes and Rural Families, 1909–1915." In *Standing on New Ground: Women in Alberta,* edited by Catherine C. Cole and Ann Milovic, 19–31. Edmonton: University of Alberta Press, 1993.

Coodley, Lauren. *Upton Sinclair: California Socialist, Celebrity Intellectual.* Lincoln: University of Nebraska Press, 2013.

Cooper, Mark Garrett. *Universal Women: Filmmaking and Institutional Change in Early Hollywood.* Urbana: University of Illinois Press, 2010.

Correia, David. *Properties of Violence: Law and Land Grant Struggle in Northern New Mexico.* Athens: University of Georgia Press, 2013.

Cramer, Michael H. "Public and Political: Documents of the Woman's Suffrage Campaign in British Columbia, 1871–1917; The View from Victoria." In *British Columbia Reconsidered: Essays on Women,* edited by Gillian Laura Creese and Veronica Jane Strong-Boag, 55–72. Vancouver: Press Gang Publishers, 1992.

Creese, Gillian. "The Politics of Dependence: Women, Work and Unemployment in the Vancouver Labour Movement before World War II." In *British Columbia Reconsidered: Essays on Women,* edited by Gillian Laura Creese and Veronica Jane Strong-Boag, 364–90. Vancouver: Press Gang Publishers, 1992.

Crifasi, Robert R. *A Land Made from Water: Appropriation and the Evolution of Colorado's Landscape, Ditches, and Water Institutions.* Boulder: University of Colorado Press, 2015.

Crockett, Norman L. *The Black Towns.* Lawrence: Regents Press of Kansas, 1979.

Cronon, William. "Foreword: Sheep Are Good to Think With." In *Dreaming of Sheep in Navajo Country,* by Marsha Weisiger. Seattle: University of Washington Press, 2009.

Daniels, Roger. *The Politics of Prejudice.* Berkeley: University of California Press, 1962.

Debo, Angie. *The Road to Disappearance: A History of the Creek Indians.* Norman: University of Oklahoma Press, 1941.

Delaney, Terrence. "'My Destiny to Wander': The Odyssey of James Stuart." PhD diss., Clark University, 2006.

Delgado, Grace Peña. "Border Control and Sexual Policing: White Slavery and Prostitution along the U.S.-Mexico Borderlands, 1903–1910." *Western Historical Quarterly* 43 (Summer 2012): 157–78.

———. *Making the Chinese Mexican: Global Migration, Localism, and Exclusion in the U.S.-Mexico Borderlands.* Palo Alto CA: Stanford University Press, 2012.

Del Mar, David Peterson. "'His Face Is Weak and Sensual': Portland and the Whipping Post Law." In *Women in Pacific Northwest History,* rev. ed., edited by Karen Blair, 59–89. Seattle: University of Washington Press, 2001.

Deloria, Philip. *Indians in Unexpected Places.* Lawrence: University Press of Kansas, 2004.

———. *Playing Indian.* New Haven CT: Yale University Press, 1998.

Dempsey, Hugh. *The Best from Alberta History.* Saskatoon SK: Historical Society Press of Alberta, 1981.

Deutsch, Sarah. "Coming Together and Coming Apart: Women's History and the West." *Montana: The Magazine of Western History* 41 (Spring 1991): 58–61.
———. "Labor, Land, and Protest Since Statehood." In *Telling New Mexico: A New History*, edited by Marta Weigle, Frances Levine, and Louise Stiver. Santa Fe: Museum of New Mexico Press, 2009.
———. "Landscapes of Enclaves: Race Relations, 1870–1980." In *Under an Open Sky: Rethinking America's Western Past*, edited by William Cronon, George Miles, and Jay Gitlin, 110–31. New York: W. W. Norton, 1992.
———. *No Separate Refuge: Culture, Class and Gender on an Anglo-Hispanic Frontier in the American Southwest, 1880–1940*. New York: Oxford University Press, 1987.
———. *Women and the City: Gender, Space, and Power in Boston, 1880–1940*. New York: Oxford University Press, 2000.
Deutsch, Sarah, George Sanchez, and Gary Okihiro. "Contemporary Peoples / Contested Places." In *The Oxford History of the American West*, edited by Clyde Milner II, Carol A. O'Connor, and Martha A. Sandweiss, 638–69. New York: Oxford University Press, 1994.
Deverell, William. *Whitewashed Adobe: The Rise of Los Angeles and the Remaking of Its Mexican Past*. Berkeley: University of California Press, 2004.
Deverell, William, and Tom Sitton, eds. *California Progressivism Revisited*. Berkeley: University of California Press, 1994.
Dewey, Alicia M. *Pesos and Dollars: Entrepreneurs in the Texas-Mexico Borderlands 1880–1940*. College Station: Texas A&M University Press, 2014.
Díaz, George T. *Border Contraband: A History of Smuggling across the Rio Grande*. Austin: University of Texas Press, 2014.
Dickson, Paul, and Thomas B. Allen. *The Bonus Army: An American Epic*. New York: Walker Publishing Company, 2005.
Dileva, Frank D. "Iowa Farm Price Revolt." *Annals of Iowa* 32, no. 3 (January 1954): 171–202.
Doman, Mahinder Kaur. "A Note on Asian Indian Women in British Columbia 1900–1935." In *Not Just Pin Money: Selected Essays on the History of Women's Work in British Columbia*, edited by Barbara K. Latham and Roberta J. Pazdro, 99–104. Victoria BC: Camosun College, 1984.
Donovan, Brian. *White Slave Crusades: Race, Gender, and Anti-vice Activism, 1887–1917*. Urbana: University of Illinois Press, 2006.
Dorsey, Kurkpatrick. *The Dawn of Conservation Diplomacy: U.S.-Canadian Wildlife Protection Treaties in the Progressive Era*. Seattle: University of Washington Press, 1998.
Doucette, Kerry. "Tucson's Love Affair with Horses: 1910s–1930s." Term paper, University of Arizona, May 6, 2003. In the author's possession.
Douglas, Ann. *The Feminization of American Culture*. New York: Alfred A. Knopf, 1977.
Dray, Philip. *There Is Power in a Union: The Epic Story of Labor in America*. New York: Doubleday, 2010.

Dubofsky, Melvyn. *We Shall Be All: A History of the Industrial Workers of the World.* Chicago: Quadrangle Books, 1969.
Dudley, Shelly. "The First Five: A Brief History of the Uncompahgre Project (Gunnison)." http://www.waterhistory.org/histories/reclamation/uncompahgre/uncompahgre.pdf. Accessed February 3, 2017.
Edwards, Rebecca. *Angels in the Machinery: Gender in American Party Politics from the Civil War to the Progressive Era.* New York: Oxford University Press, 1997.
Edwards, Wendy J. Deichmann, and Carolyn De Swarte Gifford, eds. *Gender and the Social Gospel.* Urbana: University of Illinois Press, 2003.
Ellsworth, Scott. *Death in a Promised Land: The Tulsa Race Riot of 1921.* Baton Rouge: Louisiana State University Press, 1982.
Emmons, David M. *The Butte Irish: Class and Ethnicity in an American Mining Town, 1875–1925.* Urbana: University of Illinois Press, 1989.
Enciso, Fernando Saúl Alanís. *They Should Stay There: The Story of Mexican Migration and Repatriation during the Great Depression.* Translated by Russ Davidson. Chapel Hill: University of North Carolina Press, 2017.
English, John. "Political Leadership in the First World War." In *Canada and the First World War: Essays in Honour of Robert Craig Brown,* edited by David Mackenzie, 76–95. Toronto: University of Toronto Press, 2005.
Epp-Koop, Stefan. *We're Going to Run This City: Winnipeg's Political Left after the General Strike.* Winnipeg: University of Manitoba Press, 2015.
Escobar, Edward J. *Race, Police, and the Making of a Political Identity: Mexican Americans and the Los Angeles Police Department, 1900–1945.* Berkeley: University of California Press, 1999.
Espinosa, Gastón. "'Your Daughters Shall Prophesy': A History of Women in Ministry in the Latino Pentecostal Movement in the United States." In *Women and Twentieth Century Protestantism,* edited by Margaret Lamberts Bendroth and Virginia Lieson Brereton, 25–48. Urbana: University of Illinois Press, 2002.
Espiritu, Yen Le. *Asian American Women and Men: Labor, Laws, and Love.* 2nd ed. Lanham MD: Rowman & Littlefield Publishers, 2008.
Etulain, Richard W. *The American Far West in the Twentieth Century.* New Haven CT: Yale University Press, 2008.
———. *Beyond the Missouri: The Story of the American West.* Albuquerque: University of New Mexico Press, 2006.
———. *Re-imagining the Modern American West: A Century in Fiction, History, and Art.* Tucson: University of Arizona Press, 1996.
Evans, Barbara. "'We Just Lived It as It Came Along': Stories from Jessie's Albums." In *Standing on New Ground: Women in Alberta,* edited by Catherine C. Cole and Ann Milovic, 33–54. Edmonton: University of Alberta Press, 1993.
Evans, Sterling. *Bound in Twine: The History and Ecology of the Henequen-Wheat Complex for Mexico and the American and Canadian Plains, 1880–1950.* College Station: Texas A&M University Press, 2007.

Faires, Nora. "'Talented and Charming Strangers from across the Line': Gendered Nationalism, Class Privilege, and the American Woman's Club of Calgary." In *One Step over the Line: Toward a History of Women in the North American Wests,* edited by Elizabeth Jameson and Sheila McManus, 261–92. Edmonton: University of Alberta Press, 2008.

Faue, Elizabeth. *Community of Suffering & Struggle: Women, Men, and the Labor Movement in Minneapolis, 1915–1945.* Chapel Hill: University of North Carolina Press, 1991.

Fiamengo, Janice. "Rediscovering Our Foremothers Again: Racial Ideas of Canada's Early Feminists, 1885–1945." In *Rethinking Canada: The Promise of Women's History,* 5th ed., edited by Mona Gleason and Adele Perry, 146–62. Don Mills ON: Oxford University Press, 2006.

Fiege, Mark. *Irrigated Eden: The Making of an Agricultural Landscape in the American West.* Seattle: University of Washington Press, 1999.

Field, Kendra T. "'Turn Our Faces to the West': Refugees, Pioneers, and the Roots of 'All-Black' Oklahoma." In *Freedom's Racial Frontier: African Americans in the Twentieth-Century West,* edited by Herbert G. Ruffin II and Dwayne A. Mack, 115–27. Norman: University of Oklahoma Press, 2018.

Flamming, Douglas. "African-Americans and the Politics of Race in Progressive-Era Los Angeles." In *California Progressivism Revisited,* edited by William Deverell and Tom Sitton, 203–28. Berkeley: University of California Press, 1994.

Flexner, Eleanor. *Century of Struggle: The Woman's Rights Movement in the United States.* Rev. ed. Cambridge MA: Harvard University Press, 1959.

Flores, Lori A. *Grounds for Dreaming: Mexican Americans, Mexican Immigrants, and the California Farmworker Movement.* New Haven CT: Yale University Press, 2016.

Fogo, Cheryl. "Excerpts from *Pourin' Down Rain.*" In *One Step over the Line: Toward a History of Women in the North American Wests,* edited by Elizabeth Jameson and Sheila McManus, 293–307. Edmonton: University of Alberta Press, 2008.

Foley, Neil. "Straddling the Color Line: The Legal Construction of Hispanic Identity in Texas." In *Not Just Black and White: Historical and Contemporary Perspectives on Immigration, Race, and Ethnicity in the United States,* edited by Nancy Foner and George M. Fredrickson, 341–57. New York: Russell Sage Foundation, 2004.

———. *The White Scourge: Mexicans, Blacks, and Poor Whites in Texas Cotton Culture.* Berkeley: University of California Press, 1997.

Ford, Linda. "Women on Holiday: Gender and Midwest Agrarian Activism in the Thirties." *Mid America* 77, no. 3 (August 1995): 285–302.

Foreman, Grant. *The Five Civilized Tribes.* Norman: University of Oklahoma Press, 1934.

Franklin, Jimmie Lewis. *Journey toward Hope: A History of Blacks in Oklahoma.* Norman: University of Oklahoma Press, 1982.

Frehner, Brian. "Jurisdictional No Man's Land: Choctaws, Lawyers, and the Coal Question in Indian Territory." In *Beyond the Borders of the Law: Critical Legal Histories of the North American West*, edited by Katrina Jagodinsky and Pablo Mitchell, 201–27. Lawrence: University Press of Kansas, 2018.

Fresco, Crystal. "Cannery Workers' and Farm Laborers' Union 1933–39: Their Strength in Unity." https://depts.washington.edu/civilr/cwflu.htm.

Galarza, Ernesto. *Barrio Boy*. Notre Dame IN: University of Notre Dame Press, 2011. First published in 1971 by the University of Notre Dame Press.

Gamio, Manuel. *The Mexican Immigrant: His Life Story*. Chicago: University of Chicago Press, 1931.

García, Mario T. *Mexican-Americans: Leadership, Ideology, and Identity, 1930–1960*. New Haven CT: Yale University Press, 1989.

Garcia, Matt. *A World of Its Own: Race, Labor, and Citrus in the Making of Greater Los Angeles, 1900–1970*. Chapel Hill: University of North Carolina Press, 2001.

Garcia, Richard T. *The Rise of the Mexican American Middle Class, 1929–1941*. College Station: Texas A&M University Press, 199.

Gardner, Martha. *The Qualities of a Citizen: Women, Immigration, and Citizenship, 1870–1965*. Princeton NJ: Princeton University Press, 2005.

Garrett, Nicole. "Defying Prohibition in San Jose." Term paper, Duke University, December 7, 2010. In the author's possession.

Geiger, Andrea. "Caught in the Gap: The Transit Privilege and North America's Ambiguous Borders." In *Bridging National Borders in North America: Transnational and Comparative Histories*, edited by Benjamin Johnson and Andrew R. Graybill, 199–222. Durham NC: Duke University Press, 2010.

Gerlach, Larry R. "A Battle of Empires: The Klan in Salt Lake City." In *The Invisible Empire in the West: Toward a New Historical Appraisal of the Ku Klux Klan of the 1920s*, edited by Shawn Lay, 121–52. Urbana: University of Illinois Press, 1992.

Gerstle, Gary. *American Crucible: Race and Nation in the Twentieth Century*. Princeton NJ: Princeton University Press, 2001.

Gibson, Arrell Morgan. *The American Indian: Prehistory to the Present*. Lexington MA: D. C. Heath and Company, 1980.

Gibson, Carrie. *El Norte: The Epic and Forgotten Story of Hispanic North America*. New York: Atlantic Monthly Press, 2019.

Gilbert, James. *Whose Fair? Experience, Memory, and the History of the Great St. Louis Exposition*. Chicago: University of Chicago Press, 2009.

Gilbert, Jess. "Agrarian Intellectuals in a Democratizing State: A Collective Biography of USDA Leaders in the Intended New Deal." In *The Countryside in the Age of the Modern State: Political Histories of Rural America*, edited by Catherine McNicol Stock and Robert D. Johnston, 213–39. Ithaca NY: Cornell University Press, 2001.

Glanz, Theresa A. "Federal Land Use Policy and Resettlement in the Great Plains: An Experiment in Community Development during the New Deal Years, 1933–1941." PhD diss., University of Nebraska, 2020.

Glassberg, David. *American Historical Pageantry: The Uses of Tradition in the Early Twentieth Century*. Chapel Hill: University of North Carolina Press, 1990.

Gleason, Mona, and Adele Perry, eds. *Rethinking Canada: The Promise of Women's History*. 5th ed. Don Mills ON: Oxford University Press, 2006.

Goldberg, Robert A. "Denver: Queen City of the Colorado Realm." In *The Invisible Empire in the West: Toward a New Historical Appraisal of the Ku Klux Klan of the 1920s*, edited by Shawn Lay, 39–66. Urbana: University of Illinois Press, 1992.

Goldman, Marion. *Gold Diggers and Silver Miners: Prostitution and Social Life on the Comstock Lode*. Ann Arbor: University of Michigan Press, 1981.

Goldman, Shifra M. "Siqueiros and Three Early Murals in Los Angeles." *Art Journal* 33, no. 4 (Summer 1974): 321–27.

Gómez, Laura E. *Manifest Destinies: The Making of the Mexican American Race*. 2nd ed. New York: New York University Press, 2018.

Gordon, Linda. *The Great Arizona Orphan Abduction*. Cambridge MA: Harvard University Press, 1999.

———. *The Second Coming of the KKK: The Ku Klux Klan of the 1920s and the American Political Tradition*. New York: Liveright Publishing Corporation, 2017.

Granatstein, J. L. "Conscription in the Great War." In *Canada and the First World War: Essays in Honour of Robert Craig Brown*, edited by David Mackenzie, 62–75. Toronto: University of Toronto Press, 2005.

Grandin, Greg. *The End of the Myth: From the Frontier to the Border Wall in the Mind of America*. New York: Metropolitan Books, Henry Holt and Company, 2019.

Grann, David. *Killers of the Flower Moon: The Osage Murders and the Birth of the FBI*. New York: Doubleday, 2017.

Graybill, Andrew R. *Policing the Great Plains: Rangers, Mounties and the North American Frontier, 1875–1910*. Lincoln: University of Nebraska Press, 2007.

Green, Donald E. *The Creek People*. Phoenix: Indian Tribal Series, 1973.

Green, James R. *Grass-Roots Socialism: Radical Movements in the Southwest 1895–1943*. Baton Rouge: Louisiana State University Press, 1978.

Green, Michael S. *Nevada: A History of the Silver State*. Reno: University of Nevada Press, 2015.

Greenlee, Cynthia. "Due to Her Tender Age: Black Girls and Childhood on Trial in South Carolina, 1885–1920." PhD diss., Duke University, 2014.

Greenwald, Maurine Weiner. *Women, War, and Work: The Impact of World War I on Women Workers in the United States*. Ithaca NY: Cornell University Press, 1980.

———. "Working-Class Feminism and the Family Wage Ideal: The Seattle Debate on Married Women's Right to Work, 1914–1920." In *Women in*

Pacific Northwest History, rev. ed., edited by Karen Blair, 94–134. Seattle: University of Washington Press, 2001.

Gregory, James N. *American Exodus: The Dust Bowl Migration and Okie Culture in California*. New York: Oxford University Press, 1989.

———. "Upton Sinclair's 1934 EPIC Campaign: Anatomy of a Political Movement." *Labor* 12, no. 4 (December 2015): 51–81.

Grewal, Inderpal, and Caren Kaplan, eds. *Scattered Hegemonies: Postmodernity and Transnational Feminist Practices*. Minneapolis: University of Minnesota Press, 1994.

Gross, Ariela J. *What Blood Won't Tell: A History of Race on Trial in America*. Cambridge MA: Harvard University Press, 2010.

Guerin-Gonzales, Camille. *Mexican Workers & American Dreams: Immigration, Repatriation, and California Farm Labor, 1900–1939*. New Brunswick NJ: Rutgers University Press, 1994.

Guidotti-Hernández, Nicole. *Unspeakable Violence: Remapping U.S. and Mexican National Imaginaries*. Durham NC: Duke University Press, 2011.

Gullett, Gayle. *Becoming Citizens: The Emergence and Development of the California Women's Movement, 1880–1911*. Urbana: University of Illinois Press, 2000.

Gutfeld, Arnon. *Montana's Agony: Years of War and Hysteria, 1917–1921*. Gainesville: University Press of Florida, 1979.

Gutiérrez, David G. "Antinomies of the Nation: Citizens and Non-citizens in a Transnational Age." N.d.

———. *Walls and Mirrors: Mexican Americans, Mexican Immigrants, and the Politics of Ethnicity*. Berkeley: University of California Press, 1995.

Gutiérrez, David G., and Pierrette Hondagneu-Sotelo. Introduction to *American Quarterly* 60, no. 3 (September 2008): 503–21. http://archive.oah.org/special-issues/mexico/dgutierrez.html.

Gutiérrez, Ramón A., and Elliot Young. "Transnationalizing Borderlands History." *Western Historical Quarterly* 41, no. 1 (Spring 2010): 27–53.

Haarsager, Sandra. *Organized Womanhood: Cultural Politics in the Pacific Northwest, 1840–1920*. Norman: University of Oklahoma Press, 1997.

Hahamovitch, Cindy. *No Man's Land: Jamaican Guestworkers in America and the Global History of Deportable Labor*. Princeton NJ: Princeton University Press, 2011.

Hahn, Steven. *A Nation under Our Feet: Black Political Struggles in the Rural South from Slavery to the Great Migration*. Cambridge MA: Belknap Press of Harvard University Press, 2003.

Hall, Greg. *Harvest Wobblies: The Industrial Workers of the World and Agricultural Laborers in the American West, 1905–1930*. Corvallis: Oregon State University Press, 2001.

Hansen, Karen V. *Encounter on the Great Plains: Scandinavian Settlers and the Dispossession of Dakota Indians, 1890–1930*. New York: Oxford University Press, 2013.

Harmon, Alexandra. *Rich Indians: Native People and the Problem of Wealth in American History.* Chapel Hill: University of North Carolina Press, 2010.

Harris, Charles H., III, and Louis R. Sadler. *The Secret War in El Paso: Mexican Revolutionary Intrigue, 1906–1920.* Albuquerque: University of New Mexico Press, 2009.

———. *The Texas Rangers and the Mexican Revolution: The Bloodiest Decade, 1910–1920.* Albuquerque: University of New Mexico Press, 2004.

Harris, Linda G. "The Developers Controlling the Lower Rio Grande: 1890–1980." Paper presented at the Fortieth Annual New Mexico Water Conference, Las Cruces NM, October 26–27, 1995. In *Proceedings of the Fortieth Annual New Mexico Water Conference,* 7–11. Las Cruces: New Mexico Water Resources Research Institute, 1996. https://nmwrri.nmsu.edu/wp-content/uploads/2015/watcon/proc40/Cover_TableofContents.pdf.

Hart, John Mason. *Empire and Revolution: The Americans in Mexico Since the Civil War.* Berkeley: University of California Press, 2002.

Hawley, Ellis Wayne. *The Great War and the Search for a Modern Order: A History of the American People and Their Institutions, 1917–1933.* Prospect Heights IL: Waveland Press, 1992.

———. *The New Deal and the Problem of Monopoly.* Princeton NJ: Princeton University Press, 1966.

Haywood, William D. *The Autobiography of Big Bill Haywood: William D. Haywood's Own Story of the Industrial Workers of the World (IWW).* New York: International Publishers, 1929.

Heatherton, Christina. "University of Radicalism: Ricardo Flores Magón and Leavenworth Penitentiary." *American Quarterly* 66, no. 3 (September 2014): 557–81.

Henderson, George. *California and the Fictions of Capital.* New York: Oxford University Press, 1999.

Hernández, Kelly Lytle. *City of Inmates: Conquest, Rebellion, and the Rise of Human Caging in Los Angeles, 1771–1965.* Chapel Hill: University of North Carolina Press, 2017.

———. *Migra! A History of the U.S. Border Patrol.* Berkeley: University of California Press, 2010.

Heron, Craig. "The Workers' Revolt, 1917–1925." In *Labouring Canada: Class, Gender, and Race in Canadian Working-Class History,* edited by Bryan D. Palmer and Joan Sangster, 138–58. Don Mills ON: Oxford University Press, 2008.

Hirsch, James S. *Riot and Remembrance: America's Worst Race Riot and Its Legacy.* Boston: Houghton Mifflin Company, 2002.

Hoffman, Abraham. *Unwanted Americans in the Great Depression: Repatriation Pressures.* Tucson: University of Arizona Press, 1974.

Hoganson, Kirstin L. *Fighting for Manhood: How Gender Politics Provoked the Spanish-American and Philippine-American Wars.* New Haven CT: Yale University Press, 1998.

Holley, Donald. *Uncle Sam's Farmers: The New Deal Communities in the Lower Mississippi Valley*. Urbana: University of Illinois Press, 1975.

Holmes, Todd. "Farmer's Market: Agribusiness and the Agrarian Imaginary in California and the Far West." *California History* 90, no. 2 (2013): 24–74.

Holt, Thomas C. "The First New Nations." In *Race and Nation in Modern Latin America*, edited by Nancy Appelbaum, Anne S. Macpherson, and Karin Alejandra Rosemblatt, xii–xiv. Chapel Hill: University of North Carolina Press, 2003.

Holtby, David V. *Forty-Seventh Star: Race, Politics, and New Mexico's Struggle for Statehood*. Norman: University of Oklahoma Press, 2012.

———. *Lest We Forget: World War I and New Mexico*. Norman: University of Oklahoma Press, 2018.

Horn, Michael. "Frank Underhill's Early Drafts of the Regina Manifesto 1933." *Canadian Historical Review* 54, no. 4 (December 1973): 393–418.

Horne, Gerald. *Black and Brown: African Americans and the Mexican Revolution, 1910–1920*. New York: New York University Press, 2005.

Horowitz, David A. "Order, Solidarity, and Vigilance: The Ku Klux Klan in La Grande, Oregon." In *The Invisible Empire in the West: Toward a New Historical Appraisal of the Ku Klux Klan of the 1920s*, edited by Shawn Lay, 185–216. Urbana: University of Illinois Press, 1992.

Hoxie, Frederick E. "The Curious Story of Reformers and the American Indians." In *Indians in American History: An Introduction*, edited by Frederick E. Hoxie, 205–30. Arlington Heights IL: Harlan Davidson, 1988.

———. *A Final Promise: The Campaign to Assimilate the Indians, 1880–1920*. Lincoln: University of Nebraska Press, 1984.

———, ed. *Indians in American History: An Introduction*. Arlington Heights IL: Harlan Davidson, 1988.

———. *This Indian Country: American Indian Political Activists and the Place They Made*. New York: Penguin Press, 2012.

Huebner, Karin L. "An Unexpected Alliance: Stella Atwood, the California Club Women, John Collier, and the Indians of the Southwest, 1917–1934." *Pacific Historical Review* 78, no. 3 (August 2009): 337–66.

Huginne, A. Yvette. "A New Hero Comes to Town: The Anglo Mining Engineer and 'Mexican Labor' as Contested Terrain in Southeastern Arizona, 1880–1920." *New Mexico Historical Review* 69, no. 4 (October 1994): 323–44.

Hundley, Norris, Jr. *The Great Thirst: Californians and Water, a History*. Rev. ed. Berkeley: University of California Press, 2001.

Hundley, Norris, Jr., and Donald C. Jackson. *Heavy Ground: William Mulholland and the St. Francis Dam Disaster*. Berkeley: University of California Press, 2015.

Hurt, R. Douglas. *The Big Empty: The Great Plains in the Twentieth Century*. Tucson: University of Arizona Press, 2011.

———. *Problems of Plenty: The American Farmer in the Twentieth Century*. Chicago: Ivan R. Dee, 2002.

Hurtado, Albert L., and Peter Iverson, eds. *Major Problems in American Indian History.* 2nd ed. Boston: Houghton Mifflin Company, 2001.

Hyde, Anne Farrar. *An American Vision: Far Western Landscape and National Culture, 1820–1920.* New York: New York University Press, 1990.

Hyman, Harold Melvin. *Soldiers and Spruce: Origins of the Loyal Legion of Loggers and Lumbermen.* Los Angeles: Institute of Industrial Relations, University of California, 1963.

Immerwahr, Daniel. *How to Hide an Empire: A History of the Greater United States.* New York: Farrar, Straus & Giroux, 2019.

Issel, William, and Robert W. Cherny. *San Francisco, 1865–1932: Politics, Power, and Urban Development.* Berkeley: University of California Press, 1986.

Iverson, Peter. *Barry Goldwater: Native Arizonan.* Norman: University of Oklahoma Press, 1997.

———. *The Navajo Nation.* Albuquerque: University of New Mexico Press, 1981.

———. *When Indians Became Cowboys: Native Peoples and Cattle Ranching in the American West.* Norman: University of Oklahoma Press, 1994.

Jackson, Donald C. *Building the Ultimate Dam: John S. Eastwood and the Control of Water in the West.* Lawrence: University Press of Kansas, 1995.

Jacobs, Margaret D. *Engendered Encounters: Feminism and Pueblo Cultures, 1879–1934.* Lincoln: University of Nebraska Press, 1999.

———. "The Great White Mother: Maternalism and American Indian Child Removal in the American West, 1880–1940." In *One Step over the Line: Toward a History of Women in the North American Wests,* edited by Elizabeth Jameson and Sheila McManus, 191–214. Edmonton: University of Alberta Press, 2008.

———. "Making Savages of Us All: White Women, Pueblo Indians, and the Controversy over Indian Dances in the 1920s." *Frontiers* 17, no. 3 (1996): 178–209.

Jacobson, Matthew Frye. *Whiteness of a Different Color: European Immigrants and the Alchemy of Race.* Cambridge MA: Harvard University Press, 1998.

Jacoby, Karl. "Classifying Nature: In Search of a Common Ground between Social and Environmental History." In *Situating Environmental History,* edited by Manohar Ranjan Chakrabarti, 45–58. New Delhi, India: Manohar Publishers & Distributors, 2007.

———. *Crimes against Nature: Squatters, Poachers, Thieves, and the Hidden History of American Conservation.* Berkeley: University of California Press, 2001.

Jagodinsky, Katrina, and Pablo Mitchell, eds. *Beyond the Borders of the Law: Critical Legal Histories of the North American West.* Lawrence: University Press of Kansas, 2018.

James, Harry C. *The Hopi Indians.* Caldwell ID: Caxton Printers, 1956.

Jameson, Elizabeth. *All That Glitters: Class, Conflict, and Community in Cripple Creek.* Urbana: University of Illinois Press, 1998.

———. "Connecting the Women's Wests." In *One Step over the Line: Toward a History of Women in the North American Wests*, edited by Elizabeth Jameson and Sheila McManus, 5–28. Edmonton: University of Alberta Press, 2008.

Jameson, Elizabeth, and Jeremy Mouat. "Telling Differences: The Forty-Ninth Parallel and Historiographies of the West and Nation." *Pacific Historical Review* 75, no. 2 (May 2006): 183–230.

Jameson, Elizabeth, and Sheila McManus, eds. *One Step over the Line: Toward a History of Women in the North American Wests*. Edmonton: University of Alberta Press, 2008.

Jamiolkowski, Lauren. "Feisty Locals Make Their Own Rules: Prohibition in U.S. Mexico Border Towns." Term paper, Duke University, November 20, 2012. In the author's possession.

Jensen, Joan M. *Passage from India: Asian Indian Immigrants in North America*. New Haven CT: Yale University Press, 1988.

———. "The Perils of Rural Women's History: (A Note to Storytellers Who Study the West's Unsettled Past)." In *One Step over the Line: Toward a History of Women in the North American Wests*, edited by Elizabeth Jameson and Sheila McManus, 165–88. Edmonton: University of Alberta Press, 2008.

Johnson, Benjamin, and Andrew R. Graybill, eds. *Bridging National Borders in North America: Transnational and Comparative Histories*. Durham NC: Duke University Press, 2010.

Johnson, Benjamin Heber. *Revolution in Texas: How a Forgotten Rebellion and Its Bloody Suppression Turned Mexicans into Americans*. New Haven CT: Yale University Press, 2003.

Johnson, Gaye Theresa. *Spaces of Conflict, Sounds of Solidarity: Music, Race, and Spatial Entitlement in Los Angeles*. Berkeley: University of California Press, 2013.

Johnson, Kathy. "Women in San Antonio: A Living Representation." Unpublished manuscript. In the author's possession.

Johnson, Nick. *Grass Roots: A History of Cannabis in the American West*. Corvallis: Oregon State University Press, 2017.

Johnson, Victoria. *How Many Machine Guns Does It Take to Cook One Meal? The Seattle & San Francisco General Strikes*. Seattle: University of Washington Press, 2008.

Johnston, Lauren. "The Spanish-American War and the American Quest for Empire: Racializing American Identity." Term paper, Fall 2000. In the author's possession.

Johnston, Robert D. "Beyond 'The West': Regionalism, Liberalism and the Evasion of Politics in the New Western History." *Rethinking History* 2, no. 2 (1998): 239–77.

———. "The Myth of the Harmonious City: Will Daly, Ora Little, and the Hidden Face of Progressive-Era Portland." *Oregon Historical Quarterly* 99, no. 3 (Fall 1998): 248–97.

———. *The Radical Middle Class: Populist Democracy and the Question of Capitalism in Progressive Era Portland, Oregon.* Princeton NJ: Princeton University Press, 2003.

Josephy, Alvin M., Jr. "Modern America and the Indian." In *Indians in American History: an Introduction,* edited by Frederick E. Hoxie, 251–74. Arlington Heights IL: Harlan Davidson, 1988.

Jung, Moon-Ho, ed. *The Rising Tide of Color: Race, State Violence, and Radical Movements across the Pacific.* Seattle: University of Washington Press, 2014.

———. "Seditious Subjects: Race, State Violence, and the U.S. Empire." *Journal of Asian-American Studies* 14 (June 2011): 221–47.

Kagel, John. "The General Strike: Revolution or Reaction?" *California History* 63, no. 3 (1984): 216–17.

Kang, S. Deborah. "Crossing the Line: The INS and the Federal Regulation of the Mexican Border." In *Bridging National Borders in North America: Transnational and Comparative Histories,* edited by Benjamin Johnson and Andrew R. Graybill, 167–98. Durham NC: Duke University Press, 2010.

———. *The INS on the Line: Making Immigration Law on the US-Mexico Border, 1917–1954.* New York: Oxford University Press, 2017.

Kaplan, Amy, and Donald E. Pease, eds. *Cultures of U.S. Imperialism.* Durham NC: Duke University Press, 1993.

Katz, Friedrich. *The Life and Times of Pancho Villa.* Stanford CA: Stanford University Press, 1998.

Katz, Sherry J. "A Politics of Coalition: Socialist Women and the California Suffrage Movement, 1900–1911." In *One Woman, One Vote: Rediscovering the Woman Suffrage Movement,* edited by Marjorie Wheeler Spruill, 245–62. Troutdale OR: NewSage Press, 1995.

———. "Redefining 'The Political': Socialist Women and Party Politics in California, 1900–1920." In *We Have Come to Stay: American Women and Party Politics, 1880–1960,* edited by Melanie Gustafson, Kristie Miller, and Elisabeth Israels Perry, 23–32. Albuquerque: University of New Mexico Press, 1999.

Kazin, Michael. *Barons of Labor: The San Francisco Building Trades and Union Power in the Progressive Era.* Urbana: University of Illinois Press, 1987.

Kealey, Linda, ed. *A Not Unreasonable Claim: Women and Reform in Canada 1880s–1920s.* Toronto: Women's Press, 1979.

Kehoe, Alice B. *North American Indians: A Comprehensive Account.* 2nd ed. Upper Saddle River NJ: Prentice Hall, 1981.

Keire, Mara L. *For Business & Pleasure: Red-Light Districts and the Regulation of Vice in the United States, 1890–1933.* Baltimore MD: Johns Hopkins University Press, 2010.

Kennedy, David M. *Over Here: The First World War and American Society.* New York: Oxford University Press, 1980.

Kessler, Lauren. "The Fight for Woman Suffrage and the Oregon Press." In *Women in Pacific Northwest History,* rev. ed., edited by Karen Blair, 43–58. Seattle: University of Washington Press, 2001.

———. "The Ideas of Woman Suffrage and the Mainstream Press." *Oregon Historical Quarterly* 84, no. 3 (Fall 1983): 257–75.

———. "A Siege of the Citadels: Search for a Public Forum for the Ideas of Oregon Woman Suffrage." *Oregon Historical Quarterly* 84, no. 2 (Summer 1983): 117–49.

Kinnear, Mary, ed. *First Days, Fighting Days: Women in Manitoba History*. Regina: University of Regina Press, 1987.

Klippenstein, Frieda Esau. "Scattered but Not Lost: Mennonite Domestic Servants in Winnipeg, 1920s–50s." In *Telling Tales: Essays in Western Women's History*, edited by Catherine A. Cavanaugh and Randi R. Warne, 200–232. Vancouver: University of British Columbia Press, 2000.

Kneller, Jenni. "Barrio Libre: The White Man's Intention." Unpublished essay, University of Arizona, May 2, 2000. In the author's possession.

Koshy, Susan. "Morphing Race into Ethnicity: Asian Americans and Critical Transformations of Whiteness." *Boundary* 28, no. 1 (Spring 2001): 153–94.

Kramer, Paul A. *The Blood of Government: Race, Empire, the United States, & the Philippines*. Chapel Hill: University of North Carolina Press, 2006.

Krehbiel, Randy, and Karlos K. Hill. *Tulsa, 1921: Reporting a Massacre*. Norman: University of Oklahoma Press, 2019.

Krieger, Nancy. "Queen of the Bolsheviks: The Hidden History of Dr. Marie Equi." *Radical America* 17, no. 5 (1983): 55–73.

Kropp, Phoebe S. *California Vieja: Culture and Memory in a Modern American Place*. Berkeley: University of California Press, 2006.

Krugler, David F. *1919, the Year of Racial Violence: How African Americans Fought Back*. New York: Cambridge University Press, 2015.

Kurashige, Scott. *The Shifting Grounds of Race: Black and Japanese Americans in the Making of Multiethnic Los Angeles*. Princeton NJ: Princeton University Press, 2008.

LaDow, Beth. *The Medicine Line: Life and Death on a North American Borderland*. New York: Routledge, 2001.

Laegreid, Renée M. *Riding Pretty: Rodeo Royalty in the American West*. Lincoln: University of Nebraska Press, 2006.

Lake, Marilyn, and Henry Reynolds. *Drawing the Global Colour Line: White Men's Countries and the International Challenge of Racial Equality*. Cambridge: Cambridge University Press, 2008.

Lamar, Howard R. *The Far Southwest: 1846–1912, a Territorial History*. Rev. ed. Albuquerque: University of New Mexico Press, 2000.

———, ed. *The New Encyclopedia of the American West*. New Haven CT: Yale University Press, 1998.

Langford, Nanci. "'All That Glitters': The Political Apprenticeship of Alberta Women, 1916–1930." In *Standing on New Ground: Women in Alberta*, edited by Catherine C. Cole and Ann Milovic, 71–85. Edmonton: University of Alberta Press, 1993.

———. "Childbirth on the Canadian Prairies, 1880–1930." In *Telling Tales: Essays in Western Women's History*, edited by Catherine A. Cavanaugh and Randi R. Warne, 146–73. Vancouver: University of British Columbia Press, 2000.

Langston, Nancy. *Forest Dreams, Forest Nightmares: The Paradox of Old Growth in the Inland West.* Seattle: University of Washington Press, 1995.

Lansing, Michael J. "Different Methods, Different Places: Feminist Geography and New Directions in US Western History." *Journal of Historical Geography* 19, no. 2 (2003): 230–47.

———. *Insurgent Democracy: The Nonpartisan League in North American Politics.* Chicago: University of Chicago Press, 2015.

LaPier, Rosalyn, and David R. M. Beck. "A 'One-Man Relocation Team': Scott Henry Peters and American Indian Urban Migration in the 1930s." *Western Historical Quarterly* 45, no. 1 (Spring 2014): 17–36.

Laslett, John H. M. *Sunshine Was Never Enough: Los Angeles Workers, 1880–2010.* Berkeley: University of California Press, 2012.

Latham, Barbara K., and Roberta J. Pazdro, eds. *Not Just Pin Money: Selected Essays on the History of Women's Work in British Columbia.* Victoria BC: Camosun College, 1984.

Lavender, Catherine J. *Scientists and Storytellers: Feminist Anthropologists and the Construction of the American Southwest.* Albuquerque: University of New Mexico Press, 2006.

Lay, Shawn. "Imperial Outpost on the Border: El Paso's Frontier Klan No. 100." In *The Invisible Empire in the West: Toward a New Historical Appraisal of the Ku Klux Klan of the 1920s*, edited by Shawn Lay, 67–96. Urbana: University of Illinois Press, 1992.

———, ed. *The Invisible Empire in the West: Toward a New Historical Appraisal of the Ku Klux Klan of the 1920s.* Urbana: University of Illinois Press, 1992.

Layoun, Mary. "The Female Body and 'Transnational' Reproduction; or Rape by Any Other Name." In *Scattered Hegemonies: Postmodernity and Transnational Feminist Practices*, edited by Inderpal Grewal and Caren Kaplan, 63–75. Minneapolis: University of Minnesota Press, 1994.

LeCompte, Mary Lou. *Cowgirls of the Rodeo: Pioneer Professional Athletes.* Urbana: University of Illinois Press, 1993.

Lee, Catherine. *Fictive Kinship: Family Reunification and the Meaning of Race and Nation in American Immigration.* New York: Russell Sage Foundation, 2013.

Lee, Erika. *At America's Gates: Chinese Immigration during the Exclusion Era, 1882–1943.* Chapel Hill: University of North Carolina Press, 2003.

Lee, Shelley Sang-Hee. *Claiming the Oriental Gateway: Prewar Seattle and Japanese America.* Philadelphia: Temple University Press, 2011.

Leffler, Melvyn P. "Herbert Hoover, The 'New Era,' and American Foreign Policy, 1921–1929." In *Herbert Hoover as Secretary of Commerce: Studies in New Era Thought and Practice*, edited by Ellis W. Hawley, 148–82. Iowa City: University of Iowa Press, 1981.

Leger-Anderson, Ann M. "Marriage, Family, and the Cooperative Ideal in Saskatchewan: The Telfords." In *Telling Tales: Essays in Western Women's History*, edited by Catherine A. Cavanaugh and Randi R. Warne, 281–334. Vancouver: University of British Columbia Press, 2000.

Leier, Mark. "Monopoly Capitalism and the Rise of Syndicalism: Rallying round the Standard in British Columbia." In *Labouring Canada: Class, Gender, and Race in Canadian Working-Class History*, edited by Bryan D. Palmer and Joan Sangster, 125–37. Don Mills ON: Oxford University Press, 2008.

Leiker, James N. *Racial Borders: Black Soldiers along the Rio Grande*. College Station: Texas A&M University Press, 2002.

Lentz-Smith, Adriane. *Freedom Struggles: African Americans and World War I*. Cambridge MA: Harvard University Press, 2009.

Leonard, Karen Isaksen. *Making Ethnic Choices: California's Punjabi Mexican Americans*. Philadelphia: Temple University Press, 1992.

Leuchtenburg, William E. *Herbert Hoover*. New York: Times Books, Henry Holt & Co., 2009.

Lewthwaite, Stephanie. *Race, Place, and Reform in Mexican Los Angeles: A Transnational Perspective, 1890–1940*. Tucson: University of Arizona Press, 2009.

Lew-Williams, Beth. "'Chinamen' and 'Delinquent Girls': Intimacy, Exclusion, and a Search for California's Color Line." *Journal of American History* 104, no. 3 (December 2017): 632–56.

Lim, Julian. *Porous Borders: Multiracial Migrations and the Law in the U.S.-Mexico Borderlands*. Chapel Hill: University of North Carolina Press, 2017.

Lipsitz, George. "How History Happens and Why Culture Counts: Twenty Years after *Becoming Mexican American*." *American Quarterly* 65, no. 2 (June 2013): 405–11.

Litt, Paul. "Canada Invaded! The Great War, Mass Culture, and Canadian Cultural Nationalism." In *Canada and the First World War: Essays in Honour of Robert Craig Brown*, edited by David Mackenzie, 323–49. Toronto: University of Toronto Press, 2005.

Little, Margaret Hillyard. "Claiming a Unique Place: The Introduction of Mothers' Pensions in British Columbia." In *Rethinking Canada: The Promise of Women's History*, 5th ed., edited by Mona Gleason and Adele Perry, 163–78. Don Mills ON: Oxford University Press, 2006.

Littlefield, Daniel F., and Carol A. Petty-Hunter. *The Fus Fixico Letters*. Lincoln: University of Nebraska Press, 1993.

Littlefield, Daniel F., and Lonnie E. Underhill. "The 'Crazy Snake Uprising' of 1909: A Red, Black, or White Affair?" *Arizona and the West* 20, no. 4 (Winter 1978): 307–24.

Loch-Drake, Cynthia. "Jailed Heroes and Kitchen Heroines: Class, Gender, and the Medalta Potteries Strike in Postwar Alberta." In *One Step over the Line: Toward a History of Women in the North American Wests*, edited by Elizabeth Jameson and Sheila McManus, 341–80. Edmonton: University of Alberta Press, 2008.

Lockerby, Claire E. "Owning the Intangible? A Historical Study of the Roots of Hopi Cultural Preservation and Knowledge Protection." Honors thesis, Duke University, April 16, 2012.

Long, Alecia P. *The Great Southern Babylon: Sex, Race, and Respectability in New Orleans, 1865–1920.* Baton Rouge: Louisiana State University Press, 2004.

Lozano, Rosina. *An American Language: The History of Spanish in the United States.* Berkeley: University of California Press, 2018.

Luebke, Frederick C. *Ethnicity on the Great Plains.* Lincoln: University of Nebraska Press, 1980.

Luibhéid, Eithne. *Entry Denied: Controlling Sexuality at the Border.* Minneapolis: University of Minnesota Press, 2002.

Luis-Brown, David. *Waves of Decolonization: Discourses of Race and Hemispheric Citizenship in Cuba, Mexico, and the United States.* Durham NC: Duke University Press, 2008.

Lumsden, Sarah. "The Effect of U.S. Federal and Local Policy on Mexico: A Study of El Paso and Juárez during Prohibition and the Recent Drug Wars (2000–2010)." Term paper, Duke University, December 6, 2010. In the author's possession.

Lynn-Sherow, Bonnie. *Red Earth: Race and Agriculture in Oklahoma Territory.* Lawrence: University Press of Kansas, 2004.

Lyon, Cherstin M. *Prisons and Patriots: Japanese American Wartime Citizenship, Civil Disobedience, and Historical Memory.* Philadelphia: Temple University Press, 2012.

MacDonald, Graham A. "Clare Sheridan's Western Interlude: The Importance of Being Well-Connected." In *Unsettled Pasts: Reconceiving the West through Women's History,* edited by Sarah Carter, Lesley Erickson, Patricia Roome, and Char Smith, 79–91. Calgary: University of Calgary Press, 2005.

Macías, Anna. *Against All Odds: The Feminist Movement in Mexico to 1940.* Westport CT: Greenwood Press, 1982.

Mackenzie, David, ed. *Canada and the First World War: Essays in Honour of Robert Craig Brown.* Toronto: University of Toronto Press, 2005.

———. "Introduction: Myth, Memory, and the Transformation of Canadian Society." In *Canada and the First World War: Essays in Honour of Robert Craig Brown,* edited by David Mackenzie, 3–14. Toronto: University of Toronto Press, 2005.

Mahar, Karen Ward. "Women, Filmmaking, and the Gendering of the American Film Industry, 1896–1928." PhD diss., University of Southern California, December 1995.

Manley, John. "'Starve Be Damned!': Communists and Canada's Urban Unemployed, 1929–1939." In *Labouring Canada: Class, Gender, and Race in Canadian Working-Class History,* edited by Bryan D. Palmer and Joan Sangster, 210–23. Don Mills ON: Oxford University Press, 2008.

Martelle, Scott. *Blood Passion: The Ludlow Massacre and Class War in the American West.* New Brunswick NJ: Rutgers University Press, 2007.

Martin, Joel W. *Sacred Revolt: The Muskogees' Struggle for a New World.* Boston: Beacon Press, 1991.

Martinez, Monica Muñoz. *The Injustice Never Leaves You: Anti-Mexican Violence in Texas.* Cambridge MA: Harvard University Press, 2018.

Martínez, Oscar J., ed. *Fragments of the Mexican Revolution: Personal Accounts from the Border.* Albuquerque: University of New Mexico Press, 1983.

Mason, Mary Ann. "Neither Friends nor Foes: Organized Labor and the California Progressives." In *California Progressivism Revisited,* edited by William Deverell and Tom Sitton, 57–71. Berkeley: University of California Press, 1994.

Mathieu, Sarah-Jane (Saje). "North of the Colour Line: Sleeping Car Porters and the Battle against Jim Crow on Canadian Rails, 1880–1920." In *Labouring Canada: Class, Gender, and Race in Canadian Working-Class History,* edited by Bryan D. Palmer and Joan Sangster, 176–91. Don Mills ON: Oxford University Press, 2008.

Matsumoto, Valerie J. *Farming the Home Place: A Japanese American Community in California 1919–1982.* Ithaca NY: Cornell University Press, 1993.

Mautner, Bertram, and W. Lewis Abbott. *Child Labor in Agriculture and Farm Life in the Arkansas Valley of Colorado.* New York: n.p., 1929.

May, Katja. *African-Americans and Native Americans in the Creek and Cherokee Nations, 1830s to 1920s.* New York: Routledge, 1996.

McArthur, Judith N. "Minnie Fisher Cunningham's Back Door Lobby in Texas: Political Maneuvering in a One-Party State." In *One Woman, One Vote: Rediscovering the Woman Suffrage Movement,* edited by Marjorie Wheeler Spruill, 315–31. Troutdale OR: NewSage Press, 1995.

McCalla, Douglas. "The Economic Impact of the Great War." In *Canada and the First World War: Essays in Honour of Robert Craig Brown,* edited by David Mackenzie, 138–53. Toronto: University of Toronto Press, 2005.

McCartney, Laton. *The Teapot Dome Scandal.* New York: Random House, 2008.

McCool, Daniel, Susan M. Olson, and Jennifer L. Robinson. *Native Vote: American Indians, the Voting Rights Act, and the Right to Vote.* New York: Cambridge University Press, 2007.

McDonald, Laughlin. *American Indians and the Fight for Equal Voting Rights.* Norman: University of Oklahoma Press, 2010.

McIntosh, Kenneth Waldo. "Chitto Harjo, the Crazy Snakes, and the Birth of Indian Political Activism in the Twentieth Century." PhD diss., Texas Christian University, 1993.

Mckiernan-González, John. *Fevered Measures: Public Health and Race at the Texas-Mexico Border, 1848–1942.* Durham NC: Duke University Press, 2012.

McManus, Sheila. "Gender(ed) Tensions in the Work and Politics of Alberta Farm Women, 1905–1929." In *Telling Tales: Essays in Western Women's History,* edited by Catherine A. Cavanaugh and Randi R. Warne, 123–46. Vancouver: University of British Columbia Press, 2000.

———. "Unsettled Pasts, Unsettling Borders: Women, Wests, Nations." In *One Step over the Line: Toward a History of Women in the North American Wests*, edited by Elizabeth Jameson and Sheila McManus, 29–47. Edmonton: University of Alberta Press, 2008.

McNamara, Marilyn. "Pastime Park: Veterans in Partnership with Tucson." Term paper, University of Arizona, May 1, 2001. In the author's possession.

McNickle, D'Arcy. "The Indian New Deal as Mirror of the Future." In *Major Problems in American Indian History*, 2nd ed., edited by Albert L. Hurtado and Peter Iverson, 410–17. Boston: Houghton Mifflin, 2001. First published in 1980 in *Political Organization of Native North Americans*, edited by Ernest Schusky, University Press of America.

McWilliams, Carey. *Factories in the Field: The Story of Migratory Farm Labor in California.* Boston: Little, Brown and Company, 1939.

Mead, Rebecca J. *How the Vote Was Won: Woman Suffrage in the Western United States, 1868–1914.* New York: New York University Press, 2004.

Meeks, Eric V. *Border Citizens: The Making of Indians, Mexicans, and Anglos in Arizona.* Austin: University of Texas Press, 2007.

Mercier, Laurie. "'A Union without Women Is Only Half Organized': Mine Mill, Women's Auxiliaries, and Cold War Politics in the North American Wests." In *One Step over the Line: Toward a History of Women in the North American Wests*, edited by Elizabeth Jameson and Sheila McManus, 315–40. Edmonton: University of Alberta Press, 2008.

Meriam, Lewis. "The Problem of Indian Administration." In *Major Problems in American Indian History*, 2nd ed., edited by Albert L. Hurtado and Peter Iverson, 384–87. Boston: Houghton Mifflin, 2001. First published in 1928 by Johns Hopkins Press.

Merill, Karen R. *Public Lands and Political Meaning: Ranchers, the Government, and the Property between Them.* Berkeley: University of California Press, 2002.

Mickelson, Erik. "The Loyal Legion of Loggers and Lumbermen." Seattle General Strike Project, University of Washington. https://depts.washington.edu/labhist/strike/mickelson.shtml. Accessed April 7, 2021.

Miles, Tiya. *Ties That Bind: The Story of an Afro-Cherokee Family in Slavery and Freedom.* 2nd ed. Oakland: University of California Press, 2016. https://california-universitypressscholarship.com.proxy.lib.duke.edu/view/10.1525/california/9780520285637.001.0001/upso-9780520285637-chapter-012?print=pdf.

Milner, Clyde, II, and Carol A. O'Connor. *As Big as the West: The Pioneer Life of Granville Stuart.* New York: Oxford University Press, 2008.

Mitchell, Pablo. *Coyote Nation: Sexuality, Race, and Conquest in Modernizing New Mexico, 1880–1920.* Chicago: University of Chicago Press, 2005.

Mize, Richard. "Black, White, and Read: The *Muskogee Daily Phoenix*'s Coverage of the Sequoyah Statehood Convention of 1905." *Chronicles of Oklahoma* 82, no. 2 (June 2004): 222–39.

Molina, Natalia. *Fit to Be Citizens? Public Health and Race in Los Angeles, 1879–1939*. Berkeley: University of California Press, 2006.

———. *How Race Is Made in America: Immigration, Citizenship, and the Historical Power of Racial Scripts*. Berkeley: University of California Press, 2014.

Monroy, Douglas. "Like Swallows at the Old Mission: Mexicans and the Racial Politics of Growth in Los Angeles in the Interwar Period." *Western Historical Quarterly* 14, no. 4 (October 1983): 435–58.

———. *Rebirth: Mexican Los Angeles from the Great Migration to the Great Depression*. Berkeley: University of California Press, 1999.

Montejano, David. *Anglos and Mexicans in the Making of Texas, 1836–1986*. Austin: University of Texas Press, 1987.

Montgomery, Charles. *The Spanish Redemption: Heritage, Power, and Loss on New Mexico's Upper Rio Grande*. Berkeley: University of California Press, 2002.

Montoya, María E. *Translating Property: The Maxwell Land Grant and the Conflict over Land in the American West, 1840–1900*. Berkeley: University of California Press, 2002.

Moore, Leonard J. "Historical Interpretations of the 1920s Klan: The Traditional View and Recent Revisions." In *The Invisible Empire in the West: Toward a New Historical Appraisal of the Ku Klux Klan of the 1920s*, edited by Shawn Lay, 17–38. Urbana: University of Illinois Press, 2004.

Moore, Mike. "Idaho Elects a Jewish Governor." https://thebluereview.org/moses-alexander.idaho-jewish-governor/. Accessed January 2017.

Mora, Anthony. *Border Dilemmas: Racial and National Uncertainties in New Mexico, 1848–1912*. Durham NC: Duke University Press, 2011.

———. "A Fixed Border's Shifting Meanings: The United States and Mexico, 1821 to 2007." In *Labor Market Issues along the U.S.-Mexico Border*, edited by Marie T. Mora and Alberto Dávila. Tucson: University of Arizona Press, 2009.

Moraga, Cherríe. *Loving in the War Years: Lo que nunca pasó por los labios*. Boston: South End Press, 1983.

Moreton, Bethany. *To Serve God and Wal-Mart: The Making of Christian Free Enterprise*. Cambridge MA: Harvard University Press, 2009.

Morgan, Brandon. "The Centennial of Pancho Villa's Raid on Columbus, NM: Intersections of History, Historical Memory, and Forgetting." *History of the Mexican Revolution: Violence, Myth, and Reconstruction* (blog), March 10, 2016. https://larevolucionblog.wordpress.com/2016/03/10/the-centennial-of-pancho-villas-raid-on-columbus-nm-intersections-of-history-historical-memory-and.

———. "From Brutal Ally to Humble Believer: Mormon Colonists' Image of Pancho Villa." *New Mexico Historical Review* 85, no. 2 (Spring 2010): 109–29.

Morlan, Robert L. *Political Prairie Fire: The Nonpartisan League, 1915–1922*. Minneapolis: University of Minnesota Press, 1955.

Morrissey, Katherine G. *Mental Territories: Mapping the Inland Empire*. Ithaca NY: Cornell University Press, 1997.

Morton, Desmond. "Supporting Soldiers' Families: Separation Allowance, Assigned Pay, and the Unexpected." In *Canada and the First World War: Essays in Honour of Robert Craig Brown*, edited by David Mackenzie, 194–229. Toronto: University of Toronto Press, 2005.

Mosher, Clayton J., and Scott Akins. *In the Weeds: Demonization, Legalization, and the Evolution of U.S. Marijuana Policy*. Philadelphia: Temple University Press, 2019.

Mount, Greame S. "Nuevo Mexicanos and the War of 1898." *New Mexico Historical Review* 58 (1983).

Mowry, George E. *The California Progressives*. Berkeley: University of California Press, 1951.

Moynihan, Ruth Barnes. "Of Women's Rights and Freedom: Abigail Scott Duniway." In *Women in Pacific Northwest History*, rev. ed., edited by Karen Blair, 28–42. Seattle: University of Washington Press, 2001.

———. *Rebel for Rights: Abigail Scott Duniway*. New Haven CT: Yale University Press, 1983.

Mullins, William H. *The Depression and the Urban West Coast, 1929–1933: Los Angeles, San Francisco, Seattle and Portland*. Bloomington: Indiana University Press, 1991.

Munsell, F. Darrell. *From Redstone to Ludlow: John Cleveland Osgood's Struggle against the United Mine Workers of America*. Boulder: University Press of Colorado, 2009.

Murphy, Mary. "Bootlegging Mothers and Drinking Daughters: Gender and Prohibition in Butte, Montana." *American Quarterly* 46, no. 2 (June 1994): 174–94.

———. "Latitudes and Longitudes: Teaching the History of Women in the U.S. and Canadian Wests." In *One Step over the Line: Toward a History of Women in the North American Wests*, edited by Elizabeth Jameson and Sheila McManus, 411–25. Edmonton: University of Alberta Press, 2008.

———. *Mining Cultures: Men, Women, and Leisure in Butte, 1914–1941*. Urbana: University of Illinois Press, 1997.

Nash, Gerald D. *The American West in the Twentieth Century: A Short History of an Urban Oasis*. Englewood Cliffs NJ: Prentice Hall, 1973.

———. *The Federal Landscape: An Economic History of the Twentieth Century West*. Tucson: University of Arizona Press, 1999.

Nash, Lee. "Abigail versus Harvey: Sibling Rivalry in the Oregon Campaign for Woman Suffrage." *Oregon Historical Quarterly* 98, no. 2 (Summer 1997): 134–63.

Nash, Roderick. *Wilderness and the American Mind*. Rev. ed. New Haven CT: Yale University Press, 1973.

Naylor, Celia E. *African Cherokees in Indian Territory: From Chattel to Citizens*. Chapel Hill: University of North Carolina Press, 2008.

Needham, Andrew. *Power Lines: Phoenix and the Making of the Modern Southwest*. Princeton NJ: Princeton University Press, 2014.

Nelson, Bruce. *Workers on the Waterfront: Seamen, Longshoremen, and Unionism in the 1930s.* Urbana: University of Illinois Press, 1990.

Nevins, Joseph. *Operation Gatekeeper and Beyond: The War on Illegals and the Remaking of the U.S.-Mexican Boundary.* New York: Routledge, 2010.

Nevola, Lucas. "Alcohol or Lack Thereof—Not the Solution to Every Problem: A Study of U.S. Continental Relations during Prohibition." Term paper, Duke University, n.d. In the author's possession.

Newton, Janice. "The Plight of the Working Girl." In *Labouring Canada: Class, Gender, and Race in Canadian Working-Class History,* edited by Bryan D. Palmer and Joan Sangster, 158–70. Don Mills ON: Oxford University Press, 2008.

Ngai, Mae M. *Impossible Subjects: Illegal Aliens and the Making of Modern America.* Princeton NJ: Princeton University Press, 2004.

Nickliss, Alexandra M. "Phoebe Apperson Hearst's 'Great Reserve of Power' and American Politics." Master's thesis, City College of San Francisco, 2013.

Nicolaides, Becky M. *My Blue Heaven: Life and Politics in the Working-Class Suburbs of Los Angeles, 1920–1965.* Chicago: University of Chicago Press, 2002.

Nieto-Phillips, John M. *The Language of Blood: The Making of Spanish American Identity in New Mexico, 1880s–1930s.* Albuquerque: University of New Mexico Press, 2004.

Noel, Linda C. "'I Am an American': Anglos, Mexicans, *Nativos,* and the National Debate over Arizona and New Mexico Statehood." *Pacific Historical Review* 80, no. 3 (2011): 430–67.

Noggle, Burt. *Teapot Dome: Oil and Politics in the 1920s.* Baton Rouge: Louisiana State University Press, 1962.

Nomura, Gail M. "*Tsugiki,* a Grafting: A History of a Japanese Pioneer Woman in Washington State." In *Women in Pacific Northwest History,* rev. ed., edited by Karen Blair, 284–307. Seattle: University of Washington Press, 2001.

Norcross, Elizabeth. "Mary Ellen Smith: The Right Woman in the Right Place at the Right Time." In *Not Just Pin Money: Selected Essays on the History of Women's Work in British Columbia,* edited by Barbara K. Latham and Roberta J. Pazdro, 357–64. Victoria BC: Camosun College, 1984.

North, Diane M. T. *California at War: The State and the People during World War I.* Lawrence: University Press of Kansas, 2018.

O'Connor, Carol. *A Sort of Utopia: Scarsdale, 1891–1981.* Albany: State University of New York Press, 1983.

Odem, Mary. "City Mothers and Delinquent Daughters: Female Juvenile Justice Reform in Early Twentieth-Century Los Angeles." In *California Progressivism Revisited,* edited by William Deverell and Tom Sitton, 175–99. Berkeley: University of California Press, 1994.

———. *Delinquent Daughters: Protecting and Policing Adolescent Female Sexuality in the United States, 1885–1920.* Chapel Hill: University of North Carolina Press, 1995.

Ogg, Kathryn. "'Especially When No One Agrees': An Interview with May Campbell." In *Not Just Pin Money: Selected Essays on the History of Women's Work in British Columbia*, edited by Barbara K. Latham and Roberta J. Pazdro, 237–48. Victoria BC: Camosun College, 1984.

Olcott, Jocelyn. *Revolutionary Women in Postrevolutionary Mexico.* Durham NC: Duke University Press, 2005.

Olien, Roger M., and Diana Davids Hinton. *Wildcatters: Texas Independent Oilmen.* College Station: Texas A&M University Press, 2007.

Olien, Roger M., and Diana Davids Olien. *Easy Money: Oil Promoters and Investors in the Jazz Age.* Chapel Hill: University of North Carolina Press, 1990.

Olson, Alexander I. "Heritage Schemes: The Curtis Brothers and the Indian Moment of Northwest Boosterism." *Western Historical Quarterly* 40 (Summer 2009): 159–78.

Olson, James S., and Raymond Wilson. *Native Americans in the Twentieth Century.* Urbana: University of Illinois Press, 1984.

Olsson, Tore C. *Agrarian Crossings: Reformers and the Remaking of the US and Mexican Countryside.* Princeton NJ: Princeton University Press, 2017.

O'Neill, Colleen. *Working the Navajo Way: Labor and Culture in the Twentieth Century.* Lawrence: University Press of Kansas, 2005.

Orona, Kenneth M. "Muddy Water." Unpublished manuscript, 2006. In the author's possession.

Orozco, Cynthia E. *No Mexicans, Women, or Dogs Allowed: The Rise of the Mexican American Civil Rights Movement.* Austin: University of Texas Press, 2009.

Ortiz, Alfonso. "Indian/White Relations: A View from the Other Side of the 'Frontier.'" In *Indians in American History: An Introduction*, edited by Frederick E. Hoxie, 19–46. Arlington Heights IL: Harlan Davidson, 1988.

Osselaer, Heidi J. *Winning Their Place: Arizona Women in Politics, 1883–1950.* Tucson: University of Arizona Press, 2009.

Osten, Sarah. "'Beautifying the Revolution': The Origins and the Significance of Woman Suffrage in Chiapas." Master's thesis, University of Chicago, 2004.

Otero, Lydia R. *La Calle: Spatial Conflicts and Urban Renewal in a Southwest City.* Tucson: University of Arizona Press, 2010.

———. "Refusing to Be Undocumented: Chicanas/os in Tucson during the Depression Years." In *Picturing Arizona: The Photographic Record of the 1930s*, edited by Kathrine G. Morrissey and Kirsten Jensen. Tucson: University of Arizona Press, 2005.

Otero, Miguel Antonio. *My Nine Years as Governor of the Territory of New Mexico, 1897–1906.* Albuquerque: University of New Mexico Press, 1940.

Ott, Julia C. "'The Free and Open People's Market': Political Ideology and Retail Brokerage at the New York Stock Exchange, 1913–1933." *Journal of American History* 96, no. 1 (June 2009): 44–71.

Overmyer-Velázquez, Mark. *Beyond la Frontera: The History of Mexico-U.S. Migration.* New York: Oxford University Press, 2011.

Owen, Michael. "'Lighting the Pathways for New Canadians': Methodist and United Church WMS Missions in Eastern Alberta, 1904–1940." In *Standing on New Ground: Women in Alberta,* edited by Catherine C. Cole and Ann Milovic, 1–18. Edmonton: University of Alberta Press, 1993.

Palmer, Bryan D. *Revolutionary Teamsters: The Minneapolis Truckers' Strikes of 1934.* Chicago: Haymarket Books, 2014.

Palmer, Bryan D., and Joan Sangster, eds. *Labouring Canada: Class, Gender, and Race in Canadian Working-Class History.* Don Mills ON: Oxford University Press, 2008.

Paredes, Américo. *With a Pistol in His Hand: A Border Ballad and Its Hero.* Austin: University of Texas Press, 1958.

Parnaby, Andrew. "'The Best Men That Ever Worked the Lumber': Aboriginal Longshoremen on Burrard Inlet, BC, 1863–1939." In *Labouring Canada: Class, Gender, and Race in Canadian Working-Class History,* edited by Bryan D. Palmer and Joan Sangster, 191–204. Don Mills ON: Oxford University Press, 2008.

Pascoe, Pat. *Helen Ring Robinson: Colorado Senator and Suffragist.* Boulder: University of Colorado Press, 2011.

Pascoe, Peggy. *Relations of Rescue: The Search for Female Moral Authority in the American West, 1874–1939.* New York: Oxford University Press, 1990.

———. *What Comes Naturally: Miscegenation Law and the Making of Race in America.* New York: Oxford University Press, 2009.

Peavy, Linda, and Ursula Smith. "'Leav[ing] the White[s] . . . Far behind Them': The Girls from Fort Shaw (Montana) Indian School, Basketball Champions of the 1904 World's Fair." In *The 1904 Anthropology Days and Olympic Games,* edited by Susan Brownell, 238–57. Lincoln: University of Nebraska Press, 2008.

Peck, Gunther. "The Nature of Labor: Fault Lines and Common Ground in Environmental and Labor History." *Environmental History* 11, no. 2 (April 2006): 212–38.

———. "Padrones and Protest: 'Old' Radicals and 'New' Immigrants in Bingham, Utah, 1905–1912." *Western Historical Quarterly* 24, no. 2 (May 1933): 157–78.

———. *Reinventing Free Labor: Padrones and Immigrant Workers in the North American West, 1880–1930.* Cambridge: Cambridge University Press, 2000.

Pederson, Stephanie. "The Construction and Definition of Vice: The Connection of Statehood and the Criminalization of Prostitution in Tucson 1870–1920." Term paper, University of Arizona, November 23, 2003. In the author's possession.

Peiroth, Doris H. "Bertha Knight Landes: The Woman Who Was Mayor." In *Women in Pacific Northwest History,* rev. ed., edited by Karen Blair, 135–57. Seattle: University of Washington Press, 2001.

Perales, Marian. "Teresa Urrea: Curandera and Folk Saint." In *Latina Legacies: Identity, Biography, and Community,* edited by Vicki L. Ruiz and Virginia Sánchez Korrol, 97–119. New York: Oxford University Press, 2005.

Perales, Monica. *Smeltertown: Making and Remembering a Southwest Border Community*. Chapel Hill: University of North Carolina Press, 2010.

Perdue, Theda. "Indians in Southern History." In *Indians in American History*, edited by Frederick E. Hoxie, 129–39. Chicago: Newberry Library, 1988.

Perez, Craig Santos. "Transterritorial Currents and the Imperial Terripelago." *American Quarterly* 67, no. 3 (September 2015): 619–36.

Pérez, Emma. *The Decolonial Imaginary: Writing Chicanas into History*. Bloomington: Indiana University Press, 1999.

Perry, Louis, and Richard Perry. *A History of the Los Angeles Labor Movement, 1911–1941*. Berkeley: University of California Press, 1963.

Phillips, Sarah T. *This Land, This Nation: Conservation, Rural America, and the New Deal*. New York: Cambridge University Press, 2007.

Philp, Kenneth R., ed. "Indian Self Rule: First Hand Accounts of Indian-White Relations from Roosevelt to Reagan." In *Major Problems in American Indian History*, 2nd ed., edited by Albert L. Hurtado and Peter Iverson, 391–96. Boston: Houghton Mifflin, 2001.

———. *John Collier's Crusade for Indian Reform 1920–1954*. Tucson: University of Arizona Press, 1977.

Pierce, Jason E. *Making the White Man's West: Whiteness and the Creation of the American West*. Boulder: University of Colorado Press, 2016.

Pisani, Donald J. *To Reclaim a Divided West: Water, Law, and Public Policy 1848–1902*. Albuquerque: University of New Mexico Press, 1992.

Poirier, Paula. "The Myths of Chinese and Chinatown in Tucson." Term paper, University of Arizona. In the author's possession.

Ponzo, Steve. "Disdain and Drink: The Changing Attitudes of Tucsonans towards Prohibition Laws." Term paper, University of Arizona, May 2003. In the author's possession.

Pool, Jeannie Gayle. *American Composer Zenobia Powell Perry*. Lanham MD: Scarecrow Press, 2009.

Posey, Alexander. "Journal of Creek Enrollment Field Party 1905." *Chronicles of Oklahoma* 46 (1968): 13–14.

Preston, William, Jr. *Aliens and Dissenters: Federal Suppression of Radicals, 1903–1933*. New York: Harper Torchbooks, 1963.

Price, Jennifer. *Flight Maps: Adventures with Nature in Modern America*. New York: Basic Books, 1999.

Prucha, Francis Paul. *The Great Father: The United States Government and the American Indians*. Lincoln: University of Nebraska Press, 1986.

Pruitt, Bernadette. "'Beautiful People': Community Formation in Houston, 1900–1941." In *Freedom's Racial Frontier: African Americans in the Twentieth Century West*, edited by Herbert G. Ruffin II and Dwayne A. Mack, 45–96. Norman: University of Oklahoma Press, 2018.

Putman, John C. *Class and Gender Politics in Progressive-Era Seattle*. Reno: University of Nevada Press, 2008.

Putnam, Jackson K. "The Progressive Legacy in California: Fifty Years of Politics, 1917–1967." In *California Progressivism Revisited*, edited by William Deverell and Tom Sitton, 247–68. Berkeley: University of California Press, 1994.

Raat, William Dirk. *Revoltosos! Mexico's Rebels in the United States, 1902–1923*. College Station: Texas A&M University Press, 1981.

Raftery, Judith. "Los Angeles Clubwomen and Progressive Reform." In *California Progressivism Revisited*, edited by William Deverell and Tom Sitton, 144–74. Berkeley: University of California Press, 1994.

Raptis, Helen. "Pushing Physical, Racial, and Ethnic Boundaries: Edith Lucas and Public Education in British Columbia, 1903–1989." In *One Step over the Line: Toward a History of Women in the North American Wests*, edited by Elizabeth Jameson and Sheila McManus, 215–36. Edmonton: University of Alberta Press, 2008.

Rasmussen, Linda, et al. *A Harvest Yet to Reap: A History of Prairie Women*. Lincoln: University of Nebraska Press, 1976.

Recio, Gabriela. "U.S. Prohibition and the Drug Trade in Mexico." In *Major Problems in the History of North American Borderlands: Documents and Essays*, edited by Pekka Hämäläinen and Benjamin H. Johnson, 450–59. Boston: Wadsworth, Cengage Learning, 2012. First published in the *Journal of Latin American Studies* 34 (February 2002): 21–42.

Reese, Linda Williams. *Women of Oklahoma: 1890–1920*. Norman: University of Oklahoma Press, 1997.

Reeves-Ellington, Barbara, Kathryn Kish Sklar, and Connie A. Shemo, eds. *Competing Kingdoms: Women, Mission, Nation, and the American Protestant Empire, 1812–1960*. Durham NC: Duke University Press, 2010.

Reich, Peter. "The 'Hispanic' Roots of Prior Appropriation in Arizona." In *Arizona State Law Journal* 27, no. 2 (Summer 1995): 649–62.

———. "Western Courts and the Privatization of Hispanic Mineral Rights Since 1850: An Alchemy of Title." *Columbia Journal of Environmental Law* 23, no. 1 (1998): 57–87.

Reich, Steven A. "Soldiers of Democracy: Black Texans and the Fight for Citizenship, 1917–1921." *Journal of American History* 82, no. 4 (March 1996): 1478–504.

Reid, Debra A. "African Americans, Community Building, and the Role of the State in Rural Reform in Texas, 1890s-1930s." In *The Countryside in the Age of the Modern State: Political Histories of Rural America*, edited by Catherine McNicol Stock and Robert D. Johnston, 38–65. Ithaca NY: Cornell University Press, 2001.

Reid, Joshua L. *The Sea Is My Country: The Maritime World of the Makahs*. New Haven CT: Yale University Press, 2015.

Reiner, Robert. "Kings of the Wild Frontier." In *They Went That-a-Way*, edited by Ann Lloyd. London: Orbis Publishing, 1982.

Reitman, Sharon. "The Politics of the Western Federation of Miners and the United Mine Workers of America: Uneven Development, Industry Structure, and Class Struggle." In *Bringing Class Back In: Contemporary and Historical Perspectives,* edited by Scott McNall, Rhonda F. Levine, and Rick Fantasia, 203–22. Boulder CO: Westview, 1991.

Reséndez, Andrés. *Changing National Identities at the Frontier: Texas and New Mexico, 1800–1850.* New York: Oxford University Press, 2005.

Riley, Barbara. "Six Saucepans to One: Domestic Science vs. the Home in British Columbia, 1900–1930." In *British Columbia Reconsidered: Essays on Women,* edited by Gillian Laura Creese and Veronica Jane Strong-Boag, 119–42. Vancouver: Press Gang Publishers, 1992.

Rivera, Alicia Judith. "Solidarity in the San Joaquin Valley Cotton Strike of 1933." Master's thesis, California State University, Fresno, May 2005.

Robbins, William G. *Colony and Empire: The Capitalist Transformation of the American West.* Lawrence: University Press of Kansas, 1994.

———. *A Man for All Seasons: Monroe Sweetland and the Liberal Paradox.* Corvallis: Oregon State University Press, 1915.

Robbins, William G., and Katrine Barber. *Nature's Northwest: The North Pacific Slope in the Twentieth Century.* Tucson: University of Arizona Press, 2011.

Rome, Adam. "'Political Hermaphrodites': Gender and Environmental Reform in the Progressive Era." *Environmental History* 11 (July 2006): 440–63.

Romero, Tom I., II. "Ditches and Desirability: Regulating Race through the Flow and Quality of Immigration and the Application of Western Water Law in the Nineteenth and Early Twentieth Centuries." In *Beyond the Borders of the Law: Critical Legal Histories of the North American West,* edited by Katrina Jagodinsky and Pablo Mitchell, 162–200. Lawrence: University Press of Kansas, 2018.

Romo, Ricardo. *East Los Angeles: History of a Barrio.* Austin: University of Texas Press, 1983.

Roome, Patricia A. "'From One Whose Home Is among the Indians': Henrietta Muir Edwards and Aboriginal Peoples." In *Unsettled Pasts: Reconceiving the West through Women's History,* edited by Sarah Carter, Lesley Erickson, Patricia Roome, and Char Smith, 47–78. Calgary: University of Calgary Press, 2005.

Roosevelt, Theodore. *Theodore Roosevelt: An Autobiography.* New York: Charles Scribner's Sons, 1922.

Rosen, Ruth. *The Lost Sisterhood: Prostitution in America, 1900–1918.* Baltimore MD: Johns Hopkins University Press, 1982.

Ross-Bryant, Lynn. *Pilgrimage to the National Parks: Religion and Nature in the United States.* New York: Routledge, 2013.

Ross-Nazzal, Jennifer, ed. *Winning the West for Women: The Life of Suffragist Emma Smith Devoe.* Seattle: University of Washington Press, 2011.

Rothbard, Murray N. "World War I as Fulfillment: Power and the Intellectuals." https://mises.org/library/world-war-i-fulfillment-power-and-intellectuals.

Rothman, Hal K. *Devil's Bargains: Tourism in the Twentieth-Century American West.* Lawrence: University Press of Kansas, 1998.

Rozum, Molly P. "'That Understanding with Nature': Region, Race, and Nation in Women's Stories from the Modern Canadian and American Grasslands West." In *One Step over the Line: Toward a History of Women in the North American Wests*, edited by Elizabeth Jameson and Sheila McManus, 129–64. Edmonton: University of Alberta Press, 2008.

Ruffin, Herbert G., II, and Dwayne A. Mack, eds. *Freedom's Racial Frontier: African Americans in the Twentieth-Century West.* Norman: University of Oklahoma Press, 2018.

Rutherdale, Myra. "'I Wish the Men Were Half as Good': Gender Constructions in the Canadian North Western Mission Field, 1860–1940." In *Telling Tales: Essays in Western Women's History*, edited by Catherine A. Cavanaugh and Randi R. Warne, 32–59. Vancouver: University of British Columbia Press, 2000.

Sabin, Paul. *Crude Politics: The California Oil Market 1900–1940.* Berkeley: University of California Press, 2005.

Sadowski-Smith, Claudia. "Unskilled Labor Migration and the Illegality Spiral: Chinese, European, and Mexican Indocumentados in the United States, 1882–2007." *American Quarterly* 60, no. 3 (September 2008): 779–804.

Sagarena, Roberto Ramón Lint. *Aztlán and Arcadia: Religion, Ethnicity and the Creation of Place.* New York: New York University Press, 2014.

Salas, Elizabeth. *Soldaderas in the Mexican Military: Myth and History.* Austin: University of Texas Press, 1990.

Samponaro, Frank N., and Paul J. Vanderwood. *War Scare on the Rio Grande: Robert Runyon's Photographs of the Border Conflict, 1913–1916.* Austin: Texas State Historical Association, 1992.

Sampsell, Kate. Review of *Dust Bowl, USA: Depression America and the Ecological Imagination, 1929–1941*, by Brad Lookingbill. *American Quarterly* 55, no. 4 (December 2003): 761–69.

Sánchez, George J. *Becoming Mexican American: Ethnicity, Culture, and Identity in Chicano Los Angeles, 1900–1945.* New York: Oxford University Press, 1993.

———. "The 'New Nationalism,' Mexican Style: Race and Progressivism in Chicano Political Development during the 1920s." In *California Progressivism Revisited*, edited by William Deverell and Tom Sitton, 229–44. Berkeley: University of California Press, 1994.

Sanders, Elizabeth. *Roots of Reform: Farmers, Workers, and the American State, 1877–1917.* Chicago: University of Chicago Press, 1999.

Sanders, Jeffrey C. "Public Art, Memory, and Mobility in 1920s New Mexico." In *City Dreams, Country Schemes: Community and Identity in the American West*, edited by Kathleen A. Brosnan and Amy L. Scott, 178–95. Reno: University of Nevada Press, 2011.

Sandoval, Chela. *Methodology of the Oppressed.* Minneapolis: University of Minnesota Press, 2000.

Sangster, Joan. *Dreams of Equality: Women on the Canadian Left, 1920–1950.* Toronto: McClelland and Stewart, 1989.

———. “Mobilizing Women for War.” In *Canada and the First World War: Essays in Honour of Robert Craig Brown*, edited by David Mackenzie, 157–93. Toronto: University of Toronto Press, 2005.

———. “The Softball Solution: Female Workers, Male Managers, and the Operation of Paternalism at Westclox, 1923–1960.” In *Labouring Canada: Class, Gender, and Race in Canadian Working-Class History*, edited by Bryan D. Palmer and Joan Sangster, 246–63. Don Mills ON: Oxford University Press, 2008.

Saunt, Claudio. *Black, White, and Indian: Race and the Unmaking of an American Family*. New York: Oxford University Press, 2005.

Savage, Barbara D. “Lynching, Race, and the Law: Colorado 1900–1906.” Unpublished essay, September 1992. In the author’s possession.

Saxton, Alexander. *Indispensable Enemy: Labor and the Anti-Chinese Movement in California*. Berkeley: University of California Press, 1971.

Schaffer, Ronald. “Jeannette Rankin: Progressive-Isolationist.” PhD diss., Princeton University, 1959.

Schneider, Khal. Review of *Wild Men: Ishis and Kroeber in the Wilderness of Modern America*, by Douglas Cazaux Sackman. *Western Historical Quarterly* 42, no. 2 (Summer 2011): 241–42.

Schoen, Johanna. “Fighting for Child Health: Race, Birth Control, and the State in the Jim Crow South.” In *The Countryside in the Age of the Modern State: Political Histories of Rural America*, edited by Catherine McNicol Stock and Robert D. Johnston, 113–33. Ithaca NY: Cornell University Press, 2001.

Schoonover, Thomas. *Uncle Sam’s War of 1898 and the Origins of Globalization*. Lexington: University Press of Kentucky, 2003.

Schreier, Jesse T. “Indian or Freedman? Enrollment, Race, and Identity in the Choctaw Nation, 1896–1907.” *Western Historical Quarterly* 42 (Winter 2011): 459–79.

Schulze, Jeffrey M. *Are We Not Foreigners Here? Indigenous Nationalism in the U.S.-Mexico Borderlands*. Chapel Hill: University of North Carolina Press, 2018.

Scott, Gary. “The President and the National Parks.” White House Historical Association. https://www.whitehousehistory.org/the-presidents-and-the-national-parks. Accessed November 10, 2020.

Scott, James C. *Seeing Like a State: How Certain Schemes to Improve the Human Condition Have Failed*. New Haven CT: Yale University Press, 1998.

Selvin, David F. “An Exercise in Hysteria: San Francisco’s Red Raids of 1934.” *Pacific Historical Review* 58, no. 3 (1989): 361–74.

———. *A Terrible Anger: The 1934 Waterfront and General Strikes in San Francisco*. Detroit MI: Wayne State University Press, 1996.

Sewell, Jessica Ellen. *Women and the Everyday City: Public Space in San Francisco, 1890–1915*. Minneapolis: University of Minnesota Press, 2011.

Shah, Nayan. *Contagious Divides: Epidemics and Race in San Francisco’s Chinatown*. Berkeley: University of California Press, 2001.

———. *Stranger Intimacy: Contesting Race, Sexuality, and the Law in the North American West.* Berkeley: University of California Press, 2011.

Sheehan, Nancy M. "'Women Helping Women': The WCTU and the Foreign Problem in the West, 1905–1930." *International Journal of Women's Studies* 6, no. 5 (November 1983): 395–411.

Shepard, R. Bruce. *Deemed Unsuitable: Blacks from Oklahoma Move to the Canadian Prairies in Search of Equality in the Early 20th Century Only to Find Racism in Their New Home.* Toronto: Umbrella Press, 1997.

Sheridan, Thomas E. *Los Tucsonenses: The Mexican Community in Tucson, 1854–1941.* Tucson: University of Arizona Press, 1986.

Shover, John L. "The Farmers' Holiday Association Strike, August 1932." *Agricultural History* 39, no. 4 (October 1965): 196–203.

Silverman, Elaine Leslau. "Lena Hanen and the Conflicts of Leadership in the Twentieth Century." In *Unsettled Pasts: Reconceiving the West through Women's History*, edited by Sarah Carter, Lesley Erickson, Patricia Roome, and Char Smith, 341–54. Calgary: University of Calgary Press, 2005.

Sitton, Tom. "John Randolph Haynes and the Left Wing of California Progressivism." In *California Progressivism Revisited*, edited by William Deverell and Tom Sitton, 15–33. Berkeley: University of California Press, 1994.

Sklar, Richard. *Movie-Made America: A Cultural History of American Movies.* New York: Vintage Press, 1975.

Slotkin, Richard. *Gunfighter Nation: The Myth of the Frontier in Twentieth-Century America.* Norman: University of Oklahoma Press, 1998. First published in 1992 by Atheneum.

Smith, Char. "'Crossing the Line': American Prostitutes in Western Canada, 1895–1925." In *One Step over the Line: Toward a History of Women in the North American Wests*, edited by Elizabeth Jameson and Sheila McManus, 241–60. Edmonton: University of Alberta Press, 2008.

Smith, Duane A. *Rocky Mountain Heartland: Colorado, Montana, and Wyoming in the Twentieth Century.* Tucson: University of Arizona Press, 2008.

———. "'We Are Equal': Racial Attitudes in the West." *Westerners Brand Book* 30, no. 11 (January 1974).

Smith, Karen. *The Magnificent Experiment: Building the Salt River Reclamation Project 1890–1917.* Tucson: University of Arizona Press, 1986.

Smith, Michael. *Pacific Visions: California Scientists and the Environment 1850–1915.* New Haven CT: Yale University Press, 1987.

Smith, Norma. *Jeannette Rankin: America's Conscience.* Helena: Montana Historical Society Press, 2002.

Smith, Rogers. *Civic Ideals: Conflicting Visions of Citizenship in U.S. History, 1898–1912.* New Haven CT: Yale University Press, 1997.

Smith, Sherry L. *Reimagining Indians: Native Americans through Anglo Eyes, 1880–1940.* New York: Oxford University Press, 2000.

Soden, Dale E. "The WCTU in the Pacific Northwest: A Different Side of the Social Gospel." In *Gender and the Social Gospel*, edited by Wendy J. Deichmann Edwards and Carolyn De Swarte Gifford, 103–15. Urbana: University of Illinois Press, 2003.

Sohi, Seema. *Echoes of Mutiny: Race, Surveillance and Indian Anticolonialism in North America.* New York: Oxford University Press, 2014.

———. "Race, Surveillance, and Indian Anticolonialism in the Transnational Western U.S.-Canadian Borderlands." *Journal of American History* 98, no. 2 (September 2011): 420–36.

Soja, Edward. *Thirdspace: Journeys to Los Angeles and Other Real-and-Imagined Places.* Cambridge MA: Blackwell, 1996.

Soto, Sandra. "A Run for the Border: On Representations of Nihilism in the Transnational Greater Mexico." Paper presented at "Violence and Belonging," American Studies Association, Hartford CT, October 2003.

Soto, Shirlene. *Emergence of the Modern Mexican Woman: Her Participation in Revolution and Struggle for Equality 1910–1940.* Denver CO: Arden Press, 1990.

Spargur, Justin. "Contrasting Experiences of Anglo and Hispanic Railroad Workers in the 1920s." Term paper, University of Arizona, May 2003. In the author's possession.

Spence, Mark David. *Dispossessing the Wilderness: Indian Removal and the Making of the National Parks.* New York: Oxford University Press, 1999.

Spiro, Jonathan Peter. *Defending the Master Race: Conservation, Eugenics, and the Legacy of Madison Grant.* Burlington: University of Vermont Press, 2009.

Spruill, Marjorie Wheeler, ed. *One Woman, One Vote: Rediscovering the Woman Suffrage Movement.* Troutdale OR: NewSage Press, 1995.

Starn, Orin. *Ishi's Brain: In Search of America's Last "Wild" Indian.* New York: W. W. Norton, 2004.

Starr, Kevin. *Endangered Dreams: The Great Depression in California.* New York: Oxford University Press, 1996.

Stebner, Eleanor J. "More Than Maternal Feminists and Good Samaritans: Women and the Social Gospel in Canada." In *Gender and the Social Gospel,* edited by Wendy J. Deichmann Edwards and Carolyn De Swarte Gifford, 53–67. Urbana: University of Illinois Press, 2003.

Stein, Gary C. "The Indian Citizenship Act of 1924." *New Mexico Historical Review* 47, no. 3 (July 1972): 257–74.

Steptoe, Tyina L. *Houston Bound: Culture and Color in a Jim Crow City.* Berkeley: University of California Press, 2016.

Stern, Alexandra Minna. "Buildings, Boundaries, and Blood: Medicalization and Nation-Building on the U.S. Mexico Border, 1910–1930." *Hispanic American Historical Review* 79, no. 1 (1999): 41–77.

———. *Eugenic Nation: Faults and Frontiers of Better Breeding in Modern America.* Berkeley: University of California Press, 2005.

Stern, Philip J. *The Company State: Corporate Sovereignty & the Early Modern Foundations of the British Empire in India.* New York: Oxford University Press, 2011.

Sterrett, Susan M. *Public Pensions: Gender & Civic Service in the States, 1850–1937*. Ithaca NY: Cornell University Press, 2003.

St. John, Rachel. "Divided Ranges: Trans-border Ranches and the Creation of National Space along the Western Mexico-U.S. Border." In *Bridging National Borders in North America: Transnational and Comparative Histories*, edited by Benjamin Johnson and Andrew R. Graybill, 116–40. Durham NC: Duke University Press, 2010.

———. *Line in the Sand: A History of the Western U.S.-Mexico Border*. Princeton NJ: Princeton University Press, 2011.

Stock, Catherine McNicol. *Main Street in Crisis: The Great Depression and the Old Middle Class on the Northern Plains*. Chapel Hill: University of North Carolina Press, 1992.

Stock, Catherine McNicol, and Robert D. Johnston, eds. *The Countryside in the Age of the Modern State: Political Histories of Rural America*. Ithaca NY: Cornell University Press, 2001.

Stoler, Ann Laura. "Carnal Knowledge and Imperial Power: Gender, Race, and Morality in Colonial Asia." In *Gender at the Crossroads of Knowledge: Feminist Anthropology in the Postmodern Era*, edited by Micaela di Leonardo, 51–101. Berkeley: University of California Press, 1991.

———. "Tense and Tender Ties: The Politics of Comparison in North American History and (Post)Colonial Studies." *Journal of American History* 88, no. 3 (December 2001): 829–65.

Stratton, David H. *Tempest over Teapot Dome: The Story of Albert B. Fall*. Norman: University of Oklahoma Press, 1998.

Streeby, Shelley. *Radical Sensations: World Movements, Violence, and Visual Culture*. Durham NC: Duke University Press, 2013.

Strong-Boag, Veronica, and Kathryn McPherson. "The Confinement of Women: Childbirth and Hospitalization in Vancouver, 1919–1939." In *British Columbia Reconsidered: Essays on Women*, edited by Gillian Laura Creese and Veronica Jane Strong-Boag, 143–71. Vancouver: Press Gang Publishers, 1992.

Strong-Boag, Veronica, Mona Gleason, and Adele Perry, eds. *Rethinking Canada: The Promise of Women's History*. 4th ed. Don Mills ON: Oxford University Press, 2002.

Stuckey, Melissa. Review of *Perseverance: A History of African Americans in Oregon's Marion and Polk Counties*, by Sheridan McCarthy and Stanton Nelson. *Oregon Historical Quarterly* 113, no. 2 (Summer 2012): 256.

Swatt, Steve, Susie Swatt, Jeff Raimundo, and Rebecca LaVally. *Game Changers: Twelve Elections That Transformed California*. Berkeley: California Historical Society Heyday Press, 2015.

Swindler, William F., ed. *Sources and Documents of United States Constitutions*. Vol. 8. Dobbs Ferry NY: Oceana Publications, 1979.

Swyripa, Frances. "Negotiating Sex and Gender in the Ukrainian Bloc Settlement: East Central Alberta between the Wars." In *Telling Tales: Essays in*

Western Women's History, edited by Catherine A. Cavanaugh and Randi R. Warne, 232–60. Vancouver: University of British Columbia Press, 2000.

Tamura, Eileen H. *In Defense of Justice: Joseph Kurihara and the Japanese American Struggle for Equality*. Urbana: University of Illinois Press, 2013.

Tatum, Charles. "On the Border: From the Abstract to the Specific." *Arizona Journal of Hispanic Cultural Studies* 4 (2000): 93–103.

Taylor, Leslie A. "Femininity as Strategy: A Gendered Perspective on the Farmers' Holiday." *Annals of Iowa* 51, no. 3 (January 1992): 252–77.

Taylor, Quintard. *In Search of the Racial Frontier: African Americans in the American West 1528–1990*. New York: W. W. Norton & Company, 1998.

Thistlethwaite, Frank. "Migration from Europe Overseas in the Nineteenth and Twentieth Centuries." *Historiekongressen*, 1969, 32–69.

Thompson, John. *Closing the Frontier: Radical Response in Oklahoma, 1889–1923*. Norman: University of Oklahoma Press, 1986.

Thompson, John Herd. "'The Beginning of Our Regeneration': The Great War and Western Canadian Reform Movements." *Historical Papers / Communications historiques* 7, no. 1 (1972): 227–45.

———. *Forging the Prairie West*. Toronto: Oxford University Press, 1998.

Thompson, John Herd, and Allen Seager. *Canada, 1922–1939: Decades of Discord*. Toronto: McClelland and Stewart, 1985.

Thorne, Tanis C. *The World's Richest Indian: The Scandal over Jackson Barnett's Oil Fortune*. New York: Oxford University Press, 2003.

Threlkeld, Megan. *Pan American Women: U.S. Internationalists and Revolutionary Mexico*. Philadelphia: University of Pennsylvania Press, 2014.

Tolchin, Susan. *Women in Congress*. Washington DC: Government Printing Office, 1976.

Toy, Eckard V. "Robe and Gown: The Ku Klux Klan in Eugene, Oregon." In *The Invisible Empire in the West: Toward a New Historical Appraisal of the Ku Klux Klan of the 1920s*, edited by Shawn Lay, 153–84. Urbana: University of Illinois Press, 1992.

Trafzer, Clifford E., Jean A. Keller, and Lorene Sisquoc, eds. *Boarding School Blues: Revisiting American Indian Educational Experiences*. Lincoln: University of Nebraska Press, 2006.

Troutman, John William. *Indian Blues: American Indians and the Politics of Music, 1879–1934*. Norman: University of Oklahoma Press, 2009.

Truett, Samuel. *Fugitive Landscapes: The Forgotten History of the U.S.-Mexico Borderlands*. New Haven CT: Yale University Press, 2006.

Truett, Samuel, and Elliott Young, eds. *Continental Crossroads: Remapping U.S.-Mexico Borderlands History*. Durham NC: Duke University Press, 2004.

Tsu, Cecilia M. *Garden of the World: Asian Immigrants and the Making of Agriculture in California's Santa Clara Valley*. New York: Oxford University Press, 2013.

Tuccille, Jerome. *The War against the Vets: The World War I Bonus Army during the Great Depression*. Lincoln: Potomac Books / University of Nebraska Press, 2018.

Tucker, William P. "Populism Up-to-Date: The Story of the Farmers' Union." *Agricultural History* 21, no. 4 (October 1947): 198–208.

Tygiel, Jules. *The Great Los Angeles Swindle: Oil, Stocks, and Scandal during the Roaring Twenties.* New York: Oxford University Press, 1994.

Tyrell, Ian. *Woman's World / Woman's Empire: The WCTU in International Perspective, 1880–1930.* Chapel Hill: University of North Carolina Press, 1991.

University of Washington. Civil Rights and Labor History Consortium. "IWW Strikes: 1905–1920." https://depts.washington.edu/iww/strikes.shtml. Accessed August 22, 2019.

———. "Upton Sinclair's End Poverty in California Campaign." http://depts.washington.edu/epic34/EPIW.shtml. Accessed January 4, 2017.

U.S. Bureau of Labor Statistics. *Union Scale of Wages and Hours of Labor.* Bulletin 354. May 14, 1923. https://fraser.stlouisfed.org/files/docs/publications/bls/bls_0354_1924.pdf.

U.S. Bureau of the Census. *Sixteenth Census of the United States, 1940.* Washington DC: U.S. Department of Commerce, Bureau of the Census, 1942. HathiTrust Digital Library.

———. *Thirteenth Census of the United States, 1910.* Washington DC: Government Printing Office, 1913. HathiTrust Digital Library.

U.S. Congress. House. Committee on Immigration and Naturalization. *Restriction of Immigration: Hearings on H.R. 5, H.R 101, and H.R. 561, before the Committee on Immigration and Naturalization.* 68th Cong., 1st sess., December 26, 27, 31, 1923, January 2, 3, 4, 5, 7, 8, 10, 19, 1924. Washington DC: Government Printing Office, 1924.

———. *Restriction of Immigration: Hearings on H.R. 588, before the Committee on Immigration and Naturalization.* 64th Cong., 1st sess., January 21, 1916. Washington DC: Government Printing Office, 1916.

———. *Seasonal Agricultural Laborers from Mexico: Hearings on H.R. 6741, H.R. 7559, and H.R. 9036, before the Committee on Immigration and Naturalization.* 69th Cong., 1st sess., January 28–29, February 2, 9, 11, 23, 1926. Washington DC: Government Printing Office, 1926.

———. *Statement of Sidney L. Gulick before the Committee on Immigration and Naturalization.* 66th Cong., 2nd sess., May 22, 1920. Washington DC: Government Printing Office, 1920.

U.S. Congress. House. Committee on Indian Affairs. *Alabama and Coushatta Indians of Texas: Hearings on H.R. 5479, before the Committee on Indian Affairs.* 70th Cong., 1st sess., February 23, March 1, 1928. Washington DC: Government Printing Office, 1928.

———. *Disposition of Unallotted Lands to the Omaha Indians in Nebraska, Issuance of Citizenship Certificates to Indians, and Appropriation for the Gallup and Durango Highway Lands, Hearings on H.R. 6355, before the Committee on Indian Affairs.* 68th Cong., 1st sess., May 19, 1924. Unpublished hearing. ProQuest Congressional. Accessed May 9, 2020.

———. *Modifying Osage Fund Restrictions: Hearings on H.R. 5726, before the Committee on Indian Affairs.* 68th Cong., 1st sess., January 25–February 7, 1924. Washington DC: Government Printing Office, 1924.

———. *Pima Indians and the San Carlos Irrigation Project: Hearings on S. 966, before the Committee on Indian Affairs.* 68th Cong., 1st sess., April 10, 19, 1924. Washington DC: Government Printing Office, 1924.

———. *Pueblo Indian Land Titles: Hearings on H.R. 13452 and H.R. 13674, before the Committee on Indian Affairs.* 67th Cong., 4th sess., February 1–15, 1923. Washington DC: Government Printing Office, 1923.

U.S. Congress. House. Committee on Irrigation and Reclamation. *Extension of the Time of Payment for Settlers on Government Reclamation Projects: Hearings on H.R. 8836 and H.R. 9611, before the Committee on Irrigation and Reclamation.* 68th Cong., 1st sess., May 5, 14, 16, 19, 20, 21, 23, 24, 26, 28, 1924. Washington DC: Government Printing Office, 1924.

U.S. Congress. House. Committee on the Public Lands. *Oil and Gas Lands, Red River, Oklahoma: Hearings on H.R. 12233 and H.R. 13475, before the Committee on the Public Lands.* 67th Cong., 4th sess., January 12, 15, 16, 17, 18, 19, 20, 23, 24, 25, 1923. Washington DC: Government Printing Office, 1923.

U.S. Congress. House. Industrial Commission on Immigration. *Reports of the Industrial Commission on Immigration and Education.* 57th Cong., H.R. Doc. No. 104. Washington DC: Government Printing Office, 1901.

U.S. Congress. Senate. Committee on Immigration. *Reports of the Immigration Commission: Abstracts of Reports of the Immigration Commission with Conclusions and Recommendations and Views of the Minority.* 61st Cong., 3rd sess., S. Doc. 747. Washington DC: Government Printing Office, 1911.

———. *Restriction of Western Hemisphere Immigration: Hearings on S. 1296, before the Committee on Immigration.* 70th Cong., 1st sess., February 1, 27, 28, 29, March 1, 5, 1928. Washington DC: Government Printing Office, 1928.

———. *Selective Immigration Legislation: Hearings on S. 2365 and S. 2576, before the Committee on Immigration.* 68th Cong., 1st sess., February 13, 14, 20, 21, March 8, 13, 14, April 7, 8, 1924. Washington DC: Government Printing Office, 1924.

U.S. Congress. Senate. Committee on Indian Affairs. *Ho Tul Yaholla and Ho Tul Kee Fixico.* 56th Cong., 1st sess., S. Doc. 443. United States Congressional Serial Set, Volume 3878. Washington DC: Government Printing Office, 1902.

———. *The Middle Rio Grande Conservancy District: Hearing on S. 700, before the Committee on Indian Affairs.* 70th Cong., 1st sess., January 20, February 17, 1928. Washington DC: Government Printing Office, 1928.

———. *Osage Fund Restrictions: Hearings before the Committee on Indian Affairs.* 68th Cong., 1st sess., March 28, 29, April 1, May 13, 15, 16, 19, 20, 21, 1924. Washington DC: Government Printing Office, 1924.

———. *Report of the Select Committee to Investigate Matters Connected with Affairs in the Indian Territory with Hearings, November 11, 1906–January 9, 1907.*

59th Cong., 2nd sess., S. Rep. No. 5013, vol. 1. Washington DC: Government Printing Office, 1907.

———. *To Quiet Title of Pueblo Indian Land: Hearing on S. 5828, before the Committee on Indian Affairs.* 71st Cong., 3rd sess., February 18, 1931. Washington DC: Government Printing Office, 1931.

U.S. Congress. Senate. Committee on Public Lands. *Pueblo Indian Lands: Hearings on S. 3865 and S. 4223, before a Subcommittee of the Committee on Public Lands and Surveys.* 67th Cong., 4th sess., January 15, 1923. Washington DC: Government Printing Office, 1923.

———. *Red River Oil Lands: Hearing on S. 2132, before a Subcommittee of the Committee on Public Lands and Surveys.* 68th Cong., 1st sess., June 3, 4, 1924. Washington DC: Government Printing Office, 1924.

Vallance, Michelle. "La Iglésia de San Agustín: Tucson's First Community Center." Term paper, University of Arizona, November 18, 2003. In the author's possession.

Vanderwood, Paul J. *Satan's Playground: Mobsters and Movie Stars at America's Greatest Gambling Resort.* Durham NC: Duke University Press, 2010.

Van Dieren, Karen. "The Response of the WMS to the Immigration of Asian Women 1888–1942." In *Not Just Pin Money: Selected Essays on the History of Women's Work in British Columbia,* edited by Barbara K. Latham and Roberta J. Pazdro, 79–98. Victoria BC: Camosun College, 1984.

Van Nuys, Frank. *Americanizing the West: Race, Immigrants, and Citizenship, 1890–1930.* Lawrence: University Press of Kansas, 2002.

Vargas, Zaragosa. *Crucible of Struggle: A History of Mexican Americans from Colonial Times to the Present Era.* New York: Oxford University Press, 2011.

Vizenor, Gerald. *Manifest Manners: Postindian Warriors of Survivance.* Hanover NH: University Press of New England, 1994.

Voisey, Paul. "The 'Votes for Women' Movement." In *The Best from Alberta History,* edited by Hugh Dempsey, 166–83 Saskatoon SK: Historical Society of Alberta, 1981.

Wadewitz, Lissa. "The Scales of Salmon: Diplomacy and Conservation in the Western Canada-U.S. Borderlands." In *Bridging National Borders in North America: Transnational and Comparative Histories,* edited by Benjamin Johnson and Andrew R. Graybill, 141–64. Durham NC: Duke University Press, 2010.

Wald, Priscilla. *Constituting Americans: Cultural Anxiety and Narrative Form.* Durham NC: Duke University Press, 1995.

Wall, Wendy. "Gender and the 'Citizen Indian.'" In *Writing the Range: Race, Class, and Culture in the Women's West,* edited by Elizabeth Jameson and Susan Armitage, 202–29. Norman: University of Oklahoma Press, 1997.

Wallace, Shelley Burner. "Umatilla's 'Petticoat Government,' 1916–1920." *Oregon Historical Quarterly* 88, no. 4 (Winter 1987): 385–402.

Walsh, Margaret. "Gendered Steps across the Border: Teaching the History of Women in the American and Canadian Wests." In *One Step over the*

Line: Toward a History of Women in the North American Wests, edited by Elizabeth Jameson and Sheila McManus, 385–410. Edmonton: University of Alberta Press, 2008.

Walsh, Susan. "The Peacock and the Guinea Hen: Political Profiles of Dorothy Gretchen Steeves and Grace MacInnis." In *Not Just Pin Money: Selected Essays on the History of Women's Work in British Columbia*, edited by Barbara K. Latham and Roberta J. Pazdro, 365–79. Victoria BC: Camosun College, 1984.

Warde, Mary Jane. *George Washington Grayson and the Creek Nation, 1843–1920*. Norman: University of Oklahoma Press, 1999.

Ware, Harry David. "Alcohol, Temperance, and Prohibition in Arizona." PhD diss., Arizona State University, 1995.

Warren, Louis S. *The Hunter's Game: Poachers and Conservationists in Twentieth-Century America*. New Haven CT: Yale University Press, 1997.

Washington, Booker T. "Boley, a Negro Town in the West." *Outlook*, January 4, 1908.

Watkins, Marilyn P. *Rural Democracy: Family Farmers and Politics in Western Washington, 1890–1925*. Ithaca NY: Cornell University Press, 1995.

Weber, David, ed. *Foreigners in Their Native Land: Historical Roots of the Mexican Americans*. Albuquerque: University of New Mexico Press, 1973.

Weber, Devra. *Dark Sweat, White Gold: California Farm Workers, Cotton, and the New Deal*. Berkeley: University of California Press, 1994.

Weber, Eric. "National Crimes and Southern Horrors: Trans-Atlantic Conversations about Race, Empire and Civilization, 1880–1900." PhD diss., Duke University, 2011.

Weber, John. *From South Texas to the Nation: The Exploitation of Mexican Labor in the Twentieth Century*. Chapel Hill: University of North Carolina Press, 2015.

———. "Homing Pigeons, Cheap Labor, and Frustrated Nativists: Immigration Reform and the Deportation of Mexicans from South Texas in the 1920s." *Western Historical Quarterly* 44, no. 2 (Summer 2013): 167–86.

Wefald, John. *A Voice of Protest: Norwegians in American Politics, 1890–1917*. Northfield MN: Norwegian-American Historical Association, 1971.

Weinbaum, Alys Eve, et al., eds. *The Modern Girl around the World: Consumption, Modernity, and Globalization*. Durham NC: Duke University Press, 2008.

Weise, Julie M. "Mexican Nationalisms, Southern Racisms: Mexicans and Mexican Americans in the U.S. South, 1908–1939." *American Quarterly* 60, no. 3 (September 2008): 749–77.

Weisiger, Marsha. *Dreaming of Sheep in Navajo Country*. Seattle: University of Washington Press, 2009.

Welke, Barbara Young. *Law and the Borders of Belonging in the Long Nineteenth Century United States*. New York: Cambridge University Press, 2010.

Wenger, Tisa. "Land, Culture, and Sovereignty in the Pueblo Dance Controversy." *Journal of the Southwest* 46, no. 2 (Summer 2004): 381–412.

Wernick, Robert. "Where You Went If You Really Had to Get Unhitched." *Smithsonian* 27, no. 3 (June 1996): 64.

West, Richard W., Jr., and Kevin Gover. "The Struggle for Indian Civil Rights." In *Indians in American History: An Introduction*, edited by Frederick E. Hoxie, 275–94. Arlington Heights IL: Harlan Davidson, 1988.

Whaley, Gray H. *Oregon and the Collapse of Illahee: U.S. Empire and the Transformation of an Indigenous World, 1792–1859*. Chapel Hill: University of North Carolina Press, 2010.

Wheeler-Howard Act. Pub. L. No. 73-383, 48 Stat. 984 (1934). In *Major Problems in American Indian History*, 2nd ed., edited by Albert L. Hurtado and Peter Iverson, 388–91. Boston: Houghton Mifflin, 2001.

White, Richard. *"It's Your Misfortune and None of My Own": A History of the American West.* Norman: University of Oklahoma Press, 1991.

———. *Land Use, Environment, and Social Change: The Shaping of Island County, Washington.* Seattle: University of Washington Press, 1980.

———. *The Organic Machine.* New York: Hill & Wang, 1995.

———. *Roots of Dependency: Subsistence, Environment, and Social Change among the Choctaws, Pawnees, and Navajos.* Lincoln: University of Nebraska Press, 1983.

Whyte, Kenneth. *Hoover: An Extraordinary Life in Extraordinary Times.* New York: Knopf, 2017.

Wickett, Murray R. *Contested Territory: Whites, Native Americans, and African Americans in Oklahoma 1865–1907.* Baton Rouge: Louisiana State University Press, 2000.

Wild, Mark. *Street Meeting: Multiethnic Neighborhoods in Early Twentieth-Century Los Angeles.* Berkeley: University of California Press, 2005.

Wiley, Peter, and Robert Gottlieb. *Empires in the Sun: The Rise of the New American West.* New York: G. P. Putnam's Sons, 1982.

Wilkey, James. "The Rise of Exclusive Institutions: The Tucson Golf and Country Club, 1914–1932." Term paper, University of Arizona, May 2, 2000. In the author's possession.

Williams, Walter L. "American Imperialism and the Indians." In *Indians in American History: An Introduction*, edited by Frederick E. Hoxie, 231–50. Arlington Heights IL: Harlan Davidson, 1988.

Wilson, Chris. *The Myth of Santa Fe: Creating a Modern Regional Tradition.* Albuquerque: University of New Mexico Press, 1997.

Wilson, J. Donald. "Lottie Bowron and Rural Women Teachers in British Columbia, 1928–1934." In *British Columbia Reconsidered: Essays on Women*, edited by Gillian Laura Creese and Veronica Jane Strong-Boag, 340–63. Vancouver: Press Gang Publishers, 1992.

Wilson, Joan Hoff. *Herbert Hoover: Forgotten Progressive.* Boston: Little, Brown, 1975.

———. "Herbert Hoover's Agricultural Policies, 1921–1928." In *Herbert Hoover as Secretary of Commerce: Studies in New Era Thought and Practice*, edited by Ellis W. Hawley, 115–47. Iowa City: University of Iowa Press, 1981.

Wimberly, Cory, Javier Martínez, David Muñoz, and Margarita Cavazos. "Peons and Progressives: Race and Boosterism in the Lower Rio Grande Valley, 1904–1941." *Western Historical Quarterly* 49 (Winter 2018): 437–63.

Wister, Owen. *The Virginian.* New York: Macmillan, 1902.

Woeste, Victoria Saker. *The Farmer's Benevolent Trust: Law and Agricultural Cooperation in Industrial America, 1865–1945.* Chapel Hill: University of North Carolina Press, 1998.

———. "Land Monopoly, Agribusiness, and the State: Discovering the Family Farm in Twentieth-Century California." In *The Countryside in the Age of the Modern State: Political Histories of Rural America,* edited by Catherine McNicol Stock and Robert D. Johnston, 66–87. Ithaca NY: Cornell University Press, 2001.

Wolff, David. *Industrializing the Rockies: Growth, Competition and Turmoil in the Coal Fields of Colorado and Wyoming, 1868–1914.* Boulder: University of Colorado Press, 2003.

Women's Christian Temperance Union. *Report of the Forty-Second Annual Convention of the National Women's Temperance Union.* Seattle: Plymouth Congregational Church, 1915.

Wong, K. Scott. "The 1903 Boston Chinatown Raid Revisited." *Amerasia Journal* 22, no. 3 (1996): 81–103.

Woods, Gerald. "A Penchant for Probity: California Progressives and the Disreputable Pleasures." In *California Progressivism Revisited,* edited by William Deverell and Tom Sitton, 99–113. Berkeley: University of California Press, 1994.

Work, David K. "Enforcing Neutrality: The Tenth U.S. Cavalry on the Mexican Border, 1913–1919." *Western Historical Quarterly* 40 (Summer 2009): 179–200.

Worster, Donald. *Dust Bowl: The Southern Plains in the 1930s.* New York: Oxford University Press, 1979.

———. *Rivers of Empire: Water, Aridity, and the Growth of the American West.* New York: Pantheon Books, 1985.

———. *Under Western Skies: Nature and History in the American West.* New York: Oxford University Press, 1992.

Wrobel, David M. *America's West: A History, 1890–1950.* Cambridge: Cambridge University Press, 2017.

———. *Promised Lands: Promotion, Memory, and the Creation of the American West.* Lawrence: University Press of Kansas, 2002.

Wuthnow, Robert. *Rough Country: How Texas Became America's Most Powerful Bible-Belt State.* Princeton NJ: Princeton University Press, 2014.

Yasutake, Rumi. *Transnational Women's Activism: The United States, Japan, and Japanese Immigrant Communities in California, 1859–1920.* New York: New York University Press, 2004.

Young, Elliott. *Catarino Garza's Revolution on the Texas-Mexico Border.* Durham NC: Duke University Press, 2004.

———. "Deconstructing *La Raza*: Identifying the Gente Decente of Laredo, 1904–1911." *Southwest Historical Quarterly* 98, no. 2 (October 1993): 227–59.

Young, Walter. *The Anatomy of a Party: The National CCF, 1932–61*. Toronto: University of Toronto Press, 1969.

Yung, Judy. *Unbound Feet: A Social History of Chinese Women in San Francisco*. Berkeley: University of California Press, 1995.

Zamora, Emilio. *The World of the Mexican Worker in Texas*. College Station: Texas A&M University Press, 1993.

Zellar, Gary. *African Creeks: Estelveste and the Creek Nation*. Norman: University of Oklahoma Press, 2007.

Zissu, Erik M. *Blood Matters: The Five Civilized Tribes and the Search for Unity in the Twentieth Century*. New York: Routledge, 2001.

Zitkala-Sa (Gertrude Bonnin). *American Indian Stories*. N.p., 1921.

INDEX

In the History of the American West Series

One Vast Winter Count: The American West before Lewis and Clark
by Colin G. Calloway

Empires, Nations, and Families: A History of the North American West, 1800–1860
by Anne F. Hyde

Making a Modern U.S. West: The Contested Terrain of a Region and Its Borders, 1898–1940
by Sarah Deutsch

To order or obtain more information on these or other University of Nebraska Press titles, visit nebraskapress.unl.edu.